Official publications of the Soviet Union and Eastern Europe 1945–1980

OFFICIAL PUBLICATIONS OF THE SOVIET UNION AND EASTERN EUROPE 1945–1980

A SELECT ANNOTATED BIBLIOGRAPHY

Edited by Gregory Walker

Mansell Publishing Limited

ISBN 0–7201–1641–4

Mansell Publishing Limited, 6 All Saints Street, London N1 9RL

Distributed in the United States and Canada by The H. W. Wilson Company, 950 University Avenue, Bronx, New York 10452

First published 1982

British Library Cataloguing in Publication Data

Official publications of the Soviet Union and Eastern Europe 1945–1980.
 1. Europe, Eastern—Government publications—Bibliography
 I. Walker, Gregory
 015.47   Z2483
 ISBN 0–7201–1641–4

Filmset in Monophoto Plantin by
Latimer Trend & Company Ltd, Plymouth
Printed and bound in Great Britain

CONTENTS

J YUGOSLAVIA (Garth M. Terry)

P POLAND (George Sanford) 187

U UNION OF SOVIET SOCIALIST REPUBLICS

THE CONTRIBUTORS

Jenny Brine, BA, DipLib, ALA, is Librarian of the Centre for Russian and East European Studies, University of Birmingham.

Dalibor Chrástek, BA, ALA, is on the staff of the Slavonic and East European Branch, British Library Reference Division, London.

John Freeman, MA, ALA, is Assistant Librarian, School of Slavonic and East European Studies, University of London.

Brian Hunter, BA, DipLib, is Assistant Librarian responsible for Slavonic Collections, British Library of Political and Economic Science, London School of Economics.

George Sanford, MPhil, PhD, is Lecturer in the Department of Politics, University of Bristol.

Garth M. Terry, BA, MPhil, is Librarian for Slavonic and East European Studies, University of Nottingham.

Werner Volkmer, PhD, Diplompolitologe, works as a journalist in London.

Gregory Walker, MA, PhD, FLA, is Head of the Slavonic and East European Section, Bodleian Library, University of Oxford.

PREFACE AND ACKNOWLEDGEMENTS

In the political and administrative context of the postwar Soviet Union and its East European allies, the term 'official publication' is particularly difficult of definition. The 'leading role' of the ruling parties, the high degree of control exercised over publishing activity by the authorities, and the virtual absence of central official publishing agencies on the lines of HMSO or the US Government Publications Office—all these are features which defeat the usual Western criteria for identifying 'official' documentation, and indeed suggest that the bulk of these countries' printed output could in some sense be designated as 'official'.

Nevertheless, it is perfectly feasible in most instances to isolate from the generality of Soviet and East European publications those which are issued by, or on the orders of, the established government and party authorities in the exercise of their responsibilities, and can thus properly be called official publications. In general terms, these are documents which are intended to direct and regulate the life of the country, which supply information believed to be necessary for its proper functioning, and which publicize and justify the views and policies of its rulers. In states where political, social and economic activity is subject to strongly centralized control and single-party leadership, a high degree of importance attaches to documents carrying this kind of authoritative sanction. This importance is not only a consequence of the status attributed to such material by the governments and parties which issue them, and by their supporting media. It is also in part due to the relative dearth of information and comment from non-official sources competing with, or critical of, the official line. Such a situation inevitably forces students, researchers and commentators directly to the authorized texts.

This bibliography is intended as a guide to postwar Soviet and East European official documentation, in the broad definition used above. While quite extensive as bibliographies go, it is not exhaustive. Compilers were asked to include what they regarded as the most important material within the general guidelines for coverage (described in 'Scope of the bibliography' below) and within the limitations of space available, and to give details of any existing bibliographies which offered useful additional data on official publications.

With one exception, the countries included here have had their official publications recorded with similar, though not identical, degrees of selectivity. In the case of the USSR, coverage at greater length than that given to other countries was felt to be necessary for several reasons: the far higher number of official publications issued; the desirability of adequately reflecting official publishing at union republic level; and not least, the much greater scale and variety of research now being devoted to the USSR which this bibliography could hope to assist.

The selective nature of the bibliography has meant that most of the compilers prepared entries for many official publications which could not be included in the finished volume. We are still considering, at the time of writing, how this valuable additional information can best be made publicly available. Pending a decision, enquiries relating to postwar Soviet and East European official publications not dealt with in this book may be sent in the first instance to the Editor (Slavonic Section, Bodleian Library, Oxford OX1 3BG).

Besides the general expression of thanks—in which all the contributors join— to all those libraries and individuals who have helped them in their work, the following special acknowledgements are due:

For the USSR, the compiler would particularly like to thank the staff of the Central Reference Library and the Section for the Languages of the Peoples of the USSR in the Lenin Library, Moscow, and the hard-pressed book-delivery staff. In Leningrad, the staff of the Saltykov-Shchedrin Public Library and the Library of the Academy of Sciences were most helpful. In Britain, considerable use was made of the resources of the British Library of Political and Economic Science, the British Library Reference Division and University College London, as well as Birmingham University Library. Professor W. E. Butler of University College London gave advice generously during the compilation of the bibliography. The British Council and the University of Birmingham made possible two visits to the USSR. The Centre for Russian and East European Studies at the University of Birmingham kindly allowed the compiler the time to work on the bibliography.

The compiler of the chapter on Romania wishes to express his gratitude for the help given by his fellow-librarians at the Bodleian Library, Oxford; the British Library; the British Library of Political and Economic Science; the Bulgarian National Library; the Romanian Central State Library; and the School of Slavonic and East European Studies, University of London.

The compiler of the chapter on Poland would like to acknowledge the assistance of the staff of the British Library Reference Division, and especially that of his fellow-contributor Mr Dalibor Chrástek.

The compiler of the chapter on Hungary would like to thank Mr S. de Winter, Mr T. Kachinske, Dr L. Péter, Dr G. Schöpflin, and Mr P. Sherwood.

Mr M. C. Kaser's helpful comments on the chapters for Albania, and for international and multinational publications, are gratefully acknowledged.

Gregory Walker
June 1981

INTRODUCTION

SCOPE OF THE BIBLIOGRAPHY

The bibliography aims to include the most important sources of officially issued documents, in the definition given in the Preface, emanating from the USSR and the socialist states of Eastern Europe from the end of the German occupation in 1944–5 up to 1980. Where documents are more readily accessible in Western published sources, these are stated. Translations into English (or, failing that, into French or German) are noted where they are known to exist. Other bibliographies—regardless of their channel of publication—which are likely to aid the finding and use of official publications, are also included.

The categories of publication covered, and the space devoted to each, vary in some degree from country to country, but they can be characterized as *including*:

constitutional documents;

treaties and international agreements;

formal legislation and other government and party rulings carrying the force of law;

documents of the ruling party;

publications of individual central government agencies;

regulations applying to particular areas of the economy or society;

official statements and other presentations of authoritative views on policies and events;

statistical and other reference information produced by official sources;

the speeches and other 'works' of leading individuals in the party and government hierarchy.

Publications of the following organs, despite their official or quasi-official nature, have been *excluded*:

local party and government authorities below national level, except in the cases of the USSR, Yugoslavia and Czechoslovakia, where coverage extends to the level of the union and constituent republics respectively;

trade unions;

youth, womens' and similar 'mass' organizations.

ARRANGEMENT OF ENTRIES

Each chapter begins with an introductory section intended to provide a brief outline of the political and administrative developments in the country concerned during the postwar period, with special reference to events and institutions reflected in official publishing. The bibliographical section of each chapter is arranged according to the following set of main headings:

General bibliographies and reference works.

Constitutional documents.

Law codes.

Other general legislative documents (e.g. official gazettes, parliamentary proceedings).

General party documents.

General statistics. (Subject-specialized statistics are placed under the 'subject' headings below.)

Other general sources of documentation.

International relations.

Political and ideological affairs.

Military affairs.

Economic affairs (including trade, finance, labour, industry and agriculture).

Social affairs (including health and social security).

Cultural affairs (including education, the media and religion).

Leaders' works.

Within each main heading, the arrangement of material differs between countries to follow the publishing pattern and administrative structure of each.

The arrangement of bibliographical data in individual entries is as follows:

1. Individual author(s), if any.
2. Title. This is in practice the first element in most entries.
3. Subtitle, where it supplies useful extra information.
4. English translation of title and subtitle, in square brackets.

In the case of an article, this is followed by the title of the journal, etc., containing it, volume and issue numbers, date and page reference. Otherwise the arrangement below continues:

5. Number of edition, where not the first.
6. Principal editor(s) and/or compiler(s), where given.
7. Head-of-title statement, in round brackets. This usually gives the organization(s) under whose authority the work was prepared, but is not necessarily the same as the publishing organization which issued it.
8. Title of any series within which the work was published, in round brackets.
9. Place of publication.

10. Publisher. Not generally shown if identical with 7 above.
11. Date(s) of publication.
12. Frequency (journals and other serials only).
13. Pagination* or number of volumes (non-serials only).

Where items have not been available for inspection, the data given is in some cases less complete. Items not described *de visu* are annotated [Not seen].*

LANGUAGE AND TRANSLITERATION

Authors, titles and subtitles are shown in the language in which they appear in the work—with the one exception that data on certain Soviet publications which could not be inspected have had to be given in the Russian form in which they were recorded in the source of information, with a note of their language of publication where not Russian.

Transliteration from the Cyrillic alphabet follows the system used by the Library of Congress, but omits ligatures. The following features of the system should be noted:

ю and я are transliterated by *iu* and *ia*.

г is transliterated by *h* in Ukrainian and Belorussian.

и is transliterated by *y* in Ukrainian, otherwise by *i*.

щ is transliterated by *shch* in Russian and Ukrainian, but by *sht* in Bulgarian.

ъ is transliterated by *ŭ* in Bulgarian.

Transliteration of Serbian and Macedonian does not follow the conventions for Russian, Ukrainian, Belorussian and Bulgarian, but accords with modern Yugoslav practice (e.g. ж = *ž*, ч = *č*, ш = *š*, x = *h*, ц = *c*).

* except in the chapter on the GDR.

ABBREVIATIONS

ALBANIA

bot.	botim (edition, publication); botuar/botohet (published)
CPA	Communist Party of Albania
N.SH.B.	Ndërmarrja Shtetërore e Botimeve
PLA	Party of Labour of Albania
PPSH	Partia e Punës të Shqipërisë
P(S)RA	People's (Socialist) Republic of Albania
RP(S)SH	Republika Popullore (Socialiste) të Shqipërisë
Shtëp. Bot.	Shtëpi Botonjëse
T.	Tiranë
vëll.	vëllim (volume)

BULGARIA

BCP	Bulgarian Communist Party
BKP	Bŭlgarska komunisticheska partiia
CC	Central Committee
DV	*Dŭrzhaven vestnik*
FF	Fatherland Front
IPNS	*Izvestiia na Prezidiuma na Narodnoto Sŭbranie*
PR of Bulgaria	People's Republic of Bulgaria
S.	Sofia
Sk.	Skopje

CZECHOSLOVAKIA

č., čís.	číslo
ČSR	Česká Socialistická Republika

ČSSR	Československá Socialistická Republika
KSČ	Komunistická strana Československa
KSS	Komunistická strana Slovenska
NS	Národní shromáždění
P.	Praha, Prague
ř.	řada
roč.	ročník
Sb.	*Sbírka zákonů*
SPN	Státní pedagogické nakladatelství
SSR	Slovenská Socialistická Republika
sv.	svazek
ÚV KSC	Ústřední výbor KSČ
vyd.	vydání
zv.	zväzok

GERMAN DEMOCRATIC REPUBLIC

CDU	Christlich-Demokratische Union Deutschlands
DBD	Demokratische Bauernpartei Deutschlands
KPD	Kommunistische Partei Deutschlands
LDPB	Liberal-Demokratische Partei Deutschlands
NDPD	Nationaldemokratische Partei Deutschlands
SED	Sozialistische Einheitspartei Deutschlands
ZK	Zentralkomitee

HUNGARY

Akad. K.	Akadémiai Kiadó
Áll.	Állami
átd.	átdolgozott
bev.	bevezető
bőv.	bővített
Bp.	Budapest
ell.	*See* jegyz. ell., magy. ell.
fel.	felelős
főszerk.	főszerkesztő
jegyz.	jegyzetek(et)
jegyz. ell.	jegyzetekkel ellátta
K.	Kiadó; Könyvkiadó
kiad.	kiadás
KJK	Közgazdasági és Jogi Kiadó
köt.	kötet
M.	magyar
magy.	magyarázta
magy. ell.	magyarázatokkal ellátta
MSZMP	Magyar Szocialista Munkáspárt
MTA	Magyar Tudományos Akadémia
ny.	nyomda
összeáll.	összeállította

OSZK	Országos Széchényi Könyvtár
Stat. K.	Statisztikai Kiadó
sz.	szám; számú
szerk.	szerkesztette; szerkesztő
tv.	törvény
vál.	válogatás

YUGOSLAVIA

AVNOJ	Antifašističko Vjeće Narodnog Oslobodjenja Jugoslavije
B.	Belgrade
CPY	Communist Party of Yugoslavia
FNRJ	Federativna Narodna Republika Jugoslavije
FPRY	Federal People's Republic of Yugoslavia
KPJ	Komunistička partija Jugoslavije
LCY	League of Communists of Yugoslavia
Lj.	Ljubljana
N.S.	Novi Sad
SFRJ	Socijalistička Federativna Republika Jugoslavije
SFRY	Socialist Federal Republic of Yugoslavia
Sk.	Skopje
SKJ	Savez komunista Jugoslavije
Z.	Zagreb

POLAND

BN	Biblioteka Narodowa
Dz.U.	*Dziennik ustaw*
GUS	Główny Urząd Statystyczny
KAW	Krajowa Agencja Wydawnicza
KiW	Książka i Wiedza
KPP	Komunistyczna Partia Polski
Kr.	Kraków
KRN	Krajowa Rada Narodowa
MON	Ministerstwo Obrony Narodowej
MSZ	Ministerstwo Spraw Zagranicznych
PAN	Polska Akademia Nauk
PAP	Polska Agencja Prasowa
PISM	Polski Instytut Spraw Międzynarodowych
PKWN	Polski Komitet Wyzwolenia Narodowego
PPR	Polska Partia Robotnicza
PUWP	Polish United Workers' Party
PWE	Państwowe Wydawnictwo Ekonomiczne
PWN	Państwowe Wydawnictwo Naukowe
PZPR	Polska Zjednoczona Partia Robotnicza
Wr.	Wrocław
Wwa	Warszawa
wyd.	wydanie (edition, publication), wydawnictwo (publishing house)

ROMANIA

B.	Bucureşti, Bucharest, Bucarest, Bukarest
BO	*Buletinul oficial* pt I
C.C.	Comitet Central, Central Committee
E.P.L.P.	Editura pentru literatură politică
E.S.	Editura de stat
E.S.L.J.	Editura de stat pentru literatură juridică
E.S.P.L.E.J.	Editura de stat pentru literatură economică şi juridică
E.S.P.L.P.	Editura de stat pentru literatură politică
Ed. pol.	Editura politică
Ed. şt.	Editura ştiinţifică
Ed. şt. şi enc.	Editura ştiinţifică şi enciclopedică
MO	*Monitorul oficial* pt I
P.C.R.	Partidul Comunist Român
P.M.R.	Partidul Muncitoresc Român
R.C.P.	Romanian Communist Party
R.W.P.	Romanian Workers' Party

UNION OF SOVIET SOCIALIST REPUBLICS

AN	Akademiia nauk
APN	Akademiia pedagogicheskikh nauk
Arm.	Armianskii/skaia/skoe
ASSR	Avtonomnaia Sovetskaia Sotsialisticheskaia Respublika
Az.	Azerbaidzhanskii/skaia/skoe
Bel.	Belorusskii/skaia/skoe
b-ka	biblioteka
BSSR	Belorusskaia SSR
CC	Central Committee
comp.	compiled
CP	Communist Party
CPSU	Communist Party of the Soviet Union
derzh.	derzhavnii/na/ne
dop.	dopolneniia
ekon.	ekonomicheskii/skaia/skoe
ESSR	Estonskaia SSR
Est.	Estonskii/skaia/skoe
FLPH	Foreign Languages Publishing House
gg.	gody
GIZ	Gosudarstvennoe izdatel'stvo
gl.	glavnyi/naia/noe
glav.	glavnyi/naia/noe
gos.	gosudarstvennyi/naia/noe
Gruz.	Gruzinskii/skaia/skoe

INION	Institut nauchnoi informatsii po obshchestvennym naukam
in-t	institut
issl.	issledovatel'skii/skaia/skoe
iurid.	iuridicheskii/skaia/skoe
izd.	izdanie
izd-vo	izdatel'stvo
izm.	izmeneniia
Kaz.	Kazakhskii/skaia/skoe
Kirg.	Kirgizskii/skaia/skoe
kn.	knizhnaia
KPSS	Kommunisticheskaia partiia Sovetskogo Soiuza
Latv.	Latviiskii/skaia/skoe
Lit.	Litovskii/skaia/skoe
lit-ra	literatura
M.	Moskva
Mold.	Moldavskii/skaia/skoe
MSSR	Moldavskaia SSR
M-vo	Ministerstvo
nauch.	nauchnyi/naia/noe
NII	nauchno-issledovatel'skii institut
otv.	otvetstvennyi
ped.	pedagogicheskii/skaia/skoe
perer.	pererabotannyi/noe/naia
predisl.	predislovie
pril.	prilozhenie
red.	redaktsiia, redaktor
RM	Rad Ministriv
RSFSR	Rossiiskaia Sovetskaia Federativnaia Sotsialisticheskaia Respublika
sist.	sistematizirovannyi/naia/noe
s.-kh.	sel'skokhoziaistvennyi
SM	Sovet Ministrov
sost.	sostavitel', sostoianie
sov.	sovetskii/skaia/skoe
SSR	Sovetskaia Sotsialisticheskaia Respublika
SSSR	Soiuz Sovetskikh Sotsialisticheskikh Respublik
stat.	statisticheskii/skaia/skoe
Tadzh.	Tadzhikskii/skaia/skoe
tekhn.	tekhnicheskii/skaia/skoe
tsentr.	tsentral'nyi/naia/noe
TsSU	Tsentral'noe statisticheskoe upravlenie
Turk.	Turkmenskii/skaia/skoe
Ukr.	Ukrainskii/skaia/skoe
un-t	universitet
upr.	upravlenie
URSR	Ukrains'ka Radians'ka Sotsialistychna Respublika
Uz.	Uzbekskii/skaia/skoe

vses.	vsesoiuznyi/naia/noe
VTsSPS	Vsesoiuznyi tsentral'nyi sovet
	professional'nykh soiuzov
vyp.	vypusk

INTERNATIONAL AND MULTINATIONAL OFFICIAL PUBLICATIONS

CMEA	Council for Mutual Economic Assistance
M.	Moskva/Moscow
SEV	Sovet Ekonomicheskoi Vzaimopomoshchi
WTO	Warsaw Treaty Organization

A ALBANIA

Gregory Walker

INTRODUCTION

Historical development 1944–1980

Albania was established as an independent principality by the Great Powers in 1913, and re-established after its fragmentation during the First World War, first as a republic and from 1928 as a kingdom. The country was occupied and annexed by Italy in April 1939, and German troops supplanted the Italians after Italy's withdrawal from the Axis in September 1943. Albanian resistance movements became increasingly active and successful during the occupation period. The most prominent was that organized by the Communist Party of Albania, which eventually suppressed rival groups. The CPA (Partia Komuniste të Shqipërisë), which was renamed the Party of Labour of Albania (Partia e Punës të Shqipërisë—PPSH) in 1948, was founded in November 1941. The two leading political figures in Albania today were active in the CPA resistance, Enver Hoxha (b. 1908) as its first and only secretary-general, and Mehmet Shehu (b. 1913) as a leading partisan commander, later to become Chairman of the Council of Ministers.

The CPA took control of the country as the Germans withdrew in late 1944, and announced Albania's liberation on 29 November of that year. The People's Republic of Albania (Republika Popullore e Shqipërisë—RPSH) was proclaimed on 10 January 1946 by a Constituent Assembly which approved the republic's first constitution on 14 March 1946. This constitution was closely modelled on that recently adopted by Tito's Yugoslavia (except that it did not envisage a federal structure), and exemplified the very close political and economic relations between the two countries which existed between their liberation and 1948. Indeed, it was widely believed that the Yugoslav government, at least, contemplated Albania's eventual incorporation into Yugoslavia as a constituent republic.

Albania's rejection and condemnation of Yugoslavia came on 1 July 1948, after the latter's break with the USSR and its expulsion from the Cominform. Albania then turned directly to the Soviet Union for political support and economic assistance, the first joint economic agreement being signed in September 1948. The country became a member of the CMEA (Comecon) in February 1949, shortly after the organization's foundation, and was a party to the Warsaw Treaty at its signing on 14 May 1955. However, disagreement with Soviet lines of policy began to emerge in 1956, after the USSR's *rapprochement* with Yugoslavia and Khrushchev's denunciation of Stalin. The Albanian leadership saw no grounds for a reconciliation with Tito, and refused—as it still refuses—to cast aspersions on Stalin's memory. In 1961 the USSR abrogated its economic and military agreements with Albania, withdrew Soviet advisers, and evacuated the Vlorë naval base. Relations were totally severed between the two countries in December 1961. Albania took no part in the activities of the CMEA or the Warsaw Treaty Organization after that date, formally renouncing membership of the WTO in September 1968 after the Soviet-led invasion of Czechoslovakia.

China, whose denunciation of the Soviet Union was soon to follow Albania's, quickly assumed the role of Albania's patron, and was the country's principal source of economic aid for fifteen years. The PLA launched its own 'ideological and cultural revolution' with the Central Committee's 'Open letter' of 4 March 1966, initiating reforms in the bureaucracy and changes in economic organization, but it was a revolution which remained firmly under Party control. (The English text of the 'Open letter' is printed in *Information bulletin* (A31), 18(2), 1966, pp. 18–36).

Cautious efforts to modify the country's isolation within Europe began in the late 1960s. Full diplomatic relations with Yugoslavia and Greece were re-established in 1971, and by 1978 Albania maintained relations with eighty-two countries. The leadership nevertheless remained rigidly opposed both to Western ideological influences and to what it regarded as the 'revisionist' policies of the USSR and its allies. The new constitution adopted in December 1976 emphasized the leadership's view of Albania's stand by changing the state's name to the People's Socialist Republic of Albania (Republika Popullore Socialiste të Shqipërisë—RPSSH). Albania's most recent political realignment was announced by an editorial in *Zëri i popullit* on 7 July 1977, which began a campaign of condemnation against the Chinese for cultivating better relations with the West after Mao's death. This culminated in the severance of relations and the ending of Chinese aid in July 1978.

Party and state structure

The Party of Labour of Albania has been recognized by the constitutions of 1950 and 1976 as the nation's source of political initiative and guidance. The PLA's highest organ is nominally its Congress, which has met every four or five years since 1948. The Congress elects a Central Committee (Komitet Qëndror) of—in 1976—115 members, which should meet in plenum at least three times a year.

The CC in turn elects a Politburo—of seventeen in 1976—which is regarded as the real seat of power in the country. It has for many years been under the firm control of Enver Hoxha as First Secretary (formerly Secretary-General): under the 1976 constitution, the First Secretary's post confers on him *ex officio* the supreme command of the armed forces and the chairmanship of the Defence Council. The Politburo is served by the administrative staff of the CC's Secretariat, which functions as a supervisory bureaucracy *vis-à-vis* the organs of the national government, on the same principles as those under which PLA committees at local level effectively control town and district administrations. Party resolutions and directives have in practice the force of law, even if lacking legal status in the strict sense.

The supreme organ of state—as distinct from party—power is (again nominally) the People's Assembly (Kuvëndi Popullor), a single-chamber nationally elected legislature of 250 which meets for short sessions twice a year. The Assembly appoints a fourteen-member Presidium which exercises its powers between sessions, and the Chairman of the Presidium (currently Haxhi Lleshi) is titular Head of State. The Assembly appoints the Council of Ministers (Këshilli i Ministrave), currently chaired by Mehmet Shehu, which is the highest executive organ of government. For purposes of local government, the country is divided into twenty-six districts, administered under party supervision by the executive committees of elected People's Councils.

Several other national-level bodies, administratively distinct but under party control, have 'mass-organizational' roles. Their publications are not included in this bibliography. They include the youth organization (Bashkimi i Rinisë së Punës së Shqipërisë), the women's organization (Bashkimi i Grave të Shqipërisë), the trade-union organization (Bashkimet Profesionale të Shqipërisë), and—broadest-based of all—the Democratic Front (Fronti Demokratike), which incorporates all citizens over the age of eighteen. Besides mass economic and cultural campaigns, all local and national elections are held under the aegis of the Democratic Front, not under that of the PLA.

Official publishing

Publications issued under the auspices of the government and the PLA appear through several different outlets. There is no single 'official' publishing house, although of course all publishing operations are under party and state direction. The official gazette, *Gazeta zyrtare*, issues those decrees and other formal legislation from the People's Assembly and the government which are intended for public consultation. The two main general publishing houses in Tiranë, 'Naim Frashëri' and '8 Nëntori', both include many officially sponsored publications in their output. Many of the ministries and other organs of central government also publish material within their own spheres of responsibility: for example, the Presidium of the People's Assembly (Presidiumi i Kuvëndit Popullor), the Prime Minister's Office (Kryeministria), the Statistical Directorate (Drejtoria e Statistikës), the State Planning Commission (Komisioni e Planit të Shtetit), and—before its abolition in 1966—the Ministry of Justice (Ministria e Drejtësisë). Most of the PLA's official publications are issued through the main publishing houses, but the Institute of Party History and the

3

Institute of Marxist-Leninist Studies, both attached to the Central Committee of the PLA, have themselves published collections of official documents.

Even by the standards of other East European socialist countries, and taking account of the country's small size (its 1978 population was 2,563,400), Albania issues a very restricted amount of official documents and information to the general public. Only three statistical abstracts, in particular, have been published in the last decade; and publicly available official documentation of many areas of national life exists only in an incomplete or outdated state, or has no bibliographically acknowledged existence.

GENERAL BIBLIOGRAPHIES

There are no separate bibliographies of Albanian official publications. The national bibliographies listed below are believed to include most publicly available official material falling within their terms of reference.

National bibliographies

A1 Kastrati, J. *Bibliografi shqipe (29.xi.1944–31.xii.1958)*. [Albanian bibliography (29.11.1944–31.12.1958)]. T.: Naim Frashëri, 1959. 498 pp.
   About 2,400 entries, for separately published items only but including among these many official publications. Serials are omitted except for some annuals. Personal name index only.

A2 *Bibliografia e Republikës Popullore të Shqipërisë. Vepra origjinale dhe përkthime*. [Bibliography of the People's Republic of Albania. Original and translated works]. T.: Biblioteka Kombëtare, 1960–4. Quarterly.
   Includes separately published works only. Annual author indexes from 1962, author/title index 1964. Continued by A4a.

A3 *Bibliografia e periodikut të Republikës Popullore të Shqipërisë*. [Periodical bibliography of the People's Republic of Albania]. T.: Biblioteka Kombëtare, 1961–4. Quarterly.
   Covers main articles in most journals and newspapers, including party and government announcements in *Zëri i popullit* and *Bashkimi*. Annual author indexes. Continued by A4b.

A4 *Bibliografia kombëtare e Republikës Popullore Socialiste të Shqipërisë*. [National bibliography of the People's Socialist Republic of Albania]. T.: Biblioteka Kombëtare, 1965–.
   Before 1977, title omitted 'Socialiste'. Published in two series:

A4a *Libri shqip*. [Albanian books]. Quarterly.
   Continuation of A2. Annual name/title indexes from 1976 only.

A4b *Artikujt e periodikut shqip*. [Albanian periodical articles]. Monthly.
   Continuation of A3. 6 issues in 1965. About 50 journal and newspaper titles are covered by each issue. Annual name index.

Other general bibliographies

A5a   Hetzer, A. & Roman, V. S. *Arbeitsmaterialien zu einer Landesbibliographie Albanien.* (On cover: *Albanien-Bibliographie*). [Material for a bibliography of Albania]. Bremen: Universität, Bibliothek, 1980–. To be in 6 vols.

Heft IV (law) and Heft V (economy) published in 1980. Albanian-language material strongly emphasized, especially periodical literature, but only Heft IV (so far) provides German translations of titles. Otherwise largely unannotated. Other volumes are planned as: I—generalia, II—history, III—politics, VI—indexes.

A5b   *Südosteuropa-Bibliographie.* Hrsg. von G. Krallert-Sattler. (Südost-Inst. München). München: Oldenbourg, 1956–.

Bd. I ed. by F. Valjavec. Bd. V, Teil 2 (publ. 1976), is the latest so far issued. The sections on Albania are contained in: Bd. I (1945–50), Teil 2, pp. 183–95; Bd. II (1951–5), Teil 2, pp. 363–82; Bd. III (1956–60), Teil 2, pp. 3–37; Bd. IV (1961–5), Teil 2, pp. 5–61; Bd. V (1966–70), Teil 2, pp. 5–111. Albanian and Western publications, both books and articles, are included, the scale of coverage having risen from 215 items in Bd. I to 1,601 in Bd. V. The sections 'Geschichte und Politik', 'Staat und Recht' (especially), and 'Wirtschaft und Sozialwesen' include some official publications. Gives German translations of Albanian titles. 'Alphabetical' (chiefly name) index at end of each part (each vol. for Bd. I and II).

CONSTITUTIONAL DOCUMENTS

A6   *Projekti i Statutit të Republikës Popullore të Shqipërisë.* [Draft constitution of the People's Republic of Albania]. T.: 1946. 24 pp.

The final 1946 constitution was published in *Gazeta zyrtare*, no. 19, 19 March 1946. An English translation is in *Constitutions of nations*, ed. A. J. Peaslee (1950), vol. 1, pp. 35–50. The amended constitution of 1950, which remained in force until 1976, was published separately as:

A7   *Kushtetuta e Republikës Popullore të Shqipërisë.* [The constitution of the People's Republic of Albania]. T.: Mihal Duri, 1950. 20 pp.

Frequent republication subsequently. An English translation (title as above) was published in Tiranë, 1964.

A8   *Konstitutsiia i osnovnye zakonodatel'nye akty Narodnoi Respubliki Albanii.* [Constitution and basic legislative documents of the People's Republic of Albania]. Pod red. N. Ia. Kupritsa. (Zakonodatel'stvo stran narodnoi demokratii, 6). M.: Izd-vo inostr. lit-ry, 1951. xxviii, 291 pp.

Russian translations of the 1950 constitution and 23 other measures on elections, planning, citizenship, government administration, local councils, criminal responsibility, land reform, education and the courts, all as amended to 1951.

A9 *Kushtetuta e Republikës Popullore Socialiste të Shqipërisë.* [Constitution of the People's Socialist Republic of Albania]. T.: 8 Nëntori, 1977. 59 pp.

Approved by the People's Assembly 28 December 1976, and published in *Gazeta zyrtare,* 1976(5), pp. 75–104. An English translation (title as above) was issued in 1977 by the same publisher.

LAW CODES AND OTHER GENERAL LEGISLATIVE DOCUMENTS

State legislation (as distinct from party instructions) emanates from the People's Assembly and its Presidium, from the Council of Ministers, and from individual ministries and other government organs. Such documents are designated by a variety of titles: as a law (ligj), code (kod), decree (dekret or udhëzim), resolution (vendim), directive (direktivë, dispozitë), regulation (rregullore) or order (urdhër). *Gazeta zyrtare* publishes some of this legislation, including major codes; but, judging from the serial numbers of the measures printed, a considerable number of other measures are not made public. Important documents are often also issued separately, collections of legislation on special subjects from time to time, and occasionally more general collections of legislation currently in force.

A10 *Gazeta zyrtare e Republikës Popullore Socialiste të Shqipërisë.* [Official gazette of the People's Socialist Republic of Albania]. T.: 1944–. Irregular.

1923–44 entitled *Fletorja zyrtare.* 'Socialiste' added to present title with issue 5 of 1976. Prints a selection only of measures approved by the People's Assembly, its Presidium and the Council of Ministers.

A11 *Drejtësia popullore.* [People's justice]. T.: 1947–. 6 issues p.a.

Organ of the Supreme Court and Procuracy-General, formerly of the Ministry of Justice until it abolition in 1966. Carries authoritative commentary on legislation, and from time to time the text of legal measures. Heft IV of A5a amounts to a selective index of articles published in this journal.

A12 *Indeksi i përgjithëshëm i legjislacionit të Republikës Popullore të Shqipërisë prej çlirimit deri më 31/XII/1950 simbas lëndës dhe simbas radhës alfabetike.* [General index of legislation of the PRA from the liberation to 31.12.1950, arranged by subject and alphabetically]. T.: 1953. 218 pp. [Not seen].

A13 *Ligjet kryesore civile të Republikës Popullore të Shqipërisë.* [The principal civil laws of the PRA]. (Min. e Drejtësisë). T.: N.SH.B., 1957. 231 pp. [Not seen].

A14 *Kodifikimi i përgjithëshëm i legjislacionit në fuqi të Republikës Popullore të Shqipërisë. (1945–1957).* [General codification of legislation in force of the PRA (1945–1957)]. T.: Kryeministria.

Vëllimi I. 1958. 1919 pp. [Not seen]. *Aneks 1: 1958.* 1959. 672 pp.

Aneks 2: 1959–60. 1961. 731 pp. *Kodet.* 1961. 687 pp.
The *Kodet* volume contains the Constitution and the Civil, Family, Civil Procedure, Criminal, Criminal Procedure and Customs Codes.

A15 *Përmbledhëse e përgjithshme e legjislacionit në fuqi të Republikës Popullore të Shqipërisë (1945–1971).* [General collection of legislation in force in the PRA (1945–1971)]. T.: 1971. 755 pp. *Aneks 1972.* 1973. 89 pp. *Aneksi 1973.* 1974. 84 pp. *Aneks 1976.* n.d. 83 pp. Title begins *Përmbledhje . . .* in some sources. [Not seen].

Law codes

Most of the Albanian law codes have appeared in more than one form since the liberation. The principal dates of change are as follows:
Criminal Code: 1948; 1952 with amendments 1957 and 1958; 1977.
Code of Criminal Procedure: 1953; 1979.
Civil Code: 1955–7.
Code of Civil Procedure: 1958.
Labour Code: 1947; 1956 with amendments 1965; 1966; 1980.
Family Code: 1948; 1965.

Besides publication in *Gazeta zyrtare*, and where appropriate in A14 and A15, the following are known to have been separately published:

A16 *Kodi penal i R.P. të Shqipërisë.* [Criminal Code of the PRA]. T.: Bot. i Min. së Drejtësisë, 1959. 175 pp.

A17 *Kodi penal i Republikës Popullore Socialiste të Shqipërisë.* [Criminal Code of the PSRA]. T.: 8 Nëntori, 1977. [Not seen].
German translation and commentary in *Jahrbuch für Ostrecht,* 20 (1979), pp. 223–82.

A18 *Kodi i procedurës penale i R.P. të Shqipërisë.* [Code of Criminal Procedure of the PRA]. T.: Bot. i Min. së Drejtësisë, 1959. 186 pp. [Not seen].

A19 *Ugolovnyi i ugolovno-protsessual'nyi kodeksy Narodnoi Respubliki Albanii.* [Criminal and Criminal Procedure Codes of the PRA]. Pod red. V. F. Kirichenko. (Kodeksy stran narodnoi demokratii). M.: Izd-vo inostr. lit-ry, 1954. 234 pp.
Russian translations of the 1952 Criminal Code and 1953 Criminal Procedure Code. The Criminal Code with amendments to 1958 is translated in: *Narodnaia Respublika Albaniia* (Ugolovnoe zakonodatel'stvo zarubezhnykh sots. gosudarstv). M.: Gosud. izd-vo iurid. lit-ry, 1961. 156 pp.

A20 *Kodi i procedurës civile i Republikës Popullore të Shqipërisë.* [Code of Civil Procedure of the PRA]. T.: Min. e Drejtësisë, 1958. 164 pp. [Not seen].

A21 *Kodi i punës.* [Labour Code]. T.: 1957. 340 pp. [Not seen].

A22 *Kodi i punës i Republikës Popullore të Shqipërisë.* [Labour Code of the PRA]. T.: Naim Frashëri, 1970. 71 pp.
English translation in *Information bulletin* (A31), vol. 17 (1966), special issue, pp. 29–45.

A23 *Kodi i familjes i Republikës Popullore të Shqipërisë.* [Family Code of the PRA]. T.: Naim Frashëri, [1965]. 68 pp.
German translation in *WGO*, 7(6) (1965), pp. 337–59.

Other general legislative documents

A24 *Udhëzime dhe vendime të Gjykatës së Lartë të R.P.Sh. Përmbledhje.*
[Decrees and decisions of the Supreme Court of the PRA. A collection]. T.: Naim Frashëri, 1965. 506 pp.
Contains documents issued 1958–62. Continued by A25.

A25 *Udhëzime dhe vendime të Gjykatës së Lartë të R.P.SH. (Përmbledhje të viteve 1963, 1964, 1965, 1966).* [Decrees and decisions of the Supreme Court of the PRA. (Collection for the years 1963, 1964, 1965 and 1966)]. T.: Naim Frashëri, 1972. 234 pp.
A successor volume covers the years 1967–70. The subtitle ends
... *viteve 1967, 1968, 1969 dhe 1970.* T.: 8 Nëntori, 1975. 461 pp.
[Not seen].

A26 *Ligje, rregullore dhe udhëzime për pushtetin lokal.* [Laws, regulations and decrees on local government]. T.: Kryeministria, 1952–5. 3 vols.
[Not seen].

A27 *Ligje, dekrete dhe dispozita të tjera në fuqi për këshillat popullore të fshatrave.* [Laws, decrees and other ordinances in force on village councils]. T.: Presidiumi i Kuvëndit Popullor, 1965. 120 pp. [Not seen].

A28 *Osnovnye normativnye akty o mestnykh organakh gosudarstvennoi vlasti i gosudarstvennogo upravleniia Narodnoi Respubliki Albanii.*
[Basic legal documents on local organs of state power and administration]. (Mestnye organy gosud. vlasti i upravleniia zarubezh. sots. gosudarstv). M.: Gosud. izd-vo iurid. lit-ry, 1958. 107 pp.

A29 *Zhvillimi i legjislacionit të Republikës Popullore të Shqipërisë.* [The development of legislation in the PRA]. T.: 8 Nëntori, 1975. 324 pp.
Prepared under the authority of the Supreme Court. [Not seen].

GENERAL PARTY DOCUMENTS

A30 *Rruga e partisë.* [The party road]. T.: 1953–. Monthly.
Theoretical and political organ of the PLA Central Committee.
Besides authoritatively approved views of domestic and international issues, includes the texts of many major speeches and other party documents.

A31 *Information bulletin of the Central Committee of the Party of Labour of Albania.* T.: 1949–71? Irregular.

Carried a wide variety (though a limited number) of translated communiqués, speeches, Plenum decisions, articles from *Zëri i popullit* and other material, not exclusively from PLA sources. Also published in French as *Bulletin d'information*. In many respects continued by *Albania today* (A51).

A32 *Çështje të ndërtimit të partisë. Material e dokumenta.* [Questions of party construction. Documentary material]. Pjesa I [–VIII]-të. T.: Ndërmarrja shtetërore e botimeve dhe e shpërndarjes, 1948. 8 vols. [Not seen].

A33 *Dokumente kryesore të Partisë së Punës së Shqipërisë.* [Basic documents of the PLA]. Vëllimi 1–. (Inst. i Hist. së Partisë pranë KQ të PPSH). T.: 1960–.

Title begins *Dokumenta* . . . in vëll. 1–4. Vëll. 3 and 4 issued under the auspices of the Inst. i Studimeve Marksiste-Leniniste. Includes congress, plenum and other CC documents, party–government joint declarations, and politburo and secretariat announcements and orders. Vëll. 1 (publ. 1960, expanded 2nd ed. 1971) covers 1941–8; vëll. 2 (1961), 1949–56; vëll. 3 (1970), 1957–61; vëll. 4 (1970), 1961–5; vëll. 5 (1974), 1966–70; vëll. 6 (1978), 1971–5. Continuation probable.

A34 *Tregues për Dokumentet Kryesore të PPSH.* [Index to the Basic Documents of the PLA]. Vëllimi I: 1941–8. Bot. II. T.: 1976. 107 pp. Vëllimi II: 1949–56. Bot. II. T.: 8 Nëntori, 1979. 117 pp.

Continuation probable. [Not seen].

A35 *Statuti i Partisë së Punës të Shqipërisë.* [Constitution of the PLA]. T.: Nëntor, 1948. 29 pp. [Not seen].

A36 *Statuti i Partisë së Punës të Shqipërisë. Miratuar nga Kongresi III i PPSH. Me ndryshimet e pjesshme të bëra nga Kongreset IV, V, VI dhe VII të PPSH.* [The constitution of the Party of Labour of Albania. Adopted by the 3rd Congress of the PLA. Including the amendments made at the 4th, 5th, 6th and 7th Congresses of the PLA]. T.: 1977. 150 pp.

English translation (title as above) published T.: 8 Nëntori, 1977. Earlier versions of this, the 1956 party constitution, were published after the 3rd and each subsequent congress.

Party congresses of the PLA

The PLA has so far (as of 1980) held congresses in 1948 (the only one under its original title of the Communist Party of Albania), 1952, 1956, 1961, 1966, 1971 and 1976. A substantial collection of documents (*Përmbledhje materialesh*) relating to the proceedings of each congress has been published after the event, with the exception of the 3rd congress of 1956, for which no such collection has been traced. For every congress since the 4th (1961) at least, Enver Hoxha's 'Report on the activity of the Central Committee' has been published separately ('Raport mbi veprimtarinë e Komitetit Qëndror të PPSH') and in English translation. Details of the document collections are as follows:

A37   *Kongresi i I-re i Partisë Komuniste të Shqipërisë (8–22 Nëntor 1948).* T.: M. Duri, 1950. 653 pp.
Also published in French translation, 1951. [Not seen].

A38   *Kongresi i II-të i Partisë së Punës së Shqipërisë.* T.: M. Duri, 1952. 424 pp. [Not seen].

A39   *Kongresi IV i Partisë së Punës së Shqipërisë. (Përmbledhje materialesh). 13–20 shkurt 1961.* T.: Naim Frashëri, 1961. 380 pp.

A40   *Kongresi i pestë i Partisë së Punës të Shqipërisë, 1–8 Nëndor 1966. (Përmbledhje materialesh).* T.: Naim Frashëri, 1966. 402 pp.

A41   *Kongresi VI i Partisë së Punës të Shqipërisë: 1–7 Nëndor 1971. (Përmbledhje materialesh).* T.: Naim Frashëri, 1972. 544 pp.

A42   *Kongresi VII i Partisë së Punës së Shqipërisë, 1–7 Nëntor 1976. (Përmbledhje materialesh).* T.: 8 Nëntori, 1977. 511 pp.

Party conferences were intended to be called at least annually by the Central Committee for the discussion of party policy, but only two were apparently ever held, the first in 1943 and the second in 1950. The latter is recorded by:

A43   *Konferenca e dytë nacionale e Partisë së Punës së Shqipërisë. (Përmbledhje materialesh).* T.: Mihal Duri, [1950?]. 234 pp. [Not seen].

A44   *Historia e Partisë së Punës të Shqipërisë.* [History of the Party of Labour of Albania]. (Inst. i Studimeve Marksiste-Leniniste pranë KQ të PPSH). T.: Naim Frashëri, 1969. 550 pp.
The only full, authorized party history so far published, although its view of—for example—relations with China must by now be regarded by the leadership as in need of revision. No documents, and few quotations from them, are printed. An English translation (title as above) was issued by the same publisher in 1971.

STATISTICS

The regular publication of national statistics in Albania lasted only from 1958 until 1973, with a very marked decrease in the data provided taking place for the years 1966 onwards. Since 1973, only two volumes of statistics are known to have been issued to the public, neither of them extensive.

A45   *Vjetari statistikor i R.P.SH.* [Statistical annual of the PRA]. (Drejtoria e Statistikës). T.: 1958–73. Annual vols for 1958 to 1961 and 1963 to 1966, biannual for 1967/68, 1969/70 and 1971/72.
From 1958 to 1961 entitled *Anuari statistikor....* Volumes for

1966 onwards are only about one-third the length of those for earlier years, omitting e.g. trade statistics itemized by country.

A46 *Republika Popullore Shqipërisë në jubileun e 30-vjetorit të themelimit të PPSH. Botim e veçantë në shifra.* [The PRA at the celebration of 30 years since the foundation of the PLA. A special publication of figures]. (Drejtoria e Statistikës). T.: 1971. 175 pp.
More popular presentation and even more limited data than that of the regular statistical yearbook. Latest figures are for 1970.

A47 *30 vjet Shqipëri socialiste. Shifra dhe fakte mbi zhvillimin e ekonomisë dhe kulturës.* [30 years of socialist Albania. Figures and facts on its economic and cultural development]. (Drejtoria e përgjithshme e Statistikës). T.: 1974. 240 pp.
Similar in presentation to A46. Latest figures are for 1973.

A48 *35 vjet Shqipëri socialiste të dhëna statistikore për zhvillimin e ekonomisë dhe të kulturës.* [35 years of socialist Albania in statistical data on its economic and cultural development]. (Drejtoria e Statistikës). T.: 1979. 161 pp.
Similar presentation to A46 and A47. Latest figures are for 1979.

OTHER GENERAL SOURCES OF DOCUMENTATION

A49 *Zëri i popullit.* [The voice of the people]. T.: 1942–. 6 issues per week.
The newspaper is an organ of the PLA's Central Committee, and regularly carries party statements and pronouncements of the leadership. Its editorials are often used to announce new policy initiatives, and many have been published as pamphlets in English and other languages.

A50 *Bashkimi.* [Unity]. T.: 1943–. 6 issues per week.
Newspaper of the Democratic Front, it likewise includes shorter items of official documentary material and authorized statements.

A51 *Albania today.* T.: 1971–. 6 issues p.a.
Also published in French, German, Spanish and Italian. Intended for a foreign readership, the journal carries translations of important press items and of articles and speeches by party and government leaders. In many respects a replacement for A31.

INTERNATIONAL RELATIONS

A52 *Dokumenta mbi miqësinë shqiptaro–sovjetike.* [Documents on Albanian–Soviet friendship]. (Univ. Shtet. i Tiranës; Inst. i Hist. së P.P.SH.; Shoqëria e Miqësisë Shqipëri-B.R.S.S.). T.: 1957. 551 pp.
156 of the 251 documents, speeches and articles included deal with Albanian–Soviet relations from 1945 to 1957. Published before Albania's open break with the USSR.

A53 Griffith, W. E. *Albania and the Sino-Soviet rift*. Cambridge, Mass.: MIT Press, 1963. 423 pp.

Besides an account of Soviet–Albanian relations up to November 1962, prints English translations of 34 relevant documents from the period 1960–2, chiefly Albanian speeches and communiqués, but also a few from the Soviet side.

A54 *The facts about Soviet–Albanian relations*. T.: Naim Frashëri, 1964, 165 pp.

A collection of documents (chiefly translated from items in *Zëri i popullit*) from the period October 1961–April 1963.

A55 *Documents in connection with the meeting of the Political Consultative Committee of the Warsaw Treaty, which was held from January 19 to 20, 1965*. T.: Naim Frashëri, 1965. 27 pp.

On Albania's rejection of an approach by the other WTO members.

A56 *Letter of the CC of the Party of Labour and the Government of Albania to the CC of the Communist Party and the Government of China (July 29, 1978)*. T.: 8 Nëntori, 1978. 56 pp.

Final Albanian response to the termination of Chinese economic and military aid, denouncing it as a 'perfidious and hostile act'.

MILITARY AFFAIRS

A57 *Dokumenta të Shtabit të Përgjithshëm dhe të Komandës së Përgjithëshme të Ushtrisë Nacional-Çlirimtare Shqiptare (5 korrik 1943–10 korrik 1945)*. [Documents of the General Staff and the General HQ of the Albanian National Liberation Army (5 July 1943–10 July 1945)]. T.: Inst. të Hist. së Partisë pranë KQ të PPSH, 1965–6. 2 vols.

464 documents included.

ECONOMIC AFFAIRS

A58 *Probleme ekonomike*. [Economic problems]. T.: 1954–. Quarterly.

Entitled *Ekonomia popullore* from vol. 1 to vol. 19 (1954–72), and published in 6 issues p.a. 1954–74. Until 1972 an organ of the State Planning Commission, thereafter issued under the aegis of the Institute of Economic Studies of the Academy of Sciences. From time to time prints major documents on economic affairs, and occasional statistical material.

Planning

The Albanian economy has been administered under a series of five-year plans since 1951, preceded by a Two-Year Plan in 1949–50. A report on the achievements of each plan and the prospects for its successor is presented to each party congress (a function which has always been performed by the Chairman of the Council of Ministers, Mehmet Shehu). Shehu's report, and the draft and final directives for the forthcoming plan, have usually been published separately as well as in the periodical press (usually *Ekonomia popullore*, now *Probleme ekonomike*). The separate publications which have been traced are as follows.

A59 Shehu, M. *Raport mbi planin e parë pesëvjeçar të zhvillimit të ekonomisë popullore të Republikës Popullore të Shqipërisë.* T.: Mihal Duri, 1952. 79 pp.
Also publ. in French. [Not seen].

A60 Shehu, M. *Rapport sur les résultats de la réalisation du premier plan quinquennal et des directives du deuxième plan quinquennal* [. . .]. T.: 1956. 119 pp.
Albanian original not traced as separate publication. [Not seen].

A61 *Vendimet, rezolucioni dhe direktivat mbi planin II pesëvjeçar.* [Decisions, resolutions and directives on the second Five-Year Plan]. T.: N.Sh.B., 1956. 75 pp. [Not seen].

A62 Shehu, M. *Raport mbi direktivat e Kongresit IV të P.P.SH. për planin e tretë pesëvjeçar* [. . .]. [Report on the directives of the fourth Congress of the PLA for the third Five-Year Plan]. T.: Naim Frashëri, 1961. 99 pp.

A63 *Vendimet, rezolucioni dhe direktivat mbi planin III pesëvjeçar* [. . .]. [Decisions, resolutions and directives on the third Five-Year Plan]. T.: Naim Frashëri, 1961. 84 pp. [Not seen].

A64 Shehu, M. *Raport mbi direktivat e Kongresit të V të P.P.SH. për planin e katërt pesëvjeçar* [. . .] *per vitin 1966–1970* [. . .]. [Report on the directives of the fifth Congress of the PLA for the fourth Five-Year Plan for the years 1966–1970]. T.: Naim Frashëri, 1966. 122 pp.
Also publ. in English.

A65 *Direktivat e Kongresit V të PPSH mbi planin e katërt pesëvjeçar* [. . .] *për vitet 1966–1970.* [Directives of the fifth Congress of the PLA for the fourth Five-Year Plan for the years 1966–1970]. T.: Naim Frashëri, 1966. 29 pp.
Draft directives also publ. separately as *Projekt direktivat . . .*, T.: Naim Frashëri, 1966.

A66 Shehu, M. *Raport mbi direktivat i Kongresit të 6-të të PPSH për planin e pestë pesëvjeçar (1971–1975)* [. . .]. [Report on the directives of the sixth Congress of the PLA for the fifth Five-Year Plan (1971–1975)]. T.: Naim Frashëri, 1971. 158 pp.
Also publ. in English.

A67 *Direktivat e Kongresit VI të PPSH mbi planin e pestë pesëvjeçar* [. . .] *për vitet 1971–1975.* [Directives of the sixth Congress of the PLA for the fifth Five-Year Plan for the years 1971–1975]. T.: Naim Frashëri, 1971. 47 pp.

Draft directives also publ. separately as *Projektdirektivat* ..., T.: Naim Frashëri, 1971.

A68   Shehu, M. *Raport mbi direktivat e Kongresit të 7-të të PPSH për planin e gjashtë pesëvjeçar* [...]. [Report on the directives of the seventh Congress of the PLA for the sixth Five-Year Plan]. T.: 8 Nëntori, 1976. [Not seen].

Foreign trade

A69   *Summary of principal provisions of the law on foreign trade*. T.: 1973. 91 pp. [Not seen].

SOCIAL AFFAIRS

Social security

Until December 1965, social security provision in Albania was the responsibility of the trade unions, but was then transferred to the control of the State Committee for Labour and Wages.

A70   *Sigurimet shoqërore shtetërore*. [State social security]. (Bashkimet Profesionale të Shqipërisë, Këshilli Qëndror). T.: 1958. 287 pp. [Not seen].

A71   *Sigurimet shoqërore shtetërore*. [State social security]. T.: Naim Frashëri, 1968. 126 pp.

Land reform

A72   *Osnovnye zakonodatel'nye akty po agrarnym preobrazovaniiam v zarubezhnykh sotsialisticheskikh stranakh. Vyp. 4*. [Basic legislation on land reforms in socialist countries abroad. Vol. 4]. M.: Izd-vo iurid. lit-ry, 1958. 238 pp.

Pages 5–59 contain relevant extracts from the Albanian Constitution, and the text in Russian of 15 other Albanian measures, all as at 1 January 1957.

CULTURAL AFFAIRS

A73   *Mbi riorganizimin e sistemit arësimor të R.P.SH. (Materiale dhe dokumenta)*. [On the reorganization of the educational system in the PRA. (Materials and documents)]. T.: Drejtoria e Botimeve Shkollore, 1963. 200 pp.

Prints speeches, reports and the law of June 1963 on educational reorganization.

A74   *Për revolucionarizimin e mëtejshëm të shkollës sonë*. [On the further revolutionizing of our schools]. T.: Shtëp. Bot. e Librit Shkollor, 1969. 2 vols.

Collection of documents and speeches on the educational reforms of 1969. [Not seen].

A75 *Ligji dhe vendimi 'Mbi sistemin e ri arsimor'*. [The law and resolution 'On the new educational system']. T.: 1979. 34 pp. [Not seen].

A76 *Partia e Punës e Shqipërisë për shtypin. (Dokumenta e materiale)*. [The Party of Labour of Albania on the press. (Documentary materials)]. T.: Shtëp. Bot. e Librit Politik, 1972. 264 pp.
A later collection with the same title issued 1981, 340 pp. [Not seen].

A77 *Mbrojtja e monumenteve. (Ligje, rregullore, vendime, udhëzime)*. [The protection of monuments. (Laws, regulations, resolutions, decrees)]. T.: Shtëp. Bot. e Librit Politik, 1973. 51 pp. [Not seen].

LEADER'S WORKS

Enver Hoxha has been Secretary-General of the CPA and PLA 1943–54, First Secretary of the PLA since that date, Chairman of the Council of Ministers 1944–54, Foreign Minister 1946–53, Minister of Defence 1944–53, and Commander-in-Chief of the Armed Forces since 1976. The unique status conferred on his pronouncements by the Albanian media and official opinion is consonant with Hoxha's leading role in the country's affairs for 35 years. His speeches and writings have given the lead and supplied the justification for party and government policy since 1944. No other postwar Albanian figure has appeared in print on a remotely comparable scale. In length, circulation and public prominence, the only other living communist leaders whose works approach Hoxha's are Kim Il-Sung and Nicolae Ceauşescu.

A78 Hoxha, E. *Vepra*. [Works]. T.: Naim Frashëri/8 Nëntori, 1968–.
Vol. 31, covering the period January–March 1966, was published in 1980. Indexes have been published separately as: *Tregues për Veprat e shokut Enver Hoxha*, T.: 8 Nëntori, 1975–, with 5 vols having appeared by 1980.

A79 Hoxha, E. *Selected works*. T.: 8 Nëntori, 1974–.
English translation. Vol. 3, covering the period June 1960–October 1965, was published in 1980.

A80 Hoxha, E. *Raporte e fjalime*. [Reports and speeches]. T.: Naim Frashëri, 1969–.
Not a comprehensive collection. Volumes covering 1965–6, 1967–8 (both publ. 1969), 1969–70 (publ. 1970) and 1976–7 (publ. 1980) have been traced.

A81 Hoxha, E. *Speeches, conversations and articles*. T.: 8 Nëntori, 1974–.
6 vols, covering the period 1961–73, published by 1980, the earlier ones entitled *Speeches*, then *Speeches and articles*.

A82 Hoxha, E. *Imperializmi dhe revolucioni*. [Imperialism and the revolution]. T.: 8 Nëntori, 1978. 455 pp.

Basically a polemic against Chinese 'revisionism'. Published in English (title as above), T.: 8 Nëntori, 1979.

A83   Hoxha, E. *Shënime për Kinën.* [Reflections on China]. T.: 8 Nëntori, 1979. 2 vols.

Vol. 1 covers 1962–72, vol. 2 1973–7. Published in English (title as above), T.: 8 Nëntori, 1979.

B BULGARIA

Garth M. Terry

INTRODUCTION

On 8 September 1944, the Soviet Union declared war on Bulgaria and ordered the Red Army to cross the frontier. The following day the Fatherland Front—FF (Otechestven Front)—a Bulgarian communist-dominated coalition of left-wing parties formed in 1942 in opposition to the Bulgarian government—engineered a bloodless coup and seized power. A new government was formed in which the communists occupied the key positions, most notably the ministries of the interior and justice, and, although numerically in the minority, they gradually consolidated their hold under the umbrella of the occupying Soviet armed forces.

Consolidation of power meant the wholesale liquidation of anti-communists (1944–5), the elimination of non-communists and non-conformists in the FF (1945–6), the liquidation of tolerated opposition throughout the country (1947–8), and a purge of native communists (1949–50). By 1949 the country was under formal communist control and an outright Sovietization drive began.

On 8 September 1946, a referendum was held to abolish the monarchy and a People's Republic (Narodna Republika) was proclaimed. On 27 October elections were held for a Grand National Assembly (Veliko Narodno Sŭbranie) and, despite intimidation, the opposition parties polled 30 per cent of the electorate and obtained 99 out of the 465 seats. Opposition delegates were tolerated until a Peace Treaty had been signed in 1947. Then Nikola Petkov, head of the opposition, was arrested, tried, and executed. By 1948 all opposition parties had been dissolved, the only exceptions being the Bulgarian National Agrarian Union which still exists today but under communist control, and the FF, now a monolithic political organization dominated by the communists and serving their goals of mass indoctrination and participation. On 4 December

1947, a new constitution was adopted which laid down the foundations of the new Bulgarian legal and political system. The Grand National Assembly was replaced by a National Assembly which first met in December 1949.

The 1947 'Dimitrov' constitution, which replaced the Tŭrnovo constitution in force since 1879, was closely modelled on Stalin's Soviet constitution of 1936. It provided for a unicameral National Assembly (Narodno Sŭbranie) as the sole legislative body to be elected every four years (extended to five years by the 1971 constitution). The National Assembly elects the Presidium (renamed the State Council in 1971) and appoints the government, both bodies in theory being responsible to it. In practice, however, the National Assembly meets very infrequently and has become a rubber stamp for government acts and decisions. When it is not in session, power is invested in the Presidium. This permanent body has assumed during the course of time both legislative and executive functions—it now not only promulgates and interprets laws but also legislates by decree. Supreme executive and administrative power is vested in the government or Council of Ministers (Ministerskiia Sŭvet) headed by a chairman or prime minister. In theory it is responsible to the National Assembly and Presidium.

The territory of the People's Republic of Bulgaria is divided for administrative purposes into communes (obshtini) and districts (okrŭzi); there were 1,260 and 28 respectively in December 1972. They are governed by People's Councils (Narodni Sŭveti) elected for a period of two and a half years. Executive committees carry on the work of the Councils between sessions. They take decisions on questions of local significance (economic, social and cultural) within the limits of their competence in conformity with the laws and general directives of the higher organs of government.

The judicial system is centralized under the Ministry of Justice which has extensive powers of control and appointment. Justice is administered by district, regional and military courts headed by a Supreme Court. Questions concerning the constitutionality of laws are, according to the constitution, the province of the National Assembly and the Presidium.

The 1947 constitution remained in force until a new one was adopted in May 1971. One major change was the replacement of the Presidium by a State Council (Dŭrzhaven Sŭvet; see *DV* no. 29, 18 May 1971) which received greatly increased powers. The 1971 constitution, unlike its predecessor, refers for the first time to the leading role of the Bulgarian Communist Party in society (see *DV* no. 39, 18 May 1971). The Party's influence throughout government is, in fact, all pervading. Government policies are formulated by the Politburo and channelled through the Council of Ministers. Draft bills are prepared by ministries, cleared by the chairman of the Council of Ministers, and placed before the National Assembly, or State Council, for ratification. The leading role of the party is indicated by the fact that most of the members of the State Council and Council of Ministers hold high positions in the Party. Todor Zhivkov, for instance, is not only First Secretary of the Bulgarian Communist Party but also President of the State Council.

The Bulgarian Communist Party—BCP (Bŭlgarska komunisticheska partiia—BKP) has its origins in the Bulgarian Social Democratic Party formed in 1891. At its Fifth Party Congress in December 1948 the BCP adopted its present name in place of the Bulgarian Workers' Party/Communists (Bŭlgarska rabotnicheska partiia/komunisti). The leading figures in the BCP after the seizure of power were Georgi Dimitrov (Chairman, later Secretary-General, of the CC of the BCP and Chairman of the Politburo, 1945–9; Prime Minister, 1946–9; he died in 1949 in Moscow); Vasil Kolarov (second in importance only to Dimitrov; member of the CC and Politburo; Deputy Prime Minister, 1947–9; Prime Minister, 1949–50; he died in 1950); and Traicho Kostov (member of the CC and Politburo; Deputy Prime Minister, 1946–7; tried for 'Titoism' in 1949 and executed although he was posthumously rehabilitated at the Sixth Party Congress in 1954).

Vŭlko Chervenkov, a Moscow-educated Stalinist, succeeded as Prime Minister and Secretary-General in 1950. His period of office was characterized by widescale purges (1950–3) which made Bulgaria into one of the most obedient and Sovietized satellites in Eastern Europe. At the Sixth Party Congress the post of Secretary-General was abolished and replaced by a Secretariat of three; Todor Zhivkov became First Secretary although Chervenkov retained the Politburo chairmanship. Khrushchev's rise to power, coupled with his personal antipathy towards Chervenkov, led to the latter's gradual demotion. This started at an extraordinary plenum of the CC in April, 1956, when Zhivkov attacked Chervenkov 'for encouraging the harmful cult of the individual', continued at the November 1961 plenum and ended at the Eighth Party Congress in 1962. Zhivkov was now in firm control and has remained so to this day. He served as Prime Minister from 1962 to 1971 when he relinquished the post for that of the presidency in the newly established State Council.

The Party follows the organizational pattern of the Soviet prototype. The primary organization, or lowest unit, exists in economic enterprises, government offices, the armed forces, educational institutions, etc. The hierarchical ladder ascends to the municipality, city or district, and the province levels, and ends with the national party organizations. The congress is theoretically the highest policy-making body and met once every four years (changed to once every five years at the Tenth Congress in 1971). It elects a CC which is entrusted with the administration of party work between congresses. The CC in turn elects a Politburo, a permanent body, to conduct affairs between CC plenums.

The national economy of Bulgaria is based on a five-year planning system. The seventh five-year plan covered the period 1976–80. The national economy is managed by the state through a unified plan for socio-economic development, on the basis of which the state budget is drawn up. The drafts of both plan and budget are worked out by the Council of Ministers and approved by the National Assembly. The Council of Ministers organizes, directs and controls the implementation of both plan and budget. Some local planning, profitability, and consumer demand have been admitted into the system.

In the field of international relations Bulgaria has proved to be one of the most trustworthy and obedient of the Soviet satellite countries. The Bulgarian leadership has backed Moscow unequivocally—on Comecon, the Warsaw Pact, the Vietnam war, and on all internal and domestic issues. It was the presence of the Red Army in Bulgaria in 1944–7 which enabled the communists to seize and keep power; Chervenkov's downfall was instigated by Khrushchev; Zhivkov has remained in power by closely following every Soviet move. Soviet designs have, in fact, taken official precedence over all national values in Bulgaria. For all practical purposes, the Soviet Union has annexed Bulgaria despite the absence of land contiguities. Bulgaria's relations, on the other hand, with her close neighbour Yugoslavia have constantly ebbed and flowed due in part to toeing the Moscow line during the Soviet–Yugoslav disputes of the 1950s but also due to the continuing local issue of Macedonia, a question which has vexed Bulgarian–Yugoslav relations since 1878.

Publishing

The publishing trade in Bulgaria was organized after the communist seizure of power in 1944 on a socialist basis in the form of a system of state publishers which took over the assets of the private publishing enterprises. The printing and sale of books is a monopoly of the state and social organs. The work of the publishing sector is coordinated, planned and supplied by the State Association 'Bulgarian Books' (Dŭrzhavno obedinenie 'Bŭlgarska kniga') which is part of the Committee for Art and Culture (Komitet za izkustvo i kultura). There are twenty-two Bulgarian publishing houses in all: twenty in Sofia, one in Plovdiv, and one in Varna. The work is divided amongst them on a thematic basis. For instance, Narodna Prosveta, as organ of the Ministry of Education, publishes material in the educational field whilst Dŭrzhavno Voenno Izdatelstvo publishes material for the army and the militia. The Bulgarian Communist Party itself is a publisher in its own right—Izdatelstvo na Bŭlgarskata Komunisticheska Partiia, Partizdat for short (founded in October, 1944)—and publishes material in the socio-political field. As in most communist countries, the press in Bulgaria is considered a powerful instrument of the Party and part of the educational system, and for that reason it is subject to strict control. Party intervention may be at the highest level or at the level of the individual publishing house. Bibliographical control of Bulgarian book and periodical output is maintained through *Natsionalna bibliografiia NR Bŭlgariia* which comprises eight series (*see* B1–9). Series 2, *Bŭlgarski knigopis: sluzhbeni izdaniia i disertatsii*, deals with Bulgarian official publications (*see* B11).

GENERAL BIBLIOGRAPHIES AND REFERENCE WORKS

National bibliographies

B1 *Natsionalna bibliografiia na NR Bŭlgariia.* [National bibliography of Bulgaria]. S.: Narodna biblioteka Kiril i Metodii, 1897–.

The national bibliography of Bulgaria, which provides full coverage of Bulgarian book and journal output, comprises the following eight series:

B2 Ser. 1: *Bŭlgarski knigopis: knigi, notni, graficheski i kartografski izdaniia.* [Bulgarian bibliography: books, music, prints, maps]. S.: 1969–. Biweekly.

This is the national bibliography of Bulgaria reflecting books published in the country and deposited in the National Library in Sofia. Entries are arranged by subject under 28 headings. Official publications were listed in this series until the end of 1961 when they were listed separately in B11. Through the years, its title, coverage, frequency and publisher have varied. From 1897 to 1944 it was published annually; 1945–8, quarterly; 1949–68, monthly. From 1897 to 1952 it was issued by the National Library; 1953–63, by the Bulgarian Bibliographical Institute; 1964–, by the National Library. Since 1970 an annual cumulation supersedes the biweekly issues: *Bŭlgarski knigopis: knigi . . . Obsht godishen ukazatel* [*1969–*].

B3   Ser. 2: *Bŭlgarski knigopis: sluzhbeni izdaniia i disertatsii.* [Bulgarian bibliography: official publications and dissertations].
     See B11.

B4   Ser. 3: *Bŭlgarski gramofonni plochi. Godishen ukazatel* [*1972–*]. [Bulgarian records. Annual index]. S.: 1974–. Annual. [Not seen].

B5   Ser. 4: *Bŭlgarski periodichen pechat: vestnitsi, spisaniia, biuletini i periodichni sbornitsi.* [Bulgarian periodical press: newspapers, journals, bulletins and periodical collections]. S.: 1967–. Annual.
     An annual list of all newspapers, journals and serial publications in Bulgaria. The first volume covered the year 1965. For periodical output before this date, see Spasova, M. *Bŭlgarski periodichen pechat, 1944–1969: bibliografski ukazatel.* [Bulgarian periodical press, 1944–1969: bibliographic index]. S.: Narodna biblioteka Kiril i Metodii, 1975. 3 vols. An exhaustive directory of Bulgarian journals and newspapers published in the above period. Arrangement is alphabetical by title. This is a continuation of D. P. Ivanchev's directory which covers the period 1844–1944 (S.: Nauka i izkustvo, 1962–9, 3 vols.).

B6   Ser. 5: *Letopis na statiite ot bŭlgarskite spisaniia i sbornitsi.* [Listing of articles in Bulgarian journals and collections]. S.: 1952–. Weekly.

B7   Ser. 6: *Letopis na statiite ot bŭlgarskite vestnitsi.* [Listing of articles in Bulgarian newspapers]. S.: 1952–. Monthly.
     Series 5 and 6 index articles in Bulgarian journals and newspapers respectively and include official publications.

B8   Ser. 7: *Bŭlgariia v chuzhdata literatura. Godishen ukazatel* [*1964–*]. [Bulgaria in foreign literature. Annual index]. S.: 1966–.

B9   Ser. 8: *Bibliografiia na bŭlgarskata bibliografiia. Godishen ukazatel* [*1963–*]. [Bibliography of Bulgarian bibliographies. Annual index]. S.: 1965–. Annual.
     An annual listing of all Bulgarian bibliographies published individually or in books and journals. There is also a retrospective guide covering a period of 25 years: Petkova, Z. *Bibliografiia na bŭlgarskata bibliografiia, 1944–1969.* S.: Narodna biblioteka Kiril i Metodii, 1972. 603 pp.

Bio   Kovachev, V. V., Kŭnchev, S. I. and Edreva, P. G. *Bŭlgarski knigi, 1944–1969: bibliografski ukazatel.* [Bulgarian books, 1944–1969: a bibliography]. S.: Narodna biblioteka Kiril i Metodii, 1976. 14 vols.

     A retrospective bibliography of Bulgarian books arranged alphabetically by author and spanning a period of 25 years. Unfortunately, just 20 xerox copies were produced for official use only. The National Library has also started work on a classified listing for the same period which it plans to produce in 1,500 copies. [Not seen].

Other general bibliographies and reference works

B11   *Bŭlgarski knigopis: sluzhbeni izdaniia i disertatsii.* [Bulgarian bibliography: official publications and dissertations]. S.: Narodna biblioteka Kiril i Metodii, 1962–. Monthly.

     This forms series 2 of the *Natsionalna bibliografiia na NR Bŭlgariia.* Prior to 1962, Bulgarian official publications were listed in the *Bŭlgarski knigopis: knigi . . . [see* B2]. An annual index, *Godishni pokazaltsi,* to official publications is issued containing 7 indexes to names, titles, editions in foreign languages, et al.

B12   *Südosteuropa-Bibliographie.* Vol. 1–. Munich: Oldenbourg, 1956–.

     Provides a five-year bibliographic survey of monographs and journals published in, or relating to, Eastern Europe. Five volumes have been published to date as follows: vol. 1 (1956), 1945–50 (pt. 1 contains the section on Bulgaria, pp. 57–91); vol. 2 (1962), 1951–5 (pt. 2, pp. 383–493); vol. 3 (1968), 1956–60 (pt. 2, pp. 39–199); vol. 4 (1973), 1961–5 (pt. 2, pp. 63–244); vol. 5 (1976), 1966–70 (pt. 2, pp. 113–360). Other western bibliographies with sections on Bulgarian politics, law and the state are: Pundeff, M. V. *Bulgaria: a bibliographic guide.* Washington: Library of Congress, 1965. 98 pp.; *Bibliography of social science periodicals and monograph series: Bulgaria, 1944–1960.* (Foreign social science bibliographies, Series P-92, No. 2). Washington: U.S. Bureau of the Census, 1961. 36 pp.; Horecky, P. L. 'Bulgaria' in his *Southeastern Europe: a guide to basic publications.* Chicago: Chicago U.P., 1969. Pp. 119–209.

B13   *Bibliografiia na bŭlgarskata pravna literatura, 1944–1969.* [Bibliography of Bulgarian legal literature, 1944–1969]. Comp. by M. A. Angelov et al. S.: Universitet Kliment Okhridski, 1970. 254 pp.

     A bibliography of Bulgarian legal writings on state, administrative and financial law published since the introduction of the new legal system in 1944. Supersedes the 1965 edition covering 3,440 items from the period 1944–63 (128 pp.).

B14   Sipkov, I. 'Guide to the law of the state of the People's Republic of Bulgaria', *Bulgarische Jahrbücher,* vol. 2, 1972?, pp. 423–69.

     Provides a guide to various significant acts and events of a legislative and political–historical nature, reflecting developments from the coup d'état of 9 September 1944, to the adoption of the new constitution on 18 May 1971. These acts and events are arranged systematically under 23 headings—e.g. the constitution, courts, National Assembly, official law gazette—and their history traced, together with appropriate annotations and explanations, by reference to the *Dŭrzhaven vestnik*.

B15 Sipkov, I. *Legal sources and bibliography of Bulgaria*. N.Y.: Praeger, 1956. 199 pp.

Provides a brief legal and constitutional history to both pre- and postwar Bulgaria and presents a bibliography of sources of Bulgarian law, of legal periodicals and bibliographies, and of books and articles in Bulgarian and foreign languages on Bulgarian law. Also contains a list of principal legislative enactments in the PR of Bulgaria in force as of 1 January 1956.

B16 *Directory of officials of the Bulgarian People's Republic*. Washington: 1975. 240 pp.

Issued by the American CIA, the directory covers Bulgarian officials, employees, associations, institutions, political parties, etc. An up-to-date and full list of members of the State Council, Council of Ministers, and the Politburo may be found in *The International Year Book and Statesmen's Who's Who*. Kingston upon Thames: Kelly, 1978. Similar lists are issued on an annual basis by Radio Free Europe–Radio Liberty in Munich: *Radio Free Europe Research*. See also *Kratka bŭlgarska entsiklopediia*. [Concise Bulgarian encyclopedia]. S.: Bŭlgarska akademiia na naukite, 1963–9, 5 vols., and the latest edition *Entsiklopediia Bŭlgariia*. [Encyclopedia of Bulgaria]. S.: BAN, 1978–, Vol.1–. Only the first volume has been published so far covering the letters A–V. Information on members of the Bulgarian Narodno Sŭbranie is contained in *Narodni predstaviteli ot Sedmo Narodno sŭbranie na Narodna republika Bŭlgariia: kratki biograficheski danni* [People's representatives of the Seventh National Assembly of the PR of Bulgaria: short biographical facts]. S.: Nauka i izkustvo, 1977. 444 pp. A similar dictionary was published for the 6th National Assembly (1974, 491 pp.).

CONSTITUTION

B17 *Konstitutsiia na Narodnata republika Bŭlgariia*. [Constitution of the People's Republic of Bulgaria]. S.: Dŭrzhavna pechatnitsa, 1947. 29 pp.

The text of the first constitution of communist Bulgaria. It was first published in *DV*, no. 284, 6 December 1947. An English translation was published with the above title in Sofia, December 1947 (27 pp.). Amendments to the 1947 constitution appeared in *IPNS*, no. 89, 7 November 1961; *DV*, no. 97, 10 December 1965; and *DV*, no. 89, 19 November 1969.

B18 *Konstitutsiia na Narodna republika Bŭlgariia*. [Constitution of the

People's Republic of Bulgaria]. S.: Nauka i izkustvo, 1971. 64 pp. Contains the text of Bulgaria's second constitution adopted in 1971. It appeared in *DV*, no. 39, 18 May 1971. An English translation has been published: *Constitution of the People's Republic of Bulgaria: Adopted by a national referendum on May 16, 1971*. S.: Sofia Press, 1971. 48 pp.

LAW CODES AND GENERAL COLLECTIONS OF LAWS

B19   *Nakazatelen kodeks: tekst s prilozheniia.* [Criminal code: text and appendix]. Comp. by D. Dimitrov. S.: Nauka i izkustvo, 1956. 215 pp.

Contains the new criminal code adopted in 1951 to reflect the communist concept of law and justice. The following year a new criminal and civil procedure was adopted: *Nakazatelno-protsesualen kodeks: tekst, literatura, sŭdebna praktika* [Criminal-procedural code: text, literature, judicial practice]. Comp. by N. Ruschev et al. S.: Nauka i izkustvo, 1957. 255 pp. Both the above are modelled on their Soviet counterparts. For the most recent work on this subject, see Pavlov, S. *Nakazatelen protses na Narodna republika Bŭlgariia.* [Criminal process of the PR of Bulgaria]. S.: Nauka i izkustvo, 1979. 822 pp. [Not seen].

B20   *Grazhdanski protsesualen kodeks: tekst, sŭdebna praktika, literatura.* [Civil procedural code: text, judicial practice, literature]. Comp. by N. Raichev et al. S.: Nauka i izkustvo, 1957. 542 pp. [Not seen].

B21   *Sŭdebna praktika na Vŭrkhovniia sŭd na NRB.* [Judicial practice of the Supreme Court of the PR of Bulgaria]. S.: Nauka i izkustvo, 1963–. Annual.

Contains High Court comments, decisions and interpretations of codified law. It is issued in two series: 1. *Grazhdanska kolegiia* [Civil division], (1953–63 entitled *Grazhdanski otdeleniia*) and 2. *Nakazatelna kolegiia* [Criminal division], (1953–63 entitled *Nakazatelni otdeleniia*).

B22   *Sbornik postanovleniia i tŭlkuvatelni resheniia na Vŭrkhovniia Sŭd na NR Bŭlgariia, 1953–1973.* [Collection of decrees and interpretative decisions of the Supreme Court of the PR of Bulgaria, 1953–1973]. S.: Nauka i izkustvo, 1974. 569 pp.

Supersedes the earlier edition covering the period 1953–63 (S.: 1965, 528 pp.). This basic collection of the decisions of the Bulgarian Supreme Court is continued by annual supplements covering the decisions of the court's criminal and civil law divisions (*see* B21).

B23   *Iuridecheska misŭl.* [Legal thought]. Vols. 1–6. S.: Ministerstvo na pravosŭdieto, 1946–51. Bimonthly.

Besides carrying articles on legal problems, it acts as a source of information on decisions of the Supreme Court of the Republic. In 1952 it was renamed *Sotsialistichesko pravo*. [Socialist law]. Vols. 1–19. S.: Izd. na Ministerstvoto na pravosŭdieto i Glavnata prokuratora, 1952–70. Vols. 1–3 (12 issues p.a.), vols. 4–19 (10 issues p.a.). In addition to the above, vol. 2 onwards features a running bibliography of Bulgarian legal literature in four or five issues of each volume.

OTHER LEGISLATIVE DOCUMENTS

Bibliographies and indexes

B24 Dimitrov, L. *Spravochnik po zakonodatelstvoto na Narodna republika Bŭlgariia*. [Handbook on the legislation of the People's Republic of Bulgaria]. S.: Nauka i izkustvo, 1978. 354 pp.

Supersedes earlier editions: S.: 1955, 118 pp.; S.: 1969, 217 pp.; S.: 1974, 284 pp. An index to Bulgarian normative acts arranged by subject. Covers all basic materials—laws, edicts, directives, etc.—issued by the Council of Ministers from 9 September 1944 to the present, and all other interpretative materials—rules, memoranda, regulations, etc.—issued during that period.

B25 *Spravochnik po zakonodatelstvoto na Narodna republika Bŭlgariia: zakoni, ukazi, postanovleniia, razporezhdaniia na Ministerskiia Sŭvet, pravilnitsi, naredbi i dr., obnarodvani v Dŭrzhaven vestnik i Izvestiia na Prezidiuma na Narodnoto Sŭbranie ot 9 septemvri 1944g. do 30 iuni 1957g.* [Index of the laws of the People's Republic of Bulgaria: laws, edicts, decisions, directives of the Council of Ministers, regulations, instructions, etc., published in the State Gazette and the News of the Presidium of the National Assembly from 9 September 1944 to 30 June 1957]. Ed. by Khr. Maksimov. S.: Nauka i izkustvo, 1957. 606 pp.

A detailed index to the laws of Bulgaria published in the official gazette for the period indicated. Arrangement is by subject of the laws. The index was continued for the period 1 July 1957 to 31 December 1963, under the same title, by L. Dimitrov and Z. Chalukov (S.: Nauka i izkustvo, 1965, 210 pp.).

B26 *Tŭlkuvatelni resheniia na Prezidiuma na Narodnoto Sŭbranie, 1948–1967: spravochnik.* [Interpretative decisions of the Presidium of the National Assembly, 1948–1967: a handbook]. Comp. by D. Popov. S.: 1968. 332 pp. [Not seen].

Legislative documents

B27 *Dŭrzhaven vestnik.* [State/official gazette]. S.: 1879–. Vol. 1–. Daily.

The official law gazette of Bulgaria containing Bulgarian laws, treaties, administrative regulations, and other official material.

During the years it has undergone several changes in title and numbering:

Dŭrzhaven vestnik na tsarstvo Bŭlgariia. [State gazette of the Kingdom of Bulgaria]. From 26 May 1926 (issue no. 42).

Dŭrzhaven vestnik na Narodna republika Bŭlgariia. [State gazette of the PR of Bulgaria]. From 16 September 1946 (issue no. 211). Vol. 72, no. 169 of 19 July 1950 was the last to appear bearing a volume number. No. 170 of 20 July 1950 appeared as 'Year VII' apparently expressing the number of years after the seizure of power by the new government. This series ran to no. 282 of 30 November 1950.

Izvestiia na Prezidiuma na Narodnoto Sŭbranie. [News of the Presidium of the National Assembly]. From 1 December 1950. It was numbered Year I, issue 1, and came out usually twice a week. The last issue was Year XII, issue 105. Supplements were sometimes issued containing announcements and legal notices. These were irregular and had their own numbering.

Dŭrzhaven vestnik na Narodna republika Bŭlgariia. From 4 January 1963. No. 1–. Usually appears twice a week. An index is issued to each yearly cumulation (*Sŭdŭrzhanie i spravochnik na Dŭrzhaven vestnik*).

B28   *Sbornik postanovleniia i razporezhdaniia na Ministerskiia sŭvet.* [Collection of decisions and directives of the Council of Ministers]. S.: 1951–73. Monthly.

These materials were also published in the *Dŭrzhaven vestnik.* This collection originated in 1950 as an annual publication under the title *Sbornik na po-vazhnite postanovleniia i razporezhdaniia na Ministerskiia sŭvet.* [Collection of the most important decisions and directives of the Council of Ministers]. When it was published as a cumulative volume for 1949/50, it was designed as a manual for government officials, business executives and CP leaders. From 1951 it appeared monthly. In addition to acts of the Cabinet, it carried laws enacted by the National Assembly as well as edicts passed by the Presidium. Continued by B29.

B29   *Normativni aktove.* [Normative acts]. S.: Narodno sŭbranie, 1973–.

A continuation of B28. They are issued in four series: 1. A monthly basic series which is subject to frequent modifications; 2. *Ikonomicheski mekhanizŭm.* [Economic mechanism]; 3. *Dŭrzhavno ustroistvo.* [State system]; 4. *Upravlenie na narodnoto stopanstvo.* [Management of the national economy]. The last three series appear on an irregular basis. They all contain government decrees and decisions and are issued in looseleaf binders in the style of *Keesing's contemporary archives.*

B30   *Stenografski dnevnitsi.* [Stenographic record]. S.: Narodno sŭbranie, 1944–.

The legislative background of the laws enacted and published in the *Dŭrzhaven vestnik* is found in the above, the stenographic record of the National Assembly. It is continued from its predecessor *Dnevnitsi na (Pŭrvoto) Obiknoveno Narodno Sŭbranie. Stenografski protokoli.* S.: Ia. S. Kovachev, 1879–1944. The National Assemblies lasted and had sessions as follows: 1st NA, 17 January 1950–3 November 1953 (8 regular and 4 extraordinary sessions); 2nd NA, 14 January 1954–3 December 1957 (8 regular and 9 extraordinary sessions); 3rd NA, 13 January 1958–1 November 1961 (8 regular and 7 extraordinary sessions); 4th NA, 15 March 1962–6 December 1965 (11 sessions); 5th NA, 11 March 1966–7 May 1971 (16 sessions); 6th NA, 7 July 1971–5 June 1975 (15 sessions); 7th NA, 16 June 1976–.

GENERAL PARTY DOCUMENTS

Bibliographies and indexes

B31 Dancheva, I. and Lazarov, M. *Bŭlgarskata komunisticheska partiia v chuzhdata literatura, 1885–1967: bibliografski ukazatel.* [The Bulgarian Communist Party in foreign literature, 1885–1967: a bibliography]. S.: Partizdat, 1971. 480 pp.
Contains 3,392 books and periodical articles.

B32 Diugmedzhieva, P., Vasileva, E. and Karadzhova, A. *80 godini Bŭlgarska komunisticheska partiia: bibliografski materiali i razrabotki.* [80 years of the Bulgarian Communist Party: bibliographical materials and treatments]. S.: Narodna biblioteka Kiril i Metodii, 1971. 146 pp. [Not seen].

B33 Draganov, G. G. and Spasov, E. K. *Istoricheskoto delo na Aprilskiia plenum na TsK na BKP: bibliografiia 1956–1976.* [The historical work of the April plenum of the BCP CC: a bibliography 1956–1976]. S.: Narodna biblioteka Kiril i Metodii, 1976. 319 pp.
A bibliography of materials concerning the application and development of the party line taken at the April 1956 plenum of the CC in all spheres of socio-political, economic and cultural life. The April plenum was significant in that it marked the first steps in the demotion of Chervenkov and the corresponding rise of Zhivkov. See also *Resheniiata na Aprilskiia plenum v deistvie: bibliografiia.* [Decisions of the April plenum in action: a bibliography]. Ed. P. Tsanev. S.: BKP, 1966. 211 pp. [Not seen].

B34 *Pred Desetiia kongres na Bŭlgarskata komunisticheska partiia: bibliografski i metodologichni materiali.* [Before the 10th Congress of the Bulgarian Communist Party: bibliographical and methodological materials]. S,: Narodna biblioteka Kiril i Metodii, 1970. 116 pp.
A guide to material published on the work of the BCP between the 9th and 10th congresses. Includes a chronology of CC plenums between the two congresses.

B35 Vŭlcheva, A., Minkova, Ts. and Kalaidzheva, K. *VI kongres na*

Bŭlgarskata komunisticheska partiia: preporŭch. bibliografiia. [The 6th Congress of the Bulgarian Communist Party: a recommended bibliography]. S.: Nauka i izkustvo, 1954. 56 pp.

A guide to various materials concerning the 6th Congress: party documents, addresses, statements of congress delegates, and the more important articles from newspapers and periodicals in connection with the congress. A similar guide was prepared by the National Library for the 9th Congress for use by 'librarians, propagandists and party workers': *Deveti kongres na BKP: preporŭch. bibliografiia.* Ed. S. Ivanov. S.: Narodna biblioteka Kiril i Metodii, 1967. 137 pp. [Not seen].

Party congresses and documents

To date there have been 11 congresses of the Bulgarian Communist Party. The first was held in May 1919; the second, May–June 1920; the third, May 1921; and the fourth, June 1922. The first postwar congress was the fifth held in December 1948 at which the Party changed its name from the Bŭlgarska rabotnicheska partiia (komunisti) to the Bŭlgarska komunisticheska partiia.

5th–9th Congresses

B36   *Bŭlgarskata rabotnicheska partiia (komunisti) v rezoliutsii i resheniia na kongresite, konferentsiite i plenumite na TsK.* [The Bulgarian Workers' Party (Communists) in the resolutions and decisions of its congresses, conferences, and the plenums of the CC]. Comp. by R. K. Karakolov. S.: Nauka i izkustvo, 1947–65. 5 vols.

Vols. 2–5 have the title *Bŭlgarskata komunisticheska partiia v....* The official collection of the decisions and policy statements of the BCP adopted from its founding in 1891 to 1962. Vol. 1 covers the period 1891–1918; 2, 1919–23; 3, 1924–44; 4, 1944–55; and 5, 1956–62.

B37   *Stenografski protokoli.* [Stenographic minutes]. S.: 1948–67. 5 vols.

The record of the proceedings of the Fifth (first postwar) Congress of the Bulgarian Communist Party in 1948, the Sixth in 1954, the Seventh in 1958, the Eighth in 1962, and the Ninth in 1966. Each contains the Party statutes as amended at the time. The reports to the congresses of the Party secretaries (Dimitrov, 1948; Chervenkov, 1954; Zhivkov, 1958, 1962 and 1966) are available separately in English translations. Various materials from the 8th and 9th Congresses are available in English: *Speeches and resolutions of the Eighth Congress of the Bulgarian Communist Party.* (United States Joint Publications Research Service, No. 16,416). Washington: 1962. 140 pp.; *For unity and cohesion: materials of the 9th Congress of the Bulgarian Communist Party, Sofia, November 14–19, 1966.* S.: Foreign Languages Publishing House, 1966. 303 pp.

10th Congress, 20–25 April 1971

B38 *10. kongres na BKP, 20–25.4.1971: stenografski protokoli.* [The 10th Congress of the BCP, 20–25.4.1971: stenographic record]. S.: Partizdat, 1971. 928 pp.

See also *Deseti kongres na Bŭlgarskata komunisticheska partiia: dokladi, resheniia.* [The 10th Congress of the BCP: reports, resolutions]. S.: Partizdat, 1973. 349 pp. Speeches, resolutions and other materials are also available in English in *Under the banner of socialism: materials from the 10th Congress of the Bulgarian Communist Party, April 20–25, 1971.* S.: Sofia Press, 1971. 496 pp. For Zhivkov's report to the congress see *Otcheten doklad na Tsentralniia komitet na Bŭlgarskata komunisticheska partiia pred Desetiia kongres na Partiiata—20 april 1971g. Zakliuchitelno slovo—24 april 1971g. Rech pri zakrivaneto-na kongresa—25 april 1971g.* S.: Partizdat, 1971. 224 pp. The Party's Programme is contained in *Programa na Bŭlgarskata komunisticheska partiia, prieta edinodushno ot X kongres na BKP, 24 april 1971g.* [Programme of the Bulgarian Communist Party adopted unanimously by the 10th Party Congress on 24 April 1971]. S.: Partizdat, 1971. 127 pp. An English translation was published with the above title by Sofia Press (101 pp.).

11th Congress, 29 March–2 April 1976

B39 *Dokladi i resheniia: edinadeseti kongres na Bŭlgarskata komunisticheska partiia.* [Reports and resolutions: the 11th congress of the BCP]. S.: Partizdat, 1976. 222 pp.

For Zhivkov's report on the work of the CC at the Congress see *Otchet na Tsentralniia komitet na Bŭlgarskata komunisticheska partiia za perioda mezhdu desetiia i edinadesetiia kongres i predstoiashtite zadachi.* S.: Partizdat, 1976. 206 pp. An English translation of this has been published: *Report of the Central Committee of the Bulgarian Communist Party for the period between the tenth and eleventh congresses and on the forthcoming tasks, March 29, 1976.* S.: Sofia Press, 1976. 119 pp.

Other Party documents

B40 *Bŭlgarska komunisticheska partiia: dokumenti na tsentralni rŭkovodni organi.* [The Bulgarian Communist Party: documents of the central governing bodies]. S.: Partizdat, 1972–. Vol. 1–. [Not seen].

Latest volume to appear is vol. 4 covering the period 1906–8 (1979, 495 pp.).

B41 *Materiali po istoriia na Bŭlgarskata komunisticheska partiia, 1925–1962g.* [Materials on the history of the Bulgarian Communist Party, 1925–1962]. S.: BKP, 1966. 520 pp.

This publication, complemented by another volume under the same title for the period 1885–1925 (S.: BKP, 1966. 264 pp.), is issued as an instructional aid and serves as the official history of the

Party in Bulgarian. It has appeared in 10 substantially differing versions since 1952. Current research on the subject in Bulgaria appears in *Izvestiia* [Communications] of the Institute of History of the BCP (1957–) and *Izvestiia* of the Higher Party School of the CC (1957–).

GENERAL STATISTICS

Bibliographies

B42   Dzherova, L. and Toteva, N. *Bibliografiia na bŭlgarskata statisticheska literatura, 1878–1960.* [Bibliography of Bulgarian statistical literature, 1878–1960]. S.: Tsentralno statistichesko upravlenie pri Ministerskiia sŭvet, 1961. 105 pp.

     An exhaustive bibliography of official statistical publications as well as writings on statistics in Bulgaria.

Statistical yearbooks

B43   *Statisticheski godishnik na Narodna republika Bŭlgariia.* [Statistical yearbook of Bulgaria]. S.: Tsentralno statistichesko upravlenie pri Ministerskiia sŭvet, 1947/48–. Annual.

     Issued from 1909–42 under the title *Statisticheski godishnik na Tsarstvo Bŭlgariia.* The basic statistical publication of Bulgaria. The text is provided with French and, in recent years, English translations. Some volumes have been independently translated, e.g. the 1961 edition was translated by the U.S. Joint Publications Research Service, *Statistical yearbook of the Bulgarian People's Republic, 1961.* Washington: 1962. 925 pp.

B44   *Statisticheski spravochnik na NR Bŭlgariia.* [Statistical manual of the PR of Bulgaria]. S.: Tsentralno statistichesko upravlenie pri Ministerskiia sŭvet, 1958–. Annual.

     A pocket-sized and abridged version of the *Statisticheski godishnik* (B43). An English version is published annually: *Statistical manual of the People's Republic of Bulgaria.* S.: Central Statistical Office, 1958–.

OTHER GENERAL SOURCES OF DOCUMENTATION

B45   *Bulgaria.* S.: Sofia Press Agency, 1971–. Fortnightly.

     Formerly called *Bulgaria Today* (1952–71). Contains general information on Bulgaria but includes some official material such as speeches by major Bulgarian figures, treaties, five-year economic plans, etc. See also *Sofia News.* S.: Sofia Press Agency, 1968–. Weekly. This contains similar materials.

B46   *Rabotnichesko delo.* [Worker's deed]. S.: 1927–. Daily.
This is the organ of the BCP CC and is the major Bulgarian daily newspaper. Other newspapers and journals of interest are: *Information Bulletin.* S.: 1956–. Monthly. Organ of the BCP CC. It is also published in Russian, French, German and Spanish; *Novo vreme.* [New times]. S.: 1897–. Monthly. The theoretical organ of the BCP CC; *Otechestven Front.* [Fatherland Front]. S.: 1942–. Daily. Organ of the Presidium of the National Assembly and the National Council of the Fatherland Front; *Trud.* [Labour]. S.: 1936–. Daily. Organ of the Central Council of the Trades Unions in Bulgaria.

B47   *Radio Free Europe Research. Situation report: Bulgaria.* Munich. Approx. 33 issues p.a.
Provides information and comment obtained via Bulgarian official sources, e.g. *Dŭrzhaven vestnik* and *Rabotnichesko delo,* on current socioeconomic and political activities in Bulgaria.

B48   *Selected items from the Bulgarian press.* S.: British Embassy, 1973–5. Daily.
A bulletin containing news items selected and translated by the British Embassy from the leading Bulgarian press. It was started in July 1970 under the title *Summary of Bulgarian press.* A similar bulletin is compiled by the French Embassy in Sofia: *Extraits de la presse bulgare.* 1977–. (formerly *Revue de la presse bulgare,* 1976–7) [Not seen].

INTERNATIONAL RELATIONS

General

B49   Sipkov, I. *The Soviet Union treaties and agreements with Bulgaria, 1944–1958.* Washington: Library of Congress, 1959. 43 pp.
Treaties between Bulgaria and the Soviet Union, which after 1944 played an important role in determining Bulgarian foreign and domestic policy, are contained in the above. These and other treaties and conventions concluded by Bulgaria are published in *Dŭrzhaven vestnik.* See also *Sbornik na mezhdunarodni aktove i dogovori.* [Collection of international acts and treaties]. Ed. by V. Kutikov. S.: Izd. pri 'Obsht fond za podpomagane studentite ot visshite uchebni zavedeniia v Bŭlgariia', 1948. 648 pp. This collection contains a number of treaties signed by Bulgaria between 1918 and 1948, including the peace treaty of 1947. This latter treaty appears in *DV* no. 201, 30 August 1947.

B50   *Vŭnshna politika na Narodna republika Bŭlgariia: sbornik ot dokumenti i materiali v 2 t.* [The external policy of the PR of Bulgaria: a collection of documents and materials in 2 vols.]. S.: Nauka i izkustvo, 1970–1. 2 vols.
A collection of documents and materials, including the texts of

selected treaties, on Bulgaria's external relations with foreign powers. Vol. 1 covers the period 1944–62; vol. 2, 1963–70.

Bulgarian–Soviet relations

B51 *Bŭlgaro–sŭvetski otnosheniia, 1948–1970: dokumenti i materiali.* [Bulgarian–Soviet relations, 1948–1970: documents and materials]. Ed. by L. Petrov and N. N. Rodionov. S.: Partizdat, 1974. 814 pp.

A similar work containing 180 documents in all has been compiled for the period 1971–6 under the editorship of M. Ivanov et al. (1977, 749 pp.). Relations between the two countries from the Bulgarian communists' seizure of power in 1944 to 1948 are covered in the Russian work *Sovetsko–bolgarskie otnosheniia, 1944–1948 gg.: dokumenty i materialy.* [Soviet–Bulgarian relations, 1944–1948: documents and materials]. Ed. by L. F. Il'ichev et al. Moscow: Izd. Politicheskoi literatury, 1969. 507 pp.

B52 *Bŭlgarsko–sŭvetski otnosheniia i vrŭzki: dokumenti i materiali.* [Bulgarian–Soviet relations and ties: documents and materials]. Bulgarian ed. team: Kh. Khristov et al. Russian ed. team: L. B. Valev et al. S.: BAN, 1977–. Vol. 1–.

A new publication compiled jointly by Bulgarian and Russian specialists. A Russian edition is being simultaneously published in Moscow. Only the first volume has been published so far covering the period from November 1917 to September 1944.

Bulgarian–Yugoslav relations

B53 *Titovata banda—orŭdie na imperialistite: dokumenti i materiali, 1948–1951.* [Tito's gang—tool of the imperialists: documents and materials, 1948–1951]. Comp. by D. K'osev. S.: BKP, 1951. 663 pp.

Contains Bulgarian materials concerning the dispute with Yugoslavia in the second half of the 1940s, a period when Bulgarian–Yugoslav relations were at a low ebb. Relations between Bulgaria and Yugoslavia have always been uneasy particularly over the question of Macedonia. Other significant Bulgarian sources are: Ormandzhiev, I. P. *Federatsiia na balkanskite narodi: idei i prechki.* [Federation of Balkan peoples: ideas and impediments]. S.: Zaria, 1947. 191 pp.; *Krizata v Iugoslavskata komunisticheska partiia.* [Crisis in the Yugoslav Communist Party]. S.: BKP, 1948. 28 pp.; *Documents sur la politique hostile et agressive du gouvernement yougoslave contre la République populaire de Bulgarie.* S.: 1952. 368 pp. Contains documents published by the Bulgarian Ministry of Foreign Affairs; and K'osev, D. *Makedonskiot vŭpros i Titovata klika.* [The Macedonian question and Tito's clique]. S.: Tsentr. kom-t na makedonskite kulturno–prosvetni druzhestva v Bŭlgariia, 1949. 66 pp.

B54 *Jugoslovensko–bugarskite odnosi. Politikata i aktivnostite što vo pos-*

ledno vreme NR Bugarija gi sproveduva sprema SFR Jugoslavija, a koi osobeno ja zasegaat SR Makedonija. [Yugoslav–Bulgarian relations: the policy and activity shown by the PR of Bulgaria in the past towards the SFR of Yugoslavia and especially towards the SR of Macedonia]. Sk.: Službata za informacii na Sobranieto na SRM, 1969. 128 pp.

Presents the Yugoslav side of the dispute with Bulgaria. Various Bulgarian documentary material on the Macedonian question has been selected and translated by the Macedonians to illustrate their point of view in *From recognition to repudiation; Bulgarian attitudes on the Macedonian question: articles, speeches, documents.* Comp. by V. Čašule. Sk.: Kultura, 1972. 482 pp. The attitude of the BCP to the Macedonian question is covered in two separate Macedonian publications: Mojsov, L. *Bugarskata rabotnička partija (komunisti) i makedonskoto nacionalno prašanje.* [The Bulgarian Workers' Party (Communists) and the Macedonian national question]. Sk.: 1948. 275 pp.; and Mitrev, D. *BKP i Pirinska Makedonija.* [The BCP and Pirin Macedonia]. Sk.: Kultura, 1960. 152 pp.

B55 Palmer, S. E. and King, R. *Yugoslav communism and the Macedonian question.* Hamden, Conn.: Archon Books, 1971. 247 pp.

A western analysis of the Macedonian question and its effect on Bulgarian–Yugoslav relations. See also the chapter on the Macedonian question by P. Shoup in his *Communism and the Yugoslav national question.* N.Y.: Columbia U.P., 1968. Pp. 144–83. For a detailed bibliography on the Macedonian question, see Terry, G. M. *A bibliography of Macedonian studies.* Nottingham: Nottingham University Library, 1975. 121 pp.

POLITICAL AND IDEOLOGICAL AFFAIRS

B56 *Bŭlgarska komunisticheska partiia—rŭkovoditel i organizator na izgrazhdaneto na razvito sotsialistichesko obshtestvo v Bŭlgariia.* [The Bulgarian Communist Party—leader and organizer of the building and development of a socialist society in Bulgaria]. S.: Partizdat, 1974. 632 pp. [Not seen].

B57 Nikolov, Ts. *Rabotata na BKP sled Aprilskiia plenum za vŭzpitanieto na komunistite, 1956–1962.* [The work of the BCP after the April plenum concerning the education of communists, 1956–1962]. S.: BKP, 1964. 341 pp.

Reflects the work on ideological reorientation within the Party undertaken after Chervenkov was ousted as party leader in April 1956.

B58 *Podgotovkata na propagandistite.* [The training of propagandists]. (Biblioteka na propagandista, no. 6). S.: BKP, 1966. 86 pp. [Not seen].

B59 *Spravochnik na aktivista, 1966–1968 g.* [Handbook of the activist, 1966–1968]. Comp. by T. Vodenicharov et al. S.: BKP, 1969. 608 pp.

Earlier materials are collected in the volumes for ... *1956–1961* (1961, 1051 pp.) and ... *1961–1965* (1966, 570 pp.). A collection of party and government materials (decisions of CC plenums, of the Politburo and Secretariat of the CC, decrees of the Council of Ministers, resolutions of the congresses of sociopolitical and mass organizations, etc.) to guide the work of internal propaganda and public opinion moulding. See also the weekly journal issued by the Propaganda and Agitation Department of the BCP CC: *Narŭchnik na agitatora.* [Agitator's manual]. S.: 1945–.

B60 *Spravochnik na propagandista i agitatora.* [Handbook of the propagandist and agitator]. Comp. by T. Ganchev. S.: Partizdat, 1971. 163 pp.

MILITARY AFFAIRS

B61 *Iz opita na politiko-vŭzpitatelnata rabota v Bŭlgarskata narodna armiia: sbornik statii.* [From experience in the work of political indoctrination in the Bulgarian people's army: collection of articles]. S.: Dŭrzhavno voenno izd., 1960. 272 pp.

An analysis of the work of indoctrination by the BCP in the army since 1944. See also *Narŭchnik na voenniia agitatora.* [Handbook of the armed forces agitator]. S.: 1945–66, biweekly; continued since 1966 as *Voenen agitator.*

B62 *Narodna armiia.* [People's army]. S.: 1945–. Irregular.

Organ of the Ministry of National Defence. [Not seen].

B63 *Rabotata na BKP v armiiata, 1941–1944 g.: dokumenti i materiali.* [The work of the BCP in the army, 1941–1944: documents and materials]. S.: BKP, 1959. 614 pp. [Not seen].

ECONOMIC AFFAIRS

Statistics

B64 *Statisticheski izvestiia.* [Statistical news]. S.: Tsentralno statistichesko upravlenie pri Ministerskiia sŭvet, 1957–. Monthly.

Contains current statistical data on the various branches of economic activity in Bulgaria.

B65 *Promishlenost.* [Industry]. S.: Tsentralno statistichesko upravlenie, 1958–. Irregular.

Not published every year. Contains data on production, fixed assets, labour, etc., for state and cooperative enterprises for the whole country. There are other such specialized statistical serials: *Dokhodi, razkhodi i potreblenie na nabliudavanite domaknistva.* [Incomes, expenditure, and consumption of households]. 1970–; *Naselenie.* [Population]. 1968–; *Turizŭm.* [Tourism]. 1971–.

Economy in general

B66 *Economic news of Bulgaria.* S.: 1960–. Monthly.
Published by the Bulgarian Chamber of Commerce. It is also issued in French and German.

B67 *Finansi i kredit.* [Finances and credit]. S.: 1950–. Vol. 1–. 10 issues p.a.
Organ of the Ministry of Finance. Supersedes *Finansova misŭl.*

B68 *Sbornik ot normativni aktove po finansovo pravo.* [Collection of normative acts on financial law]. Comp. by G. Petkanov. S.: SU Kliment Okhridski, 1978. 847 pp.
A collection of laws and legislation on public finance intended as an aid for students of the Law Faculty at the University of Sofia.

Planning

B69 *Planovo stopanstvo.* [Planned economics]. S.: Dŭrzhavna komissiia za planirane, 1946–. Monthly.
From 1960 to 1967 it became *Planovo stopanstvo i statistika*; from 1968 it split into *Planovo stopanstvo* and *Statistika.* It is the major economic journal of the State Planning Commission and the Central Statistical Administration containing articles and information on applied economics and statistics. The State Planning Commission is one of the most important agencies of central government and has the task of formulating economic plans in accordance with the general economic policies of the Council of Ministers.

B70 *The first Bulgarian two year economic plan.* S.: Ministry of Information and Arts, 1947. 92 pp.
The national economic plans are enacted by law and as such are published in the *Dŭrzhaven vestnik.* The two-year economic plan was superseded by five-year plans.

B71 Terpeshev, D. *Doklad za petgodishniia dŭrzhaven narodnostopanski plan pred V kongres na BRP(k) (23 dekemvri 1948).* [Report on the five-year national economic plan to the 5th Congress of the BRP(k), 23 December 1948]. S.: BKP, 1949. 77 pp.
Covers the period 1949–52. An English translation has been published: *Bulgaria's five-year-plan: report submitted to the V Congress of the Bulgarian Communist Party.* S.: Press Dept., Ministry of Foreign Affairs, 1949. 70 pp. [Not seen].

B72 *Direktiva po II petgodishen plan za razvitieto na Narodna republika Bŭlgariia prez 1953–1957 g.* [Directives on the second five-year plan for the development of the PR of Bulgaria, 1953–1957]. S.: BKP, 1955. 63 pp.

Covers the period 1953–7. An English edition is available with the above title (S.: 1954. 31 pp.). It contains the economic features of the 'new course' announced by Chervenkov in September 1953.

B73 *Direktivi na Sedmiia kongres na Bŭlgarskata komunisticheska partiia po tretiia petgodishen plan za razvitieto na Narodna republika Bŭlgariia prez perioda 1958–1962 g.* [Directives of the 7th Congress of the Bulgarian Communist Party on the third five-year plan for the development of the People's Republic of Bulgaria from 1958–1962]. S.: BKP, 1958. 23 pp.

An English translation with the above title has been published (S.: Publishing House of the Bulgarian Communist Party, 1958. 31 pp.). The BCP CC revised the economic targets upwards at the end of the year; it was known as the 'great leap forward'.

B74 *Direktivi na Tsentralniia komitet na Bŭlgarskata komunisticheska partiia po chetvŭrtiia petgodishen plan za razvitieto na Narodna republika Bŭlgariia prez perioda 1961–1965 g.* [Directives of the CC of the BCP on the fourth five-year plan for the development of the PR of Bulgaria from 1961 to 1965]. S.: BKP, 1962. 35 pp.

A 20-year development plan was also enacted at this time: *Direktivi na Osmiia kongres na Bŭlgarskata komunisticheska partiia za razvitieto na Narodna republika Bŭlgariia prez perioda 1961–1980 g.: prieti edinodushno na noemvri 1962 g.* [Directives of the 8th Congress of the Bulgarian Communist Party for the development of the People's Republic of Bulgaria, 1961–1980: unanimously adopted in November 1962]. S.: BKP, 1962. 48 pp. An English translation is available with the above title (S.: Foreign Languages Press, 1963. 71 pp.) [Not seen].

B75 *Direktivi na Devetiia kongres na Bŭlgarskata komunisticheska partiia po petgodishniia plan za razvitieto na narodnoto stopanstvo na NR Bŭlgariia prez perioda 1966–1970 g.* [Directives of the 9th Congress of the Bulgarian Communist Party on the five-year plan for the development of the national economy of Bulgaria, 1966–1970]. S.: BKP, 1966. 47 pp. [Not seen].

B76 *Direktivi za sotsialno-ikonomicheskoto razvitie na Narodna republika Bŭlgariia prez godinite na shestata petiletka 1971–1975 g.* [Directives for the socioeconomic development of the People's Republic of Bulgaria under the sixth five-year plan, 1971–1975]. S.: Partizdat, 1971. 64 pp.

An edition in English was published by Sofia Press in 1971 (50 pp.).

B77 *Osnovni nasoki na Edinadeseti kongres na BKP za obshtestveno-ikonomicheskoto razvitie na Narodna republika Bŭlgariia pred sedmata petiletka.* [Guidelines of the 11th Congress of the Bulgarian Communist Party on the socioeconomic development of the People's

Republic of Bulgaria under the seventh five-year plan]. S.: Partizdat, 1976. 77 pp.

Covers the period 1976–80. An English translation was published in 1976 by Sofia Press (92 pp.).

Trade

B78 *Tŭrgovski dogovori na Bŭlgariia.* [Bulgarian trade treaties]. Comp. by P. M. Penkov et al. S.: Bŭlgarska tŭrgovska palata, 1969–. Vol. 1–.

A collection of selected treaties, agreements and other economic pacts concluded between Bulgaria and foreign powers. Vol. 1 covers the period 1878–1944; vol. 2, 1944–67; vol. 3, 1968–August 1970.

B79 *Vŭnshna tŭrgoviia.* [Foreign trade]. S.: 1952–. Monthly.

Published by the Ministry of Foreign Trade and containing relevant articles, facts and figures.

B80 *Vŭnshna tŭrgoviia na NR Bŭlgariia: zakoni, postanovleniia, razporezhdaniia, naredbi, pravilnitsi i dr.: normativni aktove.* [Foreign trade of Bulgaria: laws, decisions, directives, regulations, rules, etc.: normative acts]. Chief ed. P. M. Penkov. S.: Nauka i izkustvo, 1969. 655 pp.

A collection of Bulgarian foreign trade laws and regulations. See also *Sbornik ot osnovni normativni aktove po vŭnshnata tŭrgoviia na NR Bŭlgariia.* [Collection of basic normative acts on the foreign trade of the PR of Bulgaria]. Comp. by B. I. Ivanchev and I. B. Laskov. Ed. P. M. Penkov. S.: Ministerstvo na vŭnshna tŭrgoviia, 1971. 296 pp.

B81 *Vŭnshna tŭrgoviia na Narodna Republika Bŭlgariia: statisticheski danni [1939–].* [Foreign trade of the People's Republic of Bulgaria: statistical facts, 1939–]. S.: Dŭrzhavno upravlenie za informatsiia, 1950/67–. Annual.

A monographic statistical review listing foreign trade data for the period 1939 to the date of each volume. The 1973 volume, for example, contains data for 1939, 1950, 1955, 1960, 1965, 1970, 1972 and 1973; the volume covering the period 1939–68 was also published in English: *Foreign trade of the People's Republic of Bulgaria: statistic survey, 1939–1968.* S.: 1970. 297 pp. [Not seen].

Labour

B82 *Kodeks na truda: zakoni, ukazi, postanovleniia, razporezhdaniia, pravilnitsi, naredbi, instruktsii, i dr.: sbornik.* [Labour code: laws, edicts, decisions, directives, rules, regulations, instructions, etc.: collection]. Comp. by D. Dimitrov. S.: Nauka i izkustvo, 1969. 427 pp.

A recent collection of Bulgarian labour laws and regulations.

B83 *Normativni aktove po trudovo pravo.* [Normative acts on labour law].

Comp. by A. Vasilev. S.: SU Kliment Okhridski, 1979. 671 pp.
A collection of labour laws and legislation intended as an aid for
students of the Law Faculty at the University of Sofia. [Not seen].

SOCIAL AFFAIRS

Population

B84 *Demografska statistika.* [Demographic statistics]. S.: Tsentralno
statistichesko upravlenie, 1960–. Annual.

Supersedes the Agency's *Statistika za dvizhenieto na naselenieto v
NR Bŭlgariia za perioda 1947–1959 g.* [Statistics on the movements
of the population of the PR of Bulgaria for the period 1947–1959]. S.:
Nauka i izkustvo, 1961. 577 pp.

B85 *Prebroiavane na naselenieto na 1. dekemvri 1956 god: obshti rezultati.*
[Population census as of 1 December 1956: general results]. S.:
Nauka i izkustvo, 1959–61. 4 vols.

Population statistics compiled by the Central Statistical Office of
Bulgaria. Previous censuses in Bulgaria were in 1926, 1934 and 1946.

B86 *Returns of the 1 December 1965 population census in the People's
Republic of Bulgaria.* S.: Central Statistical Office, 1966. 111 pp.

The official statistics for the 1965 census are contained in *Rezultati
ot prebroiavaneto na naselenieto na 1.XII.1965 g.* [Results of the
census as of 1.12.1965]. S.: Tsentralno statistichesko upravlenie,
1968. Vol. I/1–4. Provides general coverage of the census throughout
Bulgaria. A second series was published by the Central Statistical
Office providing a breakdown of the census by region: *Rezultati ot
prebroiavaneto na naselenieto na 1.XII.1965 g.: po okrŭzi.* [Results of
the census as of 1.12.1965: by region]. S.: 1967. 34 vols.

General and miscellaneous

B87 *Normativni aktove za mladezhta: sbornik.* [Normative acts concerning young people: a collection]. S.: Narodni mladezh, 1979. 280 pp.
[Not seen].

B88 *Sbornik normativni aktove po obshtestveno osiguriavane.* [Collection of
normative acts on social insurance]. S.: SU Kliment Okhridski,
1976. 2nd ed. 125 pp.

A collection of laws and legislation on social security in Bulgaria.
Intended as an aid for students of the Law Faculty at the University
of Sofia.

B89 *Sbornik ot normativni aktove i ukazaniia po predvaritelniia sanitaren
kontrol.* [Collection of normative acts and directives on public
health]. S.: Meditsina i fizkultura, 1978. 193 pp. [Not seen].

B90 *Sbornik zakoni, ukazi, pravilnitsi, naredbi, instruktsii i dr. po pensiite v*

NRB. [Collection of laws, edicts, regulations, orders, instructions, etc., on pensions in the PR of Bulgaria]. S.: Tekhnika, 1970. 264 pp.

A later collection is *Normativni materiali po pensiite: sbornik.* [Normative materials on pensions: a collection]. S.: Nauka i izkustvo, 1976. 292 pp.

B91 Sipkov, I. *The law on the People's Militia of the People's Republic of Bulgaria.* Washington: Library of Congress, 1978. 47 pp.

A translation of the Bulgarian law of 1 March 1977.

CULTURAL AFFAIRS

B92 *Plenum of the Central Committee of the Bulgarian Communist Party on problems of education, July 30–31, 1969. On the freedom and further development of education in the People's Republic of Bulgaria.* S.: Sofia Press, 1972. 123 pp. [Not seen].

B93 *Narodna prosveta.* [People's education]. S.: 1929–. Monthly.

Organ of the Ministry of People's Education and the Association of Bulgarian Teachers.

B94 *Sbornik ot zakoni, ukazi, postanovleniia i pravilnitsi za vissheto obrazovanie.* [Collection of laws, edicts, decisions and regulations on higher education]. S.: Vissh. mashinno-elektrotekhn. institut V. I. Lenin, 1976. 183 pp.

Collection of laws and legislation concerning Bulgarian universities and colleges.

B95 *Sbornik zakoni, ukazi, postanovleniia na Ministerskiia sŭvet, pravilnitsi, naredbi, instruktsii, zapovedi i dr. po narodnata prosveta.* [Collection of laws, decrees, decisions of the Council of Ministers, rules, regulations, instructions, orders, etc., on public education]. Comp. by G. D. Kostadinov. S.: Dŭrzhavno izd-vo Formuliari i registri, 1956. 851 pp.

Covers the period from the communist seizure of power to 1 August 1956.

B96 *Zakon za avtorskoto pravo.* [Law on copyright]. S.: Nauka i izkustvo, 1975. 149 pp.

LEADERS' WORKS

B97 Chervenkov, V. *Po pŭtiia na Georgi Dimitrov: izbrani dokladi i rechi, 1948–1950.* [Along the path of Georgi Dimitrov: selected reports and speeches, 1948–1950]. S.: Bŭlgarska komunisticheska partiia, 1950. 537 pp.

A selection of addresses and speeches by Vŭlko Chervenkov, Secretary-General of the CC of the Bulgarian Communist Party from 1950 to 1954. He was demoted in April 1956 for 'encouraging the harmful cult of the individual'. As Secretary-General, Chervenkov made the major speech at the party congress in 1954: *Report of the Central Committee of the Bulgarian Communist Party to the Sixth Congress of the Party*. S.: 1954. 139 pp. In government, Chervenkov had much responsibility for cultural affairs and his views are reflected in his work *Za naukata, izkustvoto i kulturata*. [On science, art and culture]. S.: Bŭlgarski pisatel, 1953. 374 pp. See also his works *Za bŭlgaro–sŭvetska druzhba*. [On Bulgarian–Soviet friendship]. S.: Izd. na Sŭiuza na bŭlgaro–sŭvetskite d-va, 1954. 239 pp.; and *Za rabotata na Komunisticheskata partiia v selo: sbornik ot dokladi i statii*. [On the work of the Communist Party in the countryside: a collection of reports and articles]. S.: Bŭlgarska komunisticheska partiia, 1951. 374 pp.

B98 Dimitrov, G. *Sŭchineniia*. [Works]. S.: Bŭlgarska komunisticheska partiia, 1951–5. 14 vols.

The official and complete edition of the works of Georgi Dimitrov, one of the greatest figures among the Bulgarian communists. An index to Dimitrov's writings is provided by E. Savova in *Spravochnik kŭm sŭchineniiata na Georgi Dimitrov*. S.: BKP, 1957. 366 pp. A selected edition of his works was published in 1972 in 8 volumes: *Izbrani proizvedeniia*. S.: Partizdat, 1972. There have been a number of English translations of his works including: *Selected speeches and articles*. London: Wishart, 1951. 275 pp.; *Selected works, 1910–1949*. S.: Foreign Languages Press, 1960. 427 pp.; and *Selected works*. S.: Sofia Press, 1980. 3 vols. For a bibliography of Dimitrov, see Mladenova, V. *Georgi Dimitrov, 1882–1949: bibliografski materiali po sluchai 77 g. ot rozhdenieto i 10 g. ot smŭrtta mu*. [Georgi Dimitrov, 1882–1949: bibliographical materials on the occasion of 77 years from his birth and 10 years from his death]. S.: Dŭrzh. bibl. V. Kolarov, 1959. 24 pp.

B99 Kolarov, V. *Izbrani proizvedeniia*. [Selected works]. S.: BKP, 1954–5. 3 vols.

Kolarov was the third leg of the tripod (Dimitrov and Kostov were the other two) which collapsed in the late 1940s. He died in 1950. His *Spomeni*. [Reminiscences]. S.: BKP, 1968. 641 pp. is an interesting autobiography, although the period covered pertains to his youth and formative years. For a bibliography and chronology of Kolarov, see Edreva, P. *Vasil Kolarov: 95 g. ot rozhdenieto mu. Letopis i preporŭch. bibliografiia*. [Vasil Kolarov: 95 years from his birth. Annals and recommended bibliography]. S.: Narodna biblioteka Kiril i Metodii, 1972. 43 pp.

B100 Kostov, T. *Izbrani statii, dokladi, rechi*. [Selected articles, reports, speeches]. S.: Bŭlgarska komunisticheska partiia, 1965. 962 pp.

Posthumous edition of the writings of a former Secretary of the Party, executed for Titoism in 1949. It contains many of his public speeches after 1944. A more recently published collection covering his last years is *Izbrani proizvedeniia, 1944–1948*. [Selected works].

S.: Partizdat, 1978. 638 pp. The record of Kostov's trial may be found in *The trial of Traicho Kostov and his group*. S.: Press Dept., 1949. 644 pp. On the accusations made against Kostov, see Kolarov, V. *Antisŭvetskata i antipartiina deinost na Tr. Kostov*. [The anti-Soviet and anti-party activities of Tr. Kostov]. S.: 1949.

B101   Zhivkov, T. *Izbrani sŭchineniia*. [Selected works]. S.: Partizdat, 1975–9. 26 vols.

Contains selected writings and speeches by Todor Zhivkov who succeeded Chervenkov as Party Secretary in 1954 and who became Prime Minister in 1962. The most recent volume to appear is vol. 26 in 1979 which covers the period January–December 1977 (678 pp.). An earlier selection of his speeches and writings was contained in the 6-volume edition entitled *Izbrani rechi, dokladi i statii*. [Selected speeches, reports and articles]. S.: 1964–5. There are a number of his writings in English translation: *Speeches, reports, articles*. S.: Foreign Languages Press, 1964. 3 vols.; *For peace, friendship and socialism*. S.: Foreign Languages Press, 1966. 695 pp.; *Problems of the construction of an advanced socialist society in Bulgaria: reports and speeches*. S.: Sofia Press, 1969. 630 pp. A French translation—*Paix et progrès: la Bulgarie et le monde contemporain*. Paris: Hachette, 1978. 423 pp.—contains a selection of Zhivkov's speeches for the period 12 October 1966–2 March 1978.

C CZECHOSLOVAKIA

Dalibor Chrástek

INTRODUCTION

With the end of the Second World War in sight, President Beneš and representatives of his London government in exile travelled to Moscow to make plans for the future of Czechoslovakia with the Czech communist politicians who had spent the war in Moscow. The meetings took place from 22–9 March 1945 with equal representation of the Czech Communist, the Czech National Socialist, the Social Democratic and the People's (Catholic) Parties. These parties under the leadership of the Communist Party later formed the National Front coalition as the only recognized political power in the postwar state. The other parties of the First Republic, mostly right wing, were not acceptable to the communists and were accused of an appeasement policy with Nazi Germany. The Slovak National Council from the liberated part of Slovakia was represented at the meetings by members of the Slovak Democratic and the Slovak Communist Parties.

The communist representatives took the initiative by presenting a draft of their programme as a basis for negotiations. Accepted without significant changes, it became the so-called Košice Programme of the first government in the homeland, announced in Košice on 5 April by the Prime Minister Z. Fierlinger. The most important points were the closest alliance with the Soviet Union and at home the government's power would be based on National Committees, elected by popular vote, at local and regional level. The members of the National Committees could be recalled at any time if accused of non-compliance with public opinion. The Slovaks were recognized as a separate nation and the administration of Slovakia was to be carried out through their own organs. Another important point of the programme was the nationalization of the land and property of Nazi Germans and the latters' transfer to Germany as

43

agreed by the Allied conference in Potsdam in 1945. The transfer was carried out during 1946.

Until the election of the National Assembly, the President's decrees, prepared by the government, had the power of laws. From May to October 1945 ninety-eight decrees were issued and subsequently approved by the Provisional National Assembly in February 1946. Proportional representation of the parties in the National Assembly and the government was agreed by the parties of the National Front. The government's decision to press on with the economic programme of reconstruction and to postpone the preparation of the general election seems to have found public approval. A major step towards the socialist state was the decree of October 1945 by which the major industries, the mines, the banks and insurance companies were nationalized. At the same time large national organizations, such as the trade unions, the agricultural workers' unions, the youth organizations and others, all with strong communist membership, built up strong political pressure on the government through their resolutions and appeals.

The first general election took place on 26 May 1946. In Bohemia and Moravia the Communist Party obtained 40 per cent and in Slovakia 30 per cent of the votes. A surprising development was the failure of the Social Democratic Party, one of the strongest before the war, which obtained only 15.6 per cent. In Slovakia the Slovak Democratic Party gained victory, obtaining 62 per cent of the votes. Accusing it of having many wartime separatists among its supporters, the national government assumed tighter control of the Slovak regional administration. As a result of the election, Klement Gottwald was the first Communist Party Prime Minister to be appointed.

Friction between the communist and the non-communist parties of the National Front coalition increased during 1946 and 1947, particularly because of the communist pressure for wholesale nationalization and the appointments of communists to key posts, especially in the army and the police. Disagreements in the government between the communist ministers and those of the other parties led eventually to the resignation of the non-communist ministers in February 1948 in order to bring about new elections. The Communist Party, however, used the government crisis to call to Prague the national congress of workers, supported by armed factory militia and the newly formed action committees in factories in support of their policies, and demanded the replacement of the ministers who had resigned by those in sympathy with communist policies. Under this pressure the President appointed a new government which secured the Communist Party an unopposed leading position and means of pursuing its programme of further nationalization.

The Social Democratic Party amalgamated with the Communist Party in June 1948. The new constitution, called the Constitution of 9 May, sanctioning all political and economic changes, was presented to the President for signature, but Beneš refused and resigned his office. In the elections in May 1948, parties of the National Front presented a united list of candidates with the communists in leading positions. The new National Assembly elected Klement Gottwald as President and Antonín Zápotocký as the new Prime Minister.

The Ninth Congress of the Communist Party in 1949 approved general guidelines for the socialist economy, especially for the collectivization of agriculture, which was also continued by the next congress in 1954. Another major programme undertaken during the 1950s was the large-scale industrialization of Slovakia, especially the building up of heavy industry. The conflict between the Roman Catholic Church and the Communist Party ended with the compulsory appropriation of church property and land and the establishment of an Office for Church Affairs. By the so-called church laws of October 1948 all churches became state institutions and the government assumed power to approve or sanction appointments of priests, ministers and other church officers. The policy of close relations with the neighbouring socialist countries led Czechoslovakia to join Comecon in 1949 and the Warsaw Pact in 1955.

In 1949 the country's administration was divided into regions, replacing the old lands of Bohemia, Moravia and Slovakia. This system was further modified in 1960 by division of the country into 10 regions and 108 districts. Antonín Zápotocký became President after Gottwald's death in 1953. He was succeeded by Antonín Novotný in 1957. The conference of the Communist Party in 1960 declared that the aim of socialization of the country had been achieved. The new constitution of 1960 embodied these changes and the country was renamed the Czechoslovak Socialist Republic.

During the 1960s there was criticism within the Communist Party of the economic and political shortcomings of the leadership, and the pressure for changes increased. The Central Committee of the Party rehabilitated many party members and others who had received long prison sentences in the political trials of the 1950s.

At the beginning of 1968 the Central Committee removed Antonín Novotný from his post of First Secretary and replaced him by Alexander Dubček. In March Novotný resigned also as President and General Ludvík Svoboda was elected in his place. The liberalizing tendencies were, however, quashed by the intervention of the Warsaw Pact countries in August 1968 and the Marxist–Leninist line was re-established. The protocol of the meeting between the Czechoslovak government and Communist Party representatives with Soviet Party leaders in Moscow in August was followed by a so-called 'November resolution' of the Central Committee of the Czechoslovak Communist Party committing the government to measures for the reintroduction of orthodox Marxist–Leninist policies on the Soviet pattern. Among other measures a revision of the membership of the Communist Party purged party members who supported the Dubček regime. Ludvík Svoboda stayed as President, Gustav Husák replaced Dubček in 1969 as First Secretary, and after Svoboda's resignation due to ill health in 1975 Husák also became President.

The history of the changing relationship between the Czechs and Slovaks would require a lengthy treatment. For the purpose of this chapter it is sufficient to start with the war period. Though the extreme National Party succeeded in separating Slovakia from the rest of Czechoslovakia during the Second World War with the help of Hitler, most of the population and political leaders always favoured union with the Czechs and were preparing for the renewal of Czechoslovakia within prewar frontiers. However, there was no return to the First Republic as one nation-state. The self-confidence of the Slovaks, enhanced by the uprising, led them to demand certain self-government in the new state. As the result of negotiations the so-called 'asymmetric system' was agreed in the

Košice programme. This meant that the national government and parliament held the legislative, administrative and executive powers both for the whole country and, at the same time, also for Bohemia and Moravia in their regional affairs. The Slovak regional government, called the Slovak National Council, received certain autonomous powers to administer the affairs of the national and the regional interests of Slovakia. This plan was modified by three 'Prague agreements' of June 1945, April and June 1946 and then by the 1960 constitution, not conceding to the Slovaks their further demands for more autonomy.

Discussions and negotiations continued intermittently until March 1968 when the Slovak National Council made a proclamation about federation. Meanwhile, in the later 1960s, the climate of opinion had changed and national ambitions were no longer considered bourgeois and anti-socialist. The national government then appointed a committee to prepare legislation for the establishment of a federal system. The work was rushed through in order to be ready for the fiftieth anniversary of the Czechoslovak Republic. The constitutional laws concerning the Czechoslovak Federation were actually passed by parliament on the anniversary day, 28 October 1968, and came into force on 1 January 1969. These laws established two independent national republics of equal rights, the Czech Socialist Republic and the Slovak Socialist Republic, which voluntarily joined together in the Federal Czechoslovak Socialist Republic. The President, the Federal Assembly and the Federal Government exercise legislative and executive powers over the whole federation in matters of mutual concern, such as foreign relations, national defence, international trade, etc. In some other fields the responsibility is shared by the federal government and the republics, such as finance, internal trade, agriculture and industry, etc. In the third group are the matters which are the responsibility of individual republics only: education, cultural affairs, health, etc. These complicated federal laws have naturally been modified in later years in the light of their practical application. There is only one President—for the federation—but there are National Assemblies (parliaments) and Governments both for the federation and the individual republics. The Federal Assembly consists of two chambers: the Assembly of the People's Representatives and the Assembly of the Nations. Each republic's parliament consists of one chamber, called respectively the Czech National Council and the Slovak National Council. In addition to ministries there are several federal agencies to which power has been transferred by the government to carry out some laws by issuing relevant orders and regulations. Each republic has several similar agencies.

The federation laws were the last major change in the country's political and economic life. The 1970s could be briefly characterized by the efforts of the Communist Party and the government to pursue the Marxist–Leninist doctrine in politics and social life, and to develop the economy through five-year plans in the framework of Comecon's close cooperation.

Biographical notes

Beneš, Eduard (1884–1948). Foreign Minister 1918–35. President of Czechoslovakia 1935–48.

Dubček, Alexander (b. 1921). Communist Party official. Studied at the Party school in Moscow 1955–8. Member of Parliament 1960–70. Member of the Presidium of the Central Committee of the Communist Party of Czechoslovakia 1963–9. First Secretary of the Central Committee January 1968–April 1969. Removed from Central Committee January 1970. Ambassador to Turkey February–June 1970. Expelled from the Party and removed from office July 1970.

Fierlinger, Zdeněk (1891–1976). In the Czech Legion in Russia during the First World War. Joined the Social Democratic Party in 1920. Czechoslovak ambassador to various countries; to the USSR 1937–9 and again from 1942 to 1945. Prime Minister in the first postwar Czechoslovak government 1945–6. Member of Parliament from 1945. Deputy Prime Minister 1948–53. Chairman of Parliament 1953–64 and member of its Presidium 1964–8.

Gottwald, Klement (1896–1953). From 1925 was a member of the Central Committee of the Czechoslovak Communist Party. Member of Parliament from 1929. During the war, head of the Moscow leadership of the Czechoslovak Communist Party. Appointed Prime Minister in 1946, President in 1948.

Husák, Gustav (b. 1913). Member of the Communist Party from 1933. During the Slovak Uprising and after the war was vice-chairman of the Slovak National Council and Commissioner for the Interior. Member of Parliament 1945–51. Expelled from the Party and arrested in 1951, and sentenced to life imprisonment in 1954. Released in 1960 and reinstated in the Party in 1963. Deputy Prime Minister April–December 1968. From August 1968 First Secretary of the Slovak Communist Party and from April 1969 General Secretary of the Central Committee of the Czechoslovak Communist Party. From 1976 also President of Czechoslovakia.

Lenárt, Jozef (b. 1923). Slovak Communist Party official. Attended Higher Party School in Moscow 1953–6. Prime Minister September 1963–April 1968. First Secretary of the Slovak Communist Party from January 1970.

Novotný, Antonin (1904–75). Joined the Communist Party in 1921. During the war was in Mauthausen concentration camp. In 1953 became Deputy Prime Minister and First Secretary of the Central Committee. Elected President of the Republic 1957. Removed from the post of First Secretary in January 1968 and resigned as President in March 1968.

Svoboda, Ludvík (1895–1979). During the war was Commander of the Czechoslovak Army Corps in the USSR. Promoted to general in 1945. Minister of National Defence 1945–50, Deputy Prime Minister 1950–1, member of the Central Committee of the Communist Party 1949–52. Stripped of all posts after the Slánský trial. Later became Head of the Military Academy 1955–8. President of the Czechoslovak Republic 1968–75.

Zápotocký, Antonín (1884–1975). Member of the Social Democratic Party and then of the Communist Party. Member of Parliament from 1925. During the war was in Oranienburg concentration camp. Chairman of the Trade Unions 1945–50. Prime Minister 1948–53. President of the Czechoslovak Republic 1953–7.

Diagram of the Federal ministries and central agencies

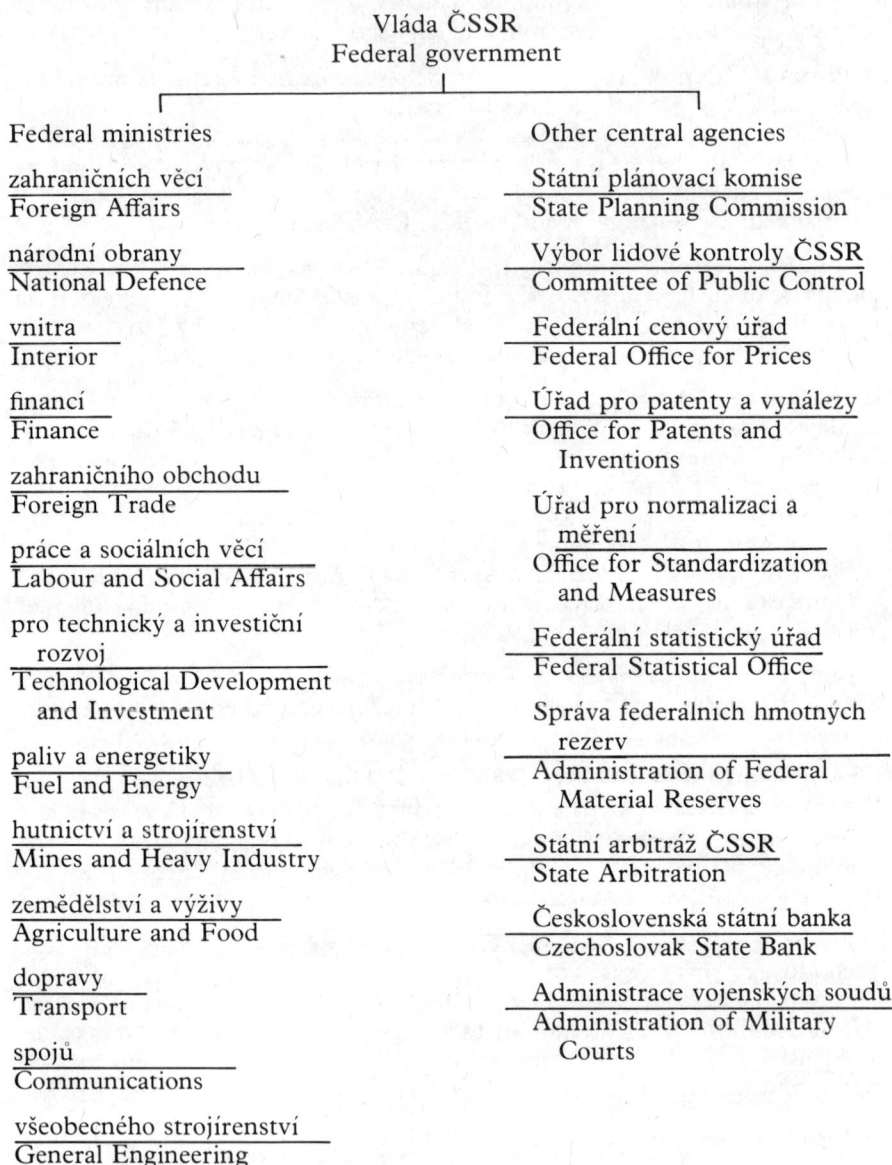

Vláda ČSSR
Federal government

Federal ministries	Other central agencies
zahraničních věcí Foreign Affairs	Státní plánovací komise State Planning Commission
národní obrany National Defence	Výbor lidové kontroly ČSSR Committee of Public Control
vnitra Interior	Federální cenový úřad Federal Office for Prices
financí Finance	Úřad pro patenty a vynálezy Office for Patents and Inventions
zahraničního obchodu Foreign Trade	Úřad pro normalizaci a měření
práce a sociálních věcí Labour and Social Affairs	Office for Standardization and Measures
pro technický a investiční rozvoj Technological Development and Investment	Federální statistický úřad Federal Statistical Office
paliv a energetiky Fuel and Energy	Správa federálních hmotných rezerv Administration of Federal Material Reserves
hutnictví a strojírenství Mines and Heavy Industry	Státní arbitráž ČSSR State Arbitration
zemědělství a výživy Agriculture and Food	Československá státní banka Czechoslovak State Bank
dopravy Transport	Administrace vojenských soudů Administration of Military Courts
spojů Communications	
všeobecného strojírenství General Engineering	

Diagram of the ministries and central agencies of the Czech Socialist Republic

Vláda ČSR
Government

Ministries	Central agencies
financí Finance	Česká plánovací komise Czech Planning Commission
práce a sociálních věcí Labour and Social Affairs	Výbor lidové kontroly ČSR Committee of the People's Control
výstavby a techniky Reconstruction and Technology	Český statistický úřad Czech Statistical Office
školství Education	Český cenový úřad Czech Office for Prices

kultury
Culture
	Český úřad geodetický
	   a kartografický
	Czech Office for Geodesy
	   and Cartography

zdravotnictví Health	Český geologický úřad Czech Geological Office
spravedlnosti Justice	Český báňský úřad Czech Office for Mines
vnitra Interior	Česká komise pro vědecké hodnosti Czech Office for Scientific Qualifications
průmyslu Industry	
stavebnictví Building Industry	Česká komise pro tisk a informace Czech Commission for Media and Information
zemědělství a výživy Agriculture and Food	
lesního a vodního hospodářství Forestry and Water	Český úřad pro bezpečnost v práci
obchodu Trade	Czech Office for Safety at Work

The diagram of these ministries and central agencies applies also to the Slovak Socialist Republic.

49

Diagram representing the hierarchy of supreme federal offices of the Czechoslovak Socialist Republic

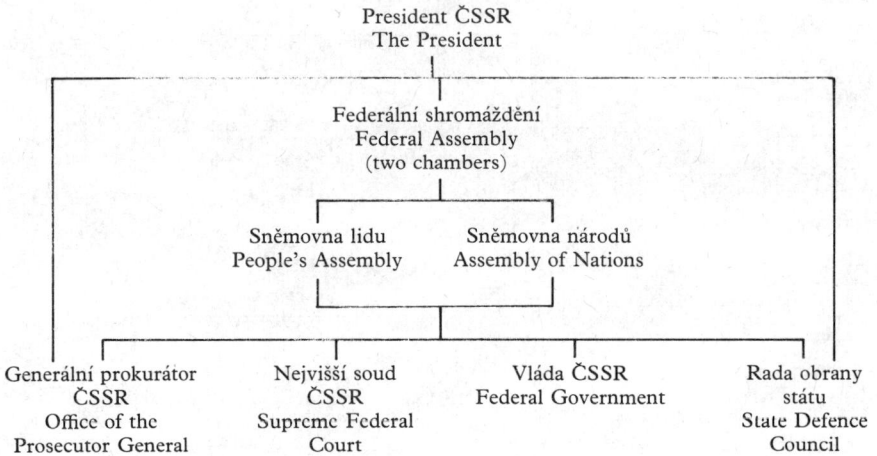

President ČSSR
The President

Federální shromáždění
Federal Assembly
(two chambers)

Sněmovna lidu
People's Assembly

Sněmovna národů
Assembly of Nations

Generální prokurátor
ČSSR
Office of the
Prosecutor General

Nejvišší soud
ČSSR
Supreme Federal
Court

Vláda ČSSR
Federal Government

Rada obrany
státu
State Defence
Council

GENERAL BIBLIOGRAPHIES AND REFERENCE WORKS

National bibliographies

C1 *Bibliografický katalog. České knihy.* [Bibliography of Czech books]. P.: Státní knihovna ČSR, 1922–. Monthly (before 1976 weekly).

An official bibliography of books and other non-periodical material published in the Czech language. In each issue the material is arranged in classified order based on the Soviet official bibliography. Annual indexes of authors, editors, titles, subjects, etc. appear after long delays.

C2 *Slovenská národná bibliografia. Knihy.* [Slovak national bibliography. Books]. Martin: Matica Slovenská, 1922–. Monthly. (Frequency varied before 1961).

Formerly called *Bibliografický katalog ČSSR. Slovenské knihy.* [Czechoslovak Bibliography. Slovak books.] An official bibliography of Slovak books and other non-periodical material. Each monthly part has personal and title indexes which are cumulated annually with additional subject indexes. Arrangement is in classified order.

C3 *Bibliografický katalog ČSSR. Články v českých časopisech.* [Czechoslovak bibliographical catalogue. Articles in Czech journals]. P.: Státní knihovna ČSR. 1954–. Monthly.

Important because it includes national newspapers which do not have indexes of their own. Classified arrangement. Each issue has an author and subject index and a list of excerpted journals.

C4 *Slovenská národná bibliografia. Články.* [Slovak national bibliography. Articles]. Martin: Matica slovenská. 1954–. Monthly.

Classified arrangement. Personal and subject indexes with a list of authors of articles and a list of excerpted newspapers and journals. Official publications are not included.

Other general bibliographies and reference works

C5 *Seznam oficiálních a poloofíciálních periodických publikací ČSSR.* [List of Czechoslovak official and semi-official serials]. P.: Státní knihovna ČSR, 1973. 66 pp.

Compiled by the Centre for the International Exchange of Publications. Titles in Czech and Slovak are followed by English translations. The list is correct to the end of 1972. A new revised and updated list is in preparation.

C6 *Bibliography of social science periodicals and monograph series: Czechoslovakia, 1948–1963.* By Foreign Demographic Analysis Division, Bureau of the Census. (Foreign Social Science Bibliographies. Series P-92, No. 19.) [Washington, D.C.]: U.S. Bureau of the Census, 1965. 129 pp.

Records periodicals and monographs published in Czechoslovakia from 1948. Includes economics, law, political science and statistics. The listed publications cover the whole range of history to the date of publication. Subject, title and author indexes.

C7   Horecky, P. L. *East Central Europe. A guide to basic publications.* Chicago, London: The University of Chicago Press, 1969. xxvi, 956 pp.

An important, but very selective bibliography. Section dealing with Czechoslovakia on pp. 137–358 contains 877 entries. Detailed annotations referring to further works on the subject compiled by experts. Official postwar publications form only a small proportion.

C8   Sturm, R. *Czechoslovakia: a bibliographic guide.* Washington: Library of Congress, 1967. xii, 157 pp.

Books and serials are recorded in a continuous evaluating narrative form under broad headings, e.g. politics and government, etc. The second part lists in alphabetical order works mentioned in the first part with the usual bibliographical information. Many works are out of date and have been superseded by more recent works or revised editions.

CONSTITUTIONAL DOCUMENTS

Pre-federation constitutions

C9   *Dokumenty o ústavnom postavení Slovenska.* [Documents concerning the constitutional position of Slovakia]. Výklad J. Kováčik a K. Král. P.: Ministerstvo informací, 1947. 53 pp.

Decrees of the president, acts of parliament and government regulations concerning the constitutional changes in the position of Slovakia in relation to the whole country and its legislative and administrative powers.

C10   *Ústava 9. května. (Ústavní zákon 'Ústava Československé Republiky' č.150/1948 Sb.)* [The Constitution of the Czechoslovak Republic of 9 May 1948, Constitutional Act no. 150/1948]. P.: Ministerstvo informací, 1949. 116 pp.

The full text of the constitution and the minutes of the meeting of the Constitutional National Assembly which passed the Act.

C11   *The Constitution of the Czechoslovak Republic. (Constitutional Act of May 9th 1948 etc.)* 2nd ed. P.: Czechoslovak Ministry of Information and Public Culture, 1948. 78 pp.

An English translation of the text of the constitution.

C12   *Ústava Československé Socialistické Republiky.* [Constitution of the

Czechoslovak Socialist Republic]. (Právnické edice. Zákony.) P.: Orbis, 1960. 47 pp.

An edition of the text of the constitution of 11 July 1960 with a commentary.

C13   *The Constitution of the Czechoslovak Socialist Republic.* P.: Orbis, 1960. 105 pp.

An English translation of the text of the constitution of 11 July 1960. With a preface by Ján Gronský. Several later editions have prefaces by different authors.

Federation

C14   Chovanec, J. & Trella, R.: *Ústava Československej Socialistickej Republiky.* [Constitution of the Czechoslovak Socialist Republic]. 5. vyd. (Ústavy európskych socialistických štátov.) Bratislava: Pravda, 1976. 168 pp.

The introduction gives a survey of the constitutional development of Czechoslovakia from 1918 with more detailed discussion of the post-1945 constitutions. The full texts of the 1960 constitution and of the constitutional law no. 143 of 27 October 1968 on the establishment of the Czechoslovak federation, and the supplementary constitutional law no. 125 of 20 December 1970 are included.

C15   *Československá federace. Zákony o federativním uspořádání ČSSR.* [The Czechoslovak federation. Laws on the federal system of Czechoslovakia]. Zpracoval J. Grospič. (Právnické edice. Zákony.) P.:Orbis, 1972. 705 pp.

A very useful book on the complex matter of the federation.

C16   *Constitutional Act no. 143 of October 27th, 1968, concerning the Czechoslovak Federation.* In: Jičínský, J. & Skála, J. *The Czechoslovak Federation.* P.: 1969, pp. 17–76.

C17   *Constitutional Act no. 144 of October 27th, 1968, concerning the status of nationalities in the Czechoslovak Socialist Republic.* In: Jičínský, J. & Skála, J. *The Czechoslovak Federation.* P.: 1969, pp. 77–9.

The rights of minorities in Czechoslovakia.

LEGISLATION

General collections

C18   *Bibliography of Czechoslovak legal literature 1945–1958.* Editor: V. Knapp. (The Institute of Law of the Czechoslovak Academy of Sciences.) P.: Publishing House of the Czechoslovak Academy of Sciences, 1959. 261 pp.

C19   Czafik, J. & Virsík, A. *Normotvorba vo federativnej ČSSR*

1969–1979. [Legislation in Federal Czechoslovakia 1969–1979]. Bratislava: Obzor, 1980. 2 vols.

Vol. 2 contains the texts of laws and regulations concerned with the legislature.

C20 *Sbírka zákonů: Československá socialistická republika, Česká socialistická republika, Slovenská socialistická republika.* [Collection of laws: Czechoslovak Socialist Republic, Czech Socialist Republic and Slovak Socialist Republic]. P.: 1918–. Irregular.

The full texts of all the laws when issued by the federal parliament and the parliaments of each of the republics. Title has varied with the official designation of the state. Also publ. in Slovak, and until 1945 in German.

Civil law

C21 *Občanský zákoník a předpisy souvisící.* [A code of civil law and relevant regulations]. Zpracoval A. Málek. (Právnické edice. Zákony.) P.: Orbis, 1964. 362 pp.

This law, dated 5 March 1964, supersedes that of 1950.

C22 *Státní občanství ČSSR. Ucelený výklad právních předpisů, upravujících československé státní občanství.* [Citizenship of Czechoslovakia. A comprehensive explanation of the legal regulations on Czechoslovak citizenship]. Zpracovali J. Černý a V. Červenka. P.: Orbis, 1963. 238 pp.

Criminal law

C23 *Trestní zákon, trestní řád a předpisy souvisící.* [Code of criminal law and criminal procedure and related regulations]. Druhé, doplněné vydání. Zpracovali K. Černý a J. Kunc. P.: Orbis, 1958. 627 pp.

C24 *Trestní zákon, trestní řád a předpisy souvisící (textové vydání).* [Criminal law and criminal procedure. Text edition]. 2. přepracované a doplněné vydání. Zpracoval J. Tolar. P.: Orbis, 1962. 748 pp.

The text of the criminal law of 29 November 1961, which replaces that of 1950, and the text of the law on criminal jurisdiction of 29 November 1961, which replaces the law of 1956.

C25 *Sbírka soudních rozhodnutí a stanovisek.* [A collection of judicial interpretations and decisions]. P.: Nejvyšší soud ČSSR, 1948–. 10 issues and 1 index vol. p.a.

Decisions by the Supreme Court on the appeals against the verdicts of lower courts. Title varies.

C26 *Občanský soudní řád, notářský řád a předpisy s nimi souvisící.* [A code of the regulations of the Civil law court proceedings and of the regulations for notaries public and relevant instructions]. Uspořádal J. Štěpán. P.: Orbis, 1964. 546 pp.

OTHER GENERAL LEGISLATIVE DOCUMENTS

C27 *Úřední list Československé Republiky*. [The official bulletin of the Czechoslovak Republic]. P.: Ministerstvo vnitra, 1920–62. Irregular.

Regulations and instructions issued by the government and various ministries. Title varies with the nomenclature of the state.

C28 *Ústřední věstník České socialistické republiky*. [Central bulletin of the Czech Socialist Republic]. P.: Ministerstvo spravedlnosti ČSR, 1969–. Irregular.

C29 *Ústredný vestník Slovenskej Socialistickej Republiky*. [Central bulletin of the Slovak Socialist Republic]. Bratislava: Ministerstvo spravodlivosti Slovenskej Socialistickej Republiky, 1969–. Irregular.

Parliamentary proceedings

C30 *Těsnopisecké zprávy o schůzích Prozatímního Národního Shromáždění Republiky Československé*. [Minutes of the sessions of the Provisional National Assembly of the Czechoslovak Republic]. P.: 1945–6.

Sessions from 28 October 1945 to 14 February 1946.

C31 *Těsnopisecké zprávy o schůzích ústavodárného Národního Shromáždění Republiky Československé*. [Minutes of the sessions of the Constitutional National Assembly of the Czechoslovak Republic]. P.: 1946–8.

Sessions from 18 June 1946 to 9 May 1948.

C32 *Těsnopisecké zprávy o schůzích Národního Shromáždění Republiky Československé*. [Minutes of the sessions of the National Assembly of the Czechoslovak Republic]. P.: Kancelář NS, 1949–68.

Sessions from June 1948 to December 1968. Drafts of proposed laws and cumulative indexes issued as supplements.

C33 *Federální shromáždění Československé Socialistické Republiky.— Zpráva o schůzi Sněmovny lidu*. [Federal Assembly of the Czechoslovak Socialist Republic.—Minutes of the sessions of the People's Assembly]. P.: Kancelář Federálního shromáždění, 1969–. Irregular.

C34 *Federální shromáždění Československé Socialistické Republiky.— Zpráva o schůzi Sněmovny národů*. [Federal Assembly of the Czechoslovak Socialist Republic.—Minutes of the sessions of the Assembly of Nations]. P.: Kancelář Federálního shromáždění, 1969–. Irregular.

Some parts are in the Slovak language: *Správa o schôdzi snemovne národov*.

C35 *Federální shromáždění Československé Socialistické Republiky.— Zpráva o společné schůzi sněmovny lidu a sněmovny národů*. [Federal

Assembly of the Czechoslovak Socialist Republic.—Minutes of the Joint sessions of the People's Assembly and the Assembly of Nations]. P.: Kancelář Federálního shromáždění, 1971–. Irregular.

C36 *Česká národní rada.—Těsnopisecká zpráva o schůzích České národní rady.* [Minutes of the meetings of the Czech National Council]. P.: Kancelář České národní rady, 1969–. Irregular.

GENERAL PARTY DOCUMENTS

Party congresses

C37 *Sněm budovatelů. Protokol VIII. řádného sjezdu Komunistické strany Československa ve dnech 28.–31. března, 1946.* [Minutes of the 8th Congress of the Czechoslovak Communist Party, 28–31 March 1946]. P.: Sekretariát Ústředního výboru KSČ, 1946. 216 pp.

C38 *Protokol IX. řádného sjezdu Komunistické strany Československa. V Praze 25.–29. května 1949.* [Minutes of the 9th Congress of the Czechoslovak Communist Party. Prague, 25–9 May 1949]. P.: Ústřední výbor KSČ, 1949. 575 pp.

C39 *X. sjezd Komunistické strany Československa [červen 1954.]* [10th Congress of the Czechoslovak Communist Party, June 1954]. (*Nová mysl*, roč. 1954, čís. 7.) P.: Rudé právo, 1954.

C40 *XI. sjezd Komunistické strany Československa.* [11th Congress of the Czechoslovak Communist Party]. (*Nová mysl*, zvláštní číslo: červen 1958). P.: Rudé právo, 1958.

C41 *XII. sjezd Komunistické strany Československa, 4.–8. prosince 1962.* [12th Congress of the Czechoslovak Communist Party, 4–8 December 1962]. P.: Ústřední výbor KSČ, 1962. 131 pp.

C42 *XIII. sjezd Komunistické strany Československa. Praha 31.V.–4.VI.1966.* [13th Congress of the Czechoslovak Communist Party. Prague, 31.5.–4.6.1966]. P.: Svoboda, 1966. 493 pp.

C43 *XIV. mimořádný sjezd KSČ. Protokol a dokumenty.* [14th Extraordinary Congress of the Czechoslovak Communist Party. Proceedings and documents]. Vienna: Europa Verlag, 1970. 292 pp.
The congress was held in Prague on 22 August 1968 immediately after the Soviet intervention. Volume edited and introduced by J. Pelikán. The English translation under the title *The Secret Vysočany Congress* was published by Allen Lane in London, 1971. The Party subsequently denied the validity of this congress.

C44 *XIV. sjezd Komunistické strany Československa. Praha 25. května–29. května 1971.* [14th Congress of the Czechoslovak Communist Party. Prague, 25–9 May 1971]. P.: Svoboda, 1971. 660 pp.

C45   *XV. sjezd Komunistické strany Československa. Praha 12.–16. dubna 1976.* [15th Congress of the Czechoslovak Communist Party. Prague, 12–16 April 1976]. P.: Svoboda, 1977. 567 pp.

C46   *Celostátní konference Komunistické strany Československa.* [National conference of the Czechoslovak Communist Party]. (*Nová mysl.* Zvláštní číslo, červen 1956.) P.: Rudé právo, 1956.

C47   *Celostátní konference Komunistické strany Československa, 5.7.–7.7.1960.* [National conference of the Czechoslovak Communist Party, 5–7 July 1960]. (*Nová mysl,* Special issue, July 1960.) P.: Rudé právo, 1960. 311 pp.
      Includes directives for the third Five-Year Plan and draft of the text of a new constitution.

C48   *Sjazd Komunistickej strany Slovenska v dňoch 12.–14. mája 1966.* [Congress of the Communist Party of Slovakia, 12–14 May 1966]. Bratislava: Vydavatelstvo politickej literatury, 1966. 345 pp.

C49   *Zjazd Komunistickej strany Slovenska, 13.–15. mája 1971.* [Congress of the Slovak Communist Party, 13–15 May 1971]. Bratislava: Pravda, 1971. 206 pp.

C49a *Zjazd Komunistickej strany Slovenska, 25.–27. marca 1976.* [Congress of the Slovak Communist Party, 25–27 March 1976]. Bratislava: 1976. [Not seen].

Other party material

C50   Kuhn, H. *Zeittafel zur Geschichte der kommunistischen Partei der Tschechoslowakei von den Anfängen der Arbeiterbewegung bis zur Gegenwart.* München: Fides-Verlagsgesellschaft, 1973. 135 pp.
      Records in chronological order up to July 1973 important meetings of the Party and the Central Committee with brief notes on the speeches and proceedings of the meetings.

C51   *Rozhodující střetnutí. Dokumenty o činnosti KSČ od slovenské politické krize do února 1948.* [Decisive conflict. Documents of the activities of the Communist Party from the Slovak political crisis to February 1948]. P.: Svoboda, 1973. 330 pp.
      The Communist Party's interpretation of the political events from June 1947 to February 1948.

C52   *Usnesení a dokumenty ÚV KSČ. Od XI. sjezdu do celostátní konference 1960.* [Resolutions and documents of the Party Central Committee. From the 11th Congress to the National Conference 1960]. P.: Stát. nakladatelství polit. lit., 1960. 864 pp.
      Covers the period from June 1958 to July 1960. Earlier vol. subtitled *Od X. do XI. sjezdu KSČ,* publ. 1958. [Not seen].

C53   *Usnesení a dokumenty ÚV KSČ, od celostátní konference KSČ 1960 do XII. sjezdu KSČ.* [Resolutions and documents of the Party Central

Committee. From the National Conference in 1960 to the 12th Congress]. P.: Nakladatelství politické literatury, 1962. 2 vols.
Covers the period from July 1960 to September 1962.

C54 *Usnesení a dokumenty ÚV KSČ. Od listopadu 1962 do konce roku 1963.* [Resolutions and documents of the Party Central Committee, November 1962–December 1963]. P.: Naklad. polit. lit., 1964. 558 pp.

C55 *Usnesení a dokumenty ÚV KSČ, 1964.* [Resolutions and documents of the Party Central Committee, 1964]. P.: Naklad. polit. lit., 1965. 420 pp.

C56 *Rok šedesátý osmý v usneseních a dokumentech ÚV KSČ.* [The year 1968 in resolutions and documents of the Party Central Committee]. P.: Svoboda, 1969. 453 pp.
Reports on the meetings which took place between 3 January and 21 December 1968, including the speeches of Dubček and other documents relating to the meetings of the Czechoslovak and the Soviet representatives. Subsequent volumes of Central Committee documents were publ. for 'internal use' only.

C57 *Akční program Komunistické strany Československa přijatý na plenárním zasedání ÚV KSČ dne 5. dubna 1968.* [A programme of action approved at the plenary meeting of the Party Central Committee on 5 April 1968]. P.:Svoboda, 1968. 63 pp.
Text of the programme, 'The road to socialism in Czechoslovakia'. The English translation, *The Action Programme of the Communist Party of Czechoslovakia*, was published by the Central Committee in April 1968.

GENERAL STATISTICS

C58 *Bibliografie československé statistiky a demografie.* [A bibliography of Czechoslovak statistics and demography]. P.: Výzkumný ústav sociálně ekonomických informací, 1965–. Annual.
Important comprehensive bibliography. It includes both monographs and articles. Some entries are annotated. Index of personal names included.

C59 *Külföldi statisztikai adatforrások. A Központi Statisztikai Hivatal könyvtárának katalógusa. 2. Czehszlovákia.* [Sources of foreign statistical data. Catalogue of the Hungarian Central Statistical Office Library. Vol. 2. Czechoslovakia]. Budapest: Központi Statisztikai Hivatal, Könyvtár és Dokumentációs Szolgálat, 1979. 102 pp.
A very useful, detailed bibliography of Czechoslovak statistical publications from 1918 up to the present. List of contents in English. Gives all changes in names of institutions with dates.

C60 *Československá statistika.* [Czechoslovak statistics]. P.: Statistický úřad, 1922–. Irregular.

The most important official statistical series. The first series (of 18 subseries) was continued (with some interruptions during the Second World War) until 1949. The last part is no. 188. The new series started in the early 1950s. It is published in annual series with irregular numbers of issues. Also includes results of censuses. Only some subseries are available abroad. However, all titles are listed in C58.

C61 *Statistická ročenka Československé Socialistické Republiky.* [Statistical yearbook of the Czechoslovak Socialist Republic]. (Federální statistický úřad, Český statistický úřad, Slovenský štatistický úrad.) P., Bratislava: 1934–. Annual.
Title varies with the nomenclature of the state. Not publ. 1939–56. An official summary of statistical information for all fields of national economy, administration, population, cultural life, etc.

C62 *Statistické přehledy.* [Statistical surveys]. P.: Federální statistický úřad, Panorama, [1967–]. Monthly.
Statistical tables showing the development of the national economy. Includes separate information on the Czech and Slovak republics.

C63 *Zpravodaj ústředních statistických orgánů: Federální statistický úřad, Český statistický úřad, Slovenský štatistický úrad.* [Bulletin of the Central statistical offices]. P.: Federální statistický úřad, 1959–. 15 issues p.a.
Formerly called *Zpravodaj Státního statistického úřadu.* Contains regulations issued by various ministries in conjunction with the statistical offices.

C64 *Slovensko 1945–1957. Hospodársky a kultúrny rozvoj.* [Slovakia 1945–1957. Economic and cultural development]. Spracoval kolektív Slovenského štatistického úradu. Bratislava: Slovenské vydavateľstvo politickej literatúry, 1958. 191 pp.
Comparative figures and tables illustrate the official policy to bring the Slovak economy and culture into line with that of the Czechs by a programme of investment and construction.

C65 *Demografie. Revue pro výzkum populačního vývoje.* [Demography. Journal for research into the population development]. P.: Federální statist. úřad, Panorama, 1959–. Quarterly.
Statistical surveys of various population changes, e.g. housing, marriages, deaths, etc.

OTHER GENERAL SOURCES OF DOCUMENTATION

C66 *Rudé právo. Orgán Ústředního výboru Komunistické strany Československa.* [The Red right. Organ of the Central Committee of the Czechoslovak Communist Party]. P.: ÚV KSČ, 1920–. Daily.

Detailed reports on party and state events. Major speeches by party officials and government ministers.

C67 *Život strany. Časopis ÚV KSČ.* [Life of the Party]. P.: Rudé právo, 1954–. Fortnightly.
Party documents and reports on party committees' meetings. Monthly bibliography of documents of ÚV KSČ, speeches, articles by leading party members.

C68 *Pravda. Orgán ústredného výboru Komunistickej strany Slovenska.* [The Truth]. Bratislava: ÚV KSS, 1921–. Daily.
The official journal of the Slovak Communist Party. Party documents, speeches of party officials and reports on Central Committee meetings reproduced in full.

INTERNATIONAL RELATIONS

C69 *Národní shromáždění a politika slovanské spolupráce. Smlouvy o spojenectví slovanských národů.* [The National Assembly and the policy of Slavonic cooperation. Treaties of alliance with other Slavonic countries]. Sestavili V. Osvald a K. Zajíček. (Publikace Národního shromáždění, sv. 5.) P.: Ministerstvo informací, 1947. 85 pp.
Includes texts of treaties with USSR, Yugoslavia and Poland on friendship, mutual assistance and cooperation.

C70 *Friendship strengthened in struggle. Speeches by the Czechoslovak and Soviet leaders at a Friendship rally in the Kremlin Palace of Congresses and the joint Soviet–Czechoslovak statement of October 27th 1969.* Moscow: Novosti Press Agency, 1969. 60 pp.

C71 *Dokumenty k československé zahraniční politice.* [Documents of Czechoslovak foreign policy]. P.: Federální ministerstvo zahraničních věcí, 1954–. Monthly.

POLITICAL AND
IDEOLOGICAL AFFAIRS

C72 *Program prvé domácí vlády republiky, vlády Národní fronty Čechů a Slováků. Sbírka dokumentů.* [Programme of the first government of the republic in the homeland, government of the National Front of Czechs and Slovaks. Collection of documents.] P.: Ministerstvo informací, 1945. 48 pp.

C73 *Budovatelský program třetí vlády Národní fronty Čechů a Slováků.* [Programme of the third government of the National Front of Czechs and Slovaks]. P.: Ministerstvo informací, 1946. 31 pp.
Programme of reconstruction presented by Prime Minister Gottwald to the National Assembly on 8 July 1946.

C74 'Akční program nové Gottwaldovy vlády. Předneseno v Ústavodárném Národním shromáždění dne 10. března 1948'. [Programme of action of the new government of K. Gottwald]. In: K. Gottwald. *Kupředu, zpátky ni krok. Sborník projevů předsedy vlády a dokumentů ze dnů 17.–29. února 1948*. P.: Orbis, 1948. Pp. 67–79.

ECONOMIC AFFAIRS

C75 *Hospodářské noviny. Ekonomický týdeník ÚV KSČ.* [Economic news]. P.: Rudé právo, 1957–. Weekly.

Issued by the Central Committee of the Czechoslovak Communist Party. Includes articles and statements of Party policy by leading members of the Party and government.

C76 *25 let Československa. Statisticko-ekonomický přehled vývoje socialistického Československa v letech 1945–1970.* [25 years of Czechoslovakia. A statistical survey of the economic development of Czechoslovakia between 1945 and 1970]. (Federální statistický úřad.) P.: Svoboda, 1970. 271 pp.

C77 *Hospodářský zákoník a předpisy souvisící.* [Economic laws and relevant regulations]. Sestavil a poznámky zpracoval K. Čapek. P.: Panorama, 1979. 573 pp.

The code of economic laws of June 1964 č. 109 Sb., as amended and supplemented by the laws č. 37/1971 Sb. and č. 144/1975 Sb. Each law is followed by references to regulations issued by the government or responsible ministries. Includes a subject index.

Economic plans

C78 *Nationalization in Czechoslovakia. Decrees of the President of the Republic of October 24, 1945 on the nationalization of mines and some industrial enterprises, some enterprises of the food industry, Joint-stock banks and private insurance companies.* P.: Orbis, 1946. 72 pp.

C79 *The first Czechoslovak economic plan. The explanatory memorandum on the bill and the text of the Two-Year Economic Plan act of 25 October 1946.* P.: Orbis, 1947. 122 pp.

C80 *Long-term planning in Czechoslovakia. A speech by Prime Minister Klement Gottwald given at the Extraordinary meeting of the Central Planning Commission of Czechoslovakia on October 10th, 1947.* P.: Czechoslovak Ministry of Information, 1947. 14 pp.

C81 *Zákon o dvouletém hospodářském plánu. Komentář.* [The law of the Two-Year Economic Plan. Commentary]. Sestavil V. Vlk. (Československé právo. ř. 2, sv. 3.) P.: Orbis, 1948. 235 pp.

C82 *První československý pětiletý plán.* [1st Czechoslovak Five-Year Plan]. P.: Ministerstvo informací a osvěty, 1948. 170 pp.

Text of the law on the Five-Year Plan č. 241/1948 Sb.

C83   *The First Czechoslovak economic five-year plan. Act and government memorandum.* P.: Czechoslovak Ministry of Information, 1949. 258 pp.
The government's statement introducing the law, 'Premises, principles and targets of the First Five-Year Plan', occupies most of the volume. It is followed by the text of the law.

Trade

C84   *Facts on Czechoslovak foreign trade.* P.: Czechoslovak Chamber of Commerce and Industry, 1967–. Annual.
Statistical tables on export and import.

Labour

C85   *Zákoník práce a předpisy souvisící.* [A code of labour laws and related regulations]. Osmé doplněné a upravené vydání. P.: Práce, 1978. 430 pp.

Finance

C86   *Finanční zpravodaj.* [Financial bulletin]. P.: Federální ministerstvo financí, Ministerstvo financí ČSR a Ministerstvo financí SSR, 1966–. Irregular.
Formerly *Věstník Ministerstva financí Republiky Československé,* 1945–1966.

C87   *Československé finanční právo.* [Czechoslovak financial laws]. Zpracoval kolektiv za hl. redakce M. Bakeše. P.: Panorama, 1979. 309 pp.

C88   *Státní banka československá. Bulletin 1968* [*etc.*]. *Report on the economic, credit and monetary development in the Czechoslovak Socialist Republic for 1968* [*etc.*]. P.: Stát. banka československá, 1968–. Annual.

Agriculture

C89   *Zákon o nové pozemkové reformě.* [The new land reform law]. Sestavili a výkladem opatřili T. Soukup a F. Petrův. (Československé právo. ř. 1. sv. 17.) P.: Orbis, 1948. 297 pp.
The complete text of the law of March 1948, č. 46/1948 Sb., with the editors' comments.

C90   *Věstník Ministerstva zemědělství a výživy České Socialistické Republiky.* [Bulletin of the Ministry of Agriculture and Food of the Czech Socialist Republic]. P.: Min. zeměděl. a výživy ČSR. 1953–. Irregular.

SOCIAL AFFAIRS

Health

C91 *ČSSR zdravotnictví.* [Czechoslovak Health Service]. P.: Ústav pro zdravotnickou statistiku. Bratislava: Ústav zdravotníckej štatistiky, 1956–. Annual.
Formerly called *Zdravotnictví ČSSR ve statistických údajích.* Statistical information on all branches of health services.

C92 *Věstník ministerstva zdravotnictví České Socialistické Republiky.* [Bulletin of the Ministry of Health of the Czech Socialist Republic]. P.: Avicenum, 1969–. 24 issues p.a.
Regulations governing the health service, including employment regulations and provisions for preventive medicine.

Social security

C93 *Czechoslovak national insurance. A contribution to the pattern of social security.* P.: Orbis, 1948. 212 pp.

C94 *Sociálné zabezpečenie pracujúcich.* [Social security for the workers]. Spracovali J. Mařík a J. Soukup. Bratislava: Práca, 1977. 458 pp.
Handbook is based on the new federal law č. 121/1975 Sb. on social security and on supplementary laws and regulations in power on 1 January 1976. Also publ. in Czech.

Social welfare

C95 *Zákon o rodině a předpisy souvisící.* [Family law and related regulations]. Sestavil M. Holub. P.: Orbis, 1977. 461 pp.
Text of all the relevant laws and regulations in power on 1 January 1976. Includes a subject index.

C96 *Sociální politika. Sociálna politika.* [Social policy]. P.: Federální ministerstvo práce a sociálních věcí a Ministerstva práce a soc. věcí ČSR a SSR, 1968–.

C97 *Social guarantees in Czechoslovakia.* Compiled by a team of the Federal Ministry of Labour and Social Affairs and the ministries of the Czech and Slovak socialist republics. P.: Práce, 1977. 151 pp.

CULTURAL AFFAIRS

C98 *Školský zákon.* [Education Laws]. Výklad zákona a prováděcích předpisů sestavil O. Chlup, F. Kahuda a K. Král. (Ceskoslovenské právo. r. 1, sv. 20.) P.: Orbis, 1949. 180 pp.
Text of the law of April 1948, č. 95/1948 Sb., on the uniform education system and related regulations.

C99 *Věstník Ministerstva školství a Ministerstva kultury České Socialis-*

tické Republiky. [Bulletin of the Ministry of Education and the Ministry of Culture of the Czech Socialist Republic]. P.: SPN, 1969–. Monthly.

C100 *Zvesti Ministerstva školstva a Ministerstva kultúry Slovenskej Socialistickej Republiky.* [Bulletin of the Ministry of Education and the Ministry of Culture of the Slovak Socialist Republic]. Bratislava: 1945–. Monthly.

C101 *Zákon zo dňa 14. októbra, 1949, ktorým sa zriaduje Štátny úrad pro cirkevné veci.* [Law on the establishment of the State office for church affairs].—*Zákon zo dňa 14. oktobra 1949 o hospodárskom zabezpečení cirkví a náboženských spoločností štátem.* [Law on the economic provisions for the churches by the state]. In: *O nový pomer cirkvi k štátu.* Druhé vydání. Bratislava: Tatran, 1950. Pp. 68–71.

C102 *Autorský zákon a předpisy souvisící.* [The law on authorship and related regulations]. 2. podstatně doplněné a přepracované vydání. Uspořádal a poznámkami opatřil K. Knap. P.: Orbis, 1975. 399 pp.

C103 *Kultura. Sborník právních předpisů.* [Culture. A collection of laws and regulations]. Uspořádal K. Neumann. P.: Orbis, 1963. 2 vols.

   Laws and regulations in force on 30 April 1963 relating to cultural activities and institutions, e.g. museums, libraries, etc.

LEADERS' WORKS

C104 Dubček, A. *K otázkam obrodzovacieho procesu v KSČ. Vybrané projevy.* [Problems of the reform process in the Czechoslovak Communist Party. Selected speeches]. Bratislava: Vydavateľstvo politickej literatúry, 1968. 245 pp.

C105 Gottwald, K. *Spisy.* [Collected works]. P.: Svoboda, 1951–61. 15 vols.

   Edited in the Historical Institute of the Communist Party.

C106 Husák, G. *State a prejavy, apríl 1969–apríl 1970.* [Speeches and articles]. Bratislava: Epocha, 1970. 390 pp.

C107 Husák, G. *Vybrané prejavy, máj 1970–dec. 1971.* [Selected speeches, May 1970–Dec. 1971]. Bratislava: Pravda, 1972. 389 pp.

C108 Husák, G. *Prejavy a state, február 1972–dec. 1978.* Speeches and articles, Feb. 1972–Dec. 1978. Bratislava: Pravda, 1976–79. 3 vols.

   Husák's works are also published in Czech.

C109 Lenárt, J. *Vybrané prejavy a state, 1949–1980.* [Selected speeches and articles]. Bratislava: Pravda, 1980–1. 2 vols.

C110 Novotný, A. *Projevy a stati, 1954–64.* [Speeches and articles]. P.: Nakladatelství politické literatury, 1964. 3 vols.

G GERMAN DEMOCRATIC REPUBLIC

Werner Volkmer

INTRODUCTION

Only in recent years, either in private or public debates, have historians and functionaries in the GDR claimed that the founding of the German Democratic Republic was intended right from the beginning in 1945. Politicians in the West with a few exceptions have always looked at the developments in the Soviet-occupied zone and later the GDR as a concerted effort by German and Soviet communists to get a foothold in Germany as a whole.

The speed with which the Soviet authorities rebuilt the political infrastructure was by any account remarkable. They could rely on the help of three groups of communist functionaries who had been flown into East Germany during the last days of the war. On 10 June 1945 the military authorities ordered that political parties and trade unions had to be refounded (Military Directive No. 2). One day later the communists published a declaration which outlined their immediate party programme.

In a semi-official history of the GDR (Dörnberg, S. *Kurze Geschichte der DDR*. Berlin (East): Dietz Verlag, 1969.) four distinct phases of political development are distinguished: 1945–9, the creation of an anti-fascist order; 1949–55, the building of the foundations of socialism; 1956–61, the final victory of socialist order of production; and 1961–4, the complete and comprehensive building of socialism. Until 1971 it was held that an advanced socialist system had been achieved and that socialism was a historic period in its own right. Since 1971 this view has been reversed and socialism is now regarded as one of the stages of communism.

The crucial dates during the first two years immediately after the war were: 3 September 1945, the agricultural reform; 30 October 1945, the nationalization of more than half of East Germany's industrial potential; 30 June 1946, the end of freedom of movement between East and West Germany; 21/22 April 1946, the amalgamation of the communist and the social democratic parties; and 20 October 1946, the regional elections which made the Socialist Unity Party (SED), the joint communist/social democrat party, the strongest party in all five states of East Germany. Only in Berlin the social democrats ran separately and won. Then, on 26 November 1947, the SED started the People's Congress Movement, which aimed, so it was claimed, at a reunified Germany. On 20 March 1948, however, the Soviet High Commander in Germany, Marshal Sokolovskii, left the Allied Control Council thus effectively ending the unity of Germany. Ten days later the Berlin blockade began, which lasted eleven months.

The actions of the Soviets and the developments in East Germany have to be seen against the background of developments in the West. The process which led to the founding of two separate German states—West Germany on 21 May 1949 and East Germany on 8 October 1949—can be seen as the attempt by the western powers to make Germany self-sufficient while preventing the Soviets from gaining any influence in West Germany. The German Democratic Republic and the Federal Republic of Germany are in this sense the products of the Cold War which developed after the end of the Second World War.

The Soviets, on the one hand, rapidly enforced changes in the administrative, political and economic system in East Germany after 1945. At the same time though, Moscow urged the reunification of Germany. Until recently GDR politicians and historians consistently claimed that the division of Germany was exlusively the reponsibility of the West.

For a western observer it may seem odd that the GDR historians reckon that only after 1949 did the building of the foundations of socialism begin. It is true, however, that only in the years up to 1954 was the continued existence of the GDR as a separate state in its own right secured. While in the West one tends to believe that the nationalization of the means of production and the political takeover by the communists between 1945 and 1949 were the crucial points, the GDR historians apparently regard the whole-hearted blessing of the GDR by Moscow as the vital factor.

In 1949 a social democrat, Otto Grotewohl, became the head of government on 12 October, and a communist, Wilhelm Pieck, became the President on 11 October. The bourgeois parties (CDU, LDPD, and the NDPD and DBD which were founded in 1948) had been taken over by 'loyal' leaders by 1949, but there were still many social democrats in the ranks of the SED who did not quite accept the party line. However, the purges throughout the 1950s (especially in August 1950, December 1952, July 1953, January 1954 and March 1957) made Walter Ulbricht, the party leader, the undisputed head of the SED and led to its consolidation. The purges had begun in full in 1948. The First Party Conference in January 1949 then decided on the creation of a party of the new type, i.e. a party following the principles of democratic centralism. This was confirmed by the Third Party Congress in 1950.

The introduction of a planned economy (in 1948 the first two-year plan was started) was also confirmed by the Third Party Congress which passed the first five-year plan. On 29 September 1950 the GDR also became a member of the Council of Mutual Economic Assistance (Comecon). In January 1952 it equipped its barracked police forces (Kasernierte Volkspolizei) with Soviet arms and decided in May to form a national army. In July of the same year the Second Party Conference announced that the foundations of socialism were going to be constructed, which meant that the administrative structure was changed, the Länder were dissolved and replaced by fourteen districts, collectivization of agriculture began, and a new ideological purge was announced.

The workers' uprising in June 1953 was in an ironic way the turning point for Ulbricht which consolidated the GDR more than anything else in these early years of its life. Stalin's security boss Beria was inclined, after Stalin's death in the spring of 1953, to drop the Ulbricht regime and come to an arrangement with the West over Germany. But the uprising played into the hands of those in Moscow who feared that this might be the beginning of unrest elsewhere in Eastern Europe and it was decided to back Ulbricht. The failure of the Foreign Minister Conference on Germany in Berlin in 1954 meant that the Soviet Union decided to go ahead with a divided Germany for the foreseeable future. The recognition of the GDR's sovereignty by the Soviet Union on 25 March 1954 was only the formalization of this decision. In May 1955 the Warsaw Pact Organization was formed and the GDR became a member. When Khrushchev returned from the Geneva Four-Power Summit meeting via East Berlin (24–7 July) he pronounced the two-states theory, which was the official declaration of the final division of Germany.

In the following period (1956–61) three dates stand out: the Third Party Conference in 1956; the end of the collectivization of agriculture in 1960; and the building of the Berlin Wall on 21 August 1961. The Third Party Conference followed the Twentieth CPSU Party Congress and was the SED's answer to de-Stalinization. The conference set the scene for greater economic efforts to catch up with the higher standard of living in West Germany and marked the beginning of countless initiatives on the German question aiming at reunification. The state treaty between the GDR and the USSR on 20 September 1955 and the creation of armed forces on 18 January 1956 together with the GDR's membership of Comecon and the Warsaw Pact excluded the option of a straightforward reunification. Therefore the idea of a confederation of the two German states was put forward (in an article in *Neues Deutschland*, 30 December 1956 by Walter Ulbricht). The attempts of the GDR in cooperation with the Soviet Union were now aimed at consolidating the GDR's existence. For this purpose pressure was exercised on Berlin. On 10 November 1958 Khrushchev set an ultimatum for making West Berlin into a free city in the vein of Danzig. The increasing number of Germans who fled East Germany, especially towards the end of the 1950s and the beginning of 1961 meant that the GDR was in danger of collapsing economically. The building of the Berlin Wall was the last resort which, from the GDR's point of view, had to be taken in order to survive. Thus the existence of the GDR as a Soviet-type state was, in a very physical way, secured.

The death of the first GDR President, Wilhelm Pieck, in 1960 led to the creation of the State Council, a collective body, which was chaired by Walter Ulbricht who thus added another important office to his already important position as party leader.

The 1960s were characterized by two main trends in the development of the GDR: the economic reforms of the middle of the decade and the struggle for international diplomatic recognition.

After the building of the wall in Berlin the economic situation stabilized, albeit at a very low level. Discontent was widespread amongst the population, not least because of the feeling of being cut off from the outside world. The answer of the party was to once more increase economic efforts. The Sixth Party Congress (15–21 January 1963) decided to go ahead with economic reforms which became known as the New Economic System. The Congress also passed the First Party Programme of the SED and a statute. After the failure of the seven-year plan in the early 1960s no further plan was adopted. But the Sixth Party Congress decided on some general outlines for economic development between 1964 and 1970. And indeed the GDR's economic fortunes improved noticeably after 1964. In June 1964 the GDR signed a friendship treaty with the USSR which was also a defence treaty. It tied the GDR very tightly to the Soviet Union. In September of the same year, it was decided to let old-age pensioners travel to the West once a year. This can be seen as the beginning of *détente* from the GDR's side. Finally a change took place in the government. After the death of Otto Grotewohl on 21 September, Willi Stoph became his successor as the head of the Council of Ministers.

The GDR pursued a double strategy in the mid- and late 1960s. On the one hand it wanted *détente*, on the other it was striving for diplomatic recognition. These two objectives sometimes became indistinguishable and at others contradictory. From 1964 onwards the GDR conducted an aggressive policy *vis-à-vis* West Germany which was preoccupied with the national question. The GDR's position was that two different peoples had developed under the umbrella of the German nation. Reunification was envisaged as being possible only after West Germany had become socialist. In 1966 several inter-German initiatives were started: an exchange of letters between the SED and the Social Democrats in the West in February, March and April and the suggestion of an exchange of public speakers in April were the most important. At the same time, the desire for international diplomatic recognition was accompanied by increasing alienation from anything which could be understood as all-German. Thus in February 1967 a separate GDR citizenship was introduced by law and the notion of reunification was declared to be 'silly waffle' (*Neues Deutschland*, 21 January 1967). The churches, which were still organized as all-German institutions, were increasingly attacked. The Protestants aligned their organizational borders with the political borders in Germany in 1969. The objective was to become equal to West Germany at the international level by forcing West Germany into direct negotiations and thus *de facto* recognition. The Seventh Party Congress (17–22 April 1967) confirmed this policy. The demands for diplomatic recognition by West Germany increased. Even the new constitution of the GDR passed on 9 April 1968 demanded in article 8 paragraph 2 the resumption of normal diplomatic relations between East Berlin and Bonn.

By 1969 relations between Bonn and Moscow had noticeably improved and Ostpolitik, the German version of *détente*, gained in momentum. West Germany's Chancellor Willy Brandt made a *de facto* recognition of the GDR in his government declaration when resuming office in October 1969. Ulbricht countered by denouncing the notion of the continued existence of the German nation in two separate states in a press conference on 19 January 1970. And even the two inter-German summit meetings between Chancellor Brandt and the Chairman of the Council of Ministers of the GDR, Willi Stoph, in Erfurt on 19 March and in Kassel on 21 May led to a cooling of relations between East and West Germany. But the progress made in the negotiations between Bonn and Moscow and Bonn and Warsaw in 1970 forced Ulbricht to show some flexibility. After the signing of the Moscow treaty on 12 August 1970, which recognized *de facto* the GDR and the post-Second-World-War borders in Europe, a treaty between Warsaw and Bonn followed which signalled the normalization of relations between West Germany and Eastern Europe. Ulbricht however was still dragging his feet about a rapprochement between East and West Germany, but was deposed in May 1971 shortly before the Eighth Party Congress of the SED. Ulbricht's successor, his crown prince for many years, Erich Honecker, followed a different policy from Ulbricht's.

The Eighth Party Congress saw a stronger alignment of the GDR's policies with those of the Soviet Union. Accordingly progress could be made in the four-power negotiations on Berlin (which were finalized on 3 September 1971) and the negotiations between Bonn and East Berlin led to a transit agreement on 3 December 1971 regulating the traffic to West Berlin. An agreement regarding visits of West Berliners to the East was signed on 20 December 1971. However the most important treaty between the two Germanies—the Basic Treaty about the future relations between the two countries—took another year to negotiate and was finalized on 26 May 1972.

The Eighth Party Congress also reversed two other policies of the Ulbricht period. Ulbricht's insistence on concentrating economic activities on growth sectors of industry had led to severe shortcomings in the late 1960s. The new policy after June 1971 (the party congress took place from 15 to 19 June 1971) put more emphasis on consumer goods and the term 'social policies' gained in importance. Further, an ideological change took place. Instead of projecting the GDR as a more advanced state than the Soviet Union (which was implied when Ulbricht talked about the 'advanced societal system of socialism' as the USSR had not reached this stage yet) the GDR fell back in line and the Soviet Union was regarded once again as the most advanced socialist country. One of the repercussions of the reversal in economic policy was the change in the head of government, Willi Stoph, who was replaced by Horst Sindermann in 1973. Stoph succeeded Walter Ulbricht as the head of the State Council.

The most successful period in GDR history followed the Eighth Party Congress. Cooperation with West Germany brought substantial amounts of hard currency to East Germany, the standard of living increased dramatically, the GDR was recognized internationally and entered the United Nations in 1973. There was also a relaxation in cultural policies. This honeymoon period ended in the mid-1970s. The first oil-price shock reached the East bloc, and the USSR increased her oil prices. The Helsinki agreement in 1975 led to stronger demands for more freedom in the GDR, mainly in the cultural field and with regard to free emigration. More than 100,000 East Germans applied for permission to emigrate to the West, as Honecker acknowledged in an interview with a West German paper. The economy did less well than expected.

This resulted in a tightening of ideological affairs, greater distancing from West Germany, and a reorganization of economic policies. The Ninth Party Congress in May 1976 passed a new statute for the SED and a new party programme. The programme incorporated the changes which had taken place at the Eighth Party Congress.

In October 1976 Willi Stoph went back to his old job as head of the Council of Ministers and Honecker took over as chairman of the State Council. Sindermann became the president of the People's Chamber. This marked a significant reversal in economic policies aimed at a cautious reintroduction of the 1964 reforms, or rather a continuation of these reforms. More decentralization in industry was the objective and by 1979 all major companies had been organized in Kombinate (a sort of socialist concern). At the same time the foreign trade companies (import/export) were reorganized so that greater flexibility was achieved. This process is not yet finished. Beginning with the expulsion of the critical singer and writer Wolf Biermann in November 1976, a harder line was taken in cultural affairs which led to a mass exodus of the best writers, actors and musicians the GDR had.

The aftermath of the Soviet invasion of Afghanistan in December 1979 and the Polish crisis which began in August 1980 put relations between the GDR and West Germany into jeopardy. The Tenth Party Congress in March 1981 was merely a 'wait and see affair'. Economically the GDR has fared better than most other East European countries, but greater efforts are necessary than before in order to sustain the social policies of the Honecker group. Energy price increases and the need for more advanced production technology are forcing the GDR to continue a policy which is open towards the West, because the Soviet Union cannot increase her oil deliveries and is herself in need of high technology. At the same time the atmosphere has become very frosty between Bonn and East Berlin. Only if the USSR and the USA resume their *détente* policy will there be any progress in the GDR's policies *vis à vis* the West. The two determining factors for a change in policy are the disarmament negotiations which the USSR is seeking and the developments in Poland.

GENERAL BIBLIOGRAPHIES
AND REFERENCE WORKS

This section contains entries from the GDR and from the Federal Republic of Germany.

National bibliography

G1 *Deutsche Nationalbibliographie*. [German national bibliography]. Leipzig: 1931–.

Reihe A, 1931–, weekly, records material available through the book trade; Reihe B, 1931–, semi-monthly, covers government, institutional and other non-trade publications; Reihe C, 1968–, monthly, lists doctoral theses. Besides acting as the national bibliography of the GDR, it aims to include German-language material published elsewhere and most (though not all) of the book output from the Federal Republic. Reihen A and B are cumulated by *Jahresverzeichnis des deutschen Schrifttums*, Leipzig: 1948–, annual, covering the years 1945/6 onward.

Other general bibliographies

G2 'Bibliographie zur deutschen Zeitgeschichte seit 1945'. [Bibliography of German politics since 1945]. In: *Zeitschrift für Geschichtswissenschaft*, vol. 7, 1959, pt. I, pp. 1414ff., pt. II, pp. 1904ff.

G3 *Bibliographie zur Zeitgeschichte* [Political bibliography], Beilage [Supplement] der *Vierteljahreshefte für Zeitgeschichte*. 1953–. Quarterly.

A West German publication which includes East German books and is one of the most comprehensive bibliographies covering the 1950s.

G4 *Literatur zur deutschen Frage*. [Literature on the German question]. Bonn: Ministry for All-German Questions, 1962.

A select bibliography listing the major publications relating to inter-German affairs and the question of reunification.

G5 *Kommunismus in Geschichte und Gegenwart*. [Communism in history and the present time]. K. H. Ruffmann et al. (eds). Bonn: Ministry for All-German Questions, 1964.

Again a select bibliography published in West Germany. It updates prior publications of the Ministry.

G6 *Börsenblatt für den Deutschen Buchhandel*. [Sales publication for the German booktrade]., Leipzig: 1946–. Several times a week. Special editions for the Leipzig Book Fairs in the spring and autumn of each year.

The most comprehensive and authoritative bibliography available. A very detailed, though abbreviated version of the special editions appears in *Deutschland Archiv* (G7) between January and March and June to August respectively.

G7 *Deutschland Archiv*. Cologne: Verlag Wissenschaft und Politik, 1968–. Monthly.

Each number contains a select bibliography of newspaper and journal articles from East Germany dealing with the main developments in politics, culture and economics as well as sociological affairs. Between 1950 and 1968 the journal was called *SBZ Archiv*.

G8 *Dokumente zur Aussenpolitik der Regierung der DDR*. [Documents on the foreign policy of the GDR]. Berlin (East): Staatsverlag der DDR, 1954–.

In part two of the volumes there is a very detailed bibliography

71

including West German publications. The subject areas are wide-ranging but exclude internal affairs. The bibliography has been included since vol. XI, when the publishers changed from Rütten und Loening to Staatsverlag.

Reference books

G9 *Handbuch der Deutschen Demokratischen Republik*. [Handbook of the German Democratic Republic]. 2nd ed. Leipzig: Enzyklopädie Verlag, 1979.
Lexigraphic handbook covering social, political and economic affairs. Mainly a propaganda publication but containing nevertheless a substantial amount of information.

G10 *DDR-Handbuch*. [GDR handbook]. C. P. Ludz et al. (eds.). 2nd ed. Cologne: Verlag Wissenschaft und Politik, 1979.
Again a lexigraphic handbook which Dr Ludz edited for the West German Ministry for Inter-German Relations (formerly All-German Questions). Although a West German publication it relies heavily on East German sources and provides, together with the three volumes of *Materialien zum Bericht zur Lage der Nation*, published by the same Ministry in 1971, 1972 and 1974, the best source of information on the GDR available. The handbook also contains a voluminous bibliography of mainly West German publications.

G11 *SBZ von A bis Z*. [An A to Z of the Soviet-occupied zone]. 2nd ed. Bonn: Ministry for All-German Questions, 1969.
A lexigraphic handbook including a large number of brief biographies of leading politicians and cultural figures in East Germany. Both editions are out of date but whenever information about the period covered is required both volumes are very reliable.

G12 *Namen und Daten*. [Names and dates]. G. Buch (ed.). 2nd ed. Berlin (West) and Bonn: Dietz Verlag, 1979.
A revised version of the A to Z series of books but excluding any other information apart from biographies which the previous volumes contained. The disadvantage of the book is that people who have died before publication are not included in the entries.

G13 *Kleines Politisches Wörterbuch*. [Small political dictionary]. 4th ed. Berlin (East): Dietz Verlag, 1979.
Authoritative publication for definitions of political terminology.

CONSTITUTIONAL DOCUMENTS

Entries are constitutional texts including some documents from the time prior to the founding of the GDR and also commentaries on the constitutional texts. Some of the entries have been published in West Germany.

G14 'Verfassung des Landes Thüringen'. [Constitution of the state of

Thuringia]. *Regierungsblatt für das Land Thüringen.* [Law gazette of the state of Thuringia]. 1947, pt. I, pp. 1ff.

The constitution came into force on 20 December 1946 and provided the model for the 1949 GDR constitution. It even mentions in its article 1 that Thuringia was part of the GDR although the GDR had not been founded.

G15 'Verfassung der DDR'. [Constitution of the GDR]. *Gesetzblatt der DDR,* 1949, p. 5ff.

The constitution came into force with the founding of the GDR on 7 October 1949. Formally it was a parliamentary system which was foreseen, and democratic principles were adhered to in the text. The constitution was regarded as a model for the whole of Germany and followed federal principles, albeit in a watered down version. At the same time the notion of the 'concentration of powers' was acknowledged in contrast to the traditional western division of powers in three branches.

G16 'Verfassung der DDR'. [Constitution of the GDR]. *Gesetzblatt der DDR,* I, 1968, pp. 432ff.

Apart from three minor constitutional changes in 1955, 1958 and 1960, the 1949 constitution remained essentially unaltered. However, a comprehensive system of legislation, without changing the actual text of the constitution, created a rather different constitutional reality than that foreseen in the 1949 text. Therefore, the new 1968 constitution became a necessity. It is a really 'socialist' constitution in that it accepts the vitally important principle of supremacy of the Party, stipulates the socialization of the means of production, democratic centralism, and the concentration of state powers.

G17 *Verfassung der Deutschen Demokratischen Republik.* [Constitution of the GDR]. K. Sorgenicht. et al. (eds.). Berlin (East): Staatsverlag der DDR, 1969. 2 vols.

Authoritative GDR interpretation of the new 1968 constitution.

G18 *Der Staatsrat der Deutschen Demokratischen Republik 1960–1970.* [The State Council of the GDR 1960–1970]. Berlin (East): Staatsverlag der DDR, 1970.

When East Germany's first and only President, Wilhelm Pieck, died in 1960 the State Council was formed in the same year. The 1968 Constitution confirms the predominant role of the State Council. After Walter Ulbricht's downfall in 1971, the State Council lost in importance.

G19 *Das System der sozialistischen Gesellschafts- und Staatsordnung der DDR.* [The System of socialist societal and state order in the GDR]. Berlin (East): Staatsverlag der DDR, 1970.

Contains the relevant documents referring to the political system as a whole and also the changes which occurred after 1960.

G20 *Grundrechte des Bürgers in der sozialistischen Gesellschaft.* [Human rights of citizens in socialist society]. E. Poppe (ed.). Berlin (East): Staatsverlag der DDR, 1980.

Elaborates on development and function of human rights in socialist society. Also includes duties of citizens. Rights and duties are put into the context of socialist international law.

G21 *Handbuch der Volkskammer der Deutschen Demokratischen Republik.* [Handbook of the People's Chamber of the German Democratic Republic]. 4th ed. Berlin (East): Volkskammer, 1968.

LAW CODES

The major law codes of the GDR are listed, excluding constitutional documents but including some specialized legislation which is of particular political importance.

G22 'Aus dem Gesetz zur Demokratisierung der deutschen Schule'. [Excerpts from the law on democratizing the German school system]. In: *Die Deutsche Demokratische Republik auf dem Wege zum Sozialismus,* P. Stulz et al. (eds.). Berlin (East): 1959, pt. I, pp.104ff.

Provided the basis for a fundamental reform of the educational system in Soviet-occupied East Germany, including the sacking of virtually all teachers from the Nazi period. The law was passed in 1946.

G23 'Gesetz über die Schaffung der Nationalen Volksarmee und des Ministeriums für Nationale Verteidigung'. [Law about the creation of the National People's Army and the Ministry of National Defence]. *Gesetzblatt der DDR,* 1956, I, p. 81.

Following the decision in West Germany to rearm, this law provided the legal basis for the creation of a professional army in the GDR.

G24 'Gesetz zur Änderung des Passgesetzes der DDR'. [Law amending the passport regulations in the GDR]. *Gesetzblatt der DDR,* 1957, I, p. 650.

The amendment made it a punishable crime to leave East Germany without official permission to do so. This permission was not usually given.

G25 'Gesetz zur Ergänzung des Strafgesetzbuches'. [Law amending the criminal code]. *Gesetzblatt der DDR,* 1957, I, pp. 643ff.

The criminal code used in the GDR was originally the same one that had been in force since the Kaiser period. A whole range of new regulations were introduced in 1957 which enabled the authorities to prosecute anybody who made critical remarks about the state, the Party or public figures. Further, the definition of espionage and collecting information for state enemies became extremely loose and thus arbitrary decisions by the courts were facilitated.

G26 'Gesetzbuch der Arbeit'. [Labour code]. *Gesetzblatt der DDR*, 1961, I, pp. 27ff.

The new labour law does not provide for the right to strike and the emphasis on discipline at work is very strong. The provisions for holidays were a step backwards.

G27 'Gesetz zur Verteidigung der DDR'. [Defence law of the GDR]. *Gesetzblatt der DDR*, 1961, I, pp. 175ff.

Provides the legal basis for defence measures in peace-time and in war-time in accordance with other legislation and the treaty obligations of the Warsaw Pact.

G28 'Gesetz über die Allgemeine Wehrpflicht'. [Law about the general national service]. *Gesetzblatt der DDR*, 1962, I, pp. 2ff.

After the building of the Berlin Wall in August 1961, the introduction of national service became possible without forcing people to leave the country. This measure also put the balance right with regard to West Germany, where national service had been introduced in 1957.

G29 'Verordnung über das Statut des Volkswirtschaftsrates der DDR'. [Directive on the statute of the National Economic Council of the GDR]. *Gesetzblatt der DDR*, 1962, II, pp. 453ff.

The National Economic Council was formed in 1961 from two departments of the State Planning Commission. It was responsible for the management of industry and commerce at national level. The regional economic councils were responsible to the National Council. The National Council became too much involved with details and grew too complex. In 1965 it was therefore dissolved and various industrial ministries were formed instead.

G30 'Verordnung über das Statut der Staatlichen Plankommission'. [Directive on the statute of the State Planning Commission]. *Gesetzblatt der DDR*, 1962, II, pp. 363ff.

Between 1961 and 1965 there were two planning authorities at national level: the National Economic Council and the State Planning Commission. This directive defined the division of responsibilities as far as it applied to the Planning Commission. After 1965 the Planning Commission became once more the only planning authority as between 1950 and 1961.

G31 'Erlass des Staatsrates der DDR über die Planung und Leitung der Volkswirtschaft durch den Ministerrat'. [Edict issued by the State Council on the planning and management of the national economy by the Council of Ministers]. *Gesetzblatt der DDR*, 1963, I, pp. 1ff.

The economic difficulties of the GDR were tackled by applying stricter planning principles and improving the organization of and cooperation between the various planning levels.

G32 'Gesetz über das einheitliche sozialistische Bildungswesen'. [Law on the unitary system of socialist education]. *Gesetzblatt der DDR*, 1965, I, pp. 83ff.

The law was intended to streamline existing educational legislation and to provide the basis for educating 'socialist personalities' in the GDR, i.e. ideologically more reliable people, by politicizing the educational system more than it was before.

G33 'Familiengesetzbuch der DDR'. [Family code of the GDR]. *Gesetzblatt der DDR*, 1966, I, pp. 2ff.

A major revision of all the prewar law codes was under way in the GDR at the time, and the first part to be rewritten following 'socialist principles' was the family law section. The protection of the institution of marriage was a central point in this new legislation. It had been discussed in public quite intensively before it was finalized. The position of wives and children was especially safeguarded by this law.

G34 'Gesetz über die Staatsbürgerschaft der DDR'. [Law on the citizenship of the GDR]. *Gesetzblatt der DDR*, 1967, I, pp. 3ff.

A new citizenship was created by this law and the all-German citizenship, which previously existed, was abandoned. However, the new law also claimed all those Germans to be GDR citizens who had left East Germany and those whose parents were GDR citizens. This meant that millions of refugees and their offspring in West Germany were GDR citizens. An amendment to the law in 1972 put this right. In practice there was a GDR citizenship since 1957 and several edicts and official statements spoke of GDR citizens during the period between 1957 and 1967.

G35 'Strafgesetzbuch der DDR'. [Criminal code of the GDR]. *Gesetzblatt der DDR*, 1968, I, pp. 7ff.

The new criminal code replaced the criminal code from 1871. It was a radical break with German legal history. The yardstick applied for judging crime was now the damage done to society.

G36 'Zivilgesetzbuch der DDR'. [Civil law code of the GDR]. *Gesetzblatt der DDR*, 1975, I, pp. 465ff.

The complete set of civil law codes was finalized in 1975 and came into force the following year. Several of the codes had already been put into force prior to that date. The civil law code not only differs from the traditional West European structure but also from that of other East European countries.

Commentaries and handbooks

G37 *Grundfragen des Strafrechts und der Strafgesetzgebung der sozialistischen Länder.* [Basic questions of criminal law and the passing of such law in socialist countries]. Potsdam-Babelsberg: Deutsche Akademie für Staats- und Rechtswissenschaft 'Walter Ulbricht', 1963.

Annotated bibliography on East German criminal law.

G38 *Gesetzessammlung zum Verwaltungsrecht der DDR.* [Collection of law codes of administrative laws of the GDR]. Akademie für Staats- und Rechtswissenschaft der DDR (ed.). Potsdam-Babelsberg: Selbstverlag, 1979. 2 vols.

G39 Acker, R. et al. *Unsere Abgeordneten—Vertrauensleute der Werktätigen.* [Our deputies—trustees of the working people]. Berlin (East): Verlag Tribüne, 1979.
   This little booklet is an introduction to the rights and responsibilities of the members of local parliaments.

G40 *Sozialistische Landeskultur.* [Socialist environmental culture]. Akademie für Staats- and Rechtswissenschaft der DDR und Ministerium für Umweltschutz und Wasserwirtschaft (eds.). Berlin (East): Staatsverlag der DDR, 1978.
   Selection of legal codes regarding environmental issues. Also includes explanatory notes.

OTHER GENERAL LEGISLATIVE DOCUMENTS

Includes the main legislative publications and juridical journals.

G41 *Gesetzblatt der DDR.* [Law gazette of the GDR]. Parts I, II and III. Publ. by the Chairman of the State Council, Berlin (East), 1960–. Irregular.
   Between 1949 and 1960 the President of the GDR published the law gazette. Since 1973 the three parts of the *Gesetzblatt* contain: part I—all laws and other legislative orders, directives, edicts and regulations except international treaties; part II—international treaties; part III—legislation which is only relevant to a limited number of people or government institutions. Between 1949 and 1955 there was only part I, between 1955 and 1972 parts I and II.

G42 *Verordnungsblatt für Gross-Berlin.* [Law gazette for Greater Berlin]. Publ. by the Magistrat von Gross-Berlin (East), 1945–.
   Local parliaments have only a very limited authority to pass legislation, mainly filling in where the People's Chamber has passed laws with general clauses for this purpose. However, the *Verordnungsblatt*, because of the Four-Power Status of Berlin, had a more important role as GDR legislation had to be formally adopted by the local parliament. This was abandoned in 1977.

G43 *Neue Justiz.* [New justice]. Publ. by the Oberstes Gericht der DDR, Berlin (East), 1946–. Fortnightly.
   Caters for the legal profession in the GDR and is more concerned with practical questions than the more theoretical and political journal *Staat und Recht* (G44).

G44 *Staat und Recht.* [State and justice]. Publ. by the Deutsche Akademie für Staats- und Rechtswissenschaft, Potsdam-Babelsberg, 1952–. Monthly.

A more academically oriented magazine than *Neue Justiz* (G43). Also concerns itself more than the former with constitutional and administrative law.

G45 *Verordnungsblatt der Deutschen Demokratischen Republik—VOBl.* [Decrees' gazette of the German Democratic Republic—VOBl.]. Berlin (East): Ministerrat der DDR, 1949–. Irregular.

GENERAL PARTY DOCUMENTS

Besides party documents this section contains some monographs and other publications related to party affairs. Also a couple of bibliographies are included.

G46 *Dokumente der Sozialistischen Einheitspartei Deutschlands.* [Documents of the Socialist Unity Party of Germany]. Berlin (East): Dietz Verlag, 1948–.
Contains decisions, statements and other important material relating to the Central Committee of the Party, the Politbureau and the Secretariat of the Central Committee. The 16th volume in the series appeared in 1980.

G47 *Protokoll des Vereinigungsparteitags der SED und der KPD.* [Protocol of the Amalgamating Congress of the SED and the KPD]. Berlin (East): Dietz Verlag, 1946.
Contains the discussions and decisions taken at the congress between the communists and social democrats in the Soviet-occupied part of Germany on the formation of the SED. This was an important step on the road to the division of Germany as the unification of the parties was resisted in the western zones.

G48 *Protokoll der Verhandlungen des . . . Parteitags der SED.* [Protocol of the discussions of the . . . Party Congress of the SED]. Berlin (East): Dietz Verlag.

2. Parteitags vom 20./24. September 1947, publ. 1947.
3. Parteitags vom 20./24. Juli 1950, publ. 1951. 2 vols.
4. Parteitags vom 30. März/6. April 1954, publ. 1954. 2 vols.
5. Parteitags vom 10./16. Juli 1958, publ. 1959. 2 vols.
6. Parteitags vom 15./21. Januar 1963, publ. 1963. 4 vols.
7. Parteitags vom 17./22. April 1967, publ. 1967. 4 vols.
8. Parteitags vom 15./19. Juni 1971, publ. 1971. 2 vols.
9. Parteitags vom 18./22. Mai 1976, publ. 1976. 2 vols.
10. Parteitags vom 11./16. April 1981, forthcoming.

Although the protocols are not always complete records of the speeches made at party congresses, they provide a vast amount of information about the work and direction of the Party. The opening report by the Secretary-General especially is a telling indicator of new trends. Since 1971 congresses take place every five instead of every four years.

G49 *Protokoll der Ersten Parteikonferenz der SED*. [Protocol of the 1st Party Conference of the SED]. Berlin (East): Dietz Verlag, 1950.

Party conferences can be held between regular congresses. So far three have taken place. They usually serve the purpose of fundamentally changing party policy or of a leadership reshuffle. The 1st Party Conference (1949) was called to make political and organizational adjustments in East Germany in view of the founding of the Federal Republic of Germany.

G50 *Protokoll der Zweiten Parteikonferenz der SED*. [Protocol of the 2nd Party Conference of the SED]. Berlin (East): Dietz Verlag, 1952.

The enforced development of the GDR towards a communist bloc country was the background to the 2nd Party Conference. It was decided to create armed forces (Kasernierte Volkspolizei)—though not an army—and collectivization of agriculture began. At the same time an ideological drive got under way with virulent attacks on Slánský, Tito and Gomułka.

G51 *Protokoll der Dritten Parteikonferenz der SED*. [Protocol of the 3rd Party Conference of the SED]. Berlin (East): Dietz Verlag, 1956.

The reason for calling the 3rd Party Conference in 1956 was the attempt to divert public interest from the process of de-Stalinization which took place in all other East bloc countries. This was done by emphasizing economic tasks and 'more' democracy.

G52 'Programm der SED'. [Programme of the SED]. In: *Protokoll der Verhandlungen des 6. Parteitags der SED*. [Protocol of the 6th Party Congress of the SED]. Berlin (East): Dietz Verlag, 1963. Vol. 4.

This was the first programme of the SED. Up to 1963 the programmatic basis for the Party had been the declaration in June 1945, reprinted in Ulbricht, W. *Geschichte der neuesten Zeit* [History of the most recent time]. Berlin (East): Dietz Verlag, 1955, vol. I. pt. 1, pp. 370ff., and the declaration of the Amalgamating Congress, reprinted in *Dokumente der Sozialistischen Einheitspartei* [Documents of the Socialist Unity Party]. Berlin (East): Dietz Verlag, 1948, vol. 1, pp. 9f. The 1963 programme was aiming at German reunification and emphasized the importance of scientific economic development.

G53 'Programm der SED'. [Programme of the SED]. In: *Protokoll der Verhandlungen des 9. Parteitags der SED 1976*. [Protocol of the 9th Party Congress of the SED]. Berlin (East): Dietz Verlag, 1976. Vol. 2.

The new party programme marks the change from the Ulbricht to the Honecker era. It shows greater emphasis on social policy than the first programme. The main task (Hauptaufgabe), the unity between economic growth and more welfare provisions and a higher standard of living, was underlined. The language is also less complicated than in the previous programme. Further, the claim that the GDR was a 'developed social system of socialism' was dropped in favour of a 'developed socialist society'.

G54 '5. Statut der Sozialistischen Einheitspartei Deutschlands'. [5th Statute of the Socialist Unity Party of Germany]. In: *Protokoll der Verhandlungen des 9. Parteitags der SED 1976*. [Protocol of the 9th Party Congress of the SED 1976]. Berlin (East): Dietz Verlag, 1976. Vol. 2.

The statute of the SED did not change very much between 1950 and 1976. The 1st Statute of 1946 accommodated the social democrats within the Party through joint leadership positions within the Party. From 1950 onwards however the changes made at the 1st Party Conference and before were formally adopted in the 2nd Statute providing for a 'party of a new type', i.e., a party on Leninist principles. The 3rd Statute from 1954 brought some minor organizational changes, as did the 4th Statute in 1963. The main points of the 5th Statute were a reversal from calling the party leader First Secretary to Secretary-General, as during the period 1950–54. Also members can now leave the Party on application while previously they had either to be expelled or struck off the party list. Most important however is the control function of the party over the state which has now been written into the statute.

Other official or semi-official publications relating to party affairs

G55 Dohlus, H. *Der Demokratische Zentralismus. Grundprinzipien der Führungstätigkeit der SED bei der Verwirklichung der Beschlüsse des Zentralkomitees*. [Democratic centralism. Basic principles of the leading role of the SED in putting decisions of the central committee into practice]. Berlin (East): Dietz Verlag, 1965.

Provides a guide to how democratic centralism works in practice within the Party. Dohlus is the CC Secretary responsible for party organization.

G56 *Nationale Front des Demokratischen Deutschland*. [National Front of Democratic Germany]. Berlin (East): Dietz Verlag, 1969.

Provides information on the history and the functioning of the National Front, the organizing and electioneering body comprising all parties and mass movements in the GDR represented in parliament.

G57 *Geschichte der Sozialistischen Einheitspartei Deutschlands*. [History of the Socialist Unity Party of Germany]. Institut für Marxismus-Leninismus beim ZK der SED (ed.). Berlin (East): Dietz Verlag, 1978.

Official history of the SED formally authorized by a commission of the Politbureau under the Secretary-General, Erich Honecker.

Papers and journals relating to party affairs

G58 *Neues Deutschland.* [New Germany]. Berlin (East): Zentralkomitee der SED, 1946–. Daily.

The most important paper in the GDR. As the central party organ, all major events, political decisions, legal changes of general importance, and economic developments are reported in it, often as the first source of publication. Also the best available paper from the GDR in the West.

G59 *Einheit.* [Unity]. Berlin (East): Zentralkomitee der SED, 1946–. Monthly.

Concerned with theoretical aspects of life in the GDR and with explaining the party line to functionaries and ordinary members. Long-term developments and changes are often discussed here before they appear in other publications.

G60 *Neuer Weg.* [New way]. Berlin (East): Organisationssekretariat beim ZK der SED, 1946–. Fortnightly.

A magazine for the Party functionary, who finds the arguments outlined which he may require for discussions in his local party organization. Organizational matters are also discussed.

Bibliographies

G61 *Wir sind die stärkste der Partei'n.* [We are the strongest of all parties]. Leipzig: Institut für Marxismus-Leninismus beim ZK der SED, 1961.

Published on the occasion of the 15th anniversary of the SED's founding. A bibliography including a lot of material on the KPD as well as on the SED.

G62 *Bibliographie zur Geschichte der kommunistischen und Arbeiterparteien.* [Bibliography on the history of communist and workers' parties]. Berlin (East): Institut für Gesellschaftswissenschaften beim ZK der SED, 1959/60. (Mimeograph).

GENERAL STATISTICS

G63 *Statistisches Jahrbuch der Deutschen Demokratischen Republik.* [Statistical yearbook of the German Democratic Republic]. Berlin (East): Staatsverlag der DDR, 1950–. Annual.

Usually published in the middle of the year following that to which it applies.

G64 *Statistisches Taschenbuch der Deutschen Demokratischen Republik.*

[Statistical pocketbook of the German Democratic Republic]. Berlin (East): Staatsverlag der DDR, 1963–. Annual.

Usually published in March of the following year. It is an abbreviated version of the statistical yearbook (G63) without methodological explanations or other comments which can be found in the yearbook. The figures given in the pocketbook are often only preliminary. An English-language version is published under the same title as translated.

G65 *Statistische Praxis*. [Statistical practice]. Zentralverwaltung für Statistik (ed.). Berlin (East): Staatsverlag der DDR, 1946–. Monthly.

The authoritative journal published in the GDR.

G66 *Neues Deutschland*. [New Germany]. Berlin (East): 1946–. Daily.

Towards the end of the year or at the beginning of the year, *Neues Deutschland* publishes the annual economic report and the plan for the following year. Half-way through the year the same is done for the half-year period. Most informative are the reports and plans for the five-year periods.

OTHER GENERAL SOURCES OF DOCUMENTATION

G67 *Allgemeiner Deutscher Nachrichtendienst—ADN*. [General German news service—ADN]. Berlin (East): 1946–. 24 hours a day.

Besides *Neues Deutschland* (G66) the most important source of official information in the GDR. Often articles carried by *ADN* are not carried by the national press because they may be intended for external consumption only.

G68 *Der Morgen*. [The morning]. Berlin (East): 1946–. Daily.

The national paper of the liberal party LDPD in the GDR. Besides *Der Morgen* there are four regional LDPD papers. The LDPD caters for private craftsmen and for members of the intelligentsia whose background is not working class. Thus political developments relating to these groups of the population are often first publicized in the liberal papers.

G69 *Neue Zeit*. [New time]. Berlin (East): 1946–. Daily.

Christians in the GDR and the churches, especially the Protestant churches, have been playing a far more active role in GDR politics since 1978. Church matters are also eminently political because of the diocese borders which, in the case of the Catholics, still do not coincide with the political borders. State–church relations are one of the subjects prominently covered in *Neue Zeit*. The paper does not discuss religious affairs, though, but the political implications of life for Christians in the GDR.

G70 *Nationalzeitung*. [National paper]. Berlin (East): 1948–. Daily.

In the same way as the LDPD and the CDU are vehicles for

integrating certain groups of the population into GDR society, the NDPD caters for former officers and other bourgeois people who would not fit into the SED. Accordingly, the *Nationalzeitung* publishes material relevant to this group.

G71 *Berliner Zeitung*. [Berlin paper]. Berlin (East): 1945–. Daily.

Most of the regional papers in the GDR are not for sale outside East Germany. The *Berliner Zeitung* is an exception in so far as it can be bought by the many western visitors who go daily to East Berlin. Sometimes the coverage of certain events differs significantly in regional papers from that in the national papers. The special status of Berlin is the reason why this is more often the case in the *Berliner Zeitung* than elsewhere.

INTERNATIONAL RELATIONS

The foreign policies of the GDR developed under the restraint of the country not being fully sovereign until 1955 and later of not being diplomatically recognized by most western countries until the early 1970s. Publications listed in this section are therefore mainly more recent ones.

G72 *Dokumente zur Aussenpolitik der Regierung der DDR*. [Documents on the foreign policies of the GDR]. Berlin (East): Staatsverlag der DDR, 1954–.

A collection of international documents, treaties and agreements. Vols. 1–10 published by Rütten & Loening. 24 vols. published by 1980. Title omits 'der Regierung' from volume 11.

G72a *Zur Aussenpolitik der Deutschen Demokratischen Republik*. [On the foreign policies of the German Democratic Republic]. Berlin (East): Staatsverlag der DDR, 1964.

G73 *Geschichte der Aussenpolitik der Deutschen Demokratischen Republik*. [History of the foreign policies of the German Democratic Republic]. Berlin (East): Dietz Verlag, 1968.

G74 Winzer, O. *Deutsche Aussenpolitik des Friedens und des Sozialismus*. [German foreign policy of peace and socialism]. Berlin (East): Staatsverlag der DDR, 1968.

Written by the then Foreign Minister of the GDR, this book reflects the attempts of the GDR leadership since the mid-1960s to become internationally recognized. The official history of GDR foreign policies (G73) is written in the same mould.

G75 Hänisch, W. *Aussenpolitik und internationale Beziehungen der DDR*. [Foreign policy and international relations of the GDR]. Berlin (East): Staatsverlag der DDR, 1972.

This first volume covers the years 1949 to 1955. Further volumes are planned but have not appeared yet.

G76 Florin, P. *Zur Aussenpolitik der Souveränen Sozialistischen Deutschen*

Demokratischen Republik. [On the foreign policy of the Sovereign Socialist German Democratic Republic]. Berlin (East): Dietz Verlag, 1967.

Florin is one of the leading GDR foreign policy experts and has been an ambassador. This book is concerned with the Warsaw Pact, Comecon and European security.

G77 *Konfrontation—Entspannung—Zusammenarbeit.* [Confrontation— *Détente*—cooperation]. Akademie für Staats- und Rechtswissenschaft der DDR und Institut für Internationale Beziehungen (eds.). Berlin (East): Staatsverlag der DDR, 1979.

G78 *DDR–UdSSR. Zusammenarbeit und Annäherung.* [GDR–USSR. Cooperation and *rapprochement*]. S. Doernberg (ed.). Berlin (East): Staatsverlag der DDR, 1979.

A rather short book (just over 200 pages), bearing in mind how important relations between the two countries are. As the title indicates—'*rapprochement*'—the emphasis is more on propaganda than on information.

G79 *Koordinierte sozialistische Aussenpolitik—Dokumente 1971–1975.* [Coordinated socialist foreign policy—documents 1971–1975]. Akademie für Staats- und Rechtswissenschaft der DDR und Institut für Internationale Beziehungen (eds.). Potsdam-Babelsberg: Selbstverlag, 1978. 2 vols.

Part 1 of vol. I contains documents relating to relations between the USSR and France, the Federal Republic of Germany and Britain. Part 2 consists of documents relating to relations of the USSR with other West European countries and Canada. Vol. II (forthcoming) will deal with relations between other socialist bloc countries and western countries.

G80 *Dokumente zur Abrüstung 1917 bis 1976.* [Documents on disarmament 1917–1976]. Institut für Internationale Politik und Wirtschaft der DDR (ed.). Berlin (East): Staatsverlag der DDR, 1978.

Although the selection of documents is largely designed to prove the USSR's love of peace, there are some surprising discoveries to be made when going through the volume. Documents which are not easily accessible can be found here.

G81 *Wörterbuch der Aussenpolitik und des Völkerrechts.* [Dictionary of foreign policy and international law]. Institut für Internationale Beziehungen der Akademie für Staats- und Rechtswissenschaft der DDR (ed.). Berlin (East): Dietz Verlag, 1979.

Papers and journals

G82 *Aussenpolitische Korrespondenz.* [Foreign policy correspondence]. Berlin (East): Ministry for Foreign Affairs, 1957–. Weekly.

Provides regular and detailed information on the activities of the ministry.

G83 *Horizont.* [Horizon]. Berlin (East): 1970–. Weekly.

Contains more background material than the *Aussenpolitische Korrespondenz* (G82) and is directed towards a more general public readership.

G84 *IPW-Berichte.* [IPW reports]. Berlin (East): Institut für Internationale Politik und Wirtschaft, 1972–. Monthly.

The institute is mainly concerned with the development of western capitalist countries and to some degree with the Third World. This is reflected in the contributions published. The tables and statistics which are irregularly published are otherwise not easily available in East Germany. Also a review of the most important literature on foreign and economic affairs can be found in the journal. Between 1950 and 1971 the journal appeared under the title *DWI-Berichte* and was published by the Deutsches Wirtschaftsinstitut, the predecessor of the Institut für Internationale Politik und Wirtschaft. Both institutes, however, were set up mainly as research bodies specializing in western countries, particularly the Federal Republic of Germany.

G85 *Deutsche Aussenpolitik.* [German foreign policy]. Institut für Internationale Beziehungen an der Deutschen Akademie für Staats- und Rechtswissenschaft (ed.). Berlin (East): Deutscher Verlag der Wissenschaft, 1956–. Bimonthly.

General foreign policy subjects are dealt with, and there is no area specialization. The articles are background material. There is also a comprehensive review section and a valuable table of events, and sometimes important documents are reprinted.

POLITICAL AND IDEOLOGICAL AFFAIRS

Literature on the two topics is numerous and only the most important titles are listed below. With the restrictions of space in mind more recent publications have been given preference.

The founding years of the GDR

G86 *Dokumente aus den Jahren 1945–1949.* [Documents from the years 1945–1949]. Berlin (East): Staatsverlag der DDR, 1968.

G87 Teller, H. *Der kalte Krieg gegen die DDR.* [The Cold War against the GDR]. Berlin (East): Akademie-Verlag, 1979.

The period dealt with ends in 1961. The work traces the origins of the division of Germany from an East German official point of view.

G88 *Die DDR in der Übergangsperiode.* [The GDR in the transitionary period]. R. Badstübner et al. (eds.). Berlin (East): Akademie-Verlag, 1980.

Again the period dealt with ends in 1961. More details are given than in *Der kalte Krieg gegen die DDR* (G87). Also the emphasis on the years after 1949 is stronger.

The German nation

G89   Kulke, H. J. et al. *Nationalität: deutsch, Staatsbürgerschaft: DDR.* [Nationality: German, citizenship: GDR]. Berlin (East): Staatsverlag der DDR, 1979.

Since the early 1970s the question of a separate GDR nation has become a widely discussed issue inside and outside East Germany. This book provides the official line of argument in a historical and legal way.

G90   Ulbricht, W. *Die nationale Frage in heutiger Sicht.* [The national question from today's point of view]. Berlin (East): Dietz Verlag, 1965.

Collection of speeches, declarations and other statements by the then party leader.

G91   Ulbricht, W. *Whither Germany?* Dresden: Zeit im Bild Verlag, 1966.

This volume in English contains speeches and essays on the national question.

G92   Ulbricht, W. *Zur Geschichte der deutschen Arbeiterbewegung.* [On the history of the German workers' movement]. Berlin (East): Dietz Verlag, 1953–66. 10 vols.

Provides the best insight into the changing position of the GDR leaders on this subject.

Socialist system

G93   *Politische Ökonomie des Sozialismus und ihre Anwendung in der DDR.* [Political economy of socialism and its application in the GDR]. Berlin (East): Dietz Verlag, 1969.

Attempts to explain that the GDR is a logical outcome and truthful reflection of Marxism put into practice. Apart from a brief historical chapter and some basic ideological points, provides a survey of economic planning and practically all economic activities.

G94   *Wissenschaftliche Entscheidungen—Historische Veränderungen—Fundamente der Zukunft.* [Scientific decisions—historical changes—foundations for the future]. Berlin (East): Staatsverlag der DDR, 1971.

Deals with the GDR in the 1960s and is, as so often in GDR political literature, preoccupied with economics.

G95   *Die gesellschaftlichen Organisationen in der DDR.* [The societal organizations in the GDR]. Berlin (East): Staatsverlag der DDR, 1980.

The position of and the cooperation with the state by organizations such as the women's federation and the farmers' federation are the subject of this book. The churches are not included.

G96 Lenz, W. *Der Stadtkreis, der Stadtbezirk und einige grundlegende Aufgaben der Volksvertretungen und ihrer Organe.* [The municipal region, the city district and some of the fundamental tasks of the parliaments and their organs]. Potsdam-Babelsberg: Selbstverlag der Akademie für Staats- und Rechtswissenschaft der DDR, 1980.

Handbooks

G97 *Wörterbuch zum sozialistischen Staat.* [Dictionary of the socialist state]. Akademie für Staats- und Rechtswissenschaft der DDR (ed.). Berlin (East): Dietz Verlag, 1980.

The first dictionary of its kind in the GDR, comprising some 400 keywords under which detailed information is given.

Kleines politisches Wörterbuch. See G13.
Handbuch der Volkskammer der Deutschen Demokratischen Republik. See G21.

Journals and papers

Einheit. See G59.
Neues Deutschland. See G58.

G98 *Sozialistische Demokratie.* [Socialist democracy]. State Council and Council of Ministers (eds.). Berlin (East): 1949–72.

MILITARY AFFAIRS

G99 *Die Nationale Volksarmee der Deutschen Demokratischen Republik.* [The National People's Army of the German Democratic Republic]. Berlin (East): 1961.

A documentation and brief history of the East German forces.

G100 *Sozialistisches Recht und Nationale Verteidigung.* [Socialist law and national defence]. Berlin (East): Deutscher Militärverlag, 1967.

A guideline for members of the armed forces.

G101 *Militärische Theorie und militärische Praxis.* [Military theory and military practice]. Berlin (East): 1972.

Contains a discussion of methodological problems of theory and practice.

G102 Hoffmann, H. *Sozialistische Landesverteidigung.* [Socialist national defence]. *Aus Reden und Aufsätzen.* [From speeches and essays]. Berlin (East): Deutscher Militärverlag, 1971 (2 vols.); and Militärverlag der DDR, 1974 and 1979. 4 vols. in all.

The first two vols. cover the period 1963–70; the third volume (although not numbered as such) 1970–74; the fourth volume (again unnumbered) 1974–78. General Hoffmann is Minister of Defence of the GDR.

G103 Schönherr, S. 'Über den Zusammenhang zwischen Wirtschaft und Landesverteidigung beim Aufbau des entwickelten gesellschaftlichen Systems des Sozialismus in der DDR'. [On the connection between the economy and national defence during the construction of the developed societal system of socialism in the GDR]. In: *Wirtschaftswissenschaft*, no. 8, 1969, pp. 115ff.
A classic essay on the subject. Especially important is the ideological dimension as it follows the Ulbricht theory of the GDR being a 'developed societal system of socialism'.

G104 *Beiträge zur Militärökonomie.* [Contributions to the Military Economy]. Berlin (East): Militärverlag der DDR, 1979.
Justifies the economic efforts for defence measures as being necessary for the construction of a socialist society.

Bibliographies and handbooks

G105 Vangermain, H. et al. *Fragen der Militärpolitik und sozialistischen Wehrerziehung.* [Questions of military policy and socialist military education]. Berlin (East): Pädagogische Zentralbibliothek Berlin, 1971.
A select bibliography.

G106 *Zeittafel zur Militärgeschichte der Deutschen Demokratischen Republik 1949–1968.* [Timetable of the military history of the German Democratic Republic 1949–1968]. Militärgeschichtliches Institut der DDR (eds.). Berlin (East): Deutscher Militärverlag, 1969.

G107 *Zeittafel zur Militärgeschichte der Deutschen Demokratischen Republik 1969–1977.* [Timetable of the military history of the German Democratic Republic 1969–1977]. Militärgeschichtliches Institut der DDR (eds.). Berlin (East): Militärverlag der DDR, 1979.

G108 *Militärlexikon.* [Military lexicon]. E. Bauer et al. (eds.). Berlin (East): Deutscher Militärverlag, 1971.

G109 *Handbuch militärischen Grundwissens.* [Handbook of basic military knowledge]. 4th ed. Ministerium für Nationale Verteidigung (ed.). Berlin (East): Militärverlag der DDR, 1973.

Journals

G110 *Volksarmee* [People's army]. Berlin (East): 1956–. Weekly.
A journal for the troops, used for propaganda purposes and the airing of ordinary soldiers' grievances.

G111 *Militärwesen.* [Military affairs]. Berlin (East): 1956–. Monthly.
A publication aimed at the officers and used for their theoretical and ideological training.

ECONOMIC AFFAIRS

Theory and practice

G112 *Politische Ökonomie des Sozialismus und ihre Anwendung in der DDR.* [Political economy of socialism and its application in the GDR]. Berlin (East): Dietz Verlag, 1969.

Contains a fair amount of Marxist-Leninist theory and its practical application. In addition, however—and this is the major part of the book—detailed analyses of economic and financial planning procedures are given and other economic activities are discussed.

G113 Steeger, H. et al. *Planung der Volkswirtschaft in der DDR.* [Planning of the national economy in the GDR]. Berlin (East): Verlag die Wirtschaft, 1970.

Deals with planning procedures at company, regional and state level.

G114 Ulbricht, W. *Grundfragen der ökonomischen und politischen Entwicklung in der Deutschen Demokratischen Republik.* [Basic questions of the economic and political development of the German Democratic Republic]. Berlin (East): Dietz Verlag, 1957.

Maps out the main problems of the GDR economy for the years 1957–60 and the targets which were set in the plan. Signals increased efforts during a particularly difficult period for the GDR economy. *See also* G137.

G115 Apel, E. *Durch sozialistische Rekonstruktion und Erhöhung der Arbeitsproduktivität zur Erfüllung des Siebenjahresplans.* [Through socialist reconstruction and increased labour productivity towards the fullfilment of the seven-year plan]. Berlin (East): Dietz Verlag, 1959.

After the premature end of the second five-year plan in 1958 a seven-year plan was passed, following the Soviet example. The emphasis was on increased labour productivity and the strengthening of basic industries. Apel was party secretary for economic affairs.

G116 Apel, E. et al. *Neues Ökonomisches System und Investitionspolitik.* [New Economic System and investment policy]. Berlin (East): Dietz Verlag, 1965.

After the seven-year plan faltered in 1962 and the Liberman essay on economic reforms had appeared in the Soviet Union, reforms recommended in the late 1950s in the GDR were implemented under the heading of the New Economic System. This book discusses how this system should be applied in practice. Two important government decrees are reprinted in the appendix: one on investment and the second on the planning of investment.

Agriculture

G117 *Recht für die Landwirtschaftspraxis.* [The law for agricultural practice]. R. Arlt et al. (eds.). Berlin (East): Staatsverlag der DDR, 1979.

A reader for students at polytechnics and specialist agricultural teaching institutions.

G118 *Die Landwirtschaft der DDR.* [The GDR's agriculture]. K. Groschoff et al. (eds.). Berlin (East): Dietz Verlag, 1980.

History of the agricultural reform and the gradual change from private to state and cooperative farming. The specialization of farms and the change towards large-scale industrial production methods are also discussed.

Lexicons

G119 *Ökonomisches Lexikon.* [Economic lexicon]. 3rd ed. Berlin (East): Verlag die Wirtschaft, 1978–81. 3 vol.

Includes all subject areas of macro- and micro-economics. A comprehensive work.

G120 *Lexikon der Wirtschaft—Berufsbildung.* [Lexicon of economics—vocational training]. Zentralinstitut für Berufsbildung (ed.). Berlin (East): Verlag die Wirtschaft, 1978.

Social–economic and pedagogic terminology.

G121 *Lexikon der Wirtschaft—Wirtschaftsrecht.* [Lexicon of economics—economic law]. Berlin (East): Cooperative production of Staatsverlag der DDR, transpress-VEB Verlag für Verkehrswesen, Verlag die Wirtschaft, Staatsverlag, 1978.

Legal terminology regarding foreign trade and Comecon relations.

G122 *Lexikon der Wirtschaft—Preise.* [Lexicon of economics—prices]. Berlin (East): Verlag die Wirtschaft, 1979.

G123 *Lexikon der Wirtschaft—Volkswirtschaftsplanung.* [Lexicon of economics—national economic planning]. H. Steeger (ed.). Berlin (East): Verlag die Wirtschaft, 1980.

Journals

G124 *Die Wirtschaft.* [The economy]. Berlin (East): 1946–. Monthly.

G125 *Wirtschaftswissenschaft.* [Economic science]. Berlin (East): 1953–. Monthly.

G126 *IPW-Berichte.* [IPW Reports]. Institut für Internationale Politik und Wirtschaft (ed.). Berlin (East): Staatsverlag der DDR, 1972–. Monthly. *See* G84.

SOCIAL AFFAIRS

G127 Friedrich, W. *Jugend heute*. [Youth today]. Berlin (East): Deutscher Verlag der Wissenschaften, 1966.
  Basic reader on youth affairs and the ideological role of the youth organizations.

G128 *Stellung der Frau in der DDR*. [The role of the woman in the GDR]. H. Kuhrig (ed.). Leipzig: Verlag für die Frau, 1978.
  A summary of all the positive discrimination in favour of women in the GDR and the ideological reasons for this preference.

G129 *Handbuch für den Gesundheits- und Arbeitsschutz*. [Handbook on the protection of health at work and outside work]. H.-G. Häublein (ed.). Berlin (East): Verlag Tribüne, 1976–1978. 2 vols.

G130 *Theorie und Praxis der Sozialpolitik in der DDR*. [Theory and practice of social policy in the GDR]. Akademie der Wissenschaften der DDR (ed.). Berlin (East): Akademie-Verlag, 1980.
  An assessment of what has been achieved and what still has to be done, according to the political–ideological goals set.

G131 *Zum Wohle des Volkes*. [For the welfare of the people]. Berlin (East): Dietz Verlag, 1980.
  A report on the implementation of the social programme announced at the 8th Party Congress in 1971 in documentary form. Ends with 1978.

CULTURAL AFFAIRS

G132 *Einheitlichkeit und Differenzierung im Bildungssystem*. [Unity and differentiation in the educational system]. Berlin (East): Verlag Volk und Wissen, 1971.
  A discussion of the principles of the GDR's educational system.

G133 *Das Bildungswesen der DDR*. [The educational system of the GDR]. K.-H. Günther et al. (eds.). Berlin (East): Verlag Volk und Wissen, 1979.
  A short general introduction to the subject.

G134 Schmidt, W. et al. *Öffentlichkeit, öffentliche Meinung und staatliche Öffentlichkeitsarbeit*. [The public, public opinion and government publicity]. Potsdam-Babelsberg: Akademie für Staats- und Rechtswissenschaft Selbstverlag, 1980.
  A university reader.

G135 Höpcke, K. *Kultur und Klassenkampf*. [Culture and class struggle]. Berlin (East): Dietz Verlag, 1968.
  Höpcke is a Deputy Minister of Culture and the most active member of his ministry. This book is an ideological tract.

G136 *Kulturpolitisches Wörterbuch*. [Cultural–political dictionary]. 2nd ed. Berlin (East): Dietz Verlag, 1978.

LEADERS' WORKS

G137 Ulbricht, W. *Grundfragen der ökonomischen und politischen Entwicklung in der Deutschen Demokratischen Republik*. [Basic questions on the economic and political development of the German Democratic Republic]. Berlin (East): Dietz Verlag, 1957.

Speech by Ulbricht to the Central Committee in which he outlined how the GDR could prove that it was superior to West Germany. The party leader Ulbricht thus made a last attempt to build a socialist society when the Berlin Wall had not yet been built. *See also* G114.

G138 Ulbricht, W. *Über die Dialektik unseres sozialistischen Aufbaus*. [On the dialectics of our socialist development]. Berlin (East): Dietz Verlag, 1959.

A collection of essays and speeches from 1953 to 1959.

G139 Ulbricht, W. *Zur sozialistischen Entwicklung der Volkswirtschaft seit 1945*. [On the socialist development of the national economy since 1945]. Berlin (East): Dietz Verlag, 1959.

A history of party policy on the German question and on economics presented in the form of essays and speeches by Ulbricht.

G140 Ulbricht, W. *Die Entwicklung des deutschen Volksdemokratischen Staates 1945 bis 1958*. [The development of the German People's Democratic State 1945–1958]. Berlin (East): Dietz Verlag, 1959.

G141 Ulbricht, W. *Die nationale Frage in heutiger Sicht*. [The National question from today's point of view]. Berlin (East): Dietz Verlag, 1965. *See* G90.

G142 Ulbricht, W. *Whither Germany?* Dresden: Zeit im Bild Verlag, 1966. *See* G91.

G143 Ulbricht, W. *Zur Geschichte der deutschen Arbeiterbewegung*. [On the history of the German workers' movement]. Berlin (East): Dietz Verlag, 1953–66. 10 vols. *See* G92.

G144 Ulbricht, W. *Die nationale Mission der DDR und das geistige Schaffen in unserem Staat*. [The national mission of the GDR and the intellectual work done in our state]. Berlin (East): Dietz Verlag, 1966.

A claim to represent the true Germany.

G145 Ulbricht, W. *Probleme des Perspektivplans bis 1970*. [Problems of the perspective planning to the year 1970]. Berlin (East): Dietz Verlag, 1966.

Justifies the economic reforms of the mid-1960s.

G146 Ulbricht, W. *Zum neuen ökonomischen System der Planung und Leitung*. [On the New Economic System for planning and managing the economy]. Berlin (East): Dietz Verlag, 1966.

A comprehensive explanation of what it was hoped the New Economic System would achieve and how it was working.

G147   Ulbricht, W. *Ausgewählte Reden und Aufsätze zur Geschichte der deutschen und internationalen Arbeiterbewegung.* [Select speeches and essays on the history of the German and the international workers' movement]. Berlin (East): Dietz Verlag, 1979.

A publication which can be seen as a rehabilitation of Ulbricht after a spell of several years when he was simply not mentioned, or at least only rarely.

G148   Pieck, W. *An die Jugend.* [Address to the young people]. 2nd ed. Berlin (East): Verlag Neues Leben, 1980.

An edited second edition of a similar publication in 1955. This time two contributions by Erich Honecker, Ulbricht's successor as party leader and Pieck's successor as head of state, are included.

G149   Pieck, W. *Reden und Aufsätze* [Speeches and Essays]. 2nd ed. Berlin (East): Deutscher Staatsverlag, 1954. 3 vols.

G150   Grotewohl, O. *Im Kampf um die einige Deutsche Demokratische Republik.* [In the fight for a united German Democratic Republic]. Berlin (East): Staatsverlag, 1959. 3 vols.

A collection of speeches and essays.

G151   Grotewohl, O. *Über Politik, Geschichte und Kultur.* [On politics, history and culture]. Berlin (East): Dietz Verlag, 1979.

Select essays and speeches.

G152   Honecker, E. *Unter dem Banner des Internationalismus.* [Under the flag of internationalism]. Berlin (East): Dietz Verlag, 1972.

A selection of essays and speeches with the emphasis on close cooperation with the Soviet Union.

G153   Honecker, E. *Zuverlässiger Schutz des Sozialismus.* [Reliable protection of socialism]. Berlin (East): Dietz Verlag, 1972.

Selection of speeches and essays on the defence policy of the East German communist party.

G154   Honecker, E. *Die Rolle der Arbeiterklasse und ihrer Partei in der sozialistischen Gesellschaft.* [The role of the working class and its party in socialist society]. Berlin (East): Dietz Verlag, 1974.

G155   Stoph, W. *Für das Erstarken unseres sozialistischen Staates.* [For the strengthening of our socialist state]. Berlin (East): Dietz Verlag, 1976.

Select speeches and essays covering the period 1974–79.

G156   Sindermann, H. *Frieden und Sozialismus—Staatsdoktrin der DDR.* [Peace and socialism—the doctrine of the GDR]. Berlin (East): Dietz Verlag, 1980.

Select speeches and essays covering the period 1970–80.

H HUNGARY

John Freeman

INTRODUCTION

Political and historical background

The foundations of postwar Hungarian political life were laid at Debrecen on 23 December 1944, when a provisional government was elected by the Provisional National Assembly which had met on 21 December. This coalition government consisted of members of the Communist Party, the Social Democratic Party, the Smallholders' Party and the National Peasant Party (the four 'democratic' parties permitted by the Soviet military authorities) which had previously formed themselves into the Hungarian National Independence Front at Szeged at the beginning of the month. By the end of the year southern and eastern Hungary had been occupied by the advancing Red Army, but the rest of the country was still controlled by the German authorities and the pro-German puppet government which they had installed in Budapest after an abortive attempt to extricate Hungary from the war on 15 October 1944. After renouncing the German alliance and declaring war on Germany representatives of the provisional government signed an armistice agreement in Moscow on 20 January 1945, with the Soviet Union, Great Britain and the United States, and at the same time an Allied Control Commission, under the direction of the Soviet High Command, was established to supervise the execution of the armistice terms. It was not until April 1945, when the whole of Hungary had been liberated from the German occupying forces, that the provisional government could move to Budapest, but meanwhile, on 15 March, it had decreed a sweeping land reform by which the large estates were broken up and the land redistributed amongst the smaller peasantry and landless agricultural labourers. On 4 November 1945, in elections for a new National Assembly, the Smallholders'

Party gained 57 per cent of the votes cast as against the 17 per cent polled by each of the left-wing parties, the communists and social democrats. Despite this result the coalition government continued in office with Zoltán Tildy, a smallholder, as Prime Minister. On 1 February 1946, Hungary was proclaimed a republic, Tildy becoming President.

Faced with the serious reverse which they had suffered at the elections the communists began a skilful campaign to acquire power by means later graphically described by their leader, Mátyás Rákosi, as 'salami tactics'. This consisted essentially of weakening their chief rivals by forcing them to repudiate 'reactionary' elements within their ranks, thereby causing a proliferation of dissident splinter groups which could the more easily be eliminated as effective political forces. The communists' drive for power was also helped by their acquiring key ministries such as that of the interior and by the support of the Soviet military authorities. The power of the smallholders was nullified in early 1947 when their leaders Ferenc Nagy, the Prime Minister, and Béla Kovács were implicated in an alleged anti-state conspiracy; Kovács was arrested and Nagy, forced to resign, went into exile. These tactics bore fruit in the elections of August 1947 when the communists emerged as the strongest single party, but the climax of their political strategy came in June 1948 with the unification of the Communist Party and the Social Democratic Party, by then purged of its right wing, in the new Hungarian Working People's Party. The way was now clear for a consolidation of communist power: the opposition of the Roman Catholic Church was removed by the arrest and trial in February 1949 of Cardinal Mindszenty, Primate of Hungary, on charges of treason and espionage, the economy assumed a decidedly socialist character with the completion of nationalization and the start of a campaign to collectivize agriculture, and absolute political control was finally achieved by the establishment in February 1949 of the Hungarian Independent People's Front, an organization which combined the government parties dominated by the communists with the remaining opposition parties, and also included mass organizations such as the National Council of Trade Unions, the Federation of Working Youth, and the Federation of Democratic Women. All opposition having been eliminated, the elections of 15 May 1949 were held on the basis of a single list of candidates, and the people's front received almost 96 per cent of the votes cast. The political transformation of Hungary was completed on 20 August 1949, on the adoption of a Soviet-type constitution declaring Hungary, already a 'people's republic', to be a 'state of workers and working peasantry' in which the leading role was assigned to the vanguard of the working class, the Communist Party.

The period from 1949 to 1953 was characterized by a ruthless imitation of Stalinist methods in an attempt to establish a dictatorship of the proletariat. Of undisputed pre-eminence was Mátyás Rákosi, General Secretary of the Party and, from August 1952, also Prime Minister, who, openly exploiting his unlimited power in what was later to be termed the 'cult of personality', was staunchly supported by Ernő Gerő, responsible for economic affairs, József Révai, the chief party ideologist, and Mihály Farkas, in charge of defence. The breach between Stalin and Tito in 1948, together with the strained international situation, led to a witch-hunt of alleged Titoists (equated with traitors after 1948), the chief victim of which was László Rajk, the Foreign Minister, who was tried and executed in October 1949. This heralded a drastic purge of communists and former social democrats between 1949 and 1953, among them János Kádár, imprisoned in 1951, and the widespread use of police terror to enforce conformity in the population at large. In the economic field the Five-Year Plan of 1950, designed to turn Hungary into a 'country of iron and steel', resulted in rapid and indiscriminate forced industrialization, which was accompanied by a ruthless campaign to collectivize agriculture. By early 1953 such policies had created severe tensions in the country, which were only relieved when, after the death of Stalin in March 1953, the new Soviet leadership forced Rákosi to resign as Prime Minister. He was succeeded by Imre Nagy, an opponent of Rákosi's policies, who, in his 'new course' of June 1953, attempted to reverse the trend towards forced industrialization and collectivization, placing greater emphasis on personal consumption and welfare, began a modest liberalization of cultural life, and released many political prisoners.

Rákosi, however, retained the leadership of the Party and between the summer of 1953 and the spring of 1955 spared no effort to discredit Nagy and bring about a restoration of Stalinist policies. He was rewarded when, after the fall of Malenkov in the Soviet Union, Nagy, accused of 'rightist deviation', was relieved of the premiership in April 1955, and Rákosi again became Prime Minister. The reimposition of Stalinism was, however, made more difficult the following year when Khrushchev's speech at the Twentieth Congress of the Soviet Communist Party denouncing Stalin's excesses emboldened Rákosi's critics within the Party to seek to reverse his policies. In July 1956 Rákosi was forced to resign the leadership of the Party, only to be replaced by Gerő, a man no less attached to a dogmatic interpretation of communism. Dissatisfaction and frustration continued to ferment in the summer of 1956, until on 23 October the attempted armed suppression by security forces of a large student demonstration provoked the outbreak of the thirteen-day revolution. Events moved swiftly: András Hegedűs, Rákosi's protégé, was succeeded as Prime Minister by Imre Nagy, and Gerő was replaced by Kádár as First Secretary of the Party. On 1 November Nagy's coalition government, responding to the demands of the revolutionaries, declared Hungary's neutrality and withdrawal from the Warsaw Pact and appealed to the United Nations for support. Policies were also formulated which would have turned Hungary into a pluralist democratic state, with a mixed economy, the abandonment of police terror, the right of peasants not to belong to the collectivized sector of agriculture, full national independence and sovereignty, and the safeguarding of fundamental civil and economic rights. Hopes that the Soviet Union would permit such sweeping changes were, however, dashed on 4 November when Soviet forces, which had previously withdrawn, launched an invasion and crushed the revolution. At the same time a new 'Revolutionary Worker–Peasant Government', which had been secretly formed on 1 November in the Soviet Union under János Kádár, assumed power with the support of the Soviet Army.

In the first few months after November 1956 it seemed that some at least of the gains of the revolution might be retained, but when opposition to the new regime continued more drastic measures were taken to restore party authority, with the abolition of the workers' councils which had emerged during the revolution, the arrest and imprisonment of many of those implicated in the 'counter-revolution' (including Nagy, who was executed in 1958) and a repressive cultural policy. In 1958 a harsh new campaign to re-collectivize agriculture began, which was only concluded in 1961.

The early 1960s witnessed a marked change in the internal policy of the regime. In December 1961, taking advantage of the more favourable political climate in the Soviet Union, Kádár launched his conciliatory 'alliance policy' with the aim of winning legitimacy by greatly increasing the opportunities of non-party members to assume positions of responsibility, provided that they were prepared to accept the Party's authority and aims. Within the Party Kádár steered a skilful course between the extremes of 'dogmatism', i.e. Stalinism, the excesses of which were recognized to have contributed to the débâcle of 1956, and 'revisionism' or 'right-wing deviation', which was held to characterize Nagy's reforms. The fruits of this policy of liberalization were to be observed in an amnesty of political prisoners, the abolition of internal exile and internment without trial, a reduction in the number of forced labour camps, a relaxation of restrictions on foreign travel, the concluding of an agreement with the Vatican in 1964, and a more tolerant attitude towards nonconformity in cultural and intellectual matters. Economic liberalization followed in 1968 with the introduction of the New Economic Mechanism (see below).

In the 1970s the general lines of policy established in the 1960s were followed with few major deviations. Challenges from more orthodox elements within the Party have been successfully contained, although continuing economic difficulties have led to a certain amount of recentralization in the economy, a re-emphasis on the economic interests of industrial workers and efforts to reassert the traditional proletarian image of the Party. There have also been attempts to curb expressions of ideological and cultural deviation, seen particularly in the expulsion from the Party in 1973 of leading 'new left' sociologists and philosophers of the 'Budapest School' and the arrests of the sociologist Iván Szelényi and the writer György Konrád in 1974. The foreign policy of the Kádár regime has been remarkably consistent: despite greatly increased contacts with western countries, particularly in the field of foreign trade, the leadership has shown undeviating support for the Soviet Union in all major areas of foreign policy.

The Hungarian Socialist Workers' Party

The Hungarian Communist Party (from September 1944 called Magyar Kommunista Párt, before that Kommunisták Magyarországi Pártja) was founded in November 1918 and had a brief foretaste of power during the period of the Republic of Councils established in March 1919. In early August 1919, however, the republic disintegrated and with the advent of a right-wing regime in Hungary the Party was declared illegal and forced underground. Some of its members went into exile in Soviet Russia, only to fall victim to Stalin's purges in the 1930s, but those who survived returned to Hungary in 1944 with the Red Army to form the nucleus of the revived Communist Party which played a leading role in the coalition government of December 1944. The 'Muscovites', the chief of whom were Rákosi, Gerő, Révai and Farkas, were joined by 'indigenous' communists who had remained in Hungary and participated in resistance activities in 1944.

At first support for the communists was very small, but as they adroitly exploited the postwar political situation and the power of their chief rivals was gradually eliminated, membership increased rapidly, reaching 884,000 by May 1948. After the unification of the Communist Party with the Social Democratic Party in June 1948 the new party, dominated by the Communists, assumed the name Hungarian Working People's Party (Magyar Dolgozók Pártja). In May 1949 the Party claimed some 1,500,000 members, but drastic purges of 'unreliable' elements, chiefly former social democrats, had reduced this number to about 862,000 by February 1951. After the 1956 revolution membership reached a very low ebb, but a vigorous recruiting drive by the reorganized party, which in November 1956 had assumed the name Hungarian Socialist Workers' Party (Magyar Szocialista Munkáspárt), brought numbers up to 346,000 by June 1957. Thereafter membership increased steadily as the Party attempted firstly to attract industrial workers and later, as a result of the 'alliance policy', intellectuals and the technical and managerial elite.

The Party adheres to the principle of 'democratic centralism', according to which lower party organs elect delegates to higher bodies, decisions are taken by majority vote and the resolutions and decisions of indirectly elected higher bodies are binding on lower organs and on party members in general. The structure of the Party is hierarchical, the base of the pyramid being formed by the primary organizations functioning in factories, cooperatives, offices, etc. Next in the hierarchy are the local and district delegates' conferences which elect representatives to county party conferences, which in turn send delegates to the national party congresses held about every five years. Theoretically the Party Congress is the highest organ of the Party; its chief function, however, is to elect the 127 members of the Central Committee of the Party, which meets in plenary session some three or four times a year, usually for two days at a time. The Central Committee elects the inner core of policy-makers: its own secretaries and the members of its chief subdivisions, the Political Committee or Politburo, the Economic Policy Committee, the Agitprop Committee and the Central Control Committee. The Politburo, which constitutes the most important decision-making body of the Party, meets about twice a month and its deliberations are kept secret. It has about fifteen members, consisting usually of the Secretaries of the Central Committee, other party and government leaders and the heads of non-party organizations such as the National Council of Trade Unions. The major executive functions of the Party are shared by the handful of Central Committee Secretaries, each responsible for a specific area of activity, and they are supported in these tasks by the permanent staff of the Secretariat, which is organized in departments whose heads report directly to the Secretaries of the Central Committee.

Parliament and state

According to the revised constitution of 1972 Parliament, or the National Assembly (Országgyűlés), is the supreme organ of state power, exercising all rights deriving from the sovereignty of the people. It is a unicameral body whose members (352 in 1980) are elected for five years by universal adult suffrage. Since 1966 electoral law has provided for single-member constituencies and permitted multiple candidacies. Parliament alone may amend the constitution, approve the state budget, and create ministries. Its legislative acts, laws (törvények), rank highest in the hierarchy of legal sources. The development of legislation is the task of standing parliamentary committees, each of which is responsible for a particular area of state activity.

At the first session of each parliament the National Assembly elects from its members the Presidential Council (Elnöki Tanács), which consists of a President, two Vice-Presidents, a Secretary and seventeen members, and functions as a collective head of state. It is responsible for calling elections, convening Parliament, concluding and ratifying treaties, appointing and recalling diplomats, appointing judges, higher state officials and officers of the armed forces, and exercising constitutional supervision over local councils. It may also annul or modify any rule or administrative resolution which it deems to be unconstitutional. In addition, it is empowered to exercise the functions of Parliament between the sessions of the latter, and since the National Assembly meets on average only four or five times a year the Presidential Council has greater importance in the legislative process than Parliament. Its legislative acts are termed decree-laws (törvényerejű rendeletek), i.e. decrees with the force but not the form of laws, and they must be presented for approval to the next session of Parliament, to which the Presidential Council is responsible.

National and local government

The highest-ranking body of the executive branch of government is the Council of Ministers (Minisztertanács). It is responsible to the National Assembly, to which it must regularly report, but it is in effect the body responsible for the direction of the social and economic life of the country, constituting the supreme organ of state administration, with the right to repeal or modify any statutory provision or resolution initiated by a subordinate administrative organ if it violates the law or conflicts with the public interest. It usually meets fortnightly, issuing decrees and resolutions, and consists of a Chairman (the Prime Minister), four Deputy Chairmen, the Ministers, the Chairman of the National Planning Office (which has the rank of a ministry) and the Secretaries of State. The number of ministries has varied considerably since 1945, their creation or abolition often indicating the relative priority attached to various policies at different times: in the early 1950s, for example, the importance attached to the development of industry resulted in the creation of several branch ministries to supervise such fields as coal-mining and the chemical industry, whereas by the beginning of 1981 a single ministry existed to oversee all branches of industry. Also responsible to the Council of Ministers are various government committees, the most important of which is the State Planning Committee (see below), and three permanent offices with specialized functions, the Secretariat, the Councils Office, and the Information Office.

Specialized administration below national level is the responsibility of local and regional councils, which were first set up in their present form in 1950. There is a two-tier system, a lower level represented by councils of towns, villages and the districts of Budapest, for which direct elections are held, and an upper level consisting of the county councils and the Budapest City Council, whose members are elected by town and village councillors and Budapest district councillors respectively. Up to the mid-1960s the sphere of activity of the councils was severely circumscribed, since the Ministry of the Interior (before 1953) and later the Council of Ministers could exercise strict control over their administrative functions, but in recent years they have been given a much greater degree of autonomy and independence.

Other organizations of national importance

Apart from the major organs of party and state, several other political, economic, social and cultural organizations play an important role in national life. The Patriotic People's Front, established in 1954, is a mass sociopolitical organization, based on local committees, whose function is to mobilize support amongst the population for the advancement of socialism. It includes both party and non-party members, and its chief activity is the organizing of parliamentary and council elections. The role of the trade unions, which in the early period of communist rule served mainly as 'transmission-belts' of party policy, has in recent years, particularly since the enactment of the 1967 Labour Code and the introduction of the New Economic Mechanism, been enhanced to include, for example, the right of veto over certain management decisions and a measure of worker participation in decisions at enterprise level. The unions' coordinating body, the National Council of Trade Unions, also plays a major part in the administration of social insurance. The cooperatives, of which the most important are those engaged in agriculture, have also benefited from measures granting them increased autonomy, particularly since the 1967 Law on Agricultural Production Cooperatives, and the National Council of Agricultural Cooperatives now actively participates in the drafting of legislation affecting agriculture. The Communist Youth League, reorganized in 1957, is the youth organization of the Communist Party, and its chief task is to instil in its members the spirit of communist ideology and prepare them for full party membership. The supreme body responsible for the direction and coordination of scientific and scholarly research is the Hungarian Academy of Sciences. It is organized in ten departments, each responsible for a particular area of science or scholarship, which supervise the work of the numerous institutes and committees of the Academy. Although formally an independent body, the appointment of its leading members is subject to close party and government scrutiny.

Economic planning

The first postwar economic plan was the Three-Year Plan begun on 1 August 1947, with the aim of restoring the economic resources of the country after the severe losses caused by the war. The Five-Year Plan, however, which came into force on 1 January 1950, was the first fully to apply the principles of rigidly centralized planning according to the Stalinist model. After studies by economic experts in the post-revolutionary period and the early 1960s had shown the inefficiency inherent in such rigid centralization, preparations were made for a thorough reform of the system of economic management, and as a result of a resolution passed by a narrow margin at the Central Committee plenary session of May 1966 the New Economic Mechanism came into force on 1 January 1968. The chief effects of this reform have been the introduction of elements of a market economy previously unknown in a communist country, with flexible pricing and investment techniques, a much greater degree of decentralization in economic decision-making and an emphasis on managerial skills, profitability, productivity and international competitiveness.

Despite these reforms, however, the basic socialist principle of the planned economy remains intact, and the central planning authorities still play a major role in economic management. The highest state organ involved in the planning process is the Council of Ministers, which is ultimately responsible for the fulfilment of national economic plans and for the approval of the short-term (annual) plans embodying measures taken on the basis of the continuous observance of economic performance within the framework of the primary medium-term (five-year) plans. The latter, which must be approved by the National Assembly and enacted as laws, are worked out by the State Planning Office, whose function is to prepare forecasts and formulate alternatives on the basis of which party and government leaders make decisions on economic policy. When the government has formally adopted a plan, the Planning Office is responsible for working out detailed suggestions to be presented to the appropriate ministries for implementation. The State Planning Committee, an organ of the Council of Ministers set up in 1973, is responsible for ensuring that economic development proceeds in accordance with the objectives of the current five-year plan, so that the Council of Ministers may recognize fluctuations in the economy and take steps, e.g. by the adjustment of economic regulators, to keep the economy on its planned course.

Official publishing since 1945

Until 1948 publishing in Hungary was the concern of individual publishing companies, but in that year the largest of these companies were nationalized and reorganized to form five state-controlled publishing houses, and in the following year the remaining firms also passed into state ownership. Most of the publishing houses were placed under the control of the newly formed Ministry of People's Culture, but some of the ministries had their own small publishing houses, the activities of which were coordinated by the Committee of Ministerial Publishers. In 1954 the General Directorate of Publishing (Kiadói Főigazgatóság) was established as a department of the Ministry of People's Culture; its task was to exercise general supervision over publishing and bookselling. In 1955 the directorate was responsible for the reorganization of several of the smaller publishing houses into larger concerns, each with its particular specialization, and since then the structure of publishing has remained essentially the same. Most of the publishing houses are supervised by the directorate, but some are controlled by other bodies.

The general trend in Hungarian official publishing since the late 1950s has been for official bodies such as ministries to issue their material through the appropriate state publishing house rather than to function directly as publishers, though the latter practice is still observed, particularly in the case of works intended for limited circulation. The major exception is that of Parliament, which publishes its proceedings and papers itself. The Council of Ministers is responsible for issuing the official gazette and the annual cumulation of statutes; the former is published by the Publishing House for Newspapers (Lapkiadó Vállalat), which is supervised by the Information Office of the Council of Ministers and is also responsible for the publication of ministerial gazettes, while the latter has the imprint of the Publishing House for Economics and Law (Közgazdasági és Jogi Kiadó), which also publishes practically all of the many collections of statutes, commentaries and judicial decisions which have appeared in the last twenty-five years, as well as individual law codes. The publishing house of the Communist Party, founded as Szikra Könyv- és Lapkiadó in 1944, has borne the name Kossuth Könyvkiadó since December 1956; it is controlled by the Department of Party Management and Administration and by the Department of Agitation and Propaganda of the Central Committee, and publishes all official party material, including periodicals and the speeches of party leaders. The publishing of official statistics is the responsibility of the Statistical Publishing House (Statisztikai Kiadó), established in 1959, which is directly supervised by the Central Statistical Office, whilst military material is the province of the Zrínyi Military Publishing House, under the control of the Ministry of Defence. The publishing house responsible for foreign-language texts is Corvina, set up in 1955.

The bibliographical coverage of Hungarian official material is somewhat uneven: there are good national bibliographies of bibliographies, books and periodical articles, and legal publications, including statutes, are well provided for. Several of the publishing houses, notably that for economics and law, have issued catalogues of their publications. There is, however, no adequate bibliography of periodicals for the period 1955–75, nor are there any regular bibliographies especially devoted to government and party publications as such; the best approach to such material is through the indexes of issuing bodies in the various national bibliographies.

GENERAL BIBLIOGRAPHIES AND REFERENCE WORKS

National bibliographies

H1   *A magyar bibliográfiák bibliográfiája.* [Bibliography of Hungarian bibliographies]. 1956/7–. Bp.: OSZK, 1960–. Irregular.

    A classified bibliography of bibliographies published in Hungary, either separately or appended to articles or other works, which contain over 50 items. Includes bibliographies listing official publications. Each volume covers from two to four years.

H2   *Magyar nemzeti bibliográfia: könyvek bibliográfiája.* [Hungarian national bibliography: bibliography of books]. Bp.: OSZK, 1946–. Semi-monthly.

    1946–60 issued monthly. Classified list of books and pamphlets published in Hungary, including official publications. Lists first issues and title changes of serials, but does not include individual standards or patents, propaganda literature or ephemera.

H3 *Magyar könyvészet: a Magyarországon megjelent könyvek bibliográfiája.* [Hungarian bibliography: bibliography of books published in Hungary]. 1961/2–. Bp.: OSZK, 1963–. Annual.
    The annual cumulation of H2. The first issue covered the years 1961–2.

H4 *Magyar könyvészet, 1945–1960: a Magyarországon nyomtatott könyvek szakosított jegyzéke.* [Hungarian bibliography, 1945–60: classified list of books printed in Hungary]. Bp.: OSZK, 1964–8. 5 vols.
    A cumulative bibliography for the postwar years not covered by annual cumulations (*see* H3).

H5 *Magyar nemzeti bibliográfia: időszaki kiadványok repertóriuma.* [Hungarian national bibliography: index of periodical publications]. Bp.: OSZK, 1946–. Monthly.
    1946–77 (no. 15) entitled *Magyar folyóiratok repertóriuma: a Magyar nemzeti bibliográfia melléklete.* 1946–77 issued semi-monthly. Indexes the most important items appearing in the major serials published in Hungary, including the chief daily newspapers; does not include reviews or material published in official gazettes.

Other general bibliographies and reference works

Bibliographies of serials

H6 Dezsényi, B., Falvy, Z. & Fejér, J. *A magyar sajtó bibliográfiája, 1945–1954.* [Bibliography of the Hungarian press, 1945–54]. (Az Országos Széchényi Könyvtár kiadványai, 36). Bp.: Művelt Nép, 1956. 160 pp.
    A bibliography of periodicals and newspapers appearing regularly at least twice a year. A supplement lists serials of which only a single number appeared. Includes official publications, e.g. the official gazettes of ministries. Records changes of title, subtitle, issuing body, publisher and editor.

H7 *Magyar hírlapok és folyóiratok jegyzéke, 1965.* [List of Hungarian newspapers and periodicals, 1965]. Bp.: OSZK, 1968. 132 pp.
    A list of serials appearing at least twice yearly in 1965, including official gazettes. Brief details only given. Includes index of issuing bodies. A previous edition appeared in 1958.

H8 *Kurrens időszaki kiadványok: a Magyarországon megjelenő időszaki kiadványok bibliográfiája.* [Current periodicals: bibliography of periodicals appearing in Hungary]. 1976–. Bp.: OSZK, 1977–. Annual.

Includes annuals. The two volumes for 1976 give full bibliographical details of periodicals current in that year, but subsequent volumes give full details of new titles only; if a title has been listed in the 1976 volumes, only the first issues of that title published in the current year are listed. Index of issuing bodies.

H9 *Bibliography of social science periodicals and monograph series; Hungary, 1947–1962.* By Foreign Demographic Analysis Division, Bureau of the Census. (Foreign social science bibliographies, series P-92, no. 13). Washington: U.S. Government Printing Office, 1964. iv, 137 pp.

An annotated bibliography, arranged by subject, of periodicals and monographs in series. Includes officially published titles. Index of issuing bodies.

Bibliographies of law and legislation

See also H137

H10 *Állam- és jogtudományi bibliográfia. Bibliographia juridica Hungarica.* 1945/51–. Közzéteszi a Magyar Tudományos Akadémia Állam- és Jogtudományi Intézete; összeáll. Nagy L. (Állam- és Jogtudományi Intézet tudományos könyvtára). Bp.: KJK, 1954–. Irregular.

Volumes for 1952–3 entitled *Jogi és államigazgatási bibliográfia.* A comprehensive bibliography of legal and administrative literature published in Hungary, including texts of collections of statutes, commentaries, monographs, periodicals and articles, official gazettes (1956–) and bibliographies. Subject arrangement. Each volume generally covers from two to four years.

H11 *Bibliography of Hungarian legal literature, 1945–1965.* Ed. by L. Nagy. Bp.: Akad. K., 1966. 315 pp.

A selective bibliography of periodicals, monographs, articles and texts and commentaries of statutes, arranged by subject. Introductions to each chapter outline the postwar legislation in each field. Supplemented by the bibliographies in H12. English translations of titles.

H12 *Acta juridica Academiae Scientiarum Hungaricae: a Magyar Tudományos Akadémia jogtudományi közleményei.* Bp.: Akad. K., 1959–. Quarterly.

The legal journal of the Hungarian Academy of Sciences. Each issue, which consists of two numbers, contains besides articles in English, French, German and Russian a selective bibliography of legal literature, including texts of statutes and commentaries, published in Hungary during the previous six months. This supplements H11 and includes English translations of titles.

H13 Bedo, A. K. & Torzsay-Biber, G. *Legal sources and bibliography of Hungary.* (Praeger publications on Russian history and world communism, 20). N.Y.: Published for the Free Europe Committee by Praeger, 1956. [xvi], 157 pp.

A partially annotated, selective bibliography of legal sources and treatises published before 1956, including collections of statutes, court decisions and texts of statutes and commentaries in individual fields. Includes a discussion of terminology and a classified list of the most important statutes of the years 1945–55. English translations of titles.

General reference works

H14 *Magyarország címtára.* [Directory of Hungary]. 3., átd. kiad. Bp.: KJK, 1968. 631 pp.

A directory of the organs of government and state administration, the Party and economic, social, cultural and scientific organizations. A supplement was published in 1969. A previous edition was published in 1961 and two editions of a directory listing state enterprises and cooperatives only appeared in 1957 and 1962 under the title *Vállalati címtár.*

H15 *A Magyar Népköztársaság helységnévtára, 1973.* [Gazetteer of the Hungarian People's Republic, 1973]. (Központi Statisztikai Hivatal). Bp.: Stat. K., 1973. 1120 pp.

A supplement was published in 1975 and an abridged version, taking into account the changes in territorial organization coming into force in April 1977, appeared in 1978 under the title *A Magyar Népköztársaság városainak és községeinek névtára, 1977.* Previous postwar editions of the full gazetteer were published for the years 1950, 1951, 1952, 1956, 1962 and 1967, all under the title *Magyarország helységnévtára.*

H16 *Directory of officials of the Hungarian People's Republic: a reference aid.* (Central Intelligence Agency. National Foreign Assessment Center). Washington: U.S. Government Printing Office, 1979. xi, 184 pp.

A regularly updated list of the officials of major government, party and other public organizations.

H17 Bölöny, J. *Magyarország kormányai, 1848–1975.* [The governments of Hungary, 1848–1975]. (A Magyar Országos Levéltár kiadványai, IV. Levéltártan és történeti forrástudományok, 2). Bp.: Akad. K., 1978. 329 pp.

A complete list of governments and ministries, with the names and dates of office holders. Gives dates of changes in the names of ministries.

CONSTITUTIONAL DOCUMENTS

Constitutions

In 1945 Hungary possessed no written constitution, and one of the first acts of the National Assembly elected in November 1945 was to pass Law No. I of 1946 (published in *Országos törvénytár*, 31 January 1946), which, though not a constitution in name, established the form of government of the new Hungarian Republic and laid down the functions of the President of the Republic, parliament and government. After the consolidation of communist power in 1948–9 a new constitution was enacted as Law No. XX of 1949. This came into force on 20 August 1949 and remained in force, with several subsequent amendments, until the political and economic changes of the late 1960s necessitated its thorough revision, and Law No. I of 1972, though formally an amendment to the 1949 Law, in fact represented a new constitution. Further amendments were made in 1975 (see *Magyar közlöny*, 1975, no. 23).

H18　*A Magyar Népköztársaság alkotmánya.* [The constitution of the Hungarian People's Republic]. Közreadja a Magyar Tudományos Akadémia Állam- és Jogtudományi Intézete. Bp.: KJK, 1959. 207 pp.

Includes annotations. Consolidated text of the 1949 constitution and amendments passed up to 1959. The first edition was published in 1949.

H19　*Constitution of the Hungarian People's Republic.* Bp.: Hungarian Review, 1959. 87 pp.

English translation of the 1949 constitution, as amended up to 1959, with introduction and concluding remarks by J. Beér. An English translation of the original 1949 text, with the same title, was published in 1949.

H20　*A Magyar Népköztársaság alkotmánya.* [The constitution of the Hungarian People's Republic]. (Kis jogszabály sorozat). Bp.: KJK, 1979. 81 pp.

The text of the 1972 revision, with the 1975 amendments.

H21　*The constitution of the Hungarian People's Republic.* Bp.: Office of the Hungarian Parliament, 1972. 70 pp.

English translation of the 1972 revision.

Local councils

The present system of local government was first established under the provisions of the Councils Act (Law No. I) of 1950 and further regulated by Law No. X of 1954. Since the mid-1960s greater autonomy and independence have been granted to the local councils, and these increased powers of self-government were confirmed in the so-called 'Third Councils Act' (Law No. I) of 1971.

H22 *A tanácstörvény és végrehajtási utasításai.* [The Councils Act and its implementing directives]. Közzéteszi a Minisztertanács titkársága. Bp.: KJK, 1955. 431 pp.

> Law No. X of 1954. A French translation of the original act (Law No. I of 1950) was published in *Revue de la législation hongroise,* 1952, 1, pp. 48–58.

H23 *Tanácstörvény: az 1971. évi I. törvény és végrehajtási rendelkezései.* [Councils Act: Law No. I of 1971 and its implementing regulations]. Új, átd. és bőv. kiad. Összeáll. Fonyó Gy. (Kis jogszabály sorozat). Bp.: KJK, 1980. 373 pp.

> An English translation of the 1971 Act was published in *Hungarian law review,* 1972, 2, pp. 47–68, with an introductory essay by J. Varga.

H24 *A tanácstörvény magyarázata.* [Commentary on the Councils Act]. Szerk. Fonyó Gy. Bp.: KJK, 1976. 899 pp.

> A commentary on the 1971 Act.

LAW CODES

Civil code

The first Hungarian civil code passed by Parliament, containing provisions on persons, rights of ownership, obligations and succession, came into force on 1 May 1960, following the enactment of Law No. IV of 1959. A new code was enacted as Law No. IV of 1977.

H25 *A Magyar Népköztársaság polgári törvénykönyve: az 1959. évi IV. törvény és törvény javaslatának miniszteri indokolása, a polgári törvénykönyv hatálybalépéséről szóló 1960. évi 11. sz. törvényerejű rendelet.* [Civil code of the Hungarian People's Republic: Law No. IV of 1959 and the ministerial motivation of the bill [and] Decree-Law No. 11 of 1960 on the coming into force of the civil code]. Bp.: KJK, 1963. 862 pp.

H26 *Civil code of the Hungarian People's Republic.* Bp.: Corvina, 1960. 200 pp.

> English translation of the 1959 code.

H27 *A polgári törvénykönyv.* [The civil code]. Összeáll. és jegyz. ell. Baranyai J. és Fluckné Papácsy E. Bp.: KJK, 1979. 627 pp.

> Text, with commentary, of the 1977 code. An English translation, with an introductory essay by J. Szilbereky, appeared in *Hungarian law review,* 1979, 1–2, pp. 21–182.

Civil procedure

H28 *A polgári perrendtartásról szóló törvény: az 1952: III. tv. és az azzal kapcsolatos egyéb polgári eljárási jogi szabályok.* [The Law on Civil

Procedure: Law No. III of 1952 and other relevant statutes on civil procedure]. Közzéteszi az Igazságügyminisztérium. Bp.: Jogi és Államigazgatási K., 1953. 184 pp.

H29 *Polgári peres eljárás (a Legfelsőbb Bíróság elvi iránymutatásaival).* [Civil procedure (with the directives of principle of the Supreme Court)]. 2., átd. kiad. Összeáll. és jegyz. ell. Gellért Gy. és Zoltán Ö. Bp.: KJK, 1976. 950 pp.
Includes a consolidated text of Law No. III of 1952 as amended by later statutes up to 31 May 1976.

H30 *A polgári perrendtartás magyarázata.* [Commentary on civil procedure]. Szerk. Szilbereky J., Névai L. Bp.: KJK, 1976. 2 vols.

Criminal code

The first Hungarian criminal code was that enacted as Law No. V of 1878. This, although later amended and supplemented, remained the basic statute until 1950, when Law No. II on the General Part of the Criminal Code was passed. The Special Part of the 1878 law was amended by several new statutes during the 1950s until superseded, with the General Part, by the criminal code established by Law No. V of 1961. This in turn was superseded by a new code enacted as Law No. IV of 1978.

H31 *A hatályos büntetőjog szabályai.* [Criminal law statutes in force]. Összeáll. Auer Gy. (A M. Igazságügyminisztérium kiadványa). Bp.: Forrás ny., 1947. xx, 468 pp.
Basic statute: Law No. V of 1878. Another edition: *A hatályos büntetőjog anyagi és alaki szabályai,* 1949.

H32 *A büntetőtörvénykönyv általános része: az 1950. évi II. törvény; az 1950: 39. sz. törvényerejű rendelet; a törvényjavaslat miniszteri indokolása.* [General part of the criminal code: Law No. II of 1950; Decree-law No. 39 of 1950; the ministerial motivation of the bill]. Magy. ell. Kádár M. Bp.: Jogi K., 1951. 238 pp.
Includes a commentary.

H33 *A hatályos anyagi büntetőjogi szabályok hivatalos összeállítása.* [Official compilation of substantive criminal statutes in force]. Közzéteszi az Igazságügyminisztérium. Bp.: Jogi K., 1952. 314 pp.
Later editions were published in 1953, 1956 and 1958.

H34 *A Magyar Népköztársaság büntető törvénykönyve.* [Criminal code of the Hungarian People's Republic]. Közzéteszi az Igazságügyminisztérium. Bp.: KJK, 1962. 632 pp.
The 1961 code.

H35 *Criminal code of the Hungarian People's Republic.* Bp.: Corvina, 1962. 134 pp.
English translation of the 1961 code.

H36　*Büntető törvénykönyv.* [Criminal code]. Összeáll. Kádár K., Moldoványi Gy. Bp.: KJK, 1979. 454 pp.
The 1978 code.

Criminal procedure

Immediately after the Second World War the basic statute in force was Law No. XXXIII of 1896, as modified by later amendments and supplementary statutes. A new code of criminal procedure was enacted as Law No. III of 1951, but the introduction of the criminal code of 1961 necessitated its complete revision, which was effected by Decree-Law No. 8 of 1962. This was superseded on the enactment of Law No. I of 1973 on Criminal Procedure.

H37　*A hatályos bűnvádi eljárási jog szabályai.* [Statutes on criminal procedure in force]. Összeáll. Auer Gy. (Az Igazságügyminisztérium kiadványa). Bp.: Forrás ny., 1948. xix, 483 pp.

H38　*A büntető perrendtartás kommentárja.* [Commentary on criminal procedure]. Összeáll. és magy. Molnár L. és közössége. Bp.: KJK, 1957. 888 pp.
Consolidated text, with commentary, of Law No. III of 1951 on Criminal Procedure as amended by Law No. V of 1954 and Decree-Law No. 8 of 1957, with associated statutes and the most important judicial decisions relating to criminal procedure.

H39　*A büntető eljárás: az 1962. évi 8. számú törvényerejű rendelet és mellékjogszabályai.* [Criminal procedure: Decree-Law No. 8 of 1962 and its supplementary statutes]. Közzéteszi az Igazságügyminisztérium. Bp.: KJK, 1962. 268 pp.

H40　*A büntető eljárás.* [Criminal procedure]. Összeáll. és jegyz. ell. László J. és Moldoványi Gy. 2., változatlan kiad. Bp.: KJK, 1977. 719 pp.
Text, with commentary, of the law on criminal procedure as amended by Law No. I of 1973. An English translation of this law, with introductory essays by I. Markója and J. László, was published in *Hungarian law review,* 1975, 1, pp. 39–153.

Labour code

The first comprehensive Hungarian labour code came into force in 1951 with the enactment of Decree-Law No. 7 of that year. It was followed by several amending and supplementary statutes and was superseded by a new code enacted as Law No. II of 1967. For other statutes on labour law see H168.

H41　*A munka törvénykönyve és végrehajtási szabályai.* [The labour code and its implementing statutes]. Összeáll. és magy. ell. Mikos F. [és mások]. Bp.: Jogi K., 1953. 632 pp.
Text, with commentary, of the 1951 code.

H42　*A munka törvénykönyve: a végrehajtásáról szóló kormányrendelettel egységes szerkezetbe foglalt szöveg, magyarázó jegyzetekkel, a Legfel-*

sőbb Bíróság elvi állásfoglalásaival és a munka törvénykönyvével kapcsolatos egyes munkaügyi jogszabályokkal. [The labour code: consolidated text [of the code and] the government decree on its implementation, with explanatory notes, advisory opinions with the force of principle of the Supreme Court and individual labour statutes associated with the labour code]. Bp.: KJK, 1975. 623 pp. Text, with commentary, of the 1967 code.

OTHER GENERAL LEGISLATIVE DOCUMENTS

Official gazette

H43 *Magyar közlöny: a Magyar Népköztársaság hivatalos lapja.* [Hungarian gazette: official journal of the Hungarian People's Republic]. Bp.: Lapkiadó, 1867–. Irregular.

1867–21 March 1919 entitled *Budapesti közlöny*; 21 March–2 August 1919 *Tanácsköztársaság*; 2–7 August 1919 *Hivatalos közlöny*; 2 August 1919–1944 *Budapesti közlöny*. From 1 January 1947 to April 1949 issued in two parts: *Magyar közlöny: hivatalos lap* and *Magyar közlöny: rendeletek tára* [Hungarian gazette: decrees]. On 1 May 1949 the latter part absorbed *Országos törvénytár (see* H44*)*, which from 7 September 1948 had been published as a supplement to *Magyar közlöny*, and assumed the title *Magyar közlöny: törvények és rendeletek tára* [Hungarian gazette: laws and decrees]. Under the constitution of 1949 a new type of statute, the decree-law, was created and as a result the gazette was divided into three parts from 30 August 1949: *Magyar közlöny: hivatalos lap; hivatalos rész* [Hungarian gazette: official journal; official part]; *Magyar közlöny: törvények és törvényerejű rendeletek tára* [Hungarian gazette: laws and decree-laws]; and *Magyar közlöny: minisztertanácsi és miniszteri rendeletek tára* [Hungarian gazette: decrees of the Council of Ministers and of ministers]. On 1 July 1950, however, a further reorganization resulted in its publication as two parts again: *Magyar közlöny: I. főrész* [Hungarian gazette: part one], containing the bulk of official material, and *Magyar közlöny: II. főrész; miniszteri rendeletek* [Hungarian gazette: part two; ministerial decrees]. From 1 May 1951 it has appeared as a single title, generally with about 100 issues p.a. It constitutes the official medium for the publication of all important statutes and other legal rules. Each issue contains two parts, the first containing a personal section, laws, parliamentary resolutions, decree-laws, resolutions of the Presidential Council and decrees and resolutions of the Council of Ministers, and the second containing decrees of ministries and other organs of specialized administration of nationwide authority which bear directly on the rights, obligations and legal interests of citizens, selected rules of the National Council of Trade Unions and announcements of the Hungarian National

Bank. Other normative acts and official communications of ministries which are not published in *Magyar közlöny* appear in the official gazettes of the ministries concerned. Numerical, title and subject indexes to statutes and other material are published in *Magyar közlöny* every 6 months.

General collections of statutes

H44 *Országos törvénytár*. [National collection of laws]. Bp.: Athenaeum ny., 1867–1949. Irregular.

The official medium for the publication of acts of parliament before 1 May 1949. From 7 September 1948 until April 1949 it appeared as a supplement to *Magyar közlöny* (*see* H43), with which it was fully merged from 1 May 1949. Also published as an annual cumulated volume until 1948.

H45 *Magyar törvénytár. Corpus juris Hungarici.* [Collection of Hungarian laws]. 1000–1948. Bp.: Franklin, 1896–1949. Annual.

The standard retrospective collection of Hungarian laws promulgated up to the end of 1948. Volume for 1905 not published. Volumes covering the postwar period are those for 1943–5, 1946, 1947 and 1948. The 1947 volume includes a supplement for the period 1630–1946 and the 1948 volume for the period 1848–1947. Succeeded by H49 from 1949.

H46 *Magyarországi rendeletek tára*. [Collection of Hungarian decrees]. 1867–1946. Bp.: Szikra, 1868–1948. Annual.

Includes government and ministerial decrees. Subsequent amendments are included in *Rendeletmódosítások gyűjteménye, 1867–1948* [Collection of amendments to decrees, 1867–1948], 1949. For decrees issued in 1947–8 *see* H47. Succeeded by H49 from 1949.

H47 *Két év hatályos jogszabályai, 1945–1946*. [Statutes of the two years 1945 and 1946 in force]. Szerk. Bacsó F. [és mások]. Bp.: Grill, 1947. vi, 407 pp.

Includes laws and government and ministerial decrees in force at the time of publication. Continued for 1947–8 in the two volumes published as *1947. [1948.] év hatályos jogszabályai* [Statutes of 1947 [1948] in force], 1948–9.

H48 *Igazságügyi zsebtörvénytár: hatályban levő igazságügyi törvények és rendeletek gyűjteménye egységes szerkezetben, kiegészítve a M. Kúria elvi jelentőségű határozataival.* [Pocket collection of laws for the administration of justice (consolidated texts), with the leading decisions of the Hungarian Curia]. Összeáll. Térfy Gy. és Térfy B. 6. kiad. Bp.: Grill, 1948. xx, 2006 pp.

Includes material deemed necessary for the work of practising judges and lawyers. Subject arrar.gement.

H49 *Törvények és rendeletek hivatalos gyűjteménye*. [Official collection of laws and decrees]. 1949–. Bp.: KJK, 1950–. Annual.

The official annual cumulation of statutes, based on the material published in *Magyar közlöny* (H43).

H50 *Hatályos jogszabályok gyűjteménye, 1945–1977.* [Collection of statutes from the years 1945–1977 in force]. Bp.: KJK, 1978–80. 7 vols.

A retrospective collection of statutes published in *Magyar közlöny* (H43) between 1945 and 1977 and in force at the time of publication of the collection. Contents: vol. 1: laws, parliamentary resolutions, decree-laws, resolutions of the Presidential Council; vol. 2: decrees and resolutions of the Council of Ministers; vols. 3–5: decrees of ministers and of the Chairman of the National Planning Office, statutory regulations of the non-ministerial organs of specialized administration of nationwide authority, and rules of the National Council of Trade Unions; vols. 6–7: international treaties. Includes subject and numerical indexes. Previous collections of similar scope with the same title covered statutes for the years 1945–58, 1945–68 and 1945–72. For the period 1945–63 the collection appeared as three separate publications: *Hatályos törvények és törvényerejű rendeletek, 1945–1963* [Laws and decree-laws from 1945–1963 in force], *Hatályos kormányrendeletek és kormányhatározatok, 1945–1963* [Government decrees and resolutions from 1945–1963 in force] and *Hatályos miniszteri rendeletek, 1945–1963* [Ministerial decrees from 1945–1963 in force].

Indexes to statutes

H51 Gerlai, K. *Rendeleti tárgymutató.* [Subject index to decrees]. 7–11. kiad. Bp.: Áll. ny., 1947–9. 5 vols. in 7.

Covers decrees issued by the organs of supreme state authority between 1945 and 1948. [Not seen].

H52 Némethy, L. *Az 1945. [1946., etc.] évi jogszabályok mutatója.* [Index to statutes of 1945 [1946, etc.]]. 1945–7. (TÉBE könyvtár. Új sorozat, [3, 5, 6]). Bp.: Globus ny., 1946–8. 3 vols. [Not seen].

H53 Nagy, L. & Zsigmond, Gy. *Hatályos jogszabálymutató 1945–49. évre.* [Index to statutes of 1945–1949 in force]. Bp.: Hernádi, 1949. 575 pp.

Covers the period 1945–15 May 1949. [Not seen].

H54 *Jogszabálymutató a felszabadulás első hat évének hatályos jogszabályairól.* [Index to statutes in force published in the first six years after the liberation]. Összeáll. az Igazságügyminisztérium törvényelőkészítő osztálya. Bp.: Jogi és Államigazgatási K., 1951. 392 pp.

Numerical and subject index to laws, decree-laws and decrees in force published between 1945 and 4 April 1951.

H55 *Hatályos jogszabályok mutatója, 1945–1957.* [Index to statutes of 1945–1957 in force]. Összeáll. az Igazságügyminisztérium törvényelőkészítő főosztálya. Bp.: KJK, 1958. 208 pp.

Numerical and subject index to statutes published in *Magyar közlöny* (H43) and to some of the statutory regulations published in the official gazettes of ministries.

Serial publications including texts of statutes

H56 *Hungarian law review.* (Hungarian Lawyers' Association). Bp.: KJK, 1961–. Semi-annual.
Each issue typically consists of an English translation of a recent piece of important legislation preceded by an introductory essay. Its French version, *Revue de droit hongrois,* began publication in 1958.

H57 *The statutes of the Hungarian People's Republic.* Bp.: Ministry of Justice, [197?]–. Irregular.
A series of English translations of the texts of important individual statutes.

Parliamentary proceedings and papers

Parliament, or the National Assembly (Országgyűlés, 1945–7 Nemzetgyűlés), has since 1949 met in plenary session on average some four or five times a year, sitting for a few days on each occasion. Since 1975 parliaments have been elected for a term of five years (before then for four years). Parliamentary proceedings and papers are issued in three main series: *Országgyűlési értesítő* (H58), a record of the proceedings of the sessions; *Országgyűlési napló* (H59a–e), retrospective collections of the material published in the *Értesítő* covering the life of each parliament; and *Országgyűlési irományok* (H60a–d), containing material relating to the activity of parliament such as bills and reports of parliamentary committees and ministries. Laws and resolutions passed by parliament are published in H43 and H49.

H58 *Országgyűlési értesítő: az Országgyűlés 1. [2., etc.] ülése.* [Bulletin of the National Assembly: the 1st [2nd, etc.] session of the National Assembly]. Bp.: Athenaeum ny., 1944–. Irregular.
1944–5 entitled *Az Ideiglenes Nemzetgyűlés értesítője* [Bulletin of the Provisional National Assembly]; 1945–7 *Nemzetgyűlési értesítő.* A new series is begun for each parliament; the numbering of the subtitle refers to each day's sitting and is continuous with the life of each parliament.

H59a *Az 1944. évi december hó 21-ére Debrecenbe összegyűlt, majd később Budapestre összehívott Ideiglenes Nemzetgyűlés naplója.* [Journal of the Provisional National Assembly meeting in Debrecen on 21 December 1944 and later summoned in Budapest]. Bp.: Athenaeum ny., 1946. 184 pp.

H59b *Az 1945. évi november hó 29-ére összehívott Nemzetgyűlés naplója.* [Journal of the National Assembly summoned for 29 November 1945]. Bp.: Athenaeum ny., 1946–52. 8 vols.

H59c *Az 1947. évi szeptember hó 16-ára összehívott Országgyűlés naplója.* [Journal of the National Assembly summoned for 16 September 1947]. Bp.: Athenaeum ny., 1948–9. 5 vols.

H59d *Az 1949. évi június hó 8-ára összehívott Országgyűlés naplója.* [Journal of the National Assembly summoned for 8 June 1949]. Bp.: Athenaeum ny., 1950–9. 2 vols.

H59e *Az 1967. évi április hó 14-ére összehívott Országgyűlés naplója.* [Journal of the National Assembly summoned for 14 April 1967]. Bp.: Athenaeum ny., 1975. 2 vols.

The retrospective collections of parliamentary proceedings which have so far been published.

H60a *Országgyűlési irományok.* [Papers of the National Assembly]. Bp.: Athenaeum ny., 1945–. Irregular.

Although the series is generally referred to by this standard title, there is no indication of it on the individual issues themselves; each issue bears the heading *1.* [*2., etc.*] *szám* [No. 1 [2, etc.]] followed by a description of the contents of the paper, and a new series is begun for each parliament. Some issues are confidential and have restricted circulation, but the Department of Printed Books of the British Library Reference Division, London, receives those that are available for general distribution outside Hungary. The following retrospective collections have been published:

H60b *Az 1945. évi november hó 29-ére összehívott Nemzetgyűlés irományai.* [Papers of the National Assembly summoned for 29 November 1945]. Bp.: Athenaeum ny., 1946–7. 3 vols.

H60c *Az 1947. évi szeptember hó 16-ára összehívott Országgyűlés iró-mányai.* [Papers of the National Assembly summoned for 16 September 1947]. Bp.: Athenaeum ny., 1948–9. 4 vols.

H60d *Az 1949. évi június hó 8-ára összehívott Országgyűlés irományai.* [Papers of the National Assembly summoned for 8 June 1949]. 1. köt. Bp.: Athenaeum ny., 1951. vi, 318 pp.

Contains issues 1–51 (8 June 1949–15 May 1951) of the series covering the 1949–53 parliament.

Judicial decisions
General collections

For the years 1946–9 judicial decisions were published in the following series:

H61a *Magánjogi és perjogi döntvénytár.* [Collection of judicial decisions on private law and civil procedure]. Új folyam. 1946–9. Kiadja a Jogtudományi közlöny szerkesztősége. Bp.: Hírlapkiadó, 1948–50. 3 vols. [Not seen].

H61b *Büntetőjogi és népbírósági döntvénytár.* [Collection of judicial decisions on criminal law and of decisions of the People's Courts]. Új folyam. 1946–9. Kiadja a Jogtudományi közlöny szerkesztősége. Bp.: Hírlapkiadó, 1948–50. 3 vols. [Not seen].

H61c *Hiteljogi döntvénytár (kereskedelmi, váltó-, csőd- és munkaügyekben).* [Collection of judicial decisions on commercial law (in commercial, exchange, bankruptcy and labour cases)]. Új folyam. 1946–8. Kiadja a Jogtudományi közlöny szerkesztősége. Bp.: Hírlapkiadó, 1948–9. 2 vols. [Not seen].

H61d Gazdasági jogi és munkajogi döntvénytár. [Collection of judicial decisions on economic and labour law]. Új folyam. 1949. Közreadja a Jogtudományi közlöny szerkesztősége. Bp.: Tudományos Folyóiratkiadó, 1950. xvi, 68, xxxi, 100 pp. [Not seen].

H61e Pénzügyi és közigazgatási döntvénytár. [Collection of judicial decisions on financial and administrative law]. Új folyam. [1946?–9?]. Bp.: Hírlapkiadó, [1948?–50?]. [Not seen].

With the setting up of the Supreme Court in 1949 the decisions of its Bench of Leading Cases (Elvi Tanács), the function of which was to reassess and pronounce on previous court judgements, were published in:

H62 A Legfelsőbb Bíróság Elvi Tanácsának határozatai. [Decisions of the Bench of Leading Cases of the Supreme Court]. Közzéteszi a Jogtudományi közlöny szerkesztősége. Bp.: Jogi K., 1951–3. 3 vols.
Covers decisions issued in 1950–2. There is no collection covering other court decisions of the years 1950–3, but reports of some cases were published in the various legal periodicals, particularly Jogtudományi közlöny [Review of legal sciences], 1946–, monthly.

H63 Bírósági határozatok. [Judicial decisions]. Közzéteszi a Magyar Népköztársaság Legfelsőbb Bírósága. Bp.: Lapkiadó, 1953–. Monthly.
Began publication in October 1953. Includes guiding principles (irányelvek) and decisions of principle (elvi döntések) of the Supreme Court, (advisory) opinions (állásfoglalások) and decisions (határozatok) of its five divisions (kollégiumok), i.e. the civil, economic, labour, criminal and military divisions, and a selection of the most important decisions of lower courts. Yearly subject index, arranged by division. A cumulation for the period October 1953–December 1955 was published in 1956 as Döntvénytár: bírósági határozatok.

Civil, economic and labour law

H64 Polgári jogi döntvénytár: bírósági határozatok. [Judicial decisions on civil law]. 1953/63–. Bp.: KJK, 1964–. Irregular.
Periodical cumulations, each covering a number of years.

H65 A Központi Döntőbizottság elvi határozatai és iránymutatásai, 1948–1962. [Leading decisions and directives of the Central Arbitration Board, 1948–1962]. [Összeáll.] Görgey M., Havasi Gy. (A Központi Döntőbizottság kiadványa). Bp.: KJK, 1964. 895 pp.
The function of the Central Arbitration Board (Központi Döntőbizottság, earlier Közületi Döntőbizottság) and of the economic arbitration committees was to pass judgements in civil law disputes arising between economic units and between the state and economic units. Under the provisions of Law No. IV of 1972 on the courts the

arbitration committees were abolished and their functions taken over, from January 1973, by the regular courts, particularly the new Economic Division (Gazdasági Kollégium) of the Supreme Court. Earlier collections of the decisions and guidelines of the Central Arbitration Board were *A Közületi Döntőbizottság elvi határozatai és közleményei*, 1951–2, 2 vols., and *A Központi Döntőbizottság elvi határozatai és közleményei*, 1956 (covering the period 1948–56).

H66 *Döntőbíráskodás: a Központi Gazdasági Döntőbizottság hivatalos értesítője.* [Arbitration: official bulletin of the Central Economic Arbitration Board]. 1960–72. Bp.: Lapkiadó, 1960–73. Monthly.

Includes reports of cases, legal studies and indexes of statutes and regulations bearing on the work of the economic arbitration committees.

H67 *Polgári, gazdasági és munkaügyi elvi határozatok: a Magyar Népköztársaság Legfelsőbb Bíróságának irányelvei, elvi döntései és állásfoglalásai.* [Leading decisions on civil, economic and labour law: guiding principles, decisions of principle and advisory opinions of the Supreme Court of the Hungarian People's Republic]. Bp.: KJK, 1976. 768 pp.

Includes decisions issued up to 31 December 1975.

H68 *Polgári és gazdasági elvi határozatok: a Magyar Népköztársaság Legfelsőbb Bíróságának irányelvei, elvi döntései és állásfoglalásai.* [Leading decisions on civil and economic law: guiding principles, decisions of principle and advisory opinions of the Supreme Court of the Hungarian People's Republic]. Bp.: KJK, 1980. 639 pp.

Includes decisions issued up to 31 December 1979.

Criminal law

H69 *Büntetőjogi döntvénytár: bírósági határozatok.* [Judicial decisions on criminal law]. 1953/63–. Bp.: KJK, 1964–. Irregular.

Periodical cumulations, each covering a number of years.

H70 *Büntetőjogi elvi határozatok: a Magyar Népköztársaság Legfelsőbb Bíróságának a büntető jogalkalmazással kapcsolatos irányelvei, elvi döntései, kollégiumi állásfoglalásai és elvi jelentőségű határozatai.* [Leading decisions on criminal law: guiding principles, decisions of principle, divisional advisory opinions and other leading decisions of the Supreme Court of the Hungarian People's Republic in the application of criminal law]. Bp.: KJK, 1973. 1254 pp.

H71 *Katonai büntetőjogi döntvénytár: bírósági határozatok.* [Judicial decisions on military criminal law]. Bp.: KJK, 1979. 441 pp.

Cumulation covering the period January 1973–October 1978. [Not seen].

Administration of justice

H72 *Igazságügyi közlöny: az Igazságügyminisztérium hivatalos lapja.* [Judicial gazette: official journal of the Ministry of Justice.] Bp.: Lapkiadó, 1892–. Monthly.
Includes official material relating to the administration of justice and judicial organization. [Not seen].

H73 *A bíróságokra vonatkozó jogszabályok.* [Statutes concerning the courts]. Összeáll. és jegyz. ell. Kertész I. és Tóthné Gy. Bp.: KJK, 1975. 318 pp.

H74 *Act IV of 1972 concerning the Courts.* (The statutes of the Hungarian People's Republic). Bp.: Ministry of Justice, 1975. 58 pp.
English translation of the 1972 law which reorganized the court system.

The legal profession

H75 *Ügyvédi közlöny: a magyar ügyvédség hivatalos lapja.* [Lawyers' gazette: official journal of the Hungarian legal profession]. Bp.: Lapkiadó, 1962–. Monthly.
A joint publication of the Ministry of Justice and the National Council of Lawyers which includes official material, including statutory regulations, on the legal profession.

State administration

H76 *Az államigazgatási eljárási törvény magyarázata.* [Commentary on the law of state administrative procedure]. Szerk. Fonyó Gy. Bp.: KJK, 1976. 759 pp. [Not seen].

H77 *Államigazgatás A-tól Z-ig.* [State administration from A to Z]. Szerk. Besnyő K. Bp.: KJK, 1973. 799 pp. [Not seen].
An alphabetical list of state agencies and institutions and of terms used in state administration. Previous editions were published in 1960 and 1966 under the title *Államigazgatási kézikönyv* [Handbook of state administration].

H78 *Állam és igazgatás: a Minisztertanács Tanácsi Hivatalának elméleti és szakmai folyóirata.* [State and administration: theoretical and technical journal of the Councils Office of the Council of Ministers]. Bp.: Lapkiadó, 1949–. Monthly,
1949–51 entitled *Állam és közigazgatás* [State and public administration]. Includes articles on state administration and the work of local councils, reviews of relevant statutes, a current bibliography, which includes collections of statutes, and a regular column on the application of the law in particular cases.

Chief Public Prosecutor

H79   *Ügyészségi közlöny: a Legfőbb Ügyészség hivatalos lapja.* [Gazette of the Public Prosecutor's Office: official journal of the Chief Public Prosecutor]. Bp.: Lapkiadó, 1953–. Monthly. [Not seen].

GENERAL PARTY DOCUMENTS

Party congresses

H80a   *A népi demokrácia útja: a Magyar Kommunista Párt Budapesten 1946. szeptember 28., 29., 30. és október 1. napján megtartott III. kongresszusának jegyzőkönyve.* [The road to people's democracy: proceedings of the 3rd Congress of the Hungarian Communist Party held in Budapest on 28–30 September and 1 October 1946]. Bp.: Szikra, 1946. 368 pp.

H80b   *A Magyar Kommunista Párt IV. kongresszusa, a Szociáldemokrata Párt XXXVII. kongresszusa, a Magyar Kommunista Párt és a Szociáldemokrata Párt egyesülési kongresszusa jegyzőkönyve.* [Proceedings of the 4th Congress of the Hungarian Communist Party, the 37th Congress of the Social Democratic Party and the unifying Congress of the Hungarian Communist Party and the Social Democratic Party]. Bp.: Szikra, 1949. 372 pp. [Not seen].

H80c   *A Magyar Dolgozók Pártja II. kongresszusának jegyzőkönyve, 1951. február 24–március 2.* [Proceedings of the 2nd Congress of the Hungarian Working People's Party, 24 February–2 March 1951]. Bp.: Szikra, 1951. 547 pp. [Not seen].

H80d   *A Magyar Dolgozók Pártja III. kongresszusának jegyzőkönyve, 1954. május 24–30.* [Proceedings of the 3rd Congress of the Hungarian Working People's Party, 24–30 May 1954]. Bp.: Szikra, 1954. 656 pp. [Not seen].

H80e   *A Magyar Szocialista Munkáspárt VII. kongresszusának jegyzőkönyve, 1959. november 30–december 5.* [Proceedings of the 7th Congress of the Hungarian Socialist Workers' Party, 30 November–5 December 1959]. (Pártmunkások könyvtára). Bp.: Kossuth, 1960. 640 pp.

H80f   *A Magyar Szocialista Munkáspárt VIII. kongresszusának jegyzőkönyve, 1962. november 20–24.* [Proceedings of the 8th Congress of the Hungarian Socialist Workers' Party, 20–24 November 1962]. Bp.: Kossuth, 1963. 530 pp.

H80g   *A Magyar Szocialista Munkáspárt IX. kongresszusának jegyzőkönyve, 1966. november 28–december 3.* [Proceedings of the 9th Congress of the Hungarian Socialist Workers' Party, 28 November–3 December 1966]. Bp.: Kossuth, 1967. 519 pp.

H80h   *A Magyar Szocialista Munkáspárt X. kongresszusának jegyzőkönyve, 1970. november 23–28.* [Proceedings of the 10th Congress of the Hungarian Socialist Workers' Party, 23–28 November 1970]. Bp.: Kossuth, 1971. 543 pp.

H80i   *A Magyar Szocialista Munkáspárt XI. kongresszusának jegyző-könyve, 1975. március 17–22.* [Proceedings of the 11th Congress of the Hungarian Socialist Workers' Party, 17–22 March 1975]. Bp.: Kossuth, 1975. 579 pp.

H80j   *A Magyar Szocialista Munkáspárt XII. kongresszusának jegyző-könyve, 1980. március 24–27.* [Proceedings of the 12th Congress of the Hungarian Socialist Workers' Party, 24–27 March 1980]. Bp.: Kossuth, 1980. 544 pp. [Not seen].

The 'seventh' congress of the Hungarian Socialist Workers' Party in 1959 was in fact the first held by the Communist Party under the name which it adopted in November 1956 and the seventh in the overall series of congresses held by the Party under its various names; the 1951 and 1954 congresses were thus regarded retrospectively as the fifth and sixth in that series. The reports of each congress include not only the proceedings but also the current texts of the organizational rules of the Party and a list of members of its central organs and of the delegates to the congress.

H81   *A Magyar Szocialista Munkáspárt kongresszusainak határozatai.* [Resolutions of the congresses of the Hungarian Socialist Workers' Party]. (Az MSZMP Központi Bizottságának Párttörténeti Intézete). Bp.: Kossuth, 1975. 253 pp.

Includes the resolutions adopted at the National Party Conference of 1957 and at the 7th, 8th, 9th and 10th congresses.

National party conferences

H82a   *Harc az újjáépítésért: a Magyar Kommunista Párt 1945. május 20-án és 21-én tartott országos értekezletének jegyzőkönyve.* [The struggle for reconstruction: proceedings of the National Conference of the Hungarian Communist Party held on 20–21 May 1945]. Bp.: Szikra, 1945. ?? pp. [Not seen].

H82b   *A Magyar Szocialista Munkáspárt országos értekezletének jegyző-könyve, 1957. június 27–29.* [Proceedings of the National Conference of the Hungarian Socialist Workers' Party, 27–29 June 1957]. Bp.: Kossuth, 1957. 302 pp. [Not seen].

Collections of documents

H83a   *A Magyar Kommunista Párt és a Szociáldemokrata Párt határozatai, 1944–1948.* [Resolutions of the Hungarian Communist Party and the Social Democratic Party, 1944–1948]. (Az MSZMP Központi Bizottságának Párttörténeti Intézete). Bp.: Kossuth, 1967. 655 pp.

H83b   *A Magyar Szocialista Munkáspárt határozatai és dokumentumai, 1956–1962.* [Resolutions and documents of the Hungarian Socialist Workers' Party, 1956–1962]. 3. kiad. Bp.: Kossuth, 1979. 744 pp.

H83c   *A Magyar Szocialista Munkáspárt határozatai és dokumentumai, 1963–1966.* Bp.: Kossuth, 1968. 599 pp.

H83d   *A Magyar Szocialista Munkáspárt határozatai és dokumentumai,*
      1967–1970. Bp.: Kossuth, 1974. 750 pp.

H83e   *A Magyar Szocialista Munkáspárt határozatai és dokumentumai,*
      1971–1975. Bp.: Kossuth, 1978. 1045 pp.

A series of collections of the most important Party documents from the years 1944–8 and 1956–75, including resolutions and other documents of the Central Committee, Politburo and Party Secretariat, resolutions of party congresses and national conferences, policy statements and organizational rules. Chronological arrangement. Texts of important party policy statements, particularly those emanating from plenary sessions of the Central Committee, are often published separately, generally in the form, e.g., *A Magyar Szocialista Munkáspárt Központi Bizottsága 1978. október 12-i ülésének dokumentumai* [Documents of the session of 12 October 1978 of the Central Committee of the Hungarian Socialist Workers' Party] or *A Magyar Szocialista Munkáspárt Központi Bizottságának határozata...-ról* [Resolution of the Central Committee of the Hungarian Socialist Workers' Party on ...], but sometimes with titles describing the topic under discussion. No collection of Party documents of similar scope to H83a–e has been published for the period 1949–56, but the gap is partly filled by:

H84   *A Magyar Dolgozók Pártja Központi Vezetőségének, Politikai Bizottságának és Szervező Bizottságának fontosabb határozatai.* [The most important resolutions of the Central Committee, Politburo and Organizing Committee of the Hungarian Working People's Party]. (Pártépítés kiskönyvtára, 25). Bp.: Szikra, 1951. 184 pp. [Not seen].

Periodicals

H85   *Népszabadság: az MSZMP központi lapja.* [People's freedom: the central journal of the Hungarian Socialist Workers' Party]. Bp.: Hírlapkiadó, 1956–. Daily.

The most important source for regular, detailed coverage of the Party's standpoint on political, social, economic and cultural affairs. Includes the texts of important party decisions and the speeches of leading members of the Party and government. It began publication on 2 November 1956 as the successor of *Szabad nép* [Free people], 1942–56, daily, the last issue of which appeared on 29 October 1956.

H86   *Társadalmi szemle: a Magyar Szocialista Munkáspárt elméleti és politikai folyóirata.* [Social review: theoretical and political journal of the Hungarian Socialist Workers' Party]. Bp.: Kossuth, 1946–. Monthly.

Includes articles on political theory and practice by leading party figures, reports and discussions of party decisions and important speeches. A subject index has been published: *A Társadalmi szemle repertóriuma, 1957–1971,* 1972.

H87   *Pártélet: a Magyar Szocialista Munkáspárt Központi Bizottságának folyóirata.* [Party life: journal of the Central Committee of the Hungarian Socialist Workers' Party]. Bp.: Kossuth, 1956–. Monthly.

Intended chiefly for party workers. Includes personalia, articles on political, social, economic and cultural affairs and questions of ideology, party life and education, texts of the more important Party decisions, and a regular index of articles published in the chief political journals. Its predecessors were: *Pártmunka* [Party work], 1945–8, monthly; *Pártmunkás* [Party worker], 1948–50, semi-monthly; and *Pártépítés* [Party building], 1950–5, monthly.

H88 *Information bulletin of the Central Committee of the Hungarian Socialist Workers' Party.* Bp.: Budapress, 1957–. Quarterly.

Includes English translations of important speeches by party leaders, communiqués of the Central Committee and articles setting out party policy. Its predecessor was: *Information bulletin published by the International Relations Department of the C[entral] C[ommittee] of the Hungarian Working People's Party*, 1948–[56?], monthly.

STATISTICS

This section lists only general statistical publications, population statistics and censuses. Statistics relating to special subjects are included in the appropriate subject section of this chapter.

Bibliography

H89 *Statisztikai adatforrások, 1945–1974: bibliográfia.* [Statistical sources, 1945–74: bibliography]. Fel. szerk. Dányi D. (Központi Statisztikai Hivatal. Könyvtár és Dokumentációs Szolgálat). Bp.: Stat. K., 1975. v, 209 pp.

A bibliography of works published by the Central Statistical Office and its agencies; does not include works intended for internal use only. Broad classified arrangement. References to title changes are given, but there are no indexes. A previous bibliography covering a longer period of time is *Statisztikai adatforrások: bibliográfia, 1867–1967*, 1967, which gives English translations of titles.

Serials and collections of general statistics

H90 *Statisztikai évkönyv.* [Statistical yearbook]. 1871–. (Központi Statisztikai Hivatal). Bp.: Stat. K., 1872–. Annual.

Volumes for the years 1871–1946 entitled *Magyar statisztikai évkönyv.* Not published for the years 1947–8. The years 1943–6 and 1949–55 are each covered by a single volume. In recent years supplements giving English translations of the headings have been published. An English translation of the 1949–55 volume, *Statistical yearbook of Hungary, 1949–1955*, was published in 1958 by the U.S. Joint Publications Research Service.

H91   *Statistical yearbook. Statisticheskii ezhegodnik.* 1957–. (Central Statistical Office). Bp.: Stat. K., 1957–. Annual.
An abridged English and Russian version of H90.

H92   *Magyar statisztikai zsebkönyv.* [Hungarian statistical pocketbook]. 1931–. (Központi Statisztikai Hivatal). Bp.: Stat. K., 1933–. Annual.
Not published for the years 1944, 1945, 1949–55 and 1957, but the volume for 1956 contains some data for the period 1949–55. Less detailed in coverage than H90, but the annual volumes are published sooner after the end of the relevant year.

H93   *Statistical pocket book of Hungary.* 1958–. (Hungarian Central Statistical Office). Bp.: Stat. K., 1959–. Annual.
The English version, slightly abridged, of H92. The 1958 volume contains the Hungarian text preceded by a section giving English translations of the headings; from the 1959 volume the whole text is in English.

H94   *Statisztikai időszaki közlemények.* [Periodical statistical reports]. (Központi Statisztikai Hivatal). Bp.: Stat. K., 1957–. Irregular.
A numbered series of collections of statistical data on a wide range of economic, social and cultural topics, averaging some 20 issues p.a. Includes both special reports and regularly or irregularly published sub-series, some of which also form part of the unnumbered series *Statisztikai negyedévi közlemények* [Quarterly statistical reports], 1956–.

H95   *Statisztikai havi közlemények.* [Monthly statistical reports]. [Új sorozat]. (Központi Statisztikai Hivatal). Bp.: Stat. K., 1957–. Monthly.
Each issue is devoted mainly to reports of the previous month's statistics, but data covering longer periods is also regularly included. Since 1966 it has included a monthly subject index to statistical data published in this and other Hungarian statistical publications. There is a regular supplement, *Monthly bulletin of statistics*, 1957–, which contains English translations of terms and headings.

H96   *Statisztikai szemle: a Központi Statisztikai Hivatal folyóirata.* [Statistical review: journal of the Central Statistical Office]. Bp.: Stat. K., 1923–. Monthly.
1923–48 entitled *Magyar statisztikai szemle.* Not published September 1944–June 1945. Includes methodological studies, statistical analyses, news and reports. Two indexes have been published: *Statisztikai szemle: repertórium*, 1963, which is a bibliography, with name and subject index, of articles published during the years 1923–62; and another, with the same title, listing articles published 1963–70; its subject and name indexes cover articles published from 1923 to 1972.

H97   *Statisztikai tájékoztató.* [Statistical bulletin]. Összeáll. a Központi Statisztikai Hivatal. Bp.: Áll. Lapkiadó, 1950–4. Quarterly.

Primarily intended to illustrate the economic development of Hungary as reflected in the quarterly plan reports; though overtly propagandistic, it helps to fill the gap in statistical data for the period 1949–55.

H98 *A mai Magyarország: a második világháború és a párizsi békeszerződés következményei.* [Hungary today: the consequences of the Second World War and the Paris Peace Treaty]. Szerk. Elekes D. (Egyetemes könyvtár). Bp.: Hungária Lloyd, 1946. 314 pp.

A semi-official compilation reflecting the immediate postwar situation. [Not seen].

Population statistics

H99 *Demográfiai évkönyv: Magyarország népesedése.* [Demographic yearbook: the population of Hungary]. 1955–. Kiadja a Központi Statisztikai Hivatal. Bp.: Stat. K., 1956–. Annual.

Volumes for 1955–64 entitled *Magyarország népesedése*; those for 1956–64 form part of the series *Statisztikai időszaki közlemények* (H94).

H100 *A népmozgalom főbb adatai községenként, 1901–1968.* [Chief data on population movements village by village, 1901–1968]. (Központi Statisztikai Hivatal). Bp.: Stat. K., 1969. 529 pp.

H101 *A Központi Statisztikai Hivatal Néptudományi Kutató Intézetének és a Magyar Tudományos Akadémia Demográfiai Bizottságának közleményei.* [Reports of the Demographic Research Institute of the Central Statistical Office and the Demographic Committee of the Hungarian Academy of Sciences]. Bp.: Stat. K., 1963–. Irregular.

A numbered series of reports on various aspects of demography such as fertility, alcoholism, population policy and divorce; some issues are in English or have English summaries.

Censuses

H102 *1949. évi népszámlálás.* [The census of 1949]. Bp.: Áll. ny., 1949–52. 15 vols. [Not seen].

A digest of the 1949 census, more widely available, is *Az 1949. évi népszámlálás*, 1952.

H103 *1960. évi népszámlálás.* [The census of 1960]. (Központi Statisztikai Hivatal). Bp.: Stat. K., 1960–5. 13 vols. in 33.

H104 *1963. évi mikrocenzus: személyi és családi adatai.* [The microcensus of 1963: personal and family data]. (Központi Statisztikai Hivatal). Bp.: Stat. K., 1964. 214 pp.

The 'microcensuses' are based on a 2 per cent sample of the population.

H105a *Az 1968. évi próbaszámlálás (mikrocenzus) személyi, család- és lakás adatai.* [Personal, family and housing data of the 1968 preliminary census (microcensus)]. (Központi Statisztikai Hivatal). Bp.: Stat. K., 1969. 78 pp.

H105b *Az 1968. évi próbaszámlálás (mikrocenzus) lakásdemográfiai adatai.* [Housing data of the 1968 preliminary census (microcensus)]. (Központi Statisztikai Hivatal). Bp.: Stat. K., 1969. 68 pp.

H106 *1970. évi népszámlálás.* [The census of 1970]. (Központi Statisztikai Hivatal). Bp.: Stat. K., 1970–7. 31 vols. in 61.

H107 *Az 1973. évi mikrocenzus adatai.* [Data of the 1973 microcensus]. (Központi Statisztikai Hivatal). Bp.: Stat. K., 1974. 349 pp.

OTHER GENERAL SOURCES OF DOCUMENTATION

Press agency publications

The official Hungarian News Agency (Magyar Távirati Iroda—MTI), is responsible for the collection, editing and dissemination of domestic and foreign news and information to subscribers inside Hungary and abroad. It has separate editorial offices for domestic and foreign material and also an office charged with supplying news to the foreign press. Urgent material is relayed to subscribers by telex, but the agency also issues about twenty series of periodical bulletins on various topics for distribution to the Hungarian press and to those concerned with economic management and state administration. Their titles may be found by referring to the index of issuing bodies in H8 under the Hungarian name of the news agency. Four bulletins of a general nature on Hungarian affairs are published at varying frequencies and are more widely available:

H108 *MTI daily bulletin: the Hungarian News Agency's news service in English.* Bp.: MTI, [1966?]–. Daily. [Not seen].

H109 *Weekly bulletin.* (Budapress Sajtószolgálat). Bp.: MTI, [1962?]–. Weekly. [Not seen].

H110 *Magyar dokumentáció.* [Hungarian documentation]. Magyar Távirati Iroda). Bp.: MTI, 1968–. Monthly.

Includes documentation from the Hungarian press on the Party, domestic politics, culture, sport, economic life and foreign policy; also contains personal news and a diary of current events. Subject index in each issue, with a cumulative name and subject index every six months.

H111 *Hungary: features, reports, information.* (Budapress Sajtószolgálat). Bp.: Budapress, 1974–. Semi-annual.

Gives current information on state administration, political and social organizations, international affairs, economic life, tourism, health, social welfare, cultural life and sport. Includes regular lists of government officials, summaries of important legislation, and a diary of current events. Also published in Hungarian, as *Magyarország*, and in other languages.

Other serial publications carrying official material

H112 *Hungarian review.* Bp.: Lapkiadó, 1947–79. Monthly.

1947–54 entitled *Hungarian bulletin: information service for the foreign press,* irregular. A journal intended to acquaint foreign readers with life in Hungary. More useful for official material in its earlier years, when it regularly included, for example, speeches by leading political figures, reports by the Central Statistical Office on the progress of the First Five-Year Plan and the texts of party resolutions, and also published special supplements, e.g. giving the texts of reports submitted to the National Assembly.

H113 *News from Hungary.* London: Press Section, Embassy of the Hungarian People's Republic, 1971–. Quarterly.

Includes news on all aspects of Hungarian life, including regular reports on such topics as parliamentary proceedings and new government appointments. Particular attention is paid to Anglo-Hungarian relations and contacts. Special supplements on particular subjects are included from time to time. The Press Section of the embassy in London also publishes occasional pamphlets on topical events and various irregular series, the chief of which are:

H114a *Agricultural news from Hungary,* 1950–.
H114b *Cultural news from Hungary,* 1949–.
H114c *Documents on foreign affairs,* 1951–.
H114d *Economic news from Hungary,* 1948–.
H114e *Everyday life in Hungary,* 1949–.
H114f *Hungarian budget,* 1950–.
H114g *Hungarian production,* 1949–.
H114h *Hungary today,* 1949–.
H114i *New Hungary,* 1953–.
H114j *News briefs,* 1957–.
H114k *National minorities in Hungary,* 1980–.
H114l *Peace movement in Hungary,* 1950–.
H114m *Special information service,* 1951–.
H114n *Trade union news from Hungary,* 1949–.

H115 *Magyar hírlap: politikai napilap.* [Hungarian newspaper: political daily]. Bp.: Lapkiadó, 1968–. Daily.

A semi-official government daily aiming particularly to provide detailed analyses of current events.

H116 *Magyar nemzet: a Hazafias Népfront lapja.* [Hungarian nation: journal of the Patriotic People's Front]. Bp.: Lapkiadó, 1945–. Daily.

Although not published by a government or party agency it

regularly includes reports of important policy statements and is particularly valuable for its coverage of intellectual issues.

H117   *New Hungarian quarterly.* Bp.: Corvina, 1960–. Quarterly.
A general periodical containing articles on political, cultural, economic and social affairs. As one of its main objects is to publicize Hungarian achievements it sometimes contains substantial articles by leading political figures such as János Kádár or the Foreign Minister summarizing the policies of the day. There is a subject index to the volumes published between 1960 and 1979.

H118   *Hungary 66 [67, etc.].* Editor-in-chief: M. Gárdos. Bp.: Pannonia Press, 1966–. Annual.
A yearbook compiled from information obtained from official sources such as the Central Statistical Office and the Hungarian News Agency. Includes regular chapters such as 'Chronicle of domestic policy', 'Diplomatic chronicle', 'Personnel of leading state and party bodies', 'State distinctions' and 'Hungarian diplomatic representation abroad' and special articles of topical interest, e.g. on the revised 1972 constitution, social legislation, the legal system, and statistical organization.

INTERNATIONAL RELATIONS

See also H244k.

H119   *Magyar külpolitikai évkönyv: a Magyar Népköztársaság külpolitikai kapcsolatai és külpolitikai tevékenysége.* [Yearbook of Hungarian foreign policy: the foreign relations and foreign policy activity of the Hungarian People's Republic]. 1968–. Bp.: Kossuth, 1969–. Annual.
Each issue contains a day-to-day account of Hungarian diplomacy and foreign policy activity during the year covered, a collection of documents reflecting this activity, e.g. communiqués of official visits and the texts of speeches by the Foreign Minister at the U.N. General Assembly, and information on diplomatic and consular activity, missions to international organizations, commercial counsellors, military and air attachés, Hungarian officials of international organizations, and cultural agreements signed by Hungary.

H120   *A párizsi magyar békeszerződés és magyarázata, az Atlanti Óceáni Alapokmány és a fegyverszüneti egyezmény teljes szövegével.* [The Hungarian Peace Treaty of Paris, with a commentary and the complete texts of the Atlantic Charter and the Armistice Agreement]. A magyarázatokat készítették Baracs J. [és mások]. (Documenta Danubiana, 3). Bp.: Gergely, 1947. 82 pp.
The Hungarian translation of the text of the peace treaty signed in Paris on 10 February 1947 between Hungary and the Allies and of the Armistice Agreement signed in Moscow on 20 January 1945. Includes a subject index to the treaty. The official text of the treaty was also published separately as *Az 1947. február 10-én aláírt magyar*

békeszerződés és mellékletei, 1947. The official English text is printed in *Treaty of Peace with Hungary,* Washington, 1947, which also includes the Russian, French and Hungarian texts and the accompanying frontier maps. The English edition of the Armistice Agreement was published as *Armistice Agreement with Hungary signed at Moscow, 20th January, 1945 (with annex and protocol),* London, 1947.

H121 *Hungary and the Conference of Paris.* Bp.: Hungarian Ministry of Foreign Affairs, 1947. vols. 2, 4.

A collection of documents prepared by the Hungarian Foreign Ministry for the Paris Peace Conference of 1946. Only two of the five volumes originally planned were published in English: vol. 2: *Hungary's international relations before the Conference of Paris: Hungaro-Czechoslovak relations; papers and documents relating to the preparation of the peace and to the exchange of population between Hungary and Czechoslovakia* and vol. 4: *Hungary at the Conference of Paris: papers and documents relating to the Czechoslovak draft amendment concerning the transfer of 200,000 Hungarians from Czechoslovakia to Hungary.* These were also published in French, as was a further volume, vol. 1: *Les rapports internationaux de la Hongrie avant la Conférence de Paris: notes concernant les relations hungaro-roumaines,* 1947. The French versions appeared under the collective title *La Hongrie et la Conférence de Paris.* Vols. 3 and 5 were not published.

H122a *Magyar–szovjet kapcsolatok, 1945–1948: dokumentumok.* [Hungarian–Soviet relations, 1945–1948: documents]. (A Magyar Népköztársaság Külügyminisztériuma és a Szovjetúnió Külügyminisztériuma). Bp.: Kossuth, 1969. 308 pp. [Not seen].

H122b *Magyar–szovjet kapcsolatok, 1948–1970: dokumentumok.* Bp.: Kossuth, 1973. 631 pp.

H122c *Magyar–szovjet kapcsolatok, 1971–1976: dokumentumok.* Bp.: Kossuth, 1977. 586 pp.

A series of collections of documents published jointly by the Hungarian and Soviet foreign ministries. They include the texts of important treaties, agreements, communiqués, declarations and party documents reflecting Hungarian–Soviet relations since 1945. Russian versions have also been published under the title *Sovetsko-vengerskie otnosheniia, 1945–1948* [*1948–1970, etc.*] *gg.,* Moscow, 1969, 1974, 1977. English translations of several important documents, including the Treaty of Friendship, Cooperation and Mutual Assistance of 1948, are printed in Naik, J. A., *Russia and the communist countries: documents, 1946–71,* Kolhapur, 1980.

POLITICAL AND IDEOLOGICAL AFFAIRS

H123 *Fehér könyv: a magyar köztársaság és demokrácia elleni összeesküvés okmányai.* [White book: documents concerning the conspiracy against the Hungarian Republic and Hungarian democracy]. Bp.: M. Tájékoztatásügyi Minisztérium, 1947. 153 pp.

Implicated in the alleged conspiracy were the Prime Minister, Ferenc Nagy, leader of the Smallholders' Party, and Béla Kovács, Secretary-General of the Party.

H124a Révai, J. *Élni tudtunk a szabadsággal*. [We were able to seize the opportunities of freedom]. Bp.: Szikra, 1949. iii, 687 pp.

H124b Révai, J. *Marxizmus, népiesség, magyarság*. [Marxism, popularism and the Hungarians]. 4. kiad. Bp.: Szikra, 1955. 503 pp.

Collections of essays, articles, etc. by the leading party ideologist of the period 1945–56.

H125 *Rajk László és társai a népbíróság előtt*. [László Rajk and his accomplices before the People's Court]. Bp.: Szikra, 1949. 271 pp.

A partial transcript of the Rajk trial of 1949. An English translation was also published: *László Rajk and his accomplices before the People's Court*, 1949.

H126 *Documents on the hostile activity of the United States government against the Hungarian People's Republic*. Bp.: Hungarian State Publishing House, 1951. 322 pp.

Documents purporting to implicate the U.S. government in sabotage, interference in Hungarian elections, the Rajk and Mindszenty affairs, etc.

H127 *Ellenforradalmi erők a magyar októberi eseményekben*. Bp.: A Magyar Népköztársaság Minisztertanácsa Tájékoztatási Hivatala, 1956–7. 4 vols.

The official version of the 1956 events as presented by the Kádár régime. There is an English translation: *The counter-revolutionary forces in the October events in Hungary*, 1957–8.

H128 *Nagy Imre és bűntársai ellenforradalmi összeesküvése*. Bp.: A Magyar Népköztársaság Minisztertanácsa Tájékoztatási Hivatala, 1958. 159 pp.

A continuation of H127 containing 'primarily the new documents found during the criminal proceedings [against Nagy and 8 others], which proved the anti-state activity of Imre Nagy and his group'. Also includes the communiqué of the Ministry of Justice on the sentences passed on Nagy and his colleagues. The English translation is: *The counter-revolutionary conspiracy of Imre Nagy and his accomplices*, 1958.

H129 *A magyar forradalom és szabadságharc a hazai rádióállomások tükrében, 1956. október 23–november 9*. [The Hungarian revolution and fight for freedom as reflected in Hungarian radio broadcasts, 23 October–9 November 1956]. New York: Free Europe Press, 1957. 376 pp.

Transcripts of many of the broadcasts made during the 1956 revolution, including those expressing the views of Nagy's government. [Not seen].

MILITARY AFFAIRS

H130 *Katonai könyvkiadás Magyarországon, 1945–1965: bibliográfia.* [Military publishing in Hungary, 1945–65: bibliography]. Összeáll. a Zrínyi Miklós Katonai Akadémia Tudományos Könyvtárának munkaközössége. Bp.: Zrínyi, 1967. 299 pp.

A subject bibliography of works on military theory, practice and policy. Current bibliographies of material on military affairs, including that contained in periodicals, are regularly published in the journal *Hadtörténelmi közlemények* [Contributions to military history], 1888–, quarterly.

H131 *A Magyar Szocialista Munkáspárt honvédelmi politikájáról, 1956. november–1973: dokumentum-, beszéd- és cikkgyűjtemény.* [On the defence policy of the Hungarian Socialist Workers' Party, November 1956–1973: collection of documents, speeches and articles]. Bev. tanulmány és vál. Zágoni E. Bp.: Zrínyi, 1974. 254 pp. [Not seen].

H132 *A honvédelmi jogszabályok kézikönyve.* [Handbook of statutes on defence]. Szerk. Somos J. Bp.: Zrínyi, 1978. 397 pp.

Text, with commentary, of Law No. I of 1976 on National Defence and other relevant statutes.

H133 *Honvédségi közlöny.* [Army gazette]. Bp.: Honvédelmi Minisztérium, 1945–52. Irregular. [Not seen].

H134 *Néphadsereg: a Honvédelmi Minisztérium központi politikai hetilapja.* [People's Army: the central political weekly of the Ministry of Defence]. Bp.: Zrínyi, 1948–. Weekly. [Not seen].

H135 *Honvédségi szemle: a Magyar Néphadsereg központi folyóirata.* [Army review: the central journal of the Hungarian People's Army]. Bp.: Zrínyi, 1960–. Monthly. [Not seen].

ECONOMIC AFFAIRS

Economic affairs in general

Bibliography

H136 *Magyar közgazdasági és statisztikai irodalom: bibliográfia. Hungarian bibliography of economics and statistics.* 1957/9–. (Központi Statisztikai Hivatal Könyvtára és Dokumentációs Szolgálata; MTA Közgazdaságtudományi Intézetének Könyvtára). Bp.: Marx Károly Közgazdaságtudományi Egyetem, 1960–. Annual.

Issue for 1957/9 entitled *Magyar közgazdasági művek: bibliográfia.* [Hungarian works on economics: bibliography]. The first two issues covered 1957–9 and 1960–2, the subsequent issues appearing annually. A selective bibliography of material published in Hungary on economic affairs and statistics. Titles are also given in English.

H137 *A Közgazdasági és Jogi Kiadó katalógusa, 1955–1970.* [Catalogue of the Publishing House for Economics and Law, 1955–70]. Szerk. Györki M., Jávor E. Bp.: KJK, 1971. 331 pp.

A further volume, covering works published between 1971 and 1974, appeared in 1975. [Not seen].

H138 Horchler, G. F. *Hungarian economic reforms: a selective, partially annotated bibliography.* (Hungarian reference shelf). New Brunswick, N.J.: Hungarian Research Center, 1977. iii, 182 pp.

Lists monographs, serial publications and periodical articles, including official material, relating to the New Economic Mechanism. Subject arrangement.

Periodicals

H139 *Tervgazdasági értesítő: az Országos Tervhivatal hivatalos lapja.* [Economic planning bulletin: official journal of the National Planning Office]. Bp.: Lapkiadó, 1949–. Irregular. [Not seen].

H140 *Figyelő: gazdaságpolitikai hetilap.* [Observer: weekly journal of economic policy]. Bp.: Hírlapkiadó, 1957–. Weekly.

1957 entitled *Gazdasági figyelő* [Economic observer], semimonthly. Includes reports and articles by economic experts on Hungarian economic policy and development and on economic legislation.

H141 *The Hungarian economy: a quarterly economic and business review.* Bp.: Hírlapkiadó, 1972–. Quarterly.

Published as a supplement to H140. Gives information on Hungarian economic life, trade, industry and products. Includes articles by economic experts and government ministers. A regular column, 'The law book', outlines current legislation on economic matters.

H142 *Közgazdasági szemle: a Magyar Tudományos Akadémia Közgazdaságtudományi Bizottságának folyóirata.* [Economic review: journal of the Economic Sciences Committee of the Hungarian Academy of Sciences]. Bp.: Akad. K., 1954–. Monthly.

The chief journal dealing with the theoretical aspects of economic policy.

H143 *Hungaropress economic information: information service of the Hungarian Chamber of Commerce.* Bp.: Hungarian Chamber of Commerce, 1959–. Semi-monthly.

Provides information on economic life, investments, new projects, products, trade agreements, exhibitions, fairs, international economic relations, inventions and patents.

H144 *Economic bulletin of the National Bank of Hungary.* Bp.: National Bank of Hungary, 1957–. Semi-annual.

Reviews economic developments in Hungary, with particular

stress on financial matters. The bank also published a *Monthly bulletin* between July 1945 and February 1949.

Economic policy

See also H242a–b.

H145 Nyers, R. *Gazdaságpolitikánk és a gazdasági mechanizmus reformja.* [Our economic policy and the reform of the economic mechanism]. Bp.: Kossuth, 1968. 397 pp.

A collection of speeches, lectures and articles from the years 1963–7 by the chief architect of the New Economic Mechanism.

Statutes

H146 *Tervgazdasági jogszabálygyűjtemény: az Országos Tervhivatal elnöke által kiadott hatályos rendeletek és utasítások gyűjteménye.* [Collections of statutes on economic planning: collection of decrees and directives in force issued by the Chairman of the National Planning Office]. Bp.: Tervgazdasági Könyvkiadó, 1953. 355 pp.

Covers the period from the establishment of the National Planning Office in 1947 to 30 June 1953. [Not seen].

H147 *A gazdasági mechanizmus jogszabályainak gyűjteménye.* [Collection of statutes relating to the economic mechanism]. Bp.: KJK, 1968–71. 4 vols.

Vols. 1–3 entitled *Az új gazdasági mechanizmus jogszabályainak gyűjteménye* [Collection of statutes relating to the new economic mechanism]. Includes statutes, directives of a more general nature and guiding principles of the Government Economic Committee relating to the introduction and operation of the New Economic Mechanism. Numerical index to statutes and subject index.

Statistics

H148 *Gazdaságstatisztikai tájékoztató: a Központi Statisztikai Hivatal folyóirata.* [Information bulletin on economic statistics: journal of the Central Statistical Office]. Bp.: Áll. Lapkiadó, December 1946–July 1949. Irregular.

Frequency varies; generally published monthly. Though chiefly concerned with economic matters it also includes statistics on social conditions, broadcasting, demography and cultural life. Contents list also in English; some issues include supplements giving English translations of headings.

H149 *Adatok és adalékok a népgazdaság fejlődésének tanulmányozásához, 1949–1955.* [Data and information for the study of the development of the national economy, 1949–1955]. (Központi Statisztikai Hivatal). Bp.: Stat. K., 1957. 460 pp.

A collection of statistical material from official sources, primarily but not exclusively reflecting economic developments during the years covered.

H150 *Report of the Central Statistical Office on the fulfilment of the . . . year plan and on the growth of the national economy.* 1973–. Bp.: Central Statistical Office, 1974–. Annual.

Title varies slightly from year to year. A volume was also issued with the title *Report by the Central Statistical Office on the development of social and economic life and the fulfilment of the national economic plan during the period of the Third Five-Year Plan, 1966–1970*, 1971.

H151 *Ágazati kapcsolatok mérlege.* [Balance of inter-industry relations]. 1957–. (Központi Statisztikai Hivatal). Bp.: Stat. K., 1959–. Irregular.

A series of publications containing input–output tables for the Hungarian economy. Volumes cover either a single year or a number of years and their titles sometimes vary: volumes for 1959, 1961 and 1965 were published as *A magyar népgazdaság ágazati kapcsolatainak mérlege*. The bibliography cited at H89 should be consulted for a complete list of the series up to 1974.

Finance

H152 *Pénzügyi közlöny: a Pénzügyminisztérium hivatalos lapja.* [Financial gazette: official journal of the Ministry of Finance]. Bp.: Lapkiadó, 1874–. Irregular.

H153 *Pénzügyi szemle.* [Financial review]. Bp.: Lapkiadó, 1954–. Monthly.

From 1957, when it absorbed *Számvitel* [Accountancy], 1950–6, monthly, to 1963 it was entitled *Pénzügy és számvitel* [Finance and accountancy]. Includes some official material, such as reports of speeches in the National Assembly, on public finance, budgetary matters and taxation.

H154 *Hatályos pénzügyi jogszabályok gyűjteménye.* [Collection of financial statutes in force]. Főszerk. Bárdos Gy. Bp.: KJK, 1972. 3 vols.

Includes laws, decrees, the most important ministerial directives and other official material issued by the Ministry of Finance and the National Bank of Hungary.

H155 *Az állami pénzügyekről szóló törvény.* [The Law on State Finances]. Összeáll. Gadó D. [és mások]. (Kis jogszabály sorozat). Bp.: KJK, 1980. 164 pp.

The text of Law No. II of 1979 and its implementing decree.

Trade

Domestic trade

H156 *Kereskedelmi értesítő: a Belkereskedelmi Minisztérium hivatalos lapja.* [Trade bulletin: official journal of the Ministry of Domestic Trade]. Bp.: Lapkiadó, 1905–. Irregular.

1905–50 entitled *Közgazdasági értesítő* [Economic bulletin]; July

1953–July 1954 *Kereskedelmi értesítő. I. főrész: Belkereskedelem* [Trade bulletin. Part I: Domestic trade]. Not published 1945–6. [Not seen].

H157 *Belkereskedelmi jogszabályok gyűjteménye.* [Collection of statutes on domestic trade]. Szerk. Korda L. Bp.: KJK, 1973. 518 pp. [Not seen].

H158 *Belkereskedelmi évkönyv.* [Yearbook of domestic trade]. 1968–. (Központi Statisztikai Hivatal). Bp.: Stat. K., 1969–. Annual.

An annual statistical collection issued as part of H94. Statistics on domestic trade are also published more regularly in the series *Belkereskedelmi adatok* (cumulative volume for 1950–6, then 1970–3, quarterly), *Belkereskedelem* (for the years 1957–8 and 1965–9, irregular), *Az 1959. év a belkereskedelemben* (annual, for 1959 only), *A belkereskedelem időszaki adatgyűjteménye* (for the years 1961–4, quarterly) and *Belkereskedelmi és idegenforgalmi adatok* [Data on domestic trade and tourism] (for the years 1974–, quarterly).

Foreign trade

H159 *Handbook of Hungarian foreign trade.* Ed. E. Farkasfalvy. Bp.: Corvina Press for the Hungarian Chamber of Commerce, 1972. 282 pp.

Contains information for foreign businessmen wishing to trade with Hungarian companies. Serving a similar purpose are the periodicals *Hungarian foreign trade*, 1949–, quarterly, and *New Hungarian exporter* (formerly *Hungarian exporter*), 1951–, monthly.

H160 *Külkereskedelmi értesítő: a Külkereskedelmi Minisztérium hivatalos lapja.* [Foreign trade bulletin: official journal of the Ministry of Foreign Trade]. Bp.: Lapkiadó, 1953–. Irregular.

August 1953–July 1954 entitled *Kereskedelmi értesítő. II. főrész: Külkereskedelem és vám* [Trade bulletin. Part II: Foreign trade and customs]; July 1954–August 1964 *Külkereskedelmi értesítő. Vámközlöny.* Before August 1953 official material on foreign trade and customs appeared in *Közgazdasági értesítő* and *Kereskedelmi értesítő* (*see* H156).

H161 *Hungarian statutes on foreign trade.* Comp. and introduced by I. Szász; commissioned by the Hungarian Chamber of Commerce. Bp.: Corvina, 1971. 242 pp.

English translations of a selection of statutes necessary for the guidance of foreigners having business contacts with Hungarian companies, with an outline of Hungarian legal sources, the basic statutory regulations of the economy, and the organization of foreign trade in Hungary. Collections of statutes were also issued in two publications entitled *A külkereskedelem hatályos jogszabályai* [Statutes on foreign trade in force], 1955 and 1965.

H162 *Magyarország külkereskedelmi tárgyú kétoldalú nemzetközi szerző-*

dései. [Bilateral international foreign trade agreements concluded by Hungary]. Összeáll. Mohi Cs., Dienes-Oehm E. Bp.: KJK, 1979. 479 pp.

An official publication of the Ministry of Foreign Trade containing sections on commercial agreements in the strict sense and cooperative agreements, each arranged by partner country.

H163　*Külkereskedelmi statisztikai évkönyv.* [Statistical yearbook of foreign trade]. 1971–. (Központi Statisztikai Hivatal). Bp.: Stat. K., 1972–. Annual.

The latest issues contain supplements with translations of table headings and lists of commodities in English. A publication covering earlier years is *Külkereskedelmi évkönyv, 1938, 1949–1958,* 1960.

Transport and communications

H164　*Közlekedésügyi értesítő: a Közlekedés- és Postaügyi Minisztérium hivatalos lapja.* [Transport bulletin: official journal of the Ministry of Transport and Communications]. Bp.: Lapkiadó, 1949–. Irregular. [Not seen].

H165　*Közlekedési és hírközlési évkönyv.* [Yearbook of transport and telecommunications]. 1970–. (Központi Statisztikai Hivatal). Bp.: Stat. K., 1971–. Annual.

A statistical yearbook which is published as a sub-series of H94. Its predecessor was *Közlekedési és hírközlési adattár, 1960/6–69, 1967–70.*

Labour affairs

See also H41, H42.

H166　*Munkaügyi közlöny: a Munkaügyi Minisztérium hivatalos lapja.* [Labour gazette: official journal of the Ministry of Labour]. Bp.: Lapkiadó, 1957–. Irregular.

H167　*Munkaügyi szemle: a Munkaügyi Minisztérium szakfolyóirata.* [Labour review: technical journal of the Ministry of Labour]. Bp.: Lapkiadó, 1957–. Monthly.

Includes material on labour affairs in general, industrial hygiene and social insurance. It has a supplement, *Munkajog* [Labour law], 1968–, which deals particularly with labour arbitration cases.

H168　*Vállalati munkajogi kézikönyv.* [Handbook of labour law for enterprises]. 3., átd. kiad. Szerk. Bogyay Gy. Bp.: KJK, 1977. 865 pp.

Texts of statutes and regulations, with commentaries, relating to labour affairs at the enterprise level.

H169　*Munkaügyi statisztikai zsebkönyv.* [Statistical pocketbook of labour affairs]. Bp.: Munkaügyi Minisztérium Számítástechnikai Intézete, 1976–. [Not seen].

H170   *Munkaügyi adattár, 1949–1966.* [Compendium of labour statistics, 1949–1966]. Szerk. Lengyel L., Öryné I. (Központi Statisztikai Hivatal). Bp.: Stat. K., 1968. 397 pp.

Industry

Official gazettes

Immediately after the Second World War industrial affairs were directed by the Ministry of Industry (Iparügyi Minisztérium), set up in 1935. Its official gazette was:

H171   *Ipari értesítő: az Iparügyi Minisztérium hivatalos közlönye.* [Industry bulletin: official gazette of the Ministry of Industry]. Bp.: Lapkiadó, 7 November 1948–May 1951. Irregular. [Not seen].

   This continued to exist after June 1949, when the functions of the ministry were divided between the new Ministries of Heavy Industry (Nehézipari Minisztérium) and of Light Industry (Könnyűipari Minisztérium), and after December 1950, when the former was further divided into the Ministries of Metallurgy and Machine Engineering (Kohó- és Gépipari Minisztérium) and of Mining and Energy (Bánya- és Energiaügyi Minisztérium). From May 1951 until 1980, responsibility for the main branches of industry shifted at frequent intervals between a variety of successively retitled ministries, each publishing its own *közlöny* or *értesítő*.

   In December 1980 the Ministries of Heavy Industry, Metallurgy and Machine Engineering and Light Industry were abolished and their functions taken over by a new Ministry of Industry (Ipari Minisztérium), which publishes:

H172   *Ipari közlöny: az Ipari Minisztérium hivatalos lapja.* [Industry gazette: official journal of the Ministry of Industry]. Bp.: Lapkiadó, 1981–. Irregular. [Not seen].

Official material on the construction industry and urban development is published in:

H173   *Építésügyi értesítő: az Építésügyi és Városfejlesztési Minisztérium hivatalos közlönye.* [Construction industry bulletin: official gazette of the Ministry of Construction and Urban Development]. Bp.: Lapkiadó, 1949–. Weekly.

   The ministry assumed its present name in April 1967. Its predecessors were the Ministry of Reconstruction (Újjáépítési Minisztérium, May 1945–October 1946), the Ministry of Construction and Public Works (Építés- és Közmunkaügyi Minisztérium, October 1946–June 1949) and the Ministry of Construction (Építésügyi Minisztérium, June 1949–April 1967). An offshoot, the Ministry of the Building Materials Industry (Építőanyagipari Minisztérium), existed between January 1952 and July 1953.

Other periodicals relating to industry in general

H174 *Magyar ipar: az Iparügyi Minisztérium lapja.* [Hungarian industry: journal of the Ministry of Industry]. Bp.: Athenaeum ny., June 1947–July 1949. Semi-monthly.

Contains reports and articles intended to show the results achieved by the ministry and to outline plans for the future.

Statistics relating to industry in general

H175 *Ipari és építőipari statisztikai értesítő: a Központi Statisztikai Hivatal Iparstatisztikai, valamint Beruházási és Építőipari Statisztikai Főosztályának lapja.* [Bulletin of statistics on industry and construction: journal of the Departments of Industrial Statistics and of Investment and Construction Statistics of the Central Statistical Office]. Bp.: Stat. K., 1949–. Monthly.

1949–55 entitled *Iparstatisztikai értesítő.* Includes articles on theory and methodology, statistical analyses and reviews.

H176 *Iparstatisztikai évkönyv.* [Yearbook of industrial statistics]. 1977–. Bp.: Stat. K., 1978–. Annual.

Also published in an English version, *Yearbook of industrial statistics,* which contains the text of the Hungarian version with a supplement giving translations of headings. Previous yearbooks with a similar scope were *Iparstatisztikai zsebkönyv, 1962* and *Ipari és építőipari statisztikai évkönyv,* published for the years 1963 and 1964.

H177 *Ipari zsebkönyv.* [Industrial pocketbook]. 1974–. (Központi Statisztikai Hivatal). Bp.: Stat. K., 1974–. Annual.

A less detailed yearbook than H176, intended to show the year-by-year results of industrial policy. From 1977 it has included a supplement with English translations of headings.

H178 *Ipari adattár.* [Compendium of industrial statistics]. (Központi Statisztikai Hivatal). Bp.: Stat. K., 1978. 512 pp.

The latest in a series of compendia which between them cover the period 1949–75. Other volumes in the same series were published under this title in 1966 and 1972, and the first was entitled *A magyar ipar: statisztikai adatgyűjtemény,* 1961. More regular statistical data on industry are provided by *Ipari adatok,* 1967–, quarterly, a sub-series of H94.

Heavy industry

See also H171, H172.

H179 *Nehézipari utasítások gyűjteménye, 1952–1975.* [Collection of directives on heavy industry, 1952–1975]. Összeáll. a Nehézipari Minisztérium közössége; szerk. Németh J. Bp.: NIMDOK, 1976. 2 vols.

A comprehensive, chronologically arranged collection of directives issued by the Ministry of Heavy Industry and its predecessors.

Metallurgy and machine engineering

See also H171, H172.

H180   Kohó- és gépipari jogszabályok gyűjteménye. [Collection of statutes on metallurgy and machine engineering]. Összeáll. a Kohó- és Gépipari Minisztérium munkaközössége; szerk. Törkenczy I. Bp.: KJK, 1976, 2 vols. [Not seen].

H181   Kohászati és gépipari adattár. [Compendium of statistics on metallurgy and machine engineering]. (Központi Statisztikai Hivatal). Bp.: Stat. K., 1971. 3 vols.
    A volume was also published in 1979 with the same title, covering the years 1970–5.

Mining and energy

See also H171, H172.

H182   Bányászati és energia adattár. [Compendium of statistics on mining and energy]. (Központi Statisztikai Hivatal). Bp.: Stat. K., 1974. 555 pp.
    A volume was also published in 1978 with the same title, covering the period 1973–5.

Chemical industry

See also H171, H172.

H183   Vegyipari adattár. [Compendium of statistics on the chemical industry]. (Központi Statisztikai Hivatal). Bp.: Stat. K., 1971. 609 pp.
    A volume was also published in 1979 with the same title, covering the period 1970–5.

Light industry

See also H171, H172.

H184   Könnyűipari szemle: a Könnyűipari Minisztérium folyóirata. [Light industry review: journal of the Ministry of Light Industry]. Bp.: Könnyűipari Minisztérium, 1974–. Semi-annual. [Not seen].

H185   Könnyűipari tájékoztató: a Könnyűipari Minisztérium hivatalos kiadványa. [Light industry information bulletin: official publication of the Ministry of Light Industry]. Bp.: Könnyűipari Minisztérium, 1974–. [Not seen].

H186   A könnyűipari és a kisipari jogszabályok gyűjteménye. [Collection of statutes on light industry and small-scale industry]. Bp.: KJK, 1971. 904 pp.

H187   Könnyűipari adattár. [Compendium of statistics on light industry]. (Központi Statisztikai Hivatal). Bp.: Stat. K., 1978. 757 pp.

The latest in a series of statistical compendia on light industry. Previous editions with the same title were published in 1967 and 1972, and the first was entitled *A magyar könnyűipar: statisztikai adatgyűjtemény*, 1962. A compendium on private small-scale industry was published under the title *Magánkisipari adattár*, *1938–1971*, 1972.

Construction and investments

See also H173.

H188 *Építésügyi jogszabályok gyűjteménye.* [Collection of statutes on construction]. Összeáll. és jegyz. ell. Madarász Gy. [és mások]. Bp.: KJK, 1977. 3 vols.

An earlier edition with the same title was published in 1972. [Not seen].

H189 *Beruházási jogszabályok.* [Collection of statutes on investment]. Összeáll. Széll A. Bp.: KJK, 1977. 562 pp. [Not seen].

H190 *Építőanyagipari adattár, 1950–1973.* [Compendium of statistics on the building materials industry, 1950–1973]. (Központi Statisztikai Hivatal). Bp.: Stat. K., 1975. 353 pp.

A volume was also published in 1979 with the same title, covering the period 1974–5.

H191 *Beruházási adattár, 1950–1977.* [Compendium of statistics on investments, 1950–1977]. (Központi Statisztikai Hivatal). Bp.: Stat. K., 1979. 330 pp.

Previous compendia with the same title were published for the years 1950–66 (in 1967) and 1950–71 (in 1973). Regular statistics on construction and investments are published in *Beruházási-építőipari adatok*, 1971–, quarterly, which appears as a sub-series of H94.

Agriculture

Official gazette

H192 *Mezőgazdasági és élelmezésügyi értesítő: a Mezőgazdasági és Élelmezésügyi Minisztérium hivatalos lapja.* [Agriculture and food bulletin: official journal of the Ministry of Agriculture and Food]. Bp.: Lapkiadó, 1950–. Irregular.

1950–67 entitled *Mezőgazdasági értesítő: a Földművelésügyi Minisztérium hivatalos lapja.* The present title was adopted as a result of the creation of the Ministry of Agriculture and Food from the former Ministry of Agriculture (Földművelésügyi Minisztérium), Ministry of Food (Élelmezésügyi Minisztérium) and National Forest Authority (Országos Erdészeti Főigazgatóság).

Other periodicals

H193 *Magyar mezőgazdaság: mezőgazdasági hetilap.* [Hungarian agriculture: agricultural weekly]. (Mezőgazdasági és Élelmezésügyi Minisztérium). Bp.: Hírlapkiadó, 1946–. Weekly.

A periodical of the Ministry of Agriculture and Food; includes articles and reports on agricultural policy, production, organization, finance, law and prices. It has a supplement, *Információk* [Information], 1969–, weekly. [Not seen].

Statutes and documentary material

H194 *A földreformra vonatkozó jogszabályok, az Országos Földbirtokrendező Tanács elvi jelentőségű határozataival.* [Statutes relating to the land reform, with the decisions with the force of principle of the National Council for the Redistribution of Land]. Bp.: Földmívelésügyi Minisztérium, 1945. 194 pp.

H195 *Földreform 1945: tanulmány és dokumentumgyűjtemény.* [Land reform 1945: essay and collection of documents]. Szerk. M. Somlyai M. (Levéltárak Országos Központja és az MTA Történettudományi Intézete). Bp.: Kossuth, 1965. 575 pp.

The documentary section, which covers the years 1944–77, includes legal sources, documents emanating from the national and local organs administering the land reform and reports of the sittings of committees set up to examine land claims. There is an index of statutes. Another collection of documents, consisting chiefly of reports made to the Ministry of Agriculture on the progress of the land reform, was published in 1977 under the title *Dokumentumok a magyar mezőgazdaság történetéből, 1945–1948* [Documents on the history of Hungarian agriculture, 1945–1948].

H196 *Földmívelésügyi jogszabályok gyűjteménye.* [Collection of statutes on agriculture]. Készítette a Földmívelésügyi Miniszter megbízása alapján működő munkaközösség. Bp.: Hernádi, 1949. 5 vols.

Subject arrangement; each volume has a numerical and subject index of statutes.

H197 *A mezőgazdasági termelőszövetkezeti jogszabályok.* [Statutes on agricultural production cooperatives]. Összeáll. Bosánszky L. [és mások]. Bp.: KJK, 1978. 465 pp.

Contains the consolidated text of Law No. III of 1967 on Agricultural Production Cooperatives and its implementing statutes, and other statutes relating to the cooperatives. An English translation of the 1967 law appeared in *Hungarian law review*, 1971, 2 and 1972, 1, pp. 90–124.

Statistics

H198 *Mezőgazdasági statisztikai zsebkönyv.* [Pocketbook of agricultural

statistics]. 1959–. (Központi Statisztikai Hivatal). Bp.: Stat. K., 1959–. Annual.
Contents list also in English.

H199 *Mezőgazdasági adattár.* [Compendium of statistics on agriculture]. (Központi Statisztikai Hivatal). Bp.: Stat. K., 1978–.

Of the three volumes published so far, volume 1 contains general statistics for the years 1961–76, volume 2 statistics on livestock and volume 3 statistics on labour affairs, mechanization and agricultural technology. An earlier edition with the same title, covering the period 1950–64, was published in two volumes in 1965. Comparative historical data is available in *Mezőgazdasági statisztikai adatgyűjtemény, 1870–1970,* 1971–, in progress, which consists of several sub-series, each covering a particular aspect of agriculture, e.g. arable farming, livestock breeding and vegetable growing. Regular statistics on agriculture are published in *Mezőgazdasági adatok,* 1966–, quarterly, a sub-series of H94.

H200 *Általános mezőgazdasági összeírás, 1972.* [General census of agriculture, 1972]. (Központi Statisztikai Hivatal). Bp.: Stat. K., 1972–5. 13 vols. [Not seen].

SOCIAL AFFAIRS

Statutes of a general nature

H201 *A hatályos anyakönyvi, házassági és vallásügyi jogszabályok: az idevonatkozó összes törvények, rendeletek, valamint az érdekelt minisztériumok fontosabb elvi jelentőségű határozatai.* [Statutes in force on civil registration, marriage and religion: complete collection of relevant laws and decrees, with the most important decisions of principle of the ministries concerned]. Összeáll. és magy. Babó Sz. Bp.: Hernádi, 1948. 760 pp. [Not seen].

H202 *A családjogi törvény: az 1974. évi I. törvény és a családjoggal kapcsolatos egyéb jogszabályok, a Legfelsőbb Bíróság elvi állásfoglalásaival.* [The Family Law: Law No. I. of 1974 and other statutes relating to family law, with the advisory opinions with the force of principle of the Supreme Court]. Összeáll. és a jegyz. írta Garay M. [és mások]. Bp.: KJK, 1975, 505 pp.

Law No. I of 1974 was a restatement and consolidation of Law No. IV of 1952 on Marriage, the family and Guardianship (the 'family code'). An English translation of the 1974 Law, with an introductory essay, was published in *Hungarian law review,* 1976, 1–2, pp. 45–71. The original 1952 code was published as *A házasságról, a családról és a gyámságról szóló törvény: az 1952: IV. tv. és a családjogra, valamint az anya- és gyermekvédelemre vonatkozó egyéb jogszabályok,* 1953.

Social statistics in general

H203 *Háztartásstatisztika.* [Statistics of households]. 1959–. (Központi Statisztikai Hivatal). Bp.: Stat. K., 1961–. Annual.
Not published for the years 1965–7, but the 1968 issue covers 1965–8. Contains data on the income and expenditure of households according to social stratum.

H204 *Társadalmi rétegződés Magyarországon (15.000 háztartás 1963. évi adatai).* (Központi Statisztikai Hivatal. Statisztikai időszaki közlemények, 90). Bp.: Stat. K., 1966. 420 pp.
A detailed statistical survey of stratification according to income, living conditions, education and other factors, and of social mobility. There is an English translation: *Social stratification in Hungary: a survey of 15,000 households carried out in 1963*, 1967.

Health

H205 *Egészségügyi közlöny: az Egészségügyi Minisztérium hivatalos lapja.* [Health gazette: official journal of the Ministry of Health]. Bp.: Lapkiadó, 1951–. Irregular. (ca. 24 issues p.a.).
Before this periodical began publication, statutes and other official material relating to public health and medicine were published in:

H206 *Népegészségügy: az Egészségügyi Minisztérium egészségpolitikai, egészségügyi szervezési folyóirata.* [People's health: journal of the Ministry of Health devoted to health policy and organization]. Bp.: Ifjúsági Lapkiadó, 1920–. Bi-monthly. [Not seen].

H207 *Egészségügyi jogszabályok gyűjteménye.* [Collection of statutes on health]. Szerk. Benedek J. [és mások]. Bp.: Egészségügyi K., 1954. 6 vols. [Not seen].
A comprehensive collection of statutes from the early postwar years. The fundamental principles of policy on public health, welfare and medicine have recently been codified in Law No. II of 1972.

H208 *Egészségügyi helyzet.* [Health situation]. 1963–. (Központi Statisztikai Hivatal). Bp.: Stat. K., 1964–. Irregular.
Periodical statistical reports published as a sub-series of H94. Volumes have been issued for the years 1963, 1966, 1968, 1972 and 1977.

Social security

H209 *A társadalombiztosítási jog kézikönyve.* [Handbook on social security law]. Összeáll. Czeglédy L. [és mások]. Bp.: Táncsics, 1979. 729 pp.
Text, with commentary, of the basic statutes and rules relating to social security, the chief of which is Law No. II of 1975. An English translation of this law, with introductory essays, was published in *Hungarian law review*, 1977, 1–2, pp. 45–69.

Housing

H210   *Lakásügyi jogszabályok.* [Statutes on housing]. Összeáll. és jegyz. ell. Temesvári L. és Kiss E. Bp.: KJK, 1971. 453 pp.

H211   *A lakás- és kommunális ellátás fontosabb adatai.* [Major data on housing and communal provision]. 1970–. (Központi Statisztikai Hivatal). Bp.: Stat. K., 1972–. Annual. [Not seen].

Youth

H212   *Törvény az ifjúságról.* [The Law on Youth]. Bp.: Országos Ifjúságpolitikai és Oktatási Tanács, 1971. 61 pp.

      The text of Law No. IV of 1971 outlining the basic principles of youth policy. An English translation is *Law on Youth*, 1972.

H213   *Statisztikai adatok az ifjúságról.* [Statistical data on youth]. Szerk. Barta B. [és mások]. (Központi Statisztikai Hivatal; Állami Ifjúsági Bizottság). Bp.: Stat. K., 1976. 152 pp.

CULTURAL AFFAIRS

Cultural affairs in general

Official gazettes

In the first few years after 1945 a single ministry, the Ministry of Religion and Public Education (Vallás- és Közoktatásügyi Minisztérium) was responsible for the supervision of educational, cultural and religious affairs. In June 1949, however, a separate Ministry of People's Culture (Népművelési Minisztérium) was set up and two years later, in May 1951, a further division of responsibilities was brought about by the establishment of the State Office for Church Affairs (Állami Egyházügyi Hivatal) to oversee religious policy, leaving a renamed Ministry of Public Education (Közoktatásügyi Minisztérium) in charge of education. A separate Ministry of Higher Education (Felsőoktatási Minisztérium) was created in December 1952, but its existence was short-lived, for in July 1953 it was abolished and the administration of education was again placed within the jurisdiction of a unified and renamed Ministry of Education (Oktatásügyi Minisztérium). In January 1957 this combined with the Ministry of People's Culture to form the Ministry of Culture (Művelődésügyi Minisztérium) and this arrangement lasted until June 1974 when the Ministry's functions were again divided between a new Ministry of Education (Oktatási Minisztérium) and the Ministry of Culture (renamed Kulturális Minisztérium). In June 1980, however, education and culture again fell under the jurisdiction of a single ministry, now called Művelődési Minisztérium.

H214   *Népművelési közlöny: a Népművelési Minisztérium hivatalos lapja.* [Cultural gazette: official journal of the Ministry of People's Culture]. Bp.: Lapkiadó, 11 July 1951–6. Semi-monthly. [Not seen].

H215 *Közoktatásügyi közlöny: a Közoktatásügyi Minisztérium hivatalos lapja.* [Public education gazette: official journal of the Ministry of Public Education]. Bp.: Tankönyvkiadó, 16 August 1951–19 June 1953. Semi-monthly. [Not seen].

H216 *Felsőoktatási közlöny: a Felsőoktatási Minisztérium hivatalos lapja.* [Higher education gazette: official journal of the Ministry of Higher Education]. Bp.: Felsőoktatási Minisztérium, March?–June? 1953. Semi-monthly. [Not seen].

H217 *Oktatásügyi közlöny: az Oktatásügyi Minisztérium hivatalos lapja.* [Education gazette: official journal of the Ministry of Education]. Bp.: Tankönyvkiadó, 16 July 1953–January? 1957. Semi-monthly. [Not seen].

H218 *Művelődési közlöny: a Művelődési Minisztérium hivatalos lapja.* [Cultural gazette: official journal of the Ministry of Culture]. Bp.: Lapkiadó, 21 March 1957–. Irregular. (ca. 24 issues p.a.).
1957–79 entitled *Művelődésügyi közlöny.* Between 1974 and 1980 this was the joint gazette of the Ministries of Culture and Education.

Cultural policy

H219 *Mai magyar művelődéspolitika: elvek, tervek, eredmények.* [Hungarian cultural policy today: principles, plans, results]. Bp.: Vallás- és Közoktatásügyi Minisztérium, 1946. 143 pp.
An official publication of the Ministry of Religious Affairs and Education outlining the cultural policy of the coalition government of November 1945.

H220 *Szocialista közművelődés: szöveggyűjtemény.* [Socialist culture: collection of documents]. Szerk. Ácsné F. Bp.: Kossuth, 1980. 1171 pp.
Contains the most important documents setting out the cultural and educational policy of the Communist Party, including guidelines, resolutions and other policy statements. Includes the text of Law No. V of 1976 on the development of culture and education. [Not seen].

H221 Aczél, Gy. *Folytatás és megújulás: válogatott kultúrpolitikai írások.* [Continuity and renewal: selected writings on cultural policy]. Bp.: Gondolat, 1980, 497 pp. [Not seen].
A collection of writings by the leading party spokesman on cultural affairs and ideology in the early 1970s. Other collections are *Eszménk erejével*, 2nd ed., 1971, *Szocialista kultúra—közösségi ember*, 1974 and *Culture and socialist democracy*, London, 1975.

Cultural administration and law

H222 Hencz, A. *A művelődési intézmények és a művelődésigazgatás fejlődése, 1945–1961.* [The development of cultural institutions and administration, 1945–1961]. Bp.: KJK, 1962. 515 pp.

A handbook which is particularly useful for its list of statutes relating to the organization and administration of cultural and scientific activities.

H223   *A kulturális igazgatás kézikönyve.* [Handbook of cultural administration]. Összeáll. a Kulturális Minisztérium szerkesztő bizottsága; vezetője Blahó P. Bp.: KJK, 1977. 1314 pp.

Includes the most important statutes and other legal provisions relating to cultural administration, arranged by subject. A previous publication of similar scope was *A művelődésügyi igazgatás kézikönyve,* 1970.

Cultural statistics in general

H224   *Közművelődési adatgyűjtemény.* [Collection of data on cultural affairs]. (Központi Statisztikai Hivatal. Statisztikai időszaki közlemények, 288). Bp.: Stat. K., 1973. 386 pp.

This is supplemented by *Közművelődés, 1972–1976,* 1978. Previous statistical collections were *Magyarország művelődési viszonyai, 1945–1958,* 1960, *Kultúrstatisztikai adattár,* 1963, and *Művelődésstatisztikai adattár,* 1968.

Education

Educational policy

See also H219, H220.

H225   *A Magyar Dolgozók Pártja fontosabb határozatai a közoktatásról.* [The major resolutions of the Hungarian Working People's Party on public education]. Közli Simon Gy. (Anyagszolgáltatás a pedagógia oktatói számára, 6). Bp.: Pedagógiai Tudományos Intézet, 1955. 112 pp. [Not seen].

Educational periodicals

See also H215–H218.

H226   *Köznevelés: a Művelődési Minisztérium oktatáspolitikai hetilapja.* [Public education: weekly journal of the Ministry of Culture on educational policy]. Bp.: Ifjúsági Lapkiadó, 1945–. Weekly.

A journal devoted to the theory and practice of general education, including educational policy and ideological, literary and artistic questions.

H227   *Köznevelésünk évkönyve.* [Yearbook of Hungarian public education]. 1974/5–. Bp.: Tankönyvkiadó, 1977–. Annual.

Includes information on the major events of educational policy and practice in the year covered, statutes relating to education and the most important statistics on schools. [Not seen].

H228 *Felsőoktatási szemle: a Művelődési Minisztérium folyóirata.*
[Higher education review: journal of the Ministry of Culture].
Bp.: Ifjúsági Lapkiadó, 1952–. Monthly.
Covers all aspects of higher education, including questions of
government and party policy.

Educational administration and law

H229 *Az oktatásügyi igazgatás kézikönyve.* [Handbook of educational
administration]. Összeáll. az Oktatási Minisztérium szerkesztő bizottsága. Bp.: KJK, 1980. 1406 pp. [Not seen].
Contains texts, with commentaries, of statutes and other legal
provisions relating to elementary and secondary education, the
organization of higher education, the teaching profession, students,
courses of study, extension training and scientific work. An earlier
collection confined to statutes on higher education is *A felsőoktatásra
vonatkozó jogszabályok*, 1972.

H230 Sólyom-Fekete, W. *Laws on public education in Hungary after World
War II.* Washington: Library of Congress, European Law Division,
1959. 133 pp.
An annotated guide to the relevant statutes, with translated
digests. [Not seen].

Libraries and museums

H231 *The Hungarian library law: fundamental principles.* Bp.: OSZK,
Könyvtártudományi és Módszertani Központ, 1979. 58 pp.
Includes the texts of Decree-Law No. 15 of 1976, the decree of the
Council of Ministers on its implementation and Decree No. 5/1978
(XII.12) of the Ministry of Culture.

H232 *Múzeumokra vonatkozó jogszabályok és szabályzatok kézikönyve.*
[Handbook of statutes and rules relating to museums]. Szerk. Kovács
I. Bp.: Népművclési Propaganda Iroda, 1971. 369 pp. [Not seen].

Religion

H233 *The trial of József Mindszenty.* Bp.: Hungarian State Publishing
House, 1949. 191 pp.
A transcript of the trial of Cardinal Mindszenty in 1949 for
treason, espionage, crimes directed at the overthrow of the republic,
and foreign currency speculation.

H234 *Documents on the Mindszenty case.* Bp.: Hungarian State Publishing
House, 1949. 96 pp.
A collection issued by the authorities before the trial, including
Cardinal Mindszenty's 'confession' and the 'many proofs [of his guilt
which the government] has at its disposal'. There are grave doubts
about the authenticity of many of these documents.

H235 *The trial of József Grősz and his accomplices*. Bp.: Hungarian State Publishing House, 1951. 411 pp.

A transcript of the trial in 1951 of the Archbishop of Kalocsa, the leader of the Catholic Church in Hungary after the imprisonment of Cardinal Mindszenty, on charges of 'leading a conspiracy aiming at the overthrow of the democratic state order and other crimes'.

H236 'Church and state in Hungary'. In: *Church and state behind the iron curtain*. Prepared under the general editorship of V. Gsovski. London: Atlantic Press, 1956. Pp. 69–157.

A detailed study of church–state relations in the period 1945–55, including translations of relevant statutes and of the agreements concluded between the churches and the government. Official material on church–state relations must also be sought in the various journals of the churches themselves, such as *Katolikus szó*, 1956–, semi-monthly, and *Új ember*, 1945–, weekly (Roman Catholic), *Református egyház*, 1949–, monthly (Reformed Church), *Evangelikus élet*, 1933–, weekly (Lutheran) and *Új élet*, 1945–, semi-monthly (Jewish). For a collection of statutes on religious affairs in force in 1948 *see* H201.

The media

H237 *A szerzői jog kézikönyve*. [Handbook of copyright law]. Szerk. Bernárd A. és Timár I. Bp.: KJK, 1973. 810 pp.

Contains an introductory section on the history of international and Hungarian copyright legislation and texts, with commentaries, of the relevant statutes, the chief of which is Law No. III of 1969. An English translation of this law was published, with an introductory essay, in *Hungarian law review*, 1969, 2 and 1970, 1, pp. 39–50.

H238 Bak, J. *Magyarország könyvkiadása, 1945–1969: statisztikai alapadatok*. [Hungarian book publishing, 1945–1969: basic statistical data]. Bp.: Magyar Könyvkiadók és Könyvterjesztők Egyesülése, 1970. 202 pp.

H239a *Könyvkiadás*. [Book publishing]. 1962–3, 1965–7, 1969, 1972. (Központi Statisztikai Hivatal). Bp.: Stat. K., 1963–73. Annual.

H239b *Könyvkiadás, könyvárak, időszaki sajtókiadás, 1964*. [Book publishing, book prices, periodical publishing, 1964]. (Központi Statisztikai Hivatal). Bp.: Stat. K., 1965. 81 pp.

H239c *Könyvkiadás, könyvárak, időszaki sajtótermékek, 1968*. (Központi Statisztikai Hivatal). Bp.: Stat. K., 1969. 84 pp.

H239d *Könyvkiadás, könyvárak, készletek és forgalmazás, 1969–1970*. [Book publishing, book prices, stocks and sales, 1969–1970]. (Központi Statisztikai Hivatal). Bp.: Stat K., 1971. 112 pp.

H239e *Könyvek, napilapok és folyóiratok*. [Books, dailies and periodicals]. 1971–. (Központi Statisztikai Hivatal). Bp.: Stat. K., 1972–. Irregular.

A series of statistical publications on publishing, mostly annual, covering the period 1962–.

H240   *A magyar könyvkiadás adatai.* [Data on Hungarian book publishing]. 1971–. Bp.: Magyar Könyvkiadók és Könyvterjesztők Egyesülése, 1972–. Annual. [Not seen].

LEADERS' WORKS

This section lists only works by the four leading political figures of the postwar period, Mátyás Rákosi, Ernő Gerő, Imre Nagy and János Kádár. Publications of other major figures on individual subjects are included in the sections covering those subjects (*see* H124a–b, H145, H221).

Mátyás Rákosi

H241a   Rákosi, M. *A magyar jövőért.* [For the future of Hungary]. 4. kiad. Bp.: Szikra, 1950. 563 pp.
Selected speeches, etc., 1942–May 1945.

H241b   Rákosi, M. *A magyar demokráciáért.* [For Hungarian democracy]. 4. kiad. Bp.: Szikra, 1948. 438 pp.
Selected speeches, etc., February 1945–May 1947.

H241c   Rákosi, M. *A fordulat éve.* [The year of decisive change]. 3. kiad. Bp.: Szikra, 1950. 454 pp.
Selected speeches, etc., May 1947–March 1948.

H241d   Rákosi, M. *Építjük a nép országát.* [We are building the people's country]. Bp.: Szikra, 1949. 511 pp.
Selected speeches, etc., March 1948–April 1949.

H241e   Rákosi, M. *A békéért és a szocializmus építéséért.* [For peace and the building of socialism]. Bp.: Szikra, 1951. 543 pp. [Not seen].

H241f   Rákosi, M. *A szocialista Magyarországért.* [For a socialist Hungary]. 2., bőv. kiad. Bp.: Szikra, 1955. 636 pp.
Selected speeches, etc., April 1951–September 1955.

H241g   Rákosi, M. *Válogatott beszédek és cikkek.* [Selected speeches and articles]. 4., bőv. kiad. Bp.: Szikra, 1955. 631 pp.
Selected speeches, etc., 1941–April 1955. Other editions were published in 1950, 1951 and 1952.

Ernő Gerő

H242a   Gerő, E. *Harcban a szocialista népgazdaságért: válogatott beszédek és cikkek, 1944–1950.* [In the struggle for a socialist economy: selected speeches and articles, 1944–1950]. Bp.: Szikra, 1950. 638 pp.

H242b   Gerő, E. *A vas, az acél, a gépek országáért.* [For a land of iron, steel and machines]. Bp.: Szikra, 1952. 361 pp. [Not seen].
Collections of speeches and articles on political and economic affairs.

Imre Nagy

See also H128.

H243a   Nagy, I. *Egy évtized: válogatott beszédek és írások.* [A decade: selected speeches and writings]. Bp.: Szikra, 1954. 2 v.
Covers the period 1945–54. [Not seen].

H243b   Nagy, I. *Speech by Imre Nagy . . . in the National Assembly on July 4, 1953.* Bp.: Hungarian Bulletin, 1953. 21 pp.
The speech outlining the 'new course' adopted by the Nagy Government of 1953–5.

H243c   Nagy, I. *Imre Nagy on communism: in defence of the new course.* London: Thames & Hudson, 1957. xlvi, 306 pp.
A translation of Nagy's apologia, written in 1955–6 after he had been forced out of office and relieved of his party functions. It is a statement of principles, policies and plans intended to justify the 'new course' of July 1953 and addressed to Nagy's former colleagues on the Central Committee of the Party. The Hungarian original, which was in mimeographed form, was printed as *A magyar nép védelmében* [In defence of the Hungarian people], 1957. The French version, *Un communisme qui n'oublie pas l'homme*, 1957, also contains excerpts from a protest by Nagy to the Central Committee in October 1954 about the sabotage of his policy.

János Kádár

H244a   Kádár, J. *Szilárd népi hatalom: független Magyarország.* [Firm people's power: independent Hungary]. Bp.: Kossuth, 1958. 429 pp.
Selected speeches, etc., January 1957–July 1958.

H244b   Kádár, J. *Socialist construction in Hungary: selected speeches and articles, 1957–1961.* Bp.: Corvina, 1962. 359 pp.

H244c   Kádár, J. *A szocializmus teljes győzelméért.* [For the complete victory of socialism]. Bp.: Kossuth, 1962. 388 pp.
Selected speeches, etc., October 1958–April 1962.

H244d   Kádár, J. *Tovább a lenini úton.* [Further on the Leninist road]. Bp.: Kossuth, 1964. 358 pp.
Selected speeches, etc., October 1958–May 1964.

H244e   Kádár, J. *On the road to socialism: selected speeches and interviews, 1960–1964.* Bp.: Corvina, 1965. 283 pp.

H244f   Kádár, J. *Hazafiság és internacionalizmus.* [Patriotism and internationalism]. Bp.: Kossuth, 1968. 530 pp.
Selected speeches, etc., September 1964–January 1968.

H244g   Kádár, J. *A szocialista Magyarországért.* [For a socialist Hungary]. Bp.: Kossuth, 1972. 547 pp.
Selected speeches, etc., February 1968–April 1972.

H244h   Kádár, J. *For a socialist Hungary: speeches, articles, interviews, 1968–1972.* Bp.: Corvina, 1974. 404 pp.
Translations of a selection of the material published in H244g.

H244i   Kádár, J. *Válogatott beszédek és cikkek, 1957–1973.* [Selected speeches and articles, 1957–1973]. Bp.: Kossuth, 1974. 448 pp.

H244j   Kádár, J. *A fejlett szocialista társadalom építésének útján.* [On the road to the construction of a developed socialist society]. Bp.: Kossuth, 1975. 211 pp.

    Selected speeches, etc., September 1974–June 1975.

H244k   Kádár, J. *Internacionalizmus, szolidaritás, szocialista hazafiság.* [Internationalism, solidarity, socialist patriotism]. Bp.: Kossuth, 1977. 449 pp.

    Selected speeches, etc., on foreign policy and international affairs, March 1957–August 1977.

H244l   Kádár, J. *A szocializmusért, a békéért.* [For socialism, for peace]. Bp.: Kossuth, 1978. 657 pp.

    Selected speeches, etc., November 1972–June 1978.

J YUGOSLAVIA

Garth M. Terry

INTRODUCTION

The origins of the modern Yugoslav state are to be found in a provisional government which Tito and his Partisans established during the war years at Bihać in November 1942 and at Jajce a year later. The government was known as the Antifascist Council of National Liberation of Yugoslavia (Antifašističko Vjeće Narodnog Oslobodjenja Jugoslavije—AVNOJ). It took the decision to establish a new state community of Yugoslavia organized on federal principles. When wartime hostilities ended the Partisans agreed to enlarge their government as a concession to Allied opinion. A new provisional government was nominated on 8 March 1945, consisting of twenty representatives of AVNOJ, three of the royalist government in exile, and five of pre-war political parties. In the following August a new Provisional National Assembly of 318 members, 80 of whom were non-communists, was formed. The main task of the new administration was to prepare for the elections to a Constituent Assembly to be held in November. During this time the country was to be governed under legislation passed by AVNOJ and the Provisional Assembly although, in fact, the day-to-day administration of the country was effectively in the hands of the Yugoslav Communist Party.

Elections for the Constituent Assembly, a bicameral parliament comprising a Federal Council and a Council of Nationalities, were held on 11 November. Voting was on a single list of candidates approved by the People's Front, an 'umbrella organization' formed in August in which those non-communist parties which still existed would collaborate with the communists. There were no effective non-communist candidates and the People's Front gained 90 per cent of the votes. Though much pressure had been used to ensure a majority for Tito there is no doubt that he and the Partisans had considerable genuine support in Yugoslavia. The new assembly first met on 29 November and immediately passed an act abolishing the monarchy and changing the name of the country from the Democratic Federative Yugoslavia (Demokratska Federativna Jugoslavija) to the Federal People's Republic of Yugoslavia—FPRY (Federativna Narodna Republika Jugoslavije—FNRJ). The federation comprised six republics: Bosnia/Hercegovina, Croatia, Macedonia, Montenegro, Slovenia and Serbia, as well as the autonomous province of Vojvodina and the autonomous region of Kosovo-Metohija as part of the Republic of Serbia. A new constitution was approved on 31 January 1946 and the Constituent Assembly then turned itself into the first parliament of the People's Republic.

The 1946 constitution was modelled on Stalin's Soviet constitution of 1936 and led to extreme centralization, both as communist policy and as a means to rapid reconstruction and rehabilitation. Industry was nationalized, collectivization established, and a five-year economic plan introduced. Tito's break with Stalin and the rest of Eastern Europe forced Yugoslavia to evolve new theories and practices of communism in the 1950s and 1960s. This became known as 'Titoism'. The essence of the new position was that each communist country must decide its own 'road to socialism' and exercise independent sovereignty. Other changes included the abandonment of cooperative farms and the return of the peasantry to private farming. The highly centralized state was abandoned. Political, administrative and economic management were decentralized, giving increased powers and responsibility first to the republics and later to the communes into which the republics were divided. Workers' councils were introduced into industry.

These changes were introduced into the new constitutions of 1953 and 1963. The 1953 constitution began the system of self-management as the basis of the entire economic, social and political system of Yugoslavia. The constitution passed on 7 April 1963 enshrined the right of the working people to self-management in a constitution and also changed the name of the country to the Socialist Federal Republic of Yugoslavia—SFRY (Socijalistička Federativna Republika Jugoslavije—SFRJ) comprising six socialist republics and two socialist autonomous provinces. These changes were accompanied by a thorough restructuring of the Yugoslav parliament and government.

Amendments made to the 1963 constitution in 1967, 1968, and especially in 1971, consolidated the leading role of the working class in society, and established new relations between the federation and the constituent republics and provinces on the basis of full equality. These amendments led to the constitutional reform which was completed with the new constitution being accepted on 21 February 1974 and was succeeded by the proclamation of respective constitutions for the socialist republics and autonomous provinces.

According to the 1974 constitution the basis of the social and political system is social ownership of the means of production and social self-government by the citizenry in the processes of production and distribution of the national income. Self-government is exercised through economic organizations and social communities—communes, districts, republics, and the federation itself. The Assembly of the SFRY (formerly Federal Assembly) is the highest organ of government and has two chambers: the Federal Chamber (composed of delegates from self-managing enterprises and communities in the republics and provinces) and the Chamber of the Republics and Provinces (composed of delegates from the republican and provincial assemblies). The Federal Executive Council is the executive body of the Assembly on which each republic and province (the latter to a lesser extent) is represented equally. Executive power is vested in the sixteen-man Presidency of the SFRY. It can promulgate federal laws; it is the supreme body in charge of the administration and command of the armed forces; it considers major matters relating to foreign policy, state security and civil defence. The Presidency elects a President of the Federal Republic, a post to which Tito was elected for an unlimited period in 1974.

With the death of Tito in May 1980, however, the office of President of the Republic ceased to exist. The Macedonian Lazar Koliševski as Vice-President of the State Presidency had taken over the reins during Tito's long illness. According to the complicated standing rules of the State Presidency which rotates the offices of president and vice-president every year, the Serb Cvijetin Mijatović was elected President on 4 May 1980, with the Slovene Sergej Kraigher as Vice-President.

At local government level, the commune (opština) is the basic self-managed sociopolitical community. The 500 commune assemblies are the basic governing units in Yugoslavia. They consist of a Chamber of Work Communities (delegates from the working population), a Chamber of Local Communities (delegates from workers and non-workers residing in organized local communities), and a Sociopolitical Chamber (delegates of sociopolitical organizations). The commune assembly elects an executive body which assumes administrative functions for the community.

The judicial system of the SFRY consists of courts of general jurisdiction, i.e. communal courts, district courts, republican and autonomous provincial supreme courts (the latter decide on appeals against the decisions of country courts), and the federal supreme court. Economic cases are brought before the Supreme Economic Arbitration Court or its republican equivalent. There is also a Constitutional Court of Yugoslavia which decides whether particular laws are in accord with the constitution and hears disputes between the federation and the republics. Constitutional courts also exist at republican and provincial level.

The First Congress of the Socialist Workers' Party of Yugoslavia/Communists (Socijalistička Radnička Partija Jugoslavije/Komunista) was held in 1919 in Belgrade. A year later at its Second Congress in Vukovar the Party changed its name to the Communist Party of Yugoslavia—CPY (Komunistička Partija Jugoslavije—KPJ), a name which it kept until the Sixth Congress in 1952 when it adopted its present title, the League of Communists of Yugoslavia—LCY (Savez Komunista Jugoslavije—SKJ). The leading figures in the LCY after the seizure of power were: Milovan Djilas (originally one of the four top-ranking Yugoslav party and government officials, he has fallen into disgrace and has spent several periods in prison from the 1950s onwards for publishing some of his works in which he criticized the very Yugoslav social order he had helped create); Boris Kidrič (a leading Slovenian communist who attained high political office at both republican and federal level; he died in 1953); Edvard Kardelj (another Slovenian who was a leading party ideologist and occupied top posts in the party and government hierarchy; he was regarded as Tito's second-in-command until his death in

February 1979); and Lazar Koliševski (the leading Macedonian communist; first Prime Minister of the Macedonian Republic, 1945; President of the Macedonian National Assembly, 1953; member of the Presidium of the LCY, 1964; member of the Presidency of the SFRY, 1972).

The most important and influential figure by far in postwar Yugoslavia, however, has been that of Josip Broz Tito. In 1937 he became Secretary-General of the CPY and led the general people's uprising and revolution in occupied Yugoslavia. As undisputed head of the Yugoslav people after the war he held the most responsible posts in the country: Prime Minister, 1945–53; President of the Republic from 1953, a post to which he was elected for life in 1974; Supreme Commander of the Armed Forces, 1953–80; President (formerly Secretary-General) of the LCY, 1937–80. Despite such crises as the Soviet–Yugoslav dispute of 1948, the Djilas affair in the 1950s and 1960s, and the purge of the Croatian Communist Party in 1971, Tito's position was never really seriously threatened or undermined. With his death on 4 May 1980, an era in postwar Yugoslav politics came to a close.

The LCY is organized on the principle of democratic centralism. It is a highly structured hierarchical organization. Its basic units are set up in industry and other self-managing and work organizations in local communities, villages, the army, etc. Its vertical structure progresses from the commune, through the district, the province, and the six socialist republics, to the level of the SFRY. The highest organ is the party congress which is convened every four years. In the interval between congresses, the LCY is run by a Central Committee—CC—which elects a twenty-three-member Presidium (Executive Bureau, 1969–74). In October 1978 the position of Chairman of the CC Presidium was created and the person who holds it (on a one-year rotating basis) deputized for Tito as the President of this body in his absence.

Unlike the position of President of the Republic which died with Tito and has been replaced by the collective leadership of the State Presidency, a new President of the LCY would have to be elected if both the party statutes (articles 72–4) and the standing rules of the CC Presidium (articles 12–15) were followed. According to a seven-point resolution arrived at at the eleventh plenary session of the LCY CC on 12 June 1980, there will be no new party president until the Twelfth Party Congress meets in 1982. Instead, the Chairman of the CC Presidium is to be renamed President of the CC Presidium and will hold the office for a one-year term.

The LCY is still the most powerful and privileged body in Yugoslavia today. No opposition was allowed to be institutionalized, although it could be expressed as long as it did not challenge the basic principles on which the state was founded. But through local government, self-management in all work places, and the participation of a high proportion of people in some form of executive government, the Yugoslavs enjoy more freedom and a greater share in government than exist in other communist countries.

In matters of foreign policy, Yugoslavia has attempted to steer a course independent of both East and West. Yugoslavia's relations *vis-à-vis* the Soviet Union and her East European satellites have constantly ebbed and flowed. In 1948 after a deterioration in Soviet–Yugoslav relations, Stalin expelled the CPY from the Cominform and Yugoslavia became isolated from the communist world. Stalin's death and Khrushchev's visit to Belgrade in 1955 marked a cautious *rapprochement* but by the end of the 1950s relations had once again turned cool. Thereafter Yugoslavia's relations with the Soviet Union fluctuated between friendship and enmity, never reaching extremes of either. On a number of world issues Yugoslavia's foreign policy was basically the same as that of the Soviet Union, e.g. her policy toward the Vietnam war and the Arab–Israeli problem; and although Yugoslavia has refused to join the Warsaw Pact or Comecon, she did sign a cooperative agreement with Comecon in 1964. On the other hand—typical of Tito's policy—Yugoslavia has joined GATT and has shown interest in both the OECD and the EEC. Yugoslavia's relations with her close neighbour, Bulgaria, have likewise been troublesome, due, in the main, to the seemingly insoluble and vexing question of Macedonia (see the chapter on Bulgaria for more details). It has been suggested in some circles that with Tito's death, the Bulgarians may stir up the Macedonian issue to provide a pretext for Soviet intervention in Yugoslavia.

A unique feature of Yugoslavia's international relations is Tito's policy of nonalignment. It aims to develop friendly relations with small, weak, or noncommitted powers to increase their joint influence in a superpower-dominated world. The first two conferences of nonaligned nations were organized by Yugoslavia in Belgrade (1961) and Cairo (1964). It is debatable whether the nonalignment movement has had any real success in terms of world influence but it has won friends for Yugoslavia and eased her position between the Soviet bloc and the West.

Publishing

The book trade in Yugoslavia was already being organized in 1918 but from 1945 this matter was dealt with systematically. Today the publishing organizations existing in the individual republics are coordinated through the Association of Yugoslav Publishers and Booksellers (Poslovna Zajednica Izdavača i Knjižara Jugoslavije). In all there are sixty-three publishing houses in the six republics registered with the Poslovna Zajednica. Outside this association there are numerous enterprises and organizations concerned with publishing and, since private persons also have the right to publish their own works themselves, it is estimated that about 50 per cent of the published books in Yugoslavia are published outside the sixty-three registered publishing houses. The Yugoslav publishing trade enjoys a greater amount of freedom than do its Eastern European counterparts and this has enabled it to establish a position of some independence and individuality. The League of Yugoslav Communists can, nevertheless, still exercise political control, a point well illustrated by a ban on the works of Milovan Djilas.

Book production has steadily risen in Yugoslavia from just over 3,000 titles published in 1948 to over 10,000 in 1973 (in 52.8 million copies) of which 3,882 were in the social science field. With regard to such statistics, however, one must always bear in mind that a large proportion of Yugoslav works are translated and published in all languages of the Yugoslav peoples and national minorities and in both variants and both scripts of the Serbo–Croatian language. Bibliographical coverage of Yugoslav book and periodical output is maintained through the

Yugoslav Bibliographical Institute's *Bibliografija Jugoslavije* (*see* J1 and J5). A separate publication, *Bibliografija zvaničnih publikacija SFRJ*, covers Yugoslav official publications (*see* J11).

GENERAL BIBLIOGRAPHIES AND REFERENCE WORKS

National bibliographies

Federal

J1   *Bibliografija Jugoslavije: knjige, brošure i muzikalije.* [Bibliography of Yugoslavia: books, pamphlets and music]. B.: Jugoslovenski bibliografski institut, 1950–. Semi-monthly.
Continued from *Jugoslovenska bibliografija.* [Yugoslav bibliography]. B.: Izd. Direkcije za informacije vlade FNRJ, 1949–51, which was published annually covering the period 1945 to 1949 with a total of five volumes. A comprehensive and systematic national bibliography listing monographs currently published in the territory of Yugoslavia. Entries are arranged by subject according to a Yugoslav variant of the UDC system. Cumulated author and subject indexes are published annually. Since 1974 Yugoslav official publications have been listed in the separate publication *Bibliografija zvaničnih publikacija SFRJ* (*see* J11) although a large amount of this material still appears in the above bibliography.

J2   *Jugoslovenska retrospektivna bibliografska gradja: knjige, brošure i muzikalije, 1945–1967.* [Yugoslav retrospective bibliography: books, pamphlets and music, 1945–1967]. B.: Jugoslovenski bibliografski institut, 1969–71. 21 vols.
A major contribution to national bibliography in that it lists in a single sequence with a span of 23 years the national output of a major European country. Vol. 5 (727 pp.) is of particular interest since it covers the proceedings of the federal and republican legislatures, collections of laws, individual laws, etc. A weakness is the lack of indexes.

J3   *Katalog knjiga na jezicima jugoslovenskih naroda, 1868–1972.* [Catalogue of books in the languages of the Yugoslav peoples, 1868–1972]. Chief ed. V. Stevanović. B.: Narodna biblioteka SR Srbije, 1975–.
Covers books, pamphlets, collections, etc., published in the territories which now form present-day Yugoslavia. Arrangement is alphabetical by author or title. Official publications are covered. The latest volume to be published is 7, Mal–Mun (1980).

J4   *Bibliografija jugoslovenskih bibliografija, 1945–1955.* [Bibliography of Yugoslav bibliographies, 1945–1955]. B.: Bibliografski institut FNRJ, 1958. 270 pp. .... *1956–1960.* B.: 1975. 295 pp.
Contains only partial coverage of official publications.

J5 *Bibliografija Jugoslavije: serijske publikacije.* [Bibliography of Yugoslavia: serial publications]. B.: Jugoslovenski bibliografski institut, 1975–. Quarterly.

Formerly called *Bibliografija jugoslovenske periodike* [Bibliography of Yugoslav periodicals]. B.: 1956–74. An alphabetical listing, with bibliographic data, of periodicals and newspapers of all kinds published in Yugoslavia.

J6 *Bibliografija Jugoslavije: članci i književni prilozi u časopisima.* [Bibliography of Yugoslavia: articles and literary contributions in periodicals]. B.: Jugoslovenski bibliografski institut, 1950–. Monthly.

Since 1952, this work has been issued in three series: A. *Društvene nauke* [Social sciences]; B. *Prirodne i primenjene nauke* [Natural and applied sciences]; C. *Filologija, umetnost, šport, književnost, muzikalije* [Philology, art, sport, literature, musical scores]. Arrangement is by UDC with annual author and subject indexes. Official publications are partially covered.

Republican

In addition to the above national bibliographies, the republics of Slovenia and Macedonia each issue their own national bibliography.

J7 *Slovenska bibliografija.* [Slovene bibliography]. Lj.: Narodna in univerzitetna knjižnica, 1947–.

An annual bibliography of Slovenian monographs, periodicals, and periodical articles. Complete coverage of Slovenian-language imprints in Yugoslavia and partial coverage of Slovenian imprints outside Yugoslavia.

J8 Bulovec, Š. *Bibliografija slovenskih bibliografij, 1561–1973.* [Bibliography of Slovene bibliographies, 1561–1973]. Lj.: Narodna in univerzitetna knjižnica, 1976. 229 pp.

J9 *Makedonska bibliografija.* [Macedonian bibliography]. Sk.: Narodna i univerzitetska biblioteka, 1951–. Annual.

An annual bibliography—although the first volume covers the years 1945–9—which is divided into two parts, monographs and periodical articles.

J10 *Kumulativna makedonska bibliografija, 1944–1969.* [Cumulative Macedonian bibliography, 1944–1969]. Chief ed. I. Katardžiev. Sk.: Narodna i univerzitetska biblioteka, 1976. 12 vols.

A retrospective index listing in a single sequence with a span of 25 years the monograph output of the Republic of Macedonia. Vol. 2 is of particular interest since it covers the proceedings of the Macedonian legislature, collections of laws, etc.

Other general bibliographies
and reference works

J11   *Bibliografija zvaničnih publikacija SFRJ; Bibliografija na oficijalnite publikacii na SFRJ; Bibliografija uradnih publikacij: knjige—knigi, periodika.* [Bibliography of official publications of the SFRY: books, periodicals]. B.: Jugoslovenski bibliografski institut, 1974–. Annual.

    A recent publication by the Yugoslav Bibliographical Institute which lists books and periodicals of a statistical nature, the official gazettes, the stenographic records of the federal and republican parliaments, reports of republican, regional and local government organs, university and school reports, etc. Part of this material is still contained in the Yugoslav national bibliography (J1 and J5). The first volume, published in 1974, covers the year 1971 and contains 806 entries (42 pp.).

J12   *Südosteuropa-Bibliographie.* München: Oldenbourg, 1956–.

    Provides a five-year bibliographic survey of monographs and journals published in or relating to Eastern Europe. Five volumes have been published to date as follows: vol. 1 (1959), 1945–50 (pt. 2 covers Yugoslavia); vol. 2 (1960), 1951–5 (pt. 1 covers Yugoslavia); vol. 3 (1968), 1956–60 (pt. 2, pp. 201–529); vol. 4 (1973), 1961–5 (pt. 2, pp. 245–595); vol. 5 (1976), 1966–70 (pt. 2, pp. 361–731). Other western bibliographies with sections on Yugoslav politics, law and the state are: Petrovich, M. B. *Yugoslavia: a bibliographic guide.* Washington: Library of Congress, 1974. 270 pp.; *Bibliography of social science periodicals and monograph series: Yugoslavia, 1945–1963.* (Foreign social science bibliographies, Series P-92, No. 18). Washington: U.S. Bureau of the Census, 1965. 152 pp.; Horecky, P. L. 'Yugoslavia'. In his *Southeastern Europe: a guide to basic publications.* Chicago: Chicago U.P., 1969, pp. 451–641; Terry, G. M. *Yugoslav studies: an annotated list of basic bibliographies and reference works.* Twickenham: A. C. Hall, 1977. 89 pp.

J13   Blagojević, B. T. *Bibliographie du droit yougoslave, 1945–1967.* 11th ed. Paris: Mouton, 1970. 155 pp.

    Unannotated bibliography of 1,727 books and articles on Yugoslav law classified under 19 headings. Each section has a short introductory note. It is a bibliography of legal writings and not sources of law.

J14   Gjupanovich, F. & Adamovitch, A. *Legal sources and bibliography of Yugoslavia.* General ed. V. Gsovski. (Praeger publications in Russian history and world communism, 21). N.Y.: Praeger, 1964. 353 pp.

    Lists a total of 2,467 legal writings and sources of law arranged under 12 headings. Each section is prefaced by a short introduction. Author, title and subject indexes. A useful section on pp. 289–306 lists individual laws of primary importance in the period 1943–62.

J15 *Südosteuropa-Handbuch. Band I: Jugoslawien.* Ed. K.-D. Grothusen. Göttingen: Vandenhoeck & Ruprecht, 1975. Pp. 465–526.

This handbook has a section listing members in the supreme organs of party and state at both federal and republican level, a calendar of the main political and historical events for the period 1954–74, a list of treaties and conventions concluded with foreign countries, biobibliographical notes on leading Yugoslav political figures as of June 1974. Further biographical information may be sought in: *Directory of Yugoslav officials.* Washington: CIA, 1972. 297 pp.; *Enciklopedija Jugoslavije.* [Yugoslav encyclopedia]. Chief ed. M. Krleža. Z.: Izd. Leksikografskog zavoda, 1955–71. 8 vols.; 2nd ed., 1980–. (Only the first volume, A–Biz, so far published); *Jugoslovenski savremenici: ko je ko u Jugoslaviji.* [Yugoslav contemporaries: who's who in Yugoslavia]. B.: Hronometar, 1970. 1208 pp. Radio Free Europe also publishes on an annual basis a list of top figures in the communist parties and governments of Eastern Europe.

J16 *Imenik mesta u Jugoslavije. Opštine u SFRJ. Opštine po republikama i pokrajinama. Opštine u SFRJ, sa teritorijalno nadležnim sudovima i tužilaštvima. Naseljena mesta, sa opštinama i nadležnim poštama. Registar pošta u SFRJ, sa karakterističnim poštanskim brojevima. Stanje 30. novembra 1972.* [Directory of places in Yugoslavia]. Comp. by B. Djordjević and B. Vašić. B.: Službeni list SFRJ, 1973. 473 pp. [Not seen].

CONSTITUTIONAL DOCUMENTS

Since the foundation of modern Yugoslavia in 1945, there have been no less than four constitutions: in 1946, 1953, 1963 and, most recently, in 1974.

J17 *Ustav Federativne Narodne Republike Jugoslavije.* [Constitution of the FPRY]. B.: Izd. Službenog lista FNRJ, 1950. 50 pp.

Text of the 1946 constitution which was closely modelled on the 1936 Soviet constitution. A translation with the above title was published by the Yugoslav Embassy Information Office in London in 1946 (24 pp.).

J18 *Novi ustav; ustavni zakon od 13.1.1953 i ustav od 31.1.1946 (delovi koji nisu ukinuti).* [New constitution; the constitutional law of 13.1.1953 and the constitution of 31.1.1946 (the parts which were not revoked)]. B.: Službeni list FNRJ, 1953. 135 pp. [Not seen].

An English translation of the 1953 constitution is available: *The constitution of the Federal People's Republic of Yugoslavia.* Trans. by B. P. Ljotić. B.: Union of Jurists' Associations of Yugoslavia, 1960. 156 pp.

J19 *Ustav Socijalističke Federativne Republike Jugoslavije.* [Constitution of the SFRY. (Zbirka saveznih propisa, 12). B.: Službeni list SFRJ, 1964. 158 pp.

Also contains the official report on the constitution by E. Kardelj in his capacity as president of the Commission for Constitutional Questions, and the text of the laws relating to the promulgation of the constitution and to the organization and functions of the Federal Executive Council and the Supreme Court. An English translation is available: *Constitution of the Socialist Federal Republic of Yugoslavia.* Ed. by B. T. Blagojević. Trans. by P. Mijušković. (Collection of Yugoslav laws, 7). B.: Sekretarijat saveznog izvršenog veća za informacije, 1963. 91 pp. An explanation of the constitution is provided in the brochure *The constitutional system of the Socialist Federative Republic of Yugoslavia.* B.: Review of International Affairs, 1963. 63 pp.

J20 *Ustav Socijalističke Federativne Republike Jugoslavije i Ustavni amandmani I–VI, Ustavni amandmani VII–XIX, Ustavni amandmani XX–XLII.* [Constitution of the SFRY and constitutional amendments I–VI, VII–XIX, and XX–XLII]. Prepared by M. Josipović. B.: Književne novine, 1971. 180 pp.

Contains the text of the 1963 constitution and the constitutional amendments adopted between the 1963 and 1974 constitutions. For an English translation see *Constitutional amendments XX–XLII.* Ed. in chief D. Djurović. (Federal Assembly series). B.: Secretariat of Information of the Federal Executive Council, 1971. 72 pp. [Not seen].

J21 *Ustav Socijalističke Federativne Republike Jugoslavije. Ustavni zakon za sprovodjenje Ustava SFRJ.* [Constitution of the SFRY. Constitutional law for putting into effect the constitution of the SFRY]. Prepared by D. Marinković. B.: Savremena administracija, 1974. 296 pp.

An English translation is available: *The constitution of the Socialist Federative Republic of Yugoslavia.* B.: Dopisna delavska univerza, 1974. 310 pp. For a commentary to the new constitution, see Kulić, D. *Ustav SFRJ: komentar.* [Constitution of the SFRY: a commentary]. B.: Privredna štampa, 1979. 495 pp.

J22 *Ustav SFRJ, ustavi socijalističkih republika i pokrajina, ustavni zakoni, registar pojmova.* [Constitution of the SFRY, constitution of the socialist republics and regions, constitutional laws, index of notions]. Ed. Z. Sofronić. B.: Prosveta, 1974. 917 pp.

In addition to the federal constitution, each of the republics and regions has its own constitution closely modelled on the federal version. The 1946, 1953 and 1964 republican and regional constitutions cannot be listed for reasons of space, but the above work collects in a single volume the 1974 federal, republican and regional constitutions.

J23 *Odluke i mišlenja Ustavnog suda Jugoslavije.* [Decisions and opinions of the Constitutional Court of Yugoslavia]. B.: Ustavni sud Jugoslavije, 1972–. Annual.

Formerly called *Saopštenja ustavnih sudova.* [Reports of the constitutional courts]. B.: Službeni list SFRJ, 1966–71. Quarterly. Covers the decisions of the federal and republican constitutional courts. Editions are also published in Slovenian and Macedonian.

J24 *Zbirka na odluki i rešenija, 1964–1972: ustaven sud na Makedonija.* [Collection of decisions and judgements: constitutional court of Macedonia]. Ed. by Stojčev et al. Sk.: Služben vesnik na SRM, 1973. Vol. 1. 328 pp. [Not seen].

J25 *Constitutional judicature.* Trans. by B. P. Ljotić. (Collection of Yugoslav laws, 14). B.: Institute of Comparative Law, 1966. 70 pp.

Commentary on Yugoslav constitutional law with a guide to the rules of the constitutional court.

GENERAL LAW COLLECTIONS AND LAW CODES

Bibliographies and indexes

J26 Bauer, I. and Gajinov, M. *Registar važećih saveznih propisa od 1945. do 31. decembra 1979. godina.* [Index of current federal regulations, 1945–31 December 1979]. B.: Službeni list SFRJ, 1980. 395 pp. [Not seen].

J27 *Informatorov registar saveznih, republičkih i pokrajinskih važećih propisa. Stanje 31.III.1974.* [Informator's index of federal, republican and regional regulations in force as of 31.3.1974]. Prepared by M. Dajčić et al. (Informatorov priručnik za kadrove). Z.: Informator, 1974. 978 pp.

Supersedes earlier compilations. The main body of the work consists of laws arranged under 20 basic groups ranging from the constitution to education and culture. Laws are listed under these in a federal, republican and regional sequence. There is also an alphabetical subject index.

J28 Mihelčić, S. *Splošni register veljavnih predpisov (zveznih in republiških), 1945–1968.* [General index to current regulations (federal and republican), 1945–1968]. Lj.: Uradni list SR Slovenije, 1969. 442 pp.

A subject arranged index to laws still in force as published in the *Službeni list SFRJ* and the *Uradni list SRS* in the years 1945 to the end of 1968. A three-year supplement has been published: ... *1969–1970–1971.* Lj.: 1972. 488 pp.

J29 Lopičić, Dj. and Memedović, N. *Bibliografija krivičnog prava*

Jugoslavije, 1851–1975. [Bibliography of Yugoslav criminal law, 1851–1975]. B.: Niro Eksport Press, 1979. 415 pp. [Not seen].

J30 *Registar sudskih odluka, objavljenih u knjigama I–XV Zbirke sudskih odluka, 1956–1970.* [Index to court decisions published in volumes I–XV of the Collection of court decisions, 1956–1970]. Ed. by M. Perović. B.: Službeni list SFRJ, 1973. 1340 pp.

J31 Toplak, L. *The Yugoslav legal system.* Lj.: Gospodarska založba, 1978. 247 pp.
Yugoslav law directory for foreign lawyers and businessmen.

J32 *Pravni leksikon.* [Legal dictionary]. Ed. by B. Blagojević. 2nd rev. and enl. ed. B.: Savremena administracija, 1970. 1376 pp.

J33 *Veliki pravni priručnik: jugoslovenski pravni sistem.* [The great legal handbook: the Yugoslav legal system]. B.: Privredni pregled, 1977. 2 vols. 1205, 1418 pp. [Not seen].

Collections and codes

J34 *Zbirka saveznih propisa.* [Collection of federal regulations]. Vols. 111–. B.: Službeni list SFRJ, 1954–.
Formerly titled *Zbirka zakona FNRJ.* [Collection of laws of the FPRY]. B.: 1947–54. Vols. 1–110. A monograph series with individual volumes devoted to particular laws on a subject.

J35 *Zbornik propisa Socijalističke [formerly Narodne] Republike Srbije.* B.: Savremena administracija, 1955–.
Each of the first five volumes is devoted to Serbian laws in a particular field for the period 1945–55. From vol. 6 onwards, each volume covers the laws passed in that year, e.g. vol. 25 covers the period 1 January–31 December 1977. Vol. 13 onwards bears an additional series number, e.g. vol. 13, New Series 1, etc.

J36 *Collection of Yugoslav laws.* Vol. 1–. B.: Institute of Comparative Law, 1962–.
A monograph series issued irregularly containing English translations of Yugoslav legislation. 24 volumes have so far appeared, many of which are listed under the relevant subject heading in the bibliography.

J37 *Krivični zakonik i Zakonik o krivičnom postupku, sa uvodnim zakonima i registrima pojmova.* [Criminal code and Code of criminal procedure with introductory laws and registers of notions]. B.: Savremena administracija, 1974. 11th rev. and enl. ed. 379 pp.
For a detailed commentary to the code, see *Komentar Krivičnog zakona Socijalističke Federativne Republike Jugoslavije.* Comp. by F. Fačić et al. B.: Savremena administracija, 1978. 813 pp. [Not seen]. A translation of the criminal code is available in the series *Collection of Yugoslav laws* (J36), no. 11, 1964, 163 pp.

J38 *Pravila gradjanskih zakonika, s naknadnim propisima, sudskom prak-som, napomenama i podacima iz literature.* [Regulations of the civil code, with supplementary regulations, court practice, remarks and datum from literature]. Ed. M. Vuhović. Z.: Školska knjiga, 1961. CXXXII, 1182 pp. [Not seen].

One of the most complete Yugoslav sources on civil law. It was published as a textbook for the University of Zagreb. For the law on civil procedure, see *Zakon o parničnom postupku: od 24.XII.1976: s napomenama i bilješkama.* [Law of legal proceedings as of 24.12.1976, with remarks and notes]. Ed. by S. Triva. (Zbirka pravnih propisa, 124). Z.: Narodne novine, 1977. 8th rev. and enl. ed. 705 pp.

Courts and legal profession

J39 *Zbirka odluka vrhovnih sudova i uputstava Vrhovnog suda FNRJ 1945–1954.* [Collection of decisions of the supreme courts and decisions of the Supreme Court of the FPRY]. B.: Arhiv za pravne i društvene nauke, 1952–54. 2 vols.

J40 *Zbirka odluka Državne arbitraže.* [Collection of decisions of Government Arbitration Boards]. B.: Službeni list FNRJ, 1949–54. 7 vols.

J41 *Zbirka odluka privrednih sudova.* [Collection of the decisions of the economic courts]. B.: Savremena administracija, 1956. 123 pp. [Not seen].

J42 *Zbirka sudskih odluka.* [Collection of court decisions]. B.: Službeni list SFRJ, 1956–.

From 1956 to 1967 (vols. 1–12) three parts were published per year; from 1968 onwards (vol. 13–) four parts were published. The text is in Croatian, Macedonian, Serbian and Slovene. It covers the decisions of the supreme, supreme military, and supreme economic courts. For an index to vols. 1–15, *see* J30.

J43 *Zbirka na sudski odluki: Vrhoven sud na Makedonija.* [Collection of court decisions: the Supreme Court of Macedonia]. Ed. by Lj. Bosilkov et al. Sk.: Služben vesnik na SRM, 1976. 542 pp. [Not seen].

J44 *Jugoslovenska advokatura.* [Yugoslav legal profession]. B.: Savez advokatskih komora Jugoslavije, 1954–75. Quarterly.

Contains articles on the interpretation of all aspects of Yugoslav law, court decisions, and practice of law.

J45 *New Yugoslav law.* B.: Union of Jurists' Associations of Yugoslavia, 1950–. Quarterly.

In addition to containing articles on legal topics, this periodical lists current documentation and quotes selections from the new laws, decisions, resolutions, etc., which have recently appeared in *Službeni list*. It is also issued in French.

OTHER LEGISLATIVE DOCUMENTS

Bibliographies and indexes

J46 Nešović, S. *Stvarni registar stenografskih beležaka vrhovnih pret-stavničkih tel Jugoslavije od 26.XI.1942 do 21.XII.1957: AVNOJ, Privremena Narodna Skupština DFJ, Ustavotvorna Skupština, Narodna Skupština SFRJ, I i II saviz, i Savezna Narodna Skupština, III saviz.* [Index to the stenographic records of the supreme representative bodies of Yugoslavia, 26.11.1942–21.12.1957: AVNOJ, Provisional National Assembly of Democratic Federative Yugoslavia, Constituent Assembly, National Assembly of the FPRY, I and II sessions, and Federal National Assembly, III session]. B.: Savezna Narodna Skupština, 1961. 1316 pp. [Not seen].

J47 *Registar pravnih propisa objavljenih u 'Službenom listu SFRJ', 1945–1977.* [Index to the legal regulations announced in the 'Official gazette of the SFRY', 1945–1977]. Comp. by M. Plazinić. B.: Službeni list SFRJ, 1978. 766 pp.

From 1945 to 1955 it appeared under the title *Registar saveznih propisa* ... [Index to federal regulations ...]. This index has been appearing usually every two years since 1945. Each volume is cumulative from that year. Laws, etc., are arranged under 23 broad subject headings with further subdivisions in each. Similar indexes are published for the republican gazettes:

Bosnia/Hercegovina—*Registar republičkih propisa objavljenih u 'Službenom listu SRBiH' 1945. do jula 1965.* [Index to republican regulations announced in the 'Official gazette of the SRB/H', 1945–July 1965]. Comp. by D. Ivanišević et al. Sarajevo: Službeni list SRBiH, 1965. 371 pp. [Not seen].

Croatia—*Registar pravnih propisa objavljenih u 'Narodnim novinama', 1945–1959.* [Index to legal regulations announced in the 'Official gazette of the SR of Croatia', 1945–1959]. Comp. by Z. Ivanković. Z.: Narodne novine, 1960. 567 pp. [Not seen].

Macedonia—*Registar na republički propisi, 1945–1971.* [Index to republican regulations, 1945–1971]. Comp. by Lj. Šukarova. Sk.: Služben vesnik na SRM, 1972. 252 pp. This supersedes earlier volumes covering 1945–60 and 1961–6 published in 1961 and 1967 respectively.

Montenegro—*Registar pravnih propisa objavljenih u 'Službenom listu SRCG', 1945–1974.* [Index to legal regulations announced in the 'Official gazette of the SRM', 1945–1974]. Titograd: Sekretarijat za zakonodavstvo, 1974. 244 pp. [Not seen].

Serbia—*Registar propisa objavljenih u 'Službenom glasniku SRS', 1945–1970.* [Index to regulations announced in the 'Official gazette of the SRS', 1945–1970]. Comp. by I. Kitarović. B.: Republički zavod za javnu upravu, 1971. 392 pp. [Not seen].

Slovenia—*Registar republiških predpisov 1945–1962, 1963.* [Index to republican regulations, 1945–1962, 1963]. Lj.: Uradni list SRS, 1963–4. 2 vols. 585, 104 pp. [Not seen].

Vojvodina—*Registar propisa objavljenih u 'Službenom listu Socijalističke Autonomne Pokrajine Vojvodine'*, *1969–1977*. [Index to regulations announced in the 'Official gazette of the Socialist Autonomous Region of Vojvodina', 1969–1977]. Main ed. J. Grnja. N.S.: Službeni list SAPV, 1978. 199 pp. [Not seen].

Indexes to the official gazettes of cities and towns are also published, e.g. *Registar propisa grada Beograda*. [Index to regulations of the city of Belgrade]. B.: Kulturen centar, 1978. 211 pp. [Not seen].

Parliamentary proceedings

J48   *Prvo i drugo zasedanje veća (26 i 27 novembra 1942, 29 i 30 novembra 1943): po stenografskim beleškama i drugim izvorima.* [First and second sessions of the Council (26 and 27 November 1942, 29 and 30 November 1943): based on the stenographic records and other sources]. General ed. M. Pijade. B.: Prezidijum Skupštine FNRJ, 1953. 332 pp.

Proceedings of the revolutionary parliaments held by the communists at Bihać and Jajce respectively during the Second World War.

J49   *Treće zasedanje Antifašističkog veća narodnog oslobodjenja Jugoslavije i zasedanje Privremene Narodne Skupštine 7–26 avgust 1945: stenografske beleške.* [The third session of the Anti-Fascist Council of National Liberation of Yugoslavia and the session of the Provisional National Assembly, 7–26 August 1945: stenographic record]. B.: 1945. 708 pp.

Similar records are available for the republican counterparts of AVNOJ: Zemaljsko antifašističko vijeće narodnog oslobodjenja Bosne i Hercegovine (ZAVNOBiH), Zemaljsko antifašističko vijeće narodnog oslobodjenja Hrvatske (ZAVNOH), Antifašističkoto sobranie na narodnoto osloboduvanje na Makedonija (ASNOM), Osvobodilna fronta Slovenije. There was no such body for Serbia.

J50   *Zasedanje Ustavotvorne Skupštine, 29 nov. 1945–1 febr. 1946 godine: stenografske beleške.* [Session of the Constituent Assembly, 29 Nov. 1945–1 Febr. 1946: stenographic record]. B.: Izd. Prezidijuma Narodne Skupštine FNRJ, 1948. 992 pp. [Not seen].

J51   *Stenografske beleške. Skupština SFRJ.* [Stenographic record. Assembly of the SFRY]. B.: Služba za dokumentaciju Skupštine SFRJ, 1946–. Irregular.

Provides a comprehensive record to the proceedings of the Federal Assembly. From 1 February to 29 November 1945, it was known as *Stenografske beleške. Narodna Skupština Demokratske Federativne Jugoslavije*. The title has varied since according to the name of the Yugoslav parliament at that time: Narodna/Savezna narodna/Savezna skupština. From 31 January 1946 to 10 September 1953, it was issued in two series each numbered separately: *redovno* and *vanredno zasedanje* (regular and extraordinary session). Complete details of the Assembly's sessions may be found in vol. 5 of J2. Similar records are published for the legislative assemblies of the republics: Bosnia/Hercegovina—*Stenografske belješke.* Sarajevo: 1946–; Croatia—*Stenografski zapisnici.* Z.: 1943–; Macedonia—*Stenografski beleški.* Sk.: 1946–; Montenegro—*Stenografske bilješke.* Cetinje: 1946–; Serbia—*Stenografske beleške.* B.: 1944–; Slovenia—*Sejni zapiski* or, as it was occasionally called, *Stenografski zapiski.* Lj.: 1947–; Vojvodina—*Stenografski zapisnici.* N.S.: 1947–.

J52 *Poslovnik Skupštine SFRJ i poslovnici vijeća.* [Procedure of the Assembly of the SFRY and procedures of the chambers]. Ed. by D. Djurović. B.: Sekretarijat za informacije Skupštine SFRJ, 1975. 211 pp.

Covers rules and procedures in the Yugoslav parliament. Similar 'poslovniki' are published for the republican parliaments.

Official gazettes

J53 *Službeni list SFRJ.* [Official gazette of the SFRY]. B.: 1945–. Irregular.

First published in 1918 as *Službene novine;* from 1945 to 1953 entitled *Službeni list FNRJ.* Official gazette of the federal government containing texts of laws, decrees, regulations and executive orders issued by the federal government; official notices of government business; reviews of the laws of the republics. Since 1953 the texts of Yugoslavia's international agreements and treaties are published in a special supplement. Each of the republics have their own official gazettes:
Bosnia/Hercegovina—*Službeni list Socijalističke Republike Bosne i Hercegovine.* Sarajevo: 1944–.
Croatia—*Narodne novine: službeni list Socijalističke Republike Hrvatske.* Z.: 1945–.
Kosovo-Metohija—*Službeni list Socijalističke Autonomne Pokrajine Kosova.* Priština, 1948–.
Macedonia—*Služben vesnik na Socijalistička Republika Makedonija.* Sk.: 1945–.
Montenegro—*Službeni list Socijalističke Republike Crne Gore.* Titograd: 1945–.
Serbia—*Službeni glasnik Socijalističke Republike Srbije.* B.: 1944–.
Slovenia—*Uradni list Socialistične Republike Slovenije.* Lj.: 1945–.
Vojvodina—*Službeni list Socijalističke Autonomne Pokrajine Vojvodine.* N.S.: 1945–.

In addition, the People's Committee of cities, towns and municipalities publish their own official gazettes, e.g. *Službeni glasnik grada Zagreba.* Z.: Informator, 1946–, but these are too numerous to list here. They may be found through the relevant bibliographies already cited.

J54 *Zakonodavni rad Pretsedništva Antifašističkog veća narodnog oslobod-jenja Jugoslavije i Pretsedništva Privremene Narodne Skupštine DFJ, 19 nov. 1944–27 okt. 1945: po stenografskim beleškama i drugim izvorima.* [Legislative activity of the Presidium of AVNOJ and the Presidium of the Provisional National Assembly of the DFY, 19 Nov. 1944–27 Oct. 1945: based on stenographic records and other sources]. Arranged by S. Nešović. B.: Izd. Prezidijuma Narodne Skupštine FNRJ, 1951. 1064 pp. [Not seen].

J55 *Izveštaj Saveznog izvršnog veća.* [Report of the Federal Executive Council]. B.: Skupština SFRJ, 1950/53–. Annual.

The first report covers the period 1950–3. Report of the Federal Executive Council to the Federal National Assembly of Yugoslavia on its political, socio-economic and administrative policies. Each of the republican Executive Councils produce similar reports.

GENERAL PARTY DOCUMENTS

Bibliographies and indexes

J56 *Bibliografija KPJ-SKJ i KPM-SKM, 1919–1979.* [Bibliography of the CPY-LCY and the CPM-LCM, 1919–1979]. Ed. by M. Jovanovik. Sk.: Narodna i univerzitetska biblioteka Kliment Ohridski, 1979. 511 pp. [Not seen].

Congresses

To date there have been eleven congresses held by the League of Communists of Yugoslavia. The first took place in Belgrade in 1919 at which the Party adopted the name Socialist Workers' Party of Yugoslavia (Communist); the second—Vukovar, 1920, at which the Party changed its name to Communist Party of Yugoslavia; the third—Vienna, 1926; the fourth—Dresden, 1928.

5th Congress, Belgrade, 21–28 July, 1948

J57 *V kongres Komunističke partije Jugoslavije, 21–28 jula: stenografske beleške.* [5th Congress of the Communist Party of Yugoslavia, 21–28 July: stenographic record]. B.: Kultura, 1948. 912 pp.

Official account of the proceedings of the 5th Congress. Official reports by Tito, Kardelj, Ranković, Djilas and others may be found in *V Kongres Komunističke partije Jugoslavije, izveštaji i referati.* [5th Congress of the Communist Party of Yugoslavia, reports and statements]. Z.: Kultura, 1958. 575 pp. The Party's programme and statutes adopted at the congress are contained in *Program i statut Komunističke partije Jugoslavije.* [Programme and statute of the Communist Party of Yugoslavia]. B.: Kultura, 1948. 97 pp. The best and most detailed account of the proceedings in a West European

language is *Le Cinquième Congrès du Parti communiste de Yougoslavie,
21–28 Juillet, 1948*. P.: Livre yougoslave, 1949. 646 pp. An English
translation of Tito's report is available: *Political report of the Central
Committee of the Communist Party of Yugoslavia: report delivered at
the V Congress of the CPY by J. B. Tito*. B.: Kultura, 1948. 136 pp.

6th Congress, Zagreb, 2–7 November, 1952

J58 *VI kongres Komunističke partije Jugoslavije (Saveza komunista
Jugoslavije), 2–7 novembra 1952: stenografske beleške*. [6th Congress
of the Communist Party of Yugoslavia (League of Yugoslav Communists), 2–7 November 1952: stenographic record]. B.: Kultura,
1953. 447 pp.

Contains the unequivocal condemnation of Stalinism by the
Yugoslav communists. The Party's statute may be found in *Statut
Saveza komunista Jugoslavije; usvojen na VI kongresu KPJ*. [Statute
of the League of Yugoslav Communists adopted at the 6th Congress
of the CPY]. B.: Kultura, 1953. 43 pp. The work *Reports of the Sixth
Congress of the Communist Party of Yugoslavia, Zagreb, November
3–7, 1952*. B.: Kultura, 1953. 128 pp., contains Tito's report to the
congress, the Party's proposed new statute, and some party organizational questions.

7th Congress, Ljubljana, 22–26 April, 1958

J59 *Stenografske beleške Sedmi kongres SKJ, 22–26 aprila, 1958, Ljubl-
jana*. [Stenographic record of the 7th Congress of the LCY, 22–26
April 1958, Ljubljana]. B.: Kultura, 1958. 1156 pp.

The Party's programme and statutes are contained in *Program
Saveza komunista Jugoslavije, usvojen na sedmom kongresu Saveza
komunista Jugoslavije*. [Programme of the League of Yugoslav
Communists adopted by the 7th Congress of the League of Yugoslav
Communists]. B.: Komunist, 1962. 216 pp. This programme re-
placed the long obsolete one of 1948 and was only the third since the
founding of the CPY. An English translation with the above title was
published in Belgrade by Edition Jugoslavija in 1958 (271 pp.).
There is also an authorized translation by S. Pribichevich,
*Yugoslavia's way: the Program of the League of the Communists of
Yugoslavia*. N.Y.: All Nations Press, 1959, 263 pp. [Not seen].

8th Congress, Belgrade, 7–13 December, 1964

J60 *VIII kongres Saveza komunista Jugoslavije, Beograd 7–13. decembra
1964: stenografske beleške*. [8th Congress of the League of Yugoslav
Communists, Belgrade, 7–13 December 1964: stenographic record].
B.: Kultura, 1965. 3 vols.

An official account is contained in the work *Osmi kongres Saveza
komunista Jugoslavije*. [8th Congress of the League of Yugoslav
Communists]. B.: Komunist, 1964. 245 pp. There is available an
English translation of this entitled *Practice and theory of socialist*

development in Yugoslavia. B.: Medjunarodna politika, 1965. 375 pp. It contains not only the full text of the major reports—by Tito, Kardelj, Ranković and others—but also an abridged version of the report on the work of the Central Committee of the League of Yugoslav Communists, the full text of the resolutions of congress, and the new statute adopted by the LCY.

9th Congress, Belgrade, 11–15 March, 1969

J61 *Deveti kongres Saveza komunista Jugoslavije, Beograd, 11–13.III.1969: stenografske beleške.* [9th Congress of the League of Yugoslav Communists, Belgrade, 11–13 March 1969: stenographic record]. B.: Komunist, 1970. 6 vols.

An official account is contained in *Deveti kongres Saveza komunista Jugoslavije.* [9th Congress of the League of Yugoslav Communists]. B.: Kultura, 1969. 442 pp. An abridged version is available in English with texts of speeches and resolutions entitled *Ninth Congress of the League of Communists of Yugoslavia.* (Socialist thought and practice). B.: Aktuelna pitanja socijalizma, 1969. 234 pp.

10th Congress, Belgrade, 27–30 May, 1974

J62 *Deseti kongres Saveza komunista Jugoslavije, 27–30. maja 1974: stenografske beleške.* [10th Congress of the League of Yugoslav Communists, 27–30 May 1974: stenographic record]. B.: Komunist, 1974. 4 vols.

Congress speeches and resolutions, and the Party's statute are contained in the following works: *Deseti kongres Saveza komunista Jugoslavije: dokumenti.* [10th Congress of the League of Yugoslav Communists: documents]. B.: Komunist, 1974, 631 pp.; *Rezolucija Desetog kongresa SKJ.* [Resolutions of the 10th Congress of the LCY]. (Mala marksistička biblioteka, kolo 3, 13). Split, Marksistički centar, 1975. 290 pp.; *Statut Saveza komunista Jugoslavije.* [Statute of the League of Yugoslav Communists]. B.: Komunist, 1974. 70 pp. [Not seen]. Some of these documents are available in English: *Tenth Congress of the League of Communists of Yugoslavia.* Ed. by D. Šolajić. (Socialist thought and practice). B.: Komunist, 1975. 225 pp. Contains the speeches by Tito, Kardelj and Dolanc.; *Programme of the League of Communists of Yugoslavia.* Ed. by N. Strugar. (Socialist thought and practice). B.: Komunist, 1977. 263 pp.

11th Congress, Belgrade, 20–23 June, 1978

J63 *XI kongres Saveza komunista Jugoslavije: dokumenti.* [11th Congress of the League of Yugoslav Communists: documents]. B.: Komunist, 1978. 585 pp.

For the work of the LCY between the 10th and 11th congresses, see *Izveštaj o radu Saveza komunista Jugoslavije i Centralnog komiteta SKJ izmedju Desetog i Jedanaestog kongresa SKJ.* [Report of the work of the League of Yugoslav Communists and the Central Committee of the LCY between the 10th and 11th congresses]. B.: Komunist, 1978. 281 pp. Other material relating to the 11th Congress may be found in: *Basic theses for the formulation of policies and documents of the Eleventh Congress of the League of Communists of Yugoslavia.* Ed. N. Strugar. (Socialist thought and practice). B.: Komunist, 1978. 289 pp.; Tito, J. B. *The League of Communists of Yugoslavia in the struggle for the further development of socialist, self-managing and nonaligned Yugoslavia: report to the 11th Congress of the LCY.* (Socialist thought and practice). B.: Komunist, 1978. 92 pp. Both these works were also published in French, German, Russian and Spanish.

J64　Djurašković, Dj. *Devet kongresa SKJ.* [Nine congresses of the League of Yugoslav Communists]. B.: Beogradski izdavačko-grafički zavod, 1974. 255 pp.

　　　The first part provides a basic history to the first nine congresses of the League and includes changes in the League's statutes, resolutions and documents of congress, etc. In the second part, texts of resolutions adopted at congress are presented on a variety of subjects. A more recent compilation containing similar material is that by Lj. Ristović and O. Prica entitled *Jedanaest kongresa: 1919–1978.* [Eleven congresses, 1919–1978]. B.: Privredni pregled, 1978. 374 pp. [Not seen].

J65　*Kongresi Saveza komunista socijalističkih republika Bosne i Hercegovine, Crne Gore, Hrvatske, Makedonije, Slovenije, Srbije.* [Congresses of the League of Communists of the socialist republics of Bosnia/Hercegovina, Montenegro, Croatia, Macedonia, Slovenia, Serbia]. B.: Sedma sila, 1965. 448 pp.

　　　Congresses are held by the League of Communists on a regular basis in each of the Yugoslav republics but they are too numerous to mention here.

Conferences

At the 9th Party Congress in 1969, an annual Conference of 280 delegates was set up to bridge the four-year gap between party congresses. It met four times between 1970 and 1973 before it was dissolved by the 10th Congress.

J66　*Konferencija Saveza komunista Jugoslavije, održana od 29. do 31. oktobra 1970.* [Conference of the League of Yugoslav Communists held from 29 to 31 October 1970]. (Dokumenti SKJ). B.: Komunist, 1970–1. 3 vols.

　　　The second conference was held in Belgrade in 1971—*Druga konferencija Saveza komunista Jugoslavije.* B.: Komunist, 1972. 536 pp.; the third in 1972—*Treća konferencija Saveza* ... B.: Komunist, 1972. 462 pp.; the fourth in May 1973—*Četvrta konferencija* ... B.: Komunist, 1973. 495 pp.

GENERAL STATISTICS

Bibliographies

J67 *Katalog izdanja.* [Catalogue of publications]. B.: Savezni zavod za statistiku, 1969. 147 pp.

Lists all the publications of the institute in subject order. A 32-page supplement covering the years 1970–4 was published in 1975. Publications of the institute are also listed at the end of *Statistički godišnjak SFRJ* (*see* J71).

J68 *Bibliografija na statistiškata dokumentacija.* [Bibliography of statistical documentation]. Sk.: Zavod za statistika, 1954. 129 pp. [Not seen].

Lists both Yugoslav and Macedonian statistical publications.

J69 *Publicistika i dokumentacija, 1945–1970.* [Publications and documentation, 1945–1970]. Ed. B. Stojčevski and V. Velkovska. Sk.: Republički zavod za statistika, 1970. 102 pp.

Celebrates the 25th anniversary of the Macedonian Statistical Institute by listing all the publications issued by that institute during the period stated.

J70 *Katalog publikacij, 1944–1974.* [Catalogue of publications, 1944–1974]. Ed. by B. Mlinar. Lj.: Zavod SR Slovenije za statistiko, 1974. 114 pp.

A catalogue of statistical publications issued by the Slovenian Statistical Institute and including a subject index to the Slovene statistical series *Statistično gradivo* and *Prikazi in študije* (*see* J73).

Statistical publications

J71 *Statistički godišnjak SFRJ.* [Statistical yearbook of the SFRY].B.: Savezni zavod za statistiku, 1954–. Annual.

The most complete source of current statistical information about Yugoslavia. For those unfamiliar with the languages of Yugoslavia, an English-language key has been published annually since 1954 entitled *Statistical yearbook of the Socialist Federal Republic of Yugoslavia*; it contains translations only of the preface, table of contents, and captions of the original. A French-language key is also available. Each of the six republics publish similar statistical yearbooks and surveys:

Bosnia/Hercegovina—*Statistički godišnjak SRBiH/Statistički pregled.* [Statistical yearbook of the SRBandH/Statistical survey]. Sarajevo: Zavod za statistiku i evidenciju SRBiH, 1945–/1945–. Annual/monthly.

Croatia—*Statistički godišnjak SR Hrvatske/Mjesečni statistički izveštaj.* [Statistical yearbook of the SR of Croatia/Monthly statistical report]. Z.: Zavod za statistiku SR Hrvatske, 1952–/1951–. Annual/monthly.

Macedonia—*Statistički godišnik na SRM/Statistički izveštaj za SRM*. [Statistical yearbook of the SRM/Statistical report of the SRM]. Sk.: Zavod za statistika, 1954–/1952–. Annual/monthly.
Montenegro—*Statistički godišnjak SR Crne Gore/Mjesečni statistički pregled*. [Statistical yearbook of the SR of Montenegro/Monthly statistical review]. Titograd: Zavod za statistiku SR Crne Gore, 1955–/1952–. Annual/monthly.
Serbia—*Statistički godišnjak SR Srbije/Mesečni statistički pregled*. [Statistical yearbook of the SR of Serbia/Monthly statistical review]. B.: Zavod za statistiku SR Srbije, 1951–/1952–. Annual/monthly.
Slovenia—*Statistični letopis SR Slovenije/Mesečni statistični pregled*. [Statistical chronicle of the SR of Slovenia/Monthly statistical review]. Lj.: Zavod SR Slovenije za statistiko, 1953–/1952–. Annual/monthly.

J72 *Statistički kalendar Jugoslavije*. [Statistical pocketbook of Yugoslavia]. B.: Savezni zavod za statistiku, 1955–. Annual.
　　An abridged version of *Statistički godišnjak SFRJ* but still full of statistics on many aspects of Yugoslavia. An English translation has been published since 1955: *Statistical pocket-book of Yugoslavia*. Translations are also available in French, German and Russian.

J73 *Statistički bilten*. [Statistical bulletin]. B.: Savezni zavod za statistiku, 1950–. Irregular.
　　Each issue—more than 900 have been issued since its inception—is devoted to the statistical presentation of a different topic in Yugoslav affairs. An index to the contents of the whole series appears on the back covers for retrospective use. Similar bulletins exist in the republics: e.g. the Slovene *Statistično gradivo*. [Statistical material]. Lj.: 1945–. Irregular; and *Prikazi in študije*. [Reviews and studies]. Lj.: 1955–. Irregular. By 1974 there had been 759 issues of the former and 612 of the latter.

J74 *Jugoslavija, 1945–1964: statistički pregled*. [Yugoslavia, 1945–1964: a statistical review]. B.: Savezni zavod za statistiku, 1965. 373 pp.
　　A statistical conspectus on all aspects of Yugoslavia for the period indicated.

OTHER GENERAL SOURCES OF DOCUMENTATION

J75 *Komunist*. [Communist]. B.: 1942–. Weekly.
　　From 1942 to April 1957 it was published monthly. Published in four editions: Serbocroatian (Cyrillic and Latin alphabets), Macedonian and Slovene. It is the official organ of the Central Committee of the League of Yugoslav Communists. See also the journals: *Socijalizam*. [Socialism]. B.: 1957–. Monthly (the journal of the League of Yugoslav Communists containing information on the activities of the Party, party policy, and Marxist ideology); and the

more recent *Yugoslav Information Bulletin*. B.: 1974–. Monthly (the bulletin of the LCY and the Socialist Alliance of Working People of Yugoslavia).

J76 *Borba*. [The struggle]. B.: 1945–. Daily.
First published in 1922 as the Yugoslav Communist Party's official organ. Since 1953 it has been sponsored by the Socialist Alliance of Working People of Yugoslavia but it is still regarded as the chief organ of the Yugoslav Government and Communist Party and is an indispensable source of information on the government and its policies. It is published in two editions: in the Cyrillic script in Belgrade and in the Latin script in Zagreb. The republican equivalents of *Borba* are: *Vjesnik*. [Messenger]. Z.; *Oslobodjenje*. [Freedom]. Sarajevo; *Nova Makedonija*. [New Macedonia]. Sk.; and *Delo*. [Work]. Lj.

J77 *Politika*. [Politics]. B.: 1945–. Daily.
First published in 1904–15 and 1919–41. In the prewar period it was an independent newspaper but since 1945 it has become a semiofficial newspaper and is now regarded as the second most important newspaper in the country.

J78 *Radio Free Europe Research. Background report: Yugoslavia*. Munich. Approx. 100 issues p.a.
Provides information and comment obtained via Yugoslav official sources, e.g. *Službeni list SFRJ* and *Borba*, on current socioeconomic and political activities in Yugoslavia.

J79 *Translation service*. B.: V. Jovanović, 1972–. Daily.
Originally run by the British and U.S. embassies in Yugoslavia (1953–72) to provide speedy access to English translations of selected articles from the chief Belgrade newspapers, in the main *Borba* and *Politika*. In 1972 it was taken over by V. Jovanović as an individual enterprise. Confined mainly to translations of political and economic articles. More easily obtainable is the newspaper *Yugoslav life*. B.: Tanjug News Agency, 1956–. Monthly. Produced for foreign consumption in English, French, German, Russian and Spanish editions, it carries news, features and articles on developments in Yugoslavia and often contains 'official' speeches and reports.

J80 *Yugoslav Survey*. B.: Jugoslovenski pregled, 1960–. Quarterly.
Translation of the Serbocroatian original *Jugoslovenski pregled*. B.: 1957–. Monthly. Contains current information on the political, social, economic and cultural developments in Yugoslavia based on official sources. Includes reports of congresses and Central Committee meetings of the LCY, constitutional changes, a list of international treaties concluded each year, and basic statistical data (each issue highlights a particular sector).

INTERNATIONAL RELATIONS

Bibliographies

J81 Damian, A. *Bibliography of selected books and articles on nonalignment*. B.: Institute of International Politics and Economics, 1975. 52 pp. [Not seen].

J82 *Jugoslovenska revija za medjunarodno pravo*. [Yugoslav review of international law]. B.: Jugoslovensko udruženje za medjunarodno pravo, 1955–. Quarterly.

In addition to articles on international law, this journal contains a running bibliography, usually in the first or second issue of each volume, entitled 'Jugoslovenska bibliografija iz medjunarodnog prava'. See also *Bibliographie des jugoslawischen Schrifttums zum Völkerrecht*. Ed. by V. Ibler. (Institut für Internationales Recht an der Universität Kiel, Bibliographien, Bd. 2). Hamburg, Hansischer Gildenverlag, 1970. 380 pp. [Not seen].

J83 *Medjunarodni politički leksikon*. [International political dictionary]. Ed. by M. Hubeny et al. Z.: Novinsko izdavačko poduzeće, 1960. 592 pp.

A lexicon of international politics covering the legal and economic aspects of international relations with detailed attention to Yugoslav institutions and concepts.

Treaties

J84 *Medjunarodni ugovori SFRJ*. [International agreements of the SFRJ]. B.: Savezni sekretarijat za unutrašnje poslova, 1945–. Irregular.

Formerly called *Medjunarodni ugovori FNRJ* (1945–63). It was issued by the Ministarstvo inostranih poslova during the period 1945–53 and by the Državni sekretarijat za unutrašnje poslova during 1953–63. Contains the texts of treaties and agreements concluded between Yugoslavia and foreign powers. From 11 February 1953, treaties concluded by Yugoslavia are contained in a special supplement to *Službeni list SFRJ: Dodatak: Medjunarodni ugovori i drugi sporazumi*. [Supplement: International treaties and other agreements].

J85 'International treaties for [1959–]'. *Yugoslav survey*. 1960–. Quarterly.

Annually lists international agreements concluded between Yugoslavia and foreign powers for that given year.

Soviet–Yugoslav relations

J86 *Pisma CK KPJ i pisma CK SKP(b)*. [The correspondence between the CC of the CPY and the CC of the All-Union Communist Party (Bolsheviks)]. B.: Jugoslovenska Knjiga, 1948. 79 pp.

Contains the full text of letters exchanged between the Yugoslav and Soviet Communist Parties on the points of dispute between Tito and Stalin. An English translation with the above title was published by Jugoslovenska knjiga in the same year (79 pp.). The most recent publication by a Yugoslav on the 1948 crisis is the three-volume work by Vladimir Dedijer, Tito's official biographer, entitled *Dokumenti 1948.* [Documents 1948]. B.: Rad, 1979. 639, 691, 806 pp. It contains 336 documents in all, many of which are published here for the first time, and includes articles and speeches by purged Yugoslav leaders such as Milovan Djilas and Aleksandar Ranković. [Not seen].

J87   *Bela knjiga o agresivnim postupcima vlada SSSR, Poljske, Čehoslov-ačke, Madjarske, Rumunije, Bugarske i Albanije prema Jugoslaviji.* [White book on the aggressive activities by the governments of the USSR, Poland, Czechoslovakia, Hungary, Rumania, Bulgaria and Albania against Yugoslavia]. B.: Ministarstvo inostranih poslova, 1951. 441 pp.

During the Soviet–Yugoslav dispute, the Soviet Union organized its East European satellites against Yugoslavia. Their activities have been fully documented by Yugoslavia in the above work. An English translation was also published in the same year (481 pp.) [Not seen].

J88   *The Soviet–Yugoslav controversy, 1948–58: a documentary record.* Ed. by R. H. Bass and E. Marbury. N.Y.: Publ. for the East Europe Institute by Prospect Books, 1959. 225 pp.

A collection of 24 public documents, speeches and press articles presenting Soviet and Yugoslav positions on matters in dispute from the initial break to the controversy over revisionism.

J89   *The second Soviet–Yugoslav dispute: full text of main documents, April–June, 1958, with an introductory analysis.* Ed. by V. L. Benes et al. (Indiana University Publications, Slavic and East European Series, 14). Bloomington: Indiana U.P., 1959. 272 pp.

J90   *Yugoslavia and the Soviet Union, 1939–1973: a documentary survey.* Ed. by S. Clissold. London: Oxford U.P. for the Royal Institute of International Affairs, 1975. 318 pp.

Presents a picture of relations between the two countries based on a variety of official documents and with an analytical commentary. Divided into three major periods: wartime relations, postwar period (including the break with Stalin), and the post-Stalin period of *rapprochement* and Yugoslav nonalignment. A useful guide to some primary and secondary sources is B. Hunter's *Soviet–Yugoslav relations, 1948–1972: a bibliography of Soviet, Western, and Yugoslav comment and analysis.* N.Y.: Garland, 1976. 223 pp.

J91   'Relations between Yugoslavia and the USSR, 1955–1969'. *Yugoslav survey*, 11, no. 3, 1970, pp. 121–56.

Presents a year-by-year account of political relations between the two countries. An appendix provides a list of treaties, agreements and protocols signed during the period indicated.

Bulgarian–Yugoslav relations

For relations between Yugoslavia and her close neighbour Bulgaria, particularly concerning the Macedonian issue, see the section 'International relations' in the chapter on Bulgaria.

Yugoslav nonalignment

J92 *Documents of the gatherings of non-aligned countries, 1961–1978.* B.: Medjunarodna politika, 1978. 339 pp. [Not seen].

The two principal architects of the original Yugoslav policy of nonalignment were Tito and Kardelj. For their views on this subject see: Tito, J. *The historical mission of non-alignment.* B.: Socialist Thought and Practice, 1979. 49 pp.; Tito, J. *Tito and non-alignment: president Tito's addresses at conferences of non-aligned countries.* B.: Socialist Thought and Practice, 1979. 119 pp. [Not seen]; Kardelj, E. *Yugoslavia in international relations and in the non-aligned movement.* B.: Socialist Thought and Practice, 1979. 234 pp. See also *The policy and movement of non alignment, 1961–1979: a survey of participants and activities.* Prepared by M. Dromnjak. B.: Medjunarodna politika, 1979. 142 pp. [Not seen].

MILITARY AFFAIRS

J93 *Zakon o Jugoslavenskoj narodnoj armiji.* [Law on the Yugoslav army]. (Zbirka saveznih propisa, 41). B.: Službeni list SFRJ, 1965. 183 pp.

Collection of laws and regulations dealing with the Yugoslav army and military courts.

J94 *Zakon o narodnoj odbrani. Zakon o vojnoj obavezi.* [Law on civil defence. Law on conscription]. B.: Narodna armija, 1969. 64 pp. [Not seen].

J95 *Zbirka vojnih propisa sa komentarom.* [Collection of military regulations with commentary]. Chief ed. I. Baruh. B.: Savremena administracija, 1966. 582 pp.

Collection of military laws and regulations covering such matters as courts martial, courts of enquiry and military discipline.

ECONOMIC AFFAIRS

Statistics

J96 *Indeks: mesečni pregled privredne statistike SFRJ.* [Index: monthly review of Yugoslav economic statistics]. B.: Savezni zavod za statistiku, April 1952–. Monthly.

A monthly review of statistics on all aspects of the Yugoslav economy. Publishes data approximately 40 days after the expiration of the month to which it relates. An English and French translation of the text is available.

J97 *OECD economic surveys: Yugoslavia.* Paris: Organisation for Economic Co-operation and Development, 1962–. Annual.

Contains an analysis of the economic policy of Yugoslavia and includes statistics relating to the economy. A useful appendix in each volume, 'Basic statistics: international comparisons', compares Yugoslavia with 24 other countries.

Economy in general

Bibliographies and indexes

J98 *Registar privredno–finansijskih propisa objavljenih u 'Službenom listu SFRJ' od 1945. do 1966. godine.* [Index to economic–financial regulations announced in the Official gazette of the SFRY 1945–1966]. Comp. by M. Plazinić. B.: Savremena administracija, 1967. 280 pp. [Not seen].

Other material

J99 *Privredni propisi.* [Economic regulations]. Ed. by T. Ralčić. B.: Prosveta, 1973. 5 vols.

Vol. 1 covers federal laws and regulations; vol. 2 covers the republican laws and regulations of Bosnia/Hercegovina and Montenegro; vol. 3, of Croatia; vol. 4, of Macedonia and Slovenia; vol. 5, of Serbia, the Vojvodina and Kosovo.

J100 *Zbirka privredno–finansijskih propisa.* [Collection of economic–financial regulations]. Chief ed. R. Filipovski. B.: Pravno–ekonomski centar, 1975. 2nd ed. 2 vols.

Vol. 1 contains Savezni propisi [federal regulations]; vol. 2, Republički i pokrajinski propisi [republican and regional regulations].

J101 *Zbirka zakona iz oblasti finansije i privrede.* [Collection of laws in the financial and economic field]. B.: Export-Press, 1977. 340 pp. [Not seen].

J102 *Financije.* [Finances]. B.: Savezni sekretarijat za poslove finansija, 1946–. Bi-monthly.

Contains information on financial theory, problems of finance, and statistical data on government income and expenditure.

J103 *Informativni bilten.* [Information bulletin]. B.: 1954–. Monthly.
Issued by the Federal Chamber of Industry. [Not seen].

J103a *The Yugoslav monetary and banking system: a collection of laws and regulations*. Ed. B. Vidas. B.: Jugoslovenska stvarnost, 1980. 226 pp. [Not seen].

Planning

J104 *Zakon o petogodišnjem planu razvitka narodne privrede Federativne Narodne Republike Jugoslavije 1947–1951 i o petogodišnjim planovima razvitka narodne privrede narodnih republika: Srbije, Hrvatske, Slovenije, Bosne i Hercegovine, Makedonije, Crne Gore. S govorima Josipa Broza Tita i dr.* [Law of the five-year plan for the development of the national economy of the FPRY 1947–1951 and of the five-year plans for the development of the national economy of the people's republics: Serbia, Croatia, Slovenia, Bosnia/Hercegovina, Macedonia, Montenegro. With speeches by J. B. Tito and others]. B.: Izd. Savezne planske komisije, 1947. 464 pp.

Contains details on the organization and policies of planning in the Yugoslav economy as well as the law which inaugurated the first postwar plan. An English translation of the law exists: *The law on the five-year plan for the development of the national economy of the Federal People's Republic of Yugoslavia in the period from 1947 to 1951; with speeches by Josip Broz Tito, Andrija Hebrang, Boris Kidrič.* B.: Office of Information, 1947. 166 pp. The five-year plan of 1947 was abandoned in the wake of the break with the Soviet Union. A new system of planning was inaugurated in the early 1950s—annual 'social plans'—but in 1957 Yugoslavia reverted to medium term 'social plans'.

J105 *Društveni plan privrednog razvoja Jugoslavije 1957–1961; ekspoze, zakon, elaborat.* [Social plan for the economic development of Yugoslavia, 1957–1961: report, law, statement]. (Politička biblioteka). B.: Kultura, 1957. 237 pp.

As well as the law for the plan, this volume also contains M. Popović's speech in the Federal Assembly on the political objectives of the plan.

J106 *Društveni plan privrednog razvoja Jugoslavije, 1961–1965: ekspoze predsednika Tita, ekspoze Avde Huma, zakon.* [Social plan for the economic development of Yugoslavia, 1961–1965: report by President Tito, report by Avdo Humo, law]. B.: Kultura, 1961. 158 pp. [Not seen].

An English translation is available: *The five year plan of economic development of Yugoslavia, 1961–1965.* B.: Secretariat for Information of the Federal Executive Council, 1961. 121 pp.

J107 *Društveni plan razvoja Jugoslavije od 1966. do 1970. godine.* [Social plan for the development of Yugoslavia, 1966–1970]. (Zbirka saveznih propisa, 58). B.: Službeni list SFRJ, 1966. 181 pp. [Not seen].

Economic reforms in 1965 heralded a new economic system which relied less on centralized planning, although the five-year plan was kept as a general guide. An English edition is available: *Yugoslavia's*

1966–1970 social development plan. B.: Federal Secretariat of Information, 1966.

J108 *Društveni plan Jugoslavije za period od 1971. do 1975. godine*. [Social plan of Yugoslavia, 1971–1975]. (Biblioteka Savezne skupštine, kolo 9, sv. 3). B.: Sekretarijat za informativnu službu, 1972. 103 pp.

J109 *Društveni plan Jugoslavije za period od 1976. do 1980. godine*. [Social plan of Yugoslavia, 1976–1980]. B.: Savezni komitet za informacije, 1976. 118 pp.

An English translation with the above title was published in 1976 by the Federal Committee of Information (146 pp.). Social plans are also produced for the republics and the lower administrative units, e.g. *Plan društveno–ekonomskog razvoja regiona Titovo Užice za period 1976–1980. godine*. [Plan for the socioeconomic development of the Titovo Užice region, 1976–1980]. Titovo Užice: Zajednica Titovo Užice, 1976. 128 pp. These are, however, too numerous to list here.

Trade

J110 Filipović, R. and Paštrović, A. *Zbirka trgovinskih i platnih sporazuma s inostranstvom*. [Collection of trade and payments agreements with foreign countries]. B.: Izd. Nova administracija, 1956. 380 pp. [Not seen].

A more up-to-date collection of Yugoslav trade treaties and agreements are provided by D. Ivković. *Zbirka spoljnotrgovinskih ugovora i sporazuma Jugoslavije*. [Collection of Yugoslav foreign trade treaties and agreements]. Z.: Edok, 1965. 465 pp.

J111 *Ekonomski odnosi Jugoslavije sa inostranstvom: zbirka zakona i podzakonskih propisa sa objašnjenjima*. [Yugoslav economic relations with foreign countries: collection of laws and regulations with commentaries]. Ed. M. Kosovac. B.: Privredna štampa, 1980. xix, 938 pp. [Not seen].

A work in English on the same theme is *Foreign trade and related operations: laws and regulations*. Chief ed. B. Djurović. B.: Jugoslovenska stvarnost, 1978. 113 pp.

J112 *Statistika spoljne trgovine SFR Jugoslavije*. [Statistics of Yugoslav foreign trade]. B.: Savezni zavod za statistiku, 1946–. Annual.

Main tables show imports and exports arranged by a commodity classification and subdivided by countries of origin and destination. There are also detailed tables showing imports and exports by countries, subdivided by commodities.

Labour

Bibliographies

J113 Aćimović, Miroslav R. *Bibliografska gradja o radničkom samouprav-*

ljanju u Jugoslaviji i oblicima - učešća proizvodjača u upravljanju preduzećima u drugim zemljama. [Bibliographical material on workers' self-management in Yugoslavia and on the form of worker participation in the management of enterprises in other countries]. B.: Institut društvenih nauka, 1966. 855 pp.

A comprehensive bibliography on the Yugoslav concept of self-management. See also: Andrić, S. & Sever-Zebec, M. *Bibliografija o učešću radnika u upravljanju poduzećima u Jugoslaviji. Bibliography on workers' participation in management in Yugoslavia.* Z.: Ekonomski institut, 1969. 47 pp.; and its supplement *Dodatek bibliografiji . . . Appendix to the bibliography . . .* Z.: 1970. 20 pp.

Other material

J114 *Osnovni zakon o upravljanju državnim privrednim poduzećima i višim privrednim udruženjima od strane radnih kolektiva.* [Basic law on the management of state economic enterprises and associations by working collectives]. (Zbirka propisa iz oblasti privrede, br. 13). B.: Izd. Službenog lista FNRJ, 1950. 38 pp. [Not seen].

The first piece of legislation passed on workers' self-management in Yugoslavia, although it was not actually introduced into the economy until 1952. Further laws were passed in 1958. The 1963 Constitution led to more legislation in 1965.

J115 *Propisi o izboru i opozivu upravljanja u radnim organizacijama: propisi s napomenama i uputima za provodjenje izbora, Osnovni zakon o izboru radničkih savjeta i drugih organa upravljanja u radnim organizacijama, Zakon o izboru i opozivu radničkih savjeta i drugih organa upravljanja u radnim organizacijama.* [Regulations on the election and cancellation of management organs in workers' organizations; Regulations with notes and instructions on the realizing of elections, Basic law on the election of workers' councils and other organs of management in workers' organizations]. Ed. J. Kovačić. (Zbirka pravnih propisa, 19). Z.: Narodne novine, 1965. 240 pp.

Contains the basic legislation relating to workers' councils in Yugoslavia. See also: *Laws on employment relationships.* (Collection of Yugoslav laws, no. 16). B.: Institute of Comparative Law, 1967. 112 pp.; *Laws of enterprises and institutions.* (Collection of Yugoslav laws, no. 13). B.: Institute of Comparative Law, 1966. 130 pp.

J116 *The associated labour act.* (The S.F.R. of Yugoslavia Assembly Series). Tr. by M. Pavičić. B.: Secretariat of Information of the SFR of Yugoslavia Assembly, 1977. 430 pp.

Contains the latest legislation on workers' self-management brought about by the 1974 constitution. A useful recent collection of documents on self-management in Yugoslavia is *Socialist self-management in Yugoslavia, 1950–1980: documents,* selected and ed. by B. Bošković and D. Dašić. B.: Socialist Thought & Practice, 1980. 466 pp.

J117   *Vjesnik rada.* [Labour gazette]. B.: 1946–. Monthly.
        Issued by the Yugoslav Ministry of Labour.

SOCIAL AFFAIRS

Bibliographies

J118   Dinić, D. K. *Bibliografija radova o svojini u jugoslovenskom pravu.*
        [Bibliography of works on property in Yugoslav law]. B.: Institut
        društvenih nauka, 1968. 316 pp. [Not seen].

Population

J119   *Demografska statistika.* [Demographic statistics]. B.: Savezni zavod
        za statistiku, 1950–. Annual.
        From 1950 to 1955, it was published under the title *Vitalna
        statistika* [Vital statistics]. Contains data on population, demog-
        raphic trends, births, deaths, marriages, divorces.

J120   *Popis stanovništva i stanova, 1971.* [Population and housing census,
        1971]. B.: Savezni zavod za statistiku, 1972–5. 19 vols.
        Vols. 1–5 contain population results by republics and provinces;
        vols. 6–12, population results by smaller communities; vols. 13–19,
        results of the housing census. A useful key to the above work is
        provided by *Popis stanovništva i stanova, 1971; program obrade i
        publikovanja: šeme tabeliranja, tabele i klasifikacije.* [Population and
        housing census, 1971; programme of work and publication: scheme
        of contents and classification]. B.: Savezni zavod za statistiku, 1975.
        332 pp. There have been three earlier population censuses:
        Census of 15 March 1948—*Konačni rezultati popisa stanovništva od
        15 marta 1948 godine.* [Final results of the population census of 15
        March 1948]. B.: Savezni zavod za statistiku, 1951–6. 10 vols.
        Census of 31 March 1953—*Popis stanovništva, 1953.* [Population
        census, 1953]. B.: Savezni zavod za statistiku, 1958–62. 16 vols.
        Census of 1961—*Popis stanovništva, 1961.* [Population census,
        1961]. B.: Savezni zavod za statistiku, 1965–8. 16 vols.

Social security

J121   *Socijalno osiguranje.* [Social security]. B.: 1955–. Monthly.
        Organ of the Federal Bureau for Social Security.

J122   *Zbirka propisa o mirovinskom osiguranju.* [Collection of regulations on
        old age pensions]. Ed. Z. Cota. 3rd ed. (Zbirka pravnih propisa, 42).
        Z.: Narodne novine, 1968. 609 pp. [Not seen].

J123   *Zbirka propisa o zdravstvenom osiguranju i organizaciji i finansiranju
        socijalnog osiguranja, sa napomenama i registrima pojmova.* [Collection
        of regulations on health insurance and the organization and financing

of social insurance, with remarks and index of notions]. (Zbirka saveznih propisa, 8). B.: Službeni list SFRJ, 1963. 421 pp.

Other material

J124 Chloros, A. G. *Yugoslav civil law: history, family, property; commentary and texts.* Oxford: Oxford U.P., 1970. 285 pp.

Contains an historical introduction to Yugoslav civil law, a detailed discussion of family and property law, and translations of the four basic texts of Yugoslav family law relating to marriage, parents and children, adoption and guardianship.

J125 *Propisi o prelaženju državne granice, kretanju i boravku stranaca i putnim ispravama.* [Regulations on the crossing of the state frontiers, on the movement and sojourn of aliens, and on passports]. Ed. B. Petković. (Zbirka pravnih propisa, 82). Z.: Narodne novine, 1974. 247 pp. [Not seen].

Collections of emigration and immigration laws and regulations.

CULTURAL AFFAIRS

Bibliographies and indexes

J126 *Registar školskih propisa u FNRJ, 1945–1953.* [Index to educational regulations in the FPRY, 1945–1953]. Comp. by M. Filipović. Subotica, Minerva, 1954. 118 pp.

Index to all legislation pertaining to education in Yugoslavia passed over a 9-year period.

Other material

J127 *Bilten.* [Bulletin]. B.: Savezno izvršno veće, Sekretarijat za prosvetu i kulturu, 1959–. Irregular.

Contains information on the public education system in Yugoslavia; activities of various institutions of higher learning; texts and explanation of laws, executive orders and instructions. The republican councils of education issue similar journals: *Glasnik* (Bosnia/Hercegovina, monthly); *Prosvjetni glasnik* (Croatia, monthly); *Prosveten glasnik* (Macedonia, bimonthly); *Prosvetni glasnik* (Serbia, monthly).

J128 *Legal status of religious minorities in Yugoslavia.* (Documents, no. 12). B.: Medjunarodna štampa-interpres, 1967. 86 pp.

Contains laws, constitutional provisions, specimens of social contracts and protocol between the Vatican and the Yugoslav government.

J129 *Zbirka novih školskih propisa.* [Collection of new school regulations]. Ed. by R. Jemuović and M. Jović. B.: Savremena administracija, 1960–3. 3 vols. 431, 552, 748 pp.

Vol. 1 contains federal and republican laws on basic schooling; vol. 2, on gymnasiums and the education service; vol. 3, on higher education, special schools and schools for national minorities. See also the work in English *General law on education in Yugoslavia*. B.: Jugoslavija, 1959. 111 pp. Later legislation is contained in *Propisi o obrazovanju i kulturi*. [Regulations on education and culture]. B.: Prosveta, 1968. 3 vols. (loose-leaf). Kept up to date by 'izmene i dopune'.

J130   *Zbirka propisa iz oblasti prosvete, nauke i kulture—savezni i republičke.* [Collection of regulations from the educational, scientific and cultural spheres—federal and republican]. Comp. by D. Aleksić et al. B.: Privredno–finansijski zavod, 1969. 356 pp. [Not seen].

J131   *Zbirka zakona o štampi, novinskim i izdavačkim preduzećima, radiodifuznim stanicama i autorskom pravu.* [Collection of laws pertaining to the press, publishing and radio, including copyright law]. Chief ed. J. Guč. B.: Savremena administracija, 1961. 171 pp.

LEADERS' WORKS

J132   Djilas, M. *Članci, 1941–1946*. [Articles, 1941–1946]. B.: Kultura, 1947. 368 pp.
Originally one of the four top-ranking Yugoslav party and government officials, Djilas fell into disfavour and spent several periods in prison in the 1950s and 1960s for his outspokenness. His works in English translation include: *Anatomy of a moral: the political essays of Milovan Djilas*. Ed. by A. Rothberg. (Praeger publications in Russian history and world communism, 84). N.Y.: Praeger, 1959. 181 pp.; *Conversations with Stalin*. Trans. by M. B. Petrovich. Harmondsworth, Penguin, 1969. 171 pp. (He was re-imprisoned for this work which violated the conditions of his release from prison in 1961 and which allegedly revealed state secrets); *Memoir of a revolutionary*. Trans. by D. Willen. N.Y.: Harcourt Brace Jovanovich, 1973. 402 pp.; *The new class: an analysis of the communist system*. N.Y.: Praeger, 1957. 214 pp. (Sentenced to six years' imprisonment for this much publicized work); *Parts of a lifetime*. Ed. by M. and D. Milenkovitch. N.Y.: Harcourt Brace Jovanovich, 1975. 442 pp. (A selection of his political and literary writings); *The unperfect society: beyond the new class*. Trans. by D. Cooke. N.Y.: Harcourt Brace Jovanovich, 1969. 267 pp.; *Wartime*. Trans. by M. B. Petrovich. N.Y.: Harcourt Brace Jovanovich, 1977. 470 pp. The most recent work by Djilas, and one which is already causing some controversy appearing so soon after Tito's death, is *Tito—eine kritische Biographie*. Wien: Fritz Molden, 1980. It is translated from the original Serbocroatian title *Druženje sa Titom*. English translation: *Tito: the story from inside*, London: Weidenfeld & Nicolson, 1981. 185 pp.

J133 Kardelj, Edvard. *Probleme naše socijalističke izgradnje*. [Problems of our socialist development]. B.: Kultura, 1946–78. 10 vols.

Collection of speeches and writings covering a wide range of topics on the internal and external affairs of Yugoslavia. Kardelj, a Slovenian by nationality, was a leading party ideologist and occupied top posts in the party and government hierarchy. He was regarded as Tito's second-in-command until his recent death. His other works include: *Izbor iz dela*. [Selected works]. B.: Komunist, 1979. 7 vols. 2719 pp.; and *Samoupravljanje*. [Self-management]. Sarajevo: Svjetlost, 1979. 2252 pp. [Not seen]. English translations of his works include: *Problems of socialist policy in the countryside*. London: Lincolns-Praeger, 1962. 303 pp.; the more recent *The nation and international relations*. B.: Komunist, 1975. 211 pp.; and *Democracy and socialism*. London: Summerfield Press, 1978. 244 pp.; *Self-management and the political system*. B.: Socialist Thought & Practice, 1980. 287 pp.

J134 Kidrič, B. *Zbrano delo: članki in razprave*. [Collected works: articles and essays]. Lj.: Cankarjeva založba, 1958–76. 4 vols.

Boris Kidrič was a leading Slovenian communist who attained high political office at both republican and federal level. He was in charge of the Yugoslav economy from 1946 until his death in 1953. His collected works, which cover his writings from 1933 to 1952, deal with many aspects of Yugoslav political and economic life before, during and after the Second Word War with special attention to Slovenia.

J135 Koliševski, L. *Politički izveštaj na Centralniot komitet na Komunistička partija na Makedonija: referat održan na I kongres na KPM*. [Political report to the CC of the Macedonian Communist Party]. Sk.: Kultura, 1949. 145 pp.

Lazar Koliševski is the leading Macedonian communist who has achieved high political and government office. Other writings of Koliševski include: *Aspekti na makedonskoto prašanje*. [Aspects of the Macedonian question]. Sk.: Kultura, 1962. 535 pp.; and *Problemi razvoja poljoprivrede i sela*. [Problems in the development of agriculture and the village]. B.: Zadružna knjiga, 1967. 152 pp. [Not seen].

J136 Pijade, M. *Izabrani govori i članci*. [Selected speeches and articles]. Z.: Kultura, 1948–50. 2 vols. 496, 384 pp.

A selection of Pijade's speeches and articles on Yugoslavia's domestic and foreign affairs. Vol. 1 covers the years 1941–7; vol. 2, 1948–9. See also his *Izabrani spisi*. [Selected papers]. Selected and ed. by R. Čolaković et al. B.: Institut za izučavanje radničkog pokreta, 1964–5. Vol. 1, 3 parts. Pijade (1890–1957) was a prominent Yugoslav communist who held high political posts during and after the war and was a member of the Central Committee and Politburo.

J137 Ranković, A. *Izabrani govori i članci, 1941–1951*. [Selected speeches and articles, 1941–1951]. Z.: Kultura, 1951. 430 pp.

Collection of Ranković's speeches and articles on a variety of subjects, but primarily on internal Yugoslav problems and the communist party's activities and policies. Aleksandar Ranković was a high-ranking communist who after the war became Minister of the Interior and head of the military and secret police. He fell from power in 1964, ostensibly for abusing his authority, and was expelled from the Party in 1966.

J138 Tito, J. B. *Sabrana dela u 50 knjiga*. [Collected works in 50 volumes]. B.: Beogradski izdavačko–grafički zavod, 1978–. Vol. 1–.

A complete collection of Tito's works, articles and speeches covering the years 1926 onwards. It is to be published in 5 series, each of 10 volumes. The first series has been published to date. Until the completion of this project, the authoritative edition still is *Govori i članci*. [Speeches and articles]. Z.: Napriied, 1959–72. 21 vols. Covers Tito's speeches and articles from 10 August 1941 to 17 October 1966. There have been a number of editions of selected works: *Vojna dela*. [Military works]. B.: Vojnoizdavački zavod, 1978. 2nd ed. 5 vols. (Covers Tito's speeches and articles on military matters during the period 1941–76); *Izbor iz dela*. [Selected works]. B.: Prosveta, 1977. 5 vols.; *Spisi*. [Papers]. B.: Kultura, 1947–57. 9 vols. (Vols. 1–4 are subtitled 'Izgradnja nove Jugoslavije'; vols. 5–7, 'Borba za socijalističku demokratiju'; vols. 8–9, 'Borba za mir i medjunarodnu saradnju'; and contain articles, speeches, interviews and declarations on a variety of subjects). A variety of translations in English are available: *Selected speeches and articles, 1941–1961*. Ed. by T. Stanojević. Trans. by D. Cooke et al. Z.: Naprijed, 1963. 459 pp.; *Selected military works*. Trans. by K. Kveder. B.: Vojnoizdav-ački zavod, 1966. 336 pp.; *The essential Tito*. Ed . . . by H. M. Christman. Newton Abbot, David & Charles, 1971. 197 pp.; *Tito on non-alignment*. B.: Federal Chamber for Information, 1976. 103 pp. For a bibliography of works about Tito, see that by M. Sentić in *Časopis za suvremenu povijest*, 2, 1972, pp. 161–203: 'Bibliografija knjiga i brošura o Josipu Brozu Titu, 1941–1972'.

P POLAND

George Sanford

INTRODUCTION

Historical and political background

The interwar Second Polish Republic, resurrected in 1918, after over a century of partition by Russia, Prussia and Austria-Hungary, started off as a parliamentary democracy. It was turned gradually into an authoritarian system by Marshal Józef Piłsudski, after his seizure of power in May 1926. Overwhelmed by the Germans in September 1939 Poland endured the smashing of her state institutions, the attempted genocide of her élites, and the brutal terrorization of her population by the Nazis. The Polish resistance, the Home Army (Armia Krajowa—AK), loyal to the government-in-exile in London, was weakened by the tragedy of the Warsaw uprising in August–September 1944. The liberation of Poland and its occupation by the Red Army in the winter of 1944–5 altered the balance of political forces dramatically. Stalin, at the Yalta and Potsdam conferences, obtained Western approval of the government sponsored by him within Poland and for the westward shift of Polish territory to a new frontier on the Oder–Neisse rivers as compensation for the Soviet annexation of her eastern territories from 1939 to 1940 onwards.

The prewar Polish Communist Party (Komunistyczna Partia Polski—KPP), set up in December 1918, had some support among industrial workers, ethnic minorities and intellectuals. It led a semi-conspiratorial existence until its dissolution by Stalin in 1938. Its successor, the Polish Workers' Party, was set up clandestinely in German-occupied Warsaw in 1942. Władysław Gomułka became its Secretary-General the following year. His group, the so-called domestic communists who spent the war in Poland, set up the National Council of Poland (Krajowa Rada Narodowa—KRN) in December 1943. After the

German invasion of the USSR in July 1941 the Soviets sponsored a Polish Army in the USSR under General Zygmunt Berling. They also fostered their own group of Polish communists on Soviet soil, the so-called Muscovites, led by Wanda Wasilewska and Bolesław Bierut. The two groups of domestic and Muscovite communists amalgamated in July 1944 to set up the Polish Committee of National Liberation (Polski Komitet Wyzwolenia Narodowego—PKWN) in Lublin, which had just been liberated. This provided the basis for the PPR-dominated Provisional Government set up on 31 December 1944 (colloquially known as the Lublin Government), which was recognized by the Western Powers in exchange for its widening to include Socialist (Polska Partia Socjalistyczna—PPS), Democratic and Peasant Party (Stronnictwo Ludowe—SL) representatives and the promise of 'free elections'.

All periodization is necessarily a highly subjective exercise. The following periods of Poland's postwar political history are, however, generally accepted in the West as having a certain unity of their own.

1. The establishment of communism as the dominant force in Poland, 1944–1948

The discrediting of old élites, massive economic and human losses caused by war and population transfer, and the radicalization of the remaining intelligentsia, produced a receptive atmosphere for radical reform in postwar Poland. The nationalization of large and medium industry, a land reform breaking up the large estates, educational and social-welfare programmes and economic recon- struction, symbolized by the rebuilding of the totally devastated capital, Warsaw, were popular and non-controversial measures. The struggle for political power, however, continued within the Provisional Government until 1947 between the PPR, supported by radical socialists and agrarians, and the main Peasant Party led by a one-time Premier of the London Government, Stanisław Mikołajczyk. The PPR increased its membership dramatically from 30,000 in January 1945 to over a million just before its amalgamation with the PPS in December 1948 to form the Polish United Workers' Party (Polska Zjednoczona Partia Robotnicza—PZPR). The absence of determined Western support, to offset the Soviet military and political domination of Poland, genuine political support, and control of crucial ministries enabled the PPR to defeat its opposition, firstly over the referendum of June 1946 and then in the elections to the Constituent Assembly of January 1947. In February 1947, the communist leader Bolesław Bierut became President of the Republic, the pro-communist PPS politician Józef Cyrankiewicz became Premier and the 'Little Constitution' was promulgated. The latter document was a transitional arrangement as it was closely modelled on the liberal constitution of April 1921. It appeared just as the communist monopoly of power was being completed through the arrest of opponents and the banning of political opposition.

2. Sovietization and Stalinization, 1948–1953

The main characteristics of the period were as elsewhere in Eastern Europe at the time: massive industrialization based on holding down living standards in order to produce huge investment rates, the beginnings of the collectivization of agriculture, conflicts with the Roman Catholic Church, and the use of police terror in order to mobilize the population and move society in a more totalitarian direction. At the same time the PZPR was purged of the more national and domestic types of communists such as Gomułka, Zenon Kliszko and Marian Spychalski. The Muscovites led by Secretary-General Bierut, the economic planner Hilary Minc and the ideology and security chief Jakub Berman, now dominated the PZPR. They carried out Stalin's directives unquestioningly. The promulgation of the more socialist constitution of 22 July 1952 marked in many respects the crystallization of the political system which, although transformed in a major way in 1956, still provides the basis for the present system. The constitution itself was not amended again to any major extent until February 1976.

3. New Course and 'October', 1953–1956

Stalin's death in March 1953 and the New Course concessions promised by his successors in the Kremlin marked the failure of the attempt to sovietize Poland and to transform it into a totalitarian system. Excessive police methods were banned. The Stalinist leaders were disorientated. Above all a reaction gradually built up within Poland during 1954–6 to unpopular Stalinist policies, firstly among intellectuals, then the party élite and eventually among the workers. It exploded into the open in such events as the Poznań uprising of June 1956. Following Bierut's death at the Twentieth Soviet Party Congress in March 1956, when Khrushchev condemned Stalin, the PZPR failed to unite around the new First Party Secretary, Edward Ochab. The division of the PZPR into a reforming 'Puławy' faction and the hardline, pro-Soviet 'Natolin' group paralysed its leading role. It allowed an unparalleled degree of intellectual freedom and popular ferment to take place. The near revolutionary situation was resolved by the recall of Gomułka and the victory of the reform programme at the eighth plenum of the PZPR in October 1956 against the initial opposition of Khrushchev and the entire Soviet leadership who flew into Warsaw during its course.

4. Gomułka's Poland, 1956–1970

The essence of Gomułka's system was the preservation of communism in Poland through its adaptation to national conditions and traditions. His orthodox interpretation of the PZPR's hegemonic role spelt disappointment for the wilder 'October' hopes of a new stage of socialist democracy but he maintained the bulk of the 1956 changes. The revised political and economic relationship with the USSR enabled the PZPR to take its own domestic decisions. Police methods were curtailed in the interests of socialist legality. Intellectual life was given very liberal treatment and continued to bloom, especially the cinema and theatre. A *modus vivendi* was achieved with the Roman Catholic Church whose leader Cardinal Stefan Wyszyński had supported the national against the Muscovite brand of communism in 1956. More open tourist, economic and cultural relations were maintained with the West. Collectivization was abandoned, leaving about 85 per cent of the land in the hands of peasant family smallholdings.

Gomułka's initial success in stabilizing political life and in raising living standards was not maintained though. By the mid-1960s Poland was regarded as stagnating after the 'Small Stabilization' of 1958–64. Popular apathy was matched by the development of a 'Partisan' faction within the PZPR whose most notable figure appeared to be the police chief Mieczysław Moczar. The complicated domestic and international situation following the Arab–Israeli war of 1967 enabled the Partisans to mount a drive for power in the form of a so-called 'Anti-Zionist' campaign. This broadened out to attack both the residual Stalinists and the liberal communists of 1956 vintage and the older generation of office-holders. Gomułka's own position was at risk after the suppression of the March 1968 student riots and the ongoing purge of party and state officials. He saved himself by ceding power to the provincial party bosses and by hanging on till the Soviet occupation of Czechoslovakia. After this Brezhnev endorsed him at the PZPR's Fifth Congress in November 1968 but the way was now open for new policies such as a positive response to Brandt's Ostpolitik and an economic reform designed to encourage material incentives.

The decision to raise food prices by up to 30 per cent just before Christmas 1970, however, caused a popular upheaval, especially in the Baltic seacoast towns. Gomułka wanted to suppress the riots by force but was instead replaced by Edward Gierek (First Party Secretary in Katowice province, 1957–70) while the phenomenally long-established Premier Cyrankiewicz (1947–70 with a short break in 1952–4) found his job taken by Piotr Jaroszewicz.

5. Gierek and the modernization of Poland, 1970–1980

Gierek aimed at producing effective political leadership in contrast to the muddle of the Gomułka period. His technocratic programme was one of specific reforms and economic expansion and modernization within the existing political framework. His original aim, which after August 1980 was decried as megalo-mania, was to build a 'Second Poland'. The economy was to be modernized through the import of advanced Western technology including the development of a new motor-car industry, by increasing labour productivity, and by recruiting more competent and better educated individuals into all walks of life. Gierek favoured what the French call the deconcentration of state activities, but not democratization in order to achieve these ends.

After stabilizing the political situation in 1971 Gierek presided over a four-year economic boom marked by over-ambitious and not always efficiently applied investment especially in vast industrial projects. His early economic success was braked by the adverse effects of a large and growing foreign-trade deficit which was aggravated by the 1973 world oil and raw materials crisis. Shortfalls in the private agricultural sector also made it difficult for Gierek to maintain the price freeze on foodstuffs. He had conceded this in early 1971, in order to calm the political situation and to get the industrial workers, who in many places had organized their own independent 'Shop-stewards' movement, back to work. The attempt to raise food prices in June 1976 proved a complete fiasco and testified to the vigorously free character of Polish society. Riots in Radom and numerous work stoppages forced Premier Jaroszewicz to withdraw the proposal within a day.

Price rises were introduced on a more one-off basis, the ones on foodstuffs, especially meat, causing recurrent popular discontent. In June 1980 they triggered off a wave of strikes right across the country. The workers' occupation of factories, especially in the Lenin Shipyard in Gdańsk, and the demands for 'Free Trade Unions' caused the downfall of Premier Babiuch and the acceptance of the Gdańsk and Szczecin agreements by the PZPR in late August 1980. Gierek was then replaced in early September 1980 by Stanisław Kania, who committed himself to a democratization programme, to integrating the independent trade union Solidarity into the revised new system, and to a Social Contract with Polish Society.

The constitution of 1952 was amended substantially in February 1976. Although the Polish People's Republic was now described as a socialist state, its name remained unchanged in contrast to all the other Socialist Republics of Eastern Europe. The PZPR's leading role was written in for the first time. Much opposition was expressed to the requirement of friendship with the USSR and a section tying the citizen's rights to his duties. After 1976 various dissident groups emerged in Poland such as the Workers' Defence Committee—KOR—formed after Radom, the more Catholic and Conservative Movement for the Defence of Human and Civil Rights and the 'Flying University'. A more confident role was also played by the Roman Catholic Church after the election of Cardinal Karol Wojtyła of Kraków as Pope John Paul II and his triumphant visit to Poland in 1979. In the late 1970s Gierek resorted to a somewhat tougher ideological line. Although he applied it very flexibly he marked time economically and politically after 1976. He was unable to prevent the workers' strikes of summer 1980 which led to his downfall and after that to the far-reaching political and economic crisis and extensive purge of the political and administrative officials associated with his rule which was still in full swing in spring 1981.

The PZPR since 1956 has had to cope with a dynamic and vigorous society. Major social crises in 1956, 1968, 1970, 1976 and 1980 demonstrated that the Polish model of communism was very different from the Soviet one. Strong national, religious, peasant and intellectual traditions, extensive links and unrealistic comparisons with the West, demographic dynamism and acute generational conflict and social pluralism rather than totalitarian control were the features of Polish society which brought it into conflict with the authoritarian political system monopolized by the PZPR.

Political institutions and parties

Two constitutions have been passed in postwar Poland. These are the 'Little Constitution' of 19 February 1947 and the constitution of 22 July 1952 which is still in force with a series of major amendments passed on 10 February 1976.

Since 1957 Poland has had a Front of National Unity (Front Jedności Narodu—FJN, previously Front Narodowy, 1952–6). The FJN provides the framework for a socialist party system which is led and dominated by the PZPR. It also includes the United Peasant Party (Zjednoczone Stronnictwo Ludowe—ZSL), which had 428,000 members in 1977; about three-quarters of them were peasants and the vast bulk of its organizations are in the countryside. The Democratic Party (Stronnictwo Demokratyczne—SD) is smaller with 96,500 members in 1977; it is an urban phenomenon largely made up of professional people and handicraftsmen. Three very different Catholic groupings also exist.

Znak (the Sign) has in the past been a semi-independent Catholic group which was often described as the closest to a permitted opposition in a communist country. PAX, which has its own publishing house and a concession to sell devotional objects, attempted to reconcile Catholic belief with loyalty to the communist system. Unlike Znak it has always been condemned by the Catholic hierarchy. The Christian-Social Union—CSU—is a worthy but small and insignificant organization. All candidates to the National Assembly (Sejm) and People's Councils are elected on the basis of single electoral lists arranged by the FJN on the directives of the Central Committee of the PZPR. They also support a common FJN electoral programme.

The unicameral National Assembly is called the Sejm according to ancient historic usage. It has had a fixed number of 460 deputies since 1960. Up till then there had been 1 deputy for every 60,000 voters. Elections are normally held every four years on the basis of direct, universal suffrage. The voting age is eighteen while twenty-one is the minimum age for eligibility for election. Eight elections have been held since 1952 (1952, 1957, 1961, 1965, 1969, 1972, 1976, 1980). The Council of State divides the country up into multi-member constituencies before each election, 67 in 1952, 116 in 1957, and 80 in every election since 1961. In 1951 the FJN list had the same number of candidates as seats although alternates were also elected at the same time. The Electoral Law of 24 October 1956, however, permitted a maximum of two-thirds more candidates than seats to be registered on the official FJN voting list. An amendment of 22 December 1960 changed this figure to a maximum of one-half. The first names on the list are those of the officially preferred candidates and voting for the unchanged list means voting for them. A voter may, however, cross their names off to benefit candidates at the bottom of the list. Crossing-off was a massive phenomenon in 1957 but has since fallen to rarely more than 5 per cent.

The Sejm is presided over by a Sejm Marshal who since 1972 has been assisted by three Vice Marshals (two before that). Together they constitute the Sejm Presidium which is responsible for the everyday running of the Sejm. One should note that this body in Poland is quite distinct from the Council of State which has some of the equivalent functions of the Presidium of the Supreme Soviet in the USSR. Since 1957 the PZPR, ZSL and SD deputies have been organized in separate political clubs while the three Catholic groups have formed political circles. Their representatives together with the Sejm Presidium form the Convent of Seniors which formally draws up the agenda and decides on the timing and duration of sessions. The Sejm had twenty-two standing committees of a specialist type during the 1970s (nineteen until 1971). These vary in size and importance but most meet far more often than the plenary sessions of the Sejm. They transact useful business, especially on the sections of the budget of the ministry which they shadow. Most bills are sent directly to committee without a first reading. They then return for a very hurried second reading debate in the Sejm where they are voted on by a show of hands, signed by the Chairman and Secretary of the Council of State and become law on formal registration in the *Dziennik Ustaw* [Bulletin of Laws]. The Sejm can also pass resolutions by a simple vote.

The seventeen-strong Council of State is elected at the first sitting of a newly elected Sejm from among its members. In formal constitutional theory it is answerable only to the Sejm. Its functions are to control the Council of Ministers when the Sejm is not in session and to exercise a general oversight over the Supreme Control Chamber (Najwyższa Izba Kontroli—NIK), the Procurator-General and the Supreme Court as well as over the People's Councils. It is the Collective Head of State. Its Chairman in effect becomes the President of the Republic although he is assisted in his duties by four Deputy-Chairmen. The Council of State appoints and recalls ambassadors, receives the letters of accreditation of foreign ambassadors, and exercises the prerogative of mercy. It has numerous other responsibilities ranging from the ratification of treaties, the organization of elections, the convening of the Sejm, and appointment to a variety of posts such as university professorships. It can also pass decree-laws and appoint or dismiss ministers subject to subsequent confirmation by the Sejm. These powers were used extensively in the Stalinist period (110 decree-laws between 1952 and 1955 as against 11 laws passed by the Sejm) but one of the most significant constitutional aspects of 1956 was the transfer of power from the Council of State back to the Sejm. Decree-laws are now rather exceptional (only 3 between 1958 and 1972 as against 326 laws passed by the Sejm). From March 1972 onwards (and as of the time of writing) the Chairman of the Council of State was the distinguished history professor and former Minister of Education, Henryk Jabłoński. His predecessors were Józef Cyrankiewicz (December 1970–March 1972), Marshal Marian Spychalski (April 1968–December 1970), Edward Ochab (August 1964–April 1968) and Aleksander Zawadzki (November 1952–August 1964). Bolesław Bierut was Head of State before that as President of the KRN from September 1944 to February 1947 and then as President of the Republic until November 1952.

The Council of Ministers is described in the constitution as the supreme executive and administrative organ of state power. It oversees the work of ministries, state agencies and People's Councils. Formally appointed and dismissed by the Sejm, it works within the framework of its laws and resolutions. Its Chairman is the senior Politburo member in charge of state administration. In Poland he appoints the Deputy-Chairmen of the Council of Ministers, of which there are normally between five and eight (the Presidium since 1969), the ministers (about twenty-six) and the chairmen of the various state agencies (about seventeen). The Council of Ministers and individual ministries can pass decrees (rozporządzenie) which have the force of executive instructions connected with the implementation of legislation, and resolutions (uchwały) which deal with other matters as well as circulars (okólniki) which clarify outstanding questions.

In an unprecedented move testifying to the gravity of the situation, General Wojciech Jaruzelski was appointed Chairman of the Council of Ministers in February 1981. His predecessors were Józef Pińkowski (August 1980–February 1981), Edward Babiuch (March–August 1980), Piotr Jaroszewicz (December 1970–February 1980), Józef Cyrankiewicz (February 1947–December 1970 with a break in 1952–4), Bolesław Bierut (November 1952–March 1954) and Edward Osóbka-Morawski, a socialist who was Premier from 31 December 1944 to February 1947.

In the two decades from 1954 to 1975 the People's Councils in Poland were organized on a three-tier basis of 22 provinces (województwa), about 300 counties (powiaty) and a large number of rural districts (gromady) and settlements (osiedla). Their work was formally overseen by the Council of State. Detailed control was exercised over their presidia by the Council of Ministers while the appropriate ministries dealt with their departments as part of the unified state system. Between 1972 and 1975 the 4,313 lower-level councils were replaced by 2,367 communes (gminy) run by better-educated managers, the counties were abolished completely while the provinces were reorganized into 49 new ones closely resembling French departments in size.

The leading force in Polish politics is the PZPR, formed in December 1948. It is the successor to the KPP and PPR described earlier. The PZPR had a membership of 1.5 million (6.26 per cent of the population) in 1948, which had fallen to 1.2 million (3.55 per cent of the population) by 1958. Since then it has risen steadily both numerically and as a percentage of the population: 1.89 million (5.6 per cent) in 1966, 2.32 million (7.1 per cent) in 1970, 2.36 million (6.94 per cent) in 1975 and 3.08 million out of a population of 35 million in January 1980. Its social composition has normally been about 40 per cent manual workers, 10 per cent peasants and 45 per cent white-collar and professionals. In 1980 the PZPR was organized in about 75,000 basic party cells (POPs), 27,000 sections and 70,000 party groups. The PZPR held eight congresses between 1948 and 1980 (the most recent ones being in December 1971, December 1975 and February 1980). The Eighth Congress elected a Central Committee of 143 full and 108 candidate members. This in turn elected a Politburo of fourteen full and five candidate members, Edward Gierek as First Party Secretary and seven other party secretaries. Gierek's fall led to a period of rapid and sweeping change in the composition of the Politburo and Secretariat.

The PZPR is a typical Leninist party which is organized and functions on the principles of democratic centralism. The main decisions are taken at Politburo and Secretariat level. An increasingly important role was played in the 1970s by heads of the Central Committee departments and commissions who oversee the work of ministries and state agencies. The Central Committee meets at carefully prepared plena three or four times a year. Its members, the bulk of whom are party organizers and representatives of other political and social organizations, normally act as the most important single channel of influence on the top party leadership. The above system was sharply criticized during the period of democratic renewal after August 1980. Kania's predecessors as first party secretaries were Edward Gierek (December 1970–September 1980), Władysław Gomułka (October 1956–December 1970), Edward Ochab (March–October 1956) and Bolesław Bierut (September 1948–March 1956). Władysław Gomułka was the First Secretary of the PPR from 1943 to 1948.

Main publishing houses

Since 1948 most official PZPR material has been published by Książka i Wiedza—KiW (Book and Knowledge). In the economic field the major sources of official material are Państwowe Wydawnictwo Ekonomiczne—PWE (State Economic Publishers) and Główny Urząd Statystyczny—GUS (Central Stat-istical Office). Wydawnictwo Prawnicze—Wyd. Prawnicze (Legal Publishers) specializes in collections of legal documents. Other major sources of official publications are Państwowe Wydawnictwo Naukowe—PWN (State Academic Publishers), perhaps the most prestigious publishing house in Poland, and its illustrious rival the Ossolineum press of Wrocław, both of which publish material for Polska Akademia Nauk—PAN (Polish Academy of Sciences). Material on foreign affairs is handled mainly by the press of the Polski Instytut Spraw Międzynarodowych—PISM (Polish Institute of International Affairs) and by Interpress, which is also the official news agency which publishes foreign-language editions. Polska Agencja Prasowa—PAP (Polish Press Agency) is the main official news agency. Many of the ministries and agencies publish their own material but the most notable general press of this type is that of the Ministerstwo Obrony Narodowej—MON (Ministry of National Defence) which is now the largest in Poland. Among the remaining presses which occasionally produce official material the most noteworthy are: Krajowa Agencja Wydawnicza—KAW (National Publishing Agency) and Wiedza Powszechna (Universal Knowledge), while there are a number of regional presses, notably in Łódź, Gdańsk, Kraków and Lublin.

Censorship was exercised on the basis of PZPR Central Committee directives by the Main Department for the Control of the Press, Publications and Entertainments—GUKPPiW. The only exceptions were *Trybuna Ludu*, the PZPR daily, and the high quality weekly *Polityka*, which appeared on their editors' responsibility.

GENERAL BIBLIOGRAPHIES AND REFERENCE WORKS

National bibliographies

P1   *Bibliografia bibliografii polskich 1951–1960.* [Bibliography of Polish bibliographies 1951–1960]. Red. H. Sawoniak. (Instytut Bibliograficzny). Wr.: Ossolineum, 1967. xxix, 484 pp.

Author and subject indexes. Lists 5,795 items together with short annotations, grouped in 7 sections. The largest section, part III, contains subject bibliographies listed under 244 subject headings— many, such as law, politics, industry and the like, are relevant to official publishing. This is a revised and updated version of two earlier editions by W. Hahn.

P2   *Przewodnik bibliograficzny: urzędowy wykaz druków wydanych w Rzeczypospolitej Polskiej.* [Bibliographic guide: official register of publications issued in the Polish Republic]. Wwa: BN, 1946–. Weekly.

Vol. 2 published 1946. Vol. 1 (for 1944–5) was published in 1955. This is the official Polish national bibliography for non-periodical publications. It is the continuation of *Urzędowy wykaz druków wydanych w Rzeczypospolitej Polskiej* (1928–39).

P3   *Bibliografia czasopism i wydawnictw zbiorowych 1958 [etc.].* [Bibliography of periodicals and collective works]. Wwa: BN, 1960–.

The volumes for 1958 to 1971 (publ. 1974) appeared annually. The most recent volume covers 1972–4 and appeared in 1978. Part of the Polish national bibliography, listing current serials including irregular series, newspapers and yearbooks.

P4 *Bibliografia zawartości czasopism.* [Bibliography of periodical contents]. Wwa: BN, 1947, 1948, 1951–. Monthly.
Published twice yearly July 1947–June 1951. Indexes selected articles (including government and party statements, speeches, communiqués, etc.) from over 400 journals and major newspapers. Annual name and subject indexes.

Other general bibliographies

P5a Wepsiec, J. *Polish serial publications 1953–1962. An annotated bibliography.* Chicago: 1964. 506 pp.
P5b Wepsiec, J. *Polish serial publications 1963–1972. An annotated bibliography.* Scarborough: 1976. 489 pp.
The two volumes between them record some 8,000 journal, newspaper and irregular series titles.

P6 *Bibliographie juridique polonaise 1944–1956.* Red. W. Czachórski. (Inst. Nauk Prawnych PAN). Varsovie: PWN, 1958. 136 pp.

P7 *Polska bibliografia prawnicza.* [Polish legal bibliography]. (Inst. Państwa i Prawa, previously Inst. Nauk Prawnych PAN). Wwa: PAN, 1962–.
The most comprehensive bibliography of Polish legal literature appearing in books and journals from 1944 onwards. Vol. XIII (publ. 1980) covers 1974–5. Some notes in French.

P8 *Legal sources and bibliography of Poland.* Ed. P. Siekanowicz. (Mid-European Law Project, Gen. Ed. V. Gsovski. Praeger Publications in World Communism, 22). New York: Praeger, 1964. 311 pp.
Includes material in Polish and other languages for the period up to 1961.

P9 *Bibliografia Ziem Zachodnich 1945–1958.* [Bibliography of the Western Territories 1945–1958]. Red. F. Czarnecki. Poznań: Inst. Zachodni, 1962. 545 pp.
Bibliography of 4,753 books and articles published on the subject of the Western Territories. Material is divided into 13 thematic chapter headings dealing with economic, demographic, cultural aspects and the like. Index.

General reference works

P10 *Polska. Informator.* [Information guide to Poland]. Wyd. 2. Red. E. Trzeciak, J. Wankowicz. Wwa: Interpress, 1977. 632 pp.

P11 *Wielka encyklopedia powszechna PWN.* [Large universal encyclopedia of the PWN]. Red. B. Suchodolski. Wwa: PWN, 1962–70. 13 vols.

The largest, academically most respectable and politically most controversial encyclopedia to appear in communist Poland. A development of the *Mała encyklopedia powszechna PWN,* Wwa: PWN, 1959, 1124 pp.

P12   *Polska Ludowa. Rocznik polityczny i gospodarczy 1948.* [People's Poland. Political and economic yearbook for 1948]. Łódź: Czytelnik, 1948. 1012 pp.

Contains political documents such as the 1947 constitution, the PKWN manifesto and detailed information on incumbents of state offices in the Sejm, Cabinet, ministries, state agencies, provinces, counties and municipalities. Detailed information on the economy, culture, etc. No more published in this series.

P13   *Rocznik polityczny i gospodarczy.* [Political and economic yearbook]. Wwa: PWE, 1958–. Annual.

The most comprehensive and authoritative Polish yearbook. It contains information about the activities, membership and leaders of all the political and social organizations as well as incumbents of state and provincial offices. It overviews the economy, social and health services, education, culture, sport and foreign relations. Normally about 800 pp.

P14   Mołdawa, T. *Skład osobowy naczelnych organów państwowych Polski Ludowej.* [The individual composition of the leading state organs in People's Poland]. Wwa: Wyd. Uniw. Warszawskiego, 1971. 139 pp.

This Warsaw University textbook lists all office-holders for the period 1944–71 for the KRN, Constituent Sejm, Sejm, Council of State, Council of Ministers and Chairmen of the Supreme Control Chamber. It is particularly useful for its lists of ministerial office-holders. Index of names.

P15   Zawadzki, T. *Obsada personalna stanowisk publicznych w Polsce.* [Personal incumbents of public offices in Poland]. Munich: Radio Free Europe, Polish Service, 1959. 237 pp.

Lists incumbents of all main offices in Party, state, local government, Roman Catholic Church, and a range of social organizations. Gives additional biographical detail (party allegiance and other offices held) for major figures. Index.

P16   *Spis miejscowości Polskiej Rzeczypospolitej Ludowej.* [Directory of towns and settlements in the Polish People's Republic]. Wwa: Wyd. Komunikacji i Łączności, 1967. 1383 pp.

The first complete directory of towns and settlements in Poland since 1928. Gives complete administrative, postal, railway and civil-registry details.

CONSTITUTIONAL DOCUMENTS

Constitutions

P17 Constitutional Law of 19 February 1947, popularly known as the 'Little Constitution' (Dz.U. 1947, no. 18, pos. 71). It is reproduced in all the major collections of Polish documents cited below.

P18 *The Provisional Constitution of 20 [sic] February 1947 and the Declaration of Rights. Documents and Reports on Poland.* New York: Polish Research and Information Service, 1947. 16 pp.
An English-language translation.

P19 Constitutional Law of 22 July 1952, popularly known as the 'July Constitution' (Dz.U. 1952, no. 33, pos. 232–5). As changes in the institutions mentioned in the constitution necessitated changes in the text, it was amended 10 times between 1952 and 1976. The above and the major constitutional changes of 1976 were published in a consolidated form in:

P20 'Obwieszczenie przewodniczącego Rady Państwa z dnia 16 lutego 1976r.', Dz.U., 21.2.1976, no. 7, pos. 36.
The constitution has been published and popularized in large editions on numerous occasions.

P21 Bierut, B. *O Konstytucji Polskiej Rzeczypospolitej Ludowej.* [About the constitution of the Polish People's Republic]. Wwa: KiW, 1952. 90 pp.
Original text of the constitution as promulgated on 22 July 1952. Introduced by Bierut's speech (title as above) delivered to the Constituent Sejm on 18 July 1952.

P22 Sokolewicz, W. *Konstytucja PRL po zmianach z 1976r.* [The constitution of the PRL after the 1976 amendments]. Wwa: PWN, 1978.
Pages 242–91 include the changes between the old and new texts.

P23 *Konstytucja PRL.* [The constitution of the PRL]. Wwa: KiW, 1976. 62 pp.
A popular edition of the amended constitution. Numerous translations into foreign languages have been published at various times.

General collections
of constitutional documents

P24 *Podstawowe źródła do nauki polskiego prawa konstytucyjnego.* [Basic sources for the study of Polish constitutional law]. Red. A. Patrzałek. Wr.: Wyd. Uniw., 1979. 529 pp.
A students' textbook collection of all the most important constitutional documents.

P25   *Konstytucja i podstawowe akty ustrojowe Polskiej Rzeczypospolitej Ludowej*. [Constitution and basic acts of the political system of the Polish People's Republic]. Red. F. Siemieński [et al.]. Wwa: Wyd. Prawnicze, 1978. 513 pp.

      Updated and extended version of P27–P29 below. Gives documents as at 1 October 1978.

P26   *Ustrój społeczno-polityczny PRL. Wybór dokumentów i materiałów*. [Social and political system of the PRL. Selection of documents and materials]. Red. J. Wielgosz. Kr.: Powielarnia AGH, 1970. 465 pp.

      History and sources for the political and social system for the post-1944 period.

P27   *Konstytucja i podstawowe akty ustawodawcze PRL. Zbiór tekstów*. [The constitution and basic legislative acts of the PRL. Collected texts]. Red. J. Zakrzewska, A. Gwiżdż. Wwa: Wyd. Prawnicze, 1952. xxi, 327 pp.

      More documents on the earlier period (from 1944) than later editions. This is the first edition of what became the most authoritative and widely used collection of documents of constitutional significance. They include the PKWN manifesto, the socio-economic reforms of 1944–50, the constitutions of 1947 and 1950, and electoral laws.

P28   *Konstytucja i podstawowe akty ustawodawcze PRL*. [The constitution and basic legislative acts of the PRL]. Wyd. 5. Red. A. Gwiżdż, J. Zakrzewska. Wwa: Wyd. Prawnicze, 1966. 350 pp.

P29   *Wybór źródeł do nauki polskiego prawa państwowego*. [Selected sources for the study of Polish state law]. Red. J. Zakrzewska, A. Gwiżdż. Wwa: PWN, 1967. 508 pp.

      Legal position as of 1 April 1967. Slightly updated and extended version of the previously cited comprehensive collection covering 1944–66. Designed for use by Polish university students.

LAW CODES

As in all communist countries, there are a large number of law codes which are frequently amended and updated.

Code of Administrative Procedure

Law of 14 June 1960 (Dz.U. 1960, no. 30, pos. 168).

P30   *Kodeks postępowania administracyjnego. Wzory pism i formularzy wraz z tekstem kodeksu i przepisów wykonawczych*. [Code of Administrative Procedure. Model documents and forms together with the text of the code and executive regulations]. Wyd. 2. Wwa: Urząd Rady Ministrów, 1961.

      A French translation appeared as: *Code de procédure administratif de la République Populaire de Pologne*. Varsovie: Office du Conseil des Ministres, 1961. 62 pp. The 10th edition of the Polish text and accompanying regulations appeared in 1975.

Civil Code

Law of 23 April 1964 (Dz.U. 1964, no. 16, pos. 93).

P31 *Kodeks Cywilny wraz z przepisami wykonawczymi i skorowidzami. Kodeks Rodzinny i Opiekuńczy i prawo prywatne międzynarodowe.* [Civil Code together with executive regulations and indexes. Family and Guardianship Code and international private law]. Red. S. Chorązkowska. Wwa: Wyd. Prawnicze, 1970. 503 pp.

P32 *Code Civil de la République Populaire de Pologne*. Red. J. S. Piątowski, E. Lętowska. Wwa: Wyd. Prawnicze, 197?. 600 pp.

French translation of the 1964 code together with selections from its introductory regulations. Another French translation, ed. by W. Czachórski and J. Wasilkowski with the same title, was published by Wyd. Prawnicze in 1966, 301 pp.

P33 *Kodeks Cywilny: piśmiennictwo i orzecznictwo*. [Civil Code: literature and legal judgements]. Red. M. Gintowt, S. Rudnicki. Wwa: Wyd. Prawnicze, 1979. 655 pp.

Useful as a bibliographic guide to sources dealing with the Civil Code, and contains the most important legal pronouncements on its implementation.

Family and Guardianship Code

Law of 25 February 1964 (Dz.U. 1964, no. 9, pos. 59). The earlier Code of Family Law was promulgated in 1950 (Dz.U. 1950, no. 34, pos. 308, 309).

P34 *Kodeks Rodzinny i Opiekuńczy*. [Family and Guardianship Code]. Wyd. 6. Wwa: Wyd. Prawnicze, 1970. 50 pp.

An English translation of this code can be found in: *Polish family law*, ed. D. Lasok, Leiden: Sijthoff, 1968, pp. 263–289. This also includes the Law of 12 November 1965 on Private International Law.

Criminal Code

Law of 19 April 1969 (Dz.U. 1969, no. 13, pos. 94).

P35 *Kodeks Karny. (Oraz przepisy wprowadzające)*. [Criminal Code, and introductory regulations]. Wyd. 6. Wwa: Wyd. Prawnicze, 1978. 115 pp.

An English translation is: *The Penal Code of the Polish People's Republic*. (The American series of foreign penal codes, 19). London: Sweet & Maxwell, 1973. 139 pp.

Code of Criminal Procedure

Law of 19 April 1969 (Dz.U. 1969, no. 13, pos. 96).

P36 *Kodeks postępowania karnego oraz przepisy wprowadzające.* [Code of Criminal Procedure as well as introductory regulations]. Wyd. 3. Wwa: Wyd. Prawnicze, 1977. 224 pp.

An English text of the code, with a glossary of Polish and English legal terms, is: *Code of Criminal Procedure of the Polish People's Republic.* 5th ed. Ed. S. Wałtos. Warsaw: Wyd. Prawnicze, 1979. 262 pp.

Executive Criminal Code

Law of 19 April 1969 (Dz.U. 1969, no. 13, pos. 98).

P37 *Kodeks Karny Wykonawczy.* [Executive Criminal Code]. Wyd. 2. Wwa: Wyd. Prawnicze, 1969. 72 pp.

Code of Misdemeanours

Law of 20 May 1971 (Dz.U. 1971, no. 12, pos. 114).

P38 *Kodeks wykroczeń oraz przepisy wprowadzające.* [Code of Misdemeanours, and introductory regulations]. Wyd. 7. Wwa: Wyd. Prawnicze, 1979. 68 pp.

Maritime Code

Law of December 1961 (Dz.U. 1961, no. 58, pos. 318).

P39 *Kodeks morski.* [The Maritime Code]. Gdynia: Wyd. Morskie, 1964.

An English translation, entitled *The Polish Maritime Code,* was issued by the same publishers in the same year.

Labour Code

Law of 26 June 1974 (Dz.U. 1974, no. 24, pos. 141). A French translation was published separately as:

P40 *Code du Travail de la République Populaire de Pologne.* Varsovie: Wyd. Prawnicze, 1978. 171 pp.

For earlier labour legislation, see: P148.

P41 *Kodeks pracy. Zbiór obowiązujących ustaw na dzień 1.xi.1947r.* [The Labour Code. A collection of laws in force on 1 November 1947]. Wyd. 2. Red. W. Beyer. Gdynia: Czytelnik, 1947. 363 pp.

About two-thirds of the material is prewar, but all the relevant early postwar legislation is also contained.

OTHER GENERAL LEGISLATIVE DOCUMENTS

Official gazettes and bulletins

P42   *Dziennik ustaw Polskiej Rzeczypospolitej Ludowej.* [Bulletin of laws of the Polish People's Republic]. Wwa: 1919–39, 1944–. Irregular.

Gives the texts of laws, of orders and decrees of the Council of Ministers, and of international treaties and conventions. Published under the auspices of the Presidium of the Council of Ministers. Until 1952 the title was *Dziennik ustaw Rzeczypospolitej Polskiej.*

P43   *Monitor polski. Dziennik urzędowy Polskiej Rzeczypospolitej Ludowej.* [Polish monitor. Official journal of the Polish People's Republic]. Wwa: 1918–39, 1945–. Irregular.

Title omitted *Ludowej* before 1952. Published in two series, A and B, from 1945 to 1954 (82). Gives the texts of resolutions of the Council of State and of the government, and the more important decrees, circulars and instructions of other central agencies and public authorities.

P44   *Skorowidz przepisów prawnych ogłoszonych w Dzienniku Ustaw oraz w Monitorze Polskim w latach 1918–1939 oraz 1944–1976.* [Index of legal regulations published in the Bulletin of Laws and the Polish Monitor during 1918–1939 and 1944–1976]. (Urząd Rady Ministrów). Wwa: 1977. 728 pp.

Updated to legal position of 30 November 1976. Catalogue-index of all Polish laws grouped by subject in alphabetical order. Also includes a table of Poland's international agreements. Earlier editions, by Z. Keck, were published in 1948, 1956, 1968 and 1974.

Ministries and other state agencies have been reorganized and renamed on numerous occasions in postwar Poland. (See the section entitled 'Ministerstwa i urzędy centralne' in P13). Orders and instructions (zarządzenia) and circulars (okólniki) of ministries appear in their individual official journal, *Dziennik urzędowy....* The more important are also published in *Monitor polski.* The publicly available *Dzienniki urzędowe ...* have been those for the economic, social and cultural ministries and agencies. Some are published at regular intervals but most have varying frequencies of publication. Most contain an annual alphabetic subject index. Some contain a variety of additional information. For example, the Ministry of Enlightenment and Higher Education published in its *Dziennik urzędowy* during the 1960s lists of legal acts concerning higher education already published in *Dziennik ustaw* and *Monitor polski.* In 1977, 23 ministries and 18 other central agencies published easily available official journals (in some cases with the title beginning *Biuletyn ...* instead of *Dziennik urzędowy Ministerstwa ...*).

Collection of legislation

P45 *The legislation of Poland. Laws, decrees, orders, ordinances.* Warsaw: 1949–59. 10 vols.
The first four volumes, ed. by Barcikowski et al., appeared in 1949–50. The remaining six (numbered 1–6 in a separate sequence), were published in an irregular series by the Polish Institute of International Affairs (PISM), 1954–9.

Journals

P46 *Państwo i prawo.* [State and law]. (Inst. państwa i prawa PAN). Wwa: 1946–. Monthly.
A major academic journal which has particularly good coverage of state law and constitutional problems. English, French and Russian summaries of the main articles.

P47 *Nowe prawo.* [New law]. Wwa: 1945–. Monthly.
Up to December 1956 this was the journal of the Ministry of Justice, the Procurator-General and the Supreme Court. Since then it has been devoted to questions concerning the implementation of justice, carrying articles and reviews, and a section which publishes Supreme Court judgements.

Electoral laws

Postwar Poland has had three major electoral laws governing national elections as well as a host of minor changes. The former have been the electoral laws of 22 October 1945, of 1 August 1952, and the most important one of 24 October 1956. The electoral laws, particularly the 1956 one with its various subsequent amendments, have been publicized at various times in large brochure editions, usually before an election. The earliest and latest are:

P48a *Ordynacja wyborcza do Sejmu Ustawodawczego.* [Electoral law to the Constituent Sejm]. Wwa: 1945. 31 pp.
P48b *Ordynacja wyborcza do Sejmu PRL i Rad Narodowych.* [Electoral laws to the Sejm of the PRL and the People's Councils]. Wwa: KiW, 1980. 64 pp.

Publicity material for elections as well as the Election Manifesto are produced by the Front of National Unity (FJN).

The Sejm

P49 *Sprawozdanie stenograficzne z posiedzeń Krajowej Rady Narodowej.* [Stenographic record of sittings of the Polish National Council]. Wwa: 1944–7.

P50 *Sprawozdanie stenograficzne z posiedzeń Sejmu Ustawodawczego.* [Stenographic record of the Constituent Sejm]. Wwa: 1947–52.

P51 *Protokóły komisji Sejmu Ustawodawczego.* [Record of sittings of the committees of the Constituent Sejm]. Wwa: 1947–52.

32 permanent committees and 7 special ones functioned at various times: see *Sejm Ustawodawczy RP*, red. M. Rybicki, Wwa: Ossolineum, 1977, pp. 328–9.

P52 *Sprawozdanie stenograficzne z posiedzeń Sejmu PRL.* [Stenographic record of the Sejm of the Polish People's Republic]. Wwa: 1952–.

P53 *Biuletyny prasowe Sejmu.* [Press bulletins of the Sejm]. Wwa: 1952–.

Mimeograph reports of Sejm committee sittings produced by the Sejm's Press Bureau for government agencies. Limited circulation, but available in the Sejm Library.

P54 *Druki Sejmowe.* [Sejm publications]. Wwa: 1952–.

Draft bills, resolutions, committee reports and the like.

The Standing Orders of the Sejm have been published at intervals, e.g.:

P55 *Regulamin Sejmu PRL uchwalony dnia 1 marca 1957r. i zmieniony uchwałą Sejmu z dnia 28 grudnia 1965r.* [Standing Orders of the Sejm promulgated on 1 March 1957 and amended by Sejm resolution of 28 December 1965]. Wwa: Sejm, 1966.

P56 *Regulamin Klubu Poselskiego PZPR ogłoszony 5.iii.1957r. ze zmianami zatwierdzonymi przez Biuro Polityczne dnia 13.ii.1958r.* [Standing Orders of the PUWP Deputies' Club published on 5 March 1957 with the changes confirmed by the Politbureau on 13 February 1958]. Wwa: Sejm, 1963.

Like the U.S. Congress, each Sejm is given a chronological number according to its term of office. Since 1956 it has been customary to publicize the work of each Sejm, presenting number of sittings, laws passed and the like, in publications such as:

P57 *Informacja o działalności Sejmu PRL (III kadencja—1961–65).* [Information about the activities of the Third Sejm of the PRL, 1961–65]. Wwa: Sejm, 1965. 108 pp.

Authoritative information about the sittings, laws and resolutions passed, committee activity and composition of the Third Sejm. Lists all 460 deputies alphabetically giving party allegiance, constituency and committee affiliation. Publications with the same title have been issued for the fourth (1965–9) and fifth (1969–72) terms of the Sejm. The sixth (1972–6) is given similar treatment in:

P58 Bednarski, S. *Sejm VI kadencji.* [The sixth-term Sejm]. Wwa: KAW, 1976. 86 pp.

P59 *Skorowidz do sprawozdań stenograficznych z posiedzeń Sejmu PRL IV kadencji od 19 marca 1972r. do 10 lutego 1976r.* [Index to stenographic reports of the Sejm of the PRL, 4th term, 19.3.1972 to 10.2.1976]. Wwa: 1976.

Section A is an index to subjects discussed by the Sejm. Section B gives information about all the deputies and the occasions on which they spoke during the Sejm's term. Similar publications have been issued for other Sejm terms.

Court judgements

P60 *Orzecznictwo Sądu Najwyższego.* Wwa: 1962–. Monthly in two series.

The two monthly series are subtitled *Izba karna i wojskowa* [Penal and Military Chamber] and *Izba cywilna oraz Izba pracy i ubezpieczeń społecznych* [Civil Chamber and Social Insurance Chamber]. From 1953 to 1962 was published as a single series under the title *Orzecznictwo Sądu Najwyższego Izby cywilnej i Izby karnej* [Judgements of the Civil Chamber and Penal Chamber of the Supreme Court], monthly.

P61 *Orzecznictwo Sądów polskich i komisji arbitrażowych.* [Judgements of the Polish courts and arbitration commissions]. (Inst. Nauk Prawnych PAN). Wwa: 1958–. Monthly.

State administration

P62 *Bibliografia Rad Narodowych 1945–1958.* [Bibliography of the People's Councils 1945–1958]. (Inst. Nauk Prawnych PAN). Wwa/Wr.: Ossolineum, 1973. x, 339 pp.

P63 *Podział administracyjny Polskiej Rzeczypospolitej Ludowej.* [Administrative division of the PRL]. Wyd. 3. Wwa: Urząd Rady Ministrów, 1965.

Earlier editions 1956, 1960.

P64 Dawidowicz, W. *Zagadnienia ustroju administracji państwowej w Polsce.* [Questions concerning the system of state administration in Poland]. Wwa: PWN, 1970. 462 pp.

A comprehensive legal-institutional description of the Polish state administration. Reproduces a wide variety of laws, resolutions and instructions concerning the subject.

P65 Dawidowicz, W. *Polskie prawo administracyjne.* [Polish administrative law]. Wwa: PWN, 1978. 664 pp.

Includes excerpts from a wide range of relevant legal regulations.

P66 *Funkcjonowanie administracji w świetle orzecznictwa.* [The functioning of the administration in the light of judicial judgements]. Red. J. Starościak, J. Łętowski. Wwa: Wyd. Prawnicze, 1967–74. 4 vols.

P67 *Orzecznictwo naczelnych organów administracji państwowych.* [Legal judgements concerning the leading state administrative organs]. Red. H. Starczewski [et al.]. (Prokuratura Generalna PRL). Wwa: Wyd. Prawnicze, 1968. 358 pp.

Legal decisions by state administrative bodies which the Procurator-General's Office considered had the character of precedents and which were initiated by it.

P68 Dawidowicz, W. *Zarys ustroju organów administracji terytorialnej w Polsce.* [Outline of the system of organs of local administration in Poland]. Wwa: PWN, 1976. 265 pp.

A detailed commentary on the reformed system of local government in Poland. Includes a comprehensive bibliographic guide to the literature on postwar People's Councils and territorial administration.

P69 *Problemy Rad Narodowych. Studia i materiały.* [Problems of People's Councils. Studies and documentation]. (Inst. Państwa i Prawa PAN). Wwa: 1963–. Irregular.

49 volumes published by 1981. Publishes the results of major research on People's Councils in Poland. It has branched out to include studies of Soviet and East European local government.

P70 *Granice państwowe PRL. Wybór przepisów.* [The state frontiers of the PRL. Selected regulations]. Red. R. Ptasiński. Wwa: Wyd. Prawnicze, 1974. 462 pp.

GENERAL PARTY DOCUMENTS

Polish Workers' Party—PPR

P71 *Materiały do bibliografii publikacji Polskiej Partii Robotniczej, 1942–48.* [Materials for a bibliography of PPR publications, 1942–48]. Red. L. Smosarski. (Centralne Archiwum KC PZPR). Wwa: 1976. 473 pp.

An extensive bibliography of PPR publications for this period.

P72 *Kształtowanie się podstaw programowych PPR w latach 1942–1945. Wybór materiałów i dokumentów.* [The shaping of the fundamentals of the PPR programme during 1942–1945. Selection of material and documents]. Red. W. Góra. (Zakład Historii Partii przy PZPR). Wwa: KiW, 1958. 590 pp.

An authoritative official collection of PPR material in the Party's first three years. Also contains a detailed guide to the institutions and political parties of the period (pp. 557–79).

P73 *PPR. Rezolucje, odezwy, instrukcje i okólniki Komitetu Centralnego PPR.* [The PPR. Resolutions, appeals, instructions and circulars of the PPR Central Committee]. (Zakład Historii Polskiego Ruchu Robotniczego). Wwa: KiW, 1959–73. 3 vols.

P74 Minc, H. *Aktualne zagadnienia i perspektywy gospodarcze demokratycznej Polski. Referat wygłoszony na I Zjeździe PPR.* [Current questions and economic perspectives of democratic Poland. Report delivered at the 1st PPR Congress]. Wwa: Książka, 1945. 92 pp.

P75 *Statut PPR uchwalony na I Zjeździe PPR.* [PPR Statute adopted at the 1st PPR Congress]. Wwa: Książka, 1948.

P76 *Głos ludu.* [The voice of the people]. Wwa: 1945–8. Daily.
The official daily of the PPR Central Committee. Amalgamated with the PPS daily *Robotnik* to form *Trybuna ludu* in 1948 (*see* P90).

Polish United Workers' Party—PZPR: Congresses and national conferences

The 1st or Unification PZPR Congress in 1948 was never published in full except for the main theme-speeches of Bolesław Bierut, Józef Cyrankiewicz and Hilary Minc. See *Nowe drogi* (P89).

P77 *Podstawy ideologiczne PZPR.* [Ideological foundations of the PZPR]. Wwa: KiW, 1952. 143 pp.
Contains the speeches delivered by Bierut and Cyrankiewicz at the 1948 congress, and the Ideological Declaration of the PZPR.

P78 *II Zjazd PZPR. Główne zadania gospodarcze dwóch ostatnich lat, 1954–55, Planu Sześcioletniego.* [2nd PZPR Congress. The main economic tasks of the last two years of the 5-Year Plan, 1954–55]. Wwa: 1954. 108 pp.
Contains the report delivered by Hilary Minc, and the final resolution of the congress. Other material of the 2nd Congress was published in *Nowe drogi*, III, no. 57, March 1954 (P89).

The proceedings of the 3rd to the 8th PZPR congresses have been published in full. Foreign-language versions have also normally been produced. The original Polish-language publications are the following:

P79 *III Zjazd Polskiej Zjednoczonej Partii Robotniczej, 10.iii–19.iii.1959r. Stenogram.* [3rd PZPR Congress. Stenographic report]. Wwa: Kiw, 1959. 1267 pp.

P80 *IV Zjazd Polskiej Zjednoczonej Partii Robotniczej. 15–20.vi.1964. Stenogram.* Wwa: KiW, 1964. 989 pp.

P81 *V Zjazd Polskiej Zjednoczonej Partii Robotniczej, 11–16 listopada 1968r. Podstawowe materiały i dokumenty.* [5th PZPR Congress. Basic materials and documents]. Wwa: KiW, 1968. 331 pp.

P82 *VI Zjazd PZPR. 6–11 grudnia 1971r. Podstawowe dokumenty i materiały.* [6th PZPR Congress. Basic documents and materials]. Wwa. KiW, 1972. 317 pp.
Also *Stenogram*, Wwa: KiW, 1972. 902 pp.

P83 *VII Zjazd PZPR. 8–12 grudnia 1975r. Stenogram z obrad plenarnych.* [7th PZPR Congress. Stenographic record of plenary proceedings]. Wwa: KiW, 1975. 1056 pp.

P84 *VIII Zjazd PZPR. 11–15 lutego 1980r. Podstawowe dokumenty i materiały*. [8th PZPR Congress. Basic documents and materials]. Wwa: KiW, 1980. 267 pp.

After coming to power Gierek adopted the practice of holding mid-term PZPR national conferences in between congresses:

P85 *I Krajowa Konferencja PZPR. 22–23 października 1973r. Podstawowe dokumenty i materiały*. [1st PZPR National Conference. Basic documents and materials]. Wwa: KiW, 1973.

P86 *II Krajowa Konferencja PZPR, 9–10.I.1978r*. [2nd PZPR National Conference]. Wwa: KiW, 1978.

The PZPR publishes its draft policy-themes before each congress. The resolutions of congresses have, since 1956, also been published and publicized separately. So have congress keynote speeches. Examples are:

P87 *O dalszy rozwój sił socjalizmu i utrwalenie pokoju; o dalsze umocnienie międzynarodowej pozycji PRL; rezolucja VII Zjazdu PZPR*. [About the further development of the forces of socialism and the preservation of peace; about the further strengthening of the international position of the PRL; resolution of the 7th PZPR Congress]. Wwa: KiW, 1975. 14 pp.

P88 *O dalszy dynamiczny rozwój budownictwa socjalistycznego—o wyższą jakość pracy i warunków życia narodu*. [About the further dynamic development of the building of socialism—about the higher quality of work and the living conditions of the nation]. Wwa: KiW, 1975. 62 pp.
     Programme-report of the Politbureau delivered by Gierek at the 7th Congress.

Polish United Workers' Party: Central Committee plena and other documents

Apart from congress and conference publications, the main sources of PZPR documents, such as the most important speeches, plena proceedings, resolutions, organizational and personnel changes, official comment on Polish domestic politics and the international Communist movement, are the two following publications:

P89 *Nowe drogi*. [New roads]. Wwa: 1947–. Monthly.
     6 issues p.a. 1947–51. The main PZPR theoretical journal and most authoritative record of PZPR developments.

P90 *Trybuna ludu*. [Tribune of the people]. Wwa: 1948–. Daily.
     Official daily of the PZPR Central Committee. Its material is reproduced by the PZPR provincial newspapers and with differing emphases by the newspapers of the subsidiary political parties, youth, students', cooperative, trade-union and women's movements. The main provincial PZPR dailies are: *Trybuna robotnicza*

(Katowice), which has the largest circulation in Poland; *Sztandar ludu* (Lublin); *Gazeta zachodna* (Poznań); *Głos Wybrzeża* (Gdańsk); and *Gazeta poludniowa* (Kraków).

One should also note the following two PZPR journals published in Warsaw:

P91   *Życie partii.* [Party life]. Wwa: 1955–. Monthly.
      Official bulletin and primer for party members.

P92   *Information bulletin of the Central Committee of the Polish United Workers' Party.* Warsaw: irregular, usually quarterly.
      Starting date not established. An English-language bulletin which reproduces the most important PZPR developments such as plena, Sejm or First Party Secretary's speeches.

Almost all the post-1956 PZPR Central Committee plena have been published in brochure form by Książka i Wiedza, the Party's publishing house. They normally include the First Party Secretary's speech, that of the Politbureau member delegated to deal in depth with the topic under discussion, the most important supporting contributions, the draft of the resolution adopted and any organizational changes carried out at the same time. The most important speeches and documents are also reprinted in *Nowe drogi* and *Trybuna ludu* (P89, P90). Between the 1st Congress in December 1948 and the 8th Congress in February 1980 the PZPR held about 94 plena. The 70 held since the beginning of 1958 have produced the bulkiest single item of PZPR official publication. Among the most significant plena have been:

P93a   The most important PZPR VIII plenum of October 1956, which was published in full in *Nowe drogi*, X, no. 10, October 1956 (P89).
P93b   *VIII Plenum KC PZPR, 6–7 lutego 1971r.* Wwa: KiW, 1971.
P93c   *XI Plenum KC PZPR, 4 września 1971r.* Wwa: KiW, 1971.
P93d   *IV Plenum KC PZPR, 9 września 1976r.* Wwa: KiW, 1976.
P93e   *IV Plenum KC PZPR, 24 sierpnia 1980r.* Wwa: KiW, 1980.
P93f   *VI Plenum KC PZPR, 5–6 września, 4–6 października 1980r.* Wwa: KiW, 1980.

The PZPR's party statute is subject to continual amendment. It is republished at intervals. Examples are:

P94a   *Deklaracja Ideowa PZPR. Statut PZPR.* [Ideological declaration and statute of the PZPR]. Wwa: KiW, 1950. 91 pp.
P94b   *Statut PZPR ze zmianami i uzupełnieniami uchwalonymi przez VII Zjazd PZPR w grudniu 1975r.* [The PZPR statute with amendments and additions adopted by the 7th PZPR Congress in December 1975]. Wwa: KiW, 1978. 121 pp.

P95   Zambrowski, R. & Świątkowski, H. *O statucie i zadaniach organizacyjnych PZPR.* [On the statute and organizational tasks of the PZPR]. Wwa: KiW, 1949.

P96   *Top authorities of the Polish United Workers' Party.* Warsaw: Interpress, 1971. 18 pp.

Lists all full and candidate members of the PZPR Central Committee, the Central Auditing Committee, and the Central Party Control Commission elected by the 6th PZPR Congress in 1971. Gives biographical detail on Politbureau and Secretariat members. Similar lists have been published by Interpress on numerous occasions.

P97 *Uchwały KC PZPR od II do III Zjazdu.* [Resolutions of the PZPR Central Committee passed between its 2nd and 3rd congresses]. Wwa: KiW, 1959.

Similar publications covering periods between congresses were published subsequently.

STATISTICS

Bibliography

P98 *Bibliografia wydawnictw Głównego Urzędu Statystycznego 1918–1968.* [Bibliography of publications of the Main Statistical Office 1918–1968]. Wwa: GUS, 1968. 466 pp.

Main annuals and series

P99 *Rocznik statystyczny.* [Statistical yearbook]. Wwa: GUS, 1930–9, 1947–. Annual.

Vols. 1–10 published as *Mały rocznik statystyczny* 1930–9, vol. 11 for 1947. No volumes published between 14 (1950) and 15 (1955). GUS's most comprehensive regular compilation of statistical material concerning Poland's economic, social, demographic, cultural and regional development. In recent years increasing space has been devoted to international comparisons. English translations have appeared only as: *Statistical yearbook of Poland 1947*, Wwa: GUS, 1948; and *Statistical yearbook 1957*, Wwa: GUS, 1957.

P100 *Mały rocznik statystyczny.* [Small statistical yearbook]. [New series]. Wwa: GUS, 1958–. Annual.

English version published as *Concise statistical yearbook of Poland*, Wwa: GUS, 1959–. Annual.

P101 *Statystyka Polski.* [Statistics of Poland]. (GUS). Wwa: 1947–. Irregular.

A succession of irregular series, most of them with variations on the above title, compose the principal Polish statistical sources outside P99 and P100. They include numerous subseries and monographic publications. The main changes are as follows. Series D of *Statystyka Polski* was published in 18 volumes, 1947–50. (Series A–C were prewar.) There was then a gap of 7 years until series E (9 volumes) appeared in 1957–8, and Series F (10 volumes) in 1958–9. The series lettering was then discontinued, and vols. 20–122 were published under the main title alone between 1959 and 1966.

Between 1966 and 1972, the main title was altered to *Statystyka Polski—materiały statystyczne*, and vol. 1(123)–121(243) appeared between 1966 and 1972. A parallel series entitled *Roczniki branżowe* [Branch yearbooks], which included statistical annuals for many sectors of the economy, was published in 64 volumes between 1966 and 1973. In 1973 the two series were merged with several others, including *Studia i prace statystyczne* (P108), once again under the original title of *Statystyka Polski*, and a fresh sequence of numbering was begun.

P102 *Mały rocznik statystyki międzynarodowej.* [Small yearbook of international statistics]. Wwa: GUS, 1972–. Annual.

P103 *Rocznik statystyki międzynarodowej.* [Yearbook of international statistics]. Wwa: GUS, 1965–. Irregular, despite the title.

Census publications

The census of 14 February 1946 had its results published within Series D of P101 above. The 1960 census was published separately as:

P104 *Spis powszechny z dnia 6 grudnia 1960r. Wyniki ostateczne.* [General census of 6 December 1960. Completed results]. (GUS).
Seria L. Ludność, gospodarka domowa. [Population, home economy]. 1964–5. 23 vols.
Seria M. Mieszkania, budynki mieszkalne. [Accommodation and dwellings]. 1965–6. 23 vols.
Seria R. Indywidualne gospodarstwa rolne. [Individual farming units]. 1963–5. 20 vols.

P105 *Narodowy spis powszechny 8.xii.1970r. Wyniki wstępne.* [National census of 8 December 1970. Preliminary results]. (GUS). Wwa: 1971–?

P106 *Narodowy spis powszechny 1970. Wyniki ostateczne.* [1970 national census. Completed results]. (GUS). Wwa: 1971–3?
Published in series L, M and R like the 1960 census, subarranged by province.

Two partial censuses in 1966, one of dwellings and buildings (*Spisy mieszkań i budynków,* 18 vols.) and one of population (*Spisy ludności,* 19 vols.) were published in 1968 within the *Statystyka Polski* (P101).

Other statistical publications

P107 *Biuletyn statystyczny.* [Statistical bulletin]. Wwa: GUS, 1957–. Monthly.
Monthly update of the most important socio-economic statistics. Its function is to publish information bringing the annual *Rocznik statystyczny* up to date. International comparisons are included in the quarterly supplement *Przegląd międzynarodowy.*

P108   *Studia i prace statystyczne.* [Statistical works and studies]. (GUS).
Wwa: 1966–73. 48 vols.
Irregular series absorbed by *Statystyka Polski* (P101) in 1973.

P109   *Wiadomości statystyczne Głównego Urzędu Statystycznego.* [Statisti-
cal news of GUS]. Wwa: GUS, 1923–39, 1945–51, 1956–. Bi-
monthly.
Vols. 1–17 publ. 1923–39, vols. 18–24 in 1945–51. Fresh num-
eration begun in 1956. The official journal of GUS, including useful
bibliographical information.

P110   *Gospodarka Polski na tle wybranych krajów europejskich 1971.* [The
Polish economy compared with selected European countries 1971].
(GUS). Wwa: 1971. 262 pp.
First of a series of statistical comparisons placing Poland in the
context of other countries. During 1977, for example, GUS published a series of volumes comparing Poland's economic development individually with that of a number of other European countries.

P111   *Polska 1975: rozwój społeczno–gospodarczy między VI i VII Zjazdem
PZPR.* [Poland 1975: social and economic development between the
6th and 7th PZPR congresses]. Wwa: GUS, 1975. 158 pp.
Economic and social statistics since 1944. A political–publicist
publication designed to spotlight the achievements of the first half of
Gierek's rule.

P112   *Tendencje rozwoju społecznego.* [The tendencies of social develop-
ment]. Wwa: GUS, 1979. 330 pp.
Statistics illustrating the main characteristics of Polish social
development since 1944.

P113   *Polska 1918–1978: dane statystyczne.* [Poland 1918–1978: statistical
information]. Wwa: GUS, 1978. 87 pp.
A statistical overview of Poland's development designed for the
general public. Revised every few years.

P114   *Polska 1944–1974: liczby i fakty.* [Poland 1944–1974: facts and
figures]. Red. N. Świdzińska. Wwa: KiW, 1974. 204 pp.

P115   *Oddziaływanie prasy, radia i telewizji.* [The influence of the press,
radio and television]. Wwa: GUS, 1969. 164 pp. [Not seen].

INTERNATIONAL RELATIONS

The main official sources are the publications of the Polish Institute of
International affairs (PISM) and the Foreign Ministry (MSZ). Current
developments are covered by the press agency Interpress while the KAW
publishing house usually covers the more publicist material.

P116   *Zbiór umów międzynarodowych Polskiej Rzeczypospolitej Ludowej
1954* [etc.]. [Collected international agreements of the PRL]. (Biblioteka 'Zbioru Dokumentów'). Wwa: PISM, 1961–7. 11 vols.

The volumes published cover the years 1954–64. The first volumes issued (in 1961) were those for 1957, 1958 and 1959. Includes some agreements not published in *Dziennik ustaw.*

P117 *Polska Ludowa—Związek Radziecki 1944–1974. Zbiór dokumentów i materiałów.* [People's Poland—Soviet Union 1944–1974. Collected documents and material]. Red. S. Trepczyński, N. Rodionow. (MSZ PRL, MSZ ZSRR). Wwa: KiW, 1974. 651 pp.

An official collection of 266 documents, published under the auspices of the Polish and Soviet foreign ministries, illustrating the development of Polish–Soviet relations 1944–74.

P118 *Dokumenty i materiały do historii stosunków polsko–radzieckich.* [Documents and materials for the history of Polish–Soviet relations]. Wwa: KiW, 1962–.

This series covers the period from 1917 onwards. Vol. 10, publ. 1980, covers 1950–5.

P119 *Umowy graniczne PRL.* [Poland's frontier agreements]. Red. F. Jarzyna. Wwa: Wyd. Prawnicze, 1974. 622 pp.

A collection of 73 of the most important agreements on Polish frontiers since 1944, up to the position as of 15 June 1974.

P120 *Dokumenty wrogiej działalności Rządu Stanów Zjednoczonych wobec Polski Ludowej.* [Documents illustrating the hostile activities of the U.S. government against People's Poland]. (MSZ PRL). Wwa: 1953. xii, 247 pp.

56 diplomatic documents, speeches, press articles and court proceedings illustrating alleged hostile American activities against Poland.

P121 *Remilitaryzacja Niemiec Zachodnich. Dokumenty i materiały.* [The remilitarization of West Germany. Documents and materials]. Red. M. Tomala. (PISM. Biblioteka Zbioru Dokumentów, 3.) Wwa: 1953. 371 pp.

75 excerpts from treaties, speeches and party declarations on German rearmament.

P122 *Plan Rapackiego. Dokumenty i materiały.* [The Rapacki Plan. Documents and materials]. Red. W. Nagórski, M. Tomala. (PISM). Wwa: KiW, 1959. 179 pp.

24 speeches, newspaper articles and documents concerning the Rapacki Plan for military disengagement in Eastern Europe.

P123 *Western frontier of Poland. Documents, statements, opinions.* Ed. W. Leśniewski. Warsaw: PISM/Western Press Agency, 1965. 302 pp.

Publishes 299 documents, speeches and press items from various countries on Poland's western frontier; subdivided into chronological historical periods since 1939 and by major country.

P124 *Polska Rzeczpospolita Ludowa—Republika Federalna Niemiec: bilans stosunków wzajemnych, problemy i perspektywy normalizacji.* [The

213

Polish People's Republic—Federal Republic of Germany: balance sheet of mutual relations, problems and perspectives for normalization]. Red. J. Sułka. Wwa: PISM, 1979. 422 pp.

Documents, chronology of events 1945–78 and bibliography. German edition published by Alfred Metzner Verlag, Frankfurt am Main.

P125 *Sprawy międzynarodowe.* [International affairs]. Wwa: PISM, 1948–. Monthly.

The major journal on foreign affairs in Poland. Publishes academic studies of diplomatic problems past and present as well as statements by party leaders and Polish Foreign Ministry spokesmen. Quarterly or bi-monthly until 1955.

P126 *Biuletyn.* [Bulletin]. (MSZ. Dept. Prasy i Informacji). Wwa: MSZ, 1970–. Irregular.

No. 1 published in November 1970 in English (entitled *Bulletin*), German and Polish. Subsequent issues in Polish and various other languages.

POLITICAL AND IDEOLOGICAL AFFAIRS

The Polish press agency Interpress publishes material on political events in Polish and usually carries English, French, German, Russian and, less often, other languages as well.

P127 *Contemporary Poland.* Wwa: Interpress, 1967–. Fortnightly.

Monthly before 1977. Regularly carries documents and speeches on political events in Poland, sometimes in separately published supplements.

P128 *Partia—państwo—społeczeństwo—propaganda.* [Party—state—society—propaganda]. Red. R. Dudek, Z. Siembirowicz. Wwa: KiW, 1978. 370 pp.

Selection of articles published in the PZPR monthly *Ideologia i polityka* during 1975–7.

P129 *Podstawy nauk politycznych: dokumenty i materiały.* [Fundamentals of political studies: documents and materials]. Red. S. Macheta. Wwa: KiW, 1977. 2 vols.

P130 *Prawa i obowiązki obywatelskie w PRL.* [Citizens' rights and duties in the PRL]. Wyd. 2. Red. M. Szczepaniak. Wwa: PWN, 1978. 492 pp.

MILITARY AFFAIRS

P131 *Państwo—patriotyzm—internacjonalizm w dokumentach PZPR, xii.1975–v.1977r.* [State—patriotism—internationalism in PZPR documents December 1975–May 1977]. Red. S. Chojnecki, M.

Starczewski. Wwa: Wojskowa Akademia Polityczna, 1978. 379 pp. [Not seen].

See also P176.

P132 *Podstawowe wiadomości o prawie wojskowym.* [Basic information regarding military law]. Wyd. 2. Red. L. Łustacz. Wwa: MON, 1970. 355 pp. [Not seen].

P133 *Kodeks wojskowego postępowania karnego i przepisy wprowadzające wraz ze skorowidzem rzeczowym oraz ważniejsze przepisy szczególne.* [Code of Military Criminal Procedure and introductory regulations together with a table of contents and the most important individual regulations]. Wyd. 2. Red. J. Modlinger. Wwa: Wyd. Prawnicze, 1962. 188 pp.

P134 *Orzecznictwo Najwyższego Sądu Wojskowego.* [Judgements of the Supreme Military Court]. Wwa: MON, 1960. 440 pp.

P135 *Regulamin służby garnizonowej i wartowniczej Sił Zbrojnych PRL.* [Regulations concerning garrison and sentry service of the Armed Forces of the PRL]. Wwa: MON, 1970. 166 pp.

P136 *Regulamin służby wewnętrznej Sił Zbrojnych PRL.* [Regulations concerning internal service of the Armed Forces of the PRL]. Wwa: MON, 1970. 182 pp.

P137 *Żołnierz wolności.* [Soldier of freedom]. Wwa: 1943–. Daily.
The official informational–political daily of the Ministry of National Defence.

P138 *Żołnierz polski.* [The Polish soldier]. Wwa: 1945–. Weekly.
More popular and illustrated weekly of the Ministry of National Defence.

ECONOMIC AFFAIRS

General

P139 *Przegląd ustawodawstwa gospodarczego.* [Review of economic legislation]. Wwa: 1948–. Monthly.
Overviews and summarizes the economic legislation appearing in the immediately preceding period.

P140 *Życie gospodarcze.* [Economic life]. Wwa: 1945–. Weekly.
A high-quality, semi-official periodical dealing with economic questions. The most easily available source for summaries and partial texts of economic plans.

Planning

The best sources for the economic plans and budgets, which are not easily available to the public, are *Monitor polski* (P43), *Druki Sejmowe* (P54), *Życie gospodarcze* (P140) and *Gospodarka planowa* (P141). It has also been customary for the First Party Secretary to report to the PZPR congress on the fulfilment of the plan and the targets set for the coming five-year plan. (See the section 'Polish United Workers' Party: congresses and national conferences'.)

P141 *Gospodarka planowa*. [Planned economy]. Wwa: 1946–. Monthly.
Quarterly to 1961. Official organ of the Planning Commission attached to the Council of Ministers, until 1956 the State Economic Planning Commission.

P142 *Planowanie gospodarki narodowej w Polsce Ludowej. Materiały do bibliografii*. [The planning of the national economy in People's Poland. Materials for a bibliography]. Wwa: Biblioteka Szkoły Głównej Planowania i Statystyki, 1960–.
Vol. 1, publ. 1960, 127 pp., covers the period 1944–9; vol. 2 (1965), 1950–5; vol. 3 (1975, 310 pp.), 1956–65. Lists many official documents.

Industry

P143 *Upaństwowienie i odbudowa przemysłu w Polsce (1944–48). Materiały źródłowe*. [Nationalization and rebuilding of industry in Poland 1944–48. Source material]. Red. H. Jędruszczak. Wwa: PWN, 1967–9. 2 vols.

Agriculture

P144 *Ustawodawstwo rolne. Zbiór przepisów prawnych*. [Agricultural legislation. Collection of legal regulations]. Red. W. Gutkowski, F. Jabłoński. Wwa: Wyd. Prawnicze, 1953. 556 pp.
A collection of 119 laws, decrees and resolutions regulating farming and landholding. Legal position as of 1 October 1953.

P145 *Reforma rolna PKWN. Materiały i dokumenty*. [The land reform of the Polish Committee of National Liberation. Materials and documents]. Wwa: 1959. [Not seen].

Contracts and arbitration

P146 *Kodeks zobowiązań ze skorowidzem rzeczowym. Przepisy ogólne prawa cywilnego, ważniejsze przepisy obligacyjne oraz międzynarodowe prawo prywatne*. [Code of contracts together with a subject index. General regulations of civil law, regulations concerning contracts and international private law]. Wyd. 3. Red. A. Lipiński, S. Jabłoński. Wwa: Wyd. Prawnicze, 1953. 456 pp.
Legal position as of 1 September 1953.

P147 *Państwowy Arbitraż Gospodarczy i obsługa prawna jednostek gospodarki uspołecznionej. Przepisy—orzecznictwo—komentarz*. [State Economic Arbitration and the legal servicing of units in the socialized economy. Regulations, judgements, commentary]. Red. Z. Klafkowski [et al.]. Wwa: Wyd. Prawnicze, 1965. 189 pp.

Section I contains excerpts from and comments upon the relevant regulations relating to state arbitration of disputed economic questions. Section II reproduces ten of the most important laws and instructions related to cooperative and state economic organizations.

Labour

P148 *Prawo pracy. Przepisy, orzecznictwo i wyjaśnienia.* [Labour law. Regulations, judgements and clarification]. Wyd. 3. Zebrał i oprac. J. Zieliński. Wwa: Wyd. Prawnicze, 1969. 2 vols.

Contains the constitutional provisions and a wide range of laws and decrees regulating labour affairs. *See also* P40, P41.

Regional and local economy

P149 *Przepisy prawne dotyczące planowania przestrzennego.* [Legal regulations concerning territorial planning]. Red. W. Sieroszewski, I. Biegańska. Wwa: Wyd. Akcydensowe, 1978. 2 vols.

Legal position as of 1 July 1977.

P150 *Planowanie regionalne. Bibliografia piśmiennictwa polskiego 1945–1955.* [Regional planning. Bibliography of Polish literature 1945–1955]. Red. S. & M. Zawadzki. (Komitet przestrzennego zagospodarowania kraju PAN, Biuletyn, 55). Wwa: 1969. 318 pp.

Cooperatives

P151 *Przepisy dotyczące spółdzielczości.* [Regulations concerning cooperatives]. Red. E. Jabłoński, Z. Rzepka. (Ustawodawstwo gospodarcze. Teksty, 8). Wwa: Polskie Wyd. Gospodarcze, 1951. xxxix, 401 pp.

Contains 124 laws, decrees, instructions and circulars by government and trade union bodies regulating cooperatives. Legal position as at 30 June 1951.

P152 *Prawo spółdzielcze. Zbiór tekstów.* [The law relating to cooperatives. Collected texts]. Wwa: Wyd. Prawnicze, 1961. 76 pp.

Legal position as of 8 August 1961.

P153 *Bibliografia orzecznictwa i piśmiennictwa z zakresu prawa spółdzielczego 1971–75.* [Bibliography of judicial decisions and literature on the law on cooperatives 1971–75]. Red. W. Jastrzębski. Wwa: Centralny Zarząd Spółdzielń Rolnych, 1979. 139 pp. [Not seen].

Inventions

P154 *Prawo wynalazcze. Zbiór podstawowych przepisów.* [Law on inventions. Collection of basic regulations]. Red. J. Kosmider. Wwa: Wyd. Związkowe CRZZ, 1964. 248 pp.

19 laws, decrees, circulars and instructions concerning the law on inventions and patents.

Standardization

P155   *Zbiór aktów prawnych dotyczących normalizacji.* [Collection of legal instruments concerning standardization]. Red. M. Ambrozewicz [et al.]. Wwa: Wyd. Normalizacji, 1969. 365 pp.

SOCIAL AFFAIRS

General

P156   *Prawne instrumenty realizacji polityki społeczno-gospodarczej PRL.* [Legal instruments for the realization of the socio-economic policies of the PRL]. Red. B. Popowska. (Seria Prawo, 76). Poznań: Uniw., 1977. 146 pp. [Not seen].

Working conditions

P157   *Zbiór przepisów ochrony pracy.* [Collection of regulations dealing with safety at work]. Wyd. 2. Red. L. Kochański, S. Lach. Wwa: CRZZ, 1976–8. 3 vols.

Housing

P158   *Prawo lokalowe. Przepisy, orzecznictwo i wyjaśnienia.* [The law on dwellings. Regulations, judgements and clarification]. Red. J. Prokopczuk. Wwa: Wyd. Prawnicze, 1963. 972 pp.

Massive collection of 289 laws, decrees, instructions and circulars relating to all aspects of dwellings—sale, leasing, maintenance, rents and administrative procedure. Subject index.

P159   *Prawo lokalowe. Przepisy o budownictwie mieszkaniowym. Zbiór tekstów.* [The law on dwellings. Regulations concerning inhabited dwellings. Collected texts]. Red. S. Jabłoński. Wwa: Wyd. Prawnicze, 1965. 991 pp.

Collection of laws and regulations covering all aspects of the renting and leasing of private dwellings. Narrower in scope than P158.

Civil registration

P160   *Prawo o aktach stanu cywilnego według stanu prawnego na dzień 1.ii.1959r.* [Laws on civil registration documents. Legal position as of 1 February 1959]. Wwa: Wyd. Prawnicze, 1959. 92 pp.

15 legal documents regulating the civil registration of marriages, divorces, births, deaths and changes of name.

CULTURAL AFFAIRS

Education

P161 *Prawo szkól wyższych. Teksty i komentarze.* [Legislation on higher education. Texts and commentary]. Red. M. Jaroszyński [et al.]. Wwa: PWN, 1955. 587 pp.

P162 *Podstawowe przepisy dotyczące szkolnictwa wyższego, wydane w okresie od dnia 1.i.1960 do 15.ix.1962r.* [Basic regulations concerning higher education issued in the period between 1.1.1960 and 15.9.1962]. Red. J. Chmielowski, W. Ćwikliński. (Min. Szkolnictwa Wyższego). Wwa: PWN, 1962. 329 pp.

P163 *Zbiór przepisów prawnych obowiązujących w szkolnictwie zawodowym.* [Collection of legal regulations applying to vocational training]. Wyd. 3. Red. J. Buczkowski, J. Wojcik. Wwa: Państwowe Wyd. Szkolnictwa Zawodowego, 1968. 663 pp.

Comprehensive collection of the legal rules governing trade and vocational schooling. Reproduces 230 decrees, instructions and circulars.

Publishing

P164 *Prawo autorskie. Przepisy i orzecznictwo.* [Law relating to authors. Regulations and judgements]. Red. E. Drabienko. Wwa: Wyd. Prawnicze, 1960. 446 pp.

60 laws, decrees, instructions and circulars regulating authors', photographers', artists' and composers' contracts, remuneration and related matters. Legal position as of 30 October 1960.

P165 *Zbiór przepisów prawnych. Dla członków ZLP.* [Collection of legal regulations. For members of the Polish Writers' Association]. Wwa: 1968. [Not seen].

P166 *Czarna księga cenzury w PRL.* [Black book of the Polish censorship]. Red. T. Strzyżewski. London: Aneks, 1977–8. 2 vols.

Hardly an official publication! A collection of instructions and discussion papers for the main censorship office in Warsaw, published abroad by an ex-censorship official.

Environment

P167 *Przepisy prawne z zakresu ochrony przyrody.* [Legal regulations concerning the preservation of nature]. Wyd. 2. Wybór L. Jastrzębski. Wwa: Liga Ochrona Przyrody, 1975. 167 pp. [Not seen].

LEADERS' WORKS

Bolesław Bierut

P168   Bierut, B. *O partii*. [About the Party]. Wyd. 2. Wwa: KiW, 1952. 340 pp.
     A selection of Bierut's speeches 1948–52.

Władysław Gomułka

P169   Gomułka, W. *Artykuły i przemówienia*. [Articles and speeches]. Wwa: KiW, 1962–4. 2 vols.
     Cover January 1943–December 1945 and January 1946–April 1948 respectively.

P170   Gomułka, W. *Przemówienia*. [Speeches]. Wwa: KiW, 1957–69. 10 vols.
     Covers the period from 1956 to 1968.

P171   Gomułka, W. *Address to the Eighth Plenary Session of the Polish United Workers' Party, October 20, 1956*. Warsaw: Polonia, 1956. 65 pp.

P172   Gomułka, W. *Węzłowe problemy polityki partii*. [Crucial problems concerning the Party's policies]. Wwa: KiW, 1957.

P173   Gomułka, W. *O naszej partii*. [About our Party]. Wwa: KiW, 1968. 705 pp.

P174   Gomułka, W. *O problemie niemieckim*. [On the German problem]. Wwa: KiW, 1969. 511 pp.
     Collection of articles and speeches. English translation (title as above) publ. KiW, 1969, 431 pp.

Many of Gomułka's speeches were published individually in brochure form in Polish. The more important were translated into the major European languages.

Edward Gierek

P175   Gierek, E. *Jesteście wielką szansą: wybór przemówień 1971–1977*. [You are a great hope: selected speeches 1971–1977]. Wwa: Młodzieżowa Agencja Wydawnicza, 1978. 171 pp.

P176   Gierek, E. *O wojsku i obronności*. [On the army and our state of defence]. Wwa: MON, 1977. 215 pp.

P177   Gierek, E. *O dalszy rozwój socjalistycznej Polski, o pomyślność narodu polskiego*. [For the further development of socialist Poland, for the prosperity of the Polish nation]. Wwa: KiW, 1980. 64 pp.

R ROMANIA

Brian Hunter

INTRODUCTION

Historical background

Of all the East European communist states, Romania is one of the least studied in the West. One may surmise that this is partly because there has been no great exodus of Romanian intellectuals to stimulate the growth of Romanian studies, and partly because in its first decade or so communist Romania presented an intrinsically unexciting picture of carbon-copy Stalinism at home and sub-servience to Soviet interests abroad. However, Romania's increasing inde-pendence in foreign affairs since the 1960s has necessitated a reappraisal of its role and has also prompted a revision by historians of some of their assumptions about the earlier period.

On 23 August 1944 King Michael with the backing of the National Democratic Bloc of the National Peasant, National Liberal, Social Democratic and Communist Parties (formed in June) deposed Antonescu and announced the cessation of hostilities against the Allies. On 26 August Romania declared war on Germany, going on to lose nearly 170,000 men in the Allied cause. The Armistice of 12 September 1944, though signed by the USA, Britain and the USSR, channelled all reparations to the latter; the USSR also annexed Bessarabia and North Bukovina. The military clauses gave the Soviet army control of Romania's territory and resources.

The geographical proximity of the Soviet Union, the presence of Soviet occupation forces, and the 'spheres of influence' diplomacy of the Allies (in October 1944 Churchill and Stalin had bargained a communist Romania for a non-communist Greece) were the crucial determinants in the establishment of communism in Romania. In August 1944 the Romanian Communist Party had only a thousand members and little influence. Its achievement of absolute power by the end of 1947 was accomplished only in stages, and with the benefit of Soviet pressure, throughout a period of subversive coexistence with traditional political forces. During this period the Party ensured its supremacy by coercion, by a massive and uncritical acceptance of new recruits (a policy associated with Ana Pauker for which she was later castigated), by securing key government posts for its members and sympathizers, and by eliminating all other political parties.

In April 1944 leadership of the Party had passed to Gheorghe Gheorghiu-Dej. Dej was of working-class origin and had been a railwayman. He joined the Party in its early days and took a prominent part in the railwaymen's action at Grivița in 1933, for which he was imprisoned until 1944. Dej and other party leaders who like him spent the war in Romania (e.g. Gheorghe Apostol, Chivu Stoica, Nicolae Ceaușescu) are identified by historians as 'Romanians' or 'domesticists', to distinguish them from the 'Muscovites' (Ana Pauker, Vasile Luca, Teohari Georgescu) who spent the war in the Soviet Union. Perhaps not too much should be made of these factions' doctrinal differences: both Dej and Pauker were acceptable to Stalin. But after Dej's elimination of the 'Muscovites' in 1952 after five years of their leadership, the nationalistic attitude of the 'Romanians' began to emerge as a formative element in Romania's unique brand of communism.

Three short-lived governments under Sănătescu and Rădescu appointed by the King were brought down between November 1944 and February 1945 largely by the agitation of the Communist Party acting through the National Democratic Front (formed with the Social Democrats and Ploughmen's Front in October 1944). At Vyshinskii's insistence a government under the pro-communist Ploughman leader Petru Groza was installed on 6 March 1945, in which the key positions were in communist hands.

In March the restoration of Transylvania to Romania was announced and an agrarian reform brought in to expropriate large estates for the benefit of some 700,000 peasants. In May an economic agreement with the USSR established the Sovroms, inequitable joint enterprises through which the USSR (until their negotiated abolition in 1954) exploited Romanian sources of income.

In August the Soviet Union recognized the Groza government, whereupon the King asked Groza to resign so that a government could be formed acceptable to the other Allies. On Groza's refusal the King 'went on strike', resuming his duties only in December after Stalin had conceded that the Groza government should include a National Peasant and a Liberal representative. When this was done the American and British governments recognized Groza in February 1946. Elections were held on 19 November 1946 in an atmosphere of communist intimidation and fraudulence. The communist-led Bloc of Democratic Parties received 376 seats, the National Peasants 33, and the Liberals 3.

The Peace Treaty was signed on 10 February 1947. In August the National Peasant and National Liberal Parties were dissolved. The Social Democratic Party was eliminated by assimilation with the Communist Party, leading to the formation of the Romanian Workers' Party in February 1948. In November 1947 Liberal ministers were dismissed and replaced by Pauker, Luca and Emil Bodnaraș. On 30 December Michael was forced to abdicate, and the People's Republic was proclaimed.

A twenty-year treaty of friendship was signed with the USSR in February 1948. The economic programme adopted at the Party's 1945 National Conference provided a blueprint for the country's transformation. In June 1948 practically the whole of the economy was nationalized. The State Planning Commission was established in July 1948, and annual planning began in 1949. The first five-year plan began in 1951, a typical Soviet model with emphasis on heavy industry. In 1949 the collectivization of agriculture was commenced, to be finally completed in 1962.

After Stalin's death Dej met the challenge of de-Stalinization by simply attributing previous shortcomings to the deposed 'Muscovite' faction. For Romania the 'new course' brought not liberalization but a drive towards national political and economic independence, the first tentative signs of which are discernible in Dej's report to the 1955 Party Congress. The striving for autarky appears in the third five-year plan (1961–5) with its introduction of the concept of 'multi-lateral development'. In March 1963 Romania vetoed the Comecon proposal for a 'division of labour' in which she would have played the part of raw materials supplier to the more industrialized members, a declaration of economic independence which was translated to the diplomatic sphere in April 1964 with the Party's 'Statement on its stand concerning the problems of the world Communist movement'.

When Dej died on 19 March 1965 his leadership had long been unchallenged, and he had been able to groom Nicolae Ceauşescu as his successor. Ceauşescu was born in 1918 of peasant stock. At eleven he went to town to seek work, at fourteen he joined a trade union and at fifteen the Communist Party. Imprisoned for political activities in 1936–9 and 1940–4, he associated with Dej in prison. After the war he performed important functions in party recruitment and the supervision of the armed forces. After the dismissal of the Pauker group he became a member of the Party Central Committee and Organization Bureau in 1952, the Secretariat in 1954 and the Political Bureau in 1955, and became second secretary after Dej in 1957. Like Stalin, he was in charge of cadre assignment, and able to build up a personal following in the Party. When he succeeded Dej as First Secretary he changed the title of the office to General Secretary. He became President of the State Council in 1967, and the office of President of the Republic was created for him in 1974. His style of leadership is marked by nepotism (key positions are held by his wife and other members of his family) and an intense cult of personality.

Dej's independent foreign-policy stand was continued with gusto by Ceauşescu, as his more than thirty state visits bear voluminous witness. A selection of events will serve to demonstrate the developing features of his policy:

1967, Romania established diplomatic relations with West Germany, and maintained relations with Israel after the Six-Day War.

February 1968, walked out of the World Meeting of Communist Parties in Budapest.

August 1968, denounced the Warsaw Pact invasion of Czechoslovakia.

November 1978, refused to integrate Romanian forces into a more unified Warsaw Pact command structure or step up its financial contributions.

July 1980, secured an agreement with the European Communities on better terms than those afforded other Comecon countries.

November 1980, on a state visit to Scandinavia condemned 'antiquated bloc politics' and called for Soviet withdrawal from Afghanistan.

Though there are geopolitical limits to it, Ceauşescu's foreign policy, coupled with his vigorous presentation of the Party as the heir to the historic nationalist aspirations of the Romanian people, serves as an additional source of legitimation for the communist régime.

Political structure

The Party

Real political power lies solely with the Communist Party, called Communist Party of Romania (Partidul Comunist din România) till February 1948, Romanian Workers' Party (Partidul Muncitoresc Român) till July 1965, and Romanian Communist Party (Partidul Comunist Român) thereafter. Membership of the Party in December 1980 was just over three million.

Romania is a one-party state, and the role of the Communist Party as 'the leading political force of all of society' is explicitly laid down in Article 3 of the 1965 constitution, and was also mentioned in the 1952 constitution (Article 86). After a brief flirtation with the doctrine of the separation of party and government powers (Article 13b of the Party Rules forbidding an individual simultaneously to hold both party and state office was adopted at the 1965 Party Congress but deleted at the 1967 National Conference), Ceauşescu introduced a policy of fusion of both functions to eliminate 'wasteful parallelism'. The Party exerts its all-pervasive control by appointing its members to government positions at every level from the Council of Ministers down.

The supreme organ of the Party is in theory the Congress (Congresul), which meets every five years. Actual leadership emanates from the organs which it elects, at the apex of which is the party leader, the General Secretary (Secretar General) (called First Secretary 1954–65). Office-holders since 1944 have been: Gheorghe Gheorghiu-Dej (until 19 April 1954); Gheorghe Apostol (until 2 October 1955); Dej again (until 19 March 1965); Nicolae Ceauşescu. National conferences (Conferinţa Naţională) are convened between congresses. The Congress elects the Central Committee (Comitetul Central) and the General Secretary. The Central Committee, which meets in quarterly plenary sessions, elects the Secretariat and the Executive Political Committee (Comitetul Politic Executiv) (before 1977 Executive Committee). This committee is the primary policy-making body. Its decisions are approved at the plena of the Central Committee. It was established at the 1965 Congress alongside the Permanent Presidium (Prezidiul Permanent) to replace the former Political Bureau (Biroul Politic). The Presidium was itself abolished at the 1974 Congress to make way for the Permanent Bureau (Biroul Permanent), an administrative organ which has no analogue in other communist countries. It is elected by and responsible to the Executive Political Committee, and is charged with coordinating party and state activities.

Local party bodies descend in a pyramidal hierarchy through county (judeţ), town (oraş) and ward (comună) committees to cells (celulă) in individual enterprises and institutions.

The government

The Constitution is of the Soviet type: it does not bind the authorities, offers no real guarantees of civil rights, and is subject to constant amendment by the Grand National Assembly.

After the cessation of hostilities with the Allies the 1923 Constitution, which had been suspended by King Carol in 1937, was restored by Decree 1626 of 31 August 1944 (MO 202). This constitution was abolished after the abdication of King Michael and the proclamation of the People's Republic (Republica Populară Română) by Law 363 of 30 December 1947 (MO 300 bis). The first communist constitution was voted by the National Assembly in April 1948. The second and third followed in September 1952 and July 1965. The latter, which dubbed Romania a 'socialist republic' (Republica Socialistă România), may be said to have inaugurated the Ceauşescu era, but does not differ fundamentally from its predecessors.

The head of state is the President (Preşedinte), an office established by Law 1 of 28 March 1974 (BO 45). Previously the head of state had been first the Chairman of the Presidium of the Grand National Assembly and thereafter the Chairman of the Presidium of the Council of State with the latter's creation in March 1961. The President is also Chairman of the Defence Council and Supreme Commander of the Armed Forces. Heads of state since the abdication of King Michael have been (with dates of cessation of office): King Michael I (30 December 1947); Constantin Parhon (2 June 1952); Petru Groza (7 January 1958); Ion Gheorghe Maurer (21 March 1961); Gheorghe Gheorghiu-Dej (19 March 1965); Chivu Stoica (9 December 1967); Nicolae Ceauşescu.

Decree-laws 2218 and 2219 of 15 July 1946 (MO 161) abolished the upper house (Senat), enfranchised women, disfranchised 'fascists', and prepared the way for the election of the Chamber of Deputies (Camera Deputaţilor) which sat in December 1946. It had a Provisional Presidium (Prezidiul provizoriu). The present Grand National Assembly (Marea Adunare Naţională) was established by the 1948 constitution following the general election of March 1948. It was elected every four years until 1972, and since then every five years to synchronize with party congresses. Since the elections of 1975 more than one candidate has been permitted to stand in each constituency but the criteria of contest are personal, not political: all candidates must support the platform of the Front of Socialist Democracy and Unity (Frontul Democraţiei şi Unităţii Socialiste).

Although on paper it is the supreme organ of state power, the assembly in fact meets only for two short sessions a year, and its day-to-day functions are exercised by the Council of State (Consiliul de Stat) (prior to March 1961 its Presidium (Prezidiul), whose functions were laid down by Decree 3 of 9 January 1948, MO 7). The Council of State and its Chairmen are elected by the Assembly, as is the Council of Ministers (Consiliul de Miniştri) (Decree 264 of 15 June 1957, BO 15, and Law 2 of 25 March 1961, BO 9), the supreme government administrative body, which since 1965 has had a Permanent Bureau (Biroul Permanent). Since 1972 ministerial policies have been shaped in consultation with deliberative panels of which each minister is chairman. The

Chairman of the Council of Ministers is the Prime Minister and is elected by the assembly. Holders of this office (with dates of cessation) have been: Constantin Sănătescu (2 December 1944); Nicolae Rădescu (28 February 1945); Petru Groza (2 June 1952); Gheorghe Gheorghiu-Dej (3 October 1955); Chivu Stoica (21 March 1961); Ion Gheorghe Maurer (28 March 1974); Manea Mănescu (29 March 1979); Ilie Verdeţ.

The assembly also elects Standing Commissions (Comisie permanentă) to advise on specialist affairs, and Law 15 of 22 October 1971 (BO 134) established the Legislative Council (Consiliul Legislativ) to advise on legislation. Other government bodies include the Defence Council (Consiliul Apărării) (set up in 1969), the Economic Council (Consiliul economic) (1969), the Central Council of Workers' Control of Economic and Social Activity (Consiliul central de control muncitoresc al activităţii economice şi sociale) (1972), the Supreme Council for Economic and Social Development (Consiliul suprem al dezvoltării economice şi sociale) (1973) and the Council of Economic and Social Organization (Consiliul organizării economico–sociale) (1977).

Legislation may be initiated by the Party's Central Committee, the Front of Socialist Democracy and Unity, the Permanent Bureau of the Council of Ministers, the Council of State or any group of thirty-five deputies (usually a Commission in practice). Legislation is most often initiated by the Council of Ministers. The Party is kept informed throughout the drafting of laws and is, it may be inferred, the most important initiator and shaper of new law. Some bills are put to public debate.

The hierarchy of courts is topped by the Supreme Court (Tribunalul suprem), whose Chairman, and the Prosecutor-General (Procuror general), are elected by the Assembly.

Participatory bodies

A simulacrum of the democratic process is provided by the various participatory bodies whose actual powers vary at the discretion of the Party. Apart from the all-embracing Front of Socialist Democracy and Unity (in all its transmutations of name), which has analogues in other communist countries, the 1974 Party Congress systematized a series of bodies including: Councils of Working People (Consiliul oamenilor muncii) organized at work-place, town and county level, and meeting since October 1977 in the National Council of the Working People (Consiliul naţional oamenilor muncii); the Congress of Councils of the Working People in Industry, Construction and Transport (Congresul consiliilor oamenilor muncii din industrie, construcţii şi transporturi); and many similar organizations in the fields of agriculture, local government and political education. Ceauşescu's 'whistle-stop' stumping of these bodies is another feature of the participatory process.

There are separate such bodies for the ethnic minorities. Though the Constitution grants the minorities equal rights, in fact a process of romanianization is in train. Only Romanian is described as an 'official language', and the Hungarian Autonomous Region, set up in 1948, was abolished in 1968. Out of a 1978 total population of 21.9 million, there were 1.7 million Hungarians and 0.4 million Germans.

Local government is carried out by People's Councils (sfat popular) at county, town and ward level.

Publications

Language

There were spelling reforms in 1953 and 1965 in which inter alia first î was substituted for â in some words and then vice versa. In official bibliographies â/î are retained if they were in use at the time of publication, but may be filed as î/â, e.g. 'Gârleanu' may follow 'Gîndacul'. Protection of î is not usually extended to the form Romîn(ia).

Mention should also be made of the Romanians' own promotion in English-language publications of the form 'Romania', which since 1965 has almost supplanted the previously more common 'Rumania/Roumania' amongst users of English.

The above orthographical variations are not treated in the bibliography as varying titles. Usage of initial capital letters has also varied in the period documented. The bibliography retains the usage of the source itself.

Many official documents are intended for foreign consumption and published in English, French, German, Spanish and Russian. Additionally, many documents appear in Hungarian, German and Serbo-Croat for the ethnic minorities. Only English, French and German versions are considered in the bibliography.

Publishing and distribution

The Party established its own publishing house (Editura Partidului Comunist din România) in 1945, and the State Publisher (Editura de stat) was set up in 1947. After the communist takeover, in 1948 all publishers, printers and booksellers were nationalized. Publishing organs are characterized as 'edituri de stat', 'edituri departmentale', 'oficii editoriale' and 'organe de prese centrale'. The 'edituri de stat' are organized by subject field. Official publications as defined here may emanate from any of the above, and are included without special distinction in the national bibliography.

Documentation areas

Generally speaking, three publicatons are indispensable for research, since many of the decisive policy-making statements and data are concentrated in one or another of them: *Scînteia*, *Buletinul oficial* (Part 1) and *Anuarul statistic*.

The articles and speeches of the leaders Gheorghiu-Dej and Ceauşescu are published in voluminous collections. Apart from Petru Groza, lesser leaders' works are to be found only scattered as pamphlets, in the records of congresses, etc. or in the pages of *Scînteia*.

Party congress proceedings are published in full. Congresses were held in 1948, 1955, 1960, 1965, 1969, 1974 and 1979. The first three are numbered first, second and third. At the 1965 Congress five prewar congresses were elevated to the canon, and the revised numbering 'ninth' was adopted.

National conference proceedings have been published in full only since 1972. Conferences were held in 1945, 1946, 1967, 1972 and 1977. They are not numbered.

Party directives take the form of Resolutions (*Rezoluția*) and Decisions (*Hotărîrea*).

Constitutions are published in MO and BO, separately, and also in draft form and in Western languages. They are subject to frequent amendments. Amendments to the 1952 constitution can be found in: BO 6 of 24.1.1954; BO 19 of 21.4.1954; BO 13 of 2.6.1955; BO 11 of 4.4.1956; BO 11 of 28.3.1957; BO 3 of 15.1.1958; BO 31 of 31.12.1959; and BO 9 of 25.3.1961. Amendments to the 1965 constitution appear in: BO 16 of 16.2.1968; BO 168 of 26.12.1968; BO 157 of 17.12.1971; BO 41 of 24.4.1972; BO 45 of 28.3.1974; BO 161 of 23.12.1974; BO 30 of 21.3.1975; and BO 104 of 19.12.1979.

Terms of reference of government bodies are laid down in the laws establishing them, e.g. State Planning Committee (Decree 119 of 2.7.1948, MO 150); Economic Council (Law 4 of 14.3.1969, BO 32); Legislative Council (Law 15 of 22.10.1971, BO 134); Supreme Council of Economic and Social Development (Law 1 of 30.3.1973, BO 43); Council for Economic and Social Organization (Law 32 of 28.10.1977, BO 112).

Judicial bodies are similarly regulated: Law 341 of 5.12.1947 (MO 282); Laws 5 and 6 of 19.6.1952 (BO 31), with amendments of 31.6.1958 (BO 29); Law 60 of 27.12.1968 (BO 169).

Statutes with the force of law appear under the terms:

Legea (law); passed by the Grand National Assembly.

Decretul Consiliului de Stat (Decree of the Council of State, before 1961 Decretul Prezidiului Marii Adunări Naționale).

Decretul Presidențial (Presidential Decree).

Hotărîrea Consiliului de Miniştri (Decision of the Council of Ministers).

Dispoziție Consiliului de Miniştri (Ordinance of the Council of Ministers).

Ordin; orders of various ministries.

The primary sources for these are the official gazettes.

Codification of communist law was gradual. The Criminal Code of 1937 was in force with substantial amendments until 1968, though a Labour Code was enacted in 1950.

Treaties are published in *Buletinul oficial* (Part 1), *Colecție de legi* and *Colecția de hotărîri ale Consiliului de Miniştri*.

After two one-year plans (1949, 1950) planning has been implemented over the periods: 1951–5, 1956–60, 1961–5, 1966–70, 1971–5 and 1976–80. Plans are outlined by directives (published in draft and finalized form) of party congresses (since the second) and brought into effect by laws. Starting in 1960 fifteen-year perspective plans have also been drawn up. Other documents associated with planning include Central Committee Decisions launching the plans, communiqués on their implementation, directives on the planning mechanism, ministerial reports, and accounts put out by the Chamber of Commerce and Industry.

GENERAL BIBLIOGRAPHIES AND REFERENCE WORKS

National bibliographies

National bibliography began only in 1952. Before then some information may be gained from:

R1   The section 'Bibliografia românească' of the journal *Orizont*, which ran from 1 February 1945 to 25 December 1947 with coverage from 23 August 1944 of books, pamphlets, theses and maps, including books in Romanian published abroad.

R2   *Buletinul cărţii româneşti*. [Bulletin of the Romanian book]. B.: Cartea românească, 1927–47. Irregular.

    A private publisher's list of books available in his bookshop, but wide in scope, and aspiring to the function of a national bibliography.

R3   *Buletinul editorial*. [Publishers' bulletin]. (Serviciul de popularizare a cărţii, Centrul de librării şi difuzare a cărţii). B.: 1950–2. Irregular.

    Annotated list of publications by publishers.

National bibliography proper begins with *Buletinul bibliografic*:

R4   *Buletinul bibliografic: seria A: cărţi, broşuri, albume, hărţi, plicuri, pliante, note muzicale*. [Bibliographical bulletin: series A: books, pamphlets, albums, maps, envelopes, folders, musical scores.] (Camera cărţii). B.: 1952–6. 2 a month.

    1952 entitled 'Buletinul bibliografic al Camerei cărţii din R.P.R.'. 1953–4 entitled 'Buletinul bibliografic al cărţii'.

R5   *Buletinul bibliografic: seria B: articole şi recenzii din presă*. [Bibliographical bulletin: series B: articles and reviews in the press]. (Camera cărţii). B.: 1953–6. 2 a month.

    1953 entitled *Buletinul bibliografic al Camerei cărţii din R.P.R.: articole şi recenzii din ziare şi reviste*. Indexed only selected articles and other material 'of general interest' in national newspapers and journals.

Soon after its foundation the Central State Library issued a cumulative bibliography of books and pamphlets based on *Buletinul bibliografic* 1952–4 but including some items published in 1951:

R6   *Anuarul cărţii din Republica Populară Romînă, 1952–1954*. [Book yearbook of the Romanian People's Republic, 1952–1954]. B.: Ed. şt., 1957. 411 pp.

    No further volumes appeared.

The Central State Library also took over the publication of current bibliography:

R7   *Bibliografia Republicii Socialiste România: cărţi, albume, hărţi*. [Bibliography of the Socialist Republic of Romania: books, albums, maps]. B.: 1957–. 2 a month. 1957–64 quarterly indexes of authors and titles of anonymous works.

1957–68 subtitled 'cărţi, albume, hărţi, note muzicale'. Continues volume numbering of *Buletinul bibliografic: seria A.* Wider in coverage than the latter. Arranged by a Marxist–Leninist classification until 1970, and then by the Dewey Decimal Classification.

R8   *Bibliografia Republicii Socialiste România: articole din publicaţii periodice şi seriale.* [Bibliography of the Socialist Republic of Romania: articles in periodical and serial publications]. B.: 1957–. 2 a month.

1957–62 entitled *Bibliografia periodicelor din Republica Populară Romînă.* Continues volume numbering of *Buletinul bibliografic: seria B.* Coverage wider than the latter; includes comprehensive listing of journal articles and a selection from national newspapers.

Other general bibliographies and reference works

Bibliographies

R9   Fischer-Galati, S. *Rumania: a bibliographic guide.* Washington: Library of Congress Slavic and Central European Division, 1963. viii, 75 pp.

Reprinted without change by Arno Press, New York, 1968.

Reference Works

R10   *Südosteuropa–Handbuch.* Vol. 2 'Rumänien'; [ed.] K.-D. Grothusen [et al.]. Göttingen: Vandenhoeck und Ruprecht, 1977. 711 pp.

R11   *Organizaţii şi instituţii din Republica Socialistă România.* [Organizations and institutions in the Socialist Republic of Romania]. (Agerpres). B.: 1980–. Annual.

Archives

R12   Mateescu, T. et al. *Publicaţiile Arhivelor statului, 1860–1977: bibliografie analitică.* [Publications of the State Archives, 1860–1977: analytical bibliography]. (Direcţia generală a Arhivelor statului). B.: 1978. 191 pp.

CONSTITUTIONAL DOCUMENTS

Constitutions

R13a   *Constituţia Republicii Populare Române: textul votat de Marea Adunare Naţională în şedinţă din 13 aprilie 1948.* [Constitution of the

Romanian People's Republic: text voted by the Grand National Assembly in session on 13 April 1948]. B.: 1948. 23 pp.

Translation together with leaders' reports on its draft stage:

R13b *Constitution of the Roumanian People's Republic; Presentation of the Draft-Constitution by Dr. Petru Groza, President of the Council of Ministers; Report on the Draft-Constitution made by Mr. Gh. Gheorghiu-Dej, first Vice-President of the Council of Ministers, General-Secretary of the Roumanian Workers' Party.* B.: Ministry of Fine Arts and Information, 1948. 78 pp.

R14 *Constituţia Republicii Populare Române.* [Constitution of the Romanian People's Republic]. B.: 1952. 47 pp.

This constitution, its draft version, and Gheorghiu-Dej's report on the latter are all available in English.

R15a *Constituţia Republicii Socialiste România.* [Constitution of the Socialist Republic of Romania]. B.: Ed. pol., 1965. 32 pp.

The draft was published separately:

R15b *Constituţia Republicii Socialiste România: proiect.* [Constitution of the Socialist Republic of Romania: draft]. B.: Ed. pol., 1965. 29 pp.

Both are available in English.

Amendments to 19 December 1979 all amalgamated in:

R15c *Constituţia Republicii Socialiste România.* [Constitution of the Socialist Republic of Romania]. B.: Consiliul de Stat, Sectorul Buletinul oficial şi publicaţie legislative, 1980. 31 pp.

All amendments to 21 March 1975 are available in English:

R15d *Constitution of the Socialist Republic of Romania.* B.: Meridiane, 1975. 32 pp.

Grand National Assembly

R16 *Standing orders of the Grand National Assembly.* (Grand National Assembly). B.: 1967. 23 pp.
Reprinted 1969 by Meridiane in the series *The Socialist Republic of Romania.*

R17 *The Grand National Assembly of the Socialist Republic of Romania: a brief outline.* B.: 1974. 104 pp.

Administration

R18 *Actele de drept administrativ.* [Acts of administrative law]; [ed.] T. Drăganu. B.: 1959. 299 pp.

R19 Ceterchi, I. *The state system of the Socialist Republic of Romania.* B.: Meridiane, 1967. 130 pp.

R20 Constitutional laws are also published separately by Serviciul (previously Sectorul, previously Colegiul redacţional) al Buletinului oficial şi al publicaţiilor legislative, under the aegis of Consiliul de Stat in the series *Legislaţie privind organizarea de stat*. [Legislation on state organizations].
See also R145.

LAW CODES

Civil

R21 *Codul civil român cu modificările la zi.* [Romanian civil code with amendments to date]; [ed. E. R. Văiteanu]. B.: 1947. 372 pp.

R22 *Codul civil coordonat cu toate textele modificatoare.* [Civil code conflated with all amending texts]; [ed.] O. Sachelarie. B.: 1947. 334 pp.

R23 *Legislaţia civilă uzuală.* [Civil legislation in force]; [ed.] P. Anca [et al.]. (Ministerul Justiţiei). B.: 1956. 2 vols.

Vol. 1 has subtitle: '*texte oficiale cu modificările pînă la data de 1 august 1956*'. [official texts with amendments to 1 August 1956]; vol. 2: '*... 1 septembrie 1956*'. Also contains the family code of 1 February 1954.

R24 *Codul civil: text oficial cu modificările pînă la data de 15 iulie 1958.* [Civil code: official text with amendments to 15 July 1958]; [ed.] P. Anca [and] O. Căpăţina. B.: Ed. şt., 1958. 510 pp.

Civil procedure

R25 *Codul de procedură civilă: text oficial cu modificările pînă la data de 1 noiembrie 1954, urmat de o anexă de acte legislative.* [Civil procedure code: official text with amendments to 1 November 1954, with an appendix of legislative acts]. (Ministerul Justiţiei). B.: E.S.P.L.E.J., 1954. 299 pp.

Revised versions with amendments to: 1 February 1955, B.: 1955, 301 pp.; 1 June 1956, B.: 1956, 310 pp.; 1 June 1958, B.: Ed. şt., 1958, 349 pp.

R26 *Codul de procedură civilă, comentat şi adnotat de Graţian Porumb.* [Civil procedure code, commentated and annotated by Graţian Porumb]. B.: Ed. şt., 1960–2. 2 vols.

Criminal

R27 *Codul penal Regele Mihai I, cu rectificările, modificările şi anexe până la 1 ianuarie 1947.* [Criminal code King Michael I, with revisions, amendments and appendices to 1 January 1947]. B.: 1947. 270 pp.

R28   *Codul penal al Republicii Populare Române; adnotat.* [Criminal code of the Romanian People's Republic; annotated] [by] V. Papadopol [et al.]. B.: E.S., 1948. 715 pp.

R29   *Codul penal şi procedură penală.* [Criminal and criminal procedure codes]. (Colecţia asesorului popular. 3). B.: E.S., 1948. 172 pp.
    A manual for lay judges.

R30   *Codul penal al Republicii Populare Române.* [Criminal code of the Romanian People's Republic]. B.: E.S., 1950. 226 pp.

R31   *Codul penal: text oficial cu modificările pînă la data de 20 mai 1955, urmat de o anexă de legi penale speciale; lucrare întocmită de un colectiv din Ministerul Justiţiei şi din Procuratura R.P.R.* [Criminal code: official text with amendments to 20 May 1955 and with an appendix of special criminal laws; prepared by a team from the Ministry of Justice and the Public Prosecutor's Office]. B.: E.S.P.L.E.J., 1955. 281 pp.

R32a   Revised version with amendments to 1 June 1958, and without subtitle 'lucrare, etc.', (Ministerul Justiţiei), B.: Ed. şt., 1958. 326 pp.

R32b   Another to 1 December 1960, 1960, 427 pp., with German translation: *Rumänisches Strafgesetzbuch: amtlicher Text, mit den Abänderungen bis zum 1. Dezember 1960.* (Sammlung ausserdeutscher Strafgesetzbücher in deutscher Übersetzung, 81). Berlin: De Gruyter, 1964.

R32c   *Excerpts from the criminal code of the Romanian People's Republic;* translated by V. Stoicoiu and R. Gheorghiu; ed. V. Gsovski. (Library of Congress. European Law Division. Studies and reports). Washington, 1959. 36 pp.

R33   *Codul penal al Republicii Socialiste România.* [Criminal code of the Socialist Republic of Romania]. B.: Ed. pol., 1968. 189 pp.
    New code passed by the Grand National Assembly 21 June 1968.

R34   *Noul cod penal şi codul penal anterior: prezentare comparativă.* [The new criminal code and the previous code: a comparative presentation]. B.: Ed. pol., 1968. 269 pp.

R35   *New Romanian penal code.* (Translations on Eastern European political, sociological and military affairs, 807). N.Y.: Macmillan, 1973. 111 pp.
    Translation of code published in BO 55/56, 23 April 1973.

R36   *Codul penal al Republicii Socialiste România; comentat şi adnotat.* [Criminal code of the Socialist Republic of Romania: commentated and annotated] [by] Teodor Vasiliu [et al.]. B.: Ed. şt. şi enciclopedică, 1975–7. 2 vols.
    Vol. 1 is the general part, vol. 2 the special.

R37   *The penal code of the Romanian Socialist Republic;* translated and with an introduction by S.-M. Vrabiescu Kleckner. (The American series of foreign penal codes, 20). South Hackensack: Rothman; London: Sweet and Maxwell, 1976. 15, 143 pp.

Criminal procedure

R38 *Codul de procedură penală al Republicii Populare Române; adnotat.* [Criminal procedure code of the Romanian People's Republic; annotated] [by] I. Stoenescu [et al.]. B.: E.S.P.L.E.J., 1948. 338 pp. Reprinted: B.: E.S., 1950.

R39 *Codul de procedură penală: text oficial cu modificările pînă la data de 1 iulie 1955, urmat de o anexă de acte legislative.* [Criminal procedure code: official text with amendments to 1 July 1955 and with an appendix of legislative acts]. B.: E.S., 1955. 243 pp.
Revised versions with amendments to: 1 June 1958, B.: Ed. şt., 1958, 276 pp.; 1 December 1960, 1960, 374 pp.

R40 *Codul de procedură penală al Republicii Socialiste România.* [Civil procedure code of the Socialist Republic of Romania]. B.: Ed. pol., 1968. 278 pp.

R41 *Noul cod de procedură penală şi codul de procedură penală anterior: prezentare comparativă.* [The new criminal procedure code and the previous code: a comparative presentation]. B.: Ed. pol., 1969. 453 pp.

R42 *Codul de procedură penală al Republicii Socialiste România.* [Criminal procedure code of the Socialist Republic of Romania]. 2nd ed. (Consiliul de Stat. Serviciul Buletinului oficial şi al publicaţiilor legislative. Legislaţie penală şi contravenţională. 5). B.: 1975. 213 pp.

See also R29.

Family

The following title is representative of publications of 1954, 1955 and 1957 of the Ministry of Justice:

R43 *Codul Familiei: Decretul nr. 31 privitor la persoanele fizice şi persoanele juridice, şi Decretul nr. 32 pentru punerea în aplicare a Codului Familiei şi a Decretului privitor la persoanele fizice şi persoanele juridice: text oficial cu modificările pînă la data de 1 septembrie 1959.* [Family Code: Decree no. 31 relating to physical and legal persons, and Decree no. 32 for putting into application the Family Code and the Decree relating to physical and legal persons: official text with amendments to 1 September 1959]. B.: Ed. şt., 1959. 92 pp.

R44 *The Family Code in the Rumanian People's Republic: Decree no. 4 of 4 January 1954, amended by Decree no. 4 of 4 April 1956, republished in the Official Bulletin of the Grand National Assembly no. 11, 4 April 1956; preface by Traian Ionaşcu.* B.: Foreign Languages Publishing House, 1958. 106 pp.

R45   *Codul Familiei; comentat și adnotat.* [Family Code, commentated and annotated] [by] S. Șerbănescu. B.: Ed. șt., 1963. 413 pp.
Includes court decisions. *See also* R23.

Labour

R46   *The Labour Code of the Rumanian People's Republic.* B.: Rumanian Institute for Cultural Relations with Foreign Countries, 1951. 69 pp.
Also contains a discussion of the scope and features of the code and G. Apostol's 'Statement on the Labour Code'.

R47   *Codul muncii: legea nr. 3 din 8 iunie 1950 cu modificările pînă la 24 iulie 1956.* [Labour code: Law no. 3 of 8 June 1950 with amendments to 24 July 1956]. B.: Ed. C.C.S., 1956. 84 pp.
English translation also published.

R48   *Codul muncii: text oficial cu modificările pînă la data de 1 iunie 1958 cu o anexă cuprinzînd acte normative uzuale în materie de muncă.* [Labour Code: official text with amendments to 1 June 1958 with an appendix of normative acts in force on labour matters]. (Ministerul Justiției). B.: 1958. 157 pp.

R49   *Codul muncii: text oficial cu modificările pînă la data de aprilie 1961.* [Labour code: official text with amendments to April 1961]. B.: Ed. șt., 1961. 59 pp.

R50   *Codul muncii adnotat pe baza prevederilor din actele normative în vigoare și a soluțiilor din deciziile Tribunalului Suprem al R.P.R.* [Labour Code annotated in accordance with provisions of normative acts in force and with solutions found in decisions of the Supreme Court of the R.P.R.]; [ed. L. Miller]. B.: Ed. șt., 1959. 404 pp.

R51   *Labour Code of the Socialist Republic of Romania.* B.: 1973. 62 pp.
Supplement to the journal *Trade Unions of Romania,* 1, 1973.

Military

R52   *Codul justiției militare.* [Code of military justice]. B.: E.S., 1948. 184 pp.
Reprinted 1950.

OTHER GENERAL LEGISLATIVE DOCUMENTS
Official gazettes

Legislation as promulgated is published in *Buletinul oficial,* which was preceded by the similar

R53   *Monitorul oficial.* [Official monitor]. B.: 1859–1949. Irregular.
In two parts: 1. Laws and decrees; 2. Ordinances of the Council of Ministers and ministerial decisions.

R54 *Buletinul oficial al Republicii Socialiste România.* [Official bulletin of the Socialist Republic of Romania]. (Consiliul de Stat, Servicuil [formerly Sectorul] Buletinului oficial şi al publicaţiilor legislative). B.: 1949–. Irregular.

In four parts:

1. Laws, decrees, decisions of the Council of Ministers, other normative acts put out by leading central organs of state administration.
2. Proceedings of the Grand National Assembly.
3. Official communiqués, acts of general interest put out by the central organs of social organizations, as well as publications and announcements.

Supplement A. List of prices issued by the Ministry of Home Trade. Supplement A dates from 1975, parts 1, 2 and 3 from 1965.

Previously in three parts:

1. Laws, decrees and decisions of the Council of Ministers.
2. Decisions of specific ministries.
3. Proceedings of the Grand National Assembly.

In 1952 it became for some years a confidential document circulated only to official bodies. 1949–52 entitled *Buletinul oficial al Republicii Populare Române*; 1952–65 entitled *Buletinul al Marii Adunări Naţionale al Republicii Populare Romîne*. There is an edition in Hungarian.

R55 *Colecţia de legi şi decrete.* [Collection of laws and decrees]. (Ministerul justiţiei). B.: 1949–. Quarterly.

1945–65 entitled *Colecţia de legi, decrete, hotărîri şi dispoziţii*; 1966–8 entitled *Colecţia de legi, decrete, hotărîri şi alte acte normative.* Frequency varies: 1949–55, monthly; 1956–68, 6 a year. In 1969 the 'hotărîri' were hived off into the resurrected journal:

R56 *Colecţie de hotărîri de Consiliului de Miniştri şi alte acte normative.* [Collection of Decisions of the Council of Ministers and other normative acts]. (Consiliul de Stat, Serviciul [formerly Sectorul] Buletinului oficial şi al publicaţiilor legislative). B.: 1951–62; 1969–. Quarterly (before 1962 weekly).

R57 *Repertoriul anual al actelor normative emise în [year].* [Annual repertoire of normative acts put out in . . .]. B.: 1970–.

Indexes R55 and R56.

General collections

May be grouped by user. For the working jurist:

R58 *Călăuza juristului: îndreptar pentru avocaţi şi jurisconsulţi.* [Jurist's guide: guide for lawyers and workers in the law]; [ed.], T. Popescu [et al.]. B.: E.S.P.L.E.J., 1956. 354 pp.

R59 *Îndreptarul legislaţiei uzuale pentru lucrătorii din justiţie: texte oficiale cu modificările.* [Guide to legislation in force for workers in the law: official texts with amendments]. B.: Ed. şt., 1957–60. 4 vols.

In the series *În ajutorul activului sindical* (*Aids to trade union activists*):

R60   *Culegere de legi, decrete şi hotărîri.* [Collection of laws, decrees and decisions]. B.: Ed. pol., 1968–79. 11 vols.

A selection of interest to Western users:

R61   *Digest of general laws of Romania.* (Legislative Council). B.: Ed. şt. şi enc., 1975–78. 7 vols.

R62   *Repertoriul general al legilor, regulamentelor şi altor dispoziţiuni de ordin legislativ.* [General repertoire of laws, regulations and other orders of legal force]. B.: 1938–47. Irregular.
    Published by Legislative Council until 1946, thereafter by Ministry of Justice.

R63   *Repertoriul general al legislaţiei în vigoare, publicată pînă la data de 1 ianuarie pe materii, cronologic, alfabetic.* [General repertoire of legislation in force published up to 1 January by subject, chronologically and alphabetically]. (Ministerul justiţiei). B.: Ed. şt., 1957. 1084 pp.
    Supplement to 1 January 1958, B.: Ed. şt., 1958, 368 pp. Another edition: B.: Ed. şt., 1966, 1104 pp.

R64   *Fişier legislativ pe probleme: lexicon.* [Legislation file by problem: lexicon]. (Procuratura generală). B.: Ed. şt., 1957–.
    Looseleaf accumulation by letters (i.e. vol. 1=A–B, vol. 2=C, etc.).

R65   *Repertoriul legislaţiei Republicii Socialiste România: legi şi decrete.* [Repertoire of legislation of the Socialist Republic of Romania: laws and decrees]. (Consiliul legislativ). B.: 1976. 592 pp.
    Supplements: covering 15 July 1976–31 December 1977, 1978; covering 1 January 1978–31 December 1978, 1979.

Arbitration

R66   *Culegere de instrucţiuni date de Primul arbitru de stat din Republica Populară Romînă, 1952–1957.* [Collection of instructions from the First State Arbitrator of the Romanian People's Republic, 1952–1957]. B.: Ed. şt., 1958. 272 pp.

R67   *Culegere de instrucţiuni date de Primul arbitru de stat: comentată şi adnotată de* [Collection of instructions from the First State Arbitrator: commented and annotated by] N. Manolescu [and] I. Cioară. B.: Ed. şt., 1966. 384 pp.

R68   *Arbitrajul de stat.* [State arbitration]. (Arbitrajul de stat). B.: 1955–73. Annual.

Continued as:

R69 *Revista de drept economic*. [Review of economic law]. (Arbitrajul de stat, Academia de ştiinţe sociale şi politice). B.: 1974–. 6 a year.

Court decisions

R70 *Culegere de decizii ale Tribunal suprem pe anul [year]*. [Collection of High Court decisions for the year . . .]. (Tribunal Suprem). B.: Ed. şt. şi enc., 1955–. Annual.

First volume entitled *Culegere de decizii ale Plenului şi Colegiilor Tribunalului suprem al R.P.R., 1 august 1952–31 decembrie 1954*. 2 vols. Vol. 1 covered civil cases, vol. 2, criminal. Single volume since 1958.

R71 *Culegere de decizii de îndrumare ale Plenului Tribunalului suprem în materie civilă pe anii 1952–1965*. [Collection of guiding decisions of the Plenum of the High Court in civil matters for the years 1952–1965]. B.: Ed. şt., 1966. 369 pp.

R72 *Îndrumările date de Plenul Tribunalului suprem şi nouă legislaţia penală: decizii de îndrumare din anii 1952–1968*. [Guidelines given by the Plenum of the High Court and new criminal legislation: guiding decisions for the years 1952–1968]. B.: Ed. şt., 1971. 400 pp.

Commentary by G. Antoniu and others.

R73 *Repertoriu alfabetic de practică judiciară*. [Alphabetical repertoire of judicial practice]; [compiled by] A. D. Dimitriu [and] C. Gall. B.: Ed. şt., 1958. 400 pp.

R74 *Repertoriu de practică judiciară*. [Repertoire of judicial practice]; [compiled by] C. Gall [and] N. Hogas. B.: Ed. şt., 1963. 595 pp.

Continues coverage of R73.

Periodicals

R75 *Legalitatea populară*. [Popular legality]. (Ministerul justiţiei, Procuratura R.P.R., Tribunal suprem). B.: 1955–62. Monthly.

Bibliographies

R76 Stoicoiu, V. *Legal sources and bibliography of Romania*. (Legal sources and bibliography of Eastern Europe; Praeger publications in Russian history and world communism, 24). N.Y.: Praeger for the Free Europe Committee, 1964. 237 pp.

One of a series of bibliographies prepared by the Mid-European Law Project of the Law Library of the Library of Congress.

R77 *Bibliographie juridique roumaine 1944–1968;* [ed. by] T. Ionasco [i.e. Ionaşcu]. (Académie de la R.S.R.). B.: 1969. 410 pp.

In French and Romanian.

Reference works

R78 *Manual juridic: drept de stat şi administrativ al R.P.R.; organizarea judecătorească; drept penal general şi special; drept civil, dreptul familiei, dreptul procesual civil şi penal; dreptul muncii.* [Juridical manual: state and administrative law of R.P.R.; organization of courts; general and special criminal law; civil law; law of the family; civil and criminal procedure law; labour law]. (Ministerul justiţiei). B.: Ed. şt., 1957. 655 pp.
Compiled by G. Penculescu and others.

R79 *Principii de drept.* [Principles of law]; [ed.] G. Penculescu [and others]. (Ministerul justiţiei). B.: Ed. şt., 1958. 960 pp.
Reprinted 1959.

GENERAL PARTY DOCUMENTS

Programme

R80 *Programme of the Romanian Communist Party for the building of the multilaterally ᵥeveloped socialist society and Romania's advance towards communism.* B.: Meridiane, 1975. 220 pp.
Adopted at the 11th Party congress, November 1974. Draft published with same title by Agerpress, 1974.

Rules

Rules were adopted at the 1945 National Conference:
R81a *Statutul.* [Rules]. B.: 1945. 8 pp.

and are published from time to time to accommodate amendments adopted at successive congresses with title:
R81b *Statutul Partidului Comunist/Muncitoresc Român.* [Rules of the Romanian Communist/Workers' Party].

English versions were published by Meridiane in 1965 and 1975 with title: *The Rules of the Romanian Communist Party.*

Party work

R82 *Primirea de noi membri în partid: îndatoriile şi drepturile comuniştilor.* [Reception of new members into the Party: the duties and rights of Communists]. B.: E.P.L.P., 1952. 85 pp.
In imprint a label '1952' covers the printed date '1953'.

R83 *Probleme ale vieţii de partid: culegere.* [Problems of party life: collected items]. B.: Ed. P.M.R., 1951. 448 pp.

See also R93.

Central Committee publications

Resolutions and decisions

R84 These are published separately in the form:
*Hotărîrea Comitetului Central al Partidului Comunist/Muncitoresc
Român cu privire* ... [Decision of the Central Committee of the
Romanian Communist/Workers' Party on ...]. B.: P.M.R. or
E.P.L.P. or Ed. pol.

Joint decisions are issued with the Council of Ministers:
R85 *Hotărîrea Consiliului de Miniştri al R.S.R. şi a C.C. al P.C.R. cu
privire* ... [Decision of the Council of Ministers of the R.S.R. and the
C[entral] C[ommittee] of the R[omanian] C[ommunist] P[arty]
on ...].

Both types may be issued also in German.

Collections were published for 1948–50:
R86 *Rezoluţii şi hotărîri ale Comitetului Central al Partidului Muncitoresc
Român, 1948–1950.* [Resolutions and decisions of the Central
Committee of the Romanian Workers' Party, 1948–1950]. B.:
E.P.L.P., 1951. 311 pp.
There was a French translation.

Collections were also published for 1951–4:
R87 *Rezoluţii şi hotărîri ale Comitetului Central al Partidului Muncitoresc
Român.* [Resolutions and decisions of the Central Committee of the
Romanian Workers' Party]. B.: E.P.L.P., 1952–5. 2 vols. Vol. 1 is a
second edition of R86.

Plenary sessions

Selected documents appear separately, e.g.
R88 *Rezoluţia Plenarei a două a Comitetului Central al Partidului
Muncitoresc Român, 10–11 iunie 1948.* [Resolution of the 2nd Plenary
Session of the Central Committee of the Romanian Workers' Party,
10–11 June 1948]. B.: P.M.R. 1948. 31 pp.
These usually have German versions.

English translations are issued of some important policy stands, e.g.
R89 *Communiqué of the Special Plenary Meeting of the Central Committee
of the Romanian Communist Party, 1 March 1968; Decision of the
Central Committee; Speech delivered by Comrade Paul Niculescu-
Mizil at the Consultative Meeting held in Budapest.* B.: Meridiane,
1968. 43 pp.

Plenary sessions are only occasionally reported in full, e.g.
R90 *Plenara Comitetului Central al Partidului Comunist Român, 3–5
noiembrie 1971.* [Plenary session of the Central Committee of the

Romanian Communist Party, 3–5 November 1971]. B.: Ed. pol., 1971. 503 pp.
Also in German.

Plenary sessions issue decisions in the form:

R91 *Hotărîrea Plenarei C.C. al P.C.R. din [date] cu privire . . . .* [Decision of the Plenary Session of the C.C. of the R.C.P. of . . . on . . .]. B.: Ed. pol.

Indexes

R92 *Indice documentar al hotărîrilor, rezoluţiilor şi rapoartelor C.C. al P.M.R., 1945–1960; lucrare întocmită de* [Documentary index of decisions, resolutions and reports of the C.C. of the R.W.P., 1945–1960; work introduced by] V. Iliescu [et al.; ed. M. Ioanid.]. B.: Biblioteca Academiei R.P.R., 1961. 154 pp.

Periodicals

R93 *Munca de partid.* [Party work]. B.: 1957–. Monthly.

R94a *Information bulletin.* B.: 1973–. Monthly.
R94b Preceded by *Bulletin d'information.* B.: 1954–. Monthly.

See also R118, R142.

Conferences

R95 *Conferinţa Naţională a Partidului Comunist Român: rezoluţie.* [National Conference of the Romanian Communist Party: resolutions]. B.: Ed. P.C.R., 1945. 8 pp.

R96a *Conferinţa Naţională a Partidului Comunist Român, 19–21 iulie 1972.* [National Conference of the Romanian Communist Party, 19–21 July 1972]. B.: Ed. pol., 1972. 565 pp.

Selected materials were issued in English:

R96b *National Conference of the Romanian Communist Party, July 19–21 1972: documents.* B.: 1972. 154 pp.

R97 *Conferinţa Naţională a Partidului Comunist Român, 7–9 decembrie 1977.* B.: Ed. pol., 1978. 493 pp.
Also in German.

Congresses

R98 *Congresul Partidului Muncitoresc Român, 21–23 februarie 1948.* [Congress of the Romanian Workers' Party, 21–23 February 1948]. B.: 1948. 263 pp.

R99 *Congresul al II-lea al Partidului Muncitoresc Romîn, 23–28 decembrie 1955.* [2nd Congress of the Romanian Workers' Party, 23–28 December 1955]. B.: E.S.P.L.P., 1956. 906 pp.

R100   *Congresul al III-lea al Partidului Muncitoresc Romîn, 20–25 iunie 1960.* [3rd Congress of the Romanian Workers' Party, 20–25 June 1960]. B.: Ed. pol., 1960. 759 pp.

R101   *Congresul al IX-lea al Partidului Comunist Român, 19–24 iulie 1965.* [9th Congress of the Romanian Communist Party, 19–24 July 1965]. B.: Ed. pol., 1965. 862 pp.
Also in German.

R102   *Congresul al X-lea al Partidului Comunist Român, 6–12 august 1969.* [10th Congress of the Romanian Communist Party, 6–12 August 1969]. B.: Ed. pol., 1969. 780 pp.
Also in German. Some materials are available in English.

R103a   *Theses of the Central Committee of the Romanian Communist Party for the tenth Party Congress.* B.: Meridiane, 1969. 58 pp.

R103b   *Resolution of the tenth Congress of the Romanian Communist Party.* B.: Meridiane, 1969. 24 pp.

R104   *Congresul al XI-lea al Partidului Comunist Român 25–28 noiembrie 1974.* [11th Congress of the Romanian Communist Party, 25–28 November, 1974]. B.: Ed. pol., 1975. 863 pp.
Also in German.

GENERAL STATISTICS
Periodical compendia and studies

R105   *Anuarul statistic al Republicii Socialiste România.* [Statistical yearbook of the Socialist Republic of Romania]. (Direcţia centrală de statistică). B.: 1904–40, 1957–. Annual.
Accompanied by separate volume of Russian, French and (since 1958) English translations of captions. 1957–65 entitled *Anuarul statistic al R.P.R.*

R106   *Statistical pocket book of the Socialist Republic of Romania.* (Direcţia centrală de statistică). B.: 1961–71. Annual.
1961–5 entitled *Rumanian statistical pocket book.*

R107   *Romania: facts and figures.* B.: Meridiane, 1964–. Annual.
Briefer and more propagandistic than R106. Since 1979 published by Ed. şt. şi enc.

R108   *Comunicări statistice.* [Statistical communications]. (Institutul central de statistică). B.: Imprimeria naţională, 1945–8. Irregular: there were 19 issues by 1948.
Includes studies.

R109   *Buletinul statistic trimestrial.* [Quarterly statistical bulletin]. (Direcţia centrală de statistică). B.: 1957–71. Quarterly.
Includes studies. Translation of texts in Russian and French.

R110   *Revista de statistică.* [Review of statistics]. (Direcţia centrală de statistică jointly with Societatea de ştiinţe economice din RSR). B.: 1952–. Monthly. Frequency varies: 1952–6, 6 p.a.

Largely studies, some statistical data. Résumés in Russian, French and English since 1964.

Reference works

R111a   *Dicţionar statistic–economic*. [Statistic–economic dictionary]; ed. M. Biji. (Direcţia centrală de statistică). B.: 1962. 486 pp.

R111b   2nd edition ed. C. Ionescu. 1969. 734 pp. Indexes in Romanian, English, French and Russian.

Population

R112   *La population de la Roumanie*. (Commission nationale de démographie). B.: Meridiane, 1974. 124 pp.

Periodical compendia and studies

R113   *Anuarul demografic al Republicii Socialiste România*. [Demographic annual of the Socialist Republic of Romania]. (Direcţia centrală de statistică). B.: 1971–4.

R114   *Buletinul demografic al României*. [Demographic bulletin of Romania]. (Institutul central de statistică). B.: 1932–50. Monthly.

1948–50 6 p.a. Résumés, tables of contents in English and French. Captions in French. Annual population statistics also published separately 1939–47 as: *Mişcarea populaţiei României în anul [year]: extras din Buletinul demografic al României: date provizorii*. [The movement of the population of Romania in the year . . .: extract from *Buletinul demografic al României*: provisional data].

Censuses

R115   *Populaţia Republicii Populare Române la 25 ianuarie 1948: rezultatele provizorii ale recensământului*. [The population of the Rumanian People's Republic on 25 January 1948: provisional census results]; [compiled by] A. Golopentia [and] D. C. Georgescu. B.: 1948. 48 pp.

Reprinted from *Probleme economice*, 2, 1948. Résumé in English.

R116   *Recensămîntul populaţiei din 21 februarie 1956: rezultate generale*. [Population census of 21 February 1956: general results]. (Direcţia centrală de statistică). B.: 1959–61. 4 vols.

Accompanied by separate volume of English translations of captions.

R117   *Recensămîntul populaţiei şi locuinţelor din 15 martie 1966: rezultate generale*. [Census of population and dwellings of 15 March 1966: general results]. (Direcţia centrală de statistică). B.: 1968–70. 8 vols.

In conjunction with the 1966 census the Direcţia worked out and published: *Nomenclator pentru codificarea categoriei sociale*. [Nomenclature for the codification of social categories]. B.: 1966. 28 pp.; *Nomenclatorul sistematic al ocupaţiilor*. [Systematic nomenclature of occupations]. B.: 1966. 360 pp.

OTHER GENERAL SOURCES OF DOCUMENTATION

R118 *Scînteia*. [The spark]. B.: Partidul Comunist Român, Comitet Central, 1932–. Daily.

The party organ, the most authoritative journal of record and policy statements.

R119 *Romania: documents, events*. B.: Agerpres, 1950–. Weekly.

1950–70 fortnightly, entitled *Documents, articles and information on Romania*. 1971–4 entitled *Romania: articles, features, information*. Publishes translations of party and government documents as occasional supplements.

R120 *Rumanian press review*. B.: 1946–54. Daily.

Translated summaries of daily press issued jointly by the US and British diplomatic missions in Romania.

INTERNATIONAL RELATIONS

Treaties

With the USSR

R121 *Tratatul româno–sovietic pentru asigurarea păcii şi securităţii*. [Romanian–Soviet treaty for the assurance of peace and security]. (Ministerul informaţiilor). B.: 1948. 31 pp.

There is a translation of the second 20-year treaty signed (after a hostile hiatus of two years) on 7 July 1970 in: Remington, R. A. *The Warsaw Pact*. Cambridge, Mass.: MIT Press, 1971. Pp. 242–5.

See also R125.

Collections

R122 *România si tratatele internaţionale: culegere de texte din tratate, convenţii şi acorduri internaţionale privind relaţiile politico-militare dintre state; texte alese, studii introductiv şi note de* [Romania and international treaties: collection of texts of international treaties, conventions and agreements on politico-military relations between states; selected texts, introductory study and notes by] T. Mitroescu [et al.]. B.: Ed. militară, 1972. 233 pp.

R123 *For a better and juster world: a collection of treaties and solemn joint declarations concluded by socialist Romania with other states*; with an introductory study by G. Macovescu, consulting editors E. Popa [et al.]. B.: Meridiane, 1975. 159 pp.

Peace settlement, 1944–1947

R124 *Convenţie între Guvernul Uniunii Republicelor Socialiste Sovietice şi Guvernul Român din 16 ianuarie 1945 cu privire la executarea Articolului 11 din Convenţia de armastiţiu din 12 septemvrie 1944.* [Agreement between the Government of the Union of Soviet Socialist Republics and the Romanian Government of 16 January 1945 on the execution of Article 11 of the Armistice agreement of 12 September 1944]. (Comisiunea română pentru aplicarea armastiţiului). B.: 1945. 38 pp.

R125 *Roumania at the peace conference.* Paris: 1946. 145 pp.
A diplomatically anonymous presentation of the Romanian case. Contains appendices of documents including the Soviet–Romanian agreement for economic collaboration of 8 May 1945 and an agreement establishing one of the joint Soviet–Romanian enterprises (Sovrompetrol).

In 1946 the Romanian Foreign Ministry published several memoranda on Romania's case at the Peace Conference. These were published in English by the State Printing Office and entitled:

R126 *Memorandum on the military and economic contributions of Roumania to the war against Germany and Hungary.* 26 pp.

R127 *Memorandum on the reparations which Roumania demands from Hungary.* 11 pp.

R128 *Memorandum on the Roumanian–Hungarian Frontier.* 28 pp.

R129 *Memorandum on Transylvania.* 48 pp.

R130 *Memorandum relative to various provisions to be inserted in the treaty with Hungary.* 16 pp.

Consular relations

R131a *Relaţiile consulare al României: culegere de tratate, convenţii şi acorduri.* [Consular relations of Romania: collection of treaties, conventions and agreements]. [Editors] N. Ecobescu [et al.]. B.: Ed. pol., 1975. 1004 pp.

R131b *Relaţiile consulare al României: culegere de texte legislative.* [Consular relations of Romania: collection of legislative texts]. B.: Ed. pol., 1977. 447 pp.
Edited by N. Ecobescu, who states 'this work and [R131a] form a single whole'.

Regulations relating to aliens and foreign companies are included in R61.

Romania's foreign policy

R132a *Dezbaterile sesiunii Marii Adunări Naţionale din 24–26 iulie 1967 cu privire la politica externă a României socialiste.* [Debates of the Grand

National Assembly session of 24–26 July 1967 on the foreign policy of socialist Romania]. B.: Ed. pol., 1967. 287 pp.

English translation also published:

R132b *Session of the Grand National Assembly of the Socialist Republic of Romania, July 24–26, 1967; Report by N. Ceauşescu, General-Secretary of the C.C. of the R.C.P., on the foreign policy of the Socialist Republic of Romania; Speeches within the debate of the report.* B.: Agerpres, 1967. lxvi, 153 pp.

The Grand National Assembly session following the Soviet invasion of Czechoslovakia was also published in a separate English translation:

R133 *Basic principles of Romania's foreign policy: joint meeting of the C.C. of the R.C.P., the State Council and the Romanian Government, August 21, 1968; special session of the Grand National Assembly of the Socialist Republic of Romania, August 22, 1968. B.: Meridiane, 1968. 100 pp.*

Collections

R134 *Agenda pe probleme internaţionale.* [Agenda for international problems]. B.: Ed. pol., 1971. 432 pp.

R135 *Contribuţii ale României la soluţionarea marilor probleme ale lumii contemporane: documente.* [Romania's contributions to the solution of the major problems of the contemporary world: documents]. B.: Ed. pol., 1975. 63 pp.

Towards China

R136 *Tradiţii ale poporului român de solidaritate şi prietenie cu poporul chinez.* [The Romanian people's traditions of solidarity and friendship with the Chinese people]. B.: Ed. pol., 1973. 477 pp.

Towards non-aligned states

R137 *Solidarity relations and broad and friendly cooperation: Romania and the non-aligned states.* B.: Agerpres, 1976. 3 vols.

In some library catalogues entry is under 'Romania and the non-aligned states'.

Towards USA

R138 *Politica agresivă şi uneltirile imperialismului american impotriva Republicii Populare Române.* [Aggressive policy and machinations of American imperialism against the Rumanian People's Republic]. (Ministerul afacerilor străine). B.: 1952. 139 pp.

Official diatribe replying to Dean Acheson's charge of 5 November 1951 of the violation of human rights in Romania. An English translation was issued by the Romanian Foreign Ministry: *Enemies of peace and freedom of the peoples: aggressive policy and machinations of United States imperialism against Rumanian People's Republic.* B.: 1952. 150 pp.

Documented state visits

The record of speeches made by Gheorghiu-Dej and Gheorghe Maurer and their opposite numbers on their visit to Indonesia, India and Burma:

R139 *În numele păcii şi prieteniei, 1–24 octombrie 1962.* [In the name of peace and friendship, 1–24 October 1962]. B.: Ed. pol., 1963. 302 pp.

Set a precedent which has been voluminously followed by Ceauşescu, who has made over thirty official visits abroad since taking office. The public records of these are published by Ed. pol., commonly occurring titles being *Sub semnul prieteniei/solidarităţii . . .* [Under the sign of friendship/solidarity . . .] and *Vizita oficială/de stat . . .* [State/official visit . . .]. Most volumes cover a single visit or round of visits and appear soon after the event, but some recapitulate a series of visits with certain countries over a span of years.

Other sources

R140 *Lumea: [The world].* Romanian foreign policy weekly. B.: 1963–. Weekly.
   In English. Includes texts of official documents and policy statements.

POLITICAL AND IDEOLOGICAL AFFAIRS

Reference works

R141 *The political system of the Socialist Republic of Romania.* B.: Ed. şt. şi enc., 1979. 280 pp.

Periodicals

R142 *Era socialistă: revista teoretică şi social-politică a Comitetului Central al Partidului Comunist Român.* [Socialist era: theoretical and socio-political review of the Central Committee of the Romanian Communist Party]. B.: 1948–. Fortnightly. Tables of contents in English, Russian, French and Spanish.
   1948–72 entitled *Lupta de clasă.* [Class struggle]. Monthly.

Historical sources

R143 *Frontul unic muncitoresc: manifesto.* [United Workers' Front: manifesto]. Single sheet published 1 May 1944.

R144   *The program of the bloc of democratic parties.* (Ministry of Information. Rumania and the forthcoming elections). B.: 1947. 19 pp.

R145   *Proclamation of the Rumanian Popular Republic.* (Ministry of Information). B.: 1948. 24 pp.
        Contains: Act of Abdication; Proclamation of the Government; Two new year messages to the country; A message from the Provisional Presidium; A message from the Government.

R146   *Documents concerning right deviation in Rumanian Workers' Party.* (Rumanian Workers' Party, Institute of Party History). B.: 1952. 84 pp.

Political education

R147   *Congresul educaţiei politice şi al culturii socialiste, 2–4 iunie 1976.* [Congress of political education and socialist culture, 2–4 June 1976]. B.: Ed. pol., 1976. 447 pp.
        Also in German.

Ethnic minorities

R148   *Rezoluţia Biroului Politic al C.C. al P.M.R. în chestiunea naţională.* [Resolution of the Political Bureau of the C.C. of the R.W.P. on the national question]. B.: P.M.R., 1948. 31 pp.

R149   *Hungarians and Germans in Romania today: plenums of the Councils of Working People of Magyar and German Nationality in the Socialist Republic of Romania, March 13–14, 1978.* B.: Meridiane, 1978. 327 pp.

R150   *The new legal status of the nationalities in Romania.* B.: State Printing Office, 1946. 13 pp.

Political trials

R151   *Antonescieni şi legionari în faţă Tribunalului poporului.* [Antonescuites and Legionaries before the People's Court]. B.: Ed. Institutului român de documentare, 1946. 30 pp.

R152   *Trial of the former National Peasant Party leaders: Maniu, Mihalache, Penescu, Grigore Niculescu-Buzesti and others; after the shorthand notes.* (Bucharest Military Tribunal). B.: Dacia traiană, 1947. 228 pp.

R153   *Trial of the group of plotters, spies and saboteurs: full account of the proceedings before the Bucharest Military Tribunal on October 27th–November 2nd, 1948.* B.: 1949. 163 pp.
        Defendants A. Popp and others.

R154   *Trial of the group of spies and traitors in the service of imperialist espionage.* (Bucharest Military Tribunal). B.: 1950. 72 pp.
        Defendant V. Ciobanu.

R155   *Trial of the group of spies and traitors in the service of the espionage of Tito's fascist clique.* (Bucharest Military Tribunal). B.: 1950. 68 pp. Defendant M. Todorov.

MILITARY AFFAIRS

R156   *Îndreptar legislativ pentru practica judiciară la tribunalele militare.* [Legislative guide to judicial practice in military courts]; [ed.] G. Geamănu [et al.]. B.: 1956. 148 pp.

R157   *Legea nr. 14/1972 privind organizarea apărării naționale a Republicii Socialiste România; Decretul nr. 544/1972 privind apărarea locală antiaeriană în Republica Socialistă România.* [Law no. 14/1972 on the organization of the national defence of the Socialist Republic of Romania; Decree no. 544/1972 on local anti-aircraft defence in the Socialist Republic of Romania]. (Consiliul de Stat, Secția redacțională a Buletinului oficial și a altor publicații legislative. Legislație privind organizarea de stat. 7). B.: 1973. 88 pp.

ECONOMIC AFFAIRS

Planning

Planning directives can be found in the Party Congress proceedings (R98–R104) and are published occasionally (both draft and as finalized) as separate items and also in English and German:

R158   *Directivele Congresului al II-lea al Partidului Muncitoresc Romîn cu privire la cel de-al doilea plan cincinal de dezvoltare a economiei naționale pe anii 1956–1960.* [Directives of the 2nd Congress of the Romanian Workers' Party on the second five-year plan for the development of the national economy for the years 1956–1960]. B.: E.S.P.L.P., 1955. 44 pp.

R159   *Directivele Congresului al III-lea al P.M.R. pentru planul de dezvoltare a economiei naționale pe anii 1960–1965 și pentru programul economic de perspectivă: proiect.* [Directives of the 3rd Congress of the R.W.P. for the plan of development of the national economy for the years 1960–1965 and for an economic perspective programme: draft]. B.: Ed. pol., 1960. 88 pp.
Also in German.

R160   *Directivele Congresului al III-lea al P.M.R. cu privire la planul de dezvoltare a economiei naționale pe anii 1960–1965 și la schița planului economic de perspectivă pe 15 ani.* [Directives of the 3rd Congress of the R.W.P. on the plan of development of the national economy for the years 1960–1965 and on the sketch of the economic perspective plan for 15 years]. B.: Ed. pol., 1960. 72 pp.
Also in English as a supplement to *Rumania today*, 6, 1960.

R161 *Directives of the Ninth Congress of the Rumanian Communist Party on the development of the national economy in the 1966–1970 period; Directives of ... on the turning to account of power resources and the country's electrification in the 1966–1975 period.* B.: Meridiane, 1965. 62 pp.

R162 *Directives of the Tenth Congress of the Romanian Communist Party concerning the 1971–1975 five-year plan and the guidelines for the development of the national economy in the 1976–1980 period: draft.* B.: Meridiane, 1969. 88 pp.

R163 *Directives of the Eleventh Congress of the Romanian Communist Party concerning the 1976–1980 five-year plan and the guidelines for Romania's economic and social development over the 1981–1990 period.* B.: Meridiane, 1975. 76 pp.

Popular expositions of the one-year plans for 1949 and 1950 were published with title:

R164 *Planul de stat pe anul 1949 [1950].* B.: 80 pp.

The 1951–5 plan was outlined in English:

R165 *Planned development of the Rumanian People's Republic.* B.: 1950. 152 pp.

R166 *Programul-directivă de dezvoltare economico-socială a României în profil teritorial în perioada 1981–1985: proiect.* [Directive-programme of economico-social development of Romania in its territorial aspect in the period 1981–1985: draft]. B.: Ed. pol., 1979. 32 pp.

R167 *Programul-directivă de creştere a nivelului de trai în perioada 1981–1985 şi de ridicare continua a calităţii vieţii: proiect.* [Directive-programme of growth in the standard of living in the period 1981–1985 and of continuous raising of the quality of life: draft]. B.: Ed. pol., 1979. 42 pp.

R168 *Hotărîrea Comitetului Central al Partidului Comunist Român cu privire la îndeplinirea planului cincinal 1971–1975; Comunicat cu privire la îndeplinirea planului naţional unic de dezvoltare economico-socială a Republicii Socialiste România în perioada 1971–1975, 3 februarie 1976.* [Decision of the Central Committee of the Romanian Communist Party on the fulfilment of the five-year plan 1971–1975; Communiqué on the fulfilment of the unified national plan of economico-social development of the Socialist Republic of Romania in the period 1971–1975, 3 February 1976]. B.: Ed. pol., 1976. 77 pp. Also in German.

R169 *Directives of the Central Committee of the Romanian Communist Party on the perfecting of management and planning of the national economy in keeping with the conditions of the new stage of Romania's socialist development: draft.* B.: Agerpres, 1967. 128 pp.

R170   Maurer, I. G. *Report on the implementation of the state plan for 1965 and on the state plan for 1966 submitted to the session of the Grand National Assembly of December 20–22, 1965.* B.: Meridiane, 1965. 33 pp.

R171   Maurer, I. G. *Report on the directives of the Tenth Congress of the Romanian Communist Party concerning the 1971–1975 five-year plan and the guidelines for the development of the national economy in the 1976–1980 period.* B.: Meridiane, 1969. 55 pp.

R172   *Dezvoltarea economică a României în anul 1966: comunicat cu privire la îndeplinarea planului de stat de dezvoltare a economiei naţionale a Republicii Socialiste România pe anul 1966.* [Economic development of Romania in the year 1966: communiqué on the implementation of the state plan of development of the national economy of the Socialist Republic of Romania]. B.: Ed. pol., 1967. 72 pp.

R173   *Comunicat cu privire la îndeplinirea planului de dezvoltare economico-socială a Republicii Socialiste România în perioada 1966–1970.* [Communiqué on the implementation of the plan of economico-social development of the Socialist Republic of Romania in the period 1966–1970]. (Direcţia centrală de statistică). B.: Ed. pol., 1971. 56 pp.
       Also in German.

R174   *Romania's economic development over 1966–1970.* (Chamber of Commerce of the Socialist Republic of Romania). B.: 1966. 38 pp.
       Supplement to *Romanian foreign trade,* 4, 1966.

R175   *Romania's development over 1971–1975.* (Chamber of Commerce of the Socialist Republic of Romania). B.: 1973. 95 pp.

R176   *Sedinţă comună a Comitetului Central al Partidului Comunist Român, Marii Adunări Naţionale şi Consiliului suprem al dezvoltării economice şi sociale cu privire la activitatea partidului şi întregului popor pentru înlăturarea urmărilor cutremurului catastrofal din 4 martie, dezvoltarea economico-socială actuală a ţării, activitatea internaţională a partidului şi statului şi situaţia politică mondială, 28–29 martie 1977.* [Joint session of the Central Committee of the Romanian Communist Party, the Grand National Assembly and the Supreme Council for Economic and Social Development on the activity of the Party and the whole people for the elimination of the consequences of the catastrophic earthquake of 4 March, the present-day economico-social development of the country, the international activity of the Party and state and the world political situation, 28–29 March 1977]. B.: Ed. pol., 1977. 263 pp.

R177   *Economia româna: buletinul Ministerului industriei şi comerţului.* [The Romanian economy: bulletin of the Ministry of Industry and Commerce]. B.: 1918–47. Monthly.

Before 1945 subtitled 'buletinul Ministerului economiei naţionale'.

For planning law see following section.

Law

R178 Economic legislation is published from time to time by Serviciul al Buletinului oficial (*see* R20) in the series *Legislaţie economică şi financiară*. [Economic and financial legislation].

R179 *Nationalization of industrial, banking, insurance, mining and transport enterprises*. (Ministry of Arts and Information). B.: 1948. 43 pp.

R180 Văiteanu, E. R. *Codul redresării economice şi al stabilizării monetare.* [Code of economic rehabilitation and monetary stabilization]. B.: 1947. 425 pp.

R181 *Îndreptar legislativ financiar–economic.* [Financial–economic legislative guide]. (Direcţia generală a serviciului muncii). B.: Ed. şt., 1957–9. 3 vols.

Vols. 1–2 cover 1948–57; vol. 3 1948–58, with an appendix 'Actele normative publicate în perioada 1 septembrie 1958–15 februarie 1959'.

R182 *Organizarea şi conducerea unităţilor economice de stat: culegere de acte normative.* [Organization and administration of state economic units: collection of normative acts]. (Consiliul de Stat, Sectorul Buletinului oficial şi al publicaţiilor legislative. Legislaţie uzuală). B.: 1976. 871 pp.

Supplements of 71 pp. and 222 pp. were published in 1977.

R183 *Călăuza economică şi financiară: legi, regulamente.* [Economic and financial guide: laws, regulations]. (Ministerul de finanţe, Biblioteca financiară. Colecţia abonamente). B.: 1949. 563 pp.

R184 *Colecţia de legi şi deciziuni ale Comisiunei ministeriale de redresare economică şi stabilizare monetară şi ale Ministerului industriei şi comerţului.* [Collection of laws and decisions of the Ministerial Commission for Economic Rehabilitation and Monetary Stabilisation and of the Ministry of Industry and Commerce]. B.: 1947–8. Irregular.

The initiating planning laws are collected in:

R185 *Legislaţia economiei planificate, 13 aprilie 1948–30 iunie 1949.* [Legislation of the planned economy, 13 April 1948–30 June 1949]. (Ministerul Justiţiei, Direcţia de coordonare legislativă. Studii şi documentare). B.: E.S.L.J., 1949. 575 pp.

Agriculture

Development

R186 *La réforme agraire en Roumanie.* (Ministère de l'information, Direction des relations culturelles avec l'étranger). B.: 1946. 58 pp.

R187 *Dezvoltarea agriculturii în Republica Populară Romîna.* [Development of agriculture in the Romanian People's Republic]; [ed.] O. Feneşan [et al.]. (Ministerul agriculturii şi silviculturii). B.: Ed. agro-silvică de stat, 1958. 226 pp.

R188 *Victoria socialismului în agricultură: lucrările sesiunii extraordinare a Marii Adunări Naţionale, 27–30 aprilie 1962.* [The victory of socialism in agriculture: proceedings of an extraordinary session of the Grand National Assembly, 27–30 April 1962]. B.: Ed.pol., 1962. 687 pp.

Party directives

R189 *Resolution of the Plenary Meeting of the Central Committee of the Romanian Communist Party of November 11–12, 1965 on the improvement of the management and planning of agriculture.* B.: Meridiane, 1965. 16 pp.

R190 *Hotărîrea Plenarei Comitetului Central al Partidului Comunist Român cu privire la îmbunătăţirea conducerii şi planificării unitare a agriculturii, crearea consiliilor agroindustriale de stat şi cooperatiste şi creşterea producţiei agricole.* [Decision of the Plenum of the Central Committee ... on the improvement of unitary planning of agriculture, the creation of joint state and cooperative agro-industrial councils and the growth of agricultural production]. Sibiu: 1979. 29 pp.

Law

R191 *Legislaţia gospodăriilor agricole colective şi a întovărăşirilor agricole.* [Legislation regarding collective farms and peasant household associations]. (Ministerul justiţiei). B.: E.S.P.L.E.J., 1956. 559 pp.

R192 *Legislaţia gospodăriilor agricole de stat.* [Legislation regarding state farms]. (Ministerul justiţiei). B.: Ed. st., 1957. 516 pp.

R193 *Culegere de acte normative privind legislaţia cu caracter general şi specific uzuală unităţilor agricole socialiste de stat.* [Collection of normative acts on legislation of general and specific character in force on state socialist agricultural units]. B.: 1967. 879 pp.

Statistics

R194 *Statistica agricolă a României.* [Agricultural statistics of Romania]. (Institutul central de statistică). B.: 1937–48. Annual. Postwar vols.: 6–8.

R195 *Dezvoltarea agriculturii Republicii Populare Romîne.* [Development of agriculture in the Romanian People's Republic]. (Direcţia centrală de statistică). B.: 1961. 418 pp.
Accompanied by separate English translation of captions.

R196 A further version 1965, with same title but subtitle *culegere de date statistice.* [collection of statistical data]. 600 pp.
Also with separate English captions.

Energy

R197 *Nuclear energy development in the Rumanian People's Republic: a brief survey.* B.: 1964. 111 pp.

R198 Chivu, S. *Report on the directives of the Ninth Congress of the Romanian Communist Party on the ten-year plan for the development of energetics, July 20 1965.* B.: Meridiane, 1965. 35 pp.

R199 *Nuclear energy in the Socialist Republic of Romania, 1966–1970.* (State Committee for Nuclear Energy). B.: 1971. 104 pp.

R200 *Programul-directivă de cercetare şi dezvoltare în domeniul energiei pe perioada 1981–1990 şi orientarile principale pînă în anul 2000: proiect.* [Directive-programme of research and development in the field of energy for the period 1981–1990 and principal orientations up to the year 2000: draft]. B.: Ed. pol., 1979. 40 pp.
Also in German.

Finance
Periodicals

R201 *Revista finanţelor.* [Review of finance]. (Ministerul finanţelor). B.: 1948–9? Monthly.

R202 *Gazeta finanţelor: organ al Ministerului finanţelor şi al Bancii de stat.* [Finance gazette: organ of the Ministry of Finance and the State Bank]. B.: 1952–? Weekly.

R203 *Finanţe şi credit.* [Finance and credit]. (Ministerul finanţelor). B.: 1955–. Monthly.

Law

R204 *Hotărîrea Consiliului de Miniştri al R.P.R. şi a Comitetului Central al P.M.R. privind măsurile necesare pentru consolidarea succesului reformei băneşti, martie 1952.* [Decision of the Council of Ministers of the R.P.R. and of the Central Committee of the R.W.P. on measures necessary for consolidating the success of the monetary reform, March 1952]. B.: P.M.R., 1952. 29 pp.
The British Legation in Bucharest produced a translation: *Resolution of the Council of Ministers of the R.P.R. and of the Central Committee.... B., 1952. 10 pp.*

R205 *Legislaţia financiară a R.P.R.: textele oficiale cu modificările pînă la data de 1 septembrie 1957.* [Financial legislation of the R.P.R.: official texts with amendments to 1 September 1957]. (Ministerul justiţiei). B.: Ed. şt., 1957. 599 pp.

R206 *Legislaţia uzuală contabilă-financiară: texte oficiale cu modificările pînă la data de 1 mai 1962.* [Accountancy and financial legislation in force: official texts with amendments to 1 May 1962]. B.: 1962. 922 pp.

Industry

R207 *Dezvoltarea industriei socialiste în R.P.R.* [Development of socialist industry in R.P.R.]. B.: Ed. şt., 1959. 597 pp.

R208 *Industria uşoară, 1950–1970.* [Light industry, 1950–1970]. (Ministerul industriei uşoare, Centrul de documentare şi publicaţii tehnice). B.: 1971. 56 pp.

Statistics

R209 *Dezvoltarea industriei Republicii Populare Romîne: culegere de date statistice.* [Development of industry in the Romanian People's Republic: collection of statistical data]. (Direcţia centrală de statistică). B.: 1964. xxiii, 415 pp.

Separate English translations of captions entitled *The growth of industry in the Rumanian People's Republic: compendium of statistics.* B.: 1964. xxii, 134 pp.

Worker representation in management

R210 *Congresul consiliilor oamenilor muncii din industrie, construcţii şi transporturi, Bucureşti, 11–13 iulie 1977.* [Congress of Workers' Councils in Industry, Building and Transport, Bucharest, 11–13 July 1977]. B.: Ed. pol., 1977. 271 pp.

R211 *Plenarele consiliilor oamenilor muncii de naţionalitate maghiară şi germană din Republica Socialistă România, 13–14 martie 1978.* [Plena of the Councils of Workers of Hungarian and German ethnic groups in the Socialist Republic of Romania, 13–14 March 1978]. B.: Ed. pol., 1978. 165 pp.

Summarizes proceedings. Also in German.

Inventions

R212 *Legislaţia invenţiilor, inovaţiilor şi raţionalizărilor: texte comentate.* [The legislation of inventions, innovations and rationalizations: texts commented] [by] Y. Eminescu. B.: Ed. şt., 1969. 301 pp.

Investment

R213 *Clasificarea fondurilor fixe din economia naţionale a Republicii Pop-*

ulare Romîne. [Classification of fixed assets in the national economy of the Romanian Peoples' Republic]. (Comisia centrală pentru inventarierea şi reevaluerea fondurilor). B.: 1964. 432 pp.

R214 *Investiţii–construcţii în Republica Socialistă Română: culegere de date statistice.* [Investment and construction in the Socialist Republic of Romania: collection of statistical data]. (Direcţia centrală de statistică). B.: 1966. 527 pp.

Labour

Law

R215 *Legea pentru reorganizarea jurisdicţiei muncii: comentată şi adnotată cu toate lucrările pregătitoare şi instrucţiunile de aplicare întocmite de Consiliul permanent al jurisdicţiei muncii de* [Law for the reorganization of the jurisdiction of labour: commented and annotated with preparatory proceedings and instructions on application introduced by the Permanent Council of Labour Jurisdiction by] O. Creangu şi I. Ciurariu. B.: 1949. 170 pp.

R216 *Culegere de acte normative în materie de muncă.* [Collection of normative acts regarding labour]. [Ed.] L. Miller şi T. Zega. B.: Ed. şt., 1957. 276 pp.
Covers June 1950–November 1956.

R217 *Legislaţia uzuală a muncii.* [Labour legislation in force] [Ed.] L. Miller. B.: Ed. şt., 1960. 632 pp.
Includes High Court rulings. 2nd ed. 1966. 685 pp.

Statistics

R218 *Forţa de muncă în Republica Socialistă România: culegere de date statistice.* [The labour force in the Socialist Republic of Romania]. (Direcţia centrală de statistică). B.: 1966. 448 pp.
Separate English translation of captions in pocketbook format: *Labour force in the Socialist Republic of Romania: compendium of statistics.* 118 pp.

Periodicals

R219 *Buletin informativ al muncii: publicaţie oficială a Ministerului muncii.* [Labour information bulletin: official publication of the Ministry of Labour]. B.: 1920–47. Monthly.

Standards

R220 *Standardizarea română: publicaţie tehnico-ştiinţifică şi oficială.* [Romanian standardization: technico-scientific and official publication]. (Institutul român de standardizare). B.: 1958–. Monthly.
1958–70 entitled *Standardizarea: publicaţie oficială a Oficiului de stat pentru standarde.*

Foreign economic relations

R221 A *Commercial guide to Rumania* appeared in 1957 and ran to 6 editions (1958, 1961, 1964, 1969 and 1974). The 5th and 6th editions were entitled *Economic and commercial guide to Romania.*

R222 In 1970 an annual *Romania: pocket commercial guide* began publication.

R223 *Economic development of the Rumanian People's Republic: an active factor in extending world trade.* B.: 1954. 151 pp.

R224 *Rumania in the [sic] international trade, 1944–1964.* B.: 1964. 261 pp.

Periodicals

Journals published by the Chamber of Commerce and Industry:

R225 *Buletinul.* [Bulletin]. B.: 1901–47. Monthly.

R226 *Information bulletin.* B.: 1955–69. Monthly.

This was replaced by:

R227 *Romanian economic news.* B.:1970–4. Monthly.

R228 *Romanian foreign trade.* B.: 1950–. Quarterly.
Publishes supplements of official documents.

Other journals include:

R229 *Informaţii de comerţ exterior.* [Foreign trade information]. (Ministerul de comerţului exterior şi cooperări: economice internaţionale, with the Chamber). B.: 1950–. Weekly.

R230 *Annual bulletin.* (Romanian Bank for Foreign Trade). B.: 1972–.

R231 *Romania and the developing countries.* [Agerpres]. B.: 1976–. Monthly.

Arbitration

R232 *Arbitrajul în comerţul exterior al R.P.R.: regulamentul de organizare şi funcţionare a Comisiei de arbitraj de pe lîngă Camera de comerţ a R.P.R., comentarii, regulamentele comisiilor de arbitraj de pe lîngă camerele de comerţ din alte ţări socialiste de* [Arbitration in the foreign trade of the R.P.R.: regulation for the organization and functioning of the Arbitration Commission under the aegis of the Chamber of Commerce of the R.P.R., commentaries, regulations for the arbitration commissions under the aegis of the chambers of commerce of other socialist countries by] I. Nestor. B.: Ed. şt., 1957. 219 pp.

Law

R233 *Curier economic–legislativ pentru uzul compartimentelor de export.*

[Economic–legislative courier for the use of exporting agencies]. B.: 1971. 504 pp.
Text also in English, French and German.

Law 1 of 17 March 1971 (BO 33) regulates relations with foreign firms, and was issued by the Chamber of Commerce and Industry with title:

R234   *Romanian foreign trade law* in 1974, 1975 and 1976.

The latest legislation on contracts with foreign firms is Law 3 of 14 July 1979 (BO 6), which updates provisions of 1969. There is an account in *Romanian foreign trade*, 2, 1980.

R235   *Guidebook on the constitution of joint companies in Romania.* (Publicom). B.: 1979. 139 pp.

Statistics

R236   *Comerţul exterior al Republicii Socialiste România, 1973: culegere de date statistice.* [Foreign trade of the Socialist Republic of Romania, 1973: collection of statistical data]. (Direcţia centrală de statistică). B.: 1974. 270 pp.
Another edition: 1975. 248 pp.

For a Sovrom agreement in English, *see* R125.

SOCIAL AFFAIRS

Ethics

The 11th Party Congress adopted an ethical code, published separately in English:

R237   *Code of the principles and norms of work and life of the Communists, of socialist ethics and equality.* B.: Meridiane, 1975. 32 pp.

Health

R238   *Law on securing the health of the population.* (Ministry of Health). B.: 1978. 55 pp.

R239   *Vademecum of medico-sanitary statistics.* (Ministry of Health, Planning, Statistics, Work-and-Wages Direction). B.: 1972–. Irregular.

R240   *Breviar de statistică sanitară.* [Pocketbook of health statistics]. (Ministerul sănătăţii, Centrul de calcul şi statistică sanitară). B.: 1976–. Irregular.

Housing

R241   *Legislaţia locativă a R.P.R.: decretele nr. 78/1952, 109/1954, 330/1953, 387/1952 şi 511/1953; hotărîrile Consiliului de Miniştri nr. 1508/1953, 3989/1953, 1509/1953 şi 739/1954.* [Housing legislation

of R.P.R.: Decrees no . . .; Decisions of the Council of Ministers . . .].
(Ministerul justiţiei). B.: E.S.P.L.E.J., 1954. 61 pp.

R242   *Regimul legal al folosirii locuinţelor în R.P.R.: culegere de acte
normative.* [Legal régime for the use of dwellings in R.P.R.:
collection of normative acts]. B.: Ed. şt., 1958. 125 pp.

R243   *Legislaţia locativă adnotată.* [Housing legislation annotated]. [by] V.
Pătulea. B.: Ed. şt., 1963. 165 pp.

Social security

Accounts are published in English from time to time by the Central
Council of Trade Unions, e.g.

R244   *Social insurance in the Rumanian People's Republic.* B.: 1957. 95 pp.

The foundations of the system are laid in:

R245   *Legea şi regulamentul pentru organizarea asigurărilor sociale de stat.*
[Law and regulations for the organization of state social security].
(Confederaţia generală a muncii). B.: 1950. 64 pp.

Later legislation is collected in:

R246   *Asigurările sociale de stat în Republica Socialistă România.* [State
social security in the Socialist Republic of Romania]. B.: Ed. pol.,
1968. 208 pp.

Pension law is amply collected and annotated, and occasionally issued in
English:

R247   *Legislaţia pensiilor din cadrul asigurărilor sociale de stat.* [Pension law
within the framework of state social security]. [Ed.] D. Margaritescu
[et al.]. B.: Ed. medicală, 1963. 275 pp.

R248   *Legislaţia pensiilor, comentată şi adnotată.* [Pension law, commented
and annotated] [by] M. Niculescu. B.: Ed. şt., 1965. 534 pp.

R249   *Law on state social insurance pensions and the supplementary pension.*
B.: Agerpres, 1967. 43 pp.

Women's rights

R250   *Prevederi ale legislaţiei actuale din Republica Socialista România
privind drepturile şi îndatorile femeii.* [Provisions in the legislation in
force in the Socialist Republic of Romania regarding women's rights
and obligations]. (Consiliul naţional al femeilor din R.S.R.). 2nd ed.
B.: 1979. 80 pp.

CULTURAL AFFAIRS

Education

R251   *Development of education in the Socialist Republic of Romania for the*

[*1957–1958, etc.*] *school year.* (Ministry of Education and Culture).
B.: 1958–. Annual.
Presented each year to the International Conference on Education,
Geneva.

R252   *Contemporanul: săptămînul al Consiliului culturii şi educaţiei socialiste.* [The contemporary: weekly of the Council of Culture and
Socialist Education]. B.: 1953–. Weekly.

R253   *Tribuna scolii.* [School tribune]. (Ministerul educaţiei şi
învăţămîntului, Uniunea sindicatelor din învăţămînt şi cultura). B.:
1971–. Monthly.
Formed from the amalgamation of R254 and R255.

R254   *Gazeta învăţămîntului.* [Education gazette]. (Ministerul
învăţămîntului, Comitetul central al Sindicatului muncitorilor din
învăţămînt). B.: 1949–71.

R255   *Colocvii despre scoală, familie şi societate* [Colloquium on school,
family and society]. (Ministerul învăţămîntului). B.: 1966–71.

Law

The foundations of the communist system were laid by Decree 175, MO 177, 3
August 1948. The present eight-year system was introduced by Decree 289, BO
24, 7 October 1961.
Decree 175/1968 of the Presidium of the Grand National Assembly is
available in English:

R256   *The education law of the Socialist Republic of Romania: bill passed by
the Grand National Assembly of the Socialist Republic of Romania on
13th May 1968.* B.: Didactical and Pedagogical Publishing House,
1968. 61 pp.

Law 28, BO 113, 26 December 1978 is available separately in
Romanian (and also in German):

R257   *Legea educaţiei şi învăţămîntului nr. 28/1978.* [Law on education . . .].
(Consiliul de Stat, Sector Buletinului oficial şi al publicaţiilor
legislative. Legislaţie privind învăţămîntului, ştiinţa şi cultura. 7).
B.: 1979. 56 pp.

LEADERS' WORKS

Petru Groza

R258   *Reconstrucţia României: discursi politice, conferenţe şi interview-uri,
1944–1946.* [The reconstruction of Romania: political speeches, talks
and interviews, 1944–1946]. B.: 1946. 391 pp.

R259   *În drum spre socialism: discursuri şi întrevederi politice, 1947–1948.*
[On the way to socialism: speeches and political interviews,
1947–1948]. B.: E.S., 1950. 260 pp.

R260 *Articole, cuvîntări, interviuri: texte alese.* [Articles, speeches, interviews: selected texts]. B.: Ed. pol., 1973. 673 pp.

Gheorghe Gheorghiu-Dej

R261 The single-volume *Articole şi cuvîntări* [Articles and speeches] ran into four editions by 1955 (B.: E.S. 863 pp.), and was then treated as the first volume of an ongoing series with the same title, with coverage:
December 1955–July 1959. B.: Ed. pol., 1959. 680 pp.
August 1959–May 1961. B.: Ed. pol., 1961. 467 pp.
June 1961–December 1962. B.: Ed. pol., 1962. 472 pp.
No more were published.

The last collected works published were also put out in English:
R262 *Articles and speeches, June 1961–December 1962.* B.: Meridiane, 1963. xii, 430 pp.

Nicolae Ceauşescu

R263 First three volumes of collected works entitled *România pe drumul desăvîrşirii construcţiei socialiste: rapoarte, cuvîntări, articole.* [Romania on the way to completing socialist construction: reports, speeches, articles]. B.: Ed. pol., 1968–9. 3 vols.
Vol. 1, publ. 1968, covers July 1965–September 1966.
Vol. 2, publ. 1968, covers September 1966–December 1967.
Vol. 3, publ. 1969, covers January 1968–March 1969.
Also available in English: *Romania on the way of completing socialist construction: reports, speeches, articles.* B.: Meridiane, 1968–9. 3 vols.

R264 Vol. 4 and subsequent volumes entitled *România pe drumul construirii societăţii socialiste multilateral dezvoltate: rapoarte, cuvîntări, interviuri, articole.* (Vols. 4–12 subtitled 'rapoarte, cuvîntări, articole'). [Romania on the way to the construction of the multilateral developed socialist society]. B.: Ed. pol., 1970–.
Vol. 4, publ. 1970, covers April 1969–June 1970.
Vol. 5, publ. 1971, covers July 1970–May 1971.
Vol. 6, publ. 1972, covers May 1971–February 1972.
Vol. 7, publ. 1973, covers March 1972–December 1972.
Vol. 8, publ. 1973, covers January 1973–July 1973.
Vol. 9, publ. 1974, covers August 1973–March 1974.
Vol. 10, publ. 1974, covers March 1974–November 1974.
Vol. 11, publ. 1975, covers November 1974–September 1975.
Vol. 12, publ. 1976, covers October 1975–May 1976.
Vol. 13, publ. 1977, covers June 1976–December 1976.
Vol. 14, publ. 1978, covers January 1977–September 1977.
Vol. 15, publ. 1978, covers September 1977–March 1978.
Vol. 16, publ. 1979, covers April 1978–August 1978.
Vol. 17, publ. 1979, covers September 1978–March 1979.

Vol. 18, publ. 1980, covers March 1979–September 1979.
Vol. 19, publ. 1980, covers September 1979–March 1980.

Also available in English: *Romania on the way of building up the multilaterally developed socialist society: reports, speeches, interviews, articles.* B.: Meridiane, 1970–. Another version of vol. 4 exists entitled *Romania on the way of completing the many-sided developed socialist society.* B.: 1970.

R265 *Romania: achievements and prospects: reports, speeches, articles, July 1965–February 1969: selected texts.* B.: Meridiane, 1969. 916 pp. 26 items from vols. 1–3.

R266 *Nicolae Ceauşescu: the man, his ideas and his socialist achievements;* presented by Stan Newens. Nottingham: Bertrand Russell Peace Foundation, 1972. 236 pp.

Also presents a selection of works, as the title of the second edition makes clear: *Nicolae Ceauşescu: speeches and writings,* selected and introduced by Stan Newens. Nottingham: Spokesman Books, 1978. 287 pp.

U UNION OF SOVIET SOCIALIST REPUBLICS

Jenny Brine

INTRODUCTION

USSR

In October 1917, the Russian Social Democratic Workers' Party (Bolshevik) led by V. I. Lenin seized power from the Provisional Government set up in February 1917 after the fall of the Tsar. The new republic was called the Russian Socialist Federal Soviet Republic (RSFSR) and was led by Lenin until his death in 1924. The Union of Soviet Socialist Republics came into being on 30 December 1922, out of the federation of the RSFSR, the Transcaucasian Socialist Federated Soviet Republic, the Belorussian Soviet Socialist Republic and the Ukrainian Soviet Socialist Republic. Later in the 1920s the Uzbek SSR and the Turkmenian SSR were set up and in 1929 the Tajik ASSR, formerly part of the Uzbek SSR, became a union republic.

In the 1930s the Transcaucasian Federation was dissolved and the Armenian, Georgian and Azerbaijani SSRs entered the Union; the number of republics was increased to eleven with the creation of the Kazakh and Kirghiz Soviet Socialist Republics. In 1940, during the period of Soviet cooperation with Nazi Germany, the three Baltic States were annexed and became the Estonian, Latvian and Lithuanian SSRs; however, as they were soon occupied by the Nazis their history as members of the USSR does not really start until 1944. Also in 1940, after the Winter War with Finland, the Karelo-Finnish SSR was set up; in 1956 it was returned to ASSR status within the RSFSR. The Moldavian SSR was created in 1940.

From the late 1920s until his death in March 1953, the USSR was led by Joseph Stalin, General Secretary of the Party from 1922 and Chairman of the Council of Ministers from 1941. He was replaced as First Secretary of the CPSU by N. S. Khrushchev. The Chairman of the Council of Ministers was G. M. Malenkov from 1953 to February 1955 and N. A. Bulganin from February 1955 to March 1958, when Khrushchev took over this position, ending a period of collective leadership. After Khrushchev's fall in October 1964, L. I. Brezhnev became General Secretary of the CPSU, and A. N. Kosygin took the post of Chairman of the Council of Ministers. Kosygin resigned the job early in 1980 and was replaced by N. A. Tikhonov. During the postwar period, the Chairmen of the Presidium of the Supreme Soviet (Head of State) have been M. I. Kalinin (to March 1946), N. M. Shvernik (March 1946–March 1953), K. E. Voroshilov (March 1953–May 1960), L. I. Brezhnev (May 1960–July 1964), A. I. Mikoian (July 1964–December 1965), N. V. Podgornyi (December 1965–June 1977) and L. I. Brezhnev since then.

The USSR is a federal state, with certain functions and rights reserved to the federal government of the USSR and others allocated to the union republics, as set out in articles 13–21 of the 1936 constitution and articles 70–81 of the 1977 constitution. The chief powers of the all-union government include: the determination of state boundaries of the USSR and between union republics; establishing general principles for the organization and functioning of union republics and local bodies of state administration; the ensurance of uniformity of legislative norms throughout the USSR and the establishment of fundamentals of the legislation of the USSR and the union republics; the pursuance of a uniform social and economic policy, including scientific and technical develop- ment, the approval of state plans, the budget and overall financial and currency control; the direction of all sectors of the economy and public life, including the administration of enterprises and associations under all-union jurisdiction and the general direction of those under union republic jurisdiction; issues of war and peace, the direction of the armed forces and state security, foreign policy, foreign trade and other forms of external commercial activity. The laws of the USSR have equal force in all the union republics, and the latter's freedom to legislate within their own territories is subject to their conforming with the all- union legislation.

Supreme Soviet

The USSR Supreme Soviet has two chambers, the Soviet of the Union and the Soviet of Nationalities, elected on different bases. It meets twice a year, with extraordinary sessions being called occasionally, as for the approval of the 1977 constitution. The sessions usually last only a few days and usually consist of the passing of laws, the confirmation of Presidium edicts, and the annual approval of the budget and the state plan for the coming year. The Supreme Soviet elects the Presidium, the Council of Ministers, the Supreme Court, the Procurator General and the members of the standing commissions (postoiannye komissii) of the Supreme Soviet. The Presidium, headed by its Chairman (at present Brezhnev, who is also the General Secretary of the CPSU), carries out the functions of the Supreme Soviet in between its sessions; its edicts are subsequently confirmed by the Supreme Soviet. The union republics (and the ASSRs) have unicameral supreme soviets; these too normally meet twice a year and have similar functions to the all-union body, but are only competent to legislate for their territory and in the areas delegated to them. The Supreme Soviet of each union republic elects its own Presidium, Council of Ministers, Supreme Court and standing commissions.

Council of Ministers, ministries and state committees

The USSR Council of Ministers is the effective executive or government of the USSR; at the time of writing, its Chairman is N. A. Tikhonov, who was preceded in this post by A. N. Kosygin, who held it from 1964 to 1980. The Council of Ministers of the USSR is formed of the ministers of the all-union and union-republican ministries, and the chairmen of the state committees. The all-union (obshchesoiuznye) ministries occur only at this level and direct the branch of state entrusted to them throughout the territory of the USSR, either directly or through bodies appointed by them. The union-republican (soiuzno-respublikanskie) ministries exist at federal level but also have counterparts at union republic level. Ministries which occur only at the republican level are called republican (respublikanskie) ministries. Until 1946, ministries were called people's commissariats. During 1957–65, there was a trend towards a reduction in the total number of all-union ministries as part of decentralization moves. Some were reduced to union-republic status and others were abolished. In 1980, other reforms of the Council of Ministers and the ministerial structure were initiated.

As of 1 July 1980, the USSR Council of Ministers consisted of the ministers of the following all-union ministries: Aviation Industry, Automotive Industry, Foreign Trade, Gas Industry, Civil Aviation, Engineering, Machine Building for Livestock Raising and Fodder Production, Machine Building for Light and Food Industry and Household Appliances, Medical Industry, Merchant Fleet, Oil Industry, Defence Industry, Defence, General Engineering, Instrument-making, Automation Equipment and Control Systems, Communications Equipment Industry, Railways, Radio Industry, Medium Machine Building, Machine Tool and Tool Building, Construction, Road and Municipal Machine Engineering, Construction in the Far East and the Trans-Baikal Area, Construction of Petroleum and Gas Industry Enterprises, Shipbuilding, Tractor and Agricultural Machinery Manufacture, Transport Construction, Heavy and Transport Machine Building, Chemical and Petroleum Machinery, Chemical Industry, Pulp and Paper Industry, Electronics Industry, Electrical Equipment Industry, Power Engineering. The union-republican ministries represented were: Higher and Secondary Specialized Education, Geology, Procurements, Health, Foreign Affairs, Culture, Light Industry, Timber and Wood-processing, Land Reclamation and Water Resources, Installation and Special Construction Work, Meat and Dairy Industry, Petrol Refining and Petrochemicals, Food Industry, Industrial Construction, Building Materials Industry, Education, Fisheries, Communications, Rural Construction, Agriculture, Construction, Construction of Heavy Industry, Trade, Coal, Finance, Non-ferrous Metallurgy, Ferrous Metallurgy, Energy and Electrification, and Justice. The USSR Council of Ministers also included the chairmen of all-union state committees, i.e. those on Science and Technology, for Inventions and Discoveries, on Standards, for Foreign Economic Relations, on Hydrometeorology and the Control of the Environment, and on Material Reserves. There are also union-republican state committees, which operate at all-union and union republic level, as do the union-republican ministries; these include the State Planning Commission (Gosplan), Committee for Construction (Gosstroi), Committee for Material and Technical Supply, Committee for Labour and Social Questions, Committee for Prices, Committee for Vocational and Technical Education, Committee for Television and Radio Broadcasting, Committee for Cinematography, Committee for Publishing, Printing and the Book Trade (Goskomizdat), Committee for Forestry, the Committee for State Security and the Committee for the Supply of Production and Technical Resources to Agriculture. Other members of the Council of Ministers include the chairman of the Committee for People's Control and the chairmen of the councils of ministers of the union republics. The heads of a number of other organizations not of ministerial status are also represented on the Council of Ministers. (For more details, see Lane, 1978.)*

The councils of ministers of the union republics consist of their counterparts to the union-republican ministries listed above, and other similar organizations represented on the all-union body, plus the republican ministries; in the RSFSR in the early 1970s these were the ministries for Automobile Transport and Roads, Household Services to the Population, Housing and Public Utilities, Local Industry, the River Fleet, Social Insurance and the Heating Industry.

Most of the ministries in the USSR are responsible for a particular branch of the economy, and so their chief function is the control and supervision of the enterprises subordinated to them. Those ministries which are not involved in economic administration are responsible for supervising the work of their subordinate organizations, issuing orders and instructions to them and enabling them to get the resources necessary to do their work. The work of the state committees generally overlaps several ministries, and the state committees are in some ways hierarchically superior to the ministries and are able to issue instructions and give orders which are binding on organizations within their field of responsibility, including the ministries. The state committees' chief functions are those of coordination, planning and supervision and are made necessary by the increasing complexity of the Soviet economic and social system.

Communist Party of the Soviet Union

The role of the CPSU is formally defined in article 6 of the 1977 constitution, where it is described as 'the leading and guiding force of Soviet society and the nucleus of all state organizations and public organizations'. It 'exists for the

* See end of this introductory section for full details of these titles.

people and serves the people [. : .] and determines the general perspectives of the development of the society and the course of the home and foreign policy of the USSR, directs the great constructive work of the Soviet people, and imparts a planned, systematic and theoretically substantiated character to their struggle for the victory of communism'. In article 126 of the 1936 constitution, it is described as 'the vanguard of the working people in their struggle to build communist society and is the leading core of all organizations of the working people, both government and non-government'. The CPSU asserts its powers and influence in several ways. First, it has a monopoly over the official value system and the establishment of what is ideologically acceptable. Second, through the 'nomenklatura' system the party is able to control the appointment and dismissal of administrators, officials and others in key posts in all types of organizations at all administrative levels. Third, there is considerable overlap at the top between the party, the government and the soviet structure; members of the Politburo are also leading members of the Council of Ministers, the Supreme Soviet and the Presidium of the Supreme Soviet. Fourth, the party takes the initiative in policy formulation at all levels and serves as the major channel for the aggregation and articulation of interests in the USSR. Finally, in a centralized system where departmentalism and bureaucratic procedures thrive, the party also plays an important coordinating role and acts as a kind of ombudsman or watchdog on the administration, particularly at the lower levels.

The Communist Party of the Soviet Union was called the All-Union Communist Party (Bolshevik) until 1952, when the new title was adopted by the 19th Party Congress. The party is governed by its rules (ustav); those currently in force were adopted in 1961 at the 22nd Party Congress. The organization of the party is both territorial and functional, with territorial subdivisions roughly parallel to the administrative subdivisions of the USSR. In accordance with the principle of democratic centralism, the party organizations of the union republics are subordinate to the CPSU, and party organs at lower levels are subordinate to them in turn. The RSFSR has no separate CP organization, although between 1956 and 1966 a Central Committee Bureau for the RSFSR did exist. The functional organization of the party is composed of hundreds of thousands of primary party organizations in industrial enterprises, state and collective farms, cultural, educational, government and other institutions. The Congress of the CPSU is constitutionally the supreme body of the CPSU and usually meets once in five years. It elects the Central Committee of the CPSU and certain other central organs of the party; the Central Committee elects the Politburo, the supreme policy-making organ of the CPSU. The Politburo was renamed the Presidium at the 19th Party Congress in 1952, but reverted to its old title in April 1966 at the 23rd Party Congress. The work of the Politburo is led by the General Secretary of the Party (called the First Secretary 1953–66). The Central Committee has a number of specialist departments which in many ways resemble government ministries; they define and clarify policy proposals to the Politburo in their special areas and provide a body of expertise upon which the members of the Politburo can draw when formulating policy and making decisions. (This is discussed more fully in Lane, 1978.)

Other organizations

A number of non-governmental organizations play an important part in the administration of the USSR, some of them carrying out functions which might be considered governmental in other countries. The trade unions, for instance, are heavily involved in industrial welfare work, social security and social insurance. Other voluntary organizations (obshchestvennye organizatsii) are the Union of Writers (and similar bodies for journalists, artists and composers), the Committee of Soviet Women, the Union of Red Cross and Red Crescent Societies, and DOSAAF (which combines the roles of a civil defence organization and the territorial army). There are many others. The publications of such organizations are not included in this bibliography, except for some of their manuals and compendiums which include significant amounts of legislation.

Official publications

As the economy and the social life of the country are basically centrally planned and directed, there are a large number of administrative agencies with powers to enact legislative acts regulating the areas under their jurisdiction. The volume of legislation produced is indeed enormous. For example, the Council of Ministers of one republic alone (Uzbekistan) from 1941 to 1964 adopted no less than 37,926 decrees and 63,425 regulations (Butler, 1976/7, p. 180). Over the last fifteen years, there has been increased emphasis placed on the need to systematize and codify legislation, introduce greater order into legislative procedures and the publishing of legislative acts, improving the public's awareness of the law and taking measures to ensure that officials, particularly in economic organizations, were better informed on legal matters. However, despite progress on law reform and codification, confusion still persists in legal terminology and the hierarchy of Soviet legislative acts has not yet been fully clarified. (For further details, see Butler, 1975.)

Soviet legislative acts are of two types: normative, i.e. containing rules of behaviour of general significance; and non-normative, i.e. acts of individual significance, such as edicts on awards, changes of administrative–territorial boundaries and personnel changes. Legislation can be further divided into acts which are currently in force, acts which have been repealed or are no longer in force, and those which have been partly cancelled or amended in part. Briefly, laws (zakony) have the highest place in the legislative hierarchy and can only be enacted by the supreme soviets. Of the laws, the constitutions (which are subtitled as 'fundamental laws') are generally considered to be superior to other laws. All other legislative acts are classed as subordinate acts (podzakonnye). A particularly important type of subordinate act are the Fundamental Principles (osnovy) which consist of basic concepts and general provisions for legislation in a particular area. The presidiums of the supreme soviets pass edicts (ukazy) and ordinances (postanovleniia); the difference between them in practice seems to be that edicts have to be confirmed by full sessions of the Supreme Soviet, but ordinances do not. Edicts are also used by the full session of the Supreme Soviet to confirm other all-union enactments, such as the osnovy. The councils of ministers of the USSR and the union republics enact ordinances and regulations (rasporiazheniia); the latter are not subject to publication in the official gazette, although acts of a normative character are. Statutes (polozheniia) are enacted by a variety of bodies and agencies at different levels. Ministries, state committees and other agencies issue orders (prikazy), instructions (instruktsii) and rules (pravila) on matters within their competence, as laid down by their statutes. The legislative activities and publications of local agencies of state authority are not relevant for this bibliography. A particularly important type of legislative act is the joint decree of the USSR Council of Ministers with the Central Committee of the CPSU; such joint decrees are sometimes also issued at union republic level. Although these ordinances do not have a higher legal significance than other ordinances of the councils of ministers, they are often used for important policy statements.

In general, a normative act cannot come into force unless it has been published. Normally the act is published in the official bulletin of the body enacting it, or in some other source designated as an official publication. The regulations governing the publication of legislative acts vary according to the enacting body. For instance, all the laws of the USSR Supreme Soviet and the edicts of its Presidium must be published within seven days of their enactment in the *Vedomosti*. However, enactments not having general significance or of a non-normative character may remain unpublished if the Presidium so decides. Such documents are sent out directly to the individuals or authorities involved. Strictly speaking, publications are official only if they appear in the official bulletin or a newspaper designated as an official publication, or bear the state crest, or include the words 'Izdanie ofitsial'noe' or 'ofitsial'nyi tekst' on their title page. However, unofficial texts are generally reliable, may be more up-to-date and are frequently more easily obtained than the official text. The following additional points should be kept in mind. First, a legal act may be published simultaneously in several sources, for instance in the *Vedomosti* and in *Izvestiia*. Second, it may be published in full, as extracts, or in the form of a summary of its main points. Third, legal acts are generally reprinted over time incorporating later amendments; it is therefore particularly important to note the effective date of the edition being used, particularly for historical work. Finally, it is not possible to gauge the extent of unpublished legislation, such as specialist documents sent out direct to enterprises, departments, and other agencies for their guidance and information ('dlia svedeniia i rukovodstva'). Much material is restricted to official use only ('dlia sluzhebnogo pol'zovaniia') or distributed to people and organizations on special circulation lists ('rassylaetsia po spisku'), often as numbered copies. Sometimes documents are marked in addition 'not for the open press' ('ne dlia otkrytoi pechati'). There are obviously higher grades of classified documents dealing with more secret material. Some acts which are published may have secret clauses. Even the act on state secrets is apparently now classified, although it was not when it was passed. Sometimes documents which were first sent out directly to the organizations affected are published subsequently, often in the general collections of legislation and manuals for administrators.

Party decisions

Party decisions are not sources of law. They are important statements of policy and generally precede significant new developments in legislation. Indeed, recent party decisions are often referred to in the preambles to legislation. Decisions of the CPSU are of different types and can be taken by several organizations within the party. The central organizations of the party, the Party Congress and the Central Committee, are responsible for only a few party decisions. As the Central Committee Plenum meets in full session several times a year, but sits for only a few days at a time, it is clear that the majority of the decisions (rezoliutsii) issued in its name are in fact issued by the Secretariat or the Politburo (or until 1953 the Orgburo too). These bodies are not explicitly identified on the document as the issuing agency. The party programme and the party rules can only be approved by the Party Congress; it too issues resolutions. Other documents issued by the central organizations of the party include appeals, lists of members elected to fill various posts, and informational communications, generally about forthcoming meetings. Party decisions are normally published in the open periodical press, or circulated directly to party secretaries in the case of secret documents. There does not appear to be a restricted circulation bulletin for party members or activists. Particularly in recent years, a number of Central Committee decisions have been made public only as summaries, often under the vague heading 'In the Central Committee of the CPSU'. As with legislative acts, decisions not published at the time they were taken are sometimes published later; *Spravochnik partiinogo rabotnika* (U551) is quite often used to publish such material. These decisions may also appear first, or first appear in full rather than in summary form, in compendiums of party decisions, or anthologies of party and government documents on particular subjects.

The communist parties of the union republics have a similar system for taking and publishing party decisions, but their decisions are binding only for members in that republic.

The bibliography

This bibliography is limited to the official publications of the USSR and the constituent republics. The official publications of lower administrative agencies are excluded. The material selected reflects the availability of official publications in certain fields; nothing is listed for the Committee for State Security, the electronics industry or crime statistics, as such topics are classified. The compiler has also excluded a wide range of journals published by ministries and state committees dealing with the areas they administer. Such journals as *Planovoe khoziaistvo* [Planned economy], *Bibliotekar'* [The Librarian], *Finansy SSSR* [Finances of the USSR] and *Chelovek i zakon* [People and the law] may be considered to be official in that they are sponsored by an official body, but they are mainly used to publish articles by people working in that field (not just officials of the issuing body). They may occasionally carry reports on the work of their sponsoring body or set out briefly recent orders and instructions from the ministry, but this is so small a part of their work that they have been excluded from this bibliography. Journals of this type which do carry a significant amount of official documentation or deal with an area for which there are few other sources have been included.

The bulk of the material included has been examined by the compiler; material not seen has been marked [Not seen]. A few statistical publications known to be held by the US Foreign Demographic Analysis Division have been marked [Not seen. FDAD]. However, the compiler was not able to examine the various editions of the constitutions and law codes, although a number of them have been seen; as in most cases it was possible to establish from bibliographies or from the *National Union Catalog* the effective date of the publications, they have not been marked [Not seen]. In addition, some of the republican party organizations' publications, particularly from the 1950s and 1960s, were not examined. These were generally identified from the catalogues of the Lenin Library in Moscow. As they are all listed briefly in any case, individual [Not seen] notes have been omitted.

Each section and subsection of the bibliography has a short introduction setting the documents described in their context in terms of the main responsible administering bodies and major pieces of legislation. In compiling these brief introductions and the overall introduction to this chapter, very heavy use was made of the *Encyclopaedia of Soviet law* (U54). In describing party decisions, U547 was used. Material from these sources was supplemented by:

Butler, W. E. 'Sources of Soviet law'. *Current legal problems*, vol. 28, 1975. Pp. 223–42.

Butler, W. E. 'Systematization of union republic legislation in the USSR: the Uzbek SSR'. *Annuaire de l'URSS et les pays socialistes européens*, 1976/7. Pp. 171–88.

Johnson, E. L. *An introduction to the Soviet legal system*. London: Methuen, 1969.

Kaser, M. 'The publication of Soviet statistics'. In *Soviet economic statistics*, ed. by V. G. Treml and J. P. Hardt. Durham, N. C.: Duke University Press, 1972. Pp. 45–65.

Lane, D. *Politics and society in the USSR*. [2nd ed.] London: Martin Robertson, 1978.

Within each section and subsection, documents are listed alphabetically unless the introduction states they are listed chronologically. In some sections and subsections, documents from the union republics are listed in the same sequence as the all-union publications. Where they are numerous, they are listed after the all-union documents, by republic. The following order has been used: RSFSR, Armenia, Azerbaijan, Belorussia, Estonia, Georgia, Karelo-Finnish SSR, Kazakhstan, Kirghizia, Latvia, Lithuania, Moldavia, Tajikistan, Turkmenistan, Ukraine and Uzbekistan.

GENERAL BIBLIOGRAPHIES AND REFERENCE WORKS

This section includes general bibliographies and reference works, whether published in the USSR or abroad, which either deal with Soviet official publications in general or have been found to be particularly useful when working with Soviet official publications. Bibliographies and reference works of a more specialized nature are to be found in the sections dealing with that subject.

National bibliographies

The USSR has a system of national bibliography at all-union and union republic level. The compilation of these bibliographies is the responsibility of the All-Union Book Chamber (for the USSR) and the book chambers in each republic.

USSR

U1 *Bibliografiia sovetskoi bibliografii.* [Bibliography of Soviet bibliography]. (Vsesoiuznaia knizhnaia palata). M.: Kniga, 1939; 1946–. Annual.

A systematized bibliography of bibliographies of over 30 items published in the USSR, separately or in books and journals. Includes bibliographies of official documents; particularly useful for tracing bibliographies in specialist areas.

U2 *Gazety SSSR, 1917–1960: bibliograficheskii spravochnik.* [Newspapers of the USSR, 1917–1960: a bibliographical guide]. (Vses. knizhnaia palata. Gos. b-ka SSSR im. V. I. Lenina. Gos. publ. b-ka SSSR im. M. E. Saltykova-Shchedrina). M.: Kniga, 1970–.

Vol. 1 of this guide covers newspapers published in Moscow, Leningrad and the capitals of the union republics, and so gives the publishing history of newspapers relevant for this bibliography; for more recent bibliographical information on newspapers *see* U5. Vol. 1 has its own indexes by title, language, place of publication, etc. The whole bibliography will consist of five volumes; vols. 2–4 will cover other towns of the USSR and vol. 5 will be an index volume.

U3 *Knizhnaia letopis'.* [Book chronicle]. (Goskomizdat. Vses. knizhnaia palata). 1907–. Weekly.

Has a supplement, *Knizhnaia letopis': dopolnitel'nyi vypusk*, which appeared monthly 1961–80. From 1981, the supplement has appeared in two parts, a monthly *Knizhnaia letopis': dopolnitel'nyi vypusk. Knigi i broshiury* and a quarterly *Knizhnaia letopis': dopolnitel'nyi vypusk. Avtoreferaty dissertatsii.* The main part of *Knizhnaia letopis'* varied in frequency before 1945, had 48 issues a year in 1947–8 and has otherwise appeared weekly. The main part and the monthly supplement have quarterly name, place and subject indexes, and an annual index of series. Books published in the weekly section are cumulated into the annual *Ezhegodnik knigi SSSR* (1925–9, 1935, 1941–), which usually appears in two volumes. The weekly part and the monthly supplement list books and pamphlets published in all languages of the USSR; descriptions are given in Russian. The quarterly supplement deals with authors' abstracts of theses. The weekly part of *Knizhnaia letopis'* lists the majority of the books and pamphlets published in the USSR; the monthly supplement is used for material intended to have only a limited or specialist circulation, such as school syllabuses, ministry instructions, and books and pamphlets published in very small editions. It does not, however, list any material which is actually restricted, classified or secret. As the bibliographies are arranged by subject, they allow users to keep up-to-date with new publications in any field, and include official publications.

U4 *Letopis' gazetnykh statei.* [Chronicle of newspaper articles]. (Gos. komitet SSSR po delam izdatel'stv, poligrafii i knizhnoi torgovli. Vses. knizhnaia palata). M.: Kniga, 1936–. Weekly.

1936–8 called *Gazetnaia letopis'.* Frequency varied to 1943; weekly 1944–6, 1949–59; 48 issues a year in 1947–8; monthly 1960–74; fortnightly 1975–6; weekly 1977–. Covers major newspaper articles in Russian from the main central and republic level newspapers, and the main daily papers from Moscow and Leningrad. Includes party and government ordinances, etc. appearing in newspaper form. There is an author and geographical index in each issue.

U5 *Letopis' periodicheskikh i prodolzhaiushchikhsia izdanii SSSR.* [Chronicle of Soviet periodicals and serial publications]. (Gos. komitet SSSR po delam izdatel'stv, poligrafii i knizhnoi torgovli). M.: Kniga, 1950/4 (publ. 1955)–.

This is the five-yearly cumulation of the annual publication of the same name which is subtitled *Novye, pereimenovannye i prekrashchennye izdaniia,* which has appeared (with gaps) since 1933. Until 1970, the title of both parts was *Letopis' periodicheskikh izdanii SSSR.* The publication history of this work is complicated because of the changes which have occurred in coverage and arrangement over the years. The annual publication lists only journals and newspapers which have changed their titles, begun or ceased publication during the period covered. The five-yearly cumulations for 1950–4 (1955, 1 vol.); 1955–60 (1962–3, 2 parts); 1960–5 (1967–73, 2 parts in 3 volumes) covered newspapers, journals, bulletins and irregular publications of the *Trudy* type. However, the 1966–70 cumulation (1972–5, 2 parts) covers only journals and newspapers, and the same appears to be true of 1971–5, of which only the journal volume (publ. 1977) has so far appeared. Coverage of sborniki (irregular serials) is being effected by the publication of annual volumes; it is intended that bulletins will be covered by a volume to be published every two years. The cumulations are arranged by subject, whereas the annual list of changes of title, new and ceased journals are arranged alphabetically. All the entries are in Russian, irrespective of language of publication. Has thorough indexes.

U6 *Letopis' zhurnal'nykh statei.* [Chronicle of journal articles]. (Gos. komitet po delam izdatel'stv, poligrafii i knizhnoi torgovli. Vses. knizhnaia palata). M.: Kniga, 1926–. Weekly.

1926–37 title was *Zhurnal'naia letopis'.* Some variations in frequency before 1943; 48 issues a year 1947–8; otherwise weekly. An index of Russian-language articles, excluding mass-circulation journals, very specialized titles and certain other small-edition journals. It excludes many official and vedomstvennye journals, but is still useful for the legal and party articles it does include. Quarterly name and geographical indexes.

U7 *Periodicheskaia pechat' SSSR, 1917–1949: bibliograficheskii ukazatel'*. [The periodical press of the USSR, 1917–1949: a bibliographical index]. M.: Izd-vo Vses. knizhnoi palaty, 1955–63, 9 vols. (in 10) and index vol.

A very detailed bibliography of Soviet journals, official bulletins and irregular serials (but not newspapers), arranged by broad subject areas. For newspapers, *see* U2; for more recent journals, *see* U5.

Union republics

Each union republic publishes its own national bibliography, listing publications which appeared on its territory and publications about the republic which appeared elsewhere in the USSR and abroad. Some republics cover all their printed output in one publication, others have separate publications for newspaper and journal articles. The publication covering books usually includes music, 'foreign' publications about the republic, graphics and an annual list of serials. The union republics' bibliographies are necessary when working with books because the entry in *Knizhnaia letopis'* (U3) gives book titles only in Russian and not in the language of the original; journal and newspaper articles in languages other than Russian are not covered at all at national level. In the list which follows, basic details only are given of each republic's national bibliographies, as they conform to the pattern described above. They all have full annual indexes.

ARMENIA

U8 *Letopis' pechati Armianskoi SSR*. [Press annals of Armenia]. Erevan, 1925–. Monthly.

1925–71 called *Knizhnaia letopis' Armianskoi SSR*. In Armenian and Russian with translations of entries in Armenian. Covers books, etc. For articles and reviews, see:

U9 *Letopis' statei i retsenzii*. [Annals of articles and reviews]. Erevan, 1972–. Monthly.

Formed out of *Letopis' zhurnal'nykh statei* (1938–71) and *Letopis' gazetnykh statei* (1934–71). In Armenian and Russian; there are no translations into Russian of entries in Armenian.

AZERBAIJAN

U10 *Azarbaijan matbuat salnamasi = Letopis' pechati Azerbaidzhana*. [Press annals of Azerbaijan]. Baku, 1926–. Monthly.

Quarterly, 1926–58; 6 issues in 1959. Since 1960, the books have been cumulated annually as *Birillik Azarbaijan kitabiiiaty = Ezhegodnik knigi Azerbaidzhana*. In Azerbaijani and Russian.

BELORUSSIA

U11 *Letapis druku Belaruskai SSR = Letopis' pechati Belorusskoi SSR.* [Press annals of Belorussia]. Minsk, 1925–. Monthly.
In Belorussian and Russian.

ESTONIA

U12 *Raamatukroonika = Knizhnaia letopis'; organ gos. bibliografii Eston-skoi SSR.* [Book annals of Estonia]. Tallinn, 1946–. Quarterly.
In Estonian and Russian. There have been two cumulations of the book section: *Nõukogude Eesti raamat, 1940–1954 = Kniga sovet-skoi Estonii, 1940–54; svodnyi ukazatel'.* Tallinn: Eesti raamat, 1956; and . . ., *1955–1965*; 1972. For journals and reviews, see:

U13 *Artiklite ja retsensioonide kroonika = Letopis' statei i retsenzii.* [Annals of articles and reviews]. Tallinn, 1952–. Monthly.
In Estonian and Russian.

GEORGIA

U14 *Knizhnaia letopis' Gruzinskoi SSR.* [Book annals of the Georgian SSR]. Tbilisi, 1917–. Monthly.
In Georgian and Russian, with sections in the languages of the minority peoples of the republic. Entries in languages other than Russian are translated into Russian. For journal articles see:

U15 *Letopis' zhurnal'nykh statei Gruzinskoi SSR.* [Annals of the journal articles of the Georgian SSR]. Tbilisi, 1939–. Monthly.
In Georgian and Russian. For newspaper articles see:

U16 *Letopis' gazetnykh statei [GSSR].* [Annals of newspaper articles]. Tbilisi, 1934–. 24 p.a.
In Georgian and Russian.

KAZAKHSTAN

U17 *Baspasoz sheziresi = Letopis' pechati; organ gos. bibliografii Ka-zakhskoi SSR.* [Press annals of the Kazakh SSR]. Alma-Ata, 1957–. Monthly.
In Kazakh, Russian and Uighur. Formed out of *Knizhnaia letopis' [Kaz SSR]* (1937–57) and *Letopis' zhurnal'nykh statei [Kaz SSR].* (1938–57). Articles and reviews were split off in 1971 to form:

U18 *Magalarar men retsenziialar shezhiresi = Letopis' statei i retsenzii; organ gos. bibliografii Kazakhskoi SSR.* [Annals of articles and reviews of the Kazakh SSR]. Alma-Ata, 1972–. Quarterly.
In Kazakh and Russian.

KIRGHIZIA

U19 *Kyrgyz SSRinin basma sozdorunun letopisi = Letopis' pechati Kirgiz-skoi SSR.* [Press annals of the Kirghiz SSR]. Frunze, 1976–. Monthly.

In Kirghiz and Russian. Formed out of *Knizhnaia letopis' Kirgiz-skoi SSR* (1948–75), *Letopis' gazetnykh statei Kirgizskoi SSR* (1973–75) and *Letopis' zhurnal'nykh statei Kirgizskoi SSR* (1973–75). The two latter were formed when *Letopis' zhurnal'nykh i gazetnykh statei [KirgSSR]* (1956–72) was split.

LATVIA

U20 *Latvijas PSR preses hronika=Letopis' pechati Latviiskoi SSR.* [Press annals of the Latvian SSR]. Riga, 1949–. Monthly.

In Latvian and Russian. Quarterly 1949–56.

LITHUANIA

U21 *Spaudos metraštis = Letopis' pechati; organ gos. bibliografii Litovskoi SSR.* [Press annals of the Lithuanian SSR]. Vilnius, 1947–. Monthly.

In Lithuanian and Russian.

MOLDAVIA

U22 *Kronika presei RSS Moldovenesht' = Letopis' pechati Moldavskoi SSR.* [Press annals of the Moldavian SSR]. Kishinev, 1963–. Monthly.

In Moldavian and Russian. Quarterly 1963–70. Formed in 1963 out of *Knizhnaia letopis' [MSSR]* (1958–62), *Letopis' gazetnykh statei [MSSR]* (1958–62), *Letopis' zhurnal'nykh statei [MSSR]* (1958–62) and *Novaia lit-ra o Moldavii* (1957–63).

TAJIKSTAN

U23 *Solnomai matbuoti RSS Tojikiston = Letopis' pechati Tadzhikskoi SSR.* [Press annals of Tajikistan]. Dushanbe, 1939–. Monthly.

In Tajik and Russian.

TURKMENISTAN

U24 *Turkmenistan SSRining metbugat letopisi=Letopis' pechati Turk-menskoi SSR.* [Press annals of Turkmenistan]. Ashkhabad, 1930–. Monthly.

In Turkmen and Russian. Quarterly 1930–57.

UKRAINE

U25 *Litopys knyh=Letopis' knig; organ gos. bibliografii Ukrainskoi SSR.* [Book annals of the Ukrainian SSR]. Khar'kov, 1924–. Monthly.

In Ukrainian and Russian. For journal articles see:

U26 *Litopys zhurnal'nykh statei = Letopis' zhurnal'nykh statei; organ gos. bibliografii Ukrainskoi SSR.* [Annals of journal articles of the Ukraine]. Khar'kov, 1936–. 24 p.a.

In Ukrainian and Russian. For newspaper articles see:

U27 *Litopys hazetnykh statei = Letopis' gazetnykh statei; organ gos.*

bibliografii Ukrainskoi SSR. [Annals of newspaper articles of the Ukraine]. Khar'kov, 1937–. 24 p.a.
In Ukrainian and Russian.

UZBEKISTAN

U28 *Uzbekiston SSR matbuoti solnomasi = Letopis' pechati Uzbekskoi SSR.* [Press annals of the Uzbek SSR]. Tashkent, 1968–. Monthly.
In Uzbek and Russian. Formed in 1968 out of *Knizhaia letopis' [UzSSR]* (1928–67) and *Letopis' zhurnal'nykh statei [UzSSR]* (1938–67). *Letopis' pechati Uzbekskoi SSR* split into five sections in 1976–7: *Knizhnaia letopis'; Letopis' periodicheskikh izdanii, Letopis' not; Letopis' zhurnal'nykh statei, Letopis pechatnykh proizvedenii izobrazitel'nykh iskusstv; Letopis' gazetnykh statei, Letopis retsenzii; Ezhegodnik knigi.* From 1978 it has been published as a single bibliography. In 1977 an annual cumulation of books began publication: *Uzbekiston SSR kitoblarining iilnomasi = Ezhegodnik knigi Uzbekskoi SSR.*

Other bibliographies

The bibliographies listed in this section are Soviet and Western bibliographies which include a significant number of official publications. Here, as elsewhere in this work, no attempt is made to list all the bibliographies which include some official publications. Some general bibliographies dealing with particular republics or areas of the USSR have been included where they give particularly good coverage of official publications, but generally readers should refer to the national bibliographies or to U1 for bibliographies of particular areas. Bibliographies dealing with particular subjects are listed in the section dealing with that subject.

U29 Antonov, V. V. 'Osnovy metodiki bibliograficheskogo razyskaniia sovetskikh pravovykh aktov'. [Basic methods of bibliographical searching for Soviet legal acts]. *Sbornik metodicheskikh statei po bibliotekovedeniiu i bibliografii* (Gos. publichnaia b-ka im. Saltykova-Shchedrina), t. 17 (38), 1965, pp. 4–213
This publication had a tirazh of only 105 copies. Most of the publications listed are also listed in U40. The main section of the article is a discussion of procedures and practices in the publication of Soviet official publications, followed by advice to librarians on search strategy. This is followed by two bibliographical supplements. Supplement 1 is a review of the official serial publications of the USSR and RSFSR Supreme Soviet and Council of Ministers and of collections of laws. Supplement 2 is a selective subject listing of 1,030 sources of normative acts of the USSR and the RSFSR, 1917–64. Subject index.

U30 Antonov, V. V. *Sovetskoe zakonodatel'stvo. Spravochnik-putevoditel' po izdaniiam.* [Soviet legislation: a guide to publications]. M.: Kniga, 1981.

This publication, announced for late 1981, would appear to be similar in scope and coverage to items U29 and U40. It will describe the major USSR and RSFSR legislative publications and collections of documents, and will include guidance on how to search for legislative materials. [Not seen].

U31 *Basic Russian publications: an annotated bibliography on Russia and the Soviet Union*; ed. by P. L. Horecky. Chicago, London: University of Chicago Press, 1962. xxvi, 313 pp.

Although nearly 20 years old, this bibliography is still valuable for publications up to the end of the 1950s. Includes many party and government publications. Has 1,396 entries.

U32 *Bibliografiia Kirgizii*. [Bibliography of Kirghizia]. (Gos. b-ka KirgSSR im. Chernyshevskogo). Frunze, 1963–. Vol. 1–.

This major bibliographical work on Kirghizia is published in Russian and Kirghiz editions. It is planned to have four volumes and cover 1918–60. The volumes are not appearing in chronological or number order. Vol. 1 (in one) covers 1918–24; vol. 2 appears to cover 1925–45 in several parts; vol. 3 covers 1946–55, probably in 6 parts; vol. 4 covers 1956–60, probably also in 6 parts. The parts in each volume are arranged by subject, and all include official publications relevant for that subject; the most important for official publications of this period are vol. 3, part 2 and vol. 4, part 2, which cover party and government development in the postwar period. The entries are not annotated. The bibliography includes journal and newspaper articles as well as books. Each volume has a name index. A more detailed description of each part so far published can be found in the annual vols. of U1.

U33 *Bibliografiia literatury i trudov po iuridicheskim naukam*. [A bibliography of books and articles on legal science]. (AN Gruzinskoi SSR. Sektor nauchnoi informatsii po obshchestvennym naukam). Tbilisi, 1971 (publ. 1972)–. Annual.

In Georgian and Russian. A subject list of legal literature published in Georgia, including dissertations and legislation.

U34 *Bibliography of social science periodicals and monograph series: USSR, 1950–1963*. By the Foreign Demographic Analysis Division, Bureau of the Census. (Foreign Social Science Bibliographies Series P-92, no. 17). [Washington]: US Dept. of Commerce, [1965]. 443 pp.

Based on the holdings of the Library of Congress. The bibliography lists over 2,000 items from all the republics of the USSR, including a number of official publications. Indexes of subjects, titles, authors and issuing bodies.

U35 Butler, W. E. 'Checklist of Soviet normative acts available in English translation'. *American Journal of Comparative Law*, vol. 23, no. 3 (1975). Pp. 530–549.

A selective compilation of principal acts, and some examples of subordinate legislation. Items listed were believed to be in force as of 1 July 1975.

U36   Butler, W. E. *Russian and Soviet law: an annotated catalogue of reference works, legislation, court reports, serials and monographs on Russian and Soviet law (including international law)*. (Bibliotheca Slavica, 8). Zug: Inter Documentation Company, 1976. xvi, 122 pp. Simultaneously published on microfiche.

A catalogue of over 1,100 titles, selected for inclusion in a commercial microfilming project. The material is divided into Russian and Soviet sections, and arranged by subject. It is useful for its authoritative annotations, but is largely confined to rarer works, some very obscure, and makes no claim to be comprehensive or recommendatory. Most of the relevant official publications in it are included in this bibliography, but it is worth consulting for its lists of monographs and other secondary sources. Author index.

U37   *Half a century of Soviet serials, 1917–1968. A bibliography and union list of serials publ. in the USSR*. Comp. by R. Smits. Washington: Library of Congress, 1968. 2 vols.

Although much of the bibliographical data in this work may also be found in U5 and U7, this summarizes it all in a convenient form with ample cross-references. In addition, it usually gives the title of publications in languages other than Russian in that language, unlike the Soviet bibliographies mentioned above. It is an alphabetical list with no subject or other indexes.

U38   Harris, C. D. *Guide to geographical bibliographies and reference works in Russian or on the Soviet Union: an annotated list of 2,660 bibliographies or reference aids*. (University of Chicago Dept. of Geography research paper, 164). Chicago, 1975. xvii, 477 pp.

A very wide-ranging bibliography, including many general reference works, statistical sources, biographical data and works dealing with all aspects of geography, broadly defined. Thorough index.

U39   *Iuridicheskaia literatura: annotirovannyi ukazatel' otechestvennykh bibliograficheskikh posobii, izdannykh v 1831–1970 gg.* [Legal literature: an annotated index of Russian bibliographies, published in 1831–1970]. Sost.: T. E. Ksenzova, red.: I. Iu. Bagrova. (Gos. b-ka SSSR im. V. I. Lenina). M.: Kniga, 1972. 144 pp.

A selective annotated bibliography of Russian-language bibliographies, both separately published and published in other works. Includes bibliographies of normative acts. Has author and title index.

U40   *Izdaniia normativnykh dokumentov sovetskogo gosudarstva (SSSR i RSFSR), 1917–1967 gg.: bibliograficheskii ukazatel' v pomoshch' bibliotekam.* [The publication of Soviet normative documents (USSR and RSFSR): a bibliographical index for libraries]. [Sost.: V.

V. Antonov]. (Gos. publichnaią b-ka). Leningrad, 1967. 232 pp.

Only 100 copies published. A duplicated guide listing some 1,500 publications, including bibliographies, encyclopaedias, dictionaries, ministry bulletins, general collections of laws, collections of normative materials on various subjects and collections of materials in the different branches of law. It also has a section on foreign policy and international law. Some entries are briefly annotated. There is a very useful introductory essay on the publication of normative acts, and a subject index.

U41 *Knigi po voprosam gosudarstva i prava, vyshedshie v SSSR v . . . godu.* [Books on the state and law published in the USSR in . . .]. (AN SSSR. In-t gosudarstva i prava). M., 1970 (publ. 1972)–1972 (publ. 1974).

A duplicated subject listing, including contents listing of sborniki and collections of legislation, etc.

U42 Korshunov, O. P. *Izdaniia i bibliografiia dokumentov Kommunis-ticheskoi partii Sovetskogo Soiuza i Sovetskogo gosudarstva.* [The publication and bibliography of documents of the CPSU and the Soviet government]. (Moskovskii gos. bibliotechnyi in-t). M.: Gos. izd-vo kul′t.-pros. lit-ry, 1955. 47 pp.

Discusses: (a) the procedures for publishing party documents and describes the main collections of documents and thematic collections; (b) the procedures for publishing Supreme Soviet and local soviet documents, and describes the main collections of laws, the law codes and laws separately published; (c) methods of bibliographical work for librarians in dealing with such materials. It is a rather thin guide, but is still useful for the 1945–53 period.

U43 *Latvijas PSR 1940–1960. Literatūras rādītājs=Latviiskaia SSR, 1940–1960: ukazatel′ literatury.* [Latvia, 1940–1960: a bibliography. Comp.: O. Pūce, J. Veinbergs]. (Latvijas PSR Valsts B-ka). Riga, 1961–.

Planned in three volumes, only one published. Covers Latvian and Russian books, journals and newspaper articles. Excludes much theoretical and local material and belles-lettres. Vol. I covers the Latvian CP and the Latvian state and government organization, including lists of publications of decrees, CP resolutions, constitution and other general official publications.

U44 *Legal sources and bibliography of the Baltic States (Estonia, Latvia, Lithuania)*; by J. Klesment, D. Krivickas, V. Riismandel, A. Rusis. General ed.: V. Gsovski. N.Y.: Praeger, 1963. xiv, 196 pp.

Sponsored by the Library of Congress Mid-European Law Project. It has a separate section for the Baltic States under the USSR, and lists official publications, monographs, journals, etc. in English, French, German, Italian, Polish and Russian as well as in Estonian, Latvian and Lithuanian. There are full author, title and subject indexes.

U45 *Literatura po sovetskomu pravu: bibliograficheskii ukazatel'* = *Literature on Soviet law: index of bibliography*. (AN SSSR. In-t gosudarstva i prava). M.: Izd-vo AN SSSR, 1960. 279 pp.

A bibliography prepared for the International Association of Legal Science and intended for foreign lawyers; only 700 copies were published. It covers works in Russian published 1917–58, with an addendum covering 1959–60. Each section has a short introduction in Russian and English and the bibliographical entries also have an English translation. Covers all aspects of law, including international law, but is selective and excludes many collections of documents, law codes, etc. There is an author and editor index.

U46 Maichel, K. *Guide to Russian reference books*; ed. by J. S. G. Simmons. (Hoover Institution bibliographical series). Stanford, Calif.: Hoover Institution on War, Revolution and Peace.
Vol. 1. General bibliographies and reference books. 1962.
Vol. 2. History, auxiliary historical sciences, ethnography and geography. 1964.
Vol. 5. Science, technology and medicine. 1967.

No more published. Covers Western- and Russian-language works and includes references to many official publications in the subject areas dealt with in these volumes.

U47 *Novaia sovetskaia literatura po obshchestvennym naukam: gosudarstvo i pravo*. [New Soviet literature on the social sciences: state and law]. (AN SSSR. INION). M., 1973–. Monthly.

1973–75 called *Novaia sovetskaia literatura po gosudarstvu i pravu*. A current listing, by subject, of Soviet literature (in all languages of the USSR) on the state and law. It excludes individual legal acts, but does include law codes and collections of documents. No indexes.

U48 Rud', M. P. *Ukrains'ka Radians'ka Sotsialistychna Respublika, 1917–1967: bibliohrafichnyi pokazhchyk literatury*. [The Ukrainian SSR, 1917–1967: a bibliography]. (AN URSR. Tsentr. naukova b-ka). Kyiv: Naukova dumka, 1969. 479 pp.

A bibliography of literature in Ukrainian and material about the Ukraine in Russian published in the USSR. Includes many general Russian works which are not primarily concerned with the Ukraine. Arranged by subject within broad chronological divisions. Covers books, collections of documents and some journal articles. Includes many party and government publications, including statistical handbooks; there are separate chronological indexes to these documents. Author index.

U49 *Russia and the Soviet Union: a bibliographic guide to Western-language publications*, ed. by P. L. Horecky. Chicago, London: University of Chicago Press, 1965. xxiv, 473 pp.

Has 1,960 entries, fully annotated. Valuable for information on translations of official documents, particularly those published as appendices to monographs.

U50 *Soviet codes and statutes in German and French: a bibliography*, comp.
by H. Nökel. (University of Chicago Law School Library publications: bibliographies and guides to research). Chicago, 1970. ix, 11
pp.

A mimeographed list of 77 items, mainly post-1945. It is restricted
to USSR and RSFSR materials, with some emphasis on private law.

U51 *Soviet legal bibliography: a classified and annotated listing of books and
serials published in the Soviet Union since 1917 as represented in the
collection of the Harvard Law School Library as of January 1, 1965*;
ed. by V. Mostecky and W. E. Butler. (Harvard Law School
Library). Cambridge, Mass., 1965. xi, 288 pp.

Lists over 4,000 Soviet books and periodicals in Russian and other
languages of the USSR, as well as translations into English published
in the USSR. Although the bulk of the items recorded are monographs about the law, it does include entries for many collections of
legal material. There are author and subject indexes.

U52 *Writings on Soviet law and Soviet international law: a bibliography of
books and articles published since 1917 in languages other than East
European*, comp. and ed. by W. E. Butler. (Harvard Law School
Library). Cambridge, Mass., 1966. xi, 165 pp.

A subject bibliography, including a few collections of Soviet
legislation and some translations into English of Soviet legislation.

See also U160.

General reference works

This section is limited to those general reference works about the USSR which
have been found to be the most useful when working with Soviet official
publications. Fuller lists of general reference works dealing with the USSR can
be found in several of the bibliographies listed above, particularly U38, U46 and
U49.

Encyclopaedias

U53 *Bol'shaia sovetskaia entsiklopediia.* [Great Soviet Encylopaedia]. 3-e
izd. M.: Sovetskaia entsiklopediia, 1969–78. 30 vols. An index vol. is
planned for 1981.

An English translation of the *BSE*, preserving the Russian
alphabet order, is available as *Great Soviet encyclopaedia: a translation of the third edition.* N.Y., London: Macmillan, 1973–. Earlier
editions of the *BSE*:
2nd ed. (51 vols., 1950–60, with two index volumes publ. 1960). Vol.
50 (1957) is an encyclopaedia of the USSR; for a translation *see* U56.
1st ed. (65 vols., 1926–48) had a special supplementary volume on the
USSR (1947).
The major official encyclopaedia of the USSR, with considerable
changes between the different editions in people included, treatment

of topics and political attitudes. Valuable for its information on people, on government and party organizations, current definitions. For its annual supplement, *see* U55.

U54   *Encyclopaedia of Soviet law*; ed. by F. J. M. Feldbrugge. (Documentation Office for East European Law, University of Leiden). Dobbs Ferry, N.Y.: Oceana Publications, Inc.: Leiden: A. W. Sijthoff, 1973. 2 vols.

An authoritative encyclopaedia compiled by leading scholars concerned with Soviet law. It provides: (a) concise accounts of the functions and procedures of Soviet legislative bodies, the CPSU and other bodies which have quasi-legal functions; (b) essays on the main branches of law; (c) shorter articles on the law relating to a wide range of subjects; (d) articles on legal procedures and the courts; (e) essays on the legal history of each of the union republics. There are useful articles on bibliography and on terminology. It is based on material in force at the end of 1972, but vol. 2 has an appendix on the most important legislation during the first 7 months of 1973. At the back of vol. 2 there is also a 'Selected list of statutory materials' which lists in chronological order the most important enactments of the USSR and the RSFSR. As well as the enacting agency and the date passed, it also lists the official source, even when this is not fully known or commonly available. There are useful articles on bibliography and terminology.

U55   *Ezhegodnik Bol'shoi sovetskoi entsiklopedii.* [Yearbook of the Great Soviet Encyclopaedia]. M.: Sovetskaia entsiklopediia, 1957–. Annual.

An important source of current official information on the USSR, reflecting changes over the previous year. As well as long articles on the economy, culture, etc., it includes articles on developments in each of the union republics. It is particularly useful for its list of: (a) members of the Presidium of the Supreme Soviet and other officials of the Supreme Soviet; (b) members of the Council of Ministers, ministers and chairmen of state committees; (c) members of the main CPSU and republican party organizations. It also includes information on the work of semi-official organizations such as the Komsomol, the trade unions and various academies. There are also sections on foreign countries and international organizations. At the back there is a section of biographical information, including not only well-known party and government officials but also those who have only recently come to prominence in cultural, economic or political life.

U56   *Information USSR: an authoritative encyclopaedia about the Union of Soviet Socialist Republics.* Ed. and comp. by Robert Maxwell. Oxford [etc.]: Pergamon, 1962. xii, 982 pp.

The bulk of the book is a translation of vol. 50 (1957) of the *BSE* (2nd ed.), supplemented by some statistical information, lists of recent books in English on the USSR, lists of higher educational establishments, notes on trading with the USSR, a summary of the work of the 22nd Party Congress, and name and subject indexes.

U57 *The modern encyclopaedia of Russian and Soviet history*; ed. by Joseph L. Wieczynski. Gulf Breeze, Fla.: Academic International Press, 1976–.

Entries are based on those in the *Sovetskaia istoricheskaia entsiklopediia*, the Granat and Brockhaus-Efron encyclopaedias, the *Sibirskaia sovetskaia entsiklopediia* as well as the general Soviet encyclopaedias and many biographical reference works; but many entries have been written or up-dated by Western scholars, and provided with a bibliography of recent publications. It includes biographies, histories of ministries and other government bodies, material on the CPSU and discussions of a variety of Soviet practices such as the plans. It covers material into the 1970s.

Gazetteer

U58 *SSSR: administrativno-territorial'noe delenie soiuznykh respublik na 1 ianvaria ... goda.* [The USSR: administrative and territorial divisions of the union republics on 1 January...]. (Prezidium Verkhovnogo Soveta SSSR). M., 1924–. Annual.

Some variations in title, 1924–8. The USSR volume gives information on administrative divisions, by oblast'(or administrative unit of similar status). Under each oblast', information is given on the raiony, towns and urban settlements within its territory. There is an index of towns, raiony and urban settlements, showing to which republic, krai or oblast' they are subordinated; an index of administrative units which have changed their names; index of towns by size of population; lists of towns which are subdivided into raiony. In addition, each union republic publishes its own *Administrativnoterritorial'noe delenie*. That for the RSFSR is now annual, but the others are published irregularly. The RSFSR volume includes the same data as the USSR volume, with the addition of lists of village soviets in each raion. The volumes for the other republics are fuller and generally include lists of villages under each sel'sovet. Within the RSFSR, individual oblasti occasionally publish their own volumes. These volumes are invaluable in sorting out the location of towns and villages within the USSR, and their administrative subordination.

Dictionaries

U59 Alekseev, D. I. *Slovar' sokrashchenii russkogo iazyka; okolo 15 000 sokrashchenii.* [A dictionary of Russian abbreviations; about 15,000 terms. By] D. I. Alekseev, I. G. Gozman, G. V. Sakharov. Izd. 2-e, ispr. i dop. M.: Russkii iazyk, 1977. 415 pp.

1st ed. publ. 1963 (486 pp.). Includes abbreviations and acronyms for Soviet organizations, institutes and concepts, with guidance on pronunciation. Where necessary, the full term is briefly supplemented with explanatory notes in italic script.

U60 Crowe, B. *Concise dictionary of Soviet terminology, institutions and abbreviations.* Oxford [etc.]: Pergamon, 1969. viii, 182 pp.

As well as translating terms and names of organizations, gives a brief explanation of their use, or (for organizations) a brief account of their origin and functions.

U61 *Iuridicheskii slovar'.* [Legal dictionary]. 2.izd. M.: Gosiurizdat, 1956. 2 vols.

1st ed. publ. 1953 (781 pp.). An authoritative dictionary, with useful bibliographical references and references to official sources in many articles.

U62 Prishchepenko, N. P. *Russian–English law dictionary*; preface by M. de Capriles. Completed and ed. by the New York University School of Law. (Praeger special studies in international politics and public affairs). N.Y., Washington, London: Praeger, 1969. vi, 146 pp.

An extremely useful dictionary, because it gives examples of the use of many terms, particularly where one Russian word covers several English terms.

U63 Smith, R. E. F. *A Russian–English dictionary of social science terms.* London: Butterworths, 1962. xii, 495 pp.

Covers the economy, industry, law, politics, agriculture and society, and includes historical terms as well as modern. It does not just provide translations; for certain terms there is a succinct note helping the reader to understand the significance of the term, or qualifying it. The appendices include list of awards and conversion coefficients for British, metric and Russian measurements.

CONSTITUTIONAL DOCUMENTS

The USSR's first constitution was largely based on the 1918 RSFSR constitution, and came into force on 31 January 1924. A new constitution—often referred to as the Stalin constitution—was passed by the USSR Congress of Soviets on 5 December 1936. The union republics then in existence passed new constitutions during 1937. In 1940, the Karelo-Finnish, Moldavian, Estonian, Latvian and Lithuanian Soviet Socialist Republics were formed and adopted similar constitutions. The constitutions of the USSR and the union republics were substantially amended during the war and the postwar period. After Stalin's death, dissatisfaction with the constitutional position grew and in 1962 a drafting commission was set up to prepare a new constitution. Brezhnev became its chairman after Khrushchev was ousted. The draft of the new constitution was finally published and after public discussion was approved, with slight amendments, at an Extraordinary Session of the USSR Supreme Soviet on 7 October 1977. It came into force on that date. In April 1978, each union republic enacted its own new constitution.

In the lists of editions of the constitutions given in the subsections which follow, details are given of Russian-language editions. The USSR constitution is also published from time to time in the languages of the other peoples of the USSR, and the union republics generally publish a version of their constitution in their national language at the same time as a revised version is issued in Russian. The lists exclude drafts of the 1977–8 constitutions; they can be found in the stenotchet of the appropriate Supreme Soviet session.

Bibliographies

U64a   *Sovetskoe gosudarstvennoe pravo: bibliografiia, 1917–1957.* [Soviet state law: a bibliography, 1917–1957]. (AN SSSR. In-t prava). M.: Gosiurizdat, 1958. 775 pp.

U64b   *Sovetskoe gosudarstvennoe (konstitutsionnoe) pravo: bibliografiia, 1957–1970.* [Soviet state (constitutional) law: a bibliography, 1957–1970]. (In-t gosudarstva i prava AN SSSR. Irkutskii gos. un-t). M., Irkutsk, 1972. 557 pp.

These two bibliographies cover constitutional questions and the state structure, and include detailed lists of the laws enacted at each session of the supreme soviets of the USSR and the union republics, details of the proceedings of other governmental organizations, laws, statutes, etc. governing the work of these bodies, and books, journals and dissertations dealing with state and constitutional law, excluding popular works. They are not indexes of the various *Vedomosti* and *Sobranie postanovlenii*, but the 1958 edition does include lists of constitutions. Some of the entries are briefly annotated. The 1958 volume lists bulletins of legislation and both volumes include lists of periodicals cited and a full editor and author index.

Collections of documents

U65a   *Istoriia sovetskoi konstitutsii. Sbornik dokumentov, 1917–1957.* [The history of the Soviet constitution. A collection of documents, 1917–1957]. Red.: D. Gaidukov, V. Kotok, S. Ronin. (AN SSSR. In-t prava). M., 1957. 551 pp.

A chronological collection of documents relating to the USSR constitution, the formation of the socialist state, and constitutional matters generally. Subject index.

U65b   *Istoriia sovetskoi konstitutsii (v dokumentakh), 1917–1956 gg.* [The history of the Soviet constitution in documents, 1917–1956]. Sost.: A. Lipatov, N. Savenkov. M.: Gosiurizdat, 1957. 1046 pp.

Includes 368 documents on the 1918, 1924 and 1936 constitutions, and a wide range of other materials from the Supreme Soviet and its Presidium on constitutional matters and the state apparatus. Alphabetical subject index.

U66   *Konstitutsiia obshchenarodnogo gosudarstva.* [The constitution of a state of the whole people]. M.: Politizdat, 1978. 247 pp.

A collection of speeches by Brezhnev on the 1977 constitution, edicts on the Constitutional Commission, and reports on its work. Includes the texts of the 1977 and earlier constitutions.

U67 *Obrazovanie i razvitie Soiuza Sovetskikh Sotsialisticheskikh Respublik (v dokumentakh)*. [The formation and development of the USSR in documents]. M.: Iurid. lit-ra, 1973. 735 pp.

A collection of documents, 1917–72, on the Soviet constitution and the organization of state administration.

U68 *Osnovnye zakonodatel'nye akty po sovetskomu gosudarstvennomu stroitel'stvu i pravu*. [Basic legislative acts on the Soviet state and law]. (Vysshaia partiinaia shkola. Kafedra gos. prava i sovetskogo stroitel'stva). M.: Mysl', 1972. 2 vols.

Vol. 1 includes the major CPSU documents on the organization of the state, and legislation on constitutional law, state power and the judiciary. Vol. 2 covers voluntary bodies, the basic rights and duties of Soviet citizens, and major legislative acts on the economy, labour, the family, health, land, etc. Original official sources are cited for each document. No indexes.

U69 *Sbornik ofitsial'nykh dokumentov (primenitel'no k kursu sovetskogo gosudarstvennogo prava)*. [A collection of official documents for the course on Soviet state law]. Pod obshchei red. A. I. Lepeshkina. M.: Iurid. lit-ra, 1964. 520 pp.

A collection of 167 documents on the Soviet constitution and Soviet state administration, 1917–63.

U70 *V. I. Lenin, KPSS o sovetskoi konstitutsii*. [V. I. Lenin and the CPSU on the Soviet constitution]. M.: Politizdat, 1979, 343 pp.

A collection for mass readers, including Lenin's views on the constitutional foundations of the Soviet state and CPSU materials, 1917–77, on constitutional issues.

USSR and union republics

1936–1940 constitutions

U71a *Konstitutsiia (Osnovnoi Zakon) SSSR. Konstitutsii (osnovnye zakony) soiuznykh sovetskikh sotsialisticheskikh respublik*. M.: Gosiurizdat, 1951. 487 pp.

U71b ... 1956. 490 pp.

U71c ... *soiuznykh i avtonomnykh sovetskikh sotsialisticheskikh respublik*. 1960. 939 pp.

U71d ... *soiuznykh sovetskikh sotsialisticheskikh respublik*. M.: Izvestiia, 1972. 496 pp.

1977–1978 constitutions

U72 *Konstitutsiia (Osnovnoi Zakon) SSSR. Konstitutsii (osnovnye zakony) soiuznykh sovetskikh sotsialisticheskikh respublik*. M.: Iurid. lit-ra, 1978. 576 pp.

USSR

1936 constitution

U73 *Konstitutsiia (Osnovnoi Zakon) SSSR (utv. 5 dek. 1936 g.).* M.: Partizdat. 31 pp.
Amended editions published after each relevant session of the Supreme Soviet.

1977 constitution

U74 *Konstitutsiia (Osnovnoi Zakon) Soiuza Sovetskikh Sotsialisticheskikh Respublik, priniata na vneocherednoi sed'moi sessii Verkhovnogo Soveta SSSR deviatogo sozyva, 7 oktiabria 1977 g.* M.: Izvestiia, 1977. 47 pp.
Later editions publ. 1978 (47 pp.) and 1979 (47 pp.).

RSFSR

1937 constitution

U75 *Konstitutsiia (Osnovnoi Zakon) RSFSR (utv. 21 ianv. 1937 g.).* M.: Partizdat, 1937. 30 pp.
Amended editions published after each relevant session of the union republic's Supreme Soviet.

1978 constitution

U76 *Konstitutsiia (Osnovnoi Zakon) Rossiiskoi Sovetskoi Federativnoi Sotsialisticheskoi Respubliki, priniata na vneocherednoi sed'moi sessii Verkhovnogo Soveta RSFSR deviatogo sozyva.* M.: Izvestiia, 1978. 47 pp.
Later edition publ. 1979. 47 pp.

Armenia

1937 constitution

U77 *Konstitutsiia (Osnovnoi Zakon) Armianskoi SSR (utv. 23 marta 1937 g. ....).* Erevan: Armpartgiz, 1937. 32 pp.
Amended editions published after each relevant session of the union republic's Supreme Soviet.

1978 constitution

U78 *Konstitutsiia (Osnovnoi Zakon) Armianskoi SSR, priniata na vneocherednoi vos'moi sessii Verkhovnogo Soveta Armianskoi SSR deviatogo sozyva, 14 aprelia 1978 g.* Erevan: Aiastan, 1978, 57 pp.
Also publ. in 1979, 48 pp.

Azerbaijan

1937 constitution

U79 *Konstitutsiia (Osnovnoi Zakon) Azerbaidzhanskoi SSR (utv. 14 marta 1937 g. . . .* Baku: Azpartnesher, 1937. 56 pp.
Amended editions published after each relevant session of the union republic's Supreme Soviet.

1978 constitution

U80 *Konstitutsiia (Osnovnoi Zakon) Azerbaidzhanskoi SSR, priniata na vneocherednoi sed'moi sessii Verkhovnogo Soveta Azerbaidzhanskoi SSR deviatogo sozyva, 21 aprelia 1978 g.* Baku: Azernesher, 1978. 67 pp.
Also publ. in 1979 with the national anthem included (221 pp.).

Belorussia

1937 constitution

U81 *Konstitutsiia (Osnovnoi Zakon) Belorusskoi SSR (utv. 19 fevr. 1937 g.).* Minsk: Belpartizdat, 1937. 31 pp.
Amended editions published after each relevant session of the union republic's Supreme Soviet.

1978 constitution

U82 *Konstitutsiia (Osnovnoi Zakon) Belorusskoi SSR, priniata na vneocherednoi vos'moi sessii Verkhovnogo Soveta Belorusskoi SSR deviatogo sozyva, 14 aprelia 1978 g.* Minsk: Belarus', 1978. 63 pp.
Amended edition publ. 1979, 61 pp.

Estonia

1940 constitution

U83 *Konstitutsiia (Osnovnoi Zakon) Estonskoi SSR (utv. . . . 25 avg. 1940 g.).* Tallin: Polit. lit., 1940, 20 pp.; 1946, 31 pp.; 1947, 32 pp.
Amended editions published after each relevant session of the union republic's Supreme Soviet.

1978 constitution

U84 *Konstitutsiia (Osnovnoi Zakon) Estonskoi SSR, priniata na vneocherednoi deviatoi sessii Verkhovnogo Soveta Estonskoi SSR deviatogo sozyva, 13 aprelia 1978 g.* Tallin: Eesti raamat, 1978. 47 pp.
Several other editions in Estonian or Russian publ. 1979–80; in 1980 an edition was published with parallel texts in Estonian, Russian and German, and one with parallel texts in Estonian, Russian and French.

Georgia

1937 constitution

U85 *Konstitutsiia (Osnovnoi Zakon) Gruzinskoi SSR (utv. 13 fevr. 1937 g.).* Tbilisi: Partizdat, 1937. 39 pp.

Amended editions published after each relevant session of the union republic's Supreme Soviet.

1978 constitution

U86 *Konstitutsiia (Osnovnoi Zakon) Gruzinskoi SSR, priniata vos'moi sessiei Verkhovnogo Soveta Gruzinskoi SSR deviatogo sozyva, 15 aprelia 1978 g.* Tbilisi: Sabchota Sakartvelo, 1978. 67 pp.

Another edition publ. 1979 (67 pp.); edition with parallel Georgian and Russian text publ. 1979 (144 pp.).

Karelo-Finnish SSR

1940 constitution

U87 *Konstitutsiia (Osnovnoi Zakon) Karelo-Finskoi SSR (utv. . . . 9 iiulia 1940 g.).* Petrozavodsk: Gosizdat Karelo-Finskoi SSR, 1940, 32 pp.; and M.: Vedomosti Verkh. Soveta RSFSR, 1940, 20 pp.

Amended editions publ. 1945, 1948, 1950 and 1955.

Kazakhstan

1937 constitution

U88 *Konstitutsiia (Osnovnoi Zakon) Kazakhskoi SSR (utv. 26 marta 1937 g. . . . .).* Alma-Ata: Kazpartizdat, 1937. 30 pp.

Amended editions published after each relevant session of the union republic's Supreme Soviet.

1978 constitution

U89 *Konstitutsiia (Osnovnoi Zakon) Kazakhskoi SSR, priniata na vneocherednoi sed'moi sessii Verkhovnogo Soveta Kazakhskoi SSR deviatogo sozyva, 20 aprelia 1978 g.* Alma-Ata: Kazakhstan, 1978. 66 pp.

Also publ. 1979 (64 pp.).

Kirghizia

1937 constitution

U90 *Konstitutsiia (Osnovnoi Zakon) Kirgizskoi SSR (utv. . . . 23 marta 1937 g.).* Frunze: Kirgizgosizdat, 1937. 30 pp.

Amended editions published after each relevant session of the union republic's Supreme Soviet.

1978 constitution

U91 *Konstitutsiia (Osnovnoi Zakon) Kirgizskoi SSR, priniata na vneocherednoi vos'moi sessii Verkhovnogo Soveta Kirgizskoi SSR deviatogo sozyva, 20 aprelia 1978 g.* Frunze: Kyrgyzstan, 1978. 94 pp. [In Kirghiz and Russian].
Amended edition publ. 1979, 62 pp.

Latvia

1940 constitution

U92 *Konstitutsiia (Osnovnoi Zakon) Latviiskoi SSR (utv. 25 avg. 1940 g. . . .).* Riga: 1940. 56 pp. [In Latvian and Russian].
Amended editions published after each relevant session of the union republic's Supreme Soviet.

1978 constitution

U93 *Konstitutsiia (Osnovnoi Zakon) Latviiskoi SSR, priniata na vneocherednoi vos'moi sessii Verkhovnogo Soveta Latviiskoi SSR deviatogo sozyva, 18 aprelia 1978 g.* Riga: Liesma, 1978. 142 pp. [In Latvian and Russian].
Other editions in Latvian or Russian publ. 1978 and 1980.

Lithuania

1940 constitution

U94 *Konstitutsiia (Osnovnoi Zakon) Litovskoi SSR (utv. 25. avg. 1940 g. . . .).* Kaunas: 1940, 51 pp.; M.: Vedomosti Verkh. Soveta RSFSR, 1940, 18 pp.
Amended editions published after each relevant session of the union republic's Supreme Soviet.

1978 constitution

U95 *Konstitutsiia (Osnovnoi Zakon) Litovskoi SSR, priniata na vneocherednoi deviatoi sessii Verkhovnogo Soveta Litovskoi SSR deviatogo sozyva, 20 aprelia 1978 g.* Vilnius: Mintis, 1978. 68 pp.
Other editions in Lithuanian or Russian publ. 1978 and 1979.

Moldavia

1941 constitution

U96 *Konstitutsiia (Osnovnoi Zakon) Moldavskoi SSR, utv. 10 fevr. 1941 g. [. . .] s izm. i dop. [. . .].* M.: Gosizdat Moldavii, 1944. 22 pp.
Amended editions published after each relevant session of the union republic's Supreme Soviet.

1978 constitution

U97 *Konstitutsiia (Osnovnoi Zakon) Moldavskoi SSR, priniata na vneocherednoi vos'moi sessii Verkhovnogo Soveta Moldavskoi SSR deviatogo sozyva, 15 aprelia 1978 g.* Kishinev: Kartia Moldoveniaske, 1978. 112 pp. [In Moldavian and Russian].
Also publ. 1979.

Tajikstan

1937 constitution

U98 *Konstitutsiia (Osnovnoi Zakon) Tadzhikskoi SSR, utv. . . . 1 marta 1937 g.* Stalinabad: Tadzhgosizdat, 1937. 35 pp.
Amended editions published after each relevant session of the union republic's Supreme Soviet.

1978 constitution

U99 *Konstitutsiia (Osnovnoi Zakon) Tadzhikskoi SSR, priniata na vneocherednoi vos'moi sessii Verkhovnogo Soveta Tadzhikskoi SSR deviatogo sozyva, 14 aprelia 1978 g.* Dushanbe: Irfon, 1978. 51 pp.
Also published in Russian and Tajik editions in 1979.

Turkmenistan

1937 constitution

U100 *Konstitutsiia (Osnovnoi Zakon) Turkmenskoi SSR (utv. 2 marta 1937 g. . . .).* Ashkhabad: Turkmengosizdat, 1937. 26 pp.
Amended editions published after each relevant session of the union republic's Supreme Soviet.

1978 constitution

U101 *Konstitutsiia (Osnovnoi Zakon) Turkmenskoi SSR, priniata na vneocherednoi deviatoi sessii Verkhovnogo Soveta Turkmenskoi SSR deviatogo sozyva, 13 aprelia 1978 g.* Ashkhabad: Turkmenistan, 1978. 52 pp.
Also published 1978 and 1979 in Russian or Turkmenian editions.

Ukraine

1937 constitution

U102 *Konstitutsiia (Osnovnoi Zakon) Ukrainskoi SSR (utv. . . . 30 ianv. 1937 g.).* Kiev: Partizdat, 1937. 29 pp.
Amended editions published after each relevant session of the union republic's Supreme Soviet.

1978 constitution

U103 *Konstitutsiia (Osnovnoi Zakon) Ukrainskoi SSR, priniata vneoche-*
rednoi sed'moi sessiei Verkhovnogo Soveta Ukrainskoi SSR deviatogo
sozyva, 20 aprelia 1978 g. Kiev: Politizdat Ukrainy, 1978. 47 pp.
Other editions in Ukrainian or Russian published 1978–79.

Uzbekistan

1937 constitution

U104 *Konstitutsiia (Osnovnoi Zakon) Uzbekskoi SSR (utv. 14 fevr. 1937*
g.). Tashkent: Izd. KP(b)Uz., 1937. 31 pp.
Amended editions published after each relevant session of the
union republic's Supreme Soviet.

1978 constitution

U105 *Konstitutsiia (Osnovnoi Zakon) Uzbekskoi SSR, priniata na*
vneocherednoi shestoi sessii Verkhovnogo Soveta Uzbekskoi SSR
deviatogo sozyva, 19 aprelia 1978 g. Tashkent: Uzbekistan, 1978. 175
pp. [In Russian and Uzbek].
Several other editions published 1978–9 with separate Russian and
Uzbek text. One published by Fan in 1978 includes the text of the
national anthem of the Uzbek SSR in Russian.

Translations

1936–1940 constitutions

Translations of the USSR constitution are published from time to time in the
USSR, e.g.

U106 *Constitution (Fundamental Law) of the USSR, as amended and added*
to at the 1st, 2nd and 4th sessions of the fourth convocation of the
Supreme Soviet of the USSR. Moscow: Foreign Languages Publ.
House, 1956. 115 pp.
Republished subsequently with amendments of later sessions.

Texts of various editions of the 1936 constitution can also be found in some of
the collections of legislation in translation, such as U156 and U160.
Translations of the union republic constitutions are less easily found;
translations of most of them were published in Moscow in 1947. The RSFSR
constitution can be found in some of the collections of legislation in translation,
such as U156 and U160. It has also been published in the USSR fairly recently:

U107 *Constitution (Fundamental Law) of the RSFSR, as amended and*
supplemented at the first session of the eighth convocation of the Supreme
Soviet of the RSFSR. M.: Progress, 1972. 100 pp.

1977–1978 constitutions

A Soviet translation was made available immediately:

U108 *Constitution (Fundamental Law) of the USSR; adopted at the seventh*
      (special) session of the Supreme Soviet of the USSR, ninth convocation
      on October 7, 1977. M.: Novosti, 1977. 123 pp.
      It can also be found in U163.

Translation of the USSR 1977 constitution and the full texts of the 1978
constitutions adopted by the union republics can be found in the constitutions
binder of the *Collected legislation* (U158). See also:

U109 *The constitutions of the USSR and the union republics: analysis, texts,*
      reports; ed. by F. J. M. Feldbrugge. Alphen aan den Rijn: Sijthoff
      and Noordhoff, 1979. xv, 366 pp.
      Contains the English-language text of the 1936 constitution in its
      final version and alongside it the 1977 constitution, showing in italics
      amendments made to the draft. The constitutions of the union
      republics are dealt with by giving in full the texts of all 15 preambles
      and the full text of the RSFSR constitution, with variations in the
      texts of the constitutions of the other union republics recorded as
      notes. Also includes the state arms and flags of the USSR and the
      union republics, the Russian-language text of the 1977 constitution,
      and two of Brezhnev's speeches on the draft. There is a long
      analytical introduction and a useful note on the translation, discuss-
      ing the different types of translation and translation problems of
      Soviet legal terminology.

Soviet state symbolism

This term covers the state arms, state flag, state anthem, awards and medals,
memorial days, holidays and jubilees.

U110 *Gosudarstvennye gerby i flagi SSSR, soiuznykh i avtonomnykh*
      respublik. [State arms and flags of the USSR, the union and
      autonomous republics]. M.: Izvestiia, 1972. 79 pp.
      Has coloured illustrations depicting each flag and state arms, with
      the article from the constitution describing them alongside.

U111 Kolesnikov, G. A. *Ordena i medali SSSR.* [Orders and medals of the
      USSR. By] G. A. Kolesnikov, A. M. Rozhkov, M.: Voenizdat, 1974.
      269 pp. plus plates.
      Gives a history of the Soviet awards and medals system, extracts
      from the regulations establishing them, and setting out the pro-
      cedures for awarding them. Has a supplement listing the main
      legislative acts on awards and medals, 1918–74. The plates consist of
      coloured reproductions of each award or medal.

U112 'Soviet state symbolism'. *Soviet statutes and decisions,* vol. 8, nos.
      1–4, 1972–3.

This issue of *SS&D* (*see* U164) covers all aspects of state symbolism in the USSR and the union republics.

The national anthem of the USSR as sung during the Stalin period was felt to be inappropriate after his death and denouncement, and for some years the words were not sung. On 27 May 1977, a new version was approved by the Supreme Soviet of the USSR and can be found in *Vedomosti Verkhovnogo Soveta 1977*, no. 24.

The flags and arms of the USSR and its constituent union republics can also be found in some of the collections of constitutions, such as U71 and U72; national anthems are also appearing in recent editions of the constitutions of some of the union republics. Translations of other legislation on Soviet state symbolism can be found in *Collected legislation* (U158), section I: 8.

LAW AND JUDICIAL SYSTEM

This section includes general collections of legislation, documents dealing with the judicial system, material on citizenship, the civil law and law of civil procedure, the law of family and marriage, criminal law and procedure, and administrative law and administrative offences. Each subsection has a short introduction briefly setting out the agencies responsible for it or noting the major legislative acts which form the basis of other legislation in that field. It is, however, appropriate here to give a brief overview of the development of the law and the judicial system in the USSR in the postwar period, as this has clearly affected the amount and nature of official publishing. The Stalin constitution of 1936 was thought to herald a new era of respect for traditional legal concepts and values and mark the end of the period of arbitrary action by state agencies on grounds of economic and political expediency and the reduction in the importance of the courts which had prevailed in the late 1920s and early 1930s. However, in practice, respect for law and legal stability under Stalin were limited. Legal safeguards and procedures were completely ignored by the NKVD, and oppressive legislation enacted and used. After Stalin's death, a number of these enactments were repealed, including the 1934 and 1937 decrees authorizing special forms of trial for 'counter-revolutionary' offences and the 1940 law restricting mobility of labour and severely punishing breaches of labour discipline. Extensive amnesties were granted in 1953, 1955 and 1957. Once some of the worst abuses of the Stalinist period had been rectified, the authorities began to consider more fundamental reforms of the legal system. The general moves towards decentralization of the administration included the abandonment of the idea of all-union criminal and civil codes which had been in preparation under Stalin. Instead it was decided that in these branches of the law Fundamental Principles should be laid down by the USSR Supreme Soviet and that each union republic would then enact its own codes based on these Principles. The first of these Fundamental Principles appeared in 1959, those dealing with criminal law and procedure, and have been followed by Fundamental Principles in a number of other branches of law throughout the 1960s and 1970s. There are differences in the provisions of the codes of the union republics, but these are much less significant generally than the differences between the codes which had developed before the Fundamental Principles were enacted. Over the last twenty years there has also been considerable progress in the codification and systematization of legislation; the results of this should be seen in the *Svod zakonov* (U118) for the USSR and the parallel publications for the union republics expected to appear during the 1980s. Other developments during the post-Stalin period have included a marked expansion of the role of voluntary organizations, including the comrades' courts and the volunteer militia (druzhinniki).

General collections of legislation

This section includes large-scale chronological and systematic collections of legislation at all-union and union-republic level, and some more compact general collections produced for the use of officials in local soviets. A number of major general collections of legislation in English translation are also described here. For official gazettes, bulletins of new normative acts and other sources of current legislative materials, see the section 'Supreme soviets and governments'.

USSR

U113 *Osnovy zakonodatel'stva Soiuza SSR i soiuznykh respublik.* [Fundamental Principles of legislation of the USSR and the union republics]. M.: Iurid. lit-ra, 1971. 376 pp.

Official texts of the Principles passed 1958–70, as of 1 January 1971. Principles included are: land law, water law, health, labour, judicial system, civil law and procedure, criminal law and procedure, corrective labour, marriage and the family. Includes the edicts and other legislation bringing them into force.

U114 *Sbornik zakonov SSSR i ukazov Prezidiuma Verkhovnogo Soveta SSSR, . . .* [A collection of the laws of the USSR and edicts of the Presidium of the USSR Supreme Soviet in . . .]. M.: Izvestiia Sovetov deputatov trudiashchikhsia SSSR.

1938–iiul' 1956. 1956. 500 pp.
1938–noiabr' 1958. 1959. 710 pp.
1938–1961. 1961. 975 pp.
1938–1967. 1968. 2 vols; vol. 3 for 1968–70 publ. 1971.
1938–1975. 1975–6. 4 vols.

The collection includes laws and edicts currently in force, in a subject arrangement. In the 1975–6 collection each volume has a subject index; vol. 4 also has a supplement listing new and amended legislation relating to material in the first three volumes. The collection excludes edicts relating to the award of medals, honours, etc., edicts on boundary changes and on promotions and retirements, and some other non-normative material.

U115 *Sobranie deistvuiushchego zakonodatel'stva SSSR.* [A collection of USSR legislation currently in force]. (M-vo iustitsii SSSR). M., [1972–].

Full publication details not available. The collection was intended for official use only and no copies are known in the West. It was planned to appear in 50–60 volumes in 1972–6 in an edition of 50,000 copies; apparently extra copies were produced in 1978. The production of this collection was part of the process of consolidation and systematization of Soviet legislation intended to culminate with the presentation of the first volume of the *Svod zakonov* (U118) to the 26th CPSU Congress in February 1981. [Not seen].

U116   *Spravochnik dlia rabotnikov sel'skikh i poselkovykh Sovetov.* [Manual for officials of village and settlements soviets]. M.: Iurid. lit-ra, 1969–70. 2 vols.

Vol. 1 covers the organization of the soviet's work and economic activities; vol. 2 covers labour, public utilities, social and cultural matters, family and marriage law, and law and order. The manual includes a wide range of CPSU resolutions and USSR and RSFSR normative materials, with some material from other republics to cover points not in the RSFSR legislation. Some documents are given in extract form, but all have full references to published sources.

U117   *Spravochnik po zakonodatel'stvu dlia sudebno-prokurorskikh rabotnikov.* [A legal manual for procuracy and legal officials]. Izd. 2-e, dop. M.: Gosiurizdat, 1949. 3 vols.

1st ed. also publ. 1949 (3 vols.). The manual covers all fields of law and includes over 1,000 acts or references to published sources of legislative material. Some material is in extract form. Designed to include the material most often needed in everyday legal work. Mainly limited to all-union materials, but includes some RSFSR legislation where this is necessary for a point not covered in the all-union material. Has an excellent subject index in vol. 3. The 1st ed. includes material in force on 1 January 1949, the 2nd on 1 September 1949.

U118   *Svod zakonov SSSR.* [Digest of laws of the USSR]. M.: Izvestiia, 1981–.

This digest is an official publication of the Presidium of the Supreme Soviet of the USSR and the USSR Council of Ministers and includes legislation, joint ordinances of the Council of Ministers of the USSR and the Central Committee of the CPSU and Council of Ministers ordinances of a normative character. The collection is produced in a loose-leaf format and new material will be sent out to subscribers regularly to up-date the text. It is planned that the collection will comprise 12 volumes and appear in 1981–5. Vol. 1 covers legislation on the social and state system; vol. 2, civil law, law of marriage and the family, labour and social security; vol. 3, health, sport and physical culture, education, science and culture and legislation on foreigners and stateless persons; vol. 4, rational use and protection of natural resources; vol. 5, the economy in general and financial law; vol. 6, construction; vol. 7, industry; vol.

8, agriculture and procurements; vol. 9, transport and communications, trade and public catering and housing; vol. 10, international relations and foreign trade, defence and the protection of state borders; vol. 11, justice, procuratorial supervision and protection of the legal order; vol. 12 will be an index. The digest covers all-union legislation; each union republic will also prepare its own *Svod zakonov* to cover its own legislation.

Union republics

RSFSR

U119 *Khronologicheskoe sobranie zakonov, ukazov Prezidiuma Verkhovnogo Soveta i postanovlenii pravitel'stva RSFSR.* [A chronological collection of laws, Supreme Soviet edicts and government ordinances of the RSFSR]. (M-vo iustitsii RSFSR). M.: Gosiurizdat, 1959. 6 vols. plus index vol.; a supplementary vol. 7 publ. in 1960.

Earlier ed. 1949, 5 vols. The main collection covers 1917–57; the supplementary volume covers 1958. It includes some material not previously published. Documents in the main part were in force on 1 January 1958. The collection excludes texts of the law codes and material no longer in force, temporary legislation, edicts relating to boundary changes, personnel changes, awards and honours and other non-normative materials.

U120 *Sbornik zakonov RSFSR i ukazov Prezidiuma Verkhovnogo Soveta RSFSR* ... [A collection of laws and edicts of the Presidium of the Supreme Soviet of the RSFSR]. M.: Izvestiia.
1938–46. 1946. 64 pp.
1946–54. 1955. 108 pp.
These collections are arranged in broad subject categories and exclude budget and election laws and edicts relating to individual people and institutions; boundary changes are given only at oblast' level.

U121 *Sistematicheskoe sobranie zakonov RSFSR, ukazov Prezidiuma Verkhovnogo Soveta RSFSR i reshenii pravitel'stva RSFSR.* [A systematic collection of the laws of the RSFSR, edicts of the Presidium of the RSFSR Supreme Soviet and decisions of the government of the RSFSR]. M.: Iurid. lit-ra, 1967–70. 15 vols.

A collection of laws, edicts, ordinances, regulations, etc. of the RSFSR Supreme Soviet and its Presidium and the RSFSR Council of Ministers. It excludes material no longer in force, material in force only temporarily, boundary changes and edicts affecting individual people and organizations. Full references to original official sources are given for each document included. The material included was in force in the late 1960s and is arranged as follows: vols. 1–2, the state; vol. 3, planning and supply; vol. 4, finance and the economy; vol. 5, industry and construction; vols. 6 and 7, agriculture; vol. 8, land use, mineral rights, hunting, fishing, forestry and conservation; vol. 9, transport, communications and trade; vol. 10, housing and health services; vol. 11; labour and insurance, social security; vol. 12, education, culture and voluntary organizations; vol. 13, civil and family law; vol. 14, criminal law, the judicial system and legal organization. Vol. 15 is an alphabetical-subject and chronological index to the whole collection.

ARMENIA

U122 *Khronologicheskoe sobranie zakonov Armianskoi SSR, ukazov Prezidiuma Verkhovnogo Soveta i postanovlenii pravitel'stva Armianskoi SSR.* [A chronological collection of the laws of the Armenian SSR, edicts of the Presidium of the Supreme Soviet and government ordinances of the Armenian SSR]. Erevan, 1961–70, 11 vols.

In Armenian. The collection covers the years 1920–66; the volumes did not appear in chronological order. [Not seen].

U123 *Sbornik nekotorykh zakonodatel'nykh aktov SSSR i Armianskoi SSR.* [A collection of selected legislative acts of the USSR and the Armenian SSR]. (V pomoshch' sovetskomu rabotniku). Erevan: Aiastan, 1976. 395 pp.

In Armenian. For officials of state organizations and local soviets. [Not seen].

U124 *Spravochnik dlia rabotnikov sel'skikh i poselkovykh Sovetov deputatov trudiashchikhsia.* [Manual for officials of village and settlement soviets]. (M-vo iustitsii Armianskoi SSR). Erevan: Aiastan, 1973–4. 2 vols.

In Armenian. [Not seen].

AZERBAIJAN

U125 *Khronologicheskoe sobranie zakonov Azerbaidzhanskoi SSR, ukazov Prezidiuma Verkhovnogo Soveta Azerbaidzhanskoi SSR i postanovlenii pravitel'stva Azerbaidzhanskoi SSR.* [Chronological collection of the laws of the Azerbaijani SSR, edicts of the Presidium of the Supreme Soviet and ordinances of the government of the Azerbaijani SSR]. (Iuridicheskaia komissiia pri SM AzSSR). Baku, 1960–.

In Azerbaijani. [Not seen].

U126 *Sbornik zakonov Azerbaidzhanskoi SSR i ukazov Prezidiuma Verkhovnogo Soveta Azerbaidzhanskoi SSR, 1938–1966.* [A collection of the laws of the Azerbaijani SSR and edicts of the Presidium of the Supreme Soviet of Azerbaijan, 1938–1966]. Baku: Izd. Verkhovnogo Soveta AzSSR, 1966–67. 2 vols.

Also publ. in Azerbaijani. Earlier ed., covering 1938–62, publ. in 1962 (542 pp.). The 1966–67 collection includes the 1937 constitution of the republic and excludes non-normative material such as personnel changes, awards and boundary changes. There is a chronological index in vol. 2.

BELORUSSIA

U127   *Sbornik zakonov Belorusskoi SSR i ukazov Prezidiuma Verkhovnogo Soveta Belorusskoi SSR, 1938–1973.* [A collection of the laws of the Belorussian SSR and edicts of the Presidium of the Supreme Soviet of the Belorussian SSR, 1938–1973]. Minsk: Belarus', 1974–6. 3 vols.

     Earlier ed. covering 1938–55 publ. 1956 (347 pp.); vol. covering 1956–8 publ. 1959 (433 pp.), also in Belorussian; ed. covering 1938–67 publ. 1968–9, 2 vols. The collections are arranged by topic, with a subject and chronological index in each volume. Excludes non-normative materials, budget and plan laws.

U128   *Spravochnik sovetskogo rabotnika.* [Manual for officials of the soviets]. (Iurid. komissiia pri SM BSSR). Minsk: Belarus', 1970–72. 2 vols.

     A collection of USSR and Belorussian materials on a wide range of topics, intended for administrators and deputies to local soviets. Subject index.

ESTONIA

U129a   *Gosudarstvenno-pravovye akty Estonskoi SSR.* [Estonian legislative acts on the state]. (Tart. gos. un-t). Tartu, 1970. 218 pp.

U129b   *Nekotorye gosudarstvenno-pravovye akty ESSR, 1953–1964.* [Some Estonian legislative acts on the state, 1953–1964]. Sost.: I. Sil'smiae. ('Tart. gos. un-t). Tartu, 1966. 247 pp.

     In Estonian. Both these publications appear to contain Estonian legislation, probably general material on the state structure and the legal system. The 1970 vol. covers 1958–69. [Not seen].

U130   *Khronologicheskoe sobranie zakonov Estonskoi SSR, ukazov Prezidiuma Verkhovnogo Soveta i postanovlenii pravitel'stva Estonskoi SSR.* [A chronological collection of the laws of the Estonian SSR, edicts of the Supreme Soviet and ordinances of the government of the Estonian SSR]. (M-vo iustitsii ESSR). Tallin: Estonskoe gos. izd-vo, 1953. 2 vols.

     Also publ. in Estonian. The collection covers 1940–7; a planned third volume to cover 1948–51 was apparently not published. Includes material in force on 1 January 1952, except edicts relating to personnel matters, boundaries, awards, edicts in force temporarily, etc.

GEORGIA

U131   *Khronologicheskoe sobranie zakonov Gruzinskoi SSR, ukazov Prezidiuma Verkhovnogo Soveta i postanovlenii pravitel'stva Gruzinskoi SSR.* [A chronological collection of laws of the Georgian SSR, edicts of the Presidium of the Supreme Soviet and ordinances of the government of the Georgian SSR]. (Iurid. komissiia GSSR). Tbilisi: Sabchota Sakartvelo.

T. 1, 1921–40. 1959.
In Georgian. Possibly only vol. 1 ever published. [Not seen].

KAZAKHSTAN

U132 *Sbornik zakonov Kazakhskoi SSR i ukazov Prezidiuma Verkhovnogo Soveta Kazakhskoi SSR, 1937–1971.* [A collection of the laws of the Kazakh SSR and the edicts of the Presidium of the Kazakh Supreme Soviet, 1937–1971]. Alma-Ata: Kazakhstan, 1971. 452 pp.

Earlier ed. publ. 1958 (670 pp.) covering 1938–57; another ed. in two volumes planned for publication late in 1981. The collections exclude budget laws and decrees affecting individual people or institutions, but include boundary changes. Chronological index.

U133 *Spravochnik po zakonodatel'stvu dlia ispolnitel'nykh komitetov mestnykh Sovetov.* [Manual on legislation for the executive committees of local soviets]. Pod red. A. Bulgakbaeva, A. Tulinova. Alma-Ata: Kazakhstan, 1971–.

Planned in three volumes; apparently only vol. 1 published so far. [Not seen].

KIRGHIZIA

U134 *Sbornik zakonov Kirgizskoi SSR i ukazov Prezidiuma Verkhovnogo Soveta Kirgizskoi SSR za 1938–1956 gg.* [A collection of the laws of the Kirghiz SSR and edicts of the Presidium of the Kirghiz Supreme Soviet 1938–1956]. Frunze: Verkhovnyi Sovet KirgSSR, 1957. 272 pp.

Earlier eds. covering 1938–49 publ. 1950 (264 pp.) and 1926–54 publ. 1956 (2 vols.). The collections are arranged by topic, with a chronological index, and exclude non-normative materials, budget law and certain other types of material.

U135 *Sobranie zakonov Kirgizskoi SSR, ukazov Prezidiuma Verkhovnogo Soveta i postanovlenii pravitel'stva Kirgizskoi SSR.* [A collection of laws of the Kirghiz SSR, edicts of the Presidium of the Supreme soviet and government ordinances of the Kirghiz SSR]. (M-vo iustitsii KirgSSR). Frunze, 1956–.

Copy seen marked 'For official use only'. Only vol. 1, covering 1926–49, seen; no further publishing details known. This is a chronological collection of material still in force; excludes non-normative materials.

U136 *Zakonodatel'stvo Kirgizskoi SSR dlia mestnykh Sovetov deputatov trudiashchikhsia.* [Kirghiz legislation for officials of local soviets]. (Iurid. komissiia pri SM KirgSSR). Frunze: Kyrgyzstan, 1968. 664 pp.

Includes Kirghiz and all-union normative materials in force on 1 July 1967 in all fields relevant to the work of local soviets.

LATVIA

U137 *Alfavitno-predmetnyi ukazatel' k postanovleniiam TsK KP Latvii i Soveta Ministrov Latviiskoi SSR za 1940–1959 gody.* [Alphabetical-subject index to the decisions of the Central Committee of the Latvian Communist Party and the ordinances of the Latvian Council of Ministers, 1940–1959]. (Upr. delami SM LatvSSR). Riga: Latv. gos. izd-vo, 1960. 406 pp.

Intended to give practical assistance to new delegates to the soviets and officials. Lists the materials by topic, giving the title of the document, issuing body and date, but with no guidance on published sources of the document.

U138 *Khronologicheskoe sobranie zakonov Latviiskoi SSR, ukazov Prezidiuma Verkhovnogo Soveta Latviiskoi SSR i postanovlenii pravitel'stva Latviiskoi SSR, 1940–1959.* [A chronological collection of the laws of the Latvian SSR, edicts of the Presidium of the Supreme Soviet and government ordinances of the Latvian SSR, 1940–1959]. (Iurid. komissiia pri SM LatvSSR). Riga: Latv. gos. izd-vo, 1960. 430 pp.

Also publ. in Latvian. Includes material in force at the end of 1959, excluding non-normative material. Includes some acts not previously published officially. Chronological and subject indexes.

U139 *Sistematicheskoe sobranie deistvuiushchego zakonodatel'stva Latviiskoi SSR.* [A systematic collection of Latvian legislation currently in force]. Riga: Zvaigzne, [197?–].

In Latvian. Full publication details not known; only vol. 10, part 2 (1976) dealing with construction has been identified. [Not seen].

U140 *Spravochnik po zakonodatel'stvu dlia ispolnitel'nykh komitetov Sovetov deputatov trudiashchikhsia.* [A manual of legislation for the executive committees of local soviets]. (Iurid. komissiia pri SM LatvSSR). Riga: Liesma, 1970–6. 3 vols.

Also publ. in Latvian. A collection of all-union and Latvian normative acts in areas within the competence of local soviets. Some legislation is given in extract form, or as a reference to another published source.

LITHUANIA

U141 *Khronologicheskoe sobranie zakonov Litovskoi SSR, ukazov Prezidiuma Verkhovnogo Soveta i postanovlenii pravitel'stva Litovskoi SSR.* [A chronological collection of the laws of the Lithuanian SSR, edicts of the Presidium of the Supreme Soviet and ordinances of the government of the Lithuanian SSR]. (M-vo iustitsii LitSSR). Vilnius: Gospolitnauchizdat, 1957–9. 6 vols.

Also publ. in Lithuanian. The collection covers 1940–57 and includes some material not previously published. Excludes material no longer in force and non-normative material. Each volume has a chronological index.

U142 *Postoiannyi alfavitno-predmetnyi ukazatel' deistvuiushchikh normat-ivnykh zakonodatel'nykh aktov Litovskoi SSR.* [A permanent alphabetical-subject index to normative legislative acts of the Lithuanian SSR currently in force]. Vilnius: Izd-vo Prezidiuma Verkhovnogo Soveta LitSSR, 1969. 201 pp.

Earlier ed. publ. 1968 (186 pp.) in Russian and Lithuanian eds. [Not seen].

MOLDAVIA

U143 *Alfavitno-predmetnyi i khronologicheskii ukazateli k opublikovannomu zakonodatel'stvu Moldavskoi SSR za 1940–1971 gg.* [An alphabetical subject and chronological index to the published legislation of the Moldavian SSR in 1940–1971]. (M-vo iustitsii MSSR). Kishinev: Kartia Moldoveniaske, 1973. 367 pp.

Intended to help users of the *Khronologicheskoe sobranie* (U144) and the *Vedomosti* (U524a). Supplies very detailed subject indexes and cross-references. Arranged by date of promulgation, and gives full information on published sources for the documents.

U144 *Khronologicheskoe sobranie zakonov Moldavskoi SSR, ukazov Prezidiuma Verkhovnogo Soveta i postanovlenii pravitel'stva Moldavskoi SSR.* [Chronological collection of the laws of the Moldavian SSR, edicts of the Presidium of the Supreme Soviet and ordinances of the government of the Moldavian SSR]. (Iurid. komissiia pri SM Moldavskoi SSR). Kishinev: Kartia Moldoveniaske, 1960. 4 vols.

Also publ. in Moldavian in 1960–1. The collection covers 1940–57, and excludes material no longer in force and acts of a non-normative character. For an index, *see* U143.

U145 *Sbornik normativnykh aktov (v pomoshch' rabotnikam mestnykh Sovetov).* [A collection of normative acts for officials of local soviets]. (Iurid. komissiia pri SM MSSR). Kishinev: Kartia Moldoveniaske, 1968. 731 pp.

Current all-union and Moldavian normative acts on economic, social and educational matters relevant to the work of local soviets, and regulations governing their work.

TAJIKISTAN

U146 *Sbornik zakonodatel'stva Tadzhikskoi SSR dlia mestnykh Sovetov deputatov trudiashchikhsia.* [A collection of Tajik legislation for local soviets]. (Iurid. komissiia pri SM TadzhSSR). Dushanbe: Irfon, 1966. 558 pp.

Also publ. in Tajik in 1967. Includes Tajik normative materials on the work of the local soviets in finance, building, education, welfare, agriculture, etc., as of 1 November 1965.

U147 *Sbornik zakonov Tadzhikskoi SSR i ukazov Prezidiuma Verkhovnogo Soveta Tadzhikskoi SSR, 1938–1968.* [A collection of the laws of the

Tajik SSR and edicts of the Presidium of the Tajik Supreme Soviet, 1938–1968]. Dushanbe: Irfon, 1970. 651 pp.

Earlier ed. covering 1938–52 publ. in Tajik and Russian in 1955 (446 pp.); another covering 1938–58 publ. 1959 (402 pp.). The collection excludes budget laws, law codes and non-normative materials. Arranged by subject with a chronological index.

U148 *Sobranie deistvuiushchego zakonodatel'stva Tadzhikskoi SSR.* [A collection of Tajik legislation currently in force]. (M-vo iustitsii TadzhSSR). Dushanbe, 197?–.

Full publication details not known. Copies seen were marked 'For official use'. This is a systematic collection; section 2 (1975) covers economic matters in general; sections 25, 26 and 27 (1976, in 1 vol.) cover administrative responsibility, corrective labour and legal administration; sections 28 and 29 (1975, in 1 vol.) cover criminal law and civil and criminal procedure. Each volume has a chronological index.

TURKMENISTAN

U149 *Khronologicheskoe sobranie zakonov Turkmenskoi SSR, ukazov Prezidiuma Verkhovnogo Soveta, postanovlenii i rasporiazhenii pravitel'stva Turkmenskoi SSR.* [A chronological collection of the laws of the Turkmenian SSR, edicts of the Presidium of the Supreme Soviet, ordinances and decisions of the government of the Turkmenian SSR]. (Iurid. komissiia pri SM TurkmSSR). Ashkhabad: Turkmengosizdat, 1960–3. 4 vols.

Covers material passed 1925–60 and still in force on 1 April 1960. Includes some materials not previously published, but excludes texts of the codes and non-normative acts. Vol. 4 has a supplement listing changes 1960–3 and a full subject index.

U150 *Sbornik deistvuiushchego zakonodatel'stva Turkmenskoi SSR, na 1 mae 1954 g.* [A collection of the legislation of the Turkmenian SSR, in force on 1 May 1954]. Ashkhabad: Turkmengosizdat, 1955. 340 pp.

Includes Turkmenian Council of Ministers ordinances as well as legislative acts. Many documents in extract form. Subject arrangement.

U151 *Sbornik zakonodatel'nykh aktov dlia rabotnikov mestnykh Sovetov i organov upravleniia.* [A collection of legislative acts for officials of local soviets and other authorities]. (M-vo iustitsii TurkmSSR). Ashkhabad: Turkmenistan, 1976. 403 pp.

Earlier ed. publ. 1967 (307 pp.). A selection of current all-union and Turkmenian legislation, regulations, etc. most used in everyday legal work and in local soviets. Subject arrangement.

UKRAINE

U152 *Khronolohichne zibrannia zakoniv, ukaziv Prezydii Verkhovnoi*

Rady, postanov i rasporiadzhen' Uriadu Ukrains'koi RSR. [A chronological collection of laws, edicts of the Supreme Soviet and
government ordinances and decisions of the Ukraine]. Kyiv: Derzh.
vyd. pol. lit-ry, 1963–6. 8 vols.

In Ukrainian. Covers 1917–61; vol. 8 is a very thorough index
volume with alphabetical subject, chronological and systematic
indexes and a list of materials included in vols. 1–7 no longer in force,
as of 1 September 1965. The collection excludes material no longer in
force or of a non-normative character. Where other published
sources are available, full references are given.

U153   *Zbirnyk zakoniv Ukrains'koi RSR i ukaziv Prezydii Verkhovnoi Rady
Ukrains'koi RSR, 1938–1973.* [A collection of the laws of the Ukraine
and edicts of the Supreme Soviet of the Ukraine]. Kyiv: Vyd. pol. lit-
ry Ukrainy, 1974. 2 vols.

In Ukrainian. A systematic collection of laws and edicts currently
in force, with a chronological index in each volume and a subject
index in vol. 2.

UZBEKISTAN

U154   *Sbornik zakonov Uzbekskoi SSR i ukazov Prezidiuma Verkhovnogo
Soveta Uzbekskoi SSR, 1938–1971 gg.* [A collection of the laws of the
Uzbek SSR and edicts of the Presidium of the Uzbek Supreme
Soviet, 1938–1971]. Tashkent: Uzbekistan, 1972. 616 pp.

Earlier eds. covering 1938–55, publ. 1958 (342 pp.) and 1938–64,
publ. 1964 (527 pp.). Exclude the law codes and non-normative
materials. Have chronological and subject indexes.

U155   *Sobranie zakonov, ukazov Prezidiuma Verkhovnogo Soveta i postanovlenii pravitel'stva Uzbekskoi SSR na 1-e ianvaria 1946 g.* [A
collection of laws, edicts of the Presidium of the Supreme Soviet and
government ordinances of the Uzbek SSR, as of 1 January 1946].
Tashkent: Upr. delami SM Uzbekskoi SSR, 1947. 2 vols.

Most of the documents included were in force on 1 January 1946,
but some amendments to 1 January 1947 are also included. Vol. 1
contains edicts, ordinances and laws; vol. 2, the texts of the law codes
of the Uzbek SSR.

Translations

This section includes the most general collections of Soviet legislation in English
translation. Selections and anthologies compiled for student use can be
particularly helpful for other users, as they bring together in one place
legislation, court decisions and other material necessary to understand a
particular area of the law. Very general sources of current official documents in
translation (including party and government documents as well as legislation)
are listed under 'Other general sources of documentation' below.

U156   *Basic laws on the structure of the Soviet state*; trans. and ed. by Harold

J. Berman and John B. Quigley, Jr. Cambridge, Mass.: Harvard University Press, 1969. xviii, 325 pp.

Part I of the collection includes the USSR and RSFSR constitutions, statutes on ministries, on elections to the Supreme Soviet and on its permanent commissions, legislation on local soviets, and the statutes of the Committee on Party-State Control. In part II are laws on the procuracy and the judiciary, military tribunals, comrades' and conciliation courts, administrative commissions, the State Notary and the legal profession. All the material is as of October 1968. The introduction includes useful notes on the translation of legal terminology, territorial subdivisions of the USSR, and sources of documents translated.

U157   *A chronicle of current events.* London: Amnesty International Publications, 1968–. Irregular.

A translation into English of the *Khronika tekushchikh sobytii*, one of the main samizdat journals. The translation also includes endnotes, a table of contents, abbreviations, photographs and a name index. Most of the material in the *Chronicle* is reports on trials, persecution and conditions in prisons and camps. It prints some official documents connected with these cases, and also the texts of some administrative instructions, decrees and orders which were marked as 'for official use' or 'not for publication', or have not been published in a complete form.

U158   *Collected legislation of the Union of Soviet Socialist Republics and the constituent union republics.* Comp., trans. and with introductory materials by W. E. Butler. (Studies of socialist legal systems. Faculty of Laws, University College London). Dobbs Ferry, N.Y.: Oceana, 1979–.

Planned as a comprehensive and up-to-date collection of Soviet legislation, including codes and legislative enactments by the legislature, the councils of ministers, ministries and department and local authorities. Each enactment selected for inclusion is specially translated and is prefaced by a brief legislative history, setting out amendments and giving references to sources of authoritative commentaries on the enactment, where available. The documents are issued in three separate series, one for constitutions, one for all-union materials, and one for union republic materials. The classification scheme in use within the series has been designed to coincide with that employed in the *Svod zakonov* (U118). The collection is being issued in loose-leaf format, and the publishers intend to supply amendment sheets and new legislation regularly to subscribers. Given the wide range of material covered, both in terms of subject and of levels of legislative body, the *Collected legislation* will become the most important English-language source of current legislation.

U159   *Fundamentals of legislation of the USSR and the union republics.* M.: Progress, 1974. 387 pp.

The texts of all the Fundamental Principles passed in 1958–73, including the 1973 Fundamental Principles on education.

U160 Hazard, J. N. *The Soviet legal system: fundamental principles and historical commentary*, by J. N. Hazard, W. E. Butler, P. B. Maggs. 3rd ed. (Parker School studies in foreign and comparative law). Dobbs Ferry, N.Y.: Oceana, 1977. xvii, 621 pp.

1st ed. publ. 1962 (3 vols.), 2nd ed. publ. 1969 (xix, 667 pp.) with title *The Soviet legal system: contemporary documentation and legal commentary.* In each edition, the emphasis is on the contemporary legal system, but includes many older documents necessary for an understanding of the legal system. The documents included are excerpts from Soviet legislation, USSR and RSFSR supreme court decisions, writing by Soviet legal experts, and some party documents. The documents are grouped into chapters (with some variations between the different editions) covering topics such as: constitutional law, state administration, public order, process of law, criminal law, land use, economic planning, cooperatives, economic law, labour law, personal property, inheritance, contracts and torts, social insurance, marriage, the family and the rights of minors. Each chapter has a useful introduction explaining the background of the documents. Each edition has a subject index and lists of documents included. The second edition has a very valuable and exhaustive bibliography of materials on Soviet legal matters in English, which includes many translations into English of individual laws and statutes and other official materials. The third edition has a checklist of Soviet normative acts in force in July 1977 available in English translation, and a bibliography of books and journals in English on the Soviet legal system, with a strong emphasis on postwar publications.

U161 *Papers on Soviet law*; editors: L. Lipson, V. Chalidze. (Institution on Socialist Law). New York, 1977–. Irregular.

Publishes dissident articles on legal questions and translations of legislation relating to dissidents and official efforts to control them. Some of the material included has been officially published, but of particular interest are the translations of articles marked 'Not for publication'.

U162 *The Soviet codes of law*; ed. by William B. Simons. (Law in Eastern Europe, 23). Alphen aan den Rijn: Sijthoff and Noordhoff, 1980. 1288 pp.

Translates the codes of law of the RSFSR and other important basic legislative acts of the RSFSR and those federal codes where there is federal jurisdiction in that field. The contents are: USSR Air Code, RSFSR Criminal and Criminal Procedure codes, RSFSR Corrective Labour Code, RSFSR Law on Court Organization, USSR Customs Code, RSFSR Law on Education, RSFSR Family Code, RSFSR Forestry Code, RSFSR Law on Health Care, RSFSR

Labour Code, RSFSR Land Code, USSR Merchant Shipping Code, RSFSR Code of Mineral Resources, RSFSR Water Code. [Not seen].

U163 *The Soviet legal system: selected contemporary legislation and documents*; comp. and trans. by W. E. Butler. (Parker School studies in foreign and contemporary law). Dobbs Ferry, N.Y.: Oceana, 1978. xiii, 733 pp.

Includes material as of 31 December 1977. Includes the last version of the 1936 constitution of the USSR, the draft and final version of the 1977 USSR constitution and all the Fundamental Principles passed since 1958. There are chapters covering the state system, economic administration, the administration of the law, civil law and procedure, family law, natural resources and conservation, administrative law, legislation on finance, labour, public health, education and religious associations, criminal law and procedure and penology. Includes many of the documents in the third edition of U160. Gives full references to the original Russian sources for all documents. No indexes.

U164 *Soviet statutes and decisions: a journal of translations.* White Plains, N.Y.: M. E. Sharpe, 1964–. Quarterly.

Vols. 1–12, 1964–76, were published by IASP. Each issue of the journal consists of translations of a law code, individual statutes, ordinances, regulations, and other legislative and normative material on a particular topic. It is not a bulletin of new statutes and decisions; an issue may include considerable amounts of older legislation still in force. The sources used include the USSR and RSFSR Supreme Soviet *Vedomosti*, the bulletins of the USSR and RSFSR supreme courts, *Sobranie postanovlenii pravitel'stva SSSR*, *Sbornik instruktivnykh ukazanii Gosarbitrazha*, *Sotsialisticheskaia zakonnost'*, *Sovetskaia iustitsiia*, the newspaper *Izvestiia* and a range of sources for the union republics. Detailed and helpful translators' notes are often included.

U165 Zile, Z. L. *Ideas and forces in Soviet legal history: statutes, decisions and other materials on the development and processes of Soviet law.* 2nd ed., enlarged. Madison: College Printing and Publishing Co., 1970. 456 pp.

1st ed. publ. 1967, 376 pp. A chronological collection of USSR laws, decrees, edicts, court cases, etc., and journal articles by Soviet scholars, illustrating the development of the Soviet legal system. Many documents in extract form.

See also U317.

Legal system

This section brings together materials on the organization of the legal system in the USSR, the ministries of justice, the courts, the procuracy, notaries, the police, the correctional labour system and amnesties. For translations of material in this section, *see* U173 and consult the general collections listed in U156–U165.

General materials on the
legal system and the ministries of justice

When in the 1950s it was decided to transfer many important legislative and other legal powers from the all-union to the union-republic levels, the USSR Ministry of Justice was considered to be superfluous, and it was abolished in 1956. Those of its functions not transferred to the union republics were carried out by the USSR Supreme Court and the newly formed Legal Commission of the USSR Council of Ministers. In 1963, the ministries of justice in the union republics were also abolished. However, in 1970 the USSR Ministry of Justice was revived and with it the ministries of justice of the union republics. The chief responsibilities of the ministries are judicial organization and the systematization of legislation, and the dissemination of legal knowledge to the mass of the population.

U166   'Law reform in the Soviet Union'. *Soviet statutes and decisions*, vol. 12, nos. 1–4, 1975–6.

This volume of *SS&D* (*see* U164) includes in nos. 1–2 general material on law reform, in no. 3 material on systematic collections of laws, and in no. 4 documents relating to the all-union governmental institutions for the preparation and reform of legislation, rules for the drafting of legislation, and material on the reform of economic legislation.

U167   *Sbornik prikazov, instruktsii i ukazanii Ministerstva iustitsii RSFSR.* [A collection of orders, instructions and directives of the RSFSR Ministry of Justice]. Pod obshchei red. Iu. D. Severina. M.: Sov. Rossiia, 1976. 399 pp.

Regulations issued to courts, notaries and registrars on organizational and procedural matters from September 1971 to November 1975.

U168   *Sbornik prikazov i instruktsii Ministerstva iustitsii SSSR, 1936–1948 gg.* [A collection of the orders and instructions of the USSR Ministry of Justice, 1936–1948]. (M-vo iustitsii SSSR. Upr. kodifikatsii i sistematizatsii zakonodatel'stva SSSR). M.: Gosiurizdat, 1949. 435 pp.

Has a full list of all orders and instructions in force as of 1 August 1948 and includes the texts of material in force, with the exclusion of temporary acts, acts on special courts, materials not for publication, sample forms for accounting and notarial work, and material relating to the work of organs of justice in the union republics and lower administrative levels.

U169   *Sbornik prikazov, postanovlenii kollegii, instruktsii i ukazanii Ministerstva iustitsii SSSR.* [A collection of orders, ordinances of the Collegium, instructions and directives of the USSR Ministry of Justice]. (M-vo iustitsii SSSR). M.: Izvestiia, 1976. 807 pp.

A collection of materials from 1970 to 1976 in force on 1 June 1976. Subject arrangement, with some documents in extract form. Includes material relating to organs of justice in the union republics. Chronological index.

U170 *Sotsialisticheskaia zakonnost'; organ Ministerstva iustitsii SSSR, Prokuratury SSSR, Verkhovnogo Suda SSSR.* [Socialist legality: organ of the USSR Ministry of Justice, the USSR Procuracy and the USSR Supreme Court]. M.: Izvestiia, 1934–. Monthly.

Called *Za sotsialisticheskuiu zakonnost'* 1934–5, no. 9. Absorbed *Sovetskaia iustitsiia* July 1941–February 1957; suspended August 1941–December 1943. Monthly 1934–June 1941 and since 1944; fequency varied 1941–2. Some variations in sponsoring bodies. As well as articles on legal matters, includes texts of some laws and ordinances, some Supreme Court rulings, and reports on the work of its sponsoring bodies.

U171 *Sovetskaia iustitsiia; zhurnal Ministerstva iustitsii RSFSR i Verkhovnogo Suda RSFSR.* [Soviet justice: journal of the RSFSR Ministry of Justice and the RSFSR Supreme Court]. M.: Iurid. lit-ra, 1922–. 24 p.a.

1922–9 title was *Ezhenedel'nik sovetskoi iustitsii.* July 1941–February 1957 merged into *Sotsialisticheskaia zakonnost'* (U170). Frequency varied before the war; monthly 1957–9; 18 issues in 1960. Some variations in sponsoring bodies. As well as articles on the interpretation and administration of the law, includes USSR and RSFSR legislative acts relating to the law and its administration, often publishing them before they appear in the official publications. It also sometimes publishes drafts of legislation, reviews of recent legislation, and commentaries on law codes. There are also regular notes summarizing the most important rulings and definitions of the Supreme Court. Annual index.

U172 *Sovetskoe gosudarstvo i pravo.* [Soviet state and law]. (AN SSSR. In-t gosudarstva i prava). M.: Nauka, 1930–April 1941; 1946–. Monthly.

Title varied before the war. Bi-monthly 1933–9, 8 per year 1953–5, 10 issues in 1956. Includes authoritative articles on all aspects of Soviet law and government, and has a useful monthly listing of recent legal literature in the USSR which includes some collections of legislation and law codes.

U173 'Soviet administration of legality'. *Soviet statutes and decisions*, vol. 10, nos. 1–4, 1973–4.

This vol. of *SS&D* (*see* U164) covers in no. 1 the bar and jurisconsults; in no. 2 the jurisconsults and the judiciary; in no. 3 the procuracy, the notariat and arbitrazh; in no. 4, administrative commissions, commissions for minors, commissions to combat drunkenness, comrades' courts, druzhinniki.

U174 *V. I. Lenin, KPSS o sotsialisticheskoi zakonnosti i pravoporiadke*

[V. I. Lenin and the CPSU on socialist legality and legal order]. M.: Politizdat, 1981. 671 pp.

Courts

Until the late 1950s, court organization in the USSR was governed by the 1938 Law on the Judicial Organization of the USSR. New Fundamental Principles on Judicial Organization were enacted on 25 December 1958 and formed the basis for republican laws on judicial organization. On 25 June 1980 the USSR Supreme Soviet made a number of amendments to the 1958 Principles, mainly arising out of the 1977 constitution.

GENERAL

U175 *Ispolnenie sudebnykh reshenii. (Spravochnik po zakonodatel'stvu i sudebnoi praktike)*. [The execution of court decisions: a manual on legislation and court practice]. Pod red. V. A. Boldyreva. (M-vo iustitsii RSFSR). M.: Gosiurizdat, 1959. 407 pp.

USSR and RSFSR laws, court precedents and departmental instructions and guidance on the execution of court judgements, including documentation, procedures, limitation periods, etc. Mainly concerned with the civil law.

U176 *Nauchno-prakticheskii kommentarii k Osnovam zakonodatel'stva o sudoustroistve Soiuza SSR, soiuznykh i avtonomnykh respublik.* [Theoretical and practical commentary on the Fundamental Principles of Legislation on Judicial Organization in the USSR and the union republics]. Pod obshchei red. i s predisl. Iu. A. Kalenova. (Vses. in-t iurid. nauk). M.: Gosiurizdat, 1961. 89 pp.

Commentary on the 1958 Principles.

U177 *Nauchno-prakticheskii kommentarii k Zakonu o sudoustroistve RSFSR*. [Theoretical and practical commentary on the RSFSR Law on Judicial Organization]. Pod red. i s predisl. Iu.A. Kalenova. M.: Gosiurizdat, 1962. 132 pp.

Commentary on the 1960 law.

U178 *Osnovy zakonodatel'stva Soiuza SSR i soiuznyky respublik o sudo-ustroistve v SSSR.* [Fundamental Principles of Legislation on Judicial Organization in the USSR]. M.: Izvestiia, 1980, 15 pp.

The 1980 edition of the Principles.

U179 *Sbornik normativnykh aktov i instruktivnyky materialov, k izucheniiu kursu 'Organizatsiia suda i prokuratury v SSSR'*. [A collection of normative acts and instructions for use during the course on the organization of the courts and the procuracy in the USSR]. Sost.: A. Reigas. (Latv. gos. un-t. Kafedra ugolovnogo prava, ugolovnogo protsessa i kriminalistiki). Riga, 1969, 204 pp.

A collection of 47 all-union and Latvian acts on the legal system, for student use.

U180 *Zakonodatel'stvo o sudoustroistve Soiuza SSR i soiuznykh respublik.*

311

[Legislation on judicial organization of the USSR and the union republics]. (Vazhneishie zakonodatel′nye akty Soiuza SSR i soiuznykh respublik). M.: Gosiurizdat, 1961. 263 pp.

Includes the 1958 Principles and the union republics' codes passed in 1959–61, with the edicts and other legislation concerned with their implementation. Alphabetical subject index.

Supreme courts

The Supreme Court of the USSR is the highest judicial body of the USSR; in addition to hearing appeals against the decisions of other high-ranking courts and the issuing of general instructions on the basis of court practice, it also issues 'leading explanations' designed to help lower courts with the interpretation of detailed points of law. The supreme courts in the union republics try cases of exceptional importance, act as courts of appeal for lower-level courts in the republic, and issue instructions on the interpretation of the republic's legislation. Collections of supreme court decisions dealing with particular areas of the law (civil, criminal, labour) can be found in the sections dealing with those subjects.

USSR

U181　*Biulleten' Verkhovnogo Suda SSSR.* [Bulletin of the Supreme Court of the USSR]. M.: Izvestiia, 1943–. 6 p.a.

1943–56 had title *Sudebnaia praktika Verkhovnogo Suda SSSR.* 6 issues in 1942–3; 10 p.a. in 1944 and 1946; 8 p.a. in 1945 and 1947; 12 p.a. in 1949–52 and 1966; 9 in 1963; 6 p.a. in 1948 and since 1967. This is the official bulletin of the USSR Supreme Court and includes: (a) general reports on the Court's work; (b) rulings on individual cases; (c) 'leading explanations'—reviews of the practice of lower courts in particular areas of the law, with criticisms of their shortcomings and detailed rulings showing how the relevant legal provisions should be interpreted and applied; (d) reports on the work of the supreme courts in the union republics; (e) some amendments to legislation; (f) brief reports on visits to the USSR by foreign legal scholars and visits abroad by Soviet delegations of lawyers. Has regular lists of new books on law, and an annual index of articles, decisions and rulings.

U182　*Sbornik postanovlenii Plenuma Verkhovnogo Suda SSSR, . . .* [A collection of decisions of the Plenum of the USSR Supreme Court in . . .]. M.: Izvestiia Sovetov narodnykh deputatov SSSR.
1924–1951. 1952. 268 pp. With title *Sbornik deistvuiushchikh postanovlenii . . .*
1924–1957. 1958. 279 pp. Title as for 1952 vol.
1958–1960. 1961. 86 pp. Title as for 1952 vol.
1924–1963. 1964. 479 pp.
1924–1970. 1970. 688 pp.
1924–1973. 1974. 758 pp.
1924–1977. 1978. 2 vols.

Collections of Supreme Court 'leading explanations', with those alterations and amendments currently in force. Arranged by branch of the law, with chronological and alphabetical subject indexes.

UNION REPUBLICS

RSFSR

U183 *Biulleten' Verkhovnogo Suda RSFSR.* [Bulletin of the RSFSR Supreme Court]. M., 1961–. Monthly.
6 issues in 1961. Reports on the work of the Supreme Court of the RSFSR, and publishes its decisions and rulings. Annual index.

U184 *Sbornik postanovlenii Plenuma Verkhovnogo Suda RSFSR, 1961–1977.* [A collection of the decisions of the RSFSR Supreme Court Plenum, 1961–1977]. M.: Iurid. lit-ra, 1978. 312 pp.
Earlier eds. publ. 1972 (168 pp.) covered 1961–71 and publ. 1967 (168 pp.) with title *Postanovleniia Plenuma . . .* covered 1961–6. The collections include only decisions currently in force and of general importance, and exclude materials relating to the internal organization of the court. Subject and chronological indexes.

Belorussia

U185 *Postanovleniia Plenuma Verkhovnogo Suda Belorusskoi SSR, 1961–1979 gg.* [Decisions of the Plenum of the Belorussian Supreme Court, 1961–1979]. 2-e izd., s izm. i dop. Minsk: Belarus', 1980. 191 pp.
Details of 1st ed. not known. [Not seen].

Estonia

U186 *Sbornik postanovlenii plenumov Verkhovnogo Suda SSSR i Estonskoi SSR, 1960–1970.* [A collection of the decisions of the plenums of the USSR and Estonian Supreme Courts, 1960–1970]. Tallin: Eesti raamat, 1971. 288 pp.
In Estonian. [Not seen].

Kazakhstan

U187 *Sbornik postanovlenii Plenuma Verkhovnogo Suda Kazakhskoi SSR, 1961–1978 gg.* [A collection of the decisions of the Plenum of the Supreme Court of the Kazakh SSR, 1961–1978]. Alma-Ata: Kazakhstan, 1980. 284 pp.
Earlier ed., covering 1961–8, publ. 1969 (287 pp.). [Not seen].

Latvia

U188 *Latvijas PSR Augstākās tiesas biletins.* [Bulletin of the Supreme Court of the Latvian SSR]. Riga, 1958–. Quarterly.
In Latvian. As well as decisions of the Latvian Supreme Court, includes some materials from the USSR Supreme Court in Latvian translation.

U189 *Latvijas PSR Augstākās tiesas plēnuma lēmuma krājums,*

1960–1972 = *Sbornik postanovlenii Plenuma Verkhovnogo Suda Lat-viiskoi SSR, 1960–1972.* [A collection of the decisions of the Plenum of the Latvian Supreme Court, 1960–1972]. Riga: Zvaigzne, 1973. 351 pp.

Earlier ed. covering 1960–8 publ. 1969 (162 pp.), with Russian text only. The 1973 ed. is in Latvian and Russian and covers all branches of law.

Lithuania

U190   *Sbornik postanovlenii Plenuma Verkhovnogo Suda Litovskoi SSR, 1961–1973 gg.* [A collection of the decisions of the Plenum of the Lithuanian Supreme Court, 1961–1973]. Vilnius, 1973. 310 pp.

In Lithuanian and Russian. [Not seen].

Ukraine

U191   *Zbirnyk postanov Plenumu Verkhovnoho Suda Ukrains'koi RSR (1962–1976 gg.)* [A collection of the decisions of the Plenum of the Supreme Court, 1962–1976. Ed.: A. N. Iakimenko]. Kyiv: Vyd. polit. lit-ry Ukrainy, 1977. 240 pp.

Earlier ed., covering 1961–5 publ. 1966 (128 pp.). In Ukrainian, covering all branches of law, and with a full index.

Comrades' courts

Comrades' courts are simple public hearings at which an accused person is judged before a tribunal of his or her fellow-workers, colleagues or neighbours. They are generally used for offences concerned with moral standards or communal rules rather than formal violations of the law; petty crime; minor violations of labour discipline; and in cases where the people's court has specifically asked the comrades' court to hear a case as being in need of conciliation and advice rather than a full civil suit. The importance given to comrades' courts have varied considerably over the years; under Khrushchev their role was enhanced, and new Regulations on the comrades' courts were passed in the union republics in 1961. Later in the 1960s their role was de-emphasised, but new regulations in 1977 have reasserted their importance.

GENERAL

U192   *Tovarishcheskie sudy: sbornik normativnykh materialov.* [Comrades' courts: a collection of normative materials]. Sost.: E. I. Filippov. M.: Iurid. lit-ra, 1974. 159 pp.

UNION REPUBLICS

RSFSR

U193   Filippov, E. I. *Kommentarii k Polozheniiu o tovarishcheskikh sudakh.* [A commentary on the Regulations on Comrades' Courts]. M.: Iurid. lit-ra, 1972. 135 pp.

Based on the 1961 RSFSR Regulations, as amended in 1965 with commentary based on materials up to 1972. Alphabetical subject index.

U194 Mikhailovskaia, I. B. *Kommentarii k Polozheniiu o tovarishcheskikh sudakh RSFSR*. [Commentary on the RSFSR Regulations on Comrades' Courts]. (Vses. in-t po izucheniiu prichin i razrabotke mer preduprezhdeniia prestupnosti). M.: Iurid. lit-ra, 1968. 183 pp.

The 1961 Regulations, as amended in January 1965, plus short sections on the regulations in each of the other union republics, showing where they differ from the RSFSR's.

Belorussia

U195 *Nauchno-prakticheskii kommentarii k Polozheniiu o tovarishcheskikh sudakh Belorusskoi SSR*. [Theoretical and practical commentary to the Belorussian Regulations on the Comrades' Courts]. Minsk: Belarus', 1980. 96 pp. [Not seen].

Latvia

U196 *Kommentarii k Polozheniiu o tovarishcheskikh sudakh Latviiskoi SSR*. [Commentary to the Latvian Regulations on the Comrades' Courts]. 3 izd., ispr. i dop. Riga: Liesma, 1973. 268 pp.

1st ed. publ. 1965 (165 pp.), 2nd 1968 (250 pp.). On the 1961 Regulations.

Ukraine

U197 *Kommentarii k Polozheniiu o tovarishcheskikh sudakh Ukrainskoi SSR*. [Commentary to the Ukrainian Regulations on the Comrades' Courts]. Kiev: Politizdat Ukrainy, 1978. 59 pp.

On the 1977 Regulations.

Notaries

Notaries in the USSR have three main functions: first, the authentification of contracts and other legal documents; second, dealing with wills and questions of inheritance; third, the provision of certified copies of official documents. Until 1973, the work of the notaries was largely regulated by legislation at union republic level, but on 19 July 1973 the USSR enacted a Law on State Notaries, which brought notarial matters under the ultimate control of the USSR Ministry of Justice. This was followed by new regulations in the union republics.

U198 *Gosudarstvennyi notariat: kommentarii k zakonodatel'stvu*. [The state notary: a commentary on the legislation]. Pod red. N. A. Osetrova. M.: Iurid. lit-ra, 1980. 199 pp.

Includes the 1973 USSR Law, the RSFSR Regulations and materials from the other union republics reflecting the changes of the mid-1970s.

U199 Iudelson, K. S. *Nauchno-prakticheskii kommentarii k Polozheniiu o gosudarstvennom notariate*. [Theoretical and practical commentary to the Regulations on the State Notary]. By K. S. Iudelson, A. K. Kats, M.: Iurid. lit-ra, 1970. 216 pp.

The 1965 Regulations for the RSFSR, with references to other republics' provision where different.

U200   *Notariat: zbirnyk normatyvnykh aktiv i zrazkiv dokumentiv dlia notarial'nykh kontor i vydonkomiv mistsevykh Rad deputativ trudiashchikh.* [Notarial work: a collection of notarial acts and sample forms for notary offices and local soviets]. Vid. red.: D. I. Chorpita. (Verkhovnyi sud URSR). Kyiv: Vyd. pol. lit-ry Ukrainy, 1969. 276 pp.

        Includes all-union and Ukrainian materials.

U201   *Spravochnik gosudarstvennogo notariusa: sbornik ofitsial'nykh materialov.* [Manual for a state notary: a collection of official materials]. Pod red. M. S. Makarova. Izd. 2-e, dop. M.: Iurid. lit-ra, 1972. 624 pp.

        1st ed. publ. 1968 (487 pp.). Includes USSR and RSFSR laws, edicts and ordinances and Supreme Court decisions relating to notarial matters.

U202   *Zakonodatel'stvo o notariate: sbornik ofitsial'nykh materialov.* [Legislation on notarial work: a collection of official materials]. Pod red. I. A. Rykhlova. (M-vo iustitsii RSFSR). M.: Gosiurizdat, 1960. 403 pp.

        Earlier eds. publ. 1940 (76 pp.), 1947 (152 pp.) and 1950 (192 pp.) with title *Notariat: sbornik ofitsial'nykh materialov.* Includes USSR and RSFSR documents relating to the work of public notaries.

Police

The police in the USSR are called the militia; they come under the jurisdiction of the Ministry of Internal Affairs. Their main functions are the maintenance of public order, the fight against crime, and the enforcement of the passport system. They are assisted in their work by volunteers, called druzhinniki (people's guards). Few collections of legislation or current bulletins of legislation appear to be publicly available on police work.

U203   *Druzhinniku: sbornik zakonodatel'nykh i inykh materialov.* [A manual of legal and other materials for the volunteer militia]. M.: Gosiurizdat, 1963. 294 pp.

        Gives the texts of rules and regulations relating to petty crime, hooliganism and drunkenness, and to more serious offences likely to be encountered when keeping order in public places. It is based on RSFSR legislation with cross-references to the relevant statutes of the laws of the other republics where this differs.

U204   *Sovetskaia militsiia: ezhemesiachnyi zhurnal Ministerstva vnutrennykh del SSSR.* [The Soviet militia: a monthly journal of the USSR Ministry of Internal Affairs]. M., 1955–. Monthly.

        Mainly a popular journal for and about the militia, but does include some MVD official materials not readily available elsewhere. Annual index.

Procuracy

The procuracy is responsible for supervising compliance with the law, through the Procurator's Office of the USSR and its organs at union republic and lower administrative levels. It supervises the legality of government acts and activities in general, supervises the observance of legality of court proceedings in civil and criminal cases, inspects places of confinement, and supervises the activities of the militia. Procurators also conduct preliminary investigations into criminal cases and act as prosecutors in the court.

U205a Berezovskaia, S. G. *Prokurorskii nadzor v SSSR: bibliografiia, 1922–1964 gg.* [Procuracy supervision in the USSR: a bibliography, 1922–1964. By] S. G. Berezovskaia [and] V. I. Remnev. (Vses. in-t po izucheniiu prichin i razrabotke mer preduprezhdeniia prestupnosti). M., 1965. 135 pp.

U205b Popova, S. I. *Prokurorskii nadzor v SSSR: bibliografiia, 1965–1970 gg.* [Procuracy supervision in the USSR: a bibliography, 1965–1970. By] S. I. Popova [and] A. P. Safanov. (Vses. in-t po izucheniiu prichin i razrabotke mer preduprezhdeniia prestupnosti). M., 1974. 168 pp.

These two bibliographies list books, articles and dissertations on the procuracy, including official documents relating to its work. Author index.

U206 *Kommentarii k Polozheniiu o prokurorskom nadzore v SSSR.* [Commentary on the Regulations on Procuracy Supervision in the USSR]. Pod red. N. V. Zhogina. (Prokuratura SSSR. Metodicheskii sovet). M.: Iurid. lit-ra, 1968. 233 pp.

Detailed commentary on the 1955 Regulations.

U207 *Sovetskaia prokuratura: sbornik vazhneishikh dokumentov.* [The Soviet procuracy: a collection of major documents]. M.: Iurid. lit-ra, 1972. 408 pp.

Earlier ed. publ. as: *Sovetskaia prokuratura v vazhneishikh dokumentakh.* M.: Gosiurizdat, 1956. 508 pp.; and *Istoriia sovetskoi prokuratury v vazhneishikh dokumentakh.* Pod red. i s predisl. K. A. Mokimeva. M.: Gosiurizdat, 1952. 583 pp. (and an earlier ed. in 1947, 544 pp.). These are all chronological collections of laws, resolutions and other normative material on the history and development of the Soviet procuracy.

U208 *The Soviet procuracy protests, 1937–1973: a collection of translations,* by Leon Boim and Glenn G. Morgan. (Law in Eastern Europe, 21) Alphen aan den Rijn: Sijthoff and Noordhoff, 1978. xvi, 603 pp.

Earlier ed.: *The protests and representations lodged by the Soviet procuracy against the legality of government enactments, 1937–1964,* trans. and introduced by L. Boim, G. Morgan, A. Rudzinski. (Law in Eastern Europe, 13). Leyden: Sijthoff, 1966. 360 pp. Documents from the 1966 ed. are included in the 1978 ed. It is a chronological translation of over 800 cases taken from *Sotsialisticheskaia zakonnost'*, *Radians'ke pravo* and *Sovety deputatov trudiashchikhsia* showing the procuracy's role as investigator of complaints and supervisor of the administration of the law. There is an index of legal citations and a subject index.

Corrective labour

Until the late 1960s, Soviet penitentiary institutions and regulations controlling punishment through corrective labour without deprivation of freedom were governed by the 1933 Corrective Labour Code of the RSFSR and similar codes passed by some of the other republics. On 11 July 1969 the USSR Supreme Soviet enacted new Fundamental Principles of Corrective Labour Legislation, which were followed in 1970–2 by the passing of new codes in all the union republics.

GENERAL COLLECTIONS

U209   *Kommentarii k Osnovam ispravitel'no-trudovogo zakonodatel'stva Soiuza SSR i soiuznykh respublik.* [Commentary on the Fundamental Principles of Corrective Labour Legislation of the USSR and the Union Republics]. Pod red. N. A. Struchkova, V. A. Kirina. M.: Iurid. lit-ra, 1972. 183 pp.
   Commentary on the 1969 Principles.

U210   *Osnovy ispravitel'no-trudovogo zakonodatel'stva Soiuza SSR i soiuz- nykh respublik.* [Fundamental Principles of Corrective Labour Legislation of the USSR and the Union Republics]. M.: Iurid. lit-ra, 1970. 39 pp.
   The 1969 Principles.

U211   *Sbornik normativnykh aktov po sovetskomu ispravitel'no-trudovomu pravu.* [A collection of normative acts on Soviet corrective labour law]. (VIuZI). M., 1976. 105 pp.
   A collection of 40 documents, mainly of recent legislation, for the use of correspondence students.

U212   *Sbornik normativnykh aktov po sovetskomu ispravitel'no-trudovomu pravu (1917–1959 gg.): istoriia zakonodatel'stva.* [A collection of normative acts on Soviet correctional labour law history, 1917–1959]. Sost.: P. M. Losev, G. I. Ragulin. M.: Gosiurizdat, 1959. 360 pp.
   A collection of 133 documents, mainly from the prewar period but still in force in the 1940s and 1950s in many cases. Includes all-union and RSFSR materials only. Subject index.

U213   *Sbornik normativnykh aktov i materialov sudebnoi praktiki po vo- prosam opredeleniia vida ispravitel'no-trudovogo uchrezhdeniia litsam, osuzhdennym k lisheniiu svobody.* [A collection of normative acts and court practice on the type of corrective labour institution suitable for criminals sentenced to deprivation of liberty]. (Vysshaia shkola MOOP RSFSR). M., 1966. 61 pp. [Not seen].

U214 *Sovetskoe ispravitel'no-trudovoe zakonodatel'stvo: sistematizirovan-nyi tekst Osnov ispravitel'no-trudovogo zakonodatel'stva SSSR i soiuznykh respublik i ispravitel'no-trudovykh kodeksov soiuznykh respublik. Posobie.* [A systematized text of the Principles of Corrective Labour Legislation and the corrective labour codes of the union republics]. Sost.: L. G. Krakhmal'nik, N. A. Struchkov. (VNII MVD SSSR). M., 1979. 95 pp.

Presumably a comparison of the 1969 Principles and the 1970–2 codes. [Not seen].

CODES

All the codes listed are the new codes based on the 1969 Principles.

RSFSR

U215a *Ispravitel'no-trudovoi kodeks RSFSR: ofitsial'nyi tekst.* M.: Iurid. lit-ra, 1972. 64 pp.

U215b ... *s izm. i dop. na 15 marta 1977 g., s pril. postateino-sist. materialov.* 1977. 88 pp.

See also U392.

Commentaries

U216a *Kommentarii k Ispravitel'no-trudovomu kodeksu RSFSR.* Pod red. V. M. Blinova. M.: Iurid. lit-ra, 1973. 279 pp.

U216b ... pod red. i s predisl. N. P. Mal'shakova. Izd. 2-e, perer. i dop. 1979. 263 pp.

Armenia

U217 *Ispravitel'no-trudovoi kodeks Armianskoi SSR.* Erevan, 1971. 96 pp. [Also publ. in Armenian].

Azerbaijan

U218 *Ispravitel'no-trudovoi kodeks Azerbaidzhanskoi SSR.* Baku: Azer-nesher, 1971. 140 pp.

Belorussia

U219a *Ispravitel'no-trudovoi kodeks Belorusskoi SSR.* Minsk: Belarus', 1971. 152 pp. [In Russian and Belorussian].

U219b ... *s izm. i dop. na 1 maia 1977 g.* 1977. 127 pp.

Commentary

U220 *Kommentarii k Ispravitel'no-trudovomu kodeksu Belorusskoi SSR.* Pod red. L. V. Bagrii-Shakhmanova. Minsk: Izd-vo BGU, 1974. 304 pp.

Estonia

U221a *Ispravitel'no-trudovoi kodeks Estonskoi SSR.* Tallin: Eesti raamat, 1970. 131 pp. [Also publ. in Estonian].

U221b ... *s izm. i dop. na 1 oktiabria 1973 g.* 1974. 131 pp.

U221c ... *na 1 dekabria 1973 g.* 1974. 112 pp. [In Estonian].

Georgia

U222 *Ispravitel'no-trudovoi kodeks Gruzinskoi SSR.* Tbilisi: Sabchota Sakartvelo, 1972. 115 pp. [Also publ. in Georgian].

Kazakhstan

U223 *Ispravitel'no-trudovoi kodeks Kazakhskoi SSR.* Alma-Ata: Kazakhstan, 1972. 242 pp. [In Kazakh and Russian].

Kirghizia

U224 *Kyrgyz SSRinin tuzotuu-emgek kodeksi = Ispravitel'no-trudovoi kodeks Kirgizskoi SSR.* Frunze, 1971. 242 pp. [In Kirghiz and Russian].

Latvia

U225 *Ispravitel'no-trudovoi kodeks Latviiskoi SSR.* Riga: Liesma, 1971. 151 pp. [Also publ. in Latvian].

Lithuania

U226 *Ispravitel'no-trudovoi kodeks Litovskoi SSR.* Vilnius: Mintis, 1972. 135 pp. [Also publ. in Lithuanian].

Moldavia

U227 *Kodul de korektare prin munke al RSS Moldovenesht' = Ispravitel'no-trudovoi kodeks Moldavskoi SSR.* Kishinev: Kartia Moldoveniaske, 1972. 219 pp. [In Moldavian and Russian].

Tajikistan

U228 *Ispravitel'no-trudovoi kodeks Tadzhikskoi SSR.* Dushanbe: Irfon, 1971. 108 pp. [Also publ. in Tajik].

Turkmenistan

U229 *Ispravitel'no-trudovoi kodeks Turkmenskoi SSR.* Ashkhabad: Turkmenistan, 1972. 84 pp.

Ukraine

U230 *Ispravitel'no-trudovoi kodeks Ukrainskoi SSR.* Kiev: Politizdat Ukrainy, 1972. 90 pp. [Also publ. in Ukrainian].

Uzbekistan

U231 *Ispravitel'no-trudovoi kodeks Uzbekskoi SSR.* Tashkent: Uzbekistan, 1970. 51 pp. [Also publ. in Uzbek].

Commentary

U232 *Kommentarii k Ispravitel'no-trudovomu kodeksu Uzbekskoi SSR.* Pod red. i s predisl. M. S. Vasikovoi. Tashkent: Uzbekistan, 1977. 288 pp.

Amnesties

U233 Romashkin, P. S. *Amnistiia i pomilovaniia v SSSR.* [Amnesties and pardons in the USSR]. M.: Gosiurizdat, 1959. 364 pp.

A long introduction on amnesty and pardons in the USSR is followed by 277 official documents or extracts from documents on the subject, some not previously published. There is also an extensive bibliography of Soviet writings on the subject.

Citizenship

U234 'Soviet citizenship law'. *Soviet statutes and decisions*, vol. 7, nos. 1–4, 1970–1.

This volume of *SS&D* (*see* U164) covers all-union and union republic normative acts and international treaties, agreements and diplomatic correspondence on citizenship, 1917–70.

U235 *Zakonodatel'stvo SSSR i mezhdunarodyne soglasheniia po voprosam grazhdanstva.* [USSR legislation and international agreements on citizenship]. Sost.: G. E. Volkov. M.: Mezhdunarodnye otnosheniia, 1964. 179 pp.

Consists of 104 documents drawn from all-union and union republic constitutions, family codes and other normative acts on citizenship. Includes clauses on citizenship from bilateral and multilateral agreements to which the USSR is a signatory.

See also U879a–c.

Civil law and law of civil procedure

The RSFSR Civil Code of 1922 was the basis of civil legislation in the USSR until the early 1960s. Codes based on the Russian model were enacted in the Ukraine, Belorussia, Armenia, Azerbaijan and Georgia; Turkmenistan, Uzbekistan, Kazakhstan, Kirghizia and the Baltic States adopted the RSFSR Code. When the Moldavian SSR was set up, it adopted the Ukrainian Code, and the Tajik SSR adopted the Uzbek Code. Over the years, considerable differences developed between the codes of the union republics, even those which had adopted the RSFSR Code. The Fundamental Principles of Civil Legislation of the USSR and Union Republics were enacted on 8 December 1961 and came into force on 1 May 1962; new republican civil codes were enacted in 1964–5. The law of civil procedure was largely based on the RSFSR Code of 1923, which was adopted by Kazakhstan, Kirghizia and the Baltic republics; the other republics had their own codes, although Moldavia used the Ukraine's Code and Tajikistan that of Uzbekistan. The Fundamental Principles of Civil Procedure were also enacted on 8 December 1961 and were followed by new codes of civil procedure in the union republics.

Bibliographies

U236 *Sovetskoe grazhdanskoe pravo. Sovetskoe semeinoe pravo. Bibliografiia, 1917–1960.* [Soviet civil law. Soviet family law. A bibliography, 1917–1960]. M.: Gosiurizdat, 1962. 664 pp.

Includes material in Russian and the languages of the union republics, and covers draft legal codes, legal codes, individual legislative acts and collections of material, as well as books, articles and dissertations. Excludes popular works. Has separate sections on family law and civil law. Full name index.

Collections of material on civil law and civil procedure

U237 *Grazhdanskii protsess. Sbornik normativnykh materialov.* [Civil procedure: a collection of normative acts]. Sost.: L. I. Gaziiants. (M-vo vysshego i srednego spetsial'nogo obrazovaniia. Vses. iurid. zaochnyi in-t). M., 1960. 250 pp.

A collection for correspondence-course students, made up of extracts from legal material, Supreme Court decisions, etc.

U238 *Grazhdanskoe protsessual'noe zakonodatel'stvo SSSR i soiuznykh respublik.* [Codes of civil procedure of the USSR and the union republics]. Otv. red.: V. P. Chapurskii. M.: Gosiurizdat, 1957. 539 pp.

Includes the civil procedure codes of the RSFSR, Ukraine, Belorussia, Uzbekistan, Georgia, Azerbaijan, Tajikistan, Armenia and Turkmenistan, as of 1 January 1957, plus all-union civil procedure legislation. There are cross-reference tables, giving page references to the all-union materials included in the collection and to the relevant articles of union republics' codes. This is the most complete collection of these codes before the reforms of the early 1960s.

U239 *Grazhdanskoe zakonodatel'stvo: sbornik normativnykh aktov.* [Civil law: a collection of normative acts]. M.: Iurid. lit-ra, 1974. 1088 pp.

A very full collection of normative acts on all aspects of civil law, including Supreme Court rulings and guidance. Some documents are reproduced in extract form; in many cases reference is made to other published sources and the text is not reproduced at all. Alphabetical subject index.

U240 *Grazhdanskoe zakonodatel'stvo SSSR i soiuznykh respublik.* [Civil law of the USSR and the union republics]. Red.: I. Novitskii. M.: Gosiurizdat, 1957. 779 pp.

Section 1 covers all-union civil law, excluding family and transport law, and has its own chronological and subject index. Section 2 comprises the civil codes of the RSFSR (with other normative materials supplementing the code), the Ukraine, Belorussia, Uzbekistan, Georgia, Azerbaijan, Tajikistan, Armenia and Turkmenistan. The codes are followed by a supplement giving ministry and state committee orders, and decisions of the Supreme Court and the State Arbitration Court on civil law matters. There are cross-reference tables, giving page references to the all-union materials and to the relevant articles of the union republics' codes. Materials included were in force on 1 January 1957. Although the collection is not exhaustive, it is the most complete collection of such materials before the reforms of the early 1960s.

U241   *Istochniki sovetskogo grazhdanskogo prava (sbornik).* [Sources of Soviet civil law: a collection]. Sost.: A. V. Dozortsev. M.: Gosiurizdat, 1961. 939 pp.

A collection of normative acts for student use, with many documents in extract form or simply referred to by title with indication of a published source. Mainly relates to property relations under civil law; includes some Supreme Court and Arbitration Court materials.

U242   *Nauchno-prakticheskii kommentarii k Osnovam grazhdanskogo sudoproizvodstva Soiuza SSR i soiuznykh respublik.* [Theoretical and practical commentary to the Fundamental Principles of Civil Procedure of the USSR and the Union Republics]. Pod red. P. I. Bardina. M.: Gosiurizdat, 1962. 230 pp.

Detailed commentary and text of the 1961 Fundamental Principles, as of April 1962.

U243   *Nauchno-prakticheskii kommentarii k Osnovam grazhdanskogo zakonodatel'stva Soiuza SSR i soiuznykh respublik.* [Theoretical and practical commentary on the Fundamental Principles of Civil Legislation of the USSR and the Union Republics]. Pod red. S. N. Bratusia, E. A. Fleishits. M.: Gosiurizdat, 1962. 419 pp.

Detailed commentary and text of the 1961 Principles, as of April 1962.

U244   *Normativnye materialy po sovetskomu grazhdanskomu pravu (sbornik).* [A collection of normative materials on Soviet civil law]. Sost.: A.Iu. Kabalkin. M.: Iurid. lit-ra, 1965. 616 pp.

A collection for student use, with many documents in extract form. All documents included or cited have full references to official sources.

U245   *Rassmotrenie grazhdanskikh del v sude. Zakonodatel'stvo i sudebnaia praktika po otdel'nym kategoriiam grazhdanskikh del.* [Hearings of civil cases in court: legislation and court practice in different categories of civil cases]. Pod red. V. A. Boldyreva. M.: Gosiurizdat, 1962. 484 pp.

A manual for court officials and lawyers.

U246   *Sbornik grazhdanskopravovykh i protsessual'nykh dokumentov.* [A collection of civil law and civil procedure documents]. M.: Gosiurizdat, 1961. 278 pp.

A collection of official forms and model documents most often needed in civil law, including registration of civil status, contracts and wills, and in the conduct of civil law cases.

U247   *Sbornik normativnykh aktov po grazhdanskomu protsessu.* [A collection of normative acts on civil procedure]. Sost.: S. N. Burova [et al.] pod red. N. G. Iurkevicha. Minsk: Vysheishaia shkola, 1978. 352 pp. [Not seen].

U248   *Sbornik normativnykh aktov po sovetskomu grazhdanskomu pravu.* [A collection of normative acts on Soviet civil law]. Sost.: V. F. Chigir. Minsk: Izd-vo BGU, 1972–4. 2 vols.

USSR and Belorussian materials as of 1 July 1972 (part 1) and 1 July 1973 (part 2), for economics and law students. Some documents are given in extract or as references to a published source. Subject index in each volume.

U249   *Sbornik postanovlenii i opredelenii Sudebnoi kollegii po grazhdanskim delam Verkhovnogo suda RSFSR, 1957–1958 gg.* [A collection of decisions and instructions of the Collegium on civil matters of the RSFSR Supreme Court, 1957–1958]. Pod red. A. T. Rubicheva. M.: Gosiurizdat, 1960. 223 pp.

A collection of decisions in individual civil law cases.

U250   *Sbornik postanovlenii Plenuma i opredelenii Sudebnoi kollegii po grazhdanskim delam Verkhovnogo Suda SSSR, 1962–1978 gg.* [A collection of the decisions of the Plenum and instructions of the Collegium on civil matters of the USSR Supreme Court, 1962–1978]. Pod red. S. I. Guseva. M.: Iurid. lit-ra, 1980. 464 pp.

A collection based on the new legislation passed after the 1961 Principles and the 1968 Principles on family law, including some decisions and instructions from the union republics. Indexed.

U251   *Sopostavitel'naia tablitsa statei grazhdanskikh protsessual'nykh kodeksov soiuznykh respublik.* [A comparative table of the articles of the civil procedure codes of the union republics]. Sost.: N. B. Svirskaia, V. V. Karganova, pod red. D. S. Kareva. (M-vo iustitsii SSSR. Upr. kodifikatsii i sistematizatsii zakonodatel'stva SSSR). M.: Gosiurizdat, 1953. 246 pp.

The table cites each article of the RSFSR's civil procedure code, and shows the corresponding article in the codes of the Ukraine, Belorussia, Azerbaijan, Georgia, Armenia, Turkmenistan, Uzbekistan and Tajikistan. A supplement gives the full text of those articles which differ from the RSFSR's provisions; Armenia's code is excluded as the compilers did not have access to a Russian translation of it.

U252   *Voprosy nasledovaniia (spravochnik po zakonodatel'stvu i sudebnoi praktike).* [A manual of legislation and court practice on inheritance]. Pod red. V. A. Boldyreva. M.: Gosiurizdat, 1959. 150 pp.

A selection of USSR and RSFSR normative acts and court rulings, intended for legal officials.

Civil codes

RSFSR

Old

U253   *Grazhdanskii kodeks RSFSR, s izm. i dop. na 1 sentiabria 1947g.* M.:

Iurizdat, 1948. 255 pp. [Republished with revisions at intervals up to 1961].

New

U254a *Grazhdanskii kodeks RSFSR; ofitsial'nyi tekst.* M.: Iurid. lit-ra, 1964. 299 pp.

U254b *Grazhdanskii kodeks RSFSR. Grazhdansko-protsessual'nyi kodeks RSFSR.* M.: Iurid. lit-ra, 1965. 504 pp.

U254c *Grazhdanskii kodeks RSFSR; ofitsial'nyi tekst s pril. postateino-sist. materialov.* M.: Iurid. lit-ra, 1968. 272 pp.

U254d *..., s izm. i dop. na 1 fevralia 1972 g. i s pril. postateino-sist. materialov.* M.: Iurid. lit-ra, 1972. 280 pp.

U254e *... na 1 dekabria 1975 g.* 1976. 295 pp.

U254f *Grazhdanskii kodeks RSFSR. Grazhdansko-protsessual'nyi kodeks RSFSR. Kodeks o brake i sem'e RSFSR.* 1979. 272 pp.

Commentaries

U255a *Nauchno-prakticheskii kommentarii k GK RSFSR,* pod red. E. A. Fleishits. M.: Iurid. lit-ra, 1966. 640 pp.

U255b *Kommentarii k Grazhdanskomu kodeksu RSFSR,* pod red. E. A. Fleishits i O. S. Ioffe. 2-e izd, dop. i perer. M.: Iurid. lit-ra, 1970. 823 pp.

ARMENIA

Old

U256 *Grazhdanskii kodeks Armianskoi SSR, s izm. i dop. na 1 sentiabria 1951 g.* Erevan: Armgiz, 1951, 190 pp. [In Armenian].

New

U257a *Grazhdanskii kodeks Armianskoi SSR.* Erevan: Aiastan, 1964. 295 pp. [Also publ. in Armenian].

U257b *..., s izm. i dop. na 1 iiunia 1977 g.* 1977. 278 pp. [In Armenian].

AZERBAIJAN

Old

U258 *Grazhdanskii kodeks Azerbaidzhanskoi SSR, s izm. i dop. na 1 ianvaria 1956 g.* Baku: Azernesher, 1956. 211 pp. [Also publ. in Azerbaijani].

New

U259a *Grazhdanskii kodeks Azerbaidzhanskoi SSR.* Baku: Izd. Verkhovnogo Soveta AzSSR, 1964. 296 pp. [Also publ. in Azerbaijani].

U259b *Grazhdanskii kodeks Azerbaidzhanskoi SSR, s izm. i dop. na 1 ianvaria 1976 g.* Baku: Azerbaidzhanskoe gosizdat, 1976. 203 pp. [Also publ. in Azerbaijani].

BELORUSSIA

Old

U260 *Grazhdanskii kodeks Belorusskoi SSR, s izm. i dop. na 1 ianvaria 1951 g.* Minsk: AN BSSR, 1951. 192 pp.

New

U261 *Grazhdanskii kodeks Belorusskoi SSR.* Minsk: Belarus', 1965. 440 pp. [In Russian and Belorussian].

Commentary

U262 *Nauchno-prakticheskii kommentarii k Grazhdanskomu kodeksu Belorusskoi SSR,* pod red. F. I. Gabze i V. F. Chigira. Minsk: Izd-vo BGU, 1972. 408 pp.

ESTONIA

Old

U263 *Grazhdanskii kodeks, deistvuiushchii na territorii Estonskoi SSR; ofitsial'nyi tekst s izm. na 1 ianvaria 1952 g., s pril. postateino-sist. materialov.* Tallin: Estgosizdat, 1952. 278 pp. [In Estonian].

New

U264a *Grazhdanskii kodeks Estonskoi SSR.* Tallin: Estgosizdat, 1964. 303 pp. [Also publ. in Estonian].

U264b *..., s izm. i dop. na 1 marta 1973 g.* Tallin: Eesti raamat, 1973. 303 pp. [Also publ. in Estonian].

U264c *... na 1 iiunia 1976 g.* 1976. 278 pp. [Also publ. in Estonian].

Commentary

U265 *Grazhdanskii kodeks Estonskoi SSR: kommentirovannoe izdanie.* Tallin: Eesti raamat, 1969, 608 pp. [In Estonian].

GEORGIA

Old

U266a *Grazhdanskii kodeks Gruzinskoi SSR, s izm. i dop. po 31 dekabria 1954 g.* Tbilisi: Gosizdat GruzSSR, 1955. 320 pp. [In Georgian].

U266b *... 1 maia 1958 g.* Tbilisi: Sabchota Sakartvelo, 1958. 232 pp.

New

U267 *Grazhdanskii kodeks Gruzinski SSR.* Tbilisi: Sabchota Sakartvelo, 1965. 379 pp. [Also publ. in Georgian].

KAZAKHSTAN

New

U268a *Grazhdanskii kodeks Kazakhskoi SSR.* Alma-Ata: Kazakhskoe gos. izd-vo, 1964. 319 pp. [Also publ. in Kazakh].

U268b *..., s izm. i dop. na 1 ianv. 1975 g.* 1975. 273 pp. [Also publ. in Kazakh].

Commentary

U269 *Kommentarii k Grazhdanskomu kodeksu Kazakhskoi SSR.* Pod red. M. A. Vaksberga, Iu. G. Basina, B. V. Pokrovskogo. Alma-Ata: Kazakhstan, 1965. 630 pp.

KIRGHIZIA

New

U270a *Kyrgyz SSRinin grazhdanyk kodeksi = Grazhdanskii kodeks Kirgiz-skoi SSR.* Frunze: Kyrgyzstan, 1964. 460 pp. [In Kirghiz and Russian].

U270b *..., s izm. i dop. na 1 ianvaria 1972 g.* 1972. 461 pp. [In Kirghiz and Russian].

LATVIA

Old

U271 *Grazhdanskii kodeks RSFSR, deistvuiushchii na territorii Latviiskoi SSR.* Riga: Latvgosizdat, 1951. 220 pp. [In Latvian].

New

U272a *Grazhdanskii kodeks Latviiskoi SSR.* Riga: Latvgosizdat, 1964. 314 pp. [Also publ. in Latvian].

U272b *Grazhdanskii kodeks Latviiskoi SSR; ofitsial'nyi tekst s pril. postateino-sist. materialov.* Riga: Liesma, 1974. 607 pp. [Also publ. in Latvian].

Commentary

U273 *Kommentarii k Grazhdanskomu kodeksu Latviiskoi SSR,* pod red. Ia. Vebersa. Riga: Liesma, 1979. 763 pp. [In Latvian].

LITHUANIA

Old

U274 *Grazhdanskii kodeks RSFSR, deistvuiushchii na territorii Litovskoi SSR; ofitsial'nyi tekst s izmeneniiami na 1 ianvaria 1954 g. i s prilozheniem postateino-sist. materialov.* Vilnius: Gospolitnauchizdat, 1954, 256 pp. [In Lithuanian].

New

U275a *Grazhdanskii kodeks Litovskoi SSR.* Vilnius: Mintis, 1964. 403 pp. [Also publ. in Lithuanian].

U275b *...; ofitsial'nyi tekst s izm. i dop. na 1 ianvaria 1968 g. i s pril. postateino-sist. materialov.* Vilnius: Mintis, 1968. 602 pp. [In Lithuanian].

U275c *... na 1 dekabria 1972 g ...* 1973. 623 pp.

Commentary

U276 *Kommentarii k Grazhdanskomu kodeksu Litovskoi SSR.* Vilnius: Mintis, 1976. 422 pp. [In Lithuanian].

MOLDAVIA

Old

U277 *Grazhdanskii kodeks USSR. Primeniaetsia na territorii Moldavskoi SSR ...; ofitsial'nyi tekst s izm. na 14 dekabria 1940 i s pril. postateino-sist. materialov.* M.: Iurizdat, 1941. 296 pp.

New
U278 *Grazhdanskii kodeks Moldavskoi SSR.* Kishinev: Partizdat, 1965.
248 pp. [Also publ. in Moldavian].

Commentary
U279 *Kommentarii k Grazhdanskomu kodeksu Moldavskoi SSR.* Kishinev:
Kartia Moldoveniaske, 1971. 533 pp.

TAJIKISTAN

Old
U280 *Grazhdanskii kodeks Tadzhikskoi SSR. S izm. i dop. na 1 aprelia 1939
g.* M.: Iurizdat, 1939. 171 pp.

New
U281a *Grazhdanskii kodeks Tadzhikskoi SSR.* Dushanbe: Irfon, 1964. 199
pp. [Also publ. in Tajik].
U281b ... 1975. 255 pp. [Also publ. in Tajik].

TURKMENISTAN

Old
U282a *Grazhdanskii kodeks Turkmenskoi SSR. S izm. i dop. na 15 fevralia
1938 g.* Ashkhabad: Turkmengosizdat, 1938. 98 pp.
U282b *... na 1 ianvaria 1957 g. i s postateinymi materialami.* 1957. 258 pp.

New
U283 *Grazhdanskii kodeks Turkmenskoi SSR.* Ashkhabad: Turkmenistan,
1964. 340 pp. [Also publ. in Turkmenian].

UKRAINE

Old
U284 *Grazhdanskii kodeks Ukrainskoi SSR, s izm. i dop. na 1 iiulia 1945 g.*
Kiev, Khar'kov: Gosizdat USSR, 1945, 238 pp. [In Ukrainian].
[Republished with amendments at intervals up to 1958].

New
U285a *Tsyvil'nyi kodeks Ukrains'koi RSR.* Kyiv: Derzh. vyd. polit. lit-ry
URSR, 1963. 213 pp. [In Ukrainian].
U285b *Grazhdanskii kodeks Ukrainskoi SSR.* Kiev: Gospolitizdat Ukrainy,
1964. 226 pp.
U285c *..., ofitsial'nyi tekst s izm. i dop. na 5 iiunia 1973 g. a takzhe s
postateinymi materialami i prilozheniem.* Kiev: Politizdat Ukrainy,
1973. 438 pp.

Commentary
U286 *Tsyvil'nyi kodeks Ukrains'koi RSR: naukovo-praktychnyi komentarii;*
pod red. O. N. Iakimenka. Kiev: Vyd. polit. lit-ry URSR, 1971. 542
pp. [In Ukrainian].

UZBEKISTAN

Old

U287a *Grazhdanskii kodeks Uzbekskoi SSR, s izm. i dop. na 1 ianvaria 1946 g.* Tashkent: Upr. delami Soveta Ministrov UzSSR, 1946. 82 pp.

U287b ... *na 1 ianvaria 1953 g.* 1953. 127 pp.

New

U288a *Grazhdanskii kodeks Uzbekskoi SSR.* Tashkent: Uzgosizdat, 1963. 243 pp. [Also publ. in Uzbek].

U288b ..., *s izm. i dop. na 1 ianvaria 1974.* 1974. 251 pp.

U288c ... 1975. 278 pp. [In Uzbek].

Commentary

U289 *Kommentarii k Grazhdanskomu kodeksu Uzbekskoi SSR.* Tashkent: Uzbekistan, 1976. 2 vols. [In Uzbek].

Civil procedure codes

RSFSR

Old

U290 *Grazhdanskii protsessual'nyi kodeks RSFSR; ofitsial'nyi tekst s izm. na 1 sentiabria 1947 g. i s pril. postateino-sist. materialov.* M.: Gosiurizdat, 1948. 326 pp. [Republished with revisions at intervals up to 1961].

New

U291a *Grazhdanskii protsessual'nyi kodeks RSFSR; ofitsial'nyi tekst.* M.: Iurid. lit-ra, 1964. 255 pp.

U291b ... *s pril. postateino-sist. materialov.* 1968. 231 pp.

U291c ..., *s izm. i dop. na 20 dekabria 1974 g. i s pril. postateino-sist. materialov.* M.: Iurid. lit-ra, 1975. 310 pp.

See also U254b, U254f.

Commentaries

U292a *Nauchno-prakticheskii kommentarii k GPK RSFSR*, pod red. R. F. Kalistratova i V. K. Puchinskogo. M.: Iurid. lit-ra, 1965. 512 pp.

U292b *Postateino-prakticheskii kommentarii k Grazhdanskomu protsessual'nomu kodeksu RSFSR*, sost.: S. S. Kipnis, P. Ia. Trubnikov, M.: Iurid. lit-ra, 1971. 568 pp.

U292c *Kommentarii k Grazhdanskomu protsessual'nomu kodeksu RSFSR.* M.: Iurid. lit-ra, 1976. 600 pp.

ARMENIA

New

U293a *Grazhdanskii protsessual'nyi kodeks Armianskoi SSR.* Erevan: Aiastan, 1964. 247 pp. [Also publ. in Armenian].

U293b ..., *s izm. i dop. na 1-e noiabria 1977 g.* 1978. 204 pp. [In Armenian].

AZERBAIJAN

Old

U294 *Grazhdanskii protsessual'nyi kodeks Azerbaidzhanskoi SSR; ofitsial'nyi tekst s izm. i dop. na 1 ianv. 1956g.* Baku: Az. gos. izd-vo, 1956. 147 pp. [Also publ. in Azerbaijani].

New

U295a *Grazhdanskii protsessual'nyi kodeks Azerbaidzhanskoi SSR.* Baku: Izd-vo Verkhovnogo Soveta AzSSR, 1964. 258 pp. [Also publ. in Azerbaijani].

U295b *... s izm. i dop. na 1 ianvaria 1976 g.* Baku: Azgosizdat 1977. 190 pp. [Also publ. in Azerbaijani].

BELORUSSIA

New

U296a *Grazhdanskii protsessual'nyi kodeks Belorusskoi SSR.* Minsk: Belarus', 1965. 359 pp. [Also publ. in Belorussian].

U296b *... ofitsial'nyi tekst s izm. i dop. na 1 ianvaria 1973 g. i s pril. postateino-sist. materialov.* Minsk: Belarus', 1973. 238 pp.

ESTONIA

New

U297a *Grazhdanskii protsessual'nyi kodeks Estonskoi SSR.* Tallin: Eesti raamat, 1964. 254 pp. [Also publ. in Estonian].

U297b *... na 1 iiulia 1976 g.* 1977. 230 pp. [In Estonian].

GEORGIA

Old

U298 *Grazhdanskii protsessual'nyi kodeks; ofitsial'nyi tekst s izm. na 1 sentiabria 1957 g.* Tbilisi: Sabchota Sakartvelo, 1958. 235 pp.

New

U299 *Grazhdanskii protsessual'nyi kodeks Gruzinskoi SSR.* Tbilisi: Sabchota Sakartvelo, 1965. 320 pp. [Also publ. in Georgian].

KAZAKHSTAN

New

U300a *Grazhdanskii protsessual'nyi kodeks Kazakhskoi SSR.* Alma-Ata: Kazgosizdat, 1964. 272 pp. [Also publ. in Kazakh].

U300b *... s izm. i dop. na 1 noiabria 1975 g.* Alma-Ata: Kazakhstan, 1977. 222 pp.

Commentary

U301 *Nauchno-prakticheskii kommentarii k GPK Kazakhskoi SSR,* pod. red Z. K. Abdullinoi, V. A. Zinchenko, R. S. Tazutdinova. Alma-Ata: Kazakhstan, 1976. 543 pp.

KIRGHIZIA

New
U302a *Kyrgyz SSRinin grazhdanyk-protsessualdyk kodeksi=Grazhdanskii protsessual'nyi kodeks Kirgizskoi SSR.* Frunze: Kyrgyzstan, 1964. 422 pp. [In Kirghiz and Russian].
U302b *... Izd. 2-e, s izm. i dop. na 1 ianvaria 1972 g.* Frunze: Kyrgyzstan, 1972. 402 pp. [In Kirghiz and Russian].

LATVIA

New
U303 *Grazhdanskii protsessual'nyi kodeks Latviiskoi SSR.* Riga: Latvgosizdat, 1964. 264 pp. [Also publ. in Latvian].

LITHUANIA

New
U304a *Grazhdanskii protsessual'nyi kodeks Litovskoi SSR.* Vilnius: Mintis, 1964. 371 pp. [Also publ. in Lithuanian].
U304b *... ofitsial'nyi tekst s izm. i dop. na 1 avgusta 1974 g. i s pril. postateinosist. materialov.* Vilnius: Mintis, 1975. 550 pp.

Commentary
U305 *Kommentarii k Grazhdanskomu protsessual'nomu kodeksu Litovskoi SSR.* Vilnius: Mintis, 1980. 400 pp. [In Lithuanian].

MOLDAVIA

New
U306a *Grazhdanskii protsessual'nyi kodeks Moldavskoi SSR.* Kishinev: Partizdat, 1965. 199 pp. [Also publ. in Moldavian].
U306b *... ofitsial'nyi tekst s izm. i dop. na 1 iiulia 1975 g. i s pril. postateinosist. materialov.* Kishinev: Kartia Moldoveniaske, 1976. 604 pp.

TAJIKISTAN

New
U307a *Grazhdanskii protsessual'nyi kodeks Tadzhikskoi SSR.* Dushanbe: Irfon, 1964. 179 pp. [Also in Tajik].
U307b *... s izm. i dop. na 1 iiulia 1975 g.* Dushanbe: Irfon, 1975. 211 pp.

TURKMENISTAN

Old
U308 *Grazhdanskii protsessual'nyi kodeks Turkmenskoi SSR; ofitsial'nyi tekst s izm. na 1 ianvaria 1957 goda i s pril. sist. materialov.* Ashkhabad: Turkmengosizdat, 1957. 202 pp.

New
U309 *Grazhdanskii protsessual'nyi kodeks Turkmenskoi SSR.* Ashkhabad: Turkmengosidzdat, 1964. 294 pp. [Also in Turkmenian].

UKRAINE

Old

U310a   *Grazhdanskii protsessual'nyi kodeks Ukrainskoi SSR; ofitsial'nyi tekst s izm. na 10 oktiabria 1954 g. i s pril. postateino-sist. materialov.* M.: Gosiurizdat, 1954. 151 pp.

U310b   ... 1958. 143 pp. [In Ukrainian].

New

U311a   *Grazhdanskii protsessual'nyi kodeks Ukrainskoi SSR.* Kiev: Politizdat Ukrainy, 1964. 194 pp. [Also publ. in Ukrainian].

U311b   ... *ofitsial'nyi tekst s izm. i dop. na 1 sentiabria 1972 g. i s pril. postateinykh materialov.* 1973. 292 pp.

Commentary

U312   *Grazhdanskii protsessual'nyi kodeks Ukrainskoi SSR: nauchno-prakticheskii kommentarii.* Kiev: Politizdat Ukrainy, 1973. 496 pp. [In Ukrainian].

UZBEKISTAN

New

U313a   *Grazhdanskii protsessual'nyi kodeks Uzbekskoi SSR.* Tashkent: Gosizdat Uzbekistana, 1963. 194 pp. [Also publ. in Uzbek].

U313b   ..., *s izm. i dop. na 1 ianvaria 1975 g.* 1975. 231 pp.

Translations

U314   *The Civil Code and the Code of Civil Procedure of the RSFSR, 1964*; trans. by A. Kiralfy. (Law in Eastern Europe, 11). Leyden: Sijthoff, 1966. 312 pp.
     Well indexed.

U315   *Civil code of the Russian Soviet Federated Socialist Republic; an English translation*; by W. Gray and R. Stults, including a photographic reproduction of the original Russian text. Ann Arbor: University of Michigan Law School, 1965. viii, 150, 5–57 pp.
     Includes a brief introduction.

U316   'Principles of Civil Legislation [and] Principles of Civil Procedure'; trans. by A. Kiralfy. *Law in Eastern Europe, 7: Miscellanea. Articles and texts.* Leyden: Sijthoff, 1963. Pp. 263–320.
     The 1961 Fundamental Principles.

U317   *Soviet civil law. Private rights and their background under the Soviet regime. Comparative survey and translation of the Civil Code; Code on Domestic Relations; Judiciary Act; Code of Civil Procedure; Laws on Nationality, Corporations, Patents, Copyright, Collective Farms, Labour; and other related laws.* [Comp. by] V. Gsovski. Foreword by Hessel E. Yntema. Ann Arbor: University of Michigan Law School, 1948–9. 2 vols.

Vol. 1 is a comparative survey and vol. 2 contains the translations. As well as the legislation on the topics mentioned in the title, the book also includes translations of legislation relating to the church and religion, foreign firms and trade missions, state secrets and the RSFSR Land Code. There is a very full bibliography, followed by chronological tables of the constitutions, law codes and statutes translated or cited in the book, plus a list of the court cases abstracted or translated. There is a good index.

U318 'Soviet civil law and procedure'. *Soviet statutes and decisions*, vol. 4, nos. 1/2 and 3, 1967–8.

These two issues of *SS&D* (*see* U164) include civil law material on compensation for harm, property, contracts and inheritance.

U319 *Soviet civil legislation*; ed. by W. Gray. Ann Arbor: University of Michigan Law School, 1965. vii, 150, 5–57 pp.

Originally planned as a loose-leaf series to include all the relevant codes; only the RSFSR Civil Code was actually published. Includes the Russian original as well as the translation.

U320 *Soviet civil legislation and procedure: official texts and commentaries.* M.: FLPH, n.d.

Texts of the 1961 Fundamental Principles with lengthy introductory commentaries.

See also *Collected legislation* (U158), section II: 1.

Family law

Until the late 1960s, family law in the USSR was regulated by the republics' codes on marriage, family and guardianship of 1926, and a decree in 1944 which altered some of its provisions. Kirghizia, Kazakhstan, Lithuania, Latvia and Estonia used the RSFSR code; Moldavia adopted the Ukraine's code and Tajikistan adopted that of Uzbekistan. The Fundamental Principles of Marriage and Family Law of the USSR and the Union republics were passed on 27 June 1968 and came into effect on 1 October 1968; after that each union republic passed its own code on marriage and the family in 1969–71. Family law also covers the registration of acts of civil status.

Bibliography

See U236.

Collections of material on family law

U321 *Kommentarii k zakonodatel'stvu o registratsii aktov grazhdanskogo sostoianiia.* [Commentary on the legislation on the registration of civil status]. M.: Iurid. lit-ra, 1977. 208 pp.

Based on the 1968 Fundamental Principles and the new codes on marriage and family law, and other legislation relating to the work of the ZAGS.

U322 *Osnovy zakonodatel'stva Soiuza SSR i soiuznykh respublik o brake i sem'e.* [Fundamental Principles of Marriage and Family Law of the USSR and the Union Republics]. M., 1968. 32 pp.

Text of the 1968 Principles.

U323 *Registratsiia aktov grazhdanskogo sostoianiia: sbornik ofitsial'nykh materialov.* [The registration of acts of civil status: a collection of official materials]. Pod red. Iu. M. Guseva. (M-vo iustitsii RSFSR). M.: Iurid. lit-ra, 1974. 328 pp.

Earlier ed.: *Zapis' aktov grazhdanskogo sostoianiia: sbornik ofitsial'nykh materialov.* M.: Gosiurizdat, 1961. 160 pp. These two collections include USSR and RSFSR materials currently in force, for the use of ZAGS and officials of local soviets.

U324 *Sbornik normativnykh aktov po semeinomu pravu.* [A collection of normative acts on family law]. Minsk: Vysheishaia shkola, 1975. 344 pp.

USSR and Belorussian SSR legislation, Supreme Court decisions, etc. on family, marriage, divorce, children, adoption and fostering, state protection of mother and child, registration of births, deaths and marriages, etc.

U325 *Sbornik normativnykh materialov po sovetskomu semeinomu pravu: uchebnoe posobie.* [A collection of normative materials on Soviet family law]. (Vses. iurid. zaochnyi in-t). M., 1965. 151 pp.

A collection of basic materials for correspondence students, including court rulings, with many documents given in extract form although all have full references to published sources.

U326 *Sbornik zakonodatel'nykh materialov o registratsii aktov grazhdanskogo sostoianiia v Ukrainskoi SSR.* [A collection of legal materials on the registration of acts of civil status in the Ukraine]. Sost.: E. I. Petrakova. (M-vo iustitsii USSR). Kiev: Politizdat Ukrainy, 1972. 106 pp.

Also publ. in Ukrainian in 1971. A collection of USSR and Ukrainian materials based on the new Fundamental Principles and the 1970 Code on Marriage and the Family of the Ukraine.

U327 *Sravnitel'nye tablitsy kodeksov o brake i sem'e soiuznykh respublik.* [Comparative tables for the family and marriage codes of the union republics]. (M-vo iustitsii SSSR. Upr. kodifikatsii i sistematizatsii zakonodatel'stva). M., 1951. 96 pp.

The tables set out the basic content of the RSFSR Code and show the relevant articles in the codes of the Ukraine, Belorussia, Uzbekistan, Georgia, Azerbaijan, Tajikistan, Armenia and Turkmenistan. Where the provisions of the codes of the other republics differs from that of the RSFSR, the text of the relevant article is given.

U328 *Voprosy braka i sem'i v sude: spravochnik dlia narodnykh sudei.* [A judge's manual on marriage and family matters]. Sost.: T. B.

Mal'tsman, V. I. Nikulina, pod red. D. S. Kareva. (M-vo iustitsii SSSR. Upr. kodifikatsii i sistematizatsii zakonodatel'stva SSSR). M.: Gosiurizdat, 1949. 152 pp.

A collection of 161 documents in force on 1 January 1949 on marriage and family law.

For material on family law as it relates to women and children, see the subsection on women, children and young people in the section 'Social Affairs'.

Codes on marriage and the family

RSFSR

Old

U329   *Kodeks zakonov o brake, sem'e i opeke, s izm. i dop. na 1 noiabria 1946 g.* M.: Gosiurizdat, 1947. 164 pp. [Republished with revisions at intervals up to 1961].

New

U330a   *Kodeks o brake i sem'e RSFSR: ofitsial'nyi tekst.* M.: Iurid. lit-ra, 1969. 64 pp.

U330b   *... ofitsial'nyi tekst s pril. postateino-sist. materialov po sost. na 20 fevralia 1975 g.* M.: Iurid. lit-ra 1975. 168 pp.

See also U254f.

Commentary

U331   *Kommentarii k kodeksu o brake i sem'e RSFSR,* pod red. S. N. Bratusia, P. E. Orlovskogo. M.: Iurid. lit-ra, 1971. 246 pp.

ARMENIA

Old

U332a   *Kodeks zakonov o brake, sem'e i opeke SSR Armenii. S izm. i dop na 1 iiulia 1951 g.* Erevan: Armgiz, 1951. 96 pp.

U332b   *... na 1-e oktiabria 1967 g. i s pril. postateino-sist. materialov.* Erevan: Aiastan, 1967. 179 pp.

New

U333   *Kodeks o brake i sem'e Armianskoi SSR.* Erevan: Aiastan, 1969. 120 pp. [Also publ. in Armenian].

AZERBAIJAN

Old

U334a   *Kodeks zakonov Azerbaidzhanskoi SSR o brake, sem'e i opeke i ob aktakh grazhdanskogo sostoianiia.* Baku: Izd-vo NKIu, 1928. 45 pp.

U334b   *... so vsemi izm. i dop. po 17 maia 1940 g.* Baku: Azernesher, 1940. 36 pp. [In Azerbaijani].

New

U335   *Kodeks o brake i sem'e Azerbaidzhanskoi SSR.* Baku: Azgosizdat, 1970. 127 pp. [Also publ. in Azerbaijani].

BELORUSSIA

Old

U336a   *Kodeks zakonov o brake, sem'e i opeke Belorusskoi SSR, s izm. i dop. na 1 ianvaria 1951 g.* Minsk: Izd-vo AN BSSR, 1951. 106 pp.

U336b   *... na 1 maia 1957 g.* Minsk: Gosizdat Belorussii, 1958. 120 pp.

New

U337a   *Kodeks o brake i sem'e Belorusskoi SSR.* Minsk: Belarus', 1969. 75 pp.

U337b   *... ofitsial'nyi tekst s izm. i dop. na 1 marta 1976 g. i s pril. postateino-sist. materialov.* 1977. 95 pp.

Commentary

U338   *Kommentarii k Kodeksu o brake i sem'e Belorusskoi SSR*, pod red. N. G. Iurkevicha. Minsk: Izd-vo BGU, 1980. 317 pp.

ESTONIA

Old

U339   *Kodeks zakonov o brake, sem'e i opeke, deistvuiushchii na territorii Estonskoi SSR, s izm. na 1 ianvaria 1952. S pril. postateino-sist. materialov.* Tallin: Estongosizdat, 1952. 152 pp. [In Estonian].

New

U340   *Kodeks Estonskoi SSR o brake i sem'e.* Tallin: Eesti raamat, 1969. 122 pp. [Also publ. in Estonian].

Commentary

U341   *Kodeks Estonskoi SSR o brake i sem'e: kommentirovannoe izdanie.* Tallin: Eesti raamat, 1974. 293 pp. [Also publ. in Estonian].

GEORGIA

Old

U342   *Kodeks zakonov o brake, sem'e i opeke Gruzinskoi SSR, s izm. na 1 maia 1947 g.* Tbilisi: Gosizdat GSSR, 1948. 180 pp.

New

U343   *Kodeks o brake i sem'e Gruzinskoi SSR.* Tbilisi: Sabchota Sakartvelo, 1971. 102 pp. [Also publ. in Georgian].

KAZAKHSTAN

Old

U344   *Kodeks zakonov o brake, sem'e i opeke. S izm. na 1-e iiulia 1938 g. S pril. postateino-sist. materialov.* M.: Iurizdat, 1939. 140 pp. [In Kazakh].

New

U345a   *Kodeks o brake i sem'e Kazakhskoi SSR.* Alma-Ata: Kazakhstan, 1969. 84 pp. [Also publ. in Kazakh].

U345b   *.... 1978.* 79 pp. [Also publ. in Kazakh].

Commentary

U346 *Kommentarii k Kodeksu o brake i sem'e Kazakhskoi SSR.* Pod red.
Iu.G. Basina, M. A. Vaksberga. Alma-Ata: Kazakhstan, 1972. 227
pp.

KIRGHIZIA

New

U347 *Kyrgyz SSRinin nike zhane ui-bulo shonundozu kodeksi = Kodeks o
brake i sem'e Kirgizskoi SSR.* Frunze: Kyrgyzstan, 1970. 248 pp. [In
Kirghiz and Russian].

LATVIA

Old

U348a *Kodeks zakonov o brake, sem'e i opeke, deistvuiushchii na territorii
Latviiskoi SSR.* Riga, 1941. 112 pp. [In Latvian].

U348b .... 1949. 179 pp. [In Latvian].

New

U349a *Kodeks o brake i sem'e Latviiskoi SSR.* Riga: Liesma, 1969. 128 pp.
[Also publ. in Latvian].

U349b ... *ofitsial'nyi tekst s prilozheniem postateino-sist. materialov,* [*po sost.
na 24 fevralia 1978 g.*]. 1978. 384 pp.

LITHUANIA

Old

U350 *Kodeks zakonov o brake, sem'e i opeke, deistvuiushchii na territorii
Litovskoi SSR. S izm. na 1 iiulia 1951 g. i s pril. postateino-sist.
materialov.* Vilnius: Gospolitnauchizdat, 1952. 125 pp. [In Lith-
uanian].

New

U351 *Kodeks o brake i sem'e Litovskoi SSR.* Vilnius: Mintis, 1970. 116 pp.
[Also publ. in Lithuanian].

MOLDAVIA

Old

U352 *Kodeks zakonov o sem'e, brake, opeke i aktakh grazhdanskogo sostoianiia USSR. Primeniaetsia na territorii Moldavskoi SSR ... S
izm. na 14 dekabria 1940 g. i s pril. postateino-sist. materialov.* M.:
Iurizdat, 1941. 136 pp.

New

U353a *Kodeks o brake i sem'e Moldavskoi SSR.* Kishinev: Kartia Moldoveniaske, 1971. 124 pp. [Also publ. in Moldavian].

U353b ... *s pril. postateino-sist. materialov po sost. na 10 sentiabria 1977 g.*
1979. 295 pp.

TAJIKISTAN

Old

U354 *Kodeks zakonov o brake, sem'e i opeke Tadzhikskoi SSR. S izm. na 1 aprelia 1939 g.* M.: Iurizdat, 1939. 50 pp.

New

U355 *Kodeks o brake i sem'e Tadzhikskoi SSR.* Dushanbe: Irfon, 1970. 103 pp. [Also publ. in Tajik].

TURKMENISTAN

Old

U356a *Kodeks zakonov o brake, sem'e, opeke i ob aktakh grazhdanskogo sostoianiia Turkmenskoi SSR, s izm. na 15 ianvaria 1938 g.* Ashkhabad: Turkmengosizdat, 1938. 40 pp.
U356b ... *na 1 oktiabria 1955 g.* 1955. 104 pp.

New

U357 *Kodeks zakonov o brake i sem'e Turkmenskoi SSR.* Ashkhabad: Turkmenistan 1970. 91 pp. [Also publ. in Turkmenian].

UKRAINE

Old

U358 *Kodeks zakonov Ukrainskoi SSR o sem'e, opeke, brake i ob aktakh grazhdanskogo sostoianiia, s izm. i dop. na 1 ianvaria 1946 g.* Kiev, Khar'kov: Gospolitizdat USSR, 1946. 109 pp. [In Ukrainian]. [Republished, in Ukrainian or Russian, with revisions at intervals up to 1958].

New

U359a *Kodeks o brake i sem'e Ukrainskoi SSR.* Kiev: Politizdat Ukrainy, 1970. 118 pp. [Also publ. in Ukrainian].
U359b ..., *s izm. i dop. na 1 ianvaria 1978 g i s postateinymi materialami.* 1978. 208 pp. [in Ukrainian].

Commentary

U360 *Kodeks o brake i sem'e Ukrainskoi SSR: nauch.- prakt. kommentarii,* pod red. A. N. Iakimenko. Kiev: Politizdat Ukrainy, 1973. 219 pp. [In Ukrainian].

UZBEKISTAN

Old

U361a *Kodeks zakonov o brake, sem'e i opeke i o zapisi aktov grazhdanskogo sostoianiia Uzbekskoi SSR, po sost. na 1 ianvaria 1946 g.* Tashkent: Upr. delami Soveta Ministrov, 1946. 25 pp.
U361b ... *na 1 sentiabria 1955 g.* Tashkent: Gosizdat UzSSR, 1955. 58 pp.

New

U362a *Kodeks o brake i sem'e Uzbekskoi SSR.* Tashkent: Uzbekistan, 1969. 119 pp. [Also publ. in Uzbek].

U362b ... *s izm. i dop. na 1 ianvaria 1979 g.* 1979. 130 pp.

Translations

U363 *Code of laws on marriage, family and guardianship of the RSFSR: official text with amendments up to February 1, 1961.* Trans. and ed. by William E. Butler. Cambridge, Mass.: Hazen Publications, 1965. 35 pp. [Not seen].

U364 *The Code of Laws of Marriage, Family and Guardianship of the Russian Socialist Federated Soviet Republic.* Trans. by Hsinwoo Chao. London: Sweet and Maxwell, 1939. 51 pp.
  The 1936 code.

U365 *The family in the USSR: documents and readings.* Ed. with an introduction by Rudolf Schlesinger. (Changing attitudes in Soviet Russia). London: Routledge and Kegan Paul, 1949. ix, 408 pp.
  Includes translations of the 1926 RSFSR Code, the 1936 Law on abortion and the 1944 Law on the family as well as a number of articles and other documents on Soviet family law.

U366 'Family law'. *Soviet statutes and decisions,* vol. 4, no. 4, 1968.
  This issue of *SS&D* (*see* U164) includes the old RSFSR code as of 12 February 1968 and the 1968 Principles.

See also *Collected legislation* (U158) section II.

Criminal law and procedure

The all-union Fundamental Principles of Criminal Law enacted in 1924 formed the basis of the criminal code enacted by the RSFSR in 1926. Other union republics either enacted their own codes, with broadly similar provisions, or adopted the RSFSR code. These codes were the basis of Soviet criminal law until the new Fundamental Principles of Criminal Law of the USSR and the Union Republics were enacted on 25 December 1958 and were followed by new criminal codes in all the union republics, enacted in 1959–62. The Fundamental Principles of Criminal Procedure of the USSR and the Union Republics were also enacted on 25 December 1958 and were followed by union republic codes of criminal procedure in 1959–62. More general material on court organization and the procuracy can be found in the sections concerned.

Bibliographies

U367 *Sovetskoe ugolovnoe pravo: bibliografiia, 1917–1960.* [Soviet criminal law: a bibliography, 1917–1960]. M.: Gosiurizdat, 1961. 323 pp.
  A bibliography of Russian-language material, covering all aspects of criminal law and criminal procedure. Includes books, journal articles and official publications. Author index.

U368 *Sovetskoe ugolovnoe pravo; sovetskoe ispravitel'no-trudovoe pravo; sovetskaia kriminologiia: bibliografiia, 1961–1968.* [Soviet criminal law; Soviet correctional labour law; Soviet criminology: a bibliography, 1961–1968]. Vladivostok: Dal'nevostochnyi gos. un-t, 1969. 2 vols.

Only 500 copies publ. Has 3,079 entries, arranged by subject, drawn from the open press, and including monographs, articles, theses, law codes, commentaries and collections of legal documents. Full name index.

General collections of material on criminal law and criminal procedure

U369 *Istoriia zakonodatel'stva SSSR i RSFSR po ugolovnomu protsessu i organizatsii suda i prokuratury, 1917–1954 gg.: sbornik dokumentov.* [History of the USSR and RSFSR legislation on criminal procedure and the organization of the courts and the procuracy, 1917–1954: a collection of documents]. Pod red. S. A. Golunskogo, sost.: L. N. Gusev. M.: Gosiurizdat, 1955. 636 pp.

RSFSR and USSR official documents up to 1 January 1955, with all documents given in their original form with later amendments appended separately. The documents are in chronological order, with cross-references and a note of the original official source.

U370 Men'shagin, V. D. *Nauchno-prakticheskii kommentarii k Zakonu ob ugolovnoi otvetstvennosti za gosudarstvennye prestupleniia.* [Theoretical and practical commentary on the Law on Criminal Responsibility for State Crimes. By] V. D. Men'shagin, V. A. Kurinov, pod red. P. S. Romashkina. (MGU. Iurid. fakul'tet). M.: Gosiurizdat, 1961. 114 pp.

1st ed. publ. 1960 (71 pp.). Text and commentary of the Law passed in December 1958, and subsequent legislation.

U371 *Nauchno-prakticheskii kommentarii k Osnovam ugolovnogo sudoproizvodstva Soiuza SSR i soiuznykh respublik.* [Theoretical and practical commentary to the Fundamental Principles of Criminal Procedure of the USSR and the Union Republics]. Pod red. i s predisl. V. A. Boldyreva. (Vses. in-t iurid. nauk). M.: Gosiurizdat, 1961. 366 pp.

1st ed. publ. 1960 (280 pp.). A detailed commentary on the 1958 Fundamental Principles.

U372 *Nauchno-prakticheskii kommentarii k Osnovam ugolovnogo zakonodatel'stva Soiuza SSR i Soiuznykh Respublik.* [Theoretical and practical commentary on the Fundamental Principles of Criminal Law of the USSR and the Union Republics]. Otv. red.: V. D. Men'shagin, P. S. Romashkin. 2-e izd. (Moskovskii gos. un-t. Iurid. fakul'tet). M.: Gosiurizdat, 1961. 204 pp.

1st ed. publ. 1960 (179 pp.). Commentary on the 1958 Fundamental Principles as of 1 November 1961 with a four-page supplement on the May 1961 edict 'On Strengthening the Struggle against Especially Dangerous Crimes'.

U373 *Nauchno-prakticheskii kommentarii k Zakonu ob ugolovnoi otvetstven-*

nosti za voinskie prestupleniia. [Theoretical and practical commentary on the Law on Criminal Responsibility for Military Crimes]. Pod red. i s predisl. A. G. Gornogo. Izd. 2-e. (Metodicheskii sovet Prokuratury SSSR. Iurid. fak. VMA). M.: Gosiurizdat, 1961. 110 pp.

1st ed. publ. 1960 (104 pp.). Includes text of the 1958 Law.

U374 *Osnovy ugolovnogo zakonodatel'stva Soiuza SSR i soiuznykh respublik. Osnovy ugolovnogo sudoproizvodstva Soiuza SSR i soiuznykh respublik.* [Fundamental Principles of Criminal Law of the USSR and the Union Republics. Fundamental Principles of Criminal Procedure of the USSR and the Union Republics]. M.: Iurid. lit-ra, 1969. 53 pp.

Texts of the 1958 Fundamental Principles.

U375 *Sbornik dokumentov po istorii ugolovnogo zakonodatel'stva SSSR i RSFSR.* [A collection of documents on the history of the USSR and RSFSR criminal law]. Pod red. I. T. Goliakova. M.: Gosiurizdat, 1953. 463 pp.

Includes most of the USSR and RSFSR normative acts on criminal law, 1917–52, plus the March 1953 Act on Amnesties. Chronological arrangement, with full references to original published source. All documents are given in their original form, with cross-references to later amendments.

U376 *Sbornik postanovlenii i opredelenii kollegii Verkhovnogo Suda SSSR po voprosam ugolovnogo protsessa, 1946–1962 gg.* [A collection of ordinances and decisions of the USSR Supreme Court Collegium on matters of criminal procedure, 1946–1962]. M.: Iurid. lit-ra, 1964. 334 pp.

Includes material based on the old 1924 Principles as well as the 1958 Fundamental Principles, with the older material retained only where it is still relevant to the interpretation of the new Fundamental Principles. No indexes.

U377a *Sbornik postanovlenii prezidiuma i opredelenii sudebnoi kollegii po ugolovnym delam Verkhovnogo Suda RSFSR, 1957–1959 gg.* [A collection of the decisions of the Presidium and instructions of the Collegium on criminal law of the RSFSR Supreme Court, 1957–1959]. Pod red. A. G. Rubicheva. M.: Gosiurizdat, 1960. 349 pp.

U377b *Sbornik postanovlenii plenuma, prezidiuma i opredelenii sudebnoi kollegii po ugolovnym delam Verkhovnogo Suda RSFSR, 1961–1963 gg.* Otv. red.: L. N. Smirnov. M.: Iurid. lit-ra, 1964. 414 pp.

U377c *Sbornik postanovlenii plenuma, prezidiuma i opredelenii sudebnoi kollegii po ugolovnym delam Verkhovnogo Suda RSFSR, 1959–1971.* Red.: G. Z. Anashkin. M.: Iurid. lit-ra, 1973. 416 pp.

U377d *Sbornik postanovlenii prezidiuma i opredelenii sudebnoi kollegii po ugolovnym delam Verkhovnogo Suda RSFSR, 1964–1972.* Red.: A. K. Orlov. M.: Iurid, lit-ra, 1974. 646 pp.

These four volumes contain decisions of the RSFSR Supreme Court's Collegium on criminal law and its guiding explanations, with some extracts from individual cases. The 1964 volume has a special section on the introduction of the 1960 RSFSR Criminal Code and the clarification of matters arising out of it.

U378 *Sbornik ugolovno-protsessual'nykh dokumentov predvaritel'nogo sled- stviia.* [A collection of documents on preliminary investigation in criminal law cases]. Otv. red.: F. M. Kudin. (Sverdlovskii iurid. in- t). Sverdlovsk, 1974. 140 pp. [Not seen].

U379 *Sbornik zakonodatel'nykh i innykh materialov k izucheniiu sovetskogo ugolovnogo prava, ugolovnogo protsessa i sudoustroistva ... uchebnoe posobie.* [A collection of legislative and other documents for the study of Soviet criminal law, criminal procedure and the judiciary]. Sost.: I. M. Gutkin. (Vysshaia shkola MOOP RSFSR). M., 1964. 402 pp.

A collection of documents for the use of the RSFSR Ministry for the Protection of Public Order. Includes USSR and RSFSR legislation, Supreme Court and Ministry of Justice materials, all previously publ.

U380 *Sistematizirovannyi tekst obshchesoiuznykh ugolovnykh zakonov i ugolovnykh kodeksov soiuznykh respublik.* [Systematized text of the all-union criminal law and the criminal codes of the union republics]. M.: Iurizdat, 1948. 544 pp.

Has tables allowing the easy comparison of clauses in the criminal law at all-union level with the codes of the union republics. Where provisions in the codes of the other union republics vary from that of the RSFSR, the relevant paragraphs are reproduced. There is a historical introduction setting out the development of the criminal law in each republic.

U381 *Sopostavitel'naia tablitsa statei ugolovno-protsessual'nykh kodeksov soiuznykh respublik.* [A comparative table of articles in the criminal procedure codes of the union republics]. Sost.: Iu.I. Mochek, E. P. Nesterova, pod red. D. S. Kareva. (M-vo iustitsii SSSR. Upr. kodifikatsii i sistematizatsii zakonodatel'stva SSSR). M.: Gosiuriz- dat, 1953. 240 pp.

The tables give the articles of the RSFSR code with the cor- responding articles from the criminal procedure codes of the Ukraine, Belorussia, Azerbaijan, Georgia, Armenia, Turkmenistan, Uzbekistan and Tajikistan. Gives the texts of articles which differ from the RSFSR code or are absent from it.

U382 *Sopostavitel'naia tablitsa statei osnov ugolovnogo sudoproizvodstva Soiuza SSR i soiuznykh respublik i ugolovno-protsessual'nykh kodeksov soiuznykh respublik.* [A comparative table of the articles of the Fundamental Principles of Criminal Procedure of the USSR and the Union Republics and the criminal procedure codes of the union republics]. Pod red. L. N. Smirnova. M.: Iurid. lit-ra, 1964. 60 pp.

Tables show articles of the RSFSR code and the corresponding articles of the Fundamental Principles and the codes of the other union republics, and list those articles in the codes of the other union republics which are absent from the RSFSR code. There is also a list of when each republic passed its code and the date it came into force.

U383 *Sopostavitel'nye tablitsy statei ugolovnogo i ugolovno-protsessual'nogo zakonodatel'stva Soiuza SSR, Uzbekskoi, Rossiiskoi, Tadzhikskoi, Turkmenskoi, Kirgizskoi i Kazakhskoi soiuznykh respublik: uchebnoe posobie.* [Comparative tables of the articles of the criminal and criminal procedure laws of the USSR, RSFSR, Uzbek, Tajik, Turkmenian, Kirghiz and Kazakh republics]. (Tashkentskaia vysshaia shkola MVD SSSR). Tashkent, 1975. 76 pp.

Tables to help students cope with the differences in layout and content of the codes of the different republics. The tables give the article numbers of the USSR, RSFSR and Uzbek legislation and the corresponding articles in the codes of the other republics covered. At the back there is a list of the articles in the Kirghiz, Kazakh, Tajik and Turkmenian codes not present in the Uzbek code.

U384 *Sovershenstvovanie ugolovnogo zakonodatel'stva USSR (1961–1975 gg.): sbornik normativnykh aktov.* [The perfecting of the criminal law of the Ukraine, 1961–1975: a collection of normative acts]. Otv. red.: A. M. Serbulov. (Kievskaia vysshaia shkola MVD SSSR). Kiev, 1976. 194 pp.

An annotated collection of legislation after the enactment of the new criminal code, recording amendments and other changes to the criminal law of the Ukraine and the USSR. Chronological index.

U385 *Sravnitel'naia tablitsa statei obshchesoiuznykh ugolovnykh zakonov i ugolovnykh kodeksov soiuznykh respublik.* [Comparative table of the articles of the all-union criminal law and the criminal codes of the union republics]. Sost.: V. N. Ivanov. M.: Iurid. lit-ra, 1973. 30 pp. [Not seen].

U386 *Ugolovno-protsessual'noe zakonodatel'stvo SSSR i soiuznykh respublik: sbornik. (Osnovnye zakonodatel'nye akty).* [Criminal procedure legislation of the USSR and union republics: a collection of basic legislative acts]. Pod red. D. S. Kareva. M.: Gosiurizdat, 1957. 507 pp.

Includes all-union statutes and other material relating to criminal procedure, followed by the criminal procedure codes of the RSFSR, the Ukraine, Belorussia, Uzbekistan, Georgia, Azerbaijan, Tajikistan, Armenia and Turkmenistan. Texts of codes given in form currently in force, not in original version. Supplements on forensic medicine and psychiatric treatment of offenders. Subject index in tabular form, referring to pages of the book for all-union legislation and to the appropriate articles of the codes of the union republics.

U387 *Ugolovnoe zakonodatel'stvo Soiuza SSR i soiuznykh respublik.* [The criminal law of the USSR and the union republics]. (Vazhneishie zakonodatel'nye akty Soiuza SSR i soiuznykh respublik). M.: Gosiurizdat, 1963. 2 vols. plus separate index vol.

Has a useful introduction discussing and explaining the main differences between the criminal codes passed 1959–61, followed by the texts of the 1959 Fundamental Principles and the codes of the union republics, as of 1 February 1963. The index is by subject and lists the relevant articles in the all-union legislation and the code of each republic.

U388 *Voprosy ugolovnogo prava i protsessa v praktike Verkhovnykh sudov SSSR i RSFSR, 1938–1978 gg.* [Problems of criminal law and procedure in the practice of the USSR and RSFSR Supreme Courts, 1938–1978]. Sost.: S. V. Borodin, G. A. Levitskii. 3-e izd., dop. i perer. M.: Iurid. lit-ra, 1980. 470 pp.

1st ed. covering 1938–67 publ. 1968 (365 pp.); 2nd ed., covering 1938–69, publ. 1971 (448 pp.) The decisions included are arranged in the order of the relevant articles of the RSFSR codes.

U389 *Zakonodatel'stvo ob ugolovnom sudoproizvodstve Soiuza SSR i soiuznykh respublik.* [Criminal procedure legislation of the USSR and the union republics]. (Vazhneishie zakonodatel'nye akty Soiuza SSR i soiuznykh respublik). M.: Gosiurizdat, 1963. 2 vols.

Includes the 1958 Fundamental Principles of Criminal Procedure and the union republics' codes of 1959–61. There is a useful introduction discussing and comparing the codes, but no index.

See also U903, U925.

Criminal codes

RSFSR

Old

U390 *Ugolovnyi kodeks RSFSR, s izm. i dop. na 1 avgusta 1944 g.* M.: Gosiurizdat, 1944. [Republished with revisions at intervals up to 1957].

New

U391a *Ugolovnyi kodeks RSFSR.* M.: Iurid. lit-ra, 1960. 174 pp.
U391b *Ugolovnyi kodeks RSFSR, s izm. i dop. na 1 avgusta 1962 g. i s pril. postateino-sist. materialov.* M.: Iurid. lit-ra, 1962. 285 pp. [Republished with revisions at intervals].

U392 *Ugolovnyi kodeks RSFSR. Ugolovno-protsessual'nyi kodeks RSFSR. Ispravitel'no-trudovoi kodeks RSFSR.* [po sost. na 1 ianv. 1979 g.]. M.: Iurid. lit-ra, 1979. 256 pp.

Commentaries

U393a *Kommentarii k Ugolovnomu kodeksu RSFSR 1960 g.* Leningrad: Izd-vo Leningradskogo un-ta, 1962. 459 pp.

U393b   *Nauchno-prakticheskii kommentarii Ugolovnogo kodeksa RSFSR.* Otv. red.: B. S. Nikiforov. M.: Iurid. lit-ra, 1963. 527 pp.

U393c   ... 2. izd. 1964. 574 pp.

U393d   *Kommentarii k Ugolovnomu kodeksu RSFSR.* M.: Iurid. lit-ra, 1971. 560 pp.

U393e   ... 1980. 480 pp.

ARMENIA

Old

U394a   *Ugolovnyi kodeks Armianskoi SSR. Ofitsial'nyi tekst s izm. na 1 fevralia 1944 g. i s pril. postateino-sist. materialov.* Erevan: Armengiz, 1944.

U394b   ... *na 1 iiulia 1951 g.* Erevan: Aipetrat, 1951.

New

U395a   *Ugolovnyi kodeks Armianskoi SSR.* Erevan, 1959.

U395b   *Ugolovnyi kodeks Armianskoi SSR, s izm. i dop. na 1 oktiabria 1965 g. i s pril. postateino-sistematizirovannykh materialov.* Erevan: Aiastan, 1965. 355 pp. [Also publ. in Armenian]. [Republished with revisions 1971 and 1978].

AZERBAIJAN

Old

U396   *Ugolovnyi kodeks Azerbaidzhanskoi SSR, ofitsial'nyi tekst so vsemi izm. po 15 aprelia 1943 g. vkliuchitel'no.* Baku, 1943.

New

U397   *Ugolovnyi kodeks Azerbaidzhanskoi SSR.* Baku: Izd. Verkhovnogo Soveta AzSSR, 1961. 151 pp. [Also publ. in Azerbaijani]. [Republished with revisions 1963, 1968 and 1976].

BELORUSSIA

Old

U398a   *Ugolovnyi kodeks Belorusskoi SSR. Ofitsial'nyi tekst s izm. na 1 dekabria 1948 g. i s pril. postateino-sist. materialov.* Minsk: Gosizdat BSSR, 1949.

U398b   ... *s izm. na 1 maia 1957 g. i s pril. postateino-sist. materialov.* 1957. 297 pp. [In Russian and Belorussian].

New

U399a   *Ugolovnyi kodeks Belorusskoi SSR.* Minsk: Belarus', 1961. 214 pp. [In Russian and Belorussian]. [Republished with revisions 1965 and 1971].

U399b   *Ugolovnyi kodeks Belorusskoi SSR. Ugolovno-protsessual'nyi kodeks Belorusskoi SSR: ofitsial'nye teksty s izm. na 1 avgusta 1977 g.* Minsk: Belarus', 1977. 319 pp.

Commentaries

U400a *Kommentarii k Ugolovnomu kodeksu Belorusskoi SSR*. Minsk: Belarus', 1960. 460 pp.
U400b ... pod obshchei red. S. T. Shardyko. 1966. 460 pp.
U400c ... Izd. 3-e, dop. Minsk: Izd-vo BGU, 1971. 392 pp.
U400d ... pod obshchei red. L. K. Zaitseva. Izd. 4-e, ispr. i dop. Minsk: Belarus', 1976. 400 pp.
U400e *Nauchno-prakticheskii kommentarii k Ugolovnomu kodeksu Belorusskoi SSR*, pod obshchei red. L. K. Zaitseva. Minsk: Belarus', 1979. 399 pp.

ESTONIA

New

U401 *Ugolovnyi kodeks Estonskoi SSR*. Tallin: Estonskoe gosizdat, 1961. 187 pp. [Also publ. in Estonian]. [Republished with revisions 1963, 1965, 1970, 1974 and 1978].

Commentaries

U402a *Ugolovnyi kodeks Estonskoi SSR: kommentirovannoe izdanie*. Red.: K. Paas. Tallin: Eesti raamat, 1962. 301 pp. [In Estonian].
U402b ... [po sost. na 1 ianv. 1968 g]. 1968. 565 pp. [Also publ. in Estonian].
U402c ... *po sost. na 1-e ianvaria 1979 g*. 1980. 685 pp. [In Estonian].

GEORGIA

Old

U403 *Ugolovnyi kodeks Gruzinskoi SSR; ofitsial'nyi tekst s izm. na 1 maia 1958 g. i s pril. postateino-sist. materialov*. Tbilisi, 1958. 255 pp.

New

U404a *Ugolovnyi kodeks Gruzinskoi SSR*. Tbilisi: Sabchota Sakartvelo, 1961. 150 pp. [Also publ. in Georgian].
U404b ..., *s izm. i dop. na 1 marta 1969 i s pril. postateino-sist. materialov*. 1969. 309 pp. [Also publ. in Georgian]. [Republished with revisions 1973 and 1977].

Commentary

U405 *Kommentarii k Ugolovnomu kodeksu Gruzinskoi SSR*. Tbilisi: Sabchota Sakartvelo, 1976. Vol. 1–. [In Georgian].

KAZAKHSTAN

New

U406 *Ugolovnyi kodeks Kazakhskoi SSR*. Alma-Ata: Kazgosizdat, 1960. 87 pp. [Also publ. in Kazakh]. [Republished with revisions at intervals].

Commentary

U407 *Kommentarii k Ugolovnomu kodeksu Kazakhskoi SSR*, pod red. V. N. Markelova, G. F. Polenova. Alma-Ata: Kazakhstan, 1966. 617 pp.

KIRGHIZIA

New

U408 *Kyrgyz SSRinin ugolovnyi kodeksi = Ugolovnyi kodeks Kirgizskoi SSR.* Frunze, 1961. 283 pp. [Also publ. in Kirghiz]. [Republished with revisions 1964, 1969 and 1977].

LATVIA

New

U409a *Ugolovnyi kodeks Latviiskoi SSR.* Riga, 1961. 86 pp. [Also publ. in Latvian].

U409b ... [*po sost. na 20 iiulia 1962 g.*]. Riga, 1962. 213 pp. [Also publ. in Latvian].

U409c ... *ofitsial'nyi tekst s prilozheniem postateino-sist. materialov.* Riga: Liesma, 1971. 387 pp. [Republished with revisions 1971 and 1977].

Commentaries

U410a *Latvijas PSR kriminālkodeksa komentāri.* Riga, 1965. 492 pp. [In Latvian].

U410b *Kommentarii Ugolovnogo kodeksa Latviiskoi SSR.* Riga: Liesma, 1967. 548 pp.

U410c *Kommentarii k Ugolovnomu kodeksu Latviiskoi SSR.* 1974. 424 pp. [In Latvian].

LITHUANIA

Old

U411a *Ugolovnyi kodeks RSFSR, deistvuiushchii na territorii Litovskoi SSR. Ofitsial'nyi tekst s izm. i dop. na 1 iiulia 1951 g. i s pril. postateino-sist. materialov.* M., 1952.

U411b ... *na 1 ianvaria 1954 g.* ... Vilnius: Gospolitnauchizdat, 1954.

New

U412 *Ugolovnyi kodeks Litovskoi SSR.* Vilnius: Gospolitnauchizdat, 1961. 194 pp. [Also publ. in Lithuanian]. [Republished with revisions at intervals].

MOLDAVIA

New

U413 *Ugolovnyi kodeks Moldavskoi SSR.* Kishinev: Kartia Moldoveniaske, 1961. 127 pp. [Republished with revisions 1962 and 1973].

Commentaries

U414a *Kommentarii k Ugolovnomu kodeksu Moldavskoi SSR.* Kishinev: Kartia Moldoveniaske, 1964. 404 pp.

U414b ... 1968. 398 pp.

TAJIKISTAN

Old

U415 *Ugolovnyi kodeks Tadzhikskoi SSR; ofitsial'nyi tekst s izm. i dop. na 1 iiulia 1951 g.* Stalinabad: Tadzhgosizdat, 1952.

New

U416 *Ugolovnyi kodeks Tadzhikskoi SSR.* Dushanbe: Irfon, 1961. [Also publ. in Tajik]. [Republished with revisions 1963, 1971 and 1975].

Commentaries

U417 Mullaev, M. *Kommentarii Ugolovnogo kodeksa Tadzhikskoi SSR (obshchaia chast').* Dushanbe: Irfon, 1969. 259 pp.

TURKMENISTAN

Old

U418 *Ugolovnyi kodeks Turkmenskoi SSR; ofitsial'nyi tekst s izm. na 1 ianvaria 1956 g. i s pril. postateino-sist. materialov.* Ashkhabad: Gosizdat Turkmenistana, 1957. 185 pp.

New

U419 *Ugolovnyi kodeks Turkmenskoi SSR.* Ashkhabad: Gosizdat Turkmenistana, 1962. 220 pp. [Also publ. in Turkmenian]. [Republished with revisions 1968, 1972 and 1979].

UKRAINE

Old

U420 *Ugolovnyi kodeks Ukrainskoi SSR; ofitsial'nyi tekst s izm. i dop. na 1 noiabria 1949 g., s postateino-sist. materialami i s pril.* Kiev: Gospolitizdat Ukrainy, 1950. [Republished with revisions 1950 and 1958].

New

U421 *Ugolovnyi kodeks Ukrainskoi SSR.* Kiev: Politizdat Ukrainy, 1961. 134 pp. [Also publ. in Ukrainian]. [Republished with revisions at intervals, sometimes in Ukrainian].

Commentaries

U422a *Ugolovnyi kodeks Ukrainskoi SSR: nauchno-prakticheskii kommentarii,* pod obshchei red. V. I. Zaichuka. Kiev: Politizdat Ukrainy, 1969. 544 pp.

U422b ... 1978. 683 pp.

UZBEKISTAN

Old

U423a *Ugolovnyi kodeks Uzbekskoi SSR po sost. na 1 sentiabria 1946 g.* Tashkent, 1946.

U423b ... *na 1 noiabria 1954 g.* Tashkent: Gosizdat Uzbekskoi SSR, 1954. 118 pp.

New

U424 *Ugolovnyi kodeks Uzbekskoi SSR*. Tashkent: Gosizdat UzbSSR, 1959. 99 pp. [Also publ. in Uzbek]. [Republished with revisions at intervals].

Commentaries

U425 *Kommentarii k Ugolovnomu kodeksu Uzbekskoi SSR*. Tashkent: Uzbekistan, 1973. 380 pp. [In Uzbek].

Criminal procedure code

RSFSR

Old

U426a *Ugolovno-protsessual'nyi kodeks RSFSR, po sost. na 1 noiabria 1946g.* M.: Gosiurizdat, 1947. 270 pp.

U426b *Ugolovno-protsessual'nyi kodeks RSFSR; ofitsial'nyi tekst s izm. na 1 iiunia 1953 g. i s pril. postateino-sist. materialov.* M.: Gosiurizdat, 1953. 131 pp. [Republished with revisions 1956 and 1957].

New

U427a *Ugolovno-protsessual'nyi kodeks RSFSR.* M.: Gosiurizdat, 1960. 247 pp.

U427b *Ugolovno-protsessual'nyi kodeks RSFSR; ofitsial'nyi tekst s izm. i dop. na ianvaria 1962 g. i s pril. postateino-sist. materialov.* M.: Iurid. lit-ra, 1962. 335 pp. [Republished with revisions at intervals].

See also U392.

Commentaries

U428a *Kommentarii k Ugolovno-protsessual'nomu kodeksu RSFSR 1960 g.* Leningrad: Izd-vo Leningradskogo un-ta, 1962. 387 pp.

U428b *Nauchno-prakticheskii kommentarii k Ugolovno-protsessual'nomu kodeksu RSFSR,* pod red. L. N. Smirnova. M.: Iurid. lit-ra, 1963. 796 pp.

U428c ... 2-e izd, ispr. i dop. 1965. 636 pp.

U428d ... 3-e izd, ispr. i dop. 1970. 558 pp.

U428e *Kommentarii k Ugolovno-protsessual'nomu kodeksu RSFSR.* M.: Iurid. lit-ra, 1976. 624 pp.

ARMENIA

New

U429a *Ugolovno-protsessual'nyi kodeks Armianskoi SSR.* Erevan: Aiastan, 1961. 262 pp. [Also publ. in Armenian].

U429b *Ugolovno-protsessual'nyi kodeks Armianskoi SSR, s izm. i dop. na 1 oktiabria 1965 goda i s pril. postateino-sist. materialov.* Erevan: Aiastan, 1965. 338 pp. [Also publ. in Armenian]. [Republished with revisions 1971 and 1978].

AZERBAIJAN

New

U430 *Ugolovno-protsessual'nyi kodeks Azerbaidzhanskoi SSR.* Baku: Azgosizdat, 1961. 387 pp. [Also publ. in Azerbaijani]. [Republished with revisions 1963, 1971 and 1977].

BELORUSSIA

Old

U431 *Ugolovno-protsessual'nyi kodeks Belorusskoi SSR, ofitsial'nyi tekst s izm. na 15 aprelia 1957 g. i s pril. sist. materialov.* Minsk: Gosizdat Belorusskoi SSR. 1957. 180 pp.

New

U432 *Ugolovno-protsessual'nyi kodeks Belorusskoi SSR.* Minsk: Belarus', 1961. 365 pp. [In Russian and Belorussian]. [Republished with revisions, 1971].

See also U399b.

Commentaries

U433a *Ugolovno-protsessual'nyi kodeks Belorusskoi SSR: kommentarii,* pod red. S. T. Shardyko, G. G. Basova, Minsk: Gosizdat Belorusskoi SSR, 1963. 315 pp.

U433b *Kommentarii k Ugolovno-protsessual'nomu kodeksu Belorusskoi SSR,* pod obshchei red. S. T. Shardyko. 2 izd. Minsk: Belarus', 1968. 586 pp.

U433c . . . pod obshchei red. A. A. Zdanovich. 3 izd., ispr. i dop. Minsk: Izd-vo BGU, 1973. 504 pp.

ESTONIA

New

U434 *Ugolovno-protsessual'nyi kodeks Estonskoi SSR.* Tallin: Estgosizdat. 1961. 249 pp. [Also publ. in Estonian]. [Republished with revisions at intervals].

GEORGIA

Old

U435 *Ugolovno-protsessual'nyi kodeks Gruzinskoi SSR; s izm. na 1 marta 1957 g. i s pril. postateino-sist. materialov.* Tbilisi, 1958. 258 pp.

New

U436 *Ugolovno-protsessual'nyi kodeks Gruzinskoi SSR.* Tbilisi: Sabchota Sakartvelo, 1961. 205 pp. [Also publ. in Georgian]. [Republished with revisions at intervals, in Russian and Georgian].

KAZAKHSTAN

New

U437 *Ugolovno-protsessual'nyi kodeks Kazakhskoi SSR.* Alma-Ata: Kazgosizdat, 1960. 148 pp. [Also publ. in Kazakh]. [Republished with revisions at intervals].

Commentary

U438 *Kommentarii k Ugolovno-protsessual'nomu kodeksu Kazakhskoi SSR,* Pod obshchei red. E. S. Zeliksona. Alma-Ata: Kazakhstan, 1969. 656 pp.

KIRGHIZIA

New

U439 *Kyrgyz SSRinin ugolovnyi-protsessualdyk kodeksi = Ugolovno-protsessual'nyi kodeks Kirgizskoi SSR.* Frunze: Gosizdat Kirgizii, 1961. 283 pp. [In Kirghiz and Russian]. [Republished with revisions 1963 and 1969].

LATVIA

New

U440a *Ugolovno-protsessual'nyi kodeks Latviiskoi SSR.* Riga, 1961. 155 pp. [Also publ. in Latvian]. [Republished with revisions 1963].

U440b *Ugolovno-protsessual'nyi kodeks Latviiskoi SSR; ofitsial'nyi tekst s pril. postateino-sist. materialov,* [po sost. na 15 dek. 1972 g.]. Riga: Liesma, 1973. 466 pp. [Also publ. in Latvian].

Commentary

U441 *Kommentarii k Ugolovno-protsessual'nomu kodeksu Latviiskoi SSR.* Red.: A. Liede. Riga: Liesma, 1968. 605 pp. [In Latvian].

LITHUANIA

New

U442a *Ugolovno-protsessual'nyi kodeks Litovskoi SSR.* Vilnius: Gospolit-nauchizdat, 1961. 337 pp. [Also publ. in Lithuanian]. [Republished with revisions 1962].

U442b *... na 1 marta 1972 g. i s pril. postateino-sist. materialov.* Vilnius: Mintis, 1972. 561 pp. [Also publ. in Lithuanian].

Commentary

U443 *Kommentarii k Ugolovno-protsessual'nomu kodeksu Litovskoi SSR.* Vilnius: Mintis, 1976. 410 pp. [In Lithuanian].

MOLDAVIA

New

U444a *Ugolovno-protsessual'nyi kodeks Moldavskoi SSR.* Kishinev: Kartia Moldoveniaske, 1961. 211 pp.

U444b *Kodul de prochedure penale al RSS Moldovenesht' = Ugolovno-protsessual'nyi kodeks Moldavskoi SSR; izm. i dop. vneseny po sost. na 1 iulia 1963 g.* Kishinev: Kartia Moldoveniaske, 1963. 371 pp. [In Moldavian and Russian].

U444c *Ugolovno-protsessual'nyi kodeks Moldavskoi SSR; ofitsial'nyi tekst s izm. i dop. na 1 iiulia 1973 g. i s pril. postateino-sist. materialov.* Kishinev: Kartia Moldoveniaske, 1974. 618 pp.

Commentary

U445 *Kommentarii k Ugolovno-protsessual'nomu kodeksu Moldavskoi SSR,* sost. i red.: A. S. Kazanir, A. I. Santalov. Kishinev: Kartia Moldoveniaske, 1966. 374 pp.

TAJIKISTAN

New

U446 *Ugolovno-protsessual'nyi kodeks Tadzhikskoi SSR.* Dushanbe: Irfon, 1961. 276 pp. [Also publ. in Tajik]. [Republished with revisions at intervals].

TURKMENISTAN

New

U447 *Ugolovno-protsessual'nyi kodeks Turkmenskoi SSR.* Ashkhabad: Turkmenistan, 1962. 336 pp. [Also publ. in Turkmenian]. [Republished with revisions 1968 and 1972].

UKRAINE

Old

U448 *Ugolovno-protsessual'nyi kodeks Ukrainskoi SSR.* Kiev: Politizdat Ukrainy, 1958. 158 pp. [In Ukrainian].

New

U449 *Ugolovno-protsessual'nyi kodeks Ukrainskoi SSR.* Kiev: Politizdat Ukrainy, 1961. 213 pp. [Also publ. in Ukrainian]. [Republished with revisions at intervals].

Commentaries

U450 *Ugolovno-protsessual'nyi kodeks Ukrainskoi SSR: nauchno-prakticheskii kommentarii.* Kiev: Politizdat Ukrainy, 1968. 400 pp. [In Ukrainian]. [Republished with revisions 1974 and 1978].

UZBEKISTAN

New

U451 *Ugolovno-protsessual'nyi kodeks Uzbekskoi SSR.* Tashkent: Gosizdat UzSSR, 1959. 176 pp. [Also publ. in Uzbek]. [Republished with revisions at invervals].

Commentary

U452 *Kommentarii k Ugolovno-protsessual'nomu kodeksu Uzbekskoi SSR,* pod red. F. S. Bakirova. 1970. 390 pp. [In Uzbek].

Translations

U453a 'Cases on criminal law and procedure, from the USSR and RSFSR Supreme Courts'. *Soviet statutes and decisions*, vol. 1, no. 4, 1965.

U453b 'Criminal code of the RSFSR, as amended to 31 December 1963'. *Soviet statutes and decisions*, vol. 1, no. 1, 1964.

U453c 'Code of criminal procedure of the RSFSR, as amended to 1 October 1964'. *Soviet statutes and decisions*, vol. 1, no. 2/3, 1965.

These three issues of *SS&D* (*see* U164) contain translations of legislation, mainly from the RSFSR.

U454 *The federal criminal law of the Soviet Union. The basic principles of the criminal legislation. The law concerning crimes against the State. The law concerning military crimes. The basic principles of criminal procedure.* Russian text with an English translation by F. J. Feldbrugge. (Law in Eastern Europe, 3). Leyden: Sijthoff, 1959. 157 pp.

After a long comparative introduction, gives the parallel Russian and English texts of this material. Annotated, with index.

U455 *Fundamentals of Soviet criminal legislation, the judicial system and criminal court procedure: official texts and commentaries.* M.: FLPH, 1960. 103 pp.

The 1958 Fundamental Principles, with short commentaries.

U456 *Soviet criminal law and procedure: the RSFSR codes.* Introduction and analysis: Harold J. Berman; translation: Harold J. Berman and James W. Spindler. 2nd ed. (Russian Research Center studies, 50). Cambridge, Mass.: Harvard University Press, 1972. xi, 399 pp.

1st ed. publ. 1966 (ix, 501 pp.). The first edition has material as of July 1965, the second as of 1 March 1972. Long, useful introduction on the RSFSR criminal codes, on changes in the law 1961–71, chapters analysing the Law on Court Organization, military law and tribunals, role of the procuracy and legal profession, and a particularly valuable discussion of the vocabulary and style of the codes. Translates the RSFSR Criminal Code, Criminal Procedure Code and Law on Court Organization, all enacted in 1960. The appendix has tables on the corresponding provisions of the all-union Fundamental Principles. Glossary and index.

For translated material, see also *Collected legislation* (U158) sections VII: 8 and VII: 9.

Administrative law and administrative offences

Administrative law covers the administrative and executive activities of various state agencies in all areas of public life, including planning, housing, education, etc. In this section, only the most general collections of material on administrative law are included; material on administration in specific spheres is to be found in the sections concerned. Material on administrative responsibility and administrative offences is included here. New Fundamental Principles of Legislation of the USSR and Union Republics on Administrative Law Violations were passed on 23 October 1980 and come into force on 1 March 1981.

Collections of material on administrative law and administrative offences

U457   *Administratiivvastutus: kehtivate normatiivaktide kogumik.* [Adminstrative responsibility: a collection of normative acts]. Tallin: Eesti raamat, 1966. 314 pp.

In Estonian. Includes Estonian and all-union materials on administrative law. Subject index.

U458   *Administrativnye shtrafy: sbornik normativnykh aktov.* [Administrative penalties: a collection of normative acts]. (Iurid. komissiia pri SM Moldavskoi SSR). Kishinev: Kartia Moldoveniaske, 1967. 144 pp. [Not seen].

U459   *Sbornik normativnykh aktov po sovetskomu administrativnomu pravu.* [A collection of normative acts on Soviet administrative law]. Sost.: A. G. Khazikov. M.: Vysshaia shkola, 1964. 580 pp.

A collection for student use of materials in force on 1 November 1963 on Soviet state organization, administrative law in general, and administrative law as it relates to industry, agriculture, housing, education, health, public order, state security, etc.

U460   *Sbornik zakonodatel'nykh aktov ob administrativnoi otvetstvennosti. Dlia rabotnikov apilinkovykh i poselkovykh Sovetov deputatov trudiashchikhsia.* [A collection of legislative acts on administrative responsibility for officials of local soviets]. Vilnius, 1971. 168 pp. In Lithuanian and Russian. [Not seen].

U461   *Sbornik zakonodatel'nykh aktov ob administrativnykh shtrafakh.* [A collection of legislative acts on administrative penalties]. Tashkent: Uzbekistan, 1971. 214 pp. [Not seen].

U462   *Sbornik zakonodatel'nykh i innykh normativnykh aktov ob administrativnoi otvetstvennosti.* [A collection of legislative and other normative acts on administrative responsibility]. M.: Iurid. lit-ra, 1978. 264 pp.

Includes general USSR and RSFSR laws, regulations and decrees on administrative responsibility, followed by sections dealing with administrative offences in industry, transport and communications, agriculture, trade and finance. There are also regulations relating to breaches of public order, drunkenness, hooliganism and violations of the regulations on passports, customs and conscription. It also covers administrative responsibility for safety, fire protection, conservation and poaching, breaches of the planning law relating to house building, and other administrative matters affecting the general public. Most of the documents included have been previously published; some are reproduced in extract only. Subject index.

U463 *Sbornik zakonodatel'nykh i normativnykh aktov ob administrativnoi otvetstvennosti.* [A collection of legislation and normative acts on administrative responsibility]. M.: Pravda, 1972. 318 pp.

Earlier ed. publ. 1971 (270 pp.) Includes USSR and RSFSR materials on the administrative rights and duties of various official bodies, and on the penalties for administrative offences.

U464 'Soviet administrative law: administrative penalties'. *Soviet statutes and decisions,* vol. 5, no. 1, 1968.

This issue of *SS&D* (*see* U164) brings together legislation on administrative penalties.

U465 *Spravochnik po administrativnomu zakonodatel'stvu dlia rabotnikov organov vnutrennikh del.* [Manual of administrative law for officials of the Ministry of Internal Affairs]. Sost.: R. I. Tevlin. (M-vo vnutrennikh del USSR). Kiev, 1972–. [Not seen].

U466 *Zakonodatel'nye akty ob administrativnoi otvetstvennosti.* [Legislative acts on administrative responsibility]. Sost.: L. L. Dedkov, N. A. Stoliar. Minsk: Belarus', 1977. 304 pp.

Earlier ed. publ. as: *Sbornik zakonodatel'nykh aktov ob administrativnoi otvetstvennosti.* 1970 (318 pp.) Both collections include all-union and Belorussian materials on administrative law.

U467 *Zakonodatel'nye i normativnye akty Kazakhskoi SSR ob administrativnoi otvetstvennosti.* [Legislative and normative acts of the Kazakh SSR on administrative responsibility]. Sost.: V. A. Zinchenko. Alma-Ata: Kazakhstan, 1977. 318 pp.

Includes all-union and Kazakh materials as of 1 January 1976, in a subject arrangement.

U468 *Zakonodatel'stvo ob administrativnoi otvetstvennosti: sbornik normativnykh aktov.* [Legislation on administrative responsibility: a collection of normative acts]. (Ispolkom Kuibyshevskogo obl. Soveta deputatov trudiashchikhsia). Kuibyshev: Kuibyshevskoe kn. izd-vo, 1975. 296 pp.

A collection of material for officials of local soviets on administrative law and administrative offences.

U469 *Zakonodavstva pro administratyvnu vidovidal'nist'.* [Legislation on administrative responsibility]. [Ed.: I. P. Kononenko]. (Iurid. komissia pri RM URSR). Kyiv: Vyd. polit. lit-ry Ukrainy, 1969. 340 pp.

In Ukrainian. 1st ed. publ. 1965 (277 pp.). A collection of all-union and Ukrainian legislation and other normative acts on administrative jurisdiction, rights and responsibilities of official bodies in all spheres of economic, political and social life.

See also U923 and U925.

SUPREME SOVIETS
AND GOVERNMENTS

In this section, details are given of the serial publications of the supreme soviets and governments (councils of ministers) of the USSR and the union republics, the proceedings of the supreme soviets, statistics on elections to the supreme soviets, and general material on the work of the soviets. Local soviets are not covered. More information on the competence of the supreme soviets, the councils of ministers and their structure is given in the introduction to this chapter, where the nature of the legislation they enact is also discussed. Collections of laws are dealt with in the subsections on general collections of legislation. Legislation on particular subjects is listed with the other materials on that subject. Translations of USSR and RSFSR materials listed in this section can often be found in the general sources of translated material described at U156–U165 and U852–U859; coverage of the other union republics is poorer but sometimes translations of their legislation too is included in these general sources.

General documents on the soviets

U470 *KPSS o rabote sovetov: sbornik dokumentov*. [The CPSU on the work of the soviets: a collection of documents]. M.: Gospolitizdat, 1959. 687 pp.

A chronological collection of CPSU resolutions, decisions, etc. on the work of the soviets at all levels, 1906–59.

U471 *Sovety narodnykh deputatov; obshchestvenno-politicheskii zhurnal.* [The soviets of people's deputies; a socio-political journal]. M.: Izvestiia, 1957–. Monthly.

1957–77, no. 10, title was *Sovety deputatov trudiashchikhsia*. Includes articles on the work of the USSR and union republic supreme soviets, and lower-level soviets, reports on the work of the Permanent Commissions of the USSR Supreme Soviet, some decrees and other acts of the USSR Supreme Soviet and reports on the work of delegates to the Supreme Soviet. Annual index.

U472 *Sovety narodnykh deputatov: status, kompetentsiia, organizatsiia deiatel'nosti; sbornik dokumentov*. [A collection of documents on the status, competence and organization of the soviets]. M.: Iurid. lit-ra, 1980. 464 pp.

Includes party documents, legislation and normative acts on the USSR Supreme Soviet, the Supreme Soviet of the union republics, and local soviets in the light of the 1977 constitution.

U473 *V. I. Lenin, KPSS o rabote sovetov*. [V. I. Lenin and the CPSU on the work of the soviets]. M.: Politizdat, 1979. 744 pp.

A collection of Lenin's writings and CPSU congress, conference and plenum decisions, plus other party and government materials on the role, functions and organization of the soviets. Subject index.

See also U573–U575.

Statistics on elections to the soviets

The collections listed here cover the USSR as a whole; where handbooks exist for the supreme soviets of the USSR or individual union republics, they are listed under that republic or in the section dealing with the Supreme Soviet of the USSR.

U474a *Sostav deputatov Verkhovnykh Sovetov soiuznykh, avtonomnykh respublik i mestnykh Sovetov deputatov trudiashchikhsia, 1959 g.: statisticheskii sbornik.* [A statistical handbook on the composition of deputies to the supreme soviets of the union and autonomous republics and to local soviets, 1959]. (Otdel po voprosam raboty Sovetov Prezidiuma Verkhovnogo Soveta SSSR). M.: Izvestiia, 1959. 99 pp.

U474b *Itogi vyborov i sostav deputatov Verkhovnykh Sovetov soiuznykh, avtonomnykh respublik i mestnykh Sovetov deputatov trudiashchikhsia 1963 g.: statisticheskii sbornik.* [Results of the elections and the composition of deputies to the supreme soviets of the union and autonomous republics and to local soviets in 1963: a statistical handbook]. (Otdel po voprosam raboty Sovetov Prezidiuma Verkhovnogo Soveta SSSR). M.: Izvestiia, 1963. 223 pp.

U474c *Itogi vyborov i sostav deputatov Verkhovnykh Sovetov soiuznykh i avtonomnykh respublik, ... g.: statisticheskii sbornik.* [Results of the elections and composition of the deputies to the supreme soviets of the union and autonomous republics in ...: statistical handbook]. (Otdel po voprosam raboty Sovetov Prezidiuma Verkhovnogo Soveta SSSR). M.: Izvestiia.

1967 g. 1967. 87 pp.
1971 g. 1971. 94 pp.

These handbooks contain figures for the union republics and autonomous republics, but exclude the USSR Supreme Soviet; the 1959 and 1963 volumes also cover the local soviets.

USSR

Supreme Soviet

The USSR Supreme Soviet now usually meets twice a year, generally in June and December, with occasional extraordinary sessions, as in October 1977 when it met to pass the 1977 constitution. The proceedings of each session of the Supreme Soviet are published, with an appendix giving the texts of legislation passed during the session. Full details of the dates of the convocations and sessions, and lists of the laws enacted at each session, can be found in the bibliographies, U64a–b. In addition to the stenographic report of the proceedings of the sessions, the USSR Supreme Soviet also publishes a gazette in all the languages of the union republics of the USSR, which includes laws passed during the sessions and edicts of the Presidium of the Supreme Soviet passed between sessions. The Supreme Soviet of the USSR also has its own newspaper. Details of these publications follow.

PROCEEDINGS

U475 [*Number of session . . .*] *sessiia Verkhovnogo Soveta SSSR,* [*number of convocation . . .*] *sozyv,* [*dates of session . . .*] *g.: stenograficheskii otchet.* [Stenographic report of the . . . session of the Supreme Soviet of the USSR, . . . convocation . . .]. M.: Izd. Verkhovnogo Soveta SSSR, 1 sessiia, 1-ogo sozyva, 12–19 ianvaria 1938 g.–.

From 1946 to 1977, the title of the proceedings took the form: *Zasedaniia Verkhovnogo Soveta SSSR . . . sozyva, . . . sessiia (. . . g.) : stenograficheskii otchet.*

GAZETTE

U476 *Vedomosti Verkhovnogo Soveta Soiuza Sovetskikh Sotsialisticheskikh Respublik.* [Gazette of the USSR Supreme Soviet]. M.: Izd. Verkhovnogo Soveta SSSR, 1938–. Weekly.

1938–53 published in newspaper format. Frequency then varied from 22 to 82 issues p.a. Published in journal form since 1954; 24 issues 1954–5, 25 in 1956, 28 in 1957, 37 in 1958, 51 in 1960 and 1965; otherwise 52 p.a. Published in all the languages of the constituent republics of the USSR, but with certain supplements appearing only in the Russian-language edition. As the official gazette of the Supreme Soviet, it publishes laws, etc. passed by the Supreme Soviet during its sessions, edicts of the Presidium of the Supreme Soviet and reports on official visits by foreign delegations, and other information on Supreme Soviet business. It lists the composition of the Presidium and the Permanent Commissions of the Supreme Soviet after each of its sessions. There are annual indexes, listing: (a) normative acts and reports of the Permanent Commissions and other bodies, by topic; (b) acts relating to the award of medals and honours and personnel changes; (c) information on changes in administrative territorial boundaries. For a cumulated subject index to the *Vedomosti* for 1938–65, and *Sobranie zakonov . . .* Part I (U479) for 1924–37, see: Lassalle, W. *Verzeichnis der Schlagwörter zur Gesetzgebung der UdSSR, 1923–1965.* (Seminarabteilung für Ostrechtsforschung an der Universität Hamburg, Hilfsmittel zum Ostrecht, 3). Hamburg: The Author, 1974. vi, 83 pp.

NEWSPAPER

U477 *Izvestiia Sovetov narodnykh deputatov SSSR.* [News from the USSR soviets of people's deputies]. M.: Izvestiia, 1917–. 6 per week.

Many changes of title, linked with changes in the name of the government and the Supreme Soviet. Frequency varied in the prewar years. This is the official newspaper of the government, containing reports on the work of the Council of Ministers, ministries and state committees. It often publishes major decrees, ordinances, etc., frequently not in full but in summary form. It is extensively translated in CDSP (U853).

STATISTICS ON ELECTIONS TO THE USSR SUPREME SOVIET

U478 *Verkhovnyi Sovet SSSR ... sozyva: statisticheskii sbornik.* [A statistical handbook on the Supreme Soviet of the USSR, ... convocation]. (Otdel po voprosam raboty Sovetov Prezidiuma Verkhovnogo Soveta SSSR). M.: Izvestiia.

6 sozyv. 1962. 37 pp.

7 sozyv. 1966. 47 pp.

8 sozyv. 1970.

9 sozyv. 1974.

10 sozyv. 1979.

Gives information on the deputies elected to the Supreme Soviet, their age, sex, educational level, party membership, nationality and employment. Also gives information on deputies elected to serve on the Presidium and various Permanent Commissions. A summary at the back gives data on the composition of previous convocations back to 1937.

Government

The USSR Council of Ministers issues a large number of ordinances and other normative acts, many of which are not published. Such acts are usually sent out to those institutions and organizations which are directly affected by these acts or will have to carry them out. Some enactments of major importance and needing wide circulation are published in *Izvestiia* and other newspapers appropriate to the subject; new legislation in particular subject fields is also often published in the specialist press for that area. The main source for government ordinances is the government gazette.

GOVERNMENT GAZETTE

U479 *Sobranie postanovlenii pravitel'stva SSSR.* [Collection of the ordinances of the government of the USSR]. M.: Upr. delami Soveta ministrov SSSR, 1924–49, 1957–. Frequency varies; usually issued every 10–14 days.

In the prewar period frequency varied considerably; 1945–9 between 8 and 12 issues p.a.; 16 issues in 1957; 20 issues 1959–60; about fortnightly since. Title: 1924–January 1938 called *Sobranie zakonov i rasporiazhenii Raboche-krestianskogo pravitel'stva SSSR;* March 1938–1946, no. 4 called *Sobranie postanovlenii i rasporiazhenii pravitel'stva SSSR;* 1946, no. 5–1949, no. 12 called *Sobranie postanovlenii i rasporiazhenii Soveta Ministrov SSSR.* Adopted its present title from 1957. It was published in two parts 1924–38; from January 1981 it is also being issued in two parts, with part I containing ordinances of general significance and having a normative character, and part II containing treaties, conventions, protocols and other agreements with foreign powers. As the official bulletin of the USSR Council of Ministers, *SP SSSR* includes: (a) joint resolutions of the Council of Ministers and the Central Committee of the CPSU; (b) ordinances of the Council of Ministers; (c) appointments to government posts and changes in ministries, state committees and other authorities subordinate to the Council of Ministers; (d) international treaties, conventions, etc. Each act is numbered, with the numbering running consecutively through the year; there is a separate sequence for part I and part II. There are annual chronological and subject indexes of enactments. A cumulated index to SP SSSR has been prepared: *Ukazatel' k Sobraniiu postanovlenii pravitel'stva SSSR, 1957–1966 gg.* Leningrad, 1969, 2 vols., but is apparently not publicly available. An index to this publication for 1924–37 is available; see the Lassalle index described under U476. *SP SSSR* was not available for export from the USSR from mid-1959 until 1972, but was available in libraries in the USSR; reprints of these years can now be obtained in the West. During 1951 to mid-1957, *SP SSSR* was produced, but it was distributed only to institutions and government departments and cannot be seen by the general reader or by foreign scholars.

Ministries and state committees

Some ministries and state committees have their own bulletins; details of these are given in the relevant sections of this bibliography. Often regulations, instructions, etc. from these bodies are sent out direct to subordinate organizations and not published at all. There is one general bulletin which publishes normative acts of some ministries and state committees:

U480   *Biulleten' normativnykh aktov ministerstv i vedomstv SSSR; organ Ministerstva iustitsii SSSR.* [A bulletin of the normative acts of USSR ministries and other departments; an organ of the USSR Ministry of Justice]. M.: Iurid. lit-ra, 1972–. Monthly.

    A bulletin of normative acts (regulations, instructions, letters, ordinances, etc.), chiefly from all-union ministries and state committees which do not have their own bulletins. Annual index.

Supreme soviets and governments of the union republics

Although each union republic has a similar constitution and state structure, there are considerable variations in publishing practice between them. Each union republic publishes regularly the stenographic report of its Supreme Soviet proceedings including the legislation passed at the session. Full details of these are given in the bibliographies, U64a–b. Some merge the Supreme Soviet gazette and the government gazette, some keep them separate, and others seem to have no publication which fulfils the function of a gazette of Council of Ministers ordinances; presumably these republics either have a restricted circulation gazette or send out their ordinances directly. A number of the union republic Supreme Soviet and government gazettes listed are not generally available outside the USSR. All the union republics publish several newspapers, usually one in Russian and one in the official language of the republic, often as joint publications with the republic's Communist Party Central Committee.

These newspapers are official publications of the republic's government and, especially for republics other than the RSFSR, can often be the most easily accessible source of official materials not included in the report of the proceedings of the republic's Supreme Soviet.

In the lists which follow on each union republic, the annotations are limited to bibliographical information; in general the scope of each publication is similar to that of the all-union equivalent, but limited to matters within the competence of the union republic.

RSFSR

SUPREME SOVIET PROCEEDINGS

U481   *Zasedaniia Verkhovnogo Soveta RSFSR ... sozyva, ... sessiia, ...g.: stenograficheskii otchet.* [Proceedings of the RSFSR Supreme Soviet, ... number of convocation, ... number of session, ... date: stenographic report]. M.: Izd. Verkhovnogo Soveta RSFSR, 1 sessiia, 1 sozyva, 15–20 iiulia 1938 g.–.

SUPREME SOVIET GAZETTE

U482   *Vedomosti Verkhovnogo Soveta RSFSR.* [Gazette of the RSFSR Supreme Soviet]. M.: Izd. Verkhovnogo Soveta RSFSR, 1957–. Weekly.

     3 issues in 1957, 20 in 1958, 48 in 1959, 50 in 1960, 59 in 1961; 52 p.a. since 1962.

GOVERNMENT GAZETTE

U483   *Sobranie postanovlenii pravitel'stva RSFSR.* [Collection of ordinances of the government of the RSFSR]. M.: Upr. delami SM RSFSR, 1917–49, 1958–. Frequency varies; about once in two weeks.

     Considerable variations in frequency in the prewar period: 7 issues in 1945, 8 in 1946, 12 in 1947–8 and 3 in 1949; 15 issues in 1959, 53 in 1960 and about fortnightly since. 1917–Jan. 1938 called *Sobranie uzakonenii i rasporiazhenii Raboche-krestianskoi pravitel'stva RSFSR;* Feb. 1938–48 called *Sobranie postanovlenii i rasporiazhenii pravitel'stva RSFSR;* 1949 called *Sobranie postanovlenii i rasporiazhenii Soveta Ministrov RSFSR.* Adopted present title from 1958. Like the USSR gazette, it was not available for export from mid-1959 to 1972.

OFFICIAL NEWSPAPER

U484   *Sovetskaia Rossiia.* [Soviet Russia]. 1956–. 6 per week.

     Published by the RSFSR Supreme Soviet and Council of Ministers with the Central Committee of the CPSU. (The RSFSR does not have its own republican party.)

OTHER DOCUMENTS

U485   *Biulleten' No. ... tekushchego zakonodatel'stva.* [Bulletin of current legislation No. . . .]. (M-vo iustitsii RSFSR. Otdel kodifikatsii). M.: Gosiurizdat, [?1955–].

Copies seen, covering March–August 1956 and numbered 1 and 2, were published 1957 and were marked 'Distributed according to circulation list'. Contain USSR and RSFSR laws, Supreme Soviet edicts, ordinances of the USSR and RSFSR Council of Ministers, and orders and letters of the RSFSR Ministry of Justice. Publication appears to have begun with an issue for July–December 1955; no more details known.

U486 *Zakonodatel'nye akty po voprosam deputatskoi deyatel'nosti; deputatu Verkhovnogo Soveta RSFSR.* [Legislative acts on the activities of deputies: a collection of documents for deputies to the RSFSR Supreme Soviet]. M.: Izvestiia, 1980. 164 pp. [Not seen].

Armenia

SUPREME SOVIET PROCEEDINGS

U487 *Zasedaniia Verkhovnogo Soveta Armianskoi SSR . . . sozyva, . . . sessiia, . . . g.: stenograficheskii otchet.* [Proceedings of the Supreme Soviet of the Armenian SSR, . . . number of convocation, . . . number of session, . . . date: stenographic report]. Erevan: Izd. Verkhovnogo Soveta ArmSSR, 1 sessiia 1-ogo sozyva, 12–14 iiulia 1938 g.–. [Also publ. in Armenian].

SUPREME SOVIET GAZETTE

U488 *Vedomosti Verkhovnogo Soveta Armianskoi SSR.* [Gazette of the Supreme Soviet of the Armenian SSR]. Erevan: Izd. Verkhovnogo Soveta ArmSSR, 1939–. Fortnightly.

Parallel Armenian and Russian texts; from 1960 also publ. in Azerbaijani. Had newspaper format 1939–52. Frequency has varied considerably.

GOVERNMENT GAZETTE

U489 *Sobranie postanovlenii i rasporiazhenii pravitel'stva Armianskoi SSR.* [Collection of the ordinances and decisions of the government of the Armenian SSR]. Erevan, 1921–41, 1945, 1947.

Frequency varied; some years available in Armenian only and others in Russian only. Publishing history for 1945–7 not clear. It is believed that a successor called *Sobranie postanovlenii pravitel'stva Armianskoi SSR* is issued, but only one issue for 1959 has been positively identified; presumably if it exists it is restricted. [No issues of the Armenian SSR government gazette seen].

NEWSPAPERS

U490 [*Sovetskaia Armeniia.* Soviet Armenia]. Erevan, 1920–. 6 issues per week.

In Armenian only. Published jointly by the Armenian Council of Ministers and the Armenian Communist Party; for a Russian-language newspaper from Armenia, *see* U591.

Azerbaijan

SUPREME SOVIET PROCEEDINGS

U491 *Zasedaniia Verkhovnogo Soveta Azerbaidzhanskoi SSR ... sozyva, ... sessiia, ... g.: stenograficheskii otchet.* [Proceedings of the Supreme Soviet of the Azerbaijani SSR, ... number of convocation, ... number of session, ... date: stenographic report]. Baku: Izd. Verkhovnogo Soveta AzSSR, 1 sessiia 1-ogo sozyva, 18–22 iiulia 1938 g.–. [Also publ. in Azerbaijani].

SUPREME SOVIET GAZETTE

U492 *Azerbaijan SSR Ali Sovetinin ma'lumaty = Vedomosti Verkhovnogo Soveta Azerbaidzhanskoi SSR.* [Gazette of the Supreme Soviet of the Azerbaijani SSR]. Baku, 1938–41, 1958–. Fortnightly.

Appeared every 10 days until 1965. In Azerbaijani and Russian. In 1957–8, its functions were carried out by U493a. [Not seen].

GOVERNMENT GAZETTE

U493a *Azerbaijan SSR hokumatinin gararlary kuliiiaty = Sobranie postanovlenii pravitel'stva Azerbaidzhanskoi SSR.* [Collection of the ordinances of the government of the Azerbaijani SSR]. Baku, 1920–39, 1941, 1957–. Fortnightly.

Since 1957, publ. in parallel Azerbaijani and Russian texts. Considerable variations in frequency in the prewar period. 1957–8, no. 13 called *Sobranie zakonov Verkhovnogo Soveta AzSSR, ukazov Prezidiuma Verkhovnogo Soveta AzSSR, postanovleniia i rasporiazhenii Soveta Ministrov AzSSR* and combined the functions of Supreme Soviet and government gazette. 1958, nos. 14–29 called *Sobranie postanovlenii i rasporiazhenii Soveta Ministrov AzSSR.*

U493b *Biulleten' tekushchego zakonodatel'stva Azerbaidzhanskoi SSR.* [Bulletin of current legislation of the Azerbaijani SSR]. (Prokuratura AzSSR. Chast' sistematizatsii zakonodatel'stva). Baku, 1956–8. Quarterly.

Contains recent Council of Ministers ordinances and other legislative materials; replaced by U493a above.

NEWSPAPER

The Supreme Soviet and Council of Ministers of Azerbaijan do not appear to publish a newspaper; for Russian and Azerbaijani newspapers published by the republic's communist party, *see* U603.

OTHER DOCUMENTS

U494 *Azerbaijan SSR Ali Sovetinin deputatlary: ieddinji chaghyrysh = Deputaty Verkhovnogo Soveta Azerbaidzhanskoi SSR, sed'moi sozyv.* [Deputies to the Supreme Soviet of the Azerbaijani SSR, seventh convocation]. Baku: Izd. Verkhovnogo Soveta AzSSR, 1968. 400 pp.

In Azerbaijani and Russian. Photographs and biographical notes on the 380 delegates, with a preface giving some statistical data.

U495 *Itogi vyborov i sostav deputatov Verkhovnykh Sovetov Azerbaidzhanskoi SSR, Nakhichevanskoi ASSR i mestnykh Sovetov deputatov trudiashchikhsia, izbrannykh v* ... [Results of the elections and composition of the deputies elected to the Supreme Soviet of the Azerbaijani SSR, Nakhichevan SSR and local soviets in ...: a statistical handbook]. Baku: Azernesher.

... *marte 1967 g.* 1969. 56 pp.

... *iiune 1975 g.* 1977. 90 pp.

[Not seen].

Belorussia

SUPREME SOVIET PROCEEDINGS

U496 ... *sesiia Viarkhounaha Saveta Belaruskai SSR* ... *sklikannia,* ... *hoda: stenahrafichnaia spravazdacha =* ... *sessiia Verkhovnogo Soveta Belorusskoi SSR* ... *sozyva,* ... *goda: stenograficheskii otchet.* [Number of session ... of the Supreme Soviet of the Belorussian SSR, ... convocation, ... date: stenographic report]. Minsk: Belarus', 1 sessiia 1-ogo sozyva, 25–8 iiulia 1938 g.–. [In Russian and Belorussian].

SUPREME SOVIET AND GOVERNMENT GAZETTE

U497 *Zbor zakonau, ukazau Prezidyuma Viarkhounaha Saveta BSSR, pastanou i rasparadzhenniau Saveta Ministrau BSSR = Sobranie zakonov, ukazov Prezidiuma Verkhovnogo Soveta BSSR, postanovlenii i rasporiazhenii Soveta Ministrov BSSR.* [Collection of laws, edicts of the Presidium of the Supreme Soviet, and ordinances and decisions of the Council of Ministers of the Belorussian SSR]. Minsk, 1922–41, 1944–9, 1957–. 36 p.a.

In Belorussian and Russian. Considerable variations in frequency. Until 1948 called *Sobranie zakonov i rasporiazhenii pravitel'stva BSSR.* In 1944–9 appeared only in Russian.

NEWSPAPERS

U498a *Sovetskaia Belorussiia.* [Soviet Belorussia]. Minsk, 1927–. 6 per week.

U498b *Zviazda.* [Star]. Minsk, 1917–. 6 per week.

Both these newspapers are issued jointly by the Central Committee of the Belorussian CP and the Belorussian Council of Ministers and Supreme Soviet; *Zviazda* is in Belorussian.

Estonia

SUPREME SOVIET PROCEEDINGS

U499 ... *sessiia Verkhovnogo Soveta Estonskoi SSR ... sozyva, ... g.: stenograficheskii otchet.* [Number of session ... of the Supreme Soviet of the Estonian SSR, ... number of convocation ... date: stenographic report]. Tallin: Eesti raamat, 1 sessiia 1-ogo sozyva, 21 iiulia–25 avgusta 1940 g.–.
Also publ. in Estonian

SUPREME SOVIET AND GOVERNMENT GAZETTES

U500a *Eesti NSV teataja. Eesti NSV seaduste, Eesti NSV Ülemnõukogu Presiidiumi seadluste, Eesti NSV Ministrite nõukogo määruste ja korralduste, Eesti NSV ministriite kaskkirjade ja juhendite kogu = Vedomosti Estonskoi SSR. Sobranie zakonov ESSR, ukazov Prezidiuma Verkhovnogo Soveta ESSR, postanovleniia i rasporiazheniia Soveta ministrov ESSR, prikazov i instruktsii ministrov ESSR.* [Gazette of the Estonian SSR. A collection of laws, edicts of the Presidium of the Supreme Soviet, ordinances and decisions of the Council of Ministers, orders and instruction of ministries of the Estonian SSR]. Tallin, 1940–1, 1944–59.
Estonian and Russian text; until 1944 publ. in separate Estonian and Russian editions. Considerable variations in frequency and some minor title changes. In 1960–5 its functions were carried out by two publications:

U500b *Eesti NSV Ülemnõukogu teataja = Vedomosti Verkhovnogo Soveta ESSR.* [Gazette of the Supreme Soviet of the Estonian SSR]. Tallin, 1960–5. Weekly. [Estonian and Russian text].

U500c *Sobranie postanovlenii i rasporiazhenii Soveta ministrov ESSR.* [A collection of ordinances and decisions of the Estonian Council of Ministers]. Tallin, 1960–5. Weekly.
In Estonian and Russian; Estonian title not known. [Not seen].

From 1966, the gazettes again appeared jointly:

U500d *Eesti NSV Ülemnõukogu ja Valitsuse teataja = Vedomosti Verkhovnogo Soveta i pravitel'stva Estonii.* [Gazette of the Estonian Supreme Soviet and government]. Tallin, 1966–. Weekly.
In Estonian and Russian.

NEWSPAPERS

U501a *Sovetskaia Estoniia.* [Soviet Estonia]. Tallin, 1940–1, 1944–. 6 per week.

U501b *Rahva Hääl.* [People's voice]. Tallin, 1940–. 6 per week.
Both newspapers are jointly published by the Central Committee of the Estonian CP, the Estonian Supreme Soviet and Council of Ministers; *Rahva Hääl* is in Estonian.

OTHER DOCUMENTS

U502   *Sovetskoe pravo: iuridicheskii biulleten'.* [Soviet law: a legal bulletin].
(M-vo iustitsii ESSR). Tallin, 1967–. 6 p.a.
    Also publ. in Estonian as *Nõukogude öigus.* Includes new normative acts of the Estonian Council of Ministers and Supreme Soviet, decisions of the Estonian Supreme Court, and materials from the Procuracy and Gosarbitrazh. Includes lists of major all-union and Estonian normative acts, and articles on all aspects of law in Estonia. The Estonian-language edition also includes the texts of some all-union legislation.

Georgia

SUPREME SOVIET PROCEEDINGS

U503   *Zasedaniia Verkhovnogo Soveta Gruzinskoi SSR ... sozyva, ... sessiia, ... g.: stenograficheskii otchet.* [Proceedings of the Supreme Soviet of the Georgian SSR ... number of convocation, ... number of session, ... date: stenographic report]. Tbilisi: Izd. Prezidiuma Verkhovnogo Soveta GSSR, 1 sessiia 1-ogo sozyva, 8–11 iiulia 1938 g.–.

SUPREME SOVIET GAZETTE

U504   *Vedomosti Verkhovnogo Soveta Gruzinskoi SSR.* [Gazette of the Supreme Soviet of the Georgian SSR]. Tbilisi, 1938–. Monthly.
    Georgian and Russian text; Georgian title not known. Until 1949, publ. in separate Georgian and Russian eds. 20 issues in 1948–50, 8 p.a. 1951–3, 6 p.a. 1954–8, 11 in 1959, 25 in 1960, 37 p.a. 1961–2, 36 p.a. 1963–4, 30 in 1965, then monthly. [Not seen].

GOVERNMENT GAZETTE

U505   *Sbornik postanovlenii i rasporiazhenii pravitel'stva Gruzinskoi SSR.* [Collection of ordinances and decisions of the government of the Georgian SSR]. Tbilisi, 1958–. 6 p.a.
    Georgian and Russian text; Georgian title not known. [Not seen].

NEWSPAPERS

U506a   *Zaria Vostoka.* [Light of the East]. Tbilisi, 1922–. 6 per week.
U506b   [*Kommunist.* The Communist]. Tbilisi, 1920–. 6 per week.
    Both newspapers are issued jointly by the Supreme Soviet of the Georgian SSR and the Central Committee of the Georgian CP. [*Kommunist*] is in Georgian.

Karelo-Finnish SSR

The Karelo-Finnish Autonomous Republic was turned into a union republic on 31 March 1940 and reverted to autonomous republic status on 16 July 1956.

SUPREME SOVIET PROCEEDINGS

U507   *...sessiia Verkhovnogo Soveta Karelo-Finskoi SSR...sozyva,...g.: stenograficheskii otchet.* [... Number of session of the Supreme Soviet of the Karelo-Finnish SSR, ... number of convocation, ... date: stenographic report]. Petrozavodsk, 1 sessiia 1-ogo sozyva, 8–11 iiulia 1940 g. – 2 sessiia 4-ogo sozyva, 1–2 fevralia 1956 g.

     Also publ. in Finnish.

GAZETTE

None published while it had union republic status.

NEWSPAPER

U508   *Leninskaia pravda* [Leninist truth]. Petrozavodsk, 1918–. 6 per week.

     Sponsored by the government and the communist party of the republic; also publ. in Finnish 1940–57.

Kazakhstan

SUPREME SOVIET PROCEEDINGS

U509   *Zasedaniia Verkhovnogo Soveta Kazakhskoi SSR, ... sozyva, ... sessiia, ... g.: stenograficheskii otchet.* [Proceedings of the Supreme Soviet of the Kazakh SSR, ... number of convocation, ... number of session, ... date: stenographic report]. Alma-Ata: Izd. Verkhovnogo Soveta KazSSR, 1 sessiia 1-ogo sozyva, 15–17 iiulia 1938 g.–.

     Sometimes publ. in separate Kazakh and Russian eds., at others both languages have been published in the same volume.

SUPREME SOVIET AND GOVERNMENT GAZETTES

U510a   *Vedomosti Verkhovnogo Soveta Kazakhskoi SSR.* [Gazette of the Supreme Soviet of the Kazakh SSR]. Alma-Ata, 1938–56, no. 6. Monthly.

     Also publ. in Kazakh as *Qazaq SSR Zhogharghy Sovetining vedomostary.* From 1958, appeared as:

U510b   *Qazaq SSR Zhogharghy Sovetimen ukimetining vedomostary = Vedomosti Verkhovnogo Soveta i pravitel'stva Kazakhskoi SSR.* [Gazette of the Supreme Soviet and government of the Kazakh SSR]. Alma-Ata, 1958, no. 7-1966. Frequency varied; generally weekly.

     In Kazakh and Russian. Split again in 1966 (or possibly 1967) to form:

U510c   *Qazaq SSR Zhogharghy Sovetining vedomostary = Vedomosti Verkhovnogo Soveta Kazakhskoi SSR.* [Gazette of the Kazakh Supreme Soviet]. Alma-Ata, 1967–. Weekly.

     In Kazakh and Russian.

U510d   *Qazaq SSR ukimetining qaulylary zhinagy = Sobranie postanovlenii pravitel'stva Kazakhskoi SSR.* [Collection of the ordinances of the Kazakh government]. Alma-Ata, 1967–. 24 p.a.

     In Kazakh and Russian. 16 issues in 1967, 23 in 1969.

NEWSPAPERS

U511a   *Kazakhstanskaia pravda*. [Kazakhstan truth]. Alma-Ata, 1923–. 6 per week.

U511b   *Sotsialistik Qazaqstan*. [Socialist Kazakhstan]. Alma-Ata, 1919–. 6 per week.

    Both newspapers sponsored by the Kazakh CP, and the Kazakh Supreme Soviet and Council of Ministers. *Sotsialistik Qazaqstan* is in Kazakh.

OTHER DOCUMENTS

The Kazakh Ministry of Justice is reported to publish a quarterly review of legislation, but this publication has not been identified by the compiler.

Kirghizia

SUPREME SOVIET PROCEEDINGS

U512   *Kyrgyz SSRinin . . . shailangan Zhogorku Sovetinin zasedanieleri, . . . sessiia, . . . zhyl: stenografiialyk otchet = Zasedaniia Verkhovnogo Soveta Kirgizskoi SSR . . . sozyva, . . . sessiia, . . . goda: stenograficheskii otchet*. [Proceedings of the Supreme Soviet of the Kirghiz SSR, . . . number of convocation, . . . number of session, . . . date: stenographic report]. Frunze: Izd. Verkhovnogo Soveta KirgSSR, 1 sessiia 1-ogo sozyva, 18–20 iiulia 1938 g.–.

    Combined Russian and Kirghiz ed.; occasionally published separately.

SUPREME SOVIET GAZETTE

U513   *Kyrgyz SSR Zhogorku Sovetinin vedomostleri = Vedomosti Verkhovnogo Soveta Kirgizskoi SSR*. [Gazette of the Supreme Soviet of the Kirghiz SSR]. Frunze, 1938–41, 1956–.

    Frequency varies; at present about once a fortnight. In Kirghiz and Russian; publ. separately 1938–63. 1959, no. 9–1960, no. 15 had title *Vedomosti Verkhovnogo Soveta i pravitel'stva Kirgizskoi SSR*.

GOVERNMENT GAZETTE

Published jointly with the Supreme Soviet in 1959–60, (*see* U513). In addition, one issue of a *Sobranie postanovlenii i rasporiazhenii* was published in 1951 in Kirghiz [not seen]; it is believed that a gazette called *Postanovleniia Soveta Ministrov Kirgizskoi SSR* is published, but this is not certain.

NEWSPAPERS

U514a   *Sovetskaia Kirgiziia*. [Soviet Kirghizia]. Frunze, 1925–. 6 per week.

U514b   *Sovettik Kyrgyzstan*. [Soviet Kirghizia]. Frunze, 1924–. 6 per week.

    Both newspapers are published jointly by the Kirghiz Supreme Soviet, Council of Ministers and the Central Committee of the Kirghiz CP. *Sovettik Kyrgyzstan* is in Kirghiz.

Latvia

SUPREME SOVIET PROCEEDINGS

U515 *Latvijas PSR ... sasaukuma Augstākās Padomes sēdes, ... sesija, gad ...: stenografisks parskats = Zasedaniia Verkhovnogo Soveta Latviiskoi SSR ... sozyva, ... sessiia, ... goda: stenograficheskii otchet.* [Proceedings of the Supreme Soviet of the Latvian SSR, ... number of convocation, ... number of session, ... date: stenographic report]. Riga: Liesma, 3 sessiia 1-ogo sozyva, 5–6 oktiabria 1944 g.–.

In Latvian and Russian; published in separate Latvian and Russian eds. until 1951.

SUPREME SOVIET AND GOVERNMENT GAZETTE

U516 *Latvijas PSR Augstākās Padomes un valdības zinotājs = Vedomosti Verkhovnogo Soveta i pravitel'stva Latviiskoi SSR.* [Gazette of the Supreme Soviet and government of Latvia]. Riga, 1940–1, 1945–. Weekly.

In Latvian and Russian. Published in newspaper format until 1955. Until 1959, no. 5 covered only the Supreme Soviet and had title *Latvijas PSR Augstākās Padomes Prezidija zinotājs = Vedomosti Prezidiuma Verkhovnogo Soveta Latviiskoi SSR.* Frequency varied up to 1959; since then weekly.

GOVERNMENT GAZETTE

U517 *Latvijas PSR valdības lēmumu un rikojumu krājums = Sobranie postanovlenii i rasporiazhenii pravitel'stva Latviiskoi SSR.* [Collection of the ordinances and decisions of the government of the Latvian SSR]. Riga, 1941, 1945–9. Irregular.

In Latvian and Russian. From 1959, its functions covered by the gazette above.

NEWSPAPERS

U518a *Sovetskaia Latviia.* [Soviet Latvia]. Riga, 1940–1, 1944–. 6 per week.
U518b *Cīņa.* [Struggle]. Riga, 1904–. 6 per week.

Both newspapers are sponsored jointly by the Central Committee of the Latvian CP and the Latvian Supreme Soviet.

OTHER DOCUMENTS

U519 *Deputaty Verkhovnogo Soveta Latviiskoi SSR, deviatyi sozyv.* [Deputies of the 9th Convocation of the Latvian SSR]. Riga: Liesma, 1976. 175 pp.

In Latvian. [Not seen].

Lithuania

SUPREME SOVIET PROCEEDINGS

U520 *... sessiia Verkhovnogo Soveta Litovskoi SSR ... sozyva, ... goda:*

stenograficheskii otchet. [. . . Number of session of the Supreme Soviet of the Lithuanian SSR, . . . number of convocation . . . date: stenographic report]. Vilnius: Mintis, 1 sessiia 1-ogo sozyva, 25–6 avgusta 1940 g.–.

Also publ. in Lithuanian. Sometimes Lithuanian and Russian texts published in same volume.

SUPREME SOVIET AND GOVERNMENT GAZETTE

U521 *Lietuvos TSR Aukščiausiosios Tarybos ir Vyriausybēs žinios.* [Gazette of the Supreme Soviet and government of the Lithuanian SSR]. Vilnius, 1940–1, 1947–. 36 p.a.

In Lithuanian. Also publ. in Russian as *Vedomosti Verkhovnogo Soveta i pravitel'stva Litovskoi SSR.* Until 1947, the *Vedomosti Verkhovnogo Soveta Litovskoi SSR* and the *Sobranie postanovlenii i rasporiazhenii pravitel'stva Litovskoi SSR* were published separately, with bilingual texts. 1948–57 the two publications merged and continued with bilingual texts. From 1958, the gazette appeared in separate Russian and Lithuanian eds.

NEWSPAPERS

U522a *Sovetskaia Litva.* [Soviet Lithuania]. Vilnius, 1940–1, 1944–. 6 per week.

U522b *Tiesa.* [Truth]. Vilnius, 1917–22, 1924–30, 1934–. 6 per week.

These two newspapers are published by the Central Committee of the Lithuanian CP, the Presidium of the Supreme Soviet and the Council of Ministers of Lithuania. *Tiesa* is in Lithuanian.

Moldavia

SUPREME SOVIET PROCEEDINGS

U523 *Shedintsele Sovetului Suprem al RSS Moldovenesht' de Lejislatura a . . ., sessiia a . . ., . . . : dare de same stenografike = Zasedaniia Verkhovnogo Soveta Moldavskoi SSR . . . sozyva, . . . sessiia, . . . goda: stenograficheskii otchet.* [Proceedings of the Supreme Soviet of the Moldavian SSR, . . . number of convocation, . . . number of session, . . . date: stenographic report]. Kishinev: Kartia Moldoveniaske, 1 sessiia 1-ogo sozyva, 8–12 fevralia 1941 g.–.

In Moldavian and Russian.

SUPREME SOVIET AND GOVERNMENT GAZETTE

U524a *Veshtile Sovetului Suprem shi ale Gubernului RSS Moldovenesht' = Vedomosti Verkhovnogo Soveta i pravitel'stva Moldavskoi SSR.* [Gazette of the Supreme Soviet and government of the Moldavian SSR]. Kishinev, 1966–. Monthly.

In Moldavian and Russian. Formed out of the merger of two publications, both also in Moldavian and Russian:

U524b *Kuleshere de khotaryr' shi dispositsii ale Sovetului Minishtrilor al RSS Moldovenesht'* = *Sobranie postanovlenii i rasporiazhenii Soveta Ministrov Moldavskoi SSR.* [Collection of ordinances and decisions of the Moldavian Council of Ministers]. Kishinev, 1958–65. Monthly.

U524c *Veshtile Sovetului Suprem al RSS Moldovenesht'* = *Vedomosti Verkhovnogo Soveta Moldavskoi SSR.* [Gazette of the Moldavian Supreme Soviet]. Kishinev, 1960–5. Every ten days.

NEWSPAPERS

U525a *Sovetskaia Moldaviia.* [Soviet Moldavia]. Kishinev, 1925–41, 1944–. 6 per week.

U525b *Moldova sochialiste.* [Socialist Moldavia]. Kishinev, 1924–. 6 per week.

Published jointly by the Moldavian Supreme Soviet and the Central Committee of the Moldavian CP. *Moldova sochialiste* is in Moldavian.

Tajikistan

SUPREME SOVIET PROCEEDINGS

U526 *Majlishoi Soveti Olii RSS Tojikiston ... nuhum, sessiiai ...: hisoboti stenografi* = *Zasedaniia Verkhovnogo Soveta Tadzhikskoi SSR, ... sozyv, ... sessiia: stenograficheskii otchet.* [Proceedings of the Supreme Soviet of the Tajik SSR, ... number of convocation, ... number of session: stenographic report]. Dushanbe: Irfon, 1 sessiia 1-ogo sozyva, 13–16 iiulia 1938 g.–.

In Tajik and Russian, sometimes also Uzbek. Sometimes published in separate eds. for each language.

SUPREME SOVIET GAZETTE

U527 *Vedomost'hoi Soveti Olii RSS Tojikiston* = *Vedomosti Verkhovnogo Soveta Tadzhikskoi SSR.* [Gazette of the Supreme Soviet of the Tajik SSR]. Dushanbe, 1939–41, 1945–. Fortnightly.

In Russian, Tajik and Uzbek. Published irregularly in newspaper format until no. 3, 1954. Until 1959 had separate Russian, Tajik and Uzbek eds. Monthly 1954–9; 28 in 1960.

GOVERNMENT GAZETTE

U528 *Majmuai Qararhoi Hukumati RSS Tojikiston* = *Sobranie postanovlenii pravitel'stva Tadzhikskoi SSR.* [Collection of ordinances of the government of the Tajik SSR]. Dushanbe, 1931–2, 1935, 1938–9, 1947, 1959–. Monthly.

1931–47 title was *Sobranie postanovlenii i rasporiazhenii pravitel'stva Tadzhikskoi SSR* and it appeared about once a month. In Tajik, Russian and Uzbek.

NEWSPAPERS

U529a *Kommunist Tadzhikistana.* [Communist of Tajikistan]. Dushanbe, 1929–. 6 per week.

U529b *Tojikistoni soveti.* [Soviet Tajikistan]. Dushanbe, 1925–. 6 per week.
Published jointly by the Central Committee of the Tajik CP and the Tajik Supreme Soviet. *Tojikistoni soveti* is in Tajik.

Turkmenistan

SUPREME SOVIET PROCEEDINGS

U530 *Turkmenistan SSR ... chagyrlysh Ekary Sovetinin mejlisleri (... sessiia), ... iylyng: stenografik khasabat = Zasedaniia Verkhovnogo Soveta Turkmenskoi SSR ... sozyva (... sessiia), ... goda: stenograficheskii otchet.* [Proceedings of the Supreme Soviet of the Turkmenian SSR, ... number of convocation (number of session ...), ... date: stenographic report]. Ashkhabad: Turkmenistan, 1 sessiia 1-ogo sozyva, 24–8 iiulia 1938 g.–.
In Russian and Turkmenian.

SUPREME SOVIET GAZETTE

U531 *Turkmenistan SSR Ekary Sovetinin vedomostlary = Vedomosti Verkhovnogo Soveta Turkmenskoi SSR.* [Gazette of the Supreme Soviet of the Turkmenian SSR]. Ashkhabad, 1960–. Fortnightly.
1960–5 36 issues p.a. In Turkmenian and Russian. [Not seen].

GOVERNMENT GAZETTE

U532 *Turkmenistan SSR Ministrler Sovetining kararlarynyng iygyndysy = Sobranie postanovlenii i rasporiazhenii Soveta Ministrov Turkmenskoi SSR.* [Collection of ordinances and decisions of the Council of Ministers of the Turkmenian SSR]. Ashkhabad, 1926–48, 1964–. Monthly.
In Turkmenian and Russian.

NEWSPAPERS

U533a *Turkmenskaia iskra.* [The Turkmenian spark]. Ashkhabad, 1924–. 6 per week.

U533b *Sovet Turkmenistany.* [Soviet Turkmenistan]. Ashkhabad, 1920–. 6 per week.
Both newspapers published jointly by the Central Committee of the Turkmenian CP and the Turkmenian Council of Ministers and Supreme Soviet. *Sovet Turkmenistany* is in Turkmenian.

Ukraine

SUPREME SOVIET PROCEEDINGS

U534 *Zasedaniia Verkhovnogo Soveta Ukrainskoi SSR ... sozyva, ...*

sessiia, . . . goda: stenograficheskii otchet. [Proceedings of the Supreme Soviet of the Ukrainian SSR, . . . number of convocation, . . . number of session, . . . date: stenographic report]. Kiev: Politizdat Ukrainy, 1 sessiia 1-ogo sozyva, 25–8 iiulia 1938 g.–.

Also publ. in Ukrainian.

SUPREME SOVIET GAZETTE

U535 *Vidomosti Verkhovnoi Rady Ukrains'koi RSR = Vedomosti Verkhovnogo Soveta Ukrainskoi SSR.* [Gazette of the Supreme Soviet of the Ukrainian SSR]. Kiev, 1941, 1944–. Weekly.

In Russian and Ukrainian. Publ. in Ukrainian alone until 1954.

GOVERNMENT GAZETTE

U536 *Zbirnyk postanov i razporiadzhen' Uriadu Ukrains'koi RSR = Sbornik postanovlenii i rasporiazhenii pravitel'stva Ukrainskoi SSR.* [Collection of the ordinances and decisions of the Ukrainian SSR]. Kiev, 1919–41, 1945–9, 1957–. Monthly.

In Ukrainian and Russian. In 1945–9 and 1957–65 publ. in Ukrainian only. Fortnightly 1945–9; 16 issues in 1957, then monthly.

NEWSPAPERS

U537a *Pravda Ukrainy.* [Truth of the Ukraine]. Kiev, 1938–. 6 per week.
U537b *Radians'ka Ukraina.* [Soviet Ukraine]. Kiev, 1918–. 6 per week.

The Central Committee of the Ukrainian CP and the Ukrainian Supreme Soviet and Council of Ministers publish these two newspapers jointly. *Radians'ka Ukraina* is in Ukrainian.

OTHER DOCUMENTS

U538 *Pidsumky vyboriv ta sklad deputativ Verkhovnoi Rady Ukrains'koi RSR i mistsevykh rad deputativ trudiashchikh 1967 r. (statystychnyi zbirnyk).* [Results of the elections and the composition of the deputies to the Supreme Soviet of the Ukraine and to local soviets in 1967: a statistical handbook]. Kyiv: Vyd. pol. lit-ry Ukrainy, 1968. 215 pp.

Gives detailed information on the deputies elected, and has summary tables on those elected in 1938–67.

Uzbekistan

SUPREME SOVIET PROCEEDINGS

U539 *Uzbekiston SSR Olii Sovetining mazhlislari, . . . chaqiriq, . . . sessiia, . . . iil: stenografik hisobot = Zasedaniia Verkhovnogo Soveta Uzbekskoi SSR . . . sozyva, . . . sessiia, . . . goda: stenograficheskii otchet.* [Proceedings of the Supreme Soviet of the Uzbek SSR . . . number of convocation, . . . number of session, . . . date: stenographic report]. Tashkent: Izd. Verkhovnogo Soveta Uzbekskoi SSR, 1 sessiia 1-ogo sozyva, 19–23 iiulia 1938 g.–.

In Uzbek and Russian.

SUPREME SOVIET GAZETTE

U540   *Uzbekiston SSR Olii Sovetining vedomostlari = Vedomosti Verkhovnogo Soveta Uzbekskoi SSR.* [Gazette of the Supreme Soviet of the Uzbek SSR]. Tashkent, 1938–41, 1949–. Usually 30–36 p.a.
In Uzbek and Russian.

GOVERNMENT GAZETTE

U541   *Uzbekiston SSR Hukumatining Qarorlari tuplami = Sobranie postanovlenii pravitel'stva Uzbekskoi SSR.* [Collection of ordinances of the Supreme Soviet of the Uzbek SSR]. Tashkent, 1972–. Irregular.
In Uzbek and Russian.

NEWSPAPERS

U542a   *Pravda Vostoka.* [Truth of the East]. Tashkent, 1917–. 6 per week.
U542b   *Sovet Uzbekistoni.* [Soviet Uzbekistan]. Tashkent, 1918–. 6 per week.

    Until June 1966, *Sovet Uzbekistoni* was called *Qizil Uzbekiston*; in Uzbek. These two newspapers are published jointly by the Central Committee of the Uzbek CP and the Uzbek Supreme Soviet and Council of Ministers.

OTHER DOCUMENTS

U543   *Sovety deputatov trudiashchikhsia Uzbekskoi SSR v tsifrakh (1925–1969 gg.).* [The Uzbek soviets in figures, 1925–1969]. (AN UzSSR. In-t filosofii i prava. Otdel sovetov Prezidiuma Verkhovnogo Soveta UzSSR). Tashkent: Fan, 1970. 395 pp.

    Tables on the composition of the delegates elected to soviets of all types in the Uzbek SSR, and on the electorate.

COMMUNIST PARTY

In this section are described the general publications of the Communist Party of the Soviet Union and the communist parties of the union republics. This includes details of their serial publications, congress proceedings, statistics on the growth and development of the party organization, and other general collections of party documents. Party documents on particular subjects have been included in the appropriate subject sections; many of the collections listed in these sections include party and government documents. Material on ideology can be found in the section 'Cultural affairs', and details of general collections of the speeches and articles of party leaders in the section 'Leaders' works'. The organization and publishing of decisions of the party are discussed more fully in the introduction to this chapter.

CPSU

General

U544   *Knizhka partiinogo aktivista.* [A party activist's notebook]. M: Politizdat, 1957–. Annual.

1957–73 called *Zapisnaia knizhka partiinogo aktivista*. A handy compendium including biographical details of members and candidate members of the Politburo and of the Secretaries of the Central Committee, statistical summaries of data on the CPSU, the Supreme Soviet and the Komsomol, and the texts of a few major recent speeches and resolutions.

U545 *KPSS: spravochnik*. [The CPSU: a handbook]. 4. izd. perer. i dop. M.: Politizdat, 1980. 399 pp.

1st ed. publ. in 1963 (343 pp.), 2nd in 1965 (336 pp.), 3rd in 1971 (414 pp.). A handbook on the party from the pre-Revolutionary period to the time of publication, singling out the major resolutions, congresses, etc. and including a chronology. The introduction to each edition gives a brief summary of party membership and assesses the current state of the party.

U546 *Kommunisticheskaia partiia Sovetskogo Soiuza v rezoliutsiiakh i resheniiakh s"ezdov, konferentsii i plenumov TsK*. [The CPSU in the resolutions and decisions of its congresses, conferences and Central Committee plenums]. (In-t marksizma-leninizma pri TsK KPSS). M.: Politizdat, 1970–.

1st ed. publ. in 1922 as *RKP(b) v rezoliutsiiakh i resheniiakh s"ezdov i konferentsii*; 2nd appeared in 1924, 3rd in 1927, 4th in 1932–3 in two volumes with the title *RKP(b) v rezoliutsiiakh i resheniiakh s"ezdov, konferentsii i plenumov TsK*, 5th in 1936 and 6th in 1940–1. 7th ed., called *Kommunisticheskaia partiia Sovetskogo Soiuza v rezoliutsiiakh i resheniiakh s"ezdov, konferentsii i plenumov TsK*, appeared as three volumes in 1954 with a fourth covering 1954–60 published in 1960. 8th ed. was planned as a 10-volume set covering 1898–1970, but is now envisaged as a continuing series with volumes published every couple of years. An index to the first 10 volumes (1898–1971) was published in 1973; it includes chronological, title, subject and thematic indexes, and indexes to organizations, places and periodicals. This is the most important and authoritative collection of party documents and resolutions, including party rules and programmes, and selections from congress proceedings. Some of the material from it is included in item U550.

U547 McNeal, R. H. *Guide to the decisions of the Communist Party of the Soviet Union, 1917–1967 = Ukazatel' reshenii Kommunisticheskoi partii Sovetskogo Soiuza, 1917–1967*. Toronto: University of Toronto Press, 1972. xlix, 329 pp.

Lists 3,265 party decisions in chronological order and provides a reference to the most readily available source of a full Russian text of the decision. Particularly useful for tracing items not included in U546, but excludes joint party and government resolutions. Has a subject index and an extremely valuable introduction defining the different types of party decisions, their dissemination and history, and their relationship to legal enactments.

U548 *Partiinaia zhizn'; zhurnal Tsentral'nogo komiteta Kommunisticheskoi partii Sovetskogo Soiuza.* [Party life; journal of the Central Committee of the CPSU]. M.: Pravda, November 1946–April 1948, March 1954–. Fortnightly.

As well as authoritative editorials and articles on various practical and theoretical aspects of the work of the CPSU, the journal publishes resolutions and other decisions of the Central Committee, including selected reports from party plenums, information on party organization and membership, and has in many issues a useful listing of new publications. It also publishes reports on the proceedings of union republic party congresses and their other activities. It has an annual index. Some articles from the journal are translated in *CDSP* (U853).

U549 *Pravda; organ Tsentral'nogo komiteta KPSS.* [Truth; organ of the Central Committee of the CPSU]. M.: Pravda, 1912–. Daily.

Founded in 1912 by Lenin in exile; after various changes in title and frequency it became the official central newspaper of the party at the time of the Revolution and moved to Moscow with the Soviet government in 1918. Frequency varied in the prewar period, but has since appeared almost every day. As the official newspaper of the Central Committee, it carries authoritative editorials and articles, publishes the text of major party resolutions requiring wide dissemination and reports on the work of the Central Committee, party plenums and congresses. Many of the important articles in it are translated in *CDSP* (U853), which also published a weekly index to it and the government newspaper *Izvestiia* during 1949–73.

U550 *Resolutions and decisions of the Communist Party of the Soviet Union.* General editor: R. H. McNeal. Toronto: University of Toronto Press, 1974.·
Vol. 1, *The Russian Social Democratic Labour Party, 1898–October 1917*, ed. by R. C. Elwood.
Vol. 2, *The early Soviet period*, ed. by R. Gregor.
Vol. 3, *The Stalin years*, ed. by R. H. McNeal.
Vol. 4, *The Khrushchev years*, ed. by G. Hodnett.

Each volume contains translations of the main party decisions, resolutions and other documents from its period, with particular emphasis on materials not readily available in English elsewhere. Some documents included do not appear in the major Russian collection, U546. Each volume has an informative introduction outlining the history of the party during its period, a name index and in vols. 2–4 an appendix giving membership of the Secretariat. Vol. 5, to cover the Brezhnev years, is planned.

U551 *Spravochnik partiinogo rabotnika.* [Manual for party workers]. M.: Politizdat, vols. 1–9, 1921–35; [new series] vol. 1–, 1957–. Annual.

Indexes to vols. 1–7 [new series] appear in vol. 7 (1967), to vols. 8–12 in vol. 12 (1972) and to vols. 13–17 in vol. 17 (1977). This is a particularly convenient and authoritative compilation of the main resolutions of the Central Committee, ordinances of the Council of Ministers, laws, edicts of the Presidium of the Supreme Soviet, and major trade union and Komsomol documents promulgated during the previous year. It also includes some statistical data. Some of the material it contains is published here for the first time. The documents are arranged in broad subject categories, making it easy to find the latest party and government pronouncements on particular topics; obviously only major documents are included.

Party congresses

Reports of the work of each CPSU congress appear in *Pravda* and are usually soon followed by the *Materialy*, which contains the major speeches and resolutions and the Directives for the next five-year plan. The Directives and major speeches are often also published as separate pamphlets. The stenographic reports of the congress appear a little later. After each congress, the Party Rules and Programme are republished, incorporating any amendments made during the congress. Major speeches and resolutions will later find their way into U546. English translations of the reports published in *Pravda* quickly appear in *CDSP* (U853); details of other translations are given in the entries for each congress. The congresses are listed in chronological order, starting with the XIX Party Congress, the first postwar congress.

XIX PARTY CONGRESS, 5–14 OCTOBER 1952

No stenographic report of this congress was published; its proceedings appear in *Pravda* for 8, 9, 12 and 14 October 1952 and are reproduced in U546, vol. 6 (1971), pp. 341–82. The speeches at the congress by Beria, Bulganin, Khrushchev, Kosygin, Malenkov, Mikoian, Saburov and Stalin were published as separate pamphlets, as were the Directives on the Fifth Five-Year Plan. The main resolutions were collected and published as:

U552a   *Rezoliutsii XIX s"ezda Kommunisticheskoi partii Sovetskogo Soiuza, 5–14 oktiabria 1952 g.* M.: Gospolitizdat, 1953, 63 pp.

For a translation, see:

U552b   *Current Soviet policies. The documentary record of the 19th Communist Party Congress and the reorganization after Stalin's death.* From the translations of the Current Digest of the Soviet Press, ed. and with an introduction by L. Gruliow. N.Y.: Praeger, 1953. vi, 268 pp.

As well as the congress resolutions and speeches, it includes articles and documents published during the run-up to the congress, the major reports and discussions in the union republics' congresses held just before the All-Union Congress, and translations of articles on the 'Doctors' plot', the speeches at Stalin's funeral, and reports on the reorganization of the Secretariat after Stalin's death. Index.

XX PARTY CONGRESS, 14–25 FEBRUARY 1956

U553a *XX s"ezd Kommunisticheskoi partii Sovetskogo Soiuza, 14–25 fevralia 1956 goda: stenograficheskii otchet.* [20th Congress of the CPSU, 14–25 February 1956: stenographic report]. M.: Gospolitizdat, 1956. 2 vols.

This is known to be incomplete, as it lacks the text of Khrushchev's 'Secret Speech' (see below). The volume includes lists of delegates, by organization and *stazh*, index of speakers and lists of members chosen for the leading bodies of the CPSU. Most of the major speeches were published as separate pamphlets, and the resolutions were also published as:

U553b *Rezoliutsii XX s"ezda Kommunisticheskoi partii Sovetskogo Soiuza, 14–25 fevralia 1956 g.* M.: Gospolitizdat, 1956. 110 pp.

The greetings from foreign communist parties were also published as a separate volume:

U553c *Privetstviia XX s"ezdu Kommunisticheskoi partii Sovetskogo Soiuza ot bratskikh kommunisticheskikh i rabochikh partii.* M.: Gospolitizdat, 1956. 175 pp.

For a translation of the congress proceedings as they appeared in *Pravda*, plus the text of the 'Secret Speech' and Soviet and foreign reactions to it, see:

U553d *Current Soviet policies, II. The documentary record of the 20th Communist Party Congress and its aftermath.* From the translations of the Current Digest of the Soviet Press, edited by L. Gruliow. N.Y.: Praeger, 1957. ii, 247 pp.

Khrushchev's speech to a closed session of the congress 'On the cult of personality and its consequences' has not been published in the USSR, although readers may like to know of a clever forgery, probably produced in West Germany and made to look like a Politizdat pamphlet with a claimed edition size of one million copies:

U553e Khrushchev, N. S. *Doklad na zakrytom zasedanii XX s"ezda KPSS 'O kul'te lichnosti i ego posledstviiakh'.* M.: Politizdat, 1959 [sic!], 80 pp.

The speech was leaked to the West through West European Communist Party leaders and was made public on 4 June 1956 by the U.S. Department of State. It was published in the *New York Times* on that day and has since been reproduced in several English-language publications, including:

U553f *The Stalin dictatorship: Khrushchev's 'Secret Speech' and other documents,* ed. with an introduction and annotations by T. H. Rigby. Sydney: Sydney University Press, 1968. 128 pp.

U553g Khrushchev, N. S. *The 'Secret' speech delivered to the closed session of* the Twentieth Congress of the Communist Party of the Soviet Union [...] with an introduction by Zhores A. Medvedev and Roy A. Medvedev. Nottingham: Spokesman, 1976. 134 pp.

U553h Khrushchev, N. S. *The crimes of the Stalin era: special report to the 20th Congress of the Communist Party of the Soviet Union.* Annotated [...] by B. I. Nicolaevsky. [N.Y.]: New Leader, [1956]. 56 pp.

XXI PARTY CONGRESS, 17 JANUARY–5 FEBRUARY 1959

U554a *Vneocherednoi XXI s"ezd Kommunisticheskoi partii Sovetskogo Soiuza, 17 ianvaria–5 fevralia 1959 goda: stenograficheskii otchet.* [Extraordinary 21st Congress of the CPSU, 17 January–5 February 1959: stenographic report]. M.: Gospolitizdat, 1959. 2 vols.

The Congress was 'Extraordinary' because it met earlier than planned; its main function was to approve the Seven-Year Plan. The stenographic report includes lists of delegates, showing organization and *partstazh*, and lists of speakers. A translation is available as:

U554b *Current Soviet policies, III. The documentary record of the Extraordinary 21st Congress of the Communist Party of the Soviet Union.* From the translations of the Current Digest of the Soviet Press, edited by L. Gruliow ... with a Who's Who of the Central Committee compiled by M. Neuweld. N.Y.: Columbia University Press, 1960. xiii, 230 pp.

XXII PARTY CONGRESS, 17–31 OCTOBER 1961

U555a *XXII s"ezd Kommunisticheskoi partii Sovetskogo Soiuza, 17–31 oktiabria 1961 goda: stenograficheskii otchet.* [22nd Congress of the CPSU, 17–31 October 1961: stenographic report]. M.: Gospolitizdat, 1961. 3 vols.

Includes lists of delegates by occupation and organization, lists of speakers, etc. The materials were published separately as:

U555b *Materialy XXII s"ezda.* M.: Gospolitizdat, 1961. 464 pp.

The speeches by Khrushchev and Kozlov and the new Programme and Rules were published as separate pamphlets. A translation of the main speeches and decision and resolutions of the congress was published in the USSR:

U555c *The road to communism: documents of the 22nd Congress of the Communist Party of the Soviet Union, October 17–31 1961.* M.: FLPH, [1962]. 634 pp.

Another translation, based on press reports, is:

U555d *Current Soviet policies, IV. The documentary record of the 22nd Congress of the Soviet Union.* Edited by C. Saikowski and L. Gruliow from the translations of the Current Digest of the Soviet Press, with a Who's Who of the Central Committee compiled by M. Neuweld. N.Y., London: Columbia University Press, 1962. vii, 248 pp.

XXIII PARTY CONGRESS, 29 MARCH–8 APRIL 1966

U556a *XXIII s"ezd Kommunisticheskoi partii Sovetskogo Soiuza, 29 marta–8 aprelia 1966 goda: stenograficheskii otchet.* [23rd Congress of the CPSU, 29 March–8 April 1966: stenographic report]. M.: Politizdat, 1966. 2 vols.

Includes lists of delegates, by profession and organization, lists of speakers, etc. Major speeches and resolutions are also available in:

U556b *Materialy XXIII s"ezda Kommunisticheskoi partii Sovetskogo Soiuza.* M.: Politizdat, 1966. 304 pp.

Translations are available in:

U556c *23rd Congress of the Communist Party of the Soviet Union, 29 March–8 April 1966.* M.: Novosti, 1966. 439 pp.

U556d *Current Soviet policies, V. The documentary record of the 23rd Congress of the Communist Party of the Soviet Union.* From the translations of the Current Digest of the Soviet Press. With a Who's Who of the Central Committee compiled by Richard Bessel. Columbus, Ohio: American Association for the Advancement of Slavic Studies, 1973. 175 pp.

XXIV PARTY CONGRESS, 30 MARCH–9 APRIL 1971

U557a *XXIV s"ezd Kommunisticheskoi partii Sovetskogo Soiuza, 30 marta–9 aprelia 1971 goda: stenograficheskii otchet.* [24th Congress of the CPSU, 30 March–9 April 1971: stenographic report]. M.: Politizdat, 1971. 2 vols.

Includes lists of delegates by *partstazh*, index of speakers, lists of members elected to the ruling bodies of the CPSU.

Major speeches and resolutions are also available in:

U557b *Materialy XXIV s"ezda Kommunisticheskoi partii Sovetskogo Soiuza.* M.: Politizdat, 1971.

Translations are available in:

U557c *24th Congress of the Communist Party of the Soviet Union, March 30–April 9, 1971: documents.* M.: Novosti, 1971. 335 pp.

U557d *Current Soviet policies, VI. The documentary record of the 24th Congress of the Communist Party of the Soviet Union.* From the translations of the Current Digest of the Soviet Press. With a Who's Who of the Central Committee, compiled by Richard Bessel. Columbus, Ohio: American Association for the Advancement of Slavic Studies, 1973. 203 pp.

XXV PARTY CONGRESS, 24 FEBRUARY–5 MARCH 1976

U558a *XXV s"ezd Kommunisticheskoi partii Sovetskogo Soiuza, 24 fevralia–5 marta 1976 goda: stenograficheskii otchet.* [25th Congress of the CPSU, 24 February–5 March 1976: stenographic report]. M.: Politizdat, 1976. 3 vols.

Vol. 2 includes lists of delegates by profession and organization, lists of members and candidate members of the Central Committee and the Central Revision Commission, and photographs of some of the leaders. Vol. 3 includes a list of foreign visitors and an index of speakers.

The materials were also published separately:

U558b   *Materialy XXV s"ezda KPSS*. M.: Politizdat, 1976. 226 pp.

There is also a separate collection of the messages and greetings from foreign communist parties:

U558c   *Privetstviia XXV s"ezdu KPSS ot kommunisticheskikh, rabochikh i natsional'no-demokraticheskikh i sotsialisticheskikh partii*. M.: Politizdat, 1976. 511 pp.

For translations, see:

U558d   *XXVth Congress of the CPSU: documents and resolutions*. M.: Novosti, 1976. 270 pp.

U558e   *Current Soviet policies, VII. The documentary record of the 25th Congress of the Communist Party of the Soviet Union*. From the translations of the Current Digest of the Soviet Press, with a Who's Who of the Central Committee, compiled by R. Gruliow. Columbus, Ohio: American Association for the Advancement of Slavic Studies, 1976. 143 pp.

XXVI PARTY CONGRESS, 23 FEBRUARY–3 MARCH 1981

U559a   *XXVI s"ezd Kommunisticheskoi partii Sovetskogo Soiuza, 23 fevralia–3 marta 1981 goda: stenograficheskii otchet*. [26th Congress of the CPSU, 23 February–3 March 1981: stenographic report]. M.: Politizdat, 1981. 3 vols.

U559b   *Materialy XXVI s"ezda Kommunisticheskoi partii Sovetskogo Soiuza*. [Materials]. M.: Politizdat, 1981. 223 pp.

U559c   *Current Soviet policies, VIII. The documentary record of the 26th Congress of the Communist Party of the Soviet Union*. Columbus, Ohio: American Association for the Advancement of Slavic Studies, 1981. [Not seen].

Central Committee Plenums

For most of the postwar period only brief reports of the Plenum proceedings, and its resolutions and decisions, have been published, generally in *Pravda* (U549) and *Partiinaia zhizn'* (U548). Major decisions are sometimes also separately published in pamphlet form; these materials are later collected to appear in the appropriate volumes of U546. However, in 1958–65 the stenographic reports of the Plenums were published in book form as:

U560   *Plenum Tsentral'nogo komiteta Kommunisticheskoi partii Sovetskogo Soiuza [. . .]: stenograficheskii otchet*. M.: Politizdat.

15–19 dekabria, 1958 g. 1958.
24–29 iiunia, 1959 g. 1959.
22–25 dekabria, 1959 g. 1960.
13–16 iiulia, 1960 g. 1960.
10–18 ianvaria 1961 g. 1961.
5–9 marta, 1962 g. 1962.
19–23 noiabria, 1962 g. 1963.
18–21 iiunia, 1963 g. 1964.
9–13 dekabria, 1963 g. 1964.
10–15 fevralia, 1964 g. 1964.
24–26 marta, 1965 g. 1965.

Statistics on the CPSU

U561 'KPSS v tsifrakh, k 60-oi godovshchine Velikoi Oktiabr'skoi sotsialisticheskoi revoliutsii'. [The CPSU in figures, for the sixtieth anniversary of the Great October Soviet Revolution]. *Partiinaia zhizn'*, 1977, no. 21, pp. 20–43.

A summary of data on party membership from 1917 to June 1977. More detailed analyses for particular periods can be found in the occasional articles called 'KPSS v tsifrakh' appearing in *Partiinaia zhizn'* as follows:

1947, no. 20, pp. 73–83.
1962, no. 1, pp. 44–54.
1965, no. 10, pp. 8–17.
1967, no. 19, pp. 8–20.
1973, no. 14, pp. 9–26.
1976, no. 10, pp. 13–23.
1981, no. 14, pp. 13–26.

Party rules and programmes

U562 *Programmy i ustavy KPSS*. [Programmes and rules of the CPSU]. M.: Politizdat, 1969. 423 pp.

Contains the texts of the party programmes adopted in 1903, 1919 and 1961 and the party rules as adopted and amended at party congresses from 1903 to 1966. There is a short introduction pointing out the main changes and their significance.

U563 *Soviet communism: programs and rules; official texts of 1919, 1952 (1956), 1961*. Ed. by Jan F. Triska. San Francisco: Chandler Publishing Co., 1962. x, 196 pp.

As well as the texts of the rules and programmes, has an introduction comparing the different versions.

For more recent texts of the party rules and programme, consult the texts of the party congress; the revised edition of the rules is published as a separate booklet after each congress.

History and organization

U564 *Istoriia Kommunisticheskoi partii Sovetskogo Soiuza.* [History of the CPSU]. Izd. 5-e, dop. M.: Politizdat, 1978. 792 pp.

    1st ed. publ. 1959 (743 pp.), 2nd 1962 (784 pp.), 3rd 1969 (736 pp.), 4th 1971 (736 pp.). The official textbook of the history of the CPSU, with considerable variations in emphasis and interpretation between editions. An English translation of the 1st ed. is available: *History of the Communist Party of the Soviet Union.* M.: FLPH, 1960. 766 pp.

U565 *Istoriia Vsesoiuznoi Kommunisticheskoi partii (bol'shevikov): kratkii kurs.* [History of the All-Union Communist Party (Bol'shevik): a short course]. Pod red. Komissii TsK VKP (b). M.: Gospolitizdat, 1945. 351 pp.

    Earlier editions were published in 1938 (350 pp.) and 1943 (350 pp.). This is the official history prepared by the Central Committee and used as a textbook under Stalin. Several translations into English exist, e.g. *History of the CPSU (bolsheviks): short course.* M.: FLPH, 1939. 364 pp.

U566 *Khrestomatiia po istorii KPSS.* [Anthology on the history of the CPSU]. M.: Gospolitizdat, 1962–3. 3 vols.

    Vol. 3 covers 1945–April 1962, and is a very full collection of party materials, including much by Khrushchev excluded from later anthologies. Each volume is annotated. A later edition, publ. in two volumes in 1965, includes material up to March 1965 but is far less useful for the postwar period.

U567 *Khrestomatiia po istorii KPSS; uchebnoe posobie dlia studentov vuzov.* [Anthology on the history of the CPSU: handbook for higher education students]. M.: Vysshaia shkola, 1971–5. 3 vols. (in 4).

    Earlier edition, covering 1883–1967, publ. in two parts in 1968–9. This edition covers 1883–1975, with 1926–58 in vol. 3, part 1, and 1959–75 in vol. 3, part 2. The collection is annotated and covers the major party documents.

U568 *Partiinoe stroitel'stvo: khrestomatiia.* [Anthology on the building of the party]. 2 izd., perer. i dop. M.: Politizdat, 1968. 527 pp.

    1st ed. publ. 1966 (624 pp.). This is an annotated collection of documents on the development of the party and on its internal organization. Short subject index.

U569 *Pervichnaia partiinaia organizatsiia: dokumenty KPSS, posleoktiabr'skii period.* [The primary party organization: documents of the CPSU after the October Revolution]. 2 izd., dop. M.: Politizdat, 1974. 527 pp.

    1st ed. publ. 1970 (448 pp.). The collection includes documents from 1919 to 1974 on the work of local party organizations, and texts of letters and instructions from the Central Committee, often commenting on the work of individual party organizations.

U570   *Spravochnik sekretaria pervichnoi partiinoi organizatsii.* [Manual for the secretary of a primary party organization]. M.: Gospolitizdat, 1960. 599 pp.

A collection of material relating to the work of primary party organizations; the first section comprises a wide range of relevant party documents and the second includes short articles, often in a question-and-answer format. Later editions of the manual, publ. in 1967, 1977 and 1980, are less useful, being mainly descriptive or in question-and-answer format.

U571   *V. I. Lenin, KPSS o edinstve partii: sbornik dokumentov.* [Lenin and the CPSU on party unity: a collection of documents]. M.: Politizdat, 1974. 552 pp.

Documents, mainly from the prewar period, on party unity and factions within the Party; includes relevant postwar material. Texts are annotated and there is a name and subject index.

U572   *V. I. Lenin, KPSS o normakh partiinoi zhizni i printsipakh partiinogo rukovodstva.* [Lenin and the CPSU on the norms of party life and the principles of party leadership]. M.: Politizdat, 1979. 575 pp.

About a third of the documents are extracts from Lenin's writings; the rest are CPSU congress and conference resolutions and Central Committee documents, up to November 1978. Subject index.

U573   *V. I. Lenin, KPSS o partiinoi i gosudarstvennoi distsipline.* [Lenin and the CPSU on party and state discipline]. M.: Politizdat, 1977. 831 pp.

Excerpts from Lenin's works, texts of party resolutions, decisions, etc. on party and state discipline and organization.

U574   *V. I. Lenin, KPSS o rabote partiinogo i gosudarstvennogo apparata.* [Lenin and the CPSU on the work of the state and party apparatus]. Izd. 2-e, dop. M.: Politizdat, 1980. 800 pp.

1st ed. publ. 1976 (623 pp.). A collection of party resolutions, decisions and instructions about the structure, principles of operation and staffing of the party and state apparatus, and methods of improving their work, up to November 1979. Chronological, name and subject indexes.

U575   *V. I. Lenin, KPSS o rabote s kadrami.* [Lenin and the CPSU on work with cadres]. M.: Politizdat, 1979. 703 pp.

A collection of documents (about 50 of them from the post-1945 period) from Lenin's works, CPSU congress, conference and Central Committee materials relating to party members, government officials and other key workers, particularly their recruitment, deployment and training. Subject index.

U576   *Voprosy organizatsionno-partiinoi raboty KPSS: sbornik dokumentov.* [Problems of party organization: a collection of documents]. 2 izd., dop. M.: Politizdat, 1978. 615 pp.

1st ed. publ. 1973 (301 pp.). Includes documents produced 1965–77 on party organization and party work at central and local level.

Party organizations of union republics

Each of the union republics except the RSFSR has its own communist party, with different histories and traditions. Each CP publishes its own journal; some also have their own newspaper, while others publish newspapers jointly with the Supreme Soviet and government of the republic. The union republic CPs usually hold their party congresses a few weeks before the CPSU. Although all except the Armenian and Georgian CPs now publish stenographic reports of their party congresses, or collections of major speeches and resolutions, in the past many published only the report of the Party Secretary on the work of the Central Committee of the Party and the major resolutions. In some cases, no separate publications were produced at all, and reports must be sought in the periodical press of the republic's CP, or in the central publications such as *Pravda* and *Partiinaia zhizn'*. Translations into English are generally limited to reports in *CDSP* (U853) based on the central press.

In the entries which follow, details are given first of the publications of the proceedings of the postwar party congresses, in chronological order; the publications described are the fullest that have been identified. Many of the individual Party Secretary's reports and pamphlets containing resolutions have not been examined by the compiler; however the larger collections of materials and the stenographic reports are generally described 'de visu'. The lists of congresses are followed by details of the party journal, party newspaper if any, and other documents containing party documents or statistics about the party; in the absence of published stenographic reports, collections of party decisions can be extremely useful to researchers as they often draw on the archives of the Party.

At the time of compilation, materials from the 1981 congresses of the union republic CPs were in most cases not available, and have not been included.

Armenia

PARTY CONGRESSES

XIV, 12–24 November 1948
U577a Arutiunov, G. A. *Otchetnyi doklad na XIV s"ezde* ... [Party Secretary's report]. Erevan, 1948. 105 pp.
U577b *Rezoliutsii XIV s"ezda KP(b) Armenii po otchetnomu dokladu TsK KP(b) Armenii.* [Party resolutions on Central Committee's report]. Erevan, 1951. 24 pp. [Also publ. in Armenian].

XV, 20–22 March 1951
U578a Arutiunov, G. A. *Otchetnyi doklad na XV s"ezde* ... [Party Secretary's report]. Erevan, 1951. 105 pp.
U578b *Rezoliutsii XV s"ezda KP(b) Armenii po otchetnomu dokladu TsK KP(b) Armenii.* [Party resolutions on Central Committee's report]. Erevan, 1952. 22 pp. [Also publ. in Armenian].

XVI, 20–22 September 1952

U579a Arutiunov, G. A. *Otchetnyi doklad na XVI s"ezde* ... [Party Secretary's report]. Erevan, 1952. 94 pp.

U579b *Rezoliutsii XVI s"ezda KP(b) Armenii po otchetnomu dokladu TsK KP(b) Armenii.* [Party resolutions on Central Committee's report]. Erevan, 1952. 27 pp. [Publ. only in Armenian].

XVII, 14–17 February 1954

U580 *Rezoliutsii XVII s"ezda Kommunisticheskoi partii Armenii po otchetnomu dokladu TsK KP Armenii.* [Party resolutions on Central Committee's report]. Erevan, 1954. 35 pp.

XVIII, 19–21 January 1956

U581a Tovmasian, S. A. *Otchetnyi doklad TsK KP Armenii XVIII s"ezdu KP Armenii.* [Party Secretary's report]. Erevan, 1956. 106 pp.

U581b *Rezoliutsii XVIII s"ezda KP Armenii po otchetnomu dokladu TsK KP Armenii.* [Party resolutions on Central Committee's report]. Erevan, 1956. 32 pp. [Also publ. in Armenian].

XIX, 25–27 January 1958

U582a Tovmasian, S. A. *Otchetnyi doklad TsK KP Armenii XIX s"ezdu KP Armenii.* [Party Secretary's report]. Erevan, 1958. 99 pp.

U582b *Rezoliutsii XIX s"ezda KP Armenii po otchetnomu dokladu TsK KP Armenii.* [Party resolutions on Central Committee's report]. Erevan, 1958. 27 pp. [Also publ. in Armenian].

XX, 10–13 January 1959

U583a Tovmasian, S. A. *Tezisy doklada tov. Khrushcheva na XXI s"ezde KPSS ... i zadachi KP Armenii; doklad na Vneoch. XX s"ezde KP Armenii.* [Party Secretary's report on Khrushchev's speech to 21st CPSU Congress]. Erevan, 1959. 74 pp.

U583b *Rezoliutsii Vneocherednoi XX s"ezda KP Armenii po tezisam doklada* ... [Resolutions of the Extraordinary 20th Congress ... on the Party Secretary's report ...]. Erevan, 1959. 28 pp. [Also publ. in Armenian].

XXI, 10–12 February 1960

U584a Tovmasian, S. A. *Otchetnyi doklad TsK KP Armenii XXI s"ezdu KP Armenii.* [Party Secretary's report]. Erevan, 1960. 74 pp.

U584b *Rezoliutsii XXII s"ezda KP Armenii po otchetnomu dokladu* ... [Resolutions on the Central Committee's report]. Erevan, 1960. 33 pp. [Also publ. in Armenian].

XXII, 21–23 September 1961

U585a Zarobian, Ia.N. *Otchetnyi doklad TsK KP Armenii XXII s"ezdu KP Armenii.* [Party Secretary's report]. Erevan, 1961. 123 pp.

U585b *Rezoliutsii XXII s"ezda KP Armenii po otchetnomu dokladu* ... [Resolutions on the Central Committee's report]. Erevan, 1961. 34 pp.

XXIII, 7–8 January 1964

U586a Zarobian, Ia.N. *Otchetnyi doklad TsK KP Armenii XXIII s"ezdu KP Armenii.* [Party Secretary's report]. Erevan, 1964. 105 pp.

U586b *Rezoliutsii XXIII s"ezda KP Armenii po otchetnomu dokladu ...* [Resolutions on the Central Committee's report]. Erevan, 1964. 37 pp.

XXIV, 3–5 March 1966

U587a Kochinian, A. E. *Otchetnyi doklad TsK KP Armenii XXIV s"ezdu KP Armenii.* [Party Secretary's report]. Erevan, 1966. 87 pp.

U587b *Rezoliutsii XXIV s"ezda KP Armenii.* [Resolutions ...]. Erevan: Aiastan, 1966. 35 pp.

XXV, 25–26 February 1971

U588a Kochinian, A. E. *Otchetnyi doklad TsK KP Armenii XXV s"ezdu KP Armenii.* [Party Secretary's report]. Erevan, 1971. 93 pp.

U588b Muradian, B. A. *O proekte direktiv XXIV s"ezda KPSS po 5-letnemu planu ... doklad na XXV s"ezde KP Armenii.* [Report on draft directives for the ninth five-year plan for the USSR]. Erevan: Aiastan, 1971. 53 pp.

U588c *Rezoliutsii XXV s"ezda KP Armenii.* [Resolutions ...]. Erevan: Aiastan, 1971. 22 pp.

XXVI, 20–22 January 1976

U589a Demirchian, K. S. *Otchetnyi doklad TsK KP Armenii XXVI s"ezdu KP Armenii.* [Party Secretary's report]. Erevan, 1976. 132 pp.

U589b Arzumian, T. A. *O proekte TsK KPSS 'Osnovnye napravleniia razvitiia narodnogo khoziaistva SSSR na 1976–1980 gg.' ..., doklad na XXVI s"ezde KP Armenii.* [Report on draft directives for the tenth five-year plan for the USSR]. Erevan: Aiastan, 1976. 59 pp.

U589c *Rezoliutsii XXVI s"ezda KP Armenii.* [Resolutions ...]. Erevan: Aiastan, 1976. 28 pp.

PARTY JOURNAL

U590 *Po leninskomu puti: teoreticheskii i politicheskii zhurnal TsK KP Armenii.* [On a Leninist path: theoretical and political journal of the Central Committee of the Armenian CP]. Erevan: Leniniian ugiov, 1923–. Monthly.

In Armenian, with Russian contents page. Publication suspended 1942–6. Several changes in title before 1941; 1947–56 called *Partiinaia zhizn'*.

PARTY NEWSPAPER

U591 *Kommunist.* [The Communist]. 1934–. 6 issues per week.

There is also an Armenian-language newspaper issued jointly by the CP and the government; *see* U490.

OTHER MATERIAL

U592 *Kommunisticheskaia partiia Armenii v tsifrakh i dokumentakh, 1920–1980: sbornik statisticheskikh i dokumental'nykh materialov.*

[The Armenian CP in figures and documents, 1920–1980: a collection of statistical and documentary material]. Erevan: Aiastan, 1980. 332 pp. [Not seen].

Azerbaijan

PARTY CONGRESSES

XVII, 25–28 January 1949
U593 *Rezoliutsii XVII s"ezda KP(b) Azerbaidzhana po otchetnomu dokladu tov. M. D. Bagirova o rabote TsK KP Azerbaidzhana.* [Resolutions on the Party Secretary's report]. Baku, 1949. 35 pp. [In Azerbaijani only].

XVIII, 24–27 May 1951
U594 *Rezoliutsii XVIII s"ezda KP(b) Azerbaidzhana po otchetnomu dokladu tov. M. D. Bagirova o rabote TsK KP(b) Azerbaidzhana.* [Resolutions on the Party Secretary's report]. Baku, 1951. 37 pp. [In Azerbaijani only].

XIX, 23–25 September 1952*

XX, 12–16 February 1954*

XXI, 25–27 January 1957*

XXII, 28–30 January 1958
U595 Mustaf'ev, I. D. *Otchetnyi doklad TsK KP Azerbaidzhana XXII s"ezdu KP Azerbaidzhana.* [Party Secretary's report]. Baku, 1958. 116 pp. [Also publ. in Azerbaijani].

XXIII, 8–10 January 1959*

XXIV, 16–18 February 1960
U596a Akhundov, V. Iu. *Otchetnyi doklad o rabote TsK KP Azerbaidzhana XXIV s"ezdu KP Azerbaidzhana.* [Party Secretary's report]. Baku: Azernesher, 1960. 86 pp. [Also publ. in Azerbaijani].
U596b *Rezoliutsii XXIV s"ezda KP Azerbaidzhana.* [Resolutions ...]. Baku: Azernesher, 1960. 46 pp. [Also publ. in Azerbaijani].

XXV, 6–9 September 1961
U597a Akhundov, V. Iu. *Otchetnyi doklad o rabote TsK KP Azerbaidzhana XXV s"ezdu KP Azerbaidzhana.* [Party Secretary's report]. Baku: Azernesher, 1961. 80 pp. [Also publ. in Azerbaijani].
U597b *Rezoliutsii XXV s"ezda KP Azerbaidzhana.* [Resolutions ...]. Baku: Azernesher, 1961. 56 pp. [Also publ. in Azerbaijani].

XXVI, 9–10 January 1964
U598a Akhundov, V.Iu. *Otchetnyi doklad o rabote TsK KP Azerbaidzhana XXVI s"ezdu KP Azerbaidzhana.* [Party Secretary's report]. Baku: Azernesher, 1964. 74 pp. [Also publ. in Azerbaijani].

* Consult periodical press.

U598b *Rezoliutsii XXVI s"ezda KP Azerbaidzhana po otchetu TsK KP Azerbaidzhana.* [Resolutions . . .]. Baku: Azernesher, 1964. 39 pp. [Also publ. in Azerbaijani].

XXVII, 23–26 February 1966
U599 *XXVII s"ezd KP Azerbaidzhana, 24–26 fevr. 1966 g.* [Materials]. Baku: Azernesher, 1966. 91 pp. [Also publ. in Azerbaijani].

XXVIII, 10–12 March 1971
U600 *Materialy XXVIII s"ezda KP Azerbaidzhana, 10–12 marta 1971 g.* [Materials]. Baku: Azernesher, 1971. 103 pp. [Also publ. in Azerbaijani].

XXIX, 28–30 January 1976
U601 *Materialy XXIX s"ezda KP Azerbaidzhana, 28–30 ianv. 1976 g.* [Materials]. Baku: Azernesher, 1976. 180 pp. [Also publ. in Azerbaijani].

PARTY JOURNAL

U602 *Azarbaijan kommunisti.* [Communist Azerbaijan]. Baku: Izd. TsK KP Azerbaidzhana, 1939–. Monthly.
　　　In Azerbaijani. 1939–57 (no. 2) called *Tablighatchy.* Frequency varied 1939–45.

PARTY NEWSPAPER

U603a *Bakinskii rabochii.* [Baku worker]. 1906–. 6 per week.
U603b *Kommunist.* [The Communist]. 1919–. 6 per week [In Azerbaijani].

OTHER MATERIAL

U604 *Kommunisticheskaia partiia Azerbaidzhana v tsifrakh: statisticheskii sbornik.* [The Azerbaijan CP in figures: statistical handbook]. (In-t istorii partii KP Azerbaidzhana). Baku: Az. gos. izd-vo, 1970. 161 pp.
　　　Over 30 tables on the membership and organization of the Azerbaijani CP, based on archival sources.

Belorussia

PARTY CONGRESSES

XIX, 15–18 February 1949
U605a Gusarov, N. I. *Otchetnyi doklad TsK KP Belorussii na XIX s"ezde KP(b) Belorussii.* [Party Secretary's report]. Minsk, 1949. 119 pp. [Also publ. in Belorussian].
U605b *Rezoliutsii XIX s"ezda KP(b) Belorussii po otchetu TsK KP Belorussii.* [Resolutions on the Central Committee report]. Minsk, 1949. 48 pp. [Also publ. in Belorussian].

XX, 20–23 September 1952
U606 Patolichev, N. S. *Otchetnyi doklad TsK KP(b) Belorussii na XX*

s"ezde KP(b) Belorussii. [Party Secretary's report]. Minsk, 1952. 96 pp. [Also publ. in Belorussian].

XXI, 10–13 February 1954
U607   Patolichev, N. S. *Otchetnyi doklad TsK KP Belorussii XXI s"ezdu KP Belorussii.* [Party Secretary's report]. Minsk, 1954. 88 pp. [Also publ. in Belorussian].

XXII, 24–27 January 1956
U608   Patolichev, N. S. *Otchetnyi doklad TsK KP Belorussii na XXII s"ezde KP Belorussii.* [Party Secretary's report]. Minsk, 1956. 82 pp. [Also publ. in Belorussian].

XXIII, 14–15 January 1959
Consult periodical press.

XXIV, 17–19 February 1960
U609   Mazurov, K. T. *Otchetnyi doklad TsK KP Belorussii na XXIV s"ezde KP Belorussii.* [Party Secretary's report]. Minsk, 1960. 96 pp. [Also publ. in Belorussian].

XXV, 26–28 September 1961
U610   Mazurov, K. T. *Otchetnyi doklad TsK KP Belorussii na XXV s"ezde KP Belorussii.* [Party Secretary's report]. Minsk, 1961. 79 pp. [Also publ. in Belorussian].

XXVI, 3–5 March 1966
U611   Masherov, P. M. *Otchetnyi doklad TsK KP Belorussii na XXVI s"ezde KP Belorussii.* [Party Secretary's report]. Minsk, 1966. 71 pp. [Also publ. in Belorussian].

XXVII, 22–24 February 1971
U612   *Materyialy 27 z'ezda KP Belarusi.* [Materials]. Minsk: Belarus', 1971. 149 pp. [Only publ. in Belorussian].

XXVIII, 4–6 February 1976
U613   *Materialy XXVIII s"ezda KP Belorussii.* [Materials]. Minsk: Belarus', 1976. 175 pp. [Also publ. in Belorussian].

PARTY JOURNAL

U614   *Kommunist Belorussii: teoreticheskii i politicheskii zhurnal TsK KP Belorussii.* [Communist of Belorussia: theoretical and political journal of the Central Committee of the Belorussian CP]. Minsk: Izd-vo TsK KPB, 1927–. Monthly.

In 1927–41 and 1945–9 published as a combined Belorussian- and Russian-language journal called *Bol'shevik Belarusi = Bol'shevik Belorussii.* In 1949 this split to form a Russian-language and a Belorussian-language journal, keeping the appropriate title. From 1952, no. 11 the titles were changed to become *Kamunist Belarusi* (Belorussian) and *Kommunist Belorussii* (Russian). The Belorussian edition closed at the end of 1962.

PARTY NEWSPAPER

Published jointly with the government, *see* U498a–b

OTHER MATERIAL

U615   *Kommunisticheskaia partiia Belorussii v rezoliutsiiakh i resheniiakh s"ezdov i plenumov TsK (1918–1970)*. [The Belorussian CP in the resolutions and decisions of its Congresses and Central Committee Plenums, 1918–1970]. (In-t istorii partii pri TsK KPB). Minsk: Belarus´, vol. 1–, 1973–.

    An annotated collection of party documents on all aspects of its work.

U616   *Kommunisticheskaia partiia Belorussii v tsifrakh, 1918–1978*. [The Belorussian CP in figures, 1918–1978]. Minsk: Belarus´, 1978. 231 pp.

    An annotated collection of 34 tables on the growth and composition of the Belorussian CP, with a list of its congresses.

Estonia

PARTY CONGRESSES

V, 23–25 December 1948

U617a   Karotamm, N. G. *Otchetnyi doklad na V s"ezde KP(b) Estonii o rabote TsK KP(b) Estonii*. [Party Secretary's report]. Tallin, 1949. 43 pp. [Also publ. in Estonian].

U617b   *Rezoliutsii V s"ezda KP(b) Estonii po otchetu TsK KP(b) Estonii*. [Resolutions]. Tallin, 1949. 32 pp. [Also publ. in Estonian].

VI, 11–14 April 1951*

VII, 16–19 September 1952*

VIII, 11–13 February 1954*

IX, 17–19 January 1956*

X, 28–30 January 1958*

XI, 8–9 January 1959*

XII, 16–17 February 1960*

XIII, 27–29 September 1961*

XIV, 7–8 January 1964*

XV, 1–3 March 1966*

XVI, 17–19 February 1971

U618   *XVI s"ezd KP Estonii, 17–19 fevralia 1971 g*. [Materials]. Tallin: Eesti raamat, 1971. 81 pp. [Also publ. in Estonian].

* Consult periodical press.

XVII, 28–30 January 1976

U619 *XVII s"ezd KP Estonii, 28–30 ianvaria 1976 g.* [Materials]. Tallin: Eesti raamat, 1976. 129 pp. [Also publ. in Estonian].

PARTY JOURNAL

U620 *Eesti kommunist.* [Estonian communist]. Tallin: Izd-vo TsK KP Estonii, 1945–. Monthly.

In Estonian. Since July 1951 it has also been published in a Russian edition called *Kommunist Estonii*. Estonian edition called *Eesti bolševik* 1945–52, no. 9; Russian edition called *Bol'shevik Estonii* 1951–2, no. 9.

PARTY NEWSPAPER

Published jointly with the government, *see* U501a–b.

Georgia

PARTY CONGRESSES

XIV, 25–29 January 1949

U621 *XIV s"ezd KP(b) Gruzii, 25–29 ianvaria 1949 g.* [Materials]. Tbilisi: Komunisti, 1949. 431 pp. [Publ. in Georgian only].

XV, 15–18 September 1952*

XVI, 16–18 February 1954*

XVII, 18–21 January 1956*

XVIII, 27–29 January 1958

U622 Mzhavanadze, V. P. *Otchet TsK KP Gruzii XVII s"ezdu KP Gruzii* [and] *Rezoliutsii XVIII s"ezda KP Gruzii po otchetnomu dokladu TsK.* [Party Secretary's report and Congress resolutions]. Tbilisi, 1958. 71 pp. [Also publ. in Georgian].

XIX, 12–13 January 1959*

XX, 25–26 January 1960

U623 Mzhavanadze, V. P. *Otchet TsK KP Gruzii XX s"ezdu KP Gruzii* [and] *Rezoliutsii XX s"ezda KP Gruzii po otchetnomu dokladu TsK.* [Party Secretary's report and congress resolutions]. Tbilisi, 1960. 97 pp.

XXI, 27–29 September 1961

U624 Mzhavanadze, V. P. *Otchet TsK KP Gruzii XXI s"ezdu KP Gruzii* [and] *Rezoliutsii XXI s"ezda KP Gruzii po otchetnomu dokladu TsK.* [Party Secretary's report and congress resolutions]. Tbilisi, 1961. 83 pp. [Also publ. in Georgian].

* Consult periodical press.

XXII, 29–30 January 1964

U625 Mzhavanadze, V. P. *Otchet TsK KP Gruzii XXII s"ezdu KP Gruzii* [and] *Rezoliutsii XXII s"ezda KP Gruzii po otchetnomu dokladu TsK*. [Party Secretary's report and congress resolutions]. Tbilisi, 1964. 82 pp. [Also publ. in Georgian].

XXIII, 2–4 March 1966

U626 Mzhavanadze, V. P. *Otchet TsK KP Gruzii XXIII s"ezdu KP Gruzii* [and] *Rezoliutsii XXIII s"ezda KP Gruzii po otchetnomu dokladu TsK*. [Party Secretary's report and congress resolutions]. Tbilisi, 1966. 72 pp. [Also publ. in Georgian].

XXIV, 27 February–1 March 1971

U627 Mzhavanadze, V. P. *Otchet TsK KP Gruzii XXIV s"ezdu KP Gruzii* [and] *Rezoliutsii XXIV s"ezda KP Gruzii po otchetnomu dokladu TsK*. [Party Secretary's report and congress resolutions]. Tbilisi, 1971. 65 pp. [Also publ. in Georgian].

XXV, 22–24 January 1976

U628 Shevardnadze, E. A. *Otchetnyi doklad TsK KP Gruzii XXV s"ezdu KP Gruzii* [and] *Rezoliutsii XXV s"ezda KP Gruzii po otchetnomu dokladu TsK*. [Party Secretary's report and congress resolutions]. Tbilisi, 1976. 150 pp. [Also publ. in Georgian].

PARTY JOURNAL

U629 *Kommunist Gruzii: teoreticheskii i politicheskii zhurnal TsK KP Gruzii*. [Georgian Communist: theoretical and political journal of the Central Committee of the Georgian CP]. Tbilisi: Izd. TsK KPG, 1930–. Monthly.

In Georgian. 1930–52, no. 10 called *Bol'shevik*.

PARTY NEWSPAPER

Published jointly with the government, *see* U506a–b.

OTHER MATERIAL

U630 *Kommunisticheskaia partiia Gruzii v rezoliutsiiakh i resheniiakh s"ezdov, konferentsii i plenumov TsK*. [The Georgian CP in the resolutions and decisions of its congresses, conferences and Central Committee plenums, 1920–76]. (In-t istorii partii pri TsK KP Gruzii). Tbilisi: Izd-vo TsK KP Gruzii, 1976–.

An annotated collection of documents, some published for the first time. This was originally planned as a three- or four-volume collection covering 1920–76, but now appears to be a continuing series with volumes published every few years.

U631 *Kommunisticheskaia partiia Gruzii v tsifrakh (1920–1970 gg.): sbornik statisticheskikh materialov*. [The Georgian CP in figures, 1920–1970: a collection of statistical materials]. Tbilisi, 1971. 338 pp.

Includes tables on the growth of the Georgian CP and changes in the composition of the membership, supplemented by various resolutions on party membership. Also includes information on delegates to the congresses of the Georgian CP and lists of local party committees from 1921 to 1970.

Karelo-Finnish SSR

PARTY CONGRESSES
The Karelo-Finnish SSR held two party congresses while it had union republic status, its second in late April 1949 and its third in late September 1952. These were briefly reported in *Pravda* (U549).

PARTY JOURNAL
Apparently none published while had union republic status.

PARTY NEWSPAPER
Published a newspaper jointly with the government of the union republic, *see* U508

Kazakhstan

PARTY CONGRESSES

IV, 25 February–1 March 1949
U632a Shaiakhmetov, Zh. *Otchetnyi doklad o rabote TsK KP(b) Kazakhstana na IV s"ezde KP(b) Kazakhstana.* [Party Secretary's report]. Alma-Ata, 1949. 93 pp. [Also publ. in Kazakh].
U632b *Rezoliutsii IV s"ezda KP(b) Kazakhstana po otchetnomu dokladu TsK KP(b) Kazakhstana.* [Resolutions . . .]. Alma-Ata, 1949. 39 pp.

V, 15–18 December 1950
U633a Shaiakhmetov, Zh. *Otchetnyi doklad o rabote TsK KP(b) Kazakhstana na V s"ezde KP(b) Kazakhstana.* [Party Secretary's report]. Alma-Ata, 1951. 80 pp. [Also publ. in Kazakh].
U633b *Rezoliutsii V s"ezda KP(b) Kazakhstana.* [Resolutions . . .]. Alma-Ata, 1951. 93 pp. [In Russian and Kazakh].

VI, 20–24 September 1951
U634a Shaiakhmetov, Zh. *Otchetnyi doklad o rabote TsK KP(b) Kazakhstana na VI s"ezde KP(b) Kazakhstana.* [Party Secretary's report]. Alma-Ata, 1951. 55 pp. [Also publ. in Kazakh].
U634b *Rezoliutsii VI s"ezda KP(b) Kazakhstana po otchetnomu dokladu TsK KP(b) Kazakhstana.* [Resolutions . . .]. Alma-Ata, 1952. 27 pp. [Also publ. in Kazakh].

VII, 16–18 February 1954
Consult periodical press.

VIII, 24–27 January 1956
U635a Brezhnev, L. I. *Otchet TsK KP Kazakhstana VII s"ezdu KP*

Kazakhstana. [Party Secretary's report]. Alma-Ata, 1956. 79 pp. [Also publ. in Kazakh].

U635b *Rezoliutsii VIII s"ezda KP Kazakhstana po otchetnomu dokladu TsK KP Kazakhstana.* [Resolutions ...]. Alma-Ata, 1956. 46 pp. [In Russian and Kazakh].

IX, 14–15 January 1959

U636 Beliaev, N. I. *Tezisy doklada tov. N.S. Khrushcheva na XXI s"ezde KPSS ... i zadachi KP Kazakhstana.* [Party Secretary's report on Khrushchev's speech to the 21st CPSU Congress]. Alma-Ata, 1959. 61 pp. [Also publ. in Kazakh].

X, 10–12 March 1960

U637a Kunaev, D. A. *Otchetnyi doklad o rabote TsK KP Kazakhstana X s"ezdu KP Kazakhstana.* [Party Secretary's report]. Alma-Ata, 1959. 61 pp. [Also publ. in Kazakh].

U637b *Rezoliutsii X s"ezda KP Kazakhstana po otchetnomu dokladu TsK KP Kazakhstana.* [Resolutions ...]. Alma-Ata, 1960. 36 pp. [Also in Kazakh].

XI, 27–29 September 1961

U638a Kunaev, D. A. *Otchetnyi doklad o rabote TsK KP Kazakhstana XI s"ezdu KP Kazakhstana.* [Party Secretary's report]. Alma-Ata, 1961. 80 pp.

U638b *Postanovlenie XI s"ezda KP Kazakhstana po otchetnomu dokladu TsK KP Kazakhstana.* [Congress decision on the report]. Alma-Ata, 1961. 39 pp. [Also in Kazakh].

XII, 10–12 March 1966

U639 Kunaev, D. A. *Otchetnyi doklad o rabote TsK KP Kazakhstana XII s"ezdu KP Kazakhstana.* [Party Secretary's report]. Alma-Ata, 1966. 100 pp. [Also publ. in Kazakh].

XIII, 24–26 February 1971

U640 *Kommunisticheskaia partiia Kazakhstana. S"ezd 13, 24–26 fevr. 1971 g.: stenograficheskii otchet.* [Stenographic report]. Alma-Ata: Kazakhstan, 1971. 407 pp. [Only publ. in Russian; Party Secretary's report and congress resolutions available as pamphlets in Kazakh].

XIV, 4–6 February 1976

U641 *XIV s"ezd KP Kazakhstana, 4–6 fevralia 1976 g.: stenograficheskii otchet.* [Stenographic report]. Alma-Ata: Kazakhstan, 1976. 423 pp. [Only publ. in Russian; Party Secretary's report and congress resolutions available as pamphlets in Kazakh].

PARTY JOURNAL

U642 *Qazaqstan kommunisi.* [Kazakh communist]. Alma-Ata: Izd. TsK KP Kazakhstana, 1931–. Monthly.

In Kazakh. Since 1931 also publ. in Russian edition with title *Partiinaia zhizn' Kazakhstana.* The edition in Kazakh changed its title several times before the war and was called *Qazaqstan bol'shevigi* 1945–52, no. 10. The Russian edition was called *Bol'shevik Kazakhstana* 1931–52, no. 10, *Kommunist Kazakhstana* until the end of 1957, and then became *Partiinaia zhizn' Kazakhstana*. Some variations in frequency in the prewar period.

PARTY NEWSPAPER

Published jointly with the government, *see* U571a–b.

OTHER MATERIAL

U643a   *Kompartiia Kazakhstana za 50 let (1921–1971 gg.): rost i regulirovanie sostava partiinoi organizatsii respubliki.* [The Kazakh CP 1921–1971: growth and composition of the republic's party organization]. (In-t istorii partii pri TsK KP Kazakhstana). Alma-Ata: Kazakhstan, 1972. 343 pp.

U643b   *Kommunisticheskaia partiia Kazakhstana v dokumentakh i tsifrakh: sbornik dokumentov i statisticheskikh materialov o roste i regulirovanii sostava partiinoi organizatsii.* [The Kazakh CP in documents and figures: a collection of documents and statistical materials on the growth and composition of the party organization]. Pod red. S. B. Beisembaeva, P. M. Pakhmurnogo. Alma-Ata: Kazakhstan, 1960. 367 pp.

     The 1960 volume covers 1921–58. Both volumes include statistical tables and are largely based on archival sources. The earlier volume also includes documents relating to party membership.

U643c   *Kommunisticheskaia partiia Kazakhstana v rezoliutsiiakh i resheniiakh s"ezdov, konferentsii i plenumov.* [The Kazakh Communist Party in the resolutions and decisions of its conferences, congresses and plenums]. (In-t istorii partii pri TsK KP Kazakhstana—filial IML pri TsK KPSS). Alma-Ata: Kazakhstan.

     Vol. 1, 1921–27. 1981. [Not seen].

Kirghizia

PARTY CONGRESSES

V, 10–14 February 1949

U644   Bogoliubov, N. S. *Otchetnyi doklad TsK KP(b) Kirgizii na V s"ezde KP(b) Kirgizii* [and] *Rezoliutsii V s"ezda KP(b) Kirgizii po otchetnomu dokladu TsK.* [Party Secretary's report and congress resolutions]. Frunze, 1949. 108 pp. [Also publ. in Kirghiz].

VI, 20–23 September 1952

U645a   Razzakov, I. R. *Otchetnyi doklad o rabote TsK KP(b) Kirgizii VI s"ezdu KP(b) Kirgizii.* [Party Secretary's report]. Frunze, 1952. 79 pp. [Also publ. in Kirghiz].

U645b   *Rezoliutsii VI s"ezda KP(b) Kirgizii po otchetnomu dokladu TsK.* [Congress resolutions]. Frunze, 1952. 39 pp. [Only publ. in Kirghiz].

VII, 10–12 February 1954
Consult periodical press.

VIII, 24–26 January 1956

U646a Razzakov, I. R. *Otchetnyi doklad VIII s"ezdu KP Kirgizii o rabote TsK KP Kirgizii.* [Party Secretary's report]. Frunze, 1956. 52 pp. [Also publ. in Kirghiz].

U646b *Rezoliutsii VIII s"ezda KP Kirgizii po otchetnomu dokladu o rabote TsK.* [Resolutions . . .]. Frunze, 1956. 26 pp. [Also publ. in Kirghiz].

IX, 21–23 March 1958

U647a Razzakov, I. R. *Otchetnyi doklad IX s"ezdu KP Kirgizii o rabote TsK KP Kirgizii.* [Party Secretary's report]. Frunze, 1958. 62 pp. [Also publ. in Kirghiz].

U647b *Rezoliutsii IX s"ezda KP Kirgizii po otchetnomu dokladu o rabote TsK.* [Resolutions . . .]. Frunze, 1958. 26 pp. [Also publ. in Kirghiz].

X, 12–13 January 1959

U648a Razzakov, I. R. *Tezisy doklada tov. Khrushcheva na XXI s"ezde . . . i zadachi partiinoi organizatsii respubliki.* [Party Secretary's report on Khrushchev's speech to 21st Party Congress]. Frunze, 1959. 70 pp. [Also publ. in Kirghiz].

U648b *Rezoliutsii Vneocherednoi X s"ezda KP Kirgizii po tezisam doklada . . .* [Congress resolutions . . .]. Frunze, 1959. 17 pp. [Also publ. in Kirghiz].

XI, 25–27 February 1960

U649a Razzakov, I. R. *Otchetnyi doklad XI s"ezdu KP Kirgizii o rabote TsK KP Kirgizii.* [Party Secretary's report] Frunze, 1960. 62 pp. [Also publ. in Kirghiz].

U649b *Rezoliutsii XI s"ezda KP Kirgizii po otchetnomu dokladu o rabote TsK KP.* [Resolutions . . .]. Frunze, 1960. 28 pp. [Also publ. in Kirghiz].

XII, 19–21 September 1961

U650a Usubaliev, T. U. *Otchetnyi doklad XII s"ezdu KP Kirgizii o rabote TsK KP Kirgizii.* [Party Secretary's report]. Frunze, 1961. 67 pp. [Also publ. in Kirghiz].

U650b *Rezoliutsii XII s"ezda KP Kirgizii po otchetnomu dokladu o rabote TsK.* [Resolutions . . .]. Frunze, 1961. 31 pp. [Also publ. in Kirghiz].

XIII, 27–28 December 1963

U651a Usubaliev, T. U. *Otchetnyi doklad XIII s"ezdu KP Kirgizii o rabote TsK KP Kirgizii.* [Party Secretary's report]. Frunze, 1964. 74 pp. [Also publ. in Kirghiz].

U651b *Rezoliutsii XIII s"ezda KP Kirgizii po otchetnomu dokladu o rabote TsK KP.* [Resolutions . . .]. Frunze, 1964. 29 pp. [Also publ. in Kirghiz].

XIV, 3–4 March 1966

U652 *XIV s"ezd KP Kirgizii, 3–4 marta 1966 g: stenograficheskii otchet.* [Stenographic report]. Frunze: Kyrgyzstan, 1980. 318 pp. [In

Russian; Party Secretary's report and the congress resolutions only are available in Kirghiz].

XV, 3–5 March 1971

U653 *XV s"ezd KP Kirgizii, 3–5 marta 1971 g.: stenograficheskii otchet.* [Stenographic report]. Frunze: Kyrgyzstan, 1971. 372 pp. [In Russian only; Party Secretary's report and congress resolutions only are available in Kirghiz].

XVI, 16–18 January 1976

U654 *XVI s"ezd KP Kirgizii, 16–18 ianvaria 1976: stenograficheskii otchet.* [Stenographic report]. Frunze: Kyrgyzstan, 1976. 412 pp. [In Russian only; Party Secretary's report and congress resolutions only are available in Kirghiz].

PARTY JOURNAL

U655 *Kommunist: Kyrgyzstan KP BK teoriialyk zhana saiasii zhurnaly.* [Communist: theoretical and political journal of the Central Committee of the Kirghiz CP]. Frunze: Izd-vo TsK KP Kirgizii, 1926–9, 1931–41, 1946–. Monthly.

In Kirghiz. Also publ. in a Russian edition called *Kommunist* since 1957. Some variations in frequency before 1945.

PARTY NEWSPAPER

Published jointly with the government, *see* U514a–b.

OTHER MATERIAL

U656 *Kommunisticheskaia partiia Kirgizii v rezoliutsiiakh i resheniiakh s"ezdov i plenumov TsK.* [The Kirghiz CP in the resolutions and decisions of its congresses and Central Committee plenums]. (In-t istorii partii pri TsK KP Kirgizii). Frunze: Kyrgyzstan, 1958–.

Vol. 1 (1958) covers 1924–36; vol. 2 (1968) 1937–55; vol. 3 (1973) 1956–61; vol. 4 (1974) 1962–71. Includes some documents not previously published. Originally planned to cover 1924–57 only, but now seems likely to continue as an irregular publication.

U657a *Kommunisticheskaia partiia Kirgizii v tsifrakh.* [The Kirghiz CP in figures]. (In-t istorii pri TsK KP Kirgizii). Frunze: Izd-vo TsK KP Kirgizii, 1976. 117 pp.

U657b *Kommunisticheskaia partiia Kirgizii (1918–1973): rost i regulirovanie sostava.* [The Kirghiz CP, 1918–1973: growth and composition]. Frunze: Kyrgyzstan, 1973. 300 pp.

U657c *Rost i regulirovanie sostava Kommunisticheskoi partii Kirgizii, 1918–1962 gg.* [Growth and composition of the Kirghiz CP, 1918–1962]. Frunze, 1963. 281 pp.

These three volumes include tables and diagrams on the size and composition of the membership of the Kirghiz CP, with lists of dates of its party congresses and data on delegates to CPSU congresses.

The 1973 volume is the fullest, particularly for the early periods, and includes the dates of the local conferences of the Kirghiz CP and of its Central Committee plenums. The 1976 volume covers 1925–75.

Latvia

PARTY CONGRESSES

X, 24–27 December 1949

U658   Kalnberzin, Ia. E. *Otchetnyi doklad o rabote TsK KP Latvii na X s"ezde KP(b) Latvii.* [Party Secretary's report]. Riga, 1949. 63 pp. [Also publ. in Latvian].

XI, 27–29 December 1951*

XII, 20–22 September 1952*

XIII, 9–11 February 1954*

XIV, 17–19 January 1956*

XV, 23–25 January 1958*

XVI, 12–13 January 1959*

XVII, 16–17 February 1960*

XVIII, 26–28 September 1961*

XIX, 24–25 December 1963*

XX, 2–3 March 1966*

XXI, 25–26 February 1971*

XXII, 22–23 January 1976

U659   *Latvijas Komunistiskās partijas XXII kongresa materiāli.* [Materials]. Riga: Liesma, 1976. 125 pp. [Only publ. in Latvian].

PARTY JOURNAL

U660   *Padomju Latvijas komunists.* [Communist of Soviet Latvia]. Riga: Izd-vo TsK KP Latvii, 1945–. Monthly.

    In Latvian. Russian edition published with title *Kommunist sovetskoi Latvii.* 1945–52, no. 15 Latvian edition called *Padomju Latvijas bolševiks* and Russian edition called *Bol'shevik sovetskoi Latvii.* Issued fortnightly 1945–May 1952.

PARTY NEWSPAPER

Issued jointly with the government, *see* U518a–b.

OTHER MATERIAL

U661   *Kommunisticheskaia partiia Latvii v tsifrakh (1904–1971 gg)* [The

* Consult periodical press.

Latvian CP in figures, 1904–1971]. (In-t istorii partii TsK KP Latvii). Riga: Liesma, 1972. 189 pp.

Tables on the growth, composition and organization of the Latvian CP, mainly drawn from party archives.

Lithuania

PARTY CONGRESSES

VI, 15–18 February 1949

U662 *Rezoliutsii VI s"ezda KP(b) Litvy po otchetnomu dokladu tov. Snechkusa o rabote TsK KP(b) Litvy.* [Resolutions on Party Secretary's report]. Vilnius, 1949. 30 pp. [Also publ. in Lithuanian].

VII, 22–25 September 1952
Consult periodical press.

VIII, 16–19 February 1954

U663 *Postanovlenie VIII s"ezda KP Litvy po otchetnomu dokladu ...* [Resolution on Party Secretary's report]. Vilnius, 1954. 36 pp. [Also publ. in Lithuanian].

IX, 24–27 January 1956

U664 *Postanovleniia IX s"ezda KP Litvy po otchetnomu dokladu ...* [Resolutions ...]. Vilnius, 1956. 15 pp. [Also publ. in Lithuanian].

X, 12–15 February 1958

U665 Snechkus, A. Iu. *Otchetnyi doklad TsK KP Litvy X s"ezdu partii* [*and*] *Postanovlenie X s"ezda KP Litvy po otchetnomu dokladu ...* [Party Secretary's report and congress resolution]. Vilnius, 1958. 103 pp. [Also publ. in Lithuanian].

XI, 14–16 January 1959

U666 Snechkus, A. Iu. *Tezisy doklada tov. N. S. Khrushcheva na XXI s"ezde KPSS ... i zadachi KP Litvy ...* [*and*] *Zakliuchitel'naia rech' tov. A. Snechkusa.* [Party Secretary's report on Khrushchev's proposals to 21st CPSU Congress, and his closing speech]. Vilnius, 1959. 100 pp. [Also publ. in Lithuanian].

XII, 1–3 March 1960

U667 Snechkus, A. Iu. *Otchetnyi doklad na XII s"ezde KP Litvy* [*and*] *Zakliuchitel'noe slovo ...* [*and*] *Rezoliutsii XII s"ezda KP Litvy po otchetnomu dokladu TsK KP Litvy.* [Party Secretary's report, closing speech and congress resolutions]. Vilnius, 1960. 119 pp. [Also publ. in Lithuanian].

XIII, 27–29 September 1961

U668 *XIII s"ezd KP Litvy.* [Materials]. Vilnius: Gospolitnauchizdat, 1961. 180 pp. [Also publ. in Lithuanian].

XIV, 9–10 January 1964

U669 *XIV s"ezd KP Litvy.* [Materials]. Vilnius: Gospolitnauchizdat, 1964. 119 pp. [Also publ. in Lithuanian].

XV, 3–5 March 1966

U670 *XV s"ezd KP Litvy.* [Materials]. Vilnius: Gospolitnauchizdat, 1966. 96 pp. [Also publ. in Lithuanian].

XVI, 3–5 March 1971

U671 *XVI s"ezd KP Litvy.* [Materials]. Vilnius: Izd-vo TsK KP Litvy, 1971. 178 pp. [Also publ. in Lithuanian].

XVII, 20–22 January 1976

U672 *Materialy XVII s"ezda KP Litvy.* [Materials]. Vilnius: Mintis, 1976. 196 pp. [Also publ. in Lithuanian].

PARTY JOURNAL

U673 *Komunistas.* [Communist]. Vilnius: Izd-vo TsK KP Litvy, 1918–32, 1941, 1945–. Monthly.

In Lithuanian. Also publ. in Russian since 1946 as *Kommunist*. The Lithuanian edition appeared irregularly and in various formats 1918–32; only two issues appeared in 1941 and four in 1945. Both editions had 6 issues in 1946.

PARTY NEWSPAPER

Published jointly with the government, *see* U522a–b.

OTHER MATERIAL

U674 *Kommunisticheskaia partiia Litvy v tsifrakh, 1918–1976: sbornik statisticheskikh dannykh.* [The Lithuanian CP in figures, 1918–1976: a collection of statistical materials]. (In-t istorii partii pri TsK KP Litvy). Vilnius: Mintis, 1977. 283 pp.

Also publ. in Lithuanian in 1976. Includes nearly 200 charts on the membership of the Lithuanian CP, party organization, etc., with a long introduction on the history and development of the party.

Moldavia

PARTY CONGRESSES

II, 5–8 February 1949

U675 Koval', N. G. *Otchet TsK KP(b) Moldavii na II s"ezde KP(b) Moldavii.* [Party Secretary's report]. Kishinev, 1949. 104 pp.

III, 30 March–1 April 1951

U676 *III s"ezd KP(b) Moldavii, 30 marta–1 aprelia 1951 g.* [Materials]. Kishinev, 1951. 95 pp. [Also publ. in Moldavian].

IV, 18–21 September 1952*

V, 16–18 February 1954*

VI, 18–20 January 1956*

* Consult periodical press.

VII, 28–29 January 1958

U677   *VII s"ezd KP Moldavii, 28–29 ianv. 1958 g.* [Materials]. Kishinev: Partizdat, 1958. 141 pp. [In Moldavian and Russian].

VIII, 13–14 January 1959

U678   Consult periodical press.

IX, 28–29 September 1960

U679   *IX s"ezd KP Moldavii, 28–29 sent. 1960 g.* [Materials]. Kishinev: Partizdat, 1960. 144 pp. [In Moldavian and Russian].

X, 27–29 September 1961

U680   *X s"ezd KP Moldavii, 27–29 sent. 1961 g.* [Materials]. Kishinev: Partizdat, 1961. 249 pp. [In Moldavian and Russian].

XI, 25–26 December 1963

U681   *XI s"ezd KP Moldavii, 25–26 dek. 1963 g.* [Materials]. Kishinev: Partizdat, 1964. 183 pp. [In Moldavian and Russian].

XII, 1–3 March 1966

U682   *XII s"ezd KP Moldavii, 1–3 marta 1966 g.* [Materials]. Kishinev: Partizdat, 1966. 214 pp. [In Russian and Moldavian].

XIII, 24–26 February 1971

U683   *XIII s"ezd KP Moldavii, 24–26 fevr. 1971 g.* [Materials]. Kishinev: Partizdat, 1971. 271 pp. [In Russian and Moldavian].

XIV, 29–31 January 1976

U684   *XIV s"ezd KP Moldavii, 29–31 ianv. 1976 g.* [Materials]. Kishinev: Partizdat, 1976. 388 pp. [In Moldavian and Russian].

PARTY JOURNAL

U685   *Komunistul Moldovai.* [Moldavian Communist]. Kishinev: Izd-vo TsK KP Moldavii, 1956–. Monthly.

    In Moldavian. Also publ. in Russian since 1956 as *Kommunist Moldavii.*

PARTY NEWSPAPER

Published jointly with the government, *see* U525a–b.

OTHER MATERIAL

U686   *Rost i organizatsionnoe ukreplenie Kommunisticheskoi partii Moldavii, 1924–1974: sbornik dokumentov i materialov.* [The growth and organizational consolidation of the Moldavian CP, 1924–1974: a collection of documents and materials]. Red. kollegiia: N. N. Bibileishvili [i dr.]. Kishinev: Shtiintsa, 1976. 360 pp. plus tables in end pocket.

    178 documents and tables on the internal development and organization of the Moldavian CP and its membership. Name index.

Tajikistan

PARTY CONGRESSES

VII, 20–23 December 1948

U687 *Resoliutsiia VII s"ezda KP(b) Tadzhikistana po otchetnomu dokladu tov. B. Gafurova o rabote TsK KP Tadzhikistana.* [Congress resolution on Party Secretary's report]. Stalinabad, 1949. 31 pp. [Also publ. in Tajik].

VIII, 19–22 September 1952*

IX, 18–20 January 1954*

X, 26–29 January 1956

U688 *Rezoliutsii X s"ezda KP Tadzhikistana.* [Resolutions . . .]. Stalinabad, 1956. 34 pp. [Also publ. in Tajik].

XI, 14–16 January 1958

U689 *XI s"ezd KP Tadzhikistana, 14–16 ianv. 1958 g.: stenograficheskii otchet.* [Stenographic reports]. Stalinabad, 1958. 327 pp. [Also publ. in Tajik].

XII, 14–15 January 1959

U690 *Vneocherednoi XII s"ezd KP Tadzhikistana: stenograficheskii otchet.* [Stenographic reports]. Stalinabad, 1959. 280 pp. [Also publ. in Tajik].

XIII, 4–6 February 1960

U691 *XIII s"ezd KP Tadzhikistana, 4–6 fevr. 1960 g.: stenograficheskii otchet.* [Stenographic reports]. Stalinabad, 1961. 342 pp. [Also publ. in Tajik].

XIV, 21–23 September 1961

U692 *XIV s"ezd KP Tadzhikistana, 21–23 sent. 1961 g.: stenograficheskii otchet.* [Stenographic reports]. Dushanbe: Tadzhgosizdat, 1962. 380 pp. [Also publ. in Tajik].

XV, 25–26 December 1963

U693 Rasulov, D. R. *Otchetnyi doklad TsK KP Tadzhikistana XV s"ezdu KP Tadzhikistana.* [Party Secretary's report]. Dushanbe: Irfon, 1964. 84 pp. [Also publ. in Tajik].

XVI, 2–3 March 1966*

XVII, 18–19 February 1971

U694 *XVII s"ezd KP Tadzhikistana, 18–19 fevr. 1971 g.: stenograficheskii otchet.* [Stenographic reports]. Dushanbe: Irfon, 1971. 327 pp.

XVIII, 27–29 January 1976

U695 *XVIII s"ezd KP Tadzhikistana, 27–29 ianv. 1976 g.: stenograficheskii otchet.* [Stenographic reports]. Dushanbe: Irfon, 1977. 355 pp.

* Consult periodical press.

PARTY JOURNAL

U696 *Kommunisti Tojikiston.* [Tajik Communist]. Dushanbe: Izd-vo TsK KP Tadzhikistana, 1936–41, 1945–. Monthly.

In Tajik. In 1936–51 called *Ba erii korkuni partiiagi.* 1945–52, no. 10 called *Bol'sheviki Tojikiston.* 9 issues in 1945, otherwise monthly.

PARTY NEWSPAPER

Published jointly with the government, *see* U529a–b.

OTHER MATERIAL

U697 *Kommunisticheskaia partiia Tadzhikistana v tsifrakh za 50 let (1924–1974 gg.): rost i regulirovanie sostava partiinoi organizatsii respubliki.* [The Tadzhik CP in figures, 1924–1974: the growth and composition of the Republic's party organization]. Dushanbe: Irfon, 1977. 99 pp.

70 tables illustrating the growth and composition of the membership of the Tadzhik CP.

Turkmenistan

PARTY CONGRESSES

X, 18–22 August 1950
U698 *Materialy X s"ezda KP(b) Turkmenistana.* [Materials]. Ashkhabad: Turkmengosizdat, 1950. 104 pp. [Also publ. in Turkmenian].

XI, 20–23 September 1952
U699 *Materialy XI s"ezda KP(b) Turkmenistana, 20–23 sent. 1952 g.* [Materials]. Ashkhabad: Turkmengosizdat, 1953. 100 pp. [Also publ. in Turkmenian].

XII, 13–15 February 1954
Consult periodical press.

XIII, 20–22 January 1956
U700 *Materialy XIII s"ezda KP Turkmenistana, 20–22 ianv. 1956 g.* [Materials]. Ashkhabad: Turkmengosizdat, 1956. 88 pp. [Also publ. in Turkmenian].

XIV, 18–20 January 1958
U701 *Materialy XIV s"ezda KP Turkmenistana, 18–20 ianv. 1958 g.* [Materials]. Ashkhabad: Turkmengosizdat, 1958. 95 pp. [Also publ. in Turkmenian].

XV, 19–20 January 1959
U702 *Materialy XV s"ezda KP Turkmenistana, 19–20 ianv. 1959 g.* [Materials]. Ashkhabad: Turkmengosizdat, 1959. 68 pp. [Also publ. in Turkmenian].

XVI, 16–17 February 1960
U703 *Materialy XVI s"ezda KP Turkmenistana, 16–17 fevralia 1960 g.*

[Materials]. Ashkhabad: Turkmengosizdat, 1960. 104 pp. [Also publ. in Turkmenian].

XVII, 12–14 September 1961

U704 *Materialy XVII s"ezda KP Turkmenistana, 12–14 sent. 1961 g.* [Materials]. Ashkhabad: Turkmengosizdat, 1961. 132 pp. [Also publ. in Turkmenian].

XVIII, 26–27 dekabria 1963

U705 *Materialy XVIII s"ezda KP Turkmenistana, 26–27 dek. 1963 g.* [Materials]. Ashkhabad: Turkmengosizdat, 1964. 105 pp. [Also publ. in Turkmenian].

XIX, 24–25 February 1966

U706 *Materialy XIX s"ezda KP Turkmenistana, 24–25 fevr. 1966 g.* [Materials]. Ashkhabad: Turkmenistan, 1966. 120 pp. [Also publ. in Turkmenian].

XX, 19–20 February 1971

U707 *Materialy XX s"ezda KP Turkmenistana, 19–20 fevr. 1971 g.* [Materials]. Ashkhabad: Turkmenistan, 1971. 100 pp. [Also publ. in Turkmenian].

XXI, 23–24 January 1976

U708 *Materialy XXI s"ezda KP Turkmenistana, 23–24 ianv. 1976 g.* [Materials]. Ashkhabad: Turkmenistan, 1976. 127 pp. [Also publ. in Turkmenian].

PARTY JOURNAL

U709 *Turkmenistan komunisti.* [Turkmenian Communist]. Ashkhabad: Izd-vo TsK KP Turkmenistana, 1925–. Monthly.

In Turkmenian. Had title *Bol'shevik* until 1952, no. 9. Also publ. in a Russian edition called *Kommunist Turkmenistana,* 1953–9. Some variation in frequency until 1934; monthly from 1935.

PARTY NEWSPAPER

Published jointly with the government, *see* U533a–b.

OTHER MATERIAL

U710 *Kommunisticheskaia partiia Turkmenistana v tsifrakh (1924–1974): statisticheskii sbornik.* [The Turkmenian CP in figures, 1924–1974: a statistical handbook]. (In-t istorii partii pri TsK KP Turkmenistana). Ashkhabad: Turkmenistan, 1975. 266 pp.

Earlier edition, covering 1925–66, publ. in 1967 (223 pp.). A short leaflet, up-dating the 1975 edition for the years 1974–7, publ. in 1979 (26 pp.). The 1975 volume includes over 400 tables on the growth of the Turkmenian CP, and the composition of its membership.

U710a *Kommunisticheskaia partiia Turkmenistana v rezoliutsiiakh i resheniiakh s"ezdov i plenumov TsK.* [The Communist Party of

Turkmenistan in the resolutions and decisions of its congresses and Central Committee plenums]. Ashkhabad: Turkmenistan.
Vol. 1, part 1, 1925–1928. 1981. [Not seen].

Ukraine

PARTY CONGRESSES

XVI, 25–28 January 1949
U711 *XVI s"ezd KP(b) Ukrainy, 25–28 ianv. 1949 g.: materialy s"ezda.* [Materials]. Kiev: Gospolitizdat USSR, 1949. 259 pp. [Also publ. in Ukrainian].

XVII, 23–27 September 1952
U712 *XVII s"ezd KP(b) Ukrainy, 23–27 sent. 1952 g.: materialy s"ezda.* [Materials]. Kiev: Gospolitizdat USSR, 1953. 232 pp. [Also publ. in Ukrainian].

XVIII, 23–26 March 1954
U713 *XVIII s"ezd KP Ukrainy, 23–26 marta 1954 g.: materialy s"ezda.* [Materials]. Kiev: Gospolitizdat USSR, 1954. 224 pp. [Also publ. in Ukrainian].

XIX, 17–21 January 1956
U714 *XIX s"ezd KP Ukrainy, 17–21 ianv. 1956 g.: materialy s"ezda.* [Materials]. Kiev: Gospolitizdat USSR, 1956. 259 pp. [Also publ. in Ukrainian].

XX, 16–17 January 1959
U715 *Vneocherednoi XX s"ezd KP Ukrainy, 16–17 ianv. 1959 g.: materialy s"ezda.* [Materials]. Kiev: Gospolitizdat USSR, 1959. 158 pp. [Also publ. in Ukrainian].

XXI, 16–19 February 1960
U716 *XXI s"ezd KP Ukrainy, 16–19 fevr. 1960 g.: materialy s"ezda.* [Materials]. Kiev: Gospolitizdat USSR, 1960. 257 pp. [Also publ. in Ukrainian].

XXII, 27–30 September 1961
U717 *XXII s"ezd KP Ukrainy, 27–30 sent. 1961 g.: materialy s"ezda.* [Materials]. Kiev: Gospolitizdat USSR, 1962. 314 pp. [Also publ. in Ukrainian].

XXIII, 15–18 March 1966
U718 *XXIII s"ezd KP Ukrainy, 15–18 marta 1966 g.: materialy s"ezda.* [Materials]. Kiev: Gospolitizdat USSR, 1966. 256 pp. [Also publ. in Ukrainian].

XXIV, 17–20 March 1971
U719 *XXIV s"ezd KP Ukrainy, 17–20 marta 1971 g.: stenograficheskii otchet.* [Stenographic reports]. Kiev: Politizdat Ukrainy, 1972. 399 pp. [Also publ. in Ukrainian].

XXV, 10–13 February 1976

U720 *XXV s"ezd KP Ukrainy, 10–13 fevr. 1976 g.: stenograficheskii otchet.* [Stenographic reports]. Kiev: Politizdat Ukrainy, 1976. 494 pp. [Also publ. in Ukrainian].

PARTY JOURNAL

U721 *Komunist Ukrainy.* [Ukrainian Communist]. Kiev: Radians'ka Ukraina, 1925–41, 1946–. Monthly.

In Ukrainian. From 1950 also publ. in Russian, with title *Bol'shevik Ukrainy* 1950–2, no. 10 and subsequently *Kommunist Ukrainy.* The Ukrainian edition was called *Bil'shovyk Ukrainy* 1925–52, no. 9. Some variations in frequency before the war; two issues in 1946, then monthly.

PARTY NEWSPAPER

Published jointly with the government, *see* U537a–b.

OTHER MATERIAL

U722 *Kommunisticheskaia partiia Ukrainy v rezoliutsiiakh i resheniiakh s"ezdov, konferentsii i plenumov TsK.* [The Ukrainian CP in the resolutions and decisions of its congresses, conferences and Central Committee plenums]. (In-t istorii partii pri TsK KP Ukrainy). Kiev: Politizdat Ukrainy, 1976–7. 2 vols.

Also publ. in Ukrainian. An earlier edition covering 1918–56 publ. in 1958 (703 pp.), in Ukrainian only. In the 1976–7 edition, vol. 1 covers 1918–41 and vol. 2 1941–76; they include all the major published documents and some archival material.

The Ukrainian Central Committee also publishes as separate pamphlets the texts of many of the major resolutions passed during the meetings of its Plenum.

Uzbekistan

PARTY CONGRESSES

X, 1–4 March 1949

U723a Iusupov, U. *Otchetnyi doklad o rabote TsK KP(b) Uzbekistana na X s"ezde KP Uzbekistana.* [Party Secretary's report]. Tashkent, 1949. 80 pp. [Also publ. in Uzbek].

U723b *Rezoliutsii X s"ezda KP Uzbekistana po otchetu TsK KP(b) Uzbekistana.* [Resolutions . . .]. Tashkent, 1949. [Also publ. in Uzbek].

XI, 20–24 September 1952*

XII, 15–17 February 1954*

XIII, 26–28 January 1956*

XIV, 7–8 January 1959*

* Consult periodical press.

XV, 10–12 February 1960

U724   *XV s"ezd KP Uzbekistana, 10–12 fevralia 1960 g.: stenograficheskii otchet.* [Stenographic reports]. Tashkent, 1961. 375 pp. [Also publ. in Uzbek].

XVI, 25–27 September 1961

U725   *Rezoliutsii XVI s"ezda KP Uzbekistana, 25–27 sent. 1961 g.* [Resolutions]. Tashkent, 1961. 46 pp. [Also publ. in Uzbek].

XVII, 3–5 March 1966*

XVIII, 2–4 March 1971*

XIX, 3–5 February 1976

U726   Rashidov, Sh. R. *Otchetnyi doklad TsK KP Uzbekistana XIX s"ezdu KP Uzbekistana.* [Party Secretary's report]. Tashkent, 1976. 78 pp. [Also publ. in Uzbek].

PARTY JOURNAL

U727   *Uzbekiston komunisti.* [Uzbek Communist]. Tashkent: Izd-vo TsK KP Uzbekistana, 1925–41, 1944–. Monthly.

In Uzbek. Since July 1960 also publ. in Russian as *Kommunist Uzbekistana.* Until the end of 1952 the Uzbek edition was called *Kommunist.* Some variations in frequency before 1945.

PARTY NEWSPAPERS

Published jointly with the government, *see* U542a–b.

OTHER MATERIAL

U728   *Kommunisticheskaia partiia Uzbekistana v tsifrakh: sbornik statisticheskikh materialov, 1924–1977 gg.* [The Uzbek CP in figures: a collection of statistical materials, 1924–1977]. (In-t istorii partii pri TsK KP Uzbekistana). Tashkent: Uzbekistan, 1979. 448 pp.

Earlier volume, covering 1918–67, publ. 1968 (248 pp.) and one covering 1924–64 publ. 1964 (212 pp.) These three collections contain detailed tables on party membership, generally arranged chronologically. The 1979 volume includes lists of all party congresses and conferences at republic, oblast' and okrug level, detailed lists of party archives and lists of the various party organizations in the republic.

U729   *Rezoliutsii i resheniia s"ezdov Kommunisticheskoi partii Uzbekistana.* [Resolutions and decisions of the congresses of the Uzbek CP]. (In-t istorii partii pri TsK KP Uzbekistana). Tashkent: Gos. izd-vo Uzbekskoi SSR, 1957. 494 pp.

The collection includes materials up to the 13th Congress in 1956. There is a brief introduction to each congress and the texts of all the resolutions and decisions it took.

* Consult periodical press.

GENERAL STATISTICS

Introduction

The collection and publication of statistical data in the USSR is primarily the responsibility of the Central Statistical Administration (TsSU) of the USSR and the central statistical administrations of the union republics. However, some other organizations do produce statistical data in their special fields, notably foreign trade statistics issued by the USSR Ministry of Foreign Trade, some health statistics produced by ministries of health, and data on party membership published by the institutes of party history of the communist parties of the union republics. However, the TsSU at all-union and union republic level are responsible for virtually all the general handbooks listed in this section, and for most of the specialized handbooks listed elsewhere.

In the immediate postwar period, the publication and circulation of statistical data was seriously impeded by official secrets legislation, and the sole regular source of statistical information was the annual and quarterly plan fulfilment report (U939, U940). After Stalin's death, the first sign of a thaw in statistical publishing came with the appearance in 1955 of a handbook on the press and publishing issued by the Ministry of Culture (U1454); TsSU handbooks reappeared from mid-1956 and there was a spate of general, republican and sectoral handbooks in the late 1950s and 1960s. Since then, regular annual publication of general statistical handbooks for the USSR and union republics has been established, with occasional jubilee editions marking particular anniversaries. The production of sectoral handbooks has continued, but declined during the 1970s, particularly at all-union level.

The use of Soviet statistics presents a number of problems to western researchers; these are discussed more fully in U735. The chief problems are, first, the concealment of politically sensitive data and information on social problems. For example, no figures are published on crime rates, and the publication of data on infant mortality ceased in the 1970s as the figures began to show an increase. Information on trade with countries no longer politically acceptable (such as Albania and South Africa) may simply be dropped from retrospective compilations. Another aspect of this problem is the restriction on export which is occasionally placed on major republican handbooks normally freely available to foreign subscribers. Second, changes may be made in definitions and in the base without informing users. Third, data may be presented as percentages without giving absolute figures. Last, the nature of the planning process and the need to meet plan targets—on paper at least—can lead to distorted returns.

In the following entries, only general handbooks and material on the censuses are listed: those handbooks dealing with a particular sector of the economy or with a special area such as education or housing are to be found in the sections dealing with that subject. In each section, the works included are listed alphabetically. Readers should note that the phrase 'Narodnoe khoziaistvo', which appears frequently in the titles of these general handbooks, is translated as 'National economy'. This phrase includes the whole range of quantifiable activities of the republic, including education, culture, the arts and welfare services as well as the economy. Each republic publishes one main annual statistical handbook, and several also publish a short annual handbook, valuable mainly because it appears months before the main one. Occasionally jubilee handbooks are published; these are less useful than the regular annual handbooks as they are usually intended to demonstrate the achievements of the republic and contain fewer hard facts and figures. It should be noted that statistical publications from krai and oblast´ level are not included here. For listings of these, *see* U731, U733 and U734.

General works and bibliographies

U730   Clarke, R. A. *Soviet economic facts, 1917–1970.* London: Macmillan, 1972. xi, 151 pp.

    A compilation of statistical data on a wide range of economic topics, collected from a number of Soviet sources.

U731   Gillula, J. W. *Bibliography of regional statistical handbooks in the U.S.S.R.* 2nd. ed. [Washington]: Bureau of the Census, Foreign Demographic Analysis Division, 1980. v, 99 pp.

    1st ed. publ. 1979 (113 pp.) A computer-produced listing of all known regional statistical handbooks published in the USSR from the mid-1950s until the middle of 1979. Indicates which items are held in the library of the Foreign Demographic Analysis Division. FDAD intends to issue updated versions of the bibliography as necessary.

U732   Kotz, S. *Russian–English dictionary of statistical terms and expressions and Russian reader in statistics.* With the collaboration of Wassily Hoeffding. Chapel Hill: University of North Carolina Press, 1964. 115 pp.

    A dictionary of statistical vocabulary, mainly the technical terminology used in texts about statistics and mathematical economics, but still useful for work on statistical handbooks.

U733   'List of Soviet statistical abstracts'. *Soviet studies,* vol. 10, 1958/59–.

    This list appears annually in the journal *Soviet studies,* usually in the third issue of the volume. As well as listing the statistical abstracts known to have been published during the previous years, it indicates holdings for certain British libraries and for the Library of Congress and United Nations Library in Geneva. It up-dates and supplements the listings in items U734, as well as providing useful information on locations.

U734   Mashikhin, E. A. *Statisticheskie publikatsii v SSSR: bibliograficheskii ukazatel´.* [Statistical publications of the USSR: a bibliography. By] E. A. Mashikhin, V. M. Simchera. M.: Statistika, 1975. 280 pp.

    Lists official statistical publications from 1918 to 1972 issued at all-union, union republic, ASSR, krai, oblast´ and town level. As well as statistical handbooks, it gives details of statistical serials and conferences of statisticians. The entries are arranged by republic, with a first section dealing with all-union materials. All the entries are given in Russian; where material is published in another language, this is not indicated. Some of the handbooks listed do not appear to be available to the general public and are not in the catalogue of the Lenin Library. The bibliography has a long introduction on the organization of the statistical service in the USSR at all levels, and a review of its publishing activities. There is no index to the bibliography.

U735   Mickiewicz, E. *Handbook of Soviet social science data.* N.Y.: The Free Press; London: Collier-Macmillan, 1973. xxvi, 225 pp.

Includes sections on demography, agriculture, production, health, housing, education, élite recruitment and mobilization, communications and international interactions (trade, economic assistance, Comecon and world communist parties). The tables in each section are based on a number of Soviet statistical handbooks and newspaper and periodical articles, selected and, in some cases, recalculated by American scholars specializing in these fields. For some sections, the Soviet data is supplemented by UN and US estimates. Each section has an introduction discussing the statistical problems and peculiarities of that field, and there is an overall introduction on the uses and potential of statistical analyses of the USSR.

U736   *Vestnik statistiki; organ TsSU SSSR.* [Journal of statistics; organ of the Central Statistical Administration of the USSR]. M.: Statistika, 1919–29, 1949–. Monthly.

Published monthly 1919–25 and from 1958; bimonthly 1926, 1949–57; quarterly 1927–9. Has a cumulative index: *Bibliograficheskii ukazatel' statei i materialov po statistike i uchetu: zhurnal 'Vestnik statistiki' za 50 let (1919–1968 gg.).* M.: Statistika, 1971. This is the official journal of the Central Statistical Administration, containing authoritative articles on statistical policy and methods, and on new developments. Since 1956 it has been particularly valuable as a source for statistical data on many fields, with most issues containing a section called 'Statisticheskie materialy'. Although it is primarily used for publishing current data, information on past years is sometimes included.

Census data

The last census before the war was held in 1939; its results were never published in full. Details of what information is available are listed here because it is relevant for the study of the USSR during the 1940s and 1950s. Subsequent censuses were held in 1959, 1970 and 1979; although fuller results were published, it is not always possible to make direct comparisons, as the presentation of information differs.

1939 census

U737 'Nekotorye itogi perepisi naseleniia 1939 g.' [Some results of the 1939 census]. *Vestnik statistiki*, 1956, no. 6. Pp. 89–90.

This brief summary is a corrected reissue of the preliminary data originally published in *Pravda* and *Izvestiia* on 2 June 1939 and 29 April 1940. Some additional information can also be gleaned from the statistical series published in later handbooks and in the results of the 1959 census.

U738 Lorimer, F. *The population of the Soviet Union: history and prospects.* Geneva: League of Nations, 1946. xiv, 290 pp.

An authoritative study of the population of the USSR up to the end of the war, summarizing and recalculating official series and census data. Particularly useful for work on demography in the 1940s and 1950s, in the absence of fuller data from the 1937 and 1939 censuses.

U739 *Sistematicheskii slovar' zaniatii: posobie dlia razrabotki materialov Vsesoiuznoi perepisi naseleniia 1939 g.* [Systematic index of occupations: an aid for the processing of the 1939 census results]. M.: Gosstatizdat, 1957. 201 pp.

A listing of trades and occupations by basic industrial or occupational group, used as the basis for the analysis of occupations in the 1939, 1959 and, to a lesser extent, 1970 censuses.

1959 census

U740 *Vsesoiuznaia perepis' naseleniia 1959 goda.* [The 1959 all-union census of population]. (TsSU SSSR). M.: Politizdat, 1958. 51 pp.

Gives the procedures for carrying out the 1959 census, including its timetable and sample census return forms.

U741 *Chislennost', sostav i razmeshchenie naseleniia SSSR: kratkie itogi Vsesoiuznoi perepisi naseleniia 1959 g.* [The number, composition and distribution of the population of the USSR: summary results of the 1959 census]. (TsSU SSSR). M.: Gosstatizdat, 1961. 64 pp.

Summary results; for fuller results *see* U742

U742 *Itogi Vsesoiuznoi perepisi naseleniia 1959 goda.* [Results of the 1959 all-union census of population]. (TsSU SSSR). M.: Gosstatizdat.
SSSR (Svodnyi tom). 1962.
RSFSR. 1963.
Armianskaia SSR. 1963.
Azerbaidzhanskaia SSR. 1963.
Belorusskaia SSR. 1963.
Estonskaia SSR. 1962.
Gruzinskaia SSR. 1963.
Kazakhskaia SSR. 1962.
Kirgizskaia SSR. 1963.
Latviiskaia SSR. 1962.

Litovskaia SSR. 1963.
Moldavskaia SSR. 1962.
Tadzhikskaia SSR. 1963.
Turkmenskaia SSR. 1963.
Ukrainskaia SSR. 1963.
Uzbekskaia SSR. 1962.

The fullest available results of the 1959 census, published with an all-union summary volume, followed by volumes for each union republic.

1970 census

U743 *Vsesoiuznaia perepis' naseleniia—vsenarodnoe delo.* [The all-union census is a matter for the whole people.]. (TsSU SSSR). M.: Statistika, 1969. 64 pp.

As well as materials explaining the importance of the census, includes sample census return forms, detailed instructions on their completion, and the text of the official instructions on the procedures for carrying out the 1970 census.

U744 *Chislennost', razmeshchenie, vozrastnaia struktura, uroven' obrazovaniia, natsional'nyi sostav, iazyki i istochniki sredstv sushchestvovaniia naseleniia SSSR, po dannym Vsesoiuznoi perepisi naseleniia 1970 goda.* [The number, distribution, age structure, educational level, national composition, languages and sources of income of the population of the USSR, from the data of the all-union census of 1970]. (TsSU SSSR). M.: Statistika, 1971. 34 pp.

A summary of the results of the 1970 census. For fuller results, *see* U745.

U745 *Itogi Vsesoiuznoi perepisi naseleniia 1970 goda.* [Results of the 1970 all-union census of population]. (TsSU SSSR). M.: Statistika.

Vol. 1. *Chislennost' naseleniia SSSR, soiuznykh i avtonomnykh respublik, kraev i oblastei.* 1972.

Vol. 2. *Pol, vozrast i sostoianie v brake naseleniia SSSR, soiuznykh i avtonomnykh respublik, kraev i oblastei.* 1972.

Vol. 3. *Uroven' obrazovaniia naseleniia SSSR, soiuznykh i avtonomnykh respublik, kraev i oblastei.* 1972.

Vol. 4. *Natsional'nyi sostav naseleniia SSSR, soiuznykh i avtonomnykh respublik, kraev, oblastei i natsional'nykh okrugov.* 1973.

Vol. 5. *Raspredelenie naseleniia SSSR, soiuznykh i avtonomnykh respublik, kraev i oblastei po obshchestvennym gruppam, istochnikam sredstv sushchestvovaniia i otrasliam narodnogo khoziaistva.* 1973.

Vol. 6. *Raspredelenie naseleniia SSSR i soiuznykh respublik po zaniatiiam.* 1973.

Vol. 7. *Migratsiia naseleniia, chislo i sostav semei v SSSR, soiuznykh i avtonomnykh respublikakh, kraiakh i oblastiakh.* 1974.

The fullest available results of the 1970 census, arranged by topic rather than by republic.

413

1979 census

U746 *Vsesoiuznaia perepis' naseleniia—vsenarodnoe delo.* [The all-union census is a matter for the whole people]. (TsSU SSSR). M.: Statistika, 1978. 70 pp.

As well as information on the history of censuses in the USSR and Russia, and other general material, includes the timetable for the 1979 census, sample census return forms, instructions for their completion, and other official instructions.

U747 *Naselenie SSSR; po dannym Vsesoiuznoi perepisi naseleniia 1979 goda.* [The population of the USSR, according to the results of the 1979 census]. (TsSU SSSR). M.: Politizdat, 1980. 32 pp.

Summary results. More detailed figures are being published in *Vestnik statistiki*, from 1980, no. 2, onwards.

All-union handbooks

U748 *Dostizheniia sovetskoi vlasti za sorok let v tsifrakh: statisticheskii sbornik.* [Forty years of Soviet power in figures: a statistical handbook]. (TsSU SSSR). M.: Gosstatizdat, 1957. 370 pp.

Contains data for 1956 and selected earlier years, with descriptions of the achievements of the USSR in various fields. English translation available as: *Forty years of Soviet power in facts and figures.* (Central Statistical Board of the USSR Council of Ministers). Moscow: FLPH, 1958. 319 pp.

U749 *Narodnoe khoziaistvo SSSR: statisticheskii sbornik.* [The national economy of the USSR: a statistical collection]. (TsSU SSSR). M.: Gosstatizdat, 1956. 262 pp.

Provides preliminary data for 1955 and for a series of years from 1913. Covers a similar range of subjects to U750. It was translated into English, with a short glossary, as: *The USSR economy: a statistical abstract.* London: Lawrence and Wishart, 1957. 264 pp.

U750 *Narodnoe khoziaistvo SSSR v ... godu: statisticheskii ezhegodnik.* [The national economy of the USSR in ...: a statistical yearbook]. (TsSU SSSR). M.: Statistika, 1956 (publ. 1957)–. Annual.

Not published in 1957 and 1966; jubilee collections (U748 and U754) were published instead. The volume for 1971 appeared as *Narodnoe khoziaistvo SSSR, 1922–1972: iubileinyi statisticheskii ezhegodnik* and the volume for 1976 as *Narodnoe khoziaistvo SSSR za 60 let: iubileinyi statisticheskii ezhegodnik.* This handbook is the main statistical summary for the whole of the USSR, covering culture, education, the arts, health and welfare as well as demography, industry, the economy and agriculture.

U751 *Naselenie SSSR (chislennost' sostav i dvizhenie naseleniia), 1973: statisticheskii sbornik.* [The population of the USSR (numbers, composition, migration) in 1973: a statistical handbook]. (TsSU SSSR). M.: Statistika, 1975. 208 pp.

A handbook of demographic data, mainly relating to 1973 but in some cases limited to the results of the 1970 census. Some 1974 figures are included.

U752   *SSSR i zarubezhnye strany posle pobedy Velikoi Oktiabr'skoi sotsialis-ticheskoi revoliutsii: statisticheskii sbornik.* [The USSR and foreign countries after the Great October Socialist Revolution: a statistical handbook]. (TsSU SSSR). M.: Statistika, 1970. 319 pp.

Despite its title, the handbook is mainly concerned with the achievements of the USSR since 1917, with tables showing developments over selected years to 1969 in the fields of economy, agriculture, industry, health, education and culture. Each group of tables is accompanied by an explanatory text highlighting the main features of developments in that field, and each section has a summary table comparing the USSR with selected European countries, the USA and Japan.

U753   *SSSR v tsifrakh v . . . godu: kratkii statisticheskii sbornik.* [The USSR in figures in . . .: a short statistical handbook]. (TsSU SSSR). M.: Statistika, [1957], (publ. 1958)–. Annual.

First issue had title *SSSR v tsifrakh: statisticheskii sbornik.* An English translation is published annually in the USSR, called *The USSR in figures.* Although less detailed than the main annual handbook (U750), this brief summary is useful because it generally appears months before U750, and is far more widely available.

U754   *Strana Sovetov za 50 let: sbornik statisticheskikh materialov.* [Fifty years of the USSR: statistical data]. (TsSU SSSR). M.: Statistika, 1967. 351 pp.

Contains data for 1966 and selected previous years, with notes amplifying the tables and demonstrating the achievements of the Soviet government.

U755   *Strana Sovetov za 60 let: statisticheskie materialy.* [Sixty years of the USSR: statistical materials]. M.: Politizdat, 1977. 111 pp.

A brief statistical summary; unlike the annual handbooks (U750) it includes data on the composition of the CPSU and the soviets, and the trade unions.

See also U939–U943.

RSFSR

U756   *Narodnoe khoziaistvo RSFSR: statisticheskii sbornik.* [The national economy of the RSFSR: a statistical handbook]. (Stat. upr. RSFSR). M.: Gosstatizdat, 1957. 371 pp.

Includes data to 1956 on the economy, culture, education, health, etc. for the RSFSR and its administrative subdivisions.

U757   *Narodnoe khoziaistvo RSFSR v . . . godu: statisticheskii ezhegodnik.* [The national economy of the RSFSR in . . .: a statistical yearbook].

(TsSU RSFSR). M.: Statistika, 1958 (publ. 1959)–. Annual.

Not published in 1966; a jubilee handbook was published instead, *see* U760. The volume for 1976 was called *Narodnoe khoziaistvo RSFSR za 60 let.* Coverage is similar to U750, but gives a fuller breakdown of some topics and a detailed coverage of the RSFSR's subdivisions.

U758 *RSFSR v tsifrakh v ... g.: kratkii statisticheskii sbornik.* [The RSFSR in figures in ...: a short statistical handbook]. (TsSU RSFSR). M.: Statistika, 1959 (publ. 1960)–. Annual.

Not published in 1960 and 1961. 1959–64 title was *RSFSR v ...g.* A brief statistical handbook of data on the RSFSR.

U759 *RSFSR za 40 let: statisticheskii sbornik.* [Forty years of the RSFSR: a statistical handbook]. (TsSU RSFSR). M.: Sovetskaia Rossiia, 1958. 223 pp.

Contains data for 1956 and selected preceding years, with descriptions of the achievements of the Soviet people.

U760 *RSFSR za 50 let: statisticheskii sbornik.* [Fifty years of the RSFSR: a statistical handbook]. (TsSU RSFSR). M.: Statistika, 1967. 255 pp.

Contains data for 1967 and selected preceding years, with notes amplifying the tables and demonstrating the achievements of the Soviet government.

Armenia

U761 *Armeniia v edinoi sem'e narodov SSSR.* [Armenia in the united family of the peoples of the USSR]. (TsSU ArmSSR). Erevan, 1972. 218 pp.

A jubilee handbook on Armenia, containing data to 1971.

U762 *Narodnoe khoziaistvo Armianskoi SSR: statisticheskii sbornik.* [The national economy of the Armenian SSR: statistical handbook]. (TsSU SSSR. Stat. upr. ArmSSR). Erevan: Gosstatizdat, 1957. 180 pp.

Most of the tables cover 1940–56; some go back to 1913. All fields are covered.

U763 *Narodnoe khoziaistvo Armianskoi SSR v ... godu: statisticheskii ezhegodnik.* [The national economy of the Armenian SSR in ...: a statistical annual]. (TsSU SSSR. TsSU Armianskoi SSR). Erevan: Aiastan, 1963 (publ. 1964)–. Annual.

The 1966 volume was called *Ekonomika i kul'tura Armenii k 50–letiiu Velikogo Oktiabria: statisticheskii sbornik*; the 1969 volume was called *Sovetskaia Armeniia za 50 let: sbornik statisticheskikh materialov.* This is the main handbook for the Armenian SSR.

Azerbaijan

U764 *Azarbaijan SSR khalg tasarrufaty: statistika kulliiiaty = Narodnoe khoziaistvo Azerbaidzhanskoi SSR: statisticheskii sbornik.* [The national economy of Azerbaijan: a statistical handbook]. (TsSU SSSR. Stat. upr. AzSSR). Baku: Gosstatizdat, 1957. 525 pp.

In Azerbaijani and Russian, containing data on the development of Azerbaijan for selected prewar years and through to 1956.

U765 *Azerbaidzhan v tsifrakh: kratkii statisticheskii sbornik.* [Azerbaijan in figures: a short statistical handbook]. (TsSU SSSR. TsSU AzSSR). Baku: Az. gos. izd-vo, 1964. 302 pp.

A summary of the achievements of Azerbaijan from 1913 to 1963.

U766 *Azerbaidzhanskaia SSR [k] 50-letiiu Velikogo Oktiabria: statisticheskii sbornik.* [Azerbaijan on the fiftieth anniversary of the October revolution: a statistical handbook]. (TsSU AzSSR). Baku: Az. otd-nie izd-va Statistika, 1967. 215 pp.

A handbook on Azerbaijan covering 1913–65, with explanatory text to the tables.

U767 *Azerbaidzhanskaia SSR v tsifrakh v . . . godu: kratkii statisticheskii sbornik.* [Azerbaijan in figures in . . .: a short statistical handbook]. (TsSU AzSSR). Baku: 1964 (publ. 1965)–. Annual.

Not published for 1966, 1975 and 1976. A short statistical summary of the year's progress in Azerbaijan.

U768 *Dostizheniia Sovetskogo Azerbaidzhana za 40 let v tsifrakh: statisticheskii sbornik.* [Forty years of Soviet Azerbaijan in figures: a statistical handbook]. (TsSU SSSR. TsSU AzSSR). Baku: Az. gos. izd-vo, 1960. 259 pp.

Statistical data on Azerbaijan in figures for 1913–59, with explanatory texts to the tables.

U769 *Narodnoe khoziaistvo Azerbaidzhanskoi SSR v . . . godu: statisticheskii sbornik.* [The national economy of Azerbaijan in . . .: statistical handbook]. (TsSU AzSSR). Baku: 1962 (publ. 1963)–. Annual.

Not published for 1966 and 1967. The 1971 volume had title: *Narodnoe khoziaistvo Azerbaidzhanskoi SSR k 50-letiiu SSSR: iubileinyi statisticheskii ezhegodnik,* and the 1976 volume: *Narodnoe khoziaistvo Azerbaidzhanskoi SSR k 60-letiiu Velikogo Oktiabria: iubileinyi statisticheskii ezhegodnik.* This is the main handbook for Azerbaijan.

U770 *Razvitie narodnogo khoziaistva Azerbaidzhanskoi SSR i rost material'nogo i kul'turnogo urovnia zhizni naroda: statisticheskii sbornik.* [The development of the economy in Azerbaijan and the growth in the material and cultural well-being of the people]. (TsSU SSSR. TsSU AzSSR). Baku: Az. gos. izd-vo, 1961. 258 pp.

General data on Azerbaijan for 1913, 1920, 1928 and 1940, and selected postwar years to 1960.

U771 *Sovetskii Azerbaidzhan ot vyborov do vyborov v Verkhovnyi Sovet SSSR.* [Soviet Azerbaijan between the elections to the USSR Supreme Soviet]. Baku, 1979. [Not seen].

U772　*Sovetskii Azerbaidzhan za 50 let: statisticheskii sbornik.* [Fifty years of Soviet Azerbaijan: a statistical handbook]. (TsSU AzSSR). Baku: Az. gos. izd-vo, 1970. 266 pp.

　　Issued to mark the 50th anniversary of the formation of the Azerbaijani SSR. Contains data to 1969.

Belorussia

U773　*Belorusskaia SSR v tsifrakh: kratkii statisticheskii sbornik.* [The Belorussian SSR in figures: a short statistical handbook]. (TsSU BSSR). Minsk: Gosstatizdat, Belorusskoe otd-nie, 1962–3.

　　Two collections of statistical data for Belorussian, with most tables starting in 1940. Includes summaries by oblast′ and for the city of Minsk.

U774　*Belorusskaia SSR v tsifrakh v ... g.: statisticheskii sbornik.* [The Belorusssian SSR in figures in ...: a statistical handbook]. (TsSU BSSR). Minsk: Statistika, Belorusskoe otd-nie, 1964 (publ. 1965); 1965 (publ. 1966); 1969 (publ. 1970).

　　A summary of statistical data for Belorussia in the year covered, with some tables broken down to town or oblast′ level.

U775　*Belorusskaia SSR za gody sovetskoi vlasti: statisticheskii sbornik.* [Belorussia under Soviet power: a statistical handbook]. (TsSU BSSR). Minsk: Belarus′, 1967. 403 pp.

　　A jubilee handbook containing data up to 1966.

U776　*Belorusskaia SSR za 50 let: statisticheskii sbornik.* [Fifty years of the Belorussian SSR: a statistical handbook]. Minsk: Belarus′, 1968. 259 pp.

　　Information on the development of Belorussia, with some tables starting in 1913 but most from 1940 or later.

U777　*Dostizheniia sovetskoi Belorussii za 40 let: statisticheskii sbornik.* [Forty years of Soviet Belorussia: a statistical handbook]. (TsSU SSSR. Stat. upr. BSSR). Minsk: Gos. stat. izd-vo, 1957. 204 pp. plus diagrams.

　　Data on Belorussia, 1917–57.

U778　*Ekonomika i kul′tura Belorusskoi SSR [1966–1970 gg.]: kratkii statisticheskii sbornik.* [The economics and culture of the Belorussian SSR, 1966–70: a short statistical handbook]. Minsk, 1971. 87 pp. [Not seen].

U779　*Narodnoe khoziaistvo Belorusskoi SSR: statisticheskii sbornik.* [The national economy of Belorussia: a statistical handbook]. (Stat. upr. BSSR). Minsk: Gosstatizdat, 1957. 319 pp. [Not seen. FDAD].

U780　*Narodnoe khoziaistvo Belorusskoi SSR v ... godu: statisticheskii sbornik.* [The national economy of Belorussia in ...: a statistical handbook]. (TsSU BSSR). Minsk: Statistika, 1968 (publ. 1969)–. Annual.

Not published for 1969. 1972 volume called *Statisticheskii ezhegodnik Belorusskoi SSR*; 1977 volume called *Narodnoe khoziaistvo Belorusskoi SSR: iubileinyi statisticheskii ezhegodnik*. The main statistical handbook for Belorussia.

U781 *Narodnoe khoziaistvo Belorusskoi SSR za 40 let: statistiko-ekonomicheskii sbornik*. [Forty years of Belorussia: a statistical and economic handbook]. (Gosplan BSSR). Minsk: Gosstatizdat, 1957. 288 pp. [Not seen. FDAD].

U782 *Narodnoe khoziaistvo BSSR: statisticheskii sbornik*. [The national economy of the Belorussian SSR: statistical handbook]. (TsSU BSSR). Minsk: Gos. izd-vo BSSR, 1963. 511 pp.

Data on all aspects of Belorussian life from 1913, 1940 and 1950 up to 1961.

U783 *Razvitie narodnogo khoziaistva Belorusskoi SSR za 20 let (1944–1963): statisticheskii sbornik*. [The development of the Belorussian economy over 20 years: a statistical handbook]. Minsk: Belarus', 1964. 215 pp.

Summaries of the development of the economy, education, agriculture, etc, since the end of the war.

Estonia

U784 *Dostizheniia Sovetskoi Estonii za 20 let: statisticheskii sbornik*. [The achievements of Estonia over 20 years: a statistical handbook]. (TsSU ESSR). Tallin: Est. gos. izd-vo, 1960. 176 pp.

Data mainly from the 1950s, but with some tables going back to 1940.

U785 *Eesti NSV rahvamajandus ... aastal: statistika aastaraamat = Narodnoe khoziaistvo Estonskoi SSR v ... godu: statisticheskii ezhegodnik*. [The national economy of Estonia: a statistical annual]. (TsSU ESSR). Tallin: Eesti raamat, 1967 (publ. 1968)–. Annual.

Usually published with Estonian and Russian text; some volumes in Russian only. The main statistical handbook for Estonia.

U786 *Eesti NSV rahvamajandus: statistikiline kogumik = Narodnoe khoziaistvo SSR: statisticheskii sbornik*. [The national economy of Estonia: a statistical collection]. Tallin: Eesti riiklik kirjastus, 1957. 307 pp.

In Estonian and Russian. Covers 1955–6, with some tables going back to 1940, 1945, 1950 and 1953.

U787 *Estonskaia SSR za gody Sovetskoi vlasti: kratkii statisticheskii sbornik*. [Estonia under Soviet power: a short statistical handbook]. (TsSU ESSR). Tallin, 1967. 245 pp.

Data from 1940 or 1950 to 1966.

U788   *Sovetskaia Estoniia za 25 let.* [25 years of Soviet Estonia]. (TsSU ESSR). Tallin: Eesti raamat, 1965. 185 pp. plus diagrams.
Data for 1940 or 1956 to 1964.

Georgia

U789   *50 let Sovetskoi Gruzii: statisticheskii sbornik.* [Fifty years of Soviet Georgia: a statistical handbook]. (TsSU GSSR). Tbilisi: Gruz. otd-nie izd-va 'Statistika', 1971. 387 pp.
A jubilee handbook with data to 1970; most series start in 1940.

U790   *Gruzinskaia SSR v tsifrakh v . . . godu: kratkii statisticheskii sbornik.* [The Georgian SSR in . . . a short statistical handbook]. (TsSU GSSR). Tbilisi: Gruz. otd-nie izd-va 'Statistika', 1968 (publ. 1969)–. Annual.
Not published for 1969 and 1970. 1968 volume had title: *Gruzinskaia SSR v 1968 g.* A short handbook of data on Georgia.

U791   *Narodnoe khoziaistvo Gruzinskoi SSR: statisticheskii sbornik.* [The national economy of the Georgian SSR: a statistical handbook]. (TsSU SSSR. TsSU GSSR). Tbilisi: Gos. stat. izd-vo, 1959. 357 pp.
Earlier volume publ. 1957 had data to 1956. This covers 1913 and selected years to 1958.

U792   *Narodnoe khoziaistvo Gruzinskoi SSR v . . . g.: statisticheskii ezhegodnik.* [The national economy of the Georgian SSR: a statistical annual]. (TsSU GSSR). Tbilisi: Sabchota Sakartvelo, 1961 (publ. 1963)–. Annual.
Not published for 1965–6, 1968–72. 1976 volume had title: *Narodnoe khoziaistvo Gruzinskoi SSR k 60-letiiu Velikogo Oktiabria: iubileinyi statisticheskii ezhegodnik.* The main statistical handbook for Georgia.

U793   *Sovetskaia Gruziia k 50-letiiu Velikoi Oktiabr'skoi sotsialisticheskoi revoliutsii.* [Soviet Georgia on the fiftieth anniversary of the October Revolution]. (TsSU GSSR). Tbilisi: Gruz. otd-nie izd-va 'Statistika', 1967. 327 pp.
Gives figures for 1966 and for a few earlier years on the development of Georgia.

U794   *Sovetskaia Gruziia po leninskomu puti: statisticheskii sbornik.* [Soviet Georgia follows Lenin's path: a statistical handbook]. (TsSU GSSR). Tbilisi: Gruz. otd-nie izd-va 'Statistika', 1970. 178 pp.
A statistical handbook demonstrating Georgia's achievements, published for the centenary of Lenin's birth.

U795   *Sovetskaia Gruziia za 40 let: statisticheskii sbornik.* [40 years of Soviet Georgia: a statistical handbook]. (TsSU GSSR). Tbilisi: Gosstatizdat, 1961. 208 pp., plus diagrams and maps

Data on Georgia 1921–60, with explanatory text, diagrams and maps.

Kazakhstan

U796 *Kazakhstan v tsifrakh: kratkii statisticheskii sbornik.* [Kazakhstan in figures: a short statistical handbook]. Alma-Ata: Kazakhstan, 1971. 147 pp. [Not seen. FDAD].

U797 *Kazakhstan za 40 let: statisticheskii sbornik.* [40 years of Kazakhstan: a statistical handbook]. (TsSU KazSSR). Alma-Ata: Gosstatizdat, 1960. 525 pp.
A statistical summary of Kazakhstan with figures up to 1959.

U798 *Kazakhstan za 50 let: statisticheskii sbornik.* [50 years of Kazakhstan: a statistical handbook]. (TsSU KazSSR). Alma-Ata, 1971. 248 pp.
A statistical summary of Kazakhstan with figures up to 1970.

U799 *Narodnoe khoziaistvo i kul'tura Kazakhskoi SSR mezhdu VIII i X s"ezdami Kommunisticheskoi partii Kazakhstana.* [The national economy and culture of Kazakhstan between the 8th and 10th congresses of the Kazakh CP]. Alma-Ata: Gosstatizdat, 1960. 211 pp. [Not seen].

U800 *Narodnoe khoziaistvo Kazakhskoi SSR: statisticheskii sbornik.* [The national economy of the Kazakh SSR: a statistical handbook]. (Stat. upr. KazSSR). Alma-Ata: Kaz. gos. izd-vo, 1957. 381 pp.
Data on the development of Kazakhstan from the pre-Revolutionary period to 1956.

U801 *Narodnoe khoziaistvo Kazakhskoi SSR v 1960 i 1961 gg.: statisticheskii sbornik.* [The national economy of the Kazakh SSR in 1960–1961: a statistical handbook]. Alma-Ata: Gosstatizdat, 1963. 544 pp.
Covers all fields; many tables broken down to oblast' level.

U802 *Narodnoe khoziaistvo Kazakhstana v ... g.: statisticheskii sbornik.* [The national economy of Kazakhstan in ...: a statistical handbook]. (TsSU KazSSR). Alma-Ata: Kazakhstan, 1966 (publ. 1968)–. Annual.
Not published for 1967 and 1969–70. The main statistical handbook for Kazakhstan.

Kirghizia

U803 *Kirgizstan v tsifrakh i faktakh, 1960–1970 gg.: kratkii statisticheskii sbornik.* [Kirghizia in facts and figures, 1960–1970: a short statistical handbook]. (TsSU KirgSSR). Frunze, 1971. 190 pp.
A collection compiled for the 15th Congress of the Kirghiz CP.

U804 *Narodnoe khoziaistvo Kirgizskoi SSR: statisticheskii sbornik.* [The national economy of Kirghizia: a statistical handbook]. (Stat. upr. KirgSSR). Frunze: Gosstatizdat, Kirg. otd-nie, 1957. 207 pp.

Data for the whole republic for 1928–55, and at oblast´ level for 1940–55.

U805 *Narodnoe khoziaistvo Kirgizskoi SSR v . . . g.: statisticheskii ezhegodnik.* [The national economy of Kirghizia in . . .: statistical annual]. (TsSU KirgSSR). Frunze: Kyrgyzstan, 1960 (publ. 1961)–. Annual.

Not published for 1968. The 1962 volume was called *Kirgiziia v tsifrakh*; the 1965 volume *Sovetskii Kirgizstan za 40 let (1926–66)*; the 1966 volume *Kirgizstan za 50 let Sovetskoi vlasti*; the 1970 volume *Kirgizstan v tsifrakh*; the 1973 volume appeared as *Kirgizstan za 50 let: iubileinyi statisticheskii sbornik* and the 1976 volume was called *Kirgizstan za gody Sovetskoi vlasti: iubileinyi statisticheskii ezhegodnik*. The main statistical handbook for Kirghizia.

U806 *Razvitie ekonomiki i kul'tury Kirgizskoi SSR (1958–1965 gg.): kratkii statisticheskii sbornik.* [The development of Kirghiz economy and culture, 1958–1965: a short statistical handbook]. (TsSU KirgSSR). Frunze, 1966. 107 pp.

A collection compiled for the 14th Congress of the Kirghiz CP.

Latvia

U807 *Latviiskaia SSR v tsifrakh v . . . godu: kratkii statisticheskii sbornik.* [Latvia in figures in . . .: a short statistical handbook]. (TsSU LatvSSR). Riga: Latv. otd-nie izd-va 'Statistika', 1960 (publ. 1961)–. Annual.

Not published for 1965 and 1967. Some variation in title; some years omit '*v tsifrakh*' or '*kratkii*'. The 1963 handbook was called *Padomju Latvija skaitlos: statistiko datu krājums = Sovetskaia Latviia v tsifrakh: kratkii statisticheskii sbornik*. 1964 volume called *Sovetskaia Latviia za 25 let* and the 1966 one *Latviia za gody Sovetskoi vlasti*. The main short statistical handbook for Latvia. Some volumes also published separately in Latvian.

U808 *Latvijas PSR tautas saimnieciba: statistiko datu krājums = Narodnoe khoziaistvo Latviiskoi SSR: statisticheskii sbornik.* [National economy of Latvia: statistical handbook]. Riga: Gosstatizdat, Latv. otd-nie, 1957. 229 pp.

Detailed figures for 1940–56. Latvian and Russian text.

U809 *Padomju Latvijas tautas saimnieciba 20 gados: statistiko datu krājums = Narodnoe khoziaistvo Sovetskoi Latvii za 20 let: statisticheskii sbornik.* [20 years of the Latvian national economy: a statistical handbook]. (TsSU LatvSSR). Riga: Gosstatizdat, Latv. otd-nie, 1960. 370 pp.

A very detailed handbook in Latvian and Russian covering 1945–59.

U810 *Latvijas PSR tautas saimnieciba . . . gada: statistikas gadā = Narodnoe khoziaistvo Latviiskoi SSR v . . .: statisticheskii ezhe-*

godnik. [National economy of the Latvian SSR: a statistical yearbook]. (TsSU LatvSSR). Riga: Liesma, 1967 (publ. 1968)–. Annual.

Some volumes publ. in Latvian and Russian, others appeared only in Russian. Not published for 1968. The main statistical handbook for Latvia.

U811 *Latvijas PSR tautas saimniecības attīstība: statistiko datu krā-jums = Razvitie narodnogo khoziaistva Latviiskoi SSR: statisticheskii sbornik.* [The development of the Latvian national economy: a statistical handbook]. (TsSU LatvSSR). Riga: Gosstatizdat, 1962. 374 pp.

In Latvian and Russian, covering 1940–61.

U812 *Padomju Latvijas ekonomika un kultūra: statistiko datu krājums= Ekonomika i kul'tura Sovetskoi Latvii: statisticheskii sbornik.* [The economy and culture of Soviet Latvia]. (TsSU LatvSSR). Riga: Latv. otd-nie izd-va 'Statistika', 1966. 508 pp.

A detailed handbook in Latvian and Russian with data for 1940–65.

Lithuania

U813 *20 let Sovetskoi Litvy: statisticheskii sbornik.* [20 years of Soviet Lithuania: a statistical handbook]. (TsSU LitSSR). Vil'nius: Gos-statizdat, Lit. otd-nie, 1960. 352 pp.

Data for 1940–59.

U814 *25 let Sovetskoi Litvy: statisticheskii sbornik.* [25 years of Soviet Lithuania: a statistical handbook]. (TsSU LitSSR). Vil'nius: Gos-statizdat, Lit. otd-nie, 1965. 271 pp.

Data for 1940–64.

U815 *Ekonomika i kul'tura Litovskoi SSR k XV s"ezdu Kommunisticheskoi partii Litvy: kratkii statisticheskii sbornik.* [The economy and culture of Lithuania: a short statistical handbook for the 15th Congress of the Lithuanian CP]. Vil'nius: Statistika, 1965. 195 pp.

Also publ. in Lithuanian. [Not seen].

U816 *Ekonomika i kul'tura Litovskoi SSR k XVI s"ezdu Kommunisticheskoi partii Litvy: kratkii statisticheskii sbornik.* [The economy and culture of Lithuania: a statistical handbook for the 16th Congress of the Lithuanian CP]. Vil'nius, 1971. 313 pp. [Not seen].

U817 *Ekonomika i kul'tura Litovskoi SSR v . . . godu: statisticheskii ezhegod-nik.* [The national economy of the Lithuanian SSR: a statistical annual]. (TsSU LitSSR). Vil'nius: Lit. otd-nie izd-va 'Statistika', 1960 (publ. 1962)–. Annual.

Some volumes also published in Lithuanian called *Lietuvos TSR ekonomika ir kultūra ... metais.* The 1962 volume was called *Litovskaia SSR v tsifrakh v 1962 g.*; the 1960, 1961 and 1965 volumes were called *Narodnoe khoziaistvo Litovskoi SSR v ... g.* The main statistical handbook for Lithuania.

U818   *Narodnoe khoziaistvo Litovskoi SSR: statisticheskii sbornik.* [The national economy of the Lithuanian SSR: statistical handbook]. (Stat. upr. LitSSR). Vil'nius: Gosstatizdat, Lit. otd-nie, 1957. 224 pp.
     Covers 1940–56.

U819   *Statisticheskie dannye ob ekonomike i kul'ture Litovskoi SSR mezhdu X i XI s"ezdami Kommunisticheskoi partii Litvy.* [Statistical data on the economy and culture of Lithuania between the 10th and 11th congresses of the Lithuanian CP]. Vilnius: Gosstatizdat, Lit. otd-nie, 1956. 96 pp.
     Also publ. in Lithuanian. [Not seen].

Moldavia

U820   *Moldavskaia SSR v tsifrakh v 1961 godu: kratkii statisticheskii sbornik.* [The Moldavian SSR in figures in 1961: a statistical handbook]. (TsSU MSSR). Kishinev: Gosstatizdat, 1962. 365 pp.
     A general handbook, with most tables covering 1950 and 1955–61 but some going back to 1940.

U821   *Narodnoe khoziaistvo Moldavskoi SSR: statisticheskii sbornik.* [The national economy of Moldavia: a statistical handbook]. (Stat. upr. MSSR). Kishinev: Gosstatizdat, 1959. 287 pp.
     Earlier edition publ. 1957 (197 pp.). Two general handbooks on the development of Moldavia since 1940.

U822   *Narodnoe khoziaistvo Moldavskoi SSR v . . . g.: statisticheskii ezhegodnik.* [The national economy of the Moldavian SSR in . . .: a statistical annual]. Kishinev: Kartia Moldoveniaske, 1960 (publ. 1961)–. Annual.
     Not published for 1961 and 1967. 1963 volume called *Sovetskaia Moldaviia za 40 let*; 1966 volume *Sovetskaia Moldaviia k 50-letiiu Velikogo Oktiabria*; 1973 volume *Narodnoe khoziaistvo Moldavskoi SSR 1924–1974*; 1976 volume *Sovetskaia Moldaviia k 60-letiiu Velikogo Oktiabria*. The main statistical handbook for Moldavia.

Tajikistan

U823   *Narodnoe khoziaistvo Tadzhikskoi SSR: statisticheskii sbornik.* [The national economy of the Tajik SSR: a statistical handbook]. (TsSU SSSR. Stat. upr. TaSSR). Stalinabad: Gosstatizdat, 1957. 387 pp.
     Also publ. in Tajik in 1958. Most tables cover 1940–56; some go back to 1913.

U824   *Narodnoe khoziaistvo Tadzhikskoi SSR v . . . godu: statisticheskii ezhegodnik.* [The national economy of the Tajik SSR: a statistical annual]. (TsSU TaSSR). Dushanbe: Irfon, 1959 (publ. 1960)–. Annual.
     Not published for 1967 and 1970. The 1963 volume was called

Tadzhikistan za 40 let: statisticheskii sbornik; the 1966 volume *Tadzhikistan za gody sovetskoi vlasti: sbornik statisticheskikh materialov*; 1973 volume *Sovetskii Tadzhikistan za 50 let: sbornik statisticheskikh materialov*. The 1966 volume was also publ. in Tajik. The main statistical handbook for Tajikistan.

Turkmenistan

U825   *Narodnoe khoziaistvo Turkmenskoi SSR: statisticheskii sbornik*. [The national economy of the Turkmen SSR: a statistical handbook]. (TsSU SSSR. Stat. upr. TuSSR). Ashkhabad: Gosstatizdat, 1962. 253 pp.
    Earlier edition publ. 1957 (171 pp.) contains figures for 1913–56; the 1962 volume covers mainly 1950–61.

U826   *Narodnoe khoziaistvo Turkmenskoi SSR v ... godu: statisticheskii ezhegodnik*. [The Turkmen national economy in ...: a statistical annual]. (TsSU TuSSR). Ashkhabad: Turkmenistan, 1974 (publ. 1976)–. Annual.
    The main statistical handbook for Turkmenistan.

U827   *Sovetskii Turkmenistan za 40 let: statisticheskii sbornik*. [40 years of Soviet Turkmenistan: a statistical handbook]. Ashkhabad: Gosstatizdat, 1964. 158 pp. plus diagrams.
    Data for 1913 and 1924–63.

U828   *Turkmenistan za 50 let: statisticheskii sbornik*. [50 years of Turkmenistan: a statistical handbook]. Ashkhabad: Turkmenistan, 1974. 223 pp.
    Also publ. in Turkmenian. Data to 1973.

U829   *Turkmenistan za gody Sovetskoi vlasti: statisticheskii sbornik*. [Turkmenistan under Soviet power: a statistical handbook]. Ashkhabad: Turkmenistan, 1967. 143 pp. plus diagrams.
    Data to 1966.

Ukraine

U830   *Dosiahnennia Radians'koi Ukrainy za sorok rokiv: statystychnyi zbirnyk*. [The achievements of the Soviet Ukraine over 40 years: a statistical handbook]. (TsSU SRSR. Stat. upr. URSR). Kyiv: Derzh. stat. vyd., 1957. 152 pp.
    In Ukrainian. Includes data for 1956 and, in some tables, selected previous years.

U831   *Narodne hospodarstvo Ukrains'koi RSR pereladni XXI z'izdu Komunistychnoi partii Ukrainy*. [The national economy of the Ukraine; for the 21st Congress of the Ukrainian CP]. Kyiv: Derzh. stat. vyd., 1960. 159 pp.
    In Ukrainian. [Not seen].

U832   *Narodne hospodarstvo Ukrains'koi RSR: statystychnyi zbirnyk.* [The national economy of the Ukraine: statistical handbook]. (TsSU SRSR. Stat. upr. URSR). Kyiv: Derzh. stat. vyd., 1957. 535 pp.
    In Ukrainian. Contains data for 1956 and selected preceding years.

U833   *Narodne hospodarstvo Ukrains'koi RSR v ... rotsi: statystychnyi shchorichnyk.* [The national economy of the Ukraine in ...: a statistical annual]. (TsSU URSR). Kyiv: Statistika, 1957 (publ. 1958)–. Annual.
    In Ukrainian. Since the 1973 volume (publ. 1974) has also been published in a Russian edition called *Narodnoe khoziaistvo Ukrainskoi SSR v ... godu: statisticheskii ezhegodnik.* Not published for 1958. The main statistical handbook for the Ukraine.

U834   *Radians'ka Ukraina v tsyfrakh: statystychnyi zbirnyk.* [Soviet Ukraine in figures: a statistical handbook]. (TsSU URSR). Kyiv, 1960. 356 pp.
    In Ukrainian. A short statistical summary for 1913–58, with the plan targets for 1959–65.

U835   *Ukraina za p'iatdesiat rokiv (1917–1967): statystychnyi dovidnyk.* [50 years of the Ukraine, 1917–1967: a statistical handbook]. (TsSU URSR). Kyiv: Vyd. polit. lit-ry Ukrainy, 1967. 271 pp.
    In Ukrainian. Charts and statistics demonstrating the development of the Ukraine since 1917.

U836   *Ukrains'ka RSR v tsyfrakh v ... rotsi: korotkyi statystychnyi dovidnyk.* [The Ukraine in figures in ...: a short statistical handbook]. (TsSU URSR). Kyiv: Tekhnika, 1961 (publ. 1962)–. Annual.
    In Ukrainian. Since the 1974 volume (publ. 1975) it has also been published in Russian as *Ukrainskaia SSR v tsifrakh v ... godu.* Since 1976 it has also appeared in English translation, with the title: *The Ukraine in figures.* The short statistical summary for the Ukraine.

Uzbekistan

U837   *Narodnoe khoziaistvo Srednei Azii v 1963 godu: statisticheskii sbornik.* [The national economy of Central Asia in 1963: a statistical handbook]. (TsSU SSR. Sredneaziatskoe stat. upr.). Tashkent: Uzbekistan, 1964. 372 pp.
    Covers the Central Asian Economic Region: Uzbekistan, Kirghizia, Tajikistan and Turkmenistan. In most of the tables the series begin in 1950.

U838   *Narodnoe khoziaistvo Uzbekskoi SSR: statisticheskii sbornik.* [The national economy of the Uzbek SSR: a statistical handbook]. (TsSU SSSR. Stat. upr. UzSSR). Tashkent: Gosstatizdat, Uzb. otd-nie, 1957. 197 pp.
    Data for the years to 1956, going back to 1940 and 1913.

U839 *Narodnoe khoziaistvo Uzbekskoi SSR v ... g.: statisticheskii ezhegod-nik.* [The national economy of the Uzbek SSR: a statistical year-book]. Tashkent: Uzbekistan, 1958 (publ. 1959)–. Annual.

Not published for 1959, 1962, 1964 and 1966. The 1960 and 1961 volumes had subtitle *kratkii statisticheskii sbornik* and are much smaller than the other annual volumes. The 1963 data appeared in a jubilee volume, *Sovetskii Uzbekistan za 40 let: statisticheskii sbornik*; the 1973 volume appeared as: *Narodnoe khoziaistvo Uzbekskoi SSR za 50 let: iubileinyi statisticheskii ezhegodnik*; the 1976 volume appeared as *Narodnoe khoziaistvo Uzbekskoi SSR za 60 let Sovetskoi vlasti*. The main statistical handbook for the Uzbek SSR.

U840 *Narodnoe khoziaistvo Uzbekskoi SSR za 50 let: sbornik statisticheskikh materialov.* [The national economy of Uzbekistan over 50 years: a collection of statistical materials]. (TsSU UzSSR). Tashkent: Uzbekistan, 1967. 240 pp.

A summary of statistical data showing the achievements since 1917; many tables however only go back to 1940 or 1950.

U841 *Osnovnye pokazateli razvitiia narodnogo khoziaistva i kul'turnogo stroitel'stva Uzbekskoi SSR za 1913–1957 gg.* [The main indicators of the development of the economy and cultural construction in the Uzbek SSR, 1913–1957]. (Stat. upr. UzSSR). Tashkent: Gosizdat UzSSR, 1958. 32 pp. [Not seen].

U842 *Uzbekistan za 7 let (1959–1965 gg.): kratkii statisticheskii sbornik.* [7 years of Uzbekistan, 1959–1965: a short statistical handbook]. (TsSU UzSSR). Tashkent: Izd-vo TsK KPUz, 1966. 250 pp.

Detailed figures on Uzbekistan's achievements during the Seven-Year Plan.

U843 *Uzbekistan za gody deviatoi piatiletki (1971–1975 gg.): kratkii statisticheskii sbornik.* [Uzbekistan during the 9th Five-Year Plan, 1971–1975: a short statistical handbook]. (TsSU UzSSR). Tashkent: Izd-vo TsK KPUz., 1976. 224 pp.

Detailed figures on Uzbekistan's achievements during the 9th Five-Year Plan.

U844 *Uzbekistan za gody vos'moi piatiletki (1966–1970 gg.): kratkii statisticheskii sbornik.* [Uzbekistan during the 8th Five-Year Plan: a short statistical handbook]. (TsSU UzSSR). Tashkent: Izd-vo TsK KPUz., 1971. 160 pp.

Detailed figures on Uzbekistan's achievements during the 8th Five-Year Plan.

OTHER GENERAL SOURCES OF DOCUMENTATION

This section includes: (a) Soviet collections of party and government materials dealing with a particular period of Soviet history; (b) collections of material on individual union republics; (c) translated sources of party and government and legal material.

Historical collections

U845   *Bor'ba KPSS za vosstanovlenie i razvitie narodnogo khoziaistva v poslevoennyi period (1945–1953 gody): dokumenty i materialy.* [The struggle of the CPSU to restore and develop the national economy in the postwar period, 1945–1953: documents and materials]. (V pomoshch´ izuchaiushchim istoriiu KPSS). M.: Gospolitizdat, 1961. 403 pp.

Includes party and government resolutions, other official material and some speeches by leading officials from 1945 to 1953. As well as material on industry and agriculture, it includes resolutions on art and culture from the 1940s, documents on the party and local party organizations, and some of the major memoranda, treaties and other statements on foreign policy. The supplements to the volume include material on labour and the development of the socialist competition movement. The texts are annotated and there is a subject index.

U846   *Bor'ba KPSS za zavershenie stroitel'stva sotsializma (1953–1958): dokumenty i materialy.* [The struggle of the CPSU to complete the building of socialism (1953–1958): documents and materials]. (V pomoshch´ izuchaiushchim istoriiu KPSS). M.: Gospolitizdat, 1961. 696 pp.

Includes materials from the 20th Party Congress and CPSU plenums in 1953–8, party and government resolutions and ordinances, and legal acts on ideological and organizational work, the economy, and improvements in pay, working conditions and pensions. It also includes some material on foreign policy and some documents from the 1957 Conference of Communist and Workers' Parties in Moscow. The supplements include materials on the early work of the sovnarkhozy and reports on other important economic developments. The texts are annotated and there is a subject index.

U847   *Partiia—vdokhnovitel' i organizator razvernutogo stroitel'stva kommunisticheskogo obshchestva (1959–1961 gody): dokumenty i materialy.* [The Party as the inspirer and organizer of the further development of the building of a communist society (1959–1961): documents and materials]. (V pomoshch´ izuchaiushchim istoriiu KPSS). M.: Gospolitizdat, 1963. 599 pp.

Includes material from the 21st Party Congress, Central Committee Plenums, and documents on industry, agriculture, welfare, science and education, and ideological work. It also includes material on foreign policy and the 1960 Conference of Communist and Workers' Parties in Moscow. As well as CPSU material, it also includes a number of speeches from the 1960 Conference on Socialist Competition and Shock-Work and similar materials on labour, and some statistical data on the CPSU and on the economy. The texts are annotated and there is a subject index.

U848   *Sbornik dokumentov i materialov po istorii SSSR sovetskogo perioda (1917–1958).* [A collection of documents and materials on the history of the USSR (1917–1958)]. (Moskovskii gos. un-t, Istoricheskii fakul'tet). M.: Izd-vo Moskovskogo un-ta, 1966. 621 pp.

A collection of documents for students studying Soviet history. Includes chapters on the political, economic and social development of the USSR from 1945, which include basic party and government decisions and directives.

Collections on the republics

U849   *KPSS i sovetskoe pravitel'stvo o Kazakhstane, 1917–1977 gg.: sbornik dokumentov i materialov.* [The CPSU and the Soviet government on Kazakhstan, 1917–1977: a collection of documents and materials]. (In-t istorii partii pri TsK Kompartii Kazakhstana). Alma-Ata: Kazakhstan, 1978. 394 pp.

A collection of 138 documents demonstrating central concern for the development of Kazakhstan. All the material included has been previously published. There is a list of relevant documents not included, subject and place indexes.

U850   *KPSS i sovetskoe pravitel'stvo o Sovetskom Kirgizstane: sbornik dokumentov, 1924–1974.* [The CPSU and the Soviet government on Kirghizia: a collection of documents, 1924–1974]. (In-t istorii partii pri TsK KP Kirgizii). Frunze: Kyrgyzstan, 1974. 380 pp.

A collection of documents on all aspects of the development of Kirghizia, mainly in full and including some not previously publ. Has a list of relevant documents not included, and a subject index.

U851   *KPSS i sovetskoe pravitel'stvo ob Uzbekistane; sbornik dokumentov (1925–1970).* [The CPSU and the Soviet government on Uzbekistan: a collection of documents, 1925–1970]. (In-t istorii partii pri TsK KP Uzbekistana). Tashkent: Uzbekistan, 1972. 656 pp.

Includes archival material as well as decrees, resolutions, etc. which have been published previously. Covers the establishment and state structure of Uzbekistan, party work, nationalities and economic policy, and cultural affairs. It also includes a list of party and government resolutions on Uzbekistan which are not included in the collection.

Translations

U852   *British Broadcasting Corporation summary of world broadcasts. Part 1. The USSR.* Reading: Monitoring Service of the BBC, 1947–. Daily.

Has a weekly supplement, *Weekly economic report.* The BBC monitors radio broadcasts from the USSR and broadcasts within the country for domestic consumption, and publishes them in English as extracts or in full. It is an extremely useful source of current official information and news, particularly in the economic field. There are no indexes.

U853   *Current digest of the Soviet press.* (American Association for the Advancement of Slavic Studies). Columbus, Ohio: AAASS, 1949–. Weekly.

Has quarterly name and subject indexes. Translates or abstracts articles in all subject fields from central and republican newspapers and some major journals. As well as articles and news reports, includes the texts of major laws, decrees, party resolutions, statistical data and other official material. Vols. 1–25 (1949–73) included a weekly index to *Pravda* and *Izvestiia*.

U854   *Materials for the study of the Soviet system: state and party constitutions, laws, decrees, decisions and official statements of the leaders in translation.* Ed. by J. H. Meisel and E. S. Kozera. 2nd ed., revised and enlarged. Ann Arbor, Mich.: George Wahr, 1953. xxxiv, 613 pp.

1st ed. publ. 1950 (xii, 495 pp.) 2nd ed. is a collection of 186 party and government documents from 1917 to 1953, including translations of the main proceedings and decisions of the 19th Party Congress. In all about 50 documents from the 1945–53 period are included reflecting the major economic and ideological developments of the period. The documents are annotated and there is a topic and subject index.

U855   Matthews, M. *Soviet government: a selection of official documents on internal policies.* London: Jonathan Cape, 1974. 472 pp.

A collection of 92 party and government documents, 1917–71, on government and administration, the party, the legal system, the land, and labour. There are brief introductory notes to each section, and a glossary. Some of the documents included are not available in translation elsewhere.

U856   *Soviet booklets.* London, 1955–. Irregular.

Series of pamphlets issued by the Soviet Embassy in London, generally consisting of popular treatments of various aspects of Soviet life but sometimes including translations of official documents.

U857   *Soviet documents.* N.Y.: Crosscurrents Press, 1963–5, vol. 1–3(22). Weekly.

Vol. 1–2(13) called *Current Soviet documents.* Consists of translations of speeches, articles and interviews by Soviet leaders and some official documents, translated by Novosti.

U858   *Soviet news.* London: Press Dept. of the Soviet Embassy in London, 1942–. Weekly.

From 1942 to 19 May 1945 called *Soviet war news.* Includes translations of speeches by Soviet leaders, reports of Soviet meetings with foreign leaders, and official articles on foreign relations. It also includes some economic and technological news, and material on international cooperation in medicine, science and technology, and on Soviet aid to the Third World. Useful because it appears almost simultaneously with the events described, and is an officially approved selection for foreign audiences.

U859 *Soviet press translations*. Seattle: University of Washington Far Eastern Institute [later Far Eastern and Russian Institute], 1946–53. Frequency varied.

Published translations of articles, editorials and reviews in major Soviet newspapers and journals. Useful for the late 1940s, before *CDSP* (U853) was available. Has annual index.

INTERNATIONAL RELATIONS

Although the union republics have certain rights in the area of foreign relations, these are in practice limited to the representation of the Ukraine and Belorussia on the UN and certain other international bodies, and links with cultural and friendship societies. The formulation of foreign policy and the conduct of international relations are formally the responsibility of the USSR Ministry of Foreign Affairs, but the influence of the Central Committee of the CPSU is clearly very important both in deciding on policy and in meetings with visiting heads of state, foreign visits, etc. In addition, the CPSU, through the Foreign Department of the Central Committee, has links with foreign communist parties outside the socialist bloc. Its Department for Socialist Countries is responsible for relations with the communist parties—and hence the governments—of the rest of Eastern Europe and other socialist countries. Thus in looking for official publications relating to foreign policy, one must look to publications of the CPSU as well as to government sources. In addition to the material listed in this section, readers interested in current developments, or searching for documents not found in the items listed here, would need to look through *Pravda* (U549) and other general CPSU material, *Izvestiia* (U477) and the *Vedomosti* of the USSR Supreme Soviet (U476). Both *Soviet news* (U858) and *CDSP* (U853) are useful for translations of foreign policy material, and the *Summary of world broadcasts* (U852) is particularly valuable for short news items often not picked up by other sources.

In this section, all the reference works and general collections of documents on international relations, foreign policy and international law are listed first followed by a listing of collections of documents dealing with one country or area. For materials on foreign affairs, peace and disarmament by Brezhnev, Gromyko and other Soviet leaders, refer to the section 'Leaders' works'. For material on Soviet international economic relations, consult the subsection on trade in the section 'Economic affairs'.

General material

U860 *50 let bor'by SSSR za razoruzhenie: sbornik dokumentov, 1917–1967*. [The USSR's fight for disarmament over 50 years, 1917–1967: a collection of documents]. M.: Nauka, 1967. 691 pp.

A chronological collection of 200 documents, including TASS reports, major speeches, communications between the Soviet government and the Western powers, and Soviet resolutions and speeches at the UN and international conferences. Annotated.

U861 *Belorusskaia SSR v mezhdunarodnykh otnosheniiakh. Mezhdunarod-nye dogovory, konventsii i soglasheniia Belorusskoi SSR s inostrannymi gosudarstvami (1944–1959).* [The Belorussian SSR in international relations. International treaties, conventions and agreements of Belorussia with foreign states, 1944–1959]. (M-vo inostrannykh del BSSR. Otdel pravovykh nauk AN BSSR). Minsk: Izd-vo AN BSSR, 1960. 1050 pp.

Mainly texts of documents signed by Belorussia as a member of the UN, ILO, WHO, Unesco and other international bodies.

U862 *Diplomaticheskii slovar'.* [Diplomatic dictionary]. Glav. red.: A. A. Gromyko [et al.]. M.: Politizdat, 1971–3. 3 vols.

Earlier editions publ. 1948–50 (2 vols.) and 1960–4 (3 vols.). The dictionary includes informative and authoritative articles on Soviet foreign policy and international relations. It is well indexed and articles discussing treaties, agreements, etc. have bibliographical references.

U863 *Dogovory ob okazanii pravovoi pomoshchi po grazhdanskim, semeinym i ugolovnym delam, zakliuchennye Sovetskim Soiuzom.* [Treaties on legal assistance in civil, family and criminal cases, signed by the USSR]. Izd. 2-e, dop. (M-vo iustitsii SSSR). M.: Iurid. lit-ra, 1973. 392 pp.

1st ed. publ. 1959 (286 pp.) covered 1958–9 only. The 1973 edition has the texts of the USSR's treaties with other socialist countries, Austria and France on mutual legal assistance, plus other Soviet legislative materials on the subject.

U864a *Konsul'skie konventsii, zakliuchennye Sovetskim Soiuzom s inostran-nymi gosudarstvami.* [Consular agreements of the USSR with foreign governments]. (M-vo inostrannykh del SSSR. Konsul'skoe upr.). M., 1977. 2 vols. [Not seen].

U864b *Soglasheniia Sovetskogo Soiuza s inostrannymi gosudarstvami po konsul'skim voprosam: sbornik.* [A collection of the USSR's agree-ments with foreign states on consular matters]. Sost.: G. E. Vilkov, I. P. Blishchenko. M.: Izd-vo IMO, 1962. 232 pp.

The 1962 volume contains a chronological collection of the USSR's consular agreements, 1921–58, and documents relating to consular representation within the USSR, foreign citizens in the USSR, and Soviet citizens abroad. Coverage of the 1977 volumes is probably similar, with documents up to the mid-1970s.

U865 *Mezhdunarodnoe pravo: bibliografiia 1917–1972 gg.* [International law: a bibliography, 1917–1972]. Otv. red.: D. I. Fel'dman. M.: Iurid. lit-ra, 1976. 598 pp.

A bibliography of books and articles on international law and diplomacy published in the USSR, including collections of official documents. Author index. This bibliography largely replaces the earlier compilation on the subject, *Sovetskaia literatura po mezhdunarodnomu pravu: bibliografiia, 1917–1957*, pod red. V. N. Durdenevskogo. M.: Gosiurizdat, 1959. 303 pp.

U866   *Mezhdunarodnoe pravo v izbrannykh dokumentakh.* [Selected documents on international law]. (In-t mezhdunarodnykh otnoshenii). M.: IMO, 1957. 3 vols.
Earlier edition publ. 1955–6. As well as UN documents and other general international materials, includes much Soviet official material on international law and international relations.

U867   *Mezhdunarodnye otnosheniia i vneshniaia politika SSSR: sbornik dokumentov (1871–1957 gg.).* [International relations and the USSR's foreign policy: a collection of documents, 1871–1957]. (Vysshaia partiinaia shkola. Kafedra mezhdunarodnykh otnoshenii). M., 1957. 430 pp.
A collection of over 130 documents, mainly given in extract form with no indication of source, including treaties, joint declarations and communiqués, and general Soviet policy statements on international affairs.

U868a   *Ot Khel'sinki do Belgrada: Sovetskii Soiuz i osushchestvlenie Zakliuchitel'nogo akta obshcheevropeiskogo soveshchaniia. Dokumenty i materialy.* [From Helsinki to Belgrade: the USSR and the implementation of the Final Act of the Helsinki Conference. Documents and materials]. M.: Politizdat, 1977. 287 pp.
U868b   *Po puti, prolozhennomu v Khel'sinki: Sovetskii Soiuz i osushchestvlenie Zakliuchitel'nogo akta obshcheevropeiskogo soveshchaniia. Dokumenty i materialy.* [Along the path laid in Helsinki: the USSR and the implementation of the Final Act of the Helsinki Conference. Documents and materials]. M.: Politizdat, 1980. 511 pp.
Each volume includes speeches and articles by Soviet leaders on aspects of the implementation of the Final Act, materials from Warsaw Pact meetings relevant to the Helsinki proposals, UN materials, joint communiqués, declarations, etc. by the USSR and other countries, texts of Soviet notices on troop movements and manoeuvres, and other articles by Soviet officials relevant to the Helsinki agreement. The 1980 volume also includes the text of the Final Act and of the statement issued at the end of the Belgrade meeting.

U869   *Sbornik deistvuiushchikh dogovorov, soglashenii i konventsii, zakliuchennykh SSSR s inostrannymi gosudarstvami.* [A collection of treaties, agreements and conventions between the USSR and foreign governments currently in force]. (M-vo inostrannykh del SSSR). M.: Mezhdunarodnye otnosheniia, 1928–. Annual.
Frequency has varied considerably, but has been annual since vol. 27 (covering 1971, publ. 1974). This is a collection of treaties,

agreements, etc. at government-to-government level signed during the period covered by the volume, or which have come into force during that period. The documents are arranged by subject. The collection is not cumulative. For a listing of the period covered by each volume, see the list in U865, pp. 29–31.

U870   *Sbornik osnovnykh aktov i dokumentov Verkhovnogo soveta SSSR po vneshne-politicheskim voprosam, 1956–1962.* [A collection of major Supreme Soviet acts and documents on foreign policy matters, 1956–1962]. M.: Izvestiia Sovetov deputatov trudiashchikhsia, 1962. 224 pp.

Texts of various Supreme Soviet appeals to foreign parliaments, especially on peace and disarmament, plus texts of some speeches by Khrushchev and Gromyko. Also publ. in English as: *Soviet foreign policy. Basic acts and documents of the Supreme Soviet of the USSR, 1956–1962.* Comp.: K. U. Chernenko. M.: FLPH, 1962. 198 pp.

U871a   Slusser, R. M. *A calendar of Soviet treaties, 1917–1957,* [by] R. M. Slusser and J. F. Triska. (Hoover Institution on War, Revolution and Peace Documentary Series, 4). Stanford, Calif.: Stanford University Press, 1959. xii, 530 pp.

U871b   Slusser, R. M. *A calendar of Soviet treaties, 1958–1973,* [by] R. M. Slusser and G. Ginsburgs. Alphen aan den Rijn: Sijthoff and Noordhoff, 1980. 990 pp. [Not seen].

The 1959 volume is a chronological list of all the international agreements—not just treaties—to which the USSR was a signatory. For each there is a brief description of its contents and a list of sources for the full text, and references. There are full title and country indexes. The 1980 volume is planned to have similar coverage.

U872   *Sovetskii ezhegodnik mezhdunarodnogo prava* = *Soviet year-book of international law.* (Sovetskaia assotsiatsiia mezhdunarodnogo prava). M.: Nauka, 1958 (publ. 1959)–. Annual.

As well as articles and reviews on international law and reports on the work of the Soviet Association for International Law, each volume includes lists of the USSR's agreements with foreign countries during that year, and lists other Soviet legislation affecting international relations. There is also a bibliography of Soviet works, and works from other socialist countries, on international law.

U873   *Sowjetunion. Verträge und Abkommen. Verzeichnis der Quellen und Nachweise, 1917–1962.* Herausgegeben von W. Markert und D. Geyer. Köln: Böhlau, 1967. 611 pp.

Lists the treaties and agreements of the USSR (and of the RSFSR and the other republics to 1923), giving for each the full title, date of signing, and sources for the text (Soviet where possible). There is a full list of all sources used, and thorough chronological and country indexes.

U874   *V. I. Lenin, KPSS o bor'be za mir.* [V. I. Lenin and the CPSU on the struggle for peace]. M.: Politizdat, 1980. 488 pp.

A collection of documents, 1917–79, on international relations and foreign policy, with most of the documents from the postwar period. Subject index.

U875 *V. I. Lenin, KPSS o proletarskom internatsionalizme: sbornik dokumentov i materialov.* [V. I. Lenin and the CPSU on proletarian internationalism: a collection of documents and materials]. M.: Politizdat, 1974. 2 vols.

Includes material, 1894–1974, on CPSU policy towards the developing countries, the international workers' movement, foreign communist parties, etc. Each volume has a subject index.

U876 *Vneshniaia politika Sovetskogo Soiuza: dokumenty i materialy.* [The foreign policy of the USSR: documents and materials]. M.: Gospolitizdat, 1945 (publ. 1949)–1950 (publ. 1953).

A chronological collection, including speeches by Soviet leaders, speeches and reports by the USSR at the UN, joint communiqués and agreements, and other Soviet documents on international relations. Each volume has a name and country index.

U877 *Vneshniaia politika Sovetskogo Soiuza i mezhdunarodnye otnosheniia: sbornik dokumentov, ... god.* [The foreign policy of the USSR and international relations: a collection of documents for the year ...]. M.: Mezhdunarodnye otnosheniia, 1961 (publ. 1962)–. Annual.

A chronological collection for the year covered, including joint communiqués with foreign governments, reports on meetings with foreign leaders, bilateral agreements and other materials. The documents are annotated and there is a subject index.

U878 *Vo imia mira na zemle: Sovetskii Soiuz v bor'be za mir i sotrudnichestvo narodov.* [For the sake of peace on earth: the USSR in the struggle for peace and international cooperation]. M.: Politizdat, 1977. 2 vols.

Includes documents, 1971–7, on foreign policy and international affairs, including speeches by Brezhnev, CPSU resolutions on foreign policy, texts of joint communiqués, international agreements and declarations, and press conferences dealing with foreign relations and disarmament.

Translations

U879a 'Diplomatic and consular law of the USSR'. *Soviet statutes and decisions*, vol. 3, nos. 2–3, 1967.

U879b 'Soviet international law: legal status of foreigners in the USSR'. *Soviet statutes and decisions*, vol. 3, no. 1, 1966.

U879c 'Soviet public international law'. *Soviet statutes and decisions*, vol. 3, no. 4, 1967.

These issues of *SS&D* (*see* U164) cover various aspects of Soviet international law.

See also U234, U235 for international materials relating to citizenship. Section V: 1 of the *Collected legislation* (U158) deals with international relations legislation.

Collections of documents on specific areas or countries

Afghanistan

U880   *Sovetsko–afganskie otnosheniia, 1919–1969 gg.: dokumenty i materialy.* [Soviet–Afghan relations, 1919–1969: documents and materials]. (M-vo inostrannykh del SSSR. M-vo inostrannykh del Afganistana). M.: Politizdat, 1971. 439 pp.

An illustrated collection of 190 treaties, agreements, communiqués and other correspondence between the two governments, many published for the first time. There is a short historical introduction.

Africa

U881   *SSSR i strany Afriki: dokumenty i materialy, 1946–1962 gg.* [The USSR and Africa: documents and materials, 1946–1962]. Red. kollegiia: V. A. Brykin [et al.]. (M-vo inostrannykh del SSSR). M.: Gospolitizdat, 1963. 2 vols.

The collection excludes documents on relations with Arab countries in Africa (*see* U882). Includes about 340 documents, chronologically arranged, chiefly Soviet notes, communiqués and memoranda, speeches by Soviet leaders, etc. plus some documents from the African states which relate directly to the Soviet documents included. Annotated, with subject and country indexes.

See also U884.

Arab world

U882   *SSSR i arabskie strany, 1917–1960: dokumenty i materialy.* [The USSR and the Arab countries, 1917–1960: documents and materials]. Red. kollegiia: V.Ia. Sipols [et al]. M.: Gospolitizdat, 1961. 855 pp.

A chronological annotated collection of over 230 documents, some published for the first time, including the USSR's treaties and agreements with Arab countries, notes, speeches and other Soviet documents, plus some documents from the Arab states which relate directly to the Soviet documents included. Subject index.

Asia

U883   Jain, R. K. *Soviet–South Asian relations, 1947–1978.* [Oxford]: Martin Robertson, 1979. 2 vols.

Documents on Soviet policy towards India, Pakistan, Bangla Desh, Nepal and Sri Lanka. Most are already available elsewhere in

English translation, but the collection is convenient and supplemented by lists of visits to each other's countries by the leaders of
the USSR and the South Asian countries, loans, trade agreements,
trade and arms supplies and economic assistance. Each volume is
indexed.

U884 *Russia in Asia and Africa: documents 1946–1971*, ed. by J. A. Naik.
Kolhapur, Maharashtra: Avinash Reference Publications, 1979. xxii,
664 pp.

A collection of treaties, communiqués, joint statements, etc. on
Soviet relations with the countries of Africa and Asia, including
China, Mongolia and Korea. Selection and translations based on
Moscow news and TASS statements.

Bulgaria

U885 *Sovetsko–bolgarskie otnosheniia, ... gg.: dokumenty i materialy.*
[Soviet–Bulgarian relations in . . .: documents and materials]. (M-vo
inostrannykh del SSSR. M-vo inostrannykh del NRB). M.: Politizdat.

1944–48 gg. 1969.
1948–1970 gg. 1974.
1971–1976 gg. 1977.

These volumes include nearly 600 documents, some published for
the first time. They include treaties, agreements, communiqués and
other correspondence between the two governments, plus agreements and correspondence between various non-governmental organizations. Each volume has a short historical introduction.

China

U886a *The Sino-Soviet rift*; analysed and documented by W. E. Griffith.
London: Allen and Unwin, 1964, xiv, 508 pp.
U886b *Sino-Soviet relations, 1964–1965*; analysed and documented by W. E.
Griffith. Cambridge, Mass.; London: MIT Press, 1967, xi. 504 pp.

Each volume has a long introduction on Soviet–Chinese relations
during the period covered, followed by government memoranda,
letters, editorials and other documents.

U887 *Sovetsko–kitaiskie otnosheniia, 1917–1957: sbornik dokumentov.*
[Soviet–Chinese relations 1917–1957: a collection of documents].
Otv. red.: I. F. Kurdiukov [et al]. M.: Izd-vo vostochnoi lit-ry, 1959.
467 pp.

A selection of over 250 documents, including treaties, agreements,
communiqués, official speeches, etc. arranged chronologically.
Name index.

U888 *Sovetskii Soiuz i Kitaiskaia Narodnaia Respublika (1949–1979 gg.):
sbornik dokumentov.* [The USSR and China, 1949–1979: a collection
of documents]. Sost.: A. A. Brezhnev, S. N. Goncharenko. M.:
Mezhdunarodnye otnosheniia. 1981.

Will include over 400 documents, about a quarter of them published for the first time, on political, economic, scientific and cultural relations. [Not seen; data based on publisher's announcement].

Czechoslovakia

U889   *Sovetsko–chekhoslovatskie otnosheniia . . . gg.: dokumenty i materialy.* [Soviet–Czechoslovak relations in . . .: documents and materials]. (M-vo inostrannykh del SSSR. M-vo inostrannykh del ChSSR). M.: Politizdat.
1945–60. 1972.
1961–71. 1975.
1972–76. 1977.
Each volume has a short historical introduction and includes treaties, agreements, communiqués and other correspondence between the two governments, plus agreements and other correspondence between various non-governmental organizations. Many documents published for the first time. The three volumes include about 600 documents in all.

Germany

U890   *Chetyrekhstoronnee soglashenie po Zapadnomu Berlinu i ego realizatsii, 1971–1977 gg.: dokumenty.* [Documents on the quadripartite agreement on Berlin and its implementation, 1971–1977]. (M-vo inostrannykh del SSSR. M-vo inostrannykh del GDR). M.: Politizdat, 1977. 358 pp.
A collection of over 200 documents issued by the USSR and other socialist bloc countries relating to West Berlin, together with some of the notes and other documents issued by the Western powers and relevant to the Soviet documents. Subject index.

U891   *Otnosheniia SSSR i GDR, 1949–1955 gg.: dokumenty i materialy.* [The relations of the USSR and GDR 1949–1955: documents and materials]. (M-vo inostrannykh del SSSR. M-vo inostrannykh del GDR). M.: Politizdat, 1974. 691 pp.
Includes 368 documents, the majority of which are published in full for the first time. The documents are in chronological order, with a name index and a short historical introduction.

U892   *Sovetskii Soiuz i berlinskii vopros (dokumenty).* [The USSR and the Berlin question: documents]. (M-vo inostrannykh del SSSR). M., 1948–9. 2 vols.
Text of Soviet notes and other messages to France, the USA and Britain on Berlin, and some Allied responses. It was also publ. in English as *The Soviet Union and the Berlin question (documents).* (Ministry of Foreign Affairs of the USSR). M., 1948. 83 pp.; and *Second series.* 1949. 84 pp.

U893   *Za antifashistskuiu demokraticheskuiu Germaniiu: sbornik dokumentov, 1945–1949 gg.* [For an anti-fascist, democratic Germany: a collection of documents, 1945–1949]. (M-vo inostrannykh del SSSR. M-vo inostrannykh del GDR). M.: Politizdat, 1969. 704 pp.

A chronological collection of letters, decrees and other materials from and to the Soviet administration in the Soviet zone of Germany, many published for the first time. Includes tables on elections in the Soviet zone and on its economic and social position. Subject index.

Hungary

U894   *Sovetsko-vengerskie otnosheniia, . . . gg.: dokumenty i materialy.* [Soviet-Hungarian relations in . . .: documents and materials]. (M-vo inostrannykh del SSSR. M-vo inostrannykh del VNR). M.: Politizdat.

1945–48 gg. 1969.
1948–70 gg. 1974.
1971–76 gg. 1977.

These volumes include about 600 documents, some published for the first time. They include treaties, agreements, communiqués and other correspondence between the two governments, plus agreements and correspondence between Hungarian and Soviet non-governmental organizations. Each volume has a short historical introduction and a chronology.

Korea

U895   *Sovetskii Soiuz i koreiskii vopros: dokumenty.* [The USSR and the Korean question: documents]. (M-vo inostrannykh del SSSR). M., 1948. 108 pp.

Soviet letters and notes to the USA, 1945–8, on Korea, plus some TASS statements and other documents. Also publ. in English as: *The Soviet Union and the Korean question (documents).* (Ministry of Foreign Affairs of the USSR). M., 1948. 84 pp.

Latin America

U896   *Soviet relations with Latin America, 1918–1968: a documentary survey.* Ed. by S. Clissold. (Royal Institute of International Affairs). London: Oxford University Press, 1970. xx, 313 pp.

A collection of documents from the countries of Latin America and (to a lesser extent) the USSR dealing with relations between the two areas. The documents are annotated; many are in extract form.

Mexico

U897   *Sbornik vneshnepoliticheskikh dokumentov po istorii sovetsko-meksikanskikh otnoshenii, 1917–1979.* [A collection of foreign policy documents on Soviet–Mexican relations, 1917–1979]. Pod red. A. I. Sizonenko. M.: Mezhdunarodnye otnosheniia, 1981.

Announced in *Novye knigi SSSR* No. 29–80 g. as including official documents, many of them little known or published here for the first time. [Not seen].

Mongolia

U898   *Sovetsko–mongol'skie otnosheniia, 1921–1974 gg.: dokumenty i materialy.* [Soviet–Mongolian relations, 1921–1974: documents and materials]. Otv. red.: F. I. Dolgikh. M.: Mezhdunarodnye otnosheniia, 1975–9. 2 vols. (in 3).

An earlier edition, covering 1921–66, publ. by Nauka in 1966 (360 pp.). An annotated collection of documents, many published for the first time, on Soviet–Mongolian relations at governmental level.

Poland

U899   *Dokumenty i materialy po istorii sovetsko–pol'skikh otnoshenii.* [Documents and materials on the history of Soviet–Polish relations]. M.: Izd-vo AN SSSR, 1963–.

A massive joint Soviet–Polish publication, also appearing in Poland in Polish, covering government and other official documents on Soviet–Polish relations, and correspondence and agreements between Soviet and Polish non-governmental organizations. Each volume includes a chronology of major events, name, geographical and organization indexes, and a short historical introduction.

U900   *Sovetskii Soiuz—Narodnaia Pol'sha, 1944–1974 gg.: dokumenty i materialy.* [Documents and materials on relations between the USSR and Poland, 1944–1974]. (M-vo inostrannykh del SSSR. M-vo inostrannykh del PNR). M.: Politizdat, 1974. 664 pp.

A chronological collection of about 270 documents, some published for the first time. Includes treaties, agreements, communiqués, etc. between the two governments, plus agreements and correspondence between non-governmental organizations.

USA

U901   Timberlake, C. E. *Detente: a documentary record.* N.Y. [etc.]: Praeger, 1978. xviii, 231 pp.

Contains most of the bilateral agreements between the USA and the USSR signed between May 1972 and November 1977. Chronological arrangement. The texts are generally reproductions of those in the *Department of State bulletin* or the *United States treaties and other international acts.* Subject index, and list of documents not included.

Yugoslavia

U902   *Noty sovetskogo pravitel'stva iugoslavskomu pravitel'stvu (11, 18, 29 avgusta, 28 sentiabria 1949 goda).* [Notes of the Soviet government to

the Yugoslav government, 11, 18, 29 August and 28 September 1949]. M.: Gospolitizdat, 1949. 47 pp.
Texts of the notes from Stalin to Tito.

MILITARY AFFAIRS

Much material relating to military matters is, of course, classified and the few documents listed here cover only general policy matters and some aspects of military law and administration. Material on military crimes is included with other documents on the criminal law. The two ministries chiefly involved in military affairs are the Ministry of Defence and the Ministry of Defence Industries, but many other branches of industry have some establishments producing goods for military use, and so are affected by the secrecy surrounding defence.

U903 *Documents on Soviet military law and administration.* Ed. and trans. by H. J. Berman and M. Kerner. Cambridge, Mass.: Harvard University Press, 1955. xi, 164 pp.

Translations of over 50 documents or excerpts from documents on the army, its administration and organizational structure, military crimes and penalties, military courts and procedure.

U904 Grechko, A. A. *Vooruzhennye sily sovetskogo gosudarstva.* [The armed forces of the Soviet state]. 2. izd., dop. M.: Voenizdat, 1975. 438 pp.

1st ed. publ. 1974 (406 pp.). A translation, incorporating some revisions, is available as: Grechko, A. A. *The armed forces of the Soviet state: a Soviet view.* (US Air Force. Soviet military thought series). Washington: US GPO, [1975]. vii, 349 pp. This is Grechko's most comprehensive work on the role, development and operation of the Soviet armed forces.

U905 *KPSS o vooruzhennykh silakh Sovetskogo Soiuza: dokumenty, 1917–1981.* [The CPSU on the Soviet armed forces: documents, 1917–81]. M.: Voenizdat, 1981. 622 pp.

Earlier edition, covering 1917–68, published 1969 (471 pp.) and one covering 1917–58 published in 1958 (420 pp.). The collections consist of party resolutions and speeches by party leaders on the organization of the armed forces and political work in the armed forces.

U906 *Krasnaia zvezda.* [Red star]. 1924–. 6 days per week.

Newspaper of the USSR Ministry of Defence, and a major source on the armed forces and the defence industries.

U907 *Obshchevoinskie ustavy vooruzhennykh sil SSSR* [. . .]. [The general military regulations of the armed forces of the USSR . . .]. (M-vo oborony SSSR). M.: Voenizdat, 1972. 480 pp.

Includes the 1960 regulations on discipline and on interior duties, the 1963 regulations on garrison and sentry duty, and the 1959 regulations on marching orders.

U908   *Selected Soviet military writing 1970–1975: a Soviet view.* Trans. under the auspices of the United States Air Force. (Soviet military thought). Washington: US GPO, [1977]. 295 pp.

       Anthology of articles and extracts from books by Grechko, Kulikov and other senior military personnel.

U909   *Slovar' osnovnykh voennykh terminov.* [A dictionary of basic military terminology]. (B-ka ofitsera) M.: Voenizdat, 1965. 248 pp.

       Translated into English as: *Dictionary of basic military terms: a Soviet view.* (United States Air Force. Soviet military thought series). Washington: US GPO, [1965]. vii, 256 pp.

       An encyclopaedia of Soviet military terminology, giving explanations as well as definitions. The English version enters terms under the Russian form of the term, but provides a full English index. There are also notes on Soviet nomenclature and terminology.

U910   *Spravochnik ofitsera.* [An officer's handbook]. (B-ka ofitsera). M.: Voennoe izd-vo M-va oborony SSSR, 1971. 400 pp.

       An English translation is available as: *The Officer's Handbook: a Soviet View,* ed. by General-Major S. N. Kozlov. (United States Air Force. Soviet military thought series). Washington: US GPO, [1971]. xii, 358 pp. The handbook includes data on the organization of the Army, its relationship with the CPSU, military theory, military psychology, the role of the armed forces, and information on the armed forces of the USSR and the Warsaw Pact. It also includes excerpts from regulations on military discipline, the award of decorations, etc.

U911   *Sputnik sekretaria partorganizatsii; konsul'tatsii po voprosam organizatsionno-partiinoi rabote v sovetskoi armii i voenno-morskom flote.* [Manual for a party secretary: advice on party organizational work in the Army and Navy]. Pod red. M. G. Solev'eva. M.: Voennoe izd-vo, 1977. 198 pp.

       Questions and answers on party work in the armed forces.

U912   *Voenno-morskoi mezhdunarodnyi-pravovyi spravochnik.* [Manual of naval international law]. Pod red. P. D. Barabolia. M.: Voenizdat, 1966. 500 pp.

       Earlier edition, edited by A. S. Bakhov, publ. 1956 (351 pp.). Manual includes many official documents on naval law not readily available elsewhere, USSR's international agreements relating to naval matters, and a short bibliography.

U913   *Voennye voprosy v dokumentakh KPSS i sovetskogo gosudarstva: annotirovannyi bibliograficheskii ukazatel'.* [Military affairs in documents of the CPSU and the Soviet government: an annotated bibliographical index]. M.: Voennoe izd-vo, 1980. 416 pp.

       Appears to be an extremely important and useful bibliography for the study of military affairs. [Not seen].

See also U373 and U1559.

Translations of legislation on the defence of the USSR and the protection of state frontiers can be found in the *Collected legislation* (U158).

ECONOMIC AFFAIRS

Each of the subsections of this section, dealing with aspects of economic affairs such as planning, natural resources, transport, trade and labour, budget and finance, has its own introduction briefly describing the agencies responsible for it or noting the major legislative acts controlling it. However, it is necessary to indicate here the major changes in the overall organization of the economy of the USSR in the postwar period. During the period from the end of the war until Stalin's death, the economy continued to function as it had in the 1930s, as essentially a command economy, very centralized and with little opportunity for local initiative. After Stalin's death, some decision-making in the economic sphere was delegated to the union republics. However, regional planning was still poorly developed and the concentration of so much power in Moscow was the source of considerable inefficiency and delay. Further, the economy was becoming increasingly complex and outgrowing the traditional planning mechanism. The 1957 reforms were also motivated by political considerations. Under these reforms, a number of ministries were abolished and the country divided into 105 economic regions, each headed by a Council of National Economy (sovnarkhoz). The role of the local party secretaries in economic affairs was also enhanced, partly in an attempt to counteract localism. In the following years, there was increasingly a return to centralized control and in 1965 the sovnarkhozy were abolished and replaced by the ministerial structure described in the introduction to this chapter. The Kosygin reforms have also given greater power to individual enterprises, allowed enterprises to keep more of their 'profits', improved the incentive system, and placed greater emphasis on consumer demand. Further changes in economic organization came in 1973 with a joint decree of the Central Committee of the CPSU and the Council of Ministers of the USSR introducing the new industrial associations (ob″edineniia) responsible for coordination, planning, organization and research and, as a rule, embracing several production enterprises or combines and research, construction and other organizations. Other developments in the early 1970s have included increased emphasis on quality control, improvements in the supply and in the range of consumer goods, and a continuing search for ways of improving incentives and making the best use of computers within the planned economy.

General reference works
on the economy as a whole

U914   *Ekonomicheskaia entsiklopediia: politicheskaia ekonomiia.* [Economic encyclopaedia: political economy]. Gl. red.: A. M. Rumiantsev. (Otd-nie ekonomiki AN SSSR). M.: Sov. entsiklopediia, 1972–.
    Covers political economy, economic theory and all aspects of socialist industry and economics. More useful for current work than

U918, because it includes new terms and concepts introduced after the 1965 economic reforms.

U915 *Ekonomicheskaia entsiklopediia: promyshlennost' i stroitel'stvo.* [Economic encyclopaedia: industry and construction]. Gl. red.: A. N. Efimov. M.: Sov. entsiklopediia, 1962–5. 3 vols.

Useful for definitions of economic and industrial terms and concepts, and for its brief and authoritative articles on economic matters before the economic reforms of the mid-1960s.

U916 *Kratkii ekonomicheskii slovar' piatiletki effektivnosti i kachestva.* [A short economic dictionary on the five-year plan of effectiveness and quality]. Kiev: Politizdat Ukrainy, 1978. 261 pp.

Defines terms used in the 10th five-year plan (1976–80) and gives brief explanations; particularly useful for new terms.

U917 *Novaia sovetskaia literatura po obschestvennym naukam: ekonomika.* [New Soviet literature on the social sciences: economics]. (AN SSSR. INION). M., 1934–. Monthly.

Title varied 1934–47; 1948–75 called *Novaia sovetskaia ekonomicheskaia literatura.* Frequency varied 1934–48; 36 per year 1949–62. This bibliography is a current listing, by subject, of Soviet literature on all aspects of economics. Includes party and government documents. No indexes.

U918 *Slovar'–spravochnik ekonomista promyshlennogo predpriiatiia.* [Dictionary and handbook for economists in industry]. Pod obshchei red. A. M. Aleksandrova [et al]. M.: Politizdat, 1965. 366 pp.

Defines terms used in planning, finance, prices, wages and other economic matters in an industrial enterprise, and includes information on the calculations and procedures used. Useful for the period before the economic reforms of the mid-1960s.

Collections of documents on the economy in general

U919 *Direktivy KPSS i sovetskogo pravitel'stva po khoziaistvennym voprosam: sbornik dokumentov.* [Directives of the CPSU and the Soviet government on economic matters: a collection of documents]. M.: Gospolitizdat, 1957–8. 4 vols.

A collection of legislation and other normative acts, and party materials, on all aspects of the economy from 1917 to 1958. Although largely replaced by U926, it does include some party and government documents from all periods not published in the later collection. Subject index in vol. 4.

U920 *Ekonomicheskaia gazeta: ezhenedel'nik TsK KPSS.* [Economic newspaper: a weekly of the Central Committee of the CPSU]. M.: Pravda, 1918–41, 1956–. Weekly.

1918–November 1937 called *Ekonomicheskaia zhizn';* November

1937–June 1941 called *Finansovaia gazeta*; 1956–May 1960 called *Promyshlenno-ekonomicheskaia gazeta*. Considerable variations in sponsoring body in the prewar period; 1956–60 was organ of the State Committee on Science and Technology of the USSR Council of Ministers. 1918–41 considerable variations in frequency; about three a week 1956–July 1961; weekly thereafter. This newspaper is one of the most important sources of current economic information, including legislation, plan targets, plan fulfilment figures, official instructions and documents, and authoritative policy statements. It is translated in part in *CDSP* (U853); many articles from it are abstracted in *ABSEES* (Univ. of Glasgow, quarterly, July 1970–Oct. 1976; Oxford Microform Publications, 3 times yearly, Sept. 1977–.)

U921 *Ekonomicheskaia nauka i khoziaistvennaia praktika: ekonomicheskii ezhegodnik*. [Economic theory and practice: an economic annual]. M.: Ekonomika, 1965–8 (publ. 1969). Annual.

Intended to provide an annual round-up of economic information for economists and the general public. As well as general information on new developments and economic performance, it includes lists of new Supreme Soviet laws and edicts and Council of Ministers ordinances and other resolutions, regulations, etc. on economic matters issued during the year. There is also a chronicle of the year's economic events.

U922 *Ekonomicheskaia zhizn' SSSR: khronika sobytii i faktov, 1917–1965*. [The economic life of the USSR: a chronicle of events and facts, 1917–1965]. Glav. red.: S. G. Strumilin. Izd. 2-e, dop. M.: Sov. entsiklopediia, 1967. 2 vols.

1st ed., covering 1917–59, publ. 1961 (780 pp.). A year-by-year listing of economic developments, including dates when factories opened, trade agreements were signed, major conferences were held, etc. It lists all the major party and government resolutions, decrees, legislation, etc. on the economy, industry and agriculture, and indicates published sources for them. The entry for each year concludes with a statistical summary for the year. At the back of vol. 2 there is a combined subject index and index of names of people, factories, farms, railway lines, etc.

U923 *Gosudarstvennaia distsiplina: sbornik normativnykh aktov*. [State discipline: a collection of normative acts]. M.: Iurid. lit-ra, 1978. 600 pp.

Includes legislation, ordinances, ministry instructions and orders and other material on disciplinary transgressions in areas such as plan-fulfilment, financial control, technical and labour matters, and the performance of contractual obligations. The collection also includes documents setting out the rights and duties of the bodies responsible for enforcing the law in these areas. The collection is designed as an aid for planners, accountants and factory adminis-

445

trators as well as for legal personnel. Most of the material included was issued in the 1960s and 1970s and comes from the Council of Ministers, various ministries and state committees.

U924   *Khoziaistvo i pravo; organ Ministerstva iustitsii SSSR i Gos-udarstvennogo arbitrazha pri Sovete Ministrov SSSR.* [The economy and the law: organ of the USSR Ministry of Justice and the State Arbitration Court of the USSR Council of Ministers]. M.: Ekonomika, 1977–. Monthly.

As well as articles on legal work in the economy, includes reports on the work of the USSR and RSFSR State Arbitration Courts and relevant Ministry of Justice decisions, and texts of legislation and other official materials on economic law.

U925   *Okhrana sotsialisticheskoi sobstvennosti: sbornik normativnykh aktov.* [The protection of socialist property: a collection of normative acts]. Otv. red.: S. A. Shishkov. M.: Iurid. lit-ra, 1980. 448 pp.

The collection includes legislation, ordinances from the Council of Ministers, and ministry instructions and orders on all aspects of the protection of socialist property (particularly in industrial enterprises, shops and farms) from all forms of theft, negligence, fraud, etc. Describes penalties, etc. under the criminal and administrative law. Broad subject arrangement.

U926   *Resheniia partii i pravitel'stva po khoziaistvennym voprosam.* [Party and government decisions on economic affairs]. M.: Politizdat, 1967–.

Originally planned as a five-volume collection to mark the 50th anniversary of the October Revolution, this has now turned into a continuing series with a new volume appearing every couple of years to bring it up to date. Includes documents from party congresses, CPSU Central Committee resolutions and Plenum materials, ordinances from the Council of Ministers, laws, edicts of the Presidium of the Supreme Soviet and joint Central Committee and Council of Ministers ordinances. It does not include documents issued at union-republic level or by individual ministries. The collection covers all aspects of the economy, industry and agriculture from 1917 onwards; although it largely replaces U919, the earlier collection does include some documents excluded from this one. Some documents are not reproduced in full, and supplements are generally omitted. The collection does include some material not previously published, but original sources of official publications are not recorded. This is probably the most important source for retrospective work on Soviet economic policy.

U927   *Sbornik normativnykh aktov po khoziaistvennomu pravu.* [A collection of normative acts on economic legislation]. M.: Iurid. lit-ra, 1979. 743 pp.

A collection of legislation in force on 1 January 1979 on the legal position of economic organizations, their financial and economic arrangements, legal aspects of innovation and credit. As well as industry, agriculture, construction and supply organizations, the collection covers disputes procedures and legal services to economic organizations. Within each section, the documents are arranged hierarchically.

U928 *Sovershenstvovanie khoziaistvennogo mekhanizma: sbornik dokumentov.* [Perfecting the economic mechanism: a collection of documents]. M.: Pravda, 1980. 319 pp. [Not seen].

U929 *Zakonodatel'nye akty po voprosam narodnogo khoziaistva SSSR.* [Legal acts on economic matters in the USSR]. M.: Gosiurizdat, 1961. 2 vols.

Includes material in force on 1 March 1961. The documents are arranged in broad subject groupings and include planning and economic organization, finance, supply, standards, capital investment, transport and communications, housing and trade. Includes laws, ordinances of the USSR Council of Ministers, and other normative acts. Some documents are published for the first time; some are published in extract only. Chronological and subject indexes.

See also U1515, U1519, U1537, U1538, U1545 and U1558.

For translations of economic legislation, consult *Collected legislation* (U158) section IV; see also the sources of translated material in the section 'Other general sources of documentation' and in the sub-section on collections of legislation in the section 'Law and judicial system'.

Plans

Planning is central to the management of all areas of Soviet public life, with schools, libraries, hospitals and artistic organizations expected to formulate and fulfil a plan, just as do factories, collective farms and construction organizations. The linchpin of the planning system is the five-year plan, which sets overall targets for the economic, social and cultural development of the USSR during the plan period. These plan targets are first published as a draft plan to be put to the congress of the Communist Party of the Soviet Union by its Central Committee. The second stage is the passing of a resolution by the CPSU congress approving the draft and requesting the State Planning Committee (Gosplan) through the Council of Ministers to draw up an annual plan, and to formulate plans for each republic, ministry, sector of the economy or area of cultural and social life. These proposals are then taken to the Supreme Soviet of the USSR by the Chairman of the USSR Council of Ministers, and on this basis the Supreme Soviet passes a law on the five-year plan. The plans for each year are presented to the Supreme Soviet annually by the Chairman of Gosplan, usually at the end of the preceding year.

The draft proposals of the Central Committee on the next five-year plan are published first in *Pravda* and are reprinted in other newspapers and journals; the final resolutions of the CPSU congress on the plan are published in the stenographic reports of the congresses (see the section 'Communist Party'). The text of the report to the Supreme Soviet, and the law on the plan appear in the appropriate volume of the stenographic reports of the Supreme Soviet proceedings (U475); both the annual plans and the five-year plans are also separately published—more details are given below. There has been considerable variation in the amount of details published of the plan indicators; U936 is an instance of the very full publishing in one volume of plan targets. However, in many cases the only way to discover the plan targets for individual branches of the economy or for services such as education and welfare is a careful study of the periodical press. For industry and agriculture, *Ekonomicheskaia gazeta* (U920) is the single most important source, as it has regular features on different branches of the economy, often including detailed plan targets.

The process of plan formulation for the union republics is similar to that for the USSR as a whole; obviously their plans are compiled within the framework set out by the all-union indicators. For sources of published information, readers should consult the appropriate sub-sections on the communist parties, supreme soviets and governments of the union republics.

Five-year plans

The publications listed chronologically here are generally the CPSU directives on the five-year plan. In the case of the 1946–50 plan there was no CPSU congress before the plan went to the Supreme Soviet, so the law is described instead. In addition to the pamphlets listed here, the resolutions on the plan also appear in the stenographic reports of the congress and in *Pravda*. Translations of these documents appear in *CDSP* (U853) and *Soviet news* (U858); sometimes they may also be separately published in the *Soviet booklets* series (U856).

U930   *Zakon o piatiletnom plane vosstanovleniia i razvitiia narodnogo khoziaistva SSSR na 1946–1950 gg.: priniat Verkhovnym Sovetom SSSR 18 marta 1946 g.* [Law on the five-year plan for the reconstruction and development of the national economy of the USSR, 1946–1950; passed by the Supreme Soviet 18 March 1946]. M.: OGIZ, 1946. 95 pp.
    Also available in U926, vol. 3, 1968 and U919, vol. 3, 1958. For an English translation, see: *Law on the five-year plan for the rehabilitation of the national economy of the USSR, 1946–1950.* London: Soviet News, 1946. 104 pp. The speech by Voznesenskii, Chairman of Gosplan, to the Supreme Soviet, was also published by Soviet News.

U931   *Direktivy XIX s"ezda partii po piatomu piatiletnemu planu razvitiia SSSR na 1951–1955 gody: rezoliutsii XIX s"exda VKP(b) po dokladu Predsedatelia Gosplana M. Z. Saburova.* [Directives of the 19th Congress of the All-union Communist Party on the five-year plan for the development of the USSR. Resolution on the report by the Chairman of Gosplan]. M.: Gospolitizdat, 1952. 32 pp.
    Also available in U926 vol. 3, 1968 and U919 vol. 3, 1958.

U932 *Direktivy XX s"ezda KPSS po shestomu piatiletnemu planu razvitiia narodnogo khoziaistva SSSR na 1956–1960 gody (priniaty 25 fevralia 1956 g.).* [Directives of the 20th Congress of the CPSU on the five-year plan for the development of the national economy of the USSR, 1956–1960]. M.: Pravda, 1956. 79 pp.

Also published in U919, vol. 4, 1958; excluded from U926. It was replaced at the 21st Party Congress by the seven-year plan, 1959–65.

U933 *Kontrol'nye tsifry razvitiia narodnogo khoziaistva SSSR na 1959–1965 gody: tezisy doklada tov. N. S. Khrushcheva na XXI s"ezde KPSS.* [The control figures for the national economy, 1959–1965: report to the 21st Congress of the CPSU by N. S. Khrushchev]. M.: Gospolitizdat, 1958. 127 pp.

Extracts from the targets of the seven-year plan are also published in U926, vol. 4, 1968.

U934 *Direktivy XXIII s"ezda KPSS po piatiletnemu planu razvitiia narodnogo khoziaistva SSSR na 1966–1970 gg.* [Directives of the 22nd CPSU Congress on the five-year plan for the development of the national economy of the USSR, 1966–1970]. M.: Politizdat, 1966. 78 pp.

Also published in U926, vol. 6, 1968.

U935 *Direktivy XXIV s"ezda KPSS po piatiletnemu planu razvitiia narodnogo khoziaistva SSSR na 1971–1975 gody.* [Directives of the 24th Congress of the CPSU on the five-year plan for the development of the national economy of the USSR, 1971–1975]. M.: Politizdat, 1971. 79 pp.

Also published in U926, vol. 8, 1972.

U936 *Gosudarstvennyi piatiletnii plan razvitiia narodnogo khoziaistva SSSR na 1971–1975 gody.* [The five-year plan for the development of the national economy of the USSR in 1971–1975]. M.: Politizdat, 1972. 455 pp.

This is the first full postwar publication of the plan targets. Includes Kosygin's speech to the Supreme Soviet, the law on the plan, and an account of the plan's targets and main new projects by branch of the economy, by union republic and for the main service sectors, such as health. The volume concludes with over 100 pages of tables giving the plan indicators for each year of the plan, for each industry and project, and for services.

U937 *Osnovnye napravleniia razvitiia narodnogo khoziaistva SSSR na 1976–1980 gg.* [Basic directions in the development of the national economy of the USSR, 1976–1980]. M.: Politizdat, 1976. 95 pp.

Also published in U926 vol. 11, 1977.

U938 *Osnovnye napravleniia ekonomicheskogo i sotsial'nogo razvitiia SSSR na 1981–1985 gody i na period do 1990 goda.* [Basic directions for the economic and social development of the USSR, 1981–1985 and for the period to 1990]. M.: Politizdat, 1981. 95 pp.

Also published in *Pravda* for 5 March 1981.

Annual plans

The annual plans are usually presented to the December meeting of the USSR Supreme Soviet by the Chairman of Gosplan, and cover plan targets for the next year; sometimes plan targets for the next two years are given. The Supreme Soviet approves the report and passes the law on the development of the national economy for the coming year; the law is generally a brief summary of the targets and projects indicated in the speech by the Chairman of Gosplan. The text of the speech and the law are published immediately in the newspapers, and in the official publications of the Supreme Soviet (*see* U475 and U476). Generally the speech and law are published as separate pamphlets as well, under the same name of the current chairman of Gosplan. Until 1977, the annual plans were usually called *Gosudarstvennyi plan razvitiia narodnogo khoziaistva SSSR*, but from 1978 the title has been *Gosudarstvennyi plan ekonomicheskogo i sotsial'nogo razvitiia*, thus laying greater emphasis on the social element in the plan.

Results of the annual plans

Since 1947, quarterly results for the first nine months of the year have been published in *Pravda* and *Izvestiia*, usually in April, June and October. Annual results for the year are published in these newspapers late in the January of the following year. These figures, with (since 1964) reports on plan fulfilment of the individual union republics, are usually reissued later in the year as a separate publication, sometimes with corrections and additions. The separately published volumes are:

U939   *Soobshcheniia Gosplana SSSR ob itogakh vypolneniia gosudarstvennogo plana vosstanovleniia i razvitiia narodnogo khoziaistva SSSR v 1946 gg.* [Gosplan report on the fulfilment of the state plan for the reconstruction and development of the Soviet economy]. M.: Gosplan SSSR, 1947. 13 pp.

U940   *Ob itogakh vypolneniia Gosudarstvennogo plana razvitiia narodnogo khoziaistva SSSR v ... g.: soobshchenie TsSU SSSR.* [Report of the Central Statistical Administration of the USSR on the fulfilment of the state plan for the development of the economy in ...]. M.: Gospolitizdat, 1949 (publ. 1950)–1961 (publ. 1962). Annual.

U941   *SSSR i soiuznye respubliki v ... g.: soobshcheniia TsSU SSSR i TsSU soiuznykh respublik ob itogakh vypolneniia gosudarstvennogo plana narodnogo khoziaistva.* [The USSR and the union republics in ...: reports of the all-union and union republic central statistical administrations on the fulfilment of the plan]. M.: Statistika, 1964 (publ. 1965)–. Annual.

     1964 volume had title *Itogi vypolneniia narodnokhoziaistvennogo plana SSSR i soiuznykh respublik v 1964 g.*

Quarterly and annual plan fulfilment figures for each union republic appear in that republic's central newspaper.

Results of the five-year plans

Summary data on the fulfilment of the whole five-year (or seven-year) plan usually appear in the directives for the following plan (see above). Results of the fourth and fifth plans were published separately; the fifth includes detailed figures for the individual republics as well as the USSR as a whole.

U942   *Soobshchenie Gosplana SSSR i TsSU SSSR ob itogakh vypolneniia chetvertogo (Pervogo poslevoennogo) piatiletnego plana SSSR na 1946–1950 gg.* M.: Gospolitizdat, 1951. 22 pp.

   Available in English as: *Results of the fourth (first post-war) plan of the USSR, 1946–1950: statement of the State Planning Committee and the Central Statistical Board of the USSR.* M.: FLPH, 1951. 32 pp.

U943   *Ob itogakh vypolneniia piatogo piatiletnego plana razvitiia SSSR i soiuznykh respublik na 1951–1955 gody.* [On the fulfilment of the fifth five-year plan for the development of the USSR and the union republics in 1951–1955]. M.: Gospolitizdat, 1956. 311 pp.

Other documents on planning

Much more material on planning can be found in the general collections of legislation and party materials, particularly U546 and U926. However, here are listed four major collections of material issued by Gosplan which are very important for understanding its operations and the way the plans are drawn up.

U944a   *Metodicheskie ukazaniia k sostavleniiu gosudarstvennogo plana razvitiia narodnogo khoziaistva SSSR.* [Rules for compiling the state economic plan]. (Gosplan SSSR). M.: Ekonomika, 1969. 781 pp.

U944b   *Metodicheskie ukazaniia k razrabotke gosudarstvennykh planov razvitiia narodnogo khoziaistva SSSR.* [Rules for the compilation of the state plans]. (Gosplan SSSR). M.: Ekonomika, 1974. 791 pp.

   These two handbooks are intended for staff of planning bodies, ministries and industrial enterprises at all levels, to help in drawing up the next five-year plan. The instructions in the 1974 volume replace those in the 1969 edition, which were valid for the 1971–5 plan. The instructions include the general principles and priorities to be observed, units of calculation, norms for the use of material, labour, capital investment, etc., and how the plan for each enterprise, sector, etc. is to be coordinated with those for the rest of the economy.

U945   *Tipovaia metodika razrabotki piatiletnego plana proizvodstvennogo ob"edineniia (kombinata), predpriiatiia, napravlena ministerstvam i vedomstvam SSSR i gosplanam soiuznykh respublik . . .* [Model rules for the compilation of the five-year plan in a production association (combine) or enterprise, sent out to ministries and other authorities of the USSR and the gosplans of the union republics . . .]. (Gosplan SSSR). M: Ekonomika, 1975. 375 pp.

   Similar to U944a–b, but for the 1976–80 plan. As well as detailed instructions on norms and methods of calculation, it includes sample documents.

U946   *Zakonodatel'nye akty o zadachakh i funktsiiakh Gosplana SSSR i organizatsii pri Gosplane SSSR (po sost. na 1 avgusta 1962 g.).* [Legislative acts on the tasks and functions of Gosplan and its organizations]. M., [1962]. 147 pp.

Copy seen marked 'For official use'. Consists of government decisions relating to Gosplan and bodies under its control, after the reorganization of Gosplan. Some documents in the collection have not been published previously.

See also U1057, U1068 and U1560.

People's control

The main functions of the organs of People's Control (formerly the Soviet Control Commission and before that Ministry of State Inspection) are: (a) systematic control over the way party and government plans and targets are carried out; (b) ensuring more effective use of raw materials and other resources; (c) combatting breaches of state discipline, bureaucratic delays, wastefulness, etc. The local party organizations are usually closely involved in the work of local people's control committees, as are local soviets, economic authorities and the trade unions.

U947   *Obrazovanie i razvitie organov sotsialisticheskogo kontrolia v SSSR (1917–1975): sbornik dokumentov i materialov.* [The formation and development of the organs of socialist control in the USSR, 1917–1975: a collection of documents and materials]. (In-t marksizma-leninizma pri TsK KPSS. Komitet narodnogo kontrolia SSSR. Glav. arkhivnoe upr. pri SM SSSR). M.: Politizdat, 1975. 624 pp.

A chronological collection of documents on the development of Rabkrin and the Central Control Commission during the prewar period and the postwar Ministry of State Inspection, Soviet Control Commission and the Committee for People's Control set up in 1965, and their organs at local level. The collection is annotated and includes a list of official bulletins published by these bodies, and a chronology.

U948   *Spravochnik narodnogo kontrolia.* [Manual for members of local People's Control Committees]. 2 izd., dop. M.: Politizdat, 1977. 311 pp.

1st ed. publ. 1976 (303 pp.). Includes more recent legislation, etc. on the work of People's Control.

Statistics on industry

For more recent figures, and figures for union republics not covered here, consult the section 'General statistics'.

USSR

U949   *Promyshlennost' SSSR: statisticheskii sbornik.* [Industry in the

USSR: a statistical handbook]. (TsSU SSSR). M.: Statistika, 1964.
494 pp.

Previous volume publ. 1957 (447 pp.). Compendium of data on all
aspects of industrial production, including figures on fuel and on the
industrial labour force. Some figures for the prewar period are
included.

RSFSR

U950 *Promyshlennost' RSFSR: statisticheskii sbornik.* [Industry in the
RSFSR: statistical handbook]. M.: Gosstatizdat, 1961. 344 pp.

Coverage similar to U949, but gives a fuller breakdown of some
topics and has more details on the regions of the RSFSR.

Armenia

U951 *Promyshlennost' Armianskoi SSR: statisticheskii sbornik.* [Industry in
Armenia: a statistical handbook]. (TsSU ArmSSR). Erevan, 1973.
235 pp.

Detailed figures on industry for 1913–71, based on annual returns
from factories, etc. and including some figures not previously
published.

Belorussia

U952 *Promyshlennost' Belorusskoi SSR: statisticheskii sbornik.* [Industry in
Belorussia: a statistical handbook]. (TsSU BSSR). Minsk: Belarus',
1976. 478 pp.

Earlier edition publ. 1965 (480 pp.). Based on detailed returns
from factories, etc. The 1976 volume has detailed figures for
1913–75, but the 1965 volume covers 1940–64 only.

Estonia

U953 *Promyshlennost' Estonskoi SSR v 1965 g.: statisticheskii ezhegodnik.*
[Estonian industry in 1965: a statistical annual]. (TsSU ESSR).
Tallin, 1966. 357 pp.

Copy seen marked 'Not for publication in the open press'. 'For
official use'. Appears to be part of an annual series. Contains very
detailed figures for 1965.

U954 *Razvitie narodnogo khoziaistva Estonskoi SSR: kratkii statisticheskii
sbornik.* [The development of the Estonian economy: a short
statistical handbook]. (TsSU ESSR). Tallin: Eesti raamat, 1967.
111 pp.

Summary of data for 1965 and selected years from 1939.

Latvia

U953 *Nalichie sredstv mekhanizatsii i avtomatizatsii v promyshlennosti
Latviiskoi SSR na 1 iiulia 1975 goda: statisticheskii sbornik.* [The

availability of mechanization and automation equipment in Latvian industry on 1 July 1975: a statistical handbook]. (TsSU LatvSSR). Riga, 1976. 293 pp.

Based on a census of Latvian industry, with figures for 1965, 1971 and 1973 on provision of automation and mechanization on production lines, in production sections and shops as well as whole factories. Most of the figures are broken down by ministry and branch of industry, and some tables reproduce figures for individual named factories.

U956 *Tekhnicheskii progress v narodnom khoziaistve Latviiskoi SSR.* [Technical progress in the Latvian economy]. Riga, 1971. 207 pp. [Not seen].

Lithuania

U957 *Podsobnaia promyshlennost' Litovskoi SSR: statisticheskii sbornik.* [Subsidiary enterprises in Lithuania: a statistical handbook]. Vilnius, 1975. 58 pp. [Not seen].

U958 *Promyshlennost' Litovskoi SSR: statisticheskii sbornik.* [Industry in Lithuania: a statistical handbook]. (TsSU LitSSR). Vilnius: Mintis, 1973. 418 pp.

Covers all branches of Lithuanian industry, 1950–70.

Collections of documents on industry

U959 *Iuridicheskii spravochnik khoziaistvennika: sobranie khoziaistvenno-pravovykh normativnykh aktov.* [A legal handbook for officials in industry: a collection of legal and normative materials on industry]. Tallin: Eesti raamat, 1969. 605 pp.

In Estonian. [Not seen].

U960 *Khoziaistvennaia reforma i prava predpriiatiia: (sbornik reshenii) pravitel'stva SSSR i pravitel'stva Kazakhskoi SSR, a takzhe ukazanii vedomstvennykh organov o khoziaistvennoi reforme.* [The economic reform and the rights of enterprises: a collection of all-union and Kazakh government decisions, with regulations from other bodies about the economic reform]. Pod red. T. Urazalieva. (Iurid. komissiia SM KazSSR). Alma-Ata: Kazakhstan, 1969–74. 3 vols.

A collection of normative acts and other materials relating to the implementation of the economic reforms of the mid-1960s, particularly in Kazakhstan. Most of the documents included were issued by the USSR and Kazakh councils of ministers and state planning committees, and the Kazakh Ministry of Agriculture. Chronological arrangement.

U961 *Khoziaistvennoe protsessual'noe zakonodatel'stvo.* [Legislation on economic procedure]. Kiev: Vyshcha shkola, 1976. 256 pp.

A collection of normative acts on industrial law and commercial law, and the procedures to be used in settling disputes between enterprises.

U962 *Khoziaistvennye dogovory: sbornik normativnykh aktov.* [Economic contracts: a collection of normative acts]. M.: Gosiurizdat, 1962. 602 pp.

A collection for lawyers and economists on industrial contracts, including supply contracts, transportation and construction contracts. Alphabetical subject index.

U963 *Kommentarii k Polozheniiu o proizvodstvennom ob"edinenii (kombinate).* [Commentary on the Regulations on the Production Association (Combine)]. Pod. red. V. V. Lapteva. M.: Iurid. lit-ra, 1979. 279 pp.

Text and detailed commentary on the 1974 Regulations and on the general legal position of the production associations. Alphabetical subject index.

U964 *Kommentarii k Polozheniiu o sotsialisticheskom gosudarstvennom proizvodstvennom predpriiatii.* [Commentary on the Regulations on the Socialist Production Enterprise]. Pod red. V. V. Lapteva. 2 izd., perer. i dop. M.: Iurid. lit-ra, 1971. 359 pp.

1st ed. publ. 1968 (303 pp.). Contains the text of the 1965 Regulations and a detailed commentary.

U965 *Nomenklatura promyshlennoi produktsii (k sostavleniiu otchetov po produktsii promyshlennymi predpriiatiiami), utverzhdena TsSU SSSR 12 maia 1959 g.* [Schedule of industrial production for use in compiling reports on production by industrial enterprises]. (TsSU SSSR. Upr. statistiki promyshlennosti). M.: Gosstatizdat, 1960. 492 pp.

Detailed classification of industrial products, with notes on the units of measurement to be used in compiling official returns.

U966 *Obshcheotraslevye rukovodiashchie metodicheskie materialy po sozdaniiu avtomatizirovannykh sistem upravleniia predpriiatiiami i proizvodstvennymi ob"edeniniiami (ASUP).* [Rules and guidance for all branches of industry on setting up automated management systems in enterprises and production associations]. (Gos. komitet SSSR po nauke i tekhnike). M.: Statistika, 1977. 264 pp.

A document issued by the State Committee on Science and Technology in July 1977 and agreed with Gosplan, Gosstroi, Gossnab, Gosstandart, the Academy of Sciences and the relevant ministries, intended to assist specialists involved in designing and introducing computerization and automation in industry.

U967 *Prava promyshlennykh predpriiatii, ob"edenii i ministerstv v reshenii khoziaistvennykh voprosov: spravochnoe posobie.* [A handbook on the rights of enterprises, associations and ministries in economic matters]. M.: Iurid. lit-ra, 1969. 248 pp.

The handbook brings together under subject or problem headings sections from the relevant normative acts, showing which actions and procedures can be done by which organization after the reforms of the mid-1960s.

U968 *Prava rukovoditelei predpriiatii i organizatsii, sovnarkhozov, ministerstv i vedomstv v reshenii khoziaistvennykh voprosov.* [The rights of industrial managers, sovnarkhozy, ministries and other bodies in deciding economic matters]. M.: Iurid. lit-ra, 1961. 279 pp.

A summary of recent legislation, normative materials and party documents produced to help administrators deal with the new economic organization after the introduction of the sovnarkhozy.

U969 *Sbornik ukazanii i instruktivnykh materialov po perevodu predpriiatii, ob"edinenii i otraslei promyshlennosti na novuiu sistemu planirovaniia i ekonomicheskogo stimulirovaniia.* [A collection of orders and instructions on the transfer of enterprises, associations and branches of industry into the new system of planning and economic incentives]. M.: Ekonomika, 1967. 270 pp.

A collection of materials from Gosplan, the USSR Ministry of Finance, State Committee on Labour and Wages, the State Bank, the Central Statistical Administration and the trade unions relating to the implementation of the 1965 economic reforms. The collection is intended for administrators and contains some material not previously published elsewhere.

U970 *Sotsialisticheskaia industriia.* [Socialist industry]. M., 1969–. 6 per week.

This newspaper is an organ of the Central Committee of the CPSU and an important source of official documents and authoritative policy statements on industry.

U971 *Zakonodavstvo pro sotsialistychne derzhavne vyborochne pidpryemstvo: zbirnyk zakonodavchikh aktiv pro prava ta obov'iavky pidpryemstv.* [Laws on the socialist state production enterprise: a collection of legislation on the rights and responsibilities of enterprises]. Pid red. O. N. Iakimenka. (Iurid. kom. pry RM URSR). Kyiv: Vyd. pol. lit-ry Ukrainy, 1969. 735 pp.

In Ukrainian. A collection of Ukrainian and all-union legislation, principally from the councils of ministers, on production, finance, labour and wages, supply, etc.

State arbitration

The State Arbitration machinery operates at all levels of the economy to adjudicate on disputes which arise between economic organizations on matters relating to contracts of supply and delivery under the plan.

U972 *Arbitrazh v sovetskom khoziaistve. Sbornik zakonov, ukazov, postanovlenii, instruktsii.* [Arbitration in the Soviet economy. A collection

of laws, decrees, ordinances and instructions]. Sost.: V. N. Mozh-
eiko, Z. I. Shkundin. Izd. 4-e. M.: Iurizdat, 1948. 666 pp.

1st ed. publ. 1936 (420 pp.), 2nd ed. publ. 1938 (400 pp.), 3rd ed.
publ. 1941 (368 pp.). Includes a long and informative introduction
by the compilers on the arbitration system in the 1940s, followed by
official documents on: (a) state arbitration at all-union and union
republic level; (b) arbitration with various ministries; (c) legislation
regulating relations between economic entities. There is an alphabetical subject index. The 4th ed. includes material in force on 1
January 1948.

U973 *Instruktivnye ukazaniia Gosudarstvennogo arbitrazha pri Sovete
ministrov SSSR (sistematizirovannyi sbornik).* [A systematic collection of instructions issued by the Court of Arbitration of the
USSR Council of Ministers]. M.: Iurid. lit-ra, 1964. 311 pp.

A collection of instructional letters, rules and regulations on the
work of the arbitration tribunals in force on 1 January 1964. Subject
and chronological index.

U974 *Sbornik instruktivnykh ukazanii Gosudarstvennogo arbitrazha pri
Sovete Ministrov SSSR.* [A collection of instructions from the State
Arbitration Court]. M.: Gosiurizdat, 1955–. Irregular.

Instructional letters from the court relating to the organization of
arbitration work, or setting out its decisions in various cases.

U975 *Sbornik polozhenii ob organakh gosudarstvennogo arbitrazha.* [A
collection of regulations on the organs of State Arbitration]. M.:
Iurid. lit-ra, 1975. 184 pp.

The 1974 Regulations govern state arbitration at all levels of the
administration.

U976 'Soviet administration of legality: the procuracy; the notariat;
arbitrazh'. *Soviet statutes and decisions,* vol. 10, no. 3, 1974.
'Soviet economic law: arbitrazh'. *Soviet statutes and decisions,* vol. 2,
no. 1, 1965.

These two issues of *SS&D* (*see* U164) contain translations of
Soviet legislation on Gosarbitrazh.

See also U924 and U962.

Procurements and supply

The State Committee on Material and Technical Supplies (Gossnab) is the body
chiefly responsible for procuring and allocating raw materials, industrial
products and machinery under the plan. This sub-section includes materials on
procurement and allocation in general, and more detailed regulations on the
contracts of supply and delivery.

U977 Klein, N. I. *Kommentarii k Polozheniiam o postavkakh produktsii i
tovarov.* [Commentary on the Regulations on the Supply of Goods

and Products. By] N. I. Klein, I. N. Petrov. Izd. 2-e, perer. i dop. M.: Iurid. lit-ra, 1978. 320 pp.

1st ed. publ. 1971 (286 pp.). A detailed commentary on the Regulations on the supply of consumer goods and industrial and technical products. Alphabetical subject index.

U978   *Polozheniia o postavkakh produktsii proizvodstvenno-tekhnicheskogo naznacheniia. Instruktsii o poriadke priemki po kolichestvu i kachestvu. Osobye usloviia postavki produktsii.* [Regulations on the Supply of Industrial and Technical Goods. Instructions on the Procedures for Accepting Goods as Conforming to Quantity and Quality. Special Conditions of Supply]. M.: Iurid. lit-ra, 1972. 254 pp.

Detailed regulations in force on 15 May 1972.

U979   *Sbornik normativnykh aktov po material'no-tekhnicheskomu snabzheniiu.* [A collection of normative acts on the supply of materials and machinery]. Pod red. G. Ia. Gorchinskogo, M. M. Braginskogo. M.: Iurid. lit-ra, 1976–7. 4 vols.

A collection of normative acts on all aspects of supply and procurements from Gossnab, Gosplan and various ministries and state committees. Vol. 4 has an index to the whole collection, and a list of amendments passed after the earlier volumes were published. A second edition has been announced for 1980.

U980   *Sbornik osnovnykh i osobykh uslovii postavki.* [A collection of regulations on general and special conditions of supply]. M.: Gosiurizdat, 1956. 3 vols.

Vols. 1–2 relate to all-union regulations and are arranged by ministry; vol. 1 covers supplies of materials and machinery to industry and vol. 2 covers finished goods for the consumer. Vol. 3 covers regulations on supply of materials and goods between enterprises, etc. at union republic level. Each volume has an alphabetical subject index.

U981   'Soviet economic law: contracts of delivery'. *Soviet statutes and decisions,* vol. 2, nos. 2 and 3, 1965–6.

These issues of *SS&D* (*see* U164) contain translations of Soviet legislation on supply questions.

See also U962.

Building and construction

Matters relating to building and construction in all sectors of the economy are coordinated through the State Committee on Construction (Gosstroi SSSR) and its counterparts at union republic level. Documents on the construction of housing and town planning can be found in the section 'Social affairs'. *See also* U1018.

U982   *Biulleten' stroitel'noi tekhniki: organ Gos. komiteta SSSR po delam stroitel'stva.* [Bulletin of building technology: organ of the USSR

State Committee on Construction]. M.: Stroiizdat, 1944–. Monthly. 24 p.a. 1945–52. Includes information, guiding materials and regulations on all aspects of building work issued by the all-union and union republics' Gosstroi and by ministries involved in construction.

U983 *Finansirovanie i raschety v stroitel'stve (sbornik zakonodatel'nykh i normativnykh materialov)*. [Finance and accounting in construction: a collection of legal and normative materials]. Kiev: Budivel'nyk, 1968. 131 pp.

A collection of recent regulations, including material from the Construction Bank (Stroibank).

U984 *Finansirovanie stroitel'stva. Sbornik vazhneishikh pravitel'stvennykh reshenii i ukazanii M-va finansov SSSR po finansirovaniiu kapitalo-vlozhenii gosudarstvennykh organizatsii.* [The financing of construction: a collection of major government decisions and directions of the USSR Ministry of Finance on financing capital investment by state organizations]. Sost.: S. V. Rubinshtein. M.: Gosfinizdat, 1948. 384 pp.

Consists of about 250 major government ordinances, instructional letters from the ministry and other regulations, plus over a hundred references to other documents not reproduced in the collection, for the guidance of officials working in the construction industry. Includes material in force on 1 January 1948. Index.

U985 *Kapital'noe stroitel'stvo: sbornik vazhneishikh rukovodiashchikh materialov.* [Capital construction: a collection of the main guiding materials]. [Sost.: V. A. Goloshchapov, S. N. Protopopov]. M.: Gosplanizdat, 1948. 455 pp.

A collection of USSR and RSFSR legislation, ordinances, instructions, etc. as of 1 January 1948, relating to the organization, planning, finance and labour involved in construction, and regulations on the acceptance of completed buildings. Alphabetical subject index.

U986 *Kapital'noe stroitel'stvo v SSSR: statisticheskii sbornik.* [Capital construction in the USSR: a statistical handbook]. (TsSU SSSR). M.: Gosstatizdat, 1961. 280 pp.

Figures on the construction industry and on new building for industry, agriculture, housing and services, for 1918–60.

U987 *Kapital'noe stroitel'stvo v Armianskoi SSR: statisticheskii sbornik.* [Capital construction in Armenia: a statistical handbook]. (TsSU SSSR. TsSU ArmSSR). Erevan, 1968. 268 pp.

Data to 1966 on construction in industry, agriculture, roads, housing and services in Armenia, and on the development of the construction industry. Most tables start in 1950 or 1959, but some go back to 1921.

U988 *Postanovleniia partii i pravitel'stva po voprosam stroitel'stva i arkhit-*

ektury, 1917–1957 gg. [Party and government ordinances on construction and architecture, 1917–1957]. (Akademiia stroitel'stva i arkhitektury SSSR. Tsentr. nauch.-tekhn. b-ka po stroitel'stvu i arkhitekture. Informatsionno-bibliogr. biulleten', no. 8). M., 1957. 27 pp.

A small edition, duplicated chronological list in four sections covering building, architecture, town planning, housing and public facilities. Includes references to some unpublished material.

U989 'Soviet economic law: contracts of construction'. *Soviet statutes and decisions*, vol. 2, no. 4, 1966.

This issue of *SS&D* (*see* U164) covers construction contracts.

U990 *Stroitel'naia gazeta.* [Construction newspaper]. M., 1924–. 2 per week.

Title 1924–37 was *Postroika*; 1937–9 *Stroitel'nyi rabochii*. Has a fortnightly supplement called *Arkhitektura*. Published by Gosstroi SSSR and the trade union for the construction and building industries.

U991 *Zakonodatel'stvo o kapital'nom stroitel'stve.* [Legislation on construction]. Otv. red.: V.Ia. Isaev. 2. izd., perer. i dop. M.: Iurid. lit-ra, 1977–.

1st ed. publ. 1969–76 (7 vols. in 9, plus one volume of subject and chronological indexes). An earlier collection with the same title was publ. in 1961 in 2 vols. This is a very full collection of CPSU resolutions, legislation, ordinances and instructions issued by Gosstroi, Gossnab, Gosplan, the State Bank, the Central Statistical Administration and other organizations with responsibilities for construction at an all-union level. The collection does not include material at union republic level or material which is no longer in force.

Other industries

This sub-section includes collections of legislation and statistical materials relating to individual industries. Many other collections must exist for the guidance of officials working in these industries, but they appear not to be publicly available. However, many documents relating to individual industries can be found in the large general collections, such as U920 and U926. It is also worth consulting the general journals about each industry for current material.

Coal

U992 *Sbornik zakonodatel'nykh i vedomstvennykh rukovodiashchikh materialov po upravleniiu ugol'noi promyshlennosti.* [A collection of legislation and other official materials on the management of the coal industry]. (M-vo ugol'noi promyshlennosti SSSR. Tsentr. NIEI ugol'). M., 1979–.

This collection is planned to appear in 8 volumes. Vol. 1 included material as of 1 July 1977 from the CPSU, Council of Ministers, legislation, instructions, orders and regulations from Gosplan, Gosstroi, Gossnab, the Ministry for the Coal Industry, the trade unions and other organizations concerned with all aspects of the coal industry. Includes much material not previously published.

U993 *Sbornik zakonodatel'nykh i vedomstvennykh materialov po upravleniiu ugol'noi promyshlennosti.* [A collection of legal and other official materials on the management of the coal industry]. M.: Nedra, 1970. 510 pp.

 Includes a wide range of official materials similar to U992, as of 1 January 1970.

Energy

U994 *Elektroenergetika i energetichnoe stroitel'stvo SSSR: statisticheskii obzor.* [Statistical survey of electroenergy and power-plant construction in the USSR]. (M-vo energetiki i elektrifikatsii SSSR). M., 1980. 115 pp.

 Earlier eds. publ. 1977 (120 pp.) and 1974 (98 pp.). The 1980 volume covers use of energy in the USSR, building of power stations and electricity supply, 1950–79. Illustrated.

U995a *Elektroenergetika SSSR v 1971–1972 gg.* [Electroenergy in the USSR in 1971–1972]. M., 1973. 48 pp. [Statistical handbook. Not seen].

U995b *Elektroenergetika SSSR v 1973 g.* [Electroenergy in the USSR in 1973]. M., 1974. 45 pp. [Statistical handbook. Not seen].

Local industry, cooperatives

U996 *Promyslovaia kooperatsiia. Sbornik vazhneishikh postanovlenii o promyslovoi kooperatsii.* [Industrial cooperatives. A collection of the major ordinances]. Sost.: I. A. Selitskii, V. S. Ogolovets. (Gl. upr. po delam promyslovoi i potrebitel'skoi kooperatsii pri SM SSSR). M.: Vses. koop. izd-vo, 1949. 340 pp.

 Earlier edition publ. 1948 (168 pp.). Includes USSR and RSFSR material as of 1 May 1949 on the general organization of producers' cooperatives, their statutes, labour and insurance regulations, complaints procedures, financial matters, etc. Index.

U997 *Sbornik zakonodatel'nykh i instruktivnykh materialov dlia predpriiatii raionnoi mestnoi promyshlennosti, promyslovoi, potrebitel'skoi kooperatsii i kooperatsii invalidov.* [A collection of legislation and instructions for local industry, producers' and consumers' cooperatives and invalids' cooperatives]. Pod obshchei red. M. A. Emel'ianova. (Rostovskii in-t mestnoi promyshlennosti. Rostovskii obl. planovaia komissiia). Rostov-na-Donu, 1948. 224 pp.

 A collection of all-union legislation and other materials regulating these small-scale producers, often specializing in handicrafts.

Oil and gas

U998   *Neftianaia i gazovaia promyshlennost' SSSR v tsifrakh: kratkii spravochnik.* [A short handbook of figures on the oil and gas industry in the USSR]. (Gos. komitet neftedobyvaiushchei promyshlennosti. TsNII tekhniko-ekon. issledovanii po neft'ianoi, neftetekhnicheskoi i gazovoi promyshlennosti). M., 1964. 326 pp.

Copy marked 'Not for the open press. Distributed by circulation list'. Includes detailed figures on oil and gas extraction and processing and transport, comparing various republics, oil and gas fields, and processing plants. Most tables cover only the early 1960s, but some go back to 1940. Some data on major foreign producers.

See also U1208 and U1209.

Financial matters

The budget

Budgetary planning is closely connected with economic planning in general, and all other financial plans are coordinated with the budget. The budget for the USSR for each year is passed as a law by the Supreme Soviet of the USSR, to which body the Minister of Finance also reports on budget fulfilment for the preceding year. As well as appearing in the Supreme Soviet's official publications (U475 and U476) the Minister of Finance's report with (since 1951) the text of the law is also published as a separate pamphlet. A full list of the budget reports and laws appears in the bibliographies on finance (U1005a–b); otherwise they may be identified in library catalogues and bibliographies under the name of the Minister of Finance—it was A. G. Zverev 1946–60 and since then has been V. F. Garbuzov. The budgets of the union republics go through their supreme soviets and are generally not separately published. However, the RSFSR does publish its budget law and minister's report as a separate pamphlet; details of these too are in U1005a–b. As details of the all-union budgets are given in the central newspapers, translations may conveniently be found in *CDSP* (U853).

STATISTICAL HANDBOOKS ON THE BUDGET

U999   *Gosudarstvennyi biudzhet SSSR i biudzhety soiuznykh respublik, ... statisticheskii sbornik.* [The state budget of the USSR and the budgets of the union republics in . . . .: a statistical handbook]. (M-vo finansov SSSR. Biudzhetnoe upr.). M.: Finansy.

1955–60, 1962, 223 pp.; *1961–5*, 1966, 224 pp.; *1966–70*, 1972, 231 pp.; *1971–5*, 1976, 214 pp. An extremely useful cumulation of the annual budget returns for the USSR and the union republics, covering income and expenditure.

U1000   *Raskhody na sotsial'no-kul'turnye meropriiatiia po gosudarstvennomu biudzhetu SSSR: statisticheskii sbornik.* [Budget expenditure on social and cultural measures in the USSR: a statistical handbook]. (M-vo finansov SSSR. Biudzhetnoe upr.). M.: Gosfinizdat, 1958. 91 pp.

Details of government expenditure on health, education, sport and social insurance. Does not include funds channelled through the trade unions and factories. Figures are given for 1940 and 1950–6, and preliminary data for 1957. Most tables are broken down by republic.

COLLECTIONS OF LEGISLATION ON THE BUDGET

U1001   *Biudzhetnaia sistema Soiuza SSR. Sbornik zakonodatel'nykh materialov.* [The budgetary system of the USSR: a collection of legislative materials]. Sost.: S. Glezin, pod red. K. N. Plotnikova. 4 izd., perer. i dop. M.: Gosfinizdat, 1947. xv, 723 pp.

Earlier editions, with varying subtitles, publ. by Vlast' sovetov in 1932 (318 pp.), 1933 (380 pp.), 1937 (416 pp.). Includes laws and normative materials on the budgetary system in the USSR at all levels, including income, expenditure and budgetary control. Subject index.

U1002   *Biudzhetnyi uchet: sbornik normativnykh materialov.* [Budgetary accounting: a collection of normative materials]. M.: Finansy, 1975. 336 pp.

A collection of regulations, instructions and other documents from the Ministry of Finance on budgetary matters.

U1003   *O biudzhetnykh pravakh Soiuza SSR, soiuznykh respublik i mestnykh Sovetov deputatov trudiashchikhsia.* [On the budget rights of the USSR, the union republics and local soviets]. (Vazhneishie zakonodatel'nye akty Soiuza SSR i soiuznykh respublik). M.: Iurid. lit-ra, 1963. 342 pp.

U1004   *Zakony o biudzhetnykh pravakh Soiuza SSR, soiuznykh i avtonomnykh respublik i mestnykh Sovetov deputatov trudiashchikhsia.* [Laws on the budget rights of the USSR, union and autonomous republics and local soviets]. M.: Gosfinizdat, 1962. 368 pp.

These two collections both include the all-union legislation on budget rights passed in 1959–60 and the laws on the budget rights of the union republics passed by the union republics in 1960–1.

Bibliographies on financial matters

U1005a   *Finansy, den'gi i kredit SSSR: bibliograficheskii ukazatel', 1946–1966.* [Finance, money and credit in the USSR: a bibliographical index, 1946–1966]. (Nauch. b-ka M-va finansov SSSR). M.: Finansy, 1967. 479 pp.

1005b   *Finansy, den'gi i kredit SSSR: bibliograficheskii ukazatel', 1967–1975.* [Finance, money and credit in the USSR: a bibliographical index, 1967–1975]. (Nauch. b-ka M-va finansov SSSR). M.: Finansy, 1977. 320 pp.

These two bibliographies include Soviet books and articles on all aspects of the finances of the USSR, including material in languages other than Russian and covering material on the financing of welfare, education, etc. as well as industry and agriculture. They list collections of legislation and individual official acts on financial matters. Author index.

General collections of materials on finance

U1006 *Finansirovanie kapital'nykh vlozhenii. Sbornik zakonodatel'nykh i drugikh normativnykh dokumentov.* [The financing of capital investment. A collection of legislative and other normative materials]. M.: Gosfinizdat, 1958. 822 pp. [Not seen].

U1007 *Finansirovanie prosveshcheniia i zdravookhraneniia: sbornik postanovlenii, rasporiazhenii i instruktsii.* [Financing education and health: a collection of ordinances, decisions and instructions]. Sost.: N. A. Pomanskii. M.: Gosfinizdat, 1949. 472 pp.

Covers materials from 1928 to September 1948 issued by the all-union ministries of finance, education and health on all aspects of financing their services.

U1008 *Finansirovanie prosveshcheniia: sbornik zakonodatel'nykh i instruktivnykh materialov.* [The financing of education: a collection of legislative and instructional materials]. Sost.: A. R. Arkhipov, N. A. Pomanskii. M.: Gosfinizdat, 1957. 883 pp.

Earlier edition subtitled *sbornik zakonodatel'nykh materialov*, comp. by P. I. Zubok et al. and ed. by Ia. I. Goleva, publ. 1946 (276 pp.). The 1957 volume is a very full collection of USSR and RSFSR legislation, Council of Ministers, Ministry of Education and Ministry of Finance ordinances and instructions on financial matters, including wages and stipends, relating to schools, nurseries, children's homes, higher educational and scientific institutions, and cultural organizations. Thorough index and list of all documents included.

U1009 *Sbornik normativnykh aktov po sovetskomu finansovomu pravu.* [A collection of normative acts on Soviet financial law]. M.: Iurid. lit-ra, 1967. 375 pp.

Earlier edition called *Sbornik osnovnykh normativnykh aktov...* publ. 1961 (337 pp.). Both cover the budget, state income and expenditure, credit, finance for investment, circulation of money and foreign currency matters.

U1010 *Sbornik po finansovomu zakonodatel'stvu.* [A collection of financial legislation]. M.: Iurid. lit-ra, 1980. 664 pp.

A classified collection of documents for lawyers and finance officials covering budget law, money, insurance, taxes, expenditure and auditing. Many documents in extract only. No index.

U1011 *Sbornik prikazov i instruktsii po finansovo-khoziaistvennym voprosam.* [A collection of orders and instructions on financial and economic matters]. M.: Gosfinizdat, 1925–49, 1958–62. Monthly.

1925–35 called *Biulleten' finansovogo i khoziaistvennogo*

zakonodatel'stva; 1938–40 called *Finansovyi i khoziaistvennyi biulleten'*. An important official bulletin of financial and economic legislation, including material from the Supreme Soviet, Council of Ministers and orders, instructions, etc. from the Ministry of Finance and other ministries. Annual index of documents.

U1012 *Spravochnik nalogovogo rabotnika*. [Tax-workers' manual]. Pod red. V. I. Babushkina. M.: Gosfinizdat, 1958. 367 pp.

Earlier editions publ. 1949 (310 pp.) and 1951 (344 pp.), ed. by D. V. Burmistrov. The manual details the regulations currently in force for imposing and collecting taxes and fees, and gives examples of cases and procedures.

U1013 *Spravochnik po nalogam i sboram s naseleniia*. [Manual of taxes and fees]. M.: Finansy, 1973. 320 pp.

Earlier edition publ. 1968 (279 pp.). The 1973 edition includes legal and instructional material in force on 1 January 1973 on the calculation and collection of taxes and fees.

U1014 *Spravochnik raionnogo finansovogo rabotnika*. [Manual for a local finance official]. Pod red. P. A. Maletina. M.: Gosfinizdat, 1952–3. 2 vols.

Earlier edition publ. 1943 (768 pp.). Gives guidance on a wide range of financial and taxation matters, including local budgets, social insurance, savings banks, capital investment and the administration of the legal system. Vol. 1 covers material in force on 1 March 1952, vol. 2 goes up to 1 September 1953. At the end of each subject section, there is a list of the official materials used in compiling it, which includes references to some unpublished documents. Each volume has a subject index.

Prices

The State Committee on Prices (Goskomtsen) works closely with Gosplan in fixing prices to be charged for goods and services by state or public agencies.

U1015 *Biulleten' roznichnykh tsen*. [Bulletin of retail prices]. (Gosplan. Biuro tsen). M., 1935–59. 3 per month.

1935–58 issued by the USSR Ministry of Trade. Title varied before the war; 1941–6 called *Sbornik prikazov i preiskurantov Narkom torgovli SSSR*; 1946–57 called *Sbornik prikazov M-va torgovli*. Considerable variations in frequency pre-1945; 36 issues 1943–56, 1958–9; 16 issues in 1957. The bulletin consists of orders issued by the USSR and union republic ministries of trade relating to prices for consumer goods and food.

U1016 *Biulleten' tsen na tovary narodnogo potrebleniia*. [Bulletin of prices for consumer goods]. (Gos. komitet SSSR po tsenam). M.: Pre-iskurantizdat, 1967–. 24 p.a.

Details of prices for consumer goods, but not for food products. Annual index.

U1017a   *Sbornik normativnykh aktov Goskomtsena SSSR po voprosam ustanov-leniia i primeneniia tsen, po sostoianiiu na 1 iiulia 1977g.* [A collection of normative acts of the USSR State Committee on Prices on the fixing and application of prices, as of 1 July 1977]. (Goskomtsen SSSR). M.: Preiskurantizdat, 1978. 64 pp.

A collection of material issued in 1975–6 revising existing price lists etc.; up-dated by:

U1017b   *Sbornik normativnykh aktov Goskomtsena SSSR . . . za period s 1 iiulia 1977 g. po 1 iiulia 1978 g.* 1979. 141 pp.

U1018   *Spravochnik tsen na stroitel'nye materialy i oborudovanie, deistvu-iushchikh s 1 iiulia 1955g.* [Handbook of prices for building materials and for equipment, in force from 1 July 1955]. M.: Gosfinizdat, 1956. 2 vols.

Intended for workers in finance and supply organizations, listing wholesale prices for building materials and the prices for the most commonly used agricultural, industrial, construction and other types of tools and equipment. A third section covers prices for purchases from local industries. Each volume is indexed.

U1019   *Tseny na tovary narodnogo potrebleniia: sbornik dokumentov.* [Prices of consumer goods: a collection of documents]. M.: Gos. izd-vo torgovoi lit-ry, 1963. 335 pp.

Includes material in force on 1 November 1962 and is intended for staff in trading organizations and in ministries of trade. Includes many circulars and other ministry materials not previously published.

See also U1487.

Accountancy and book-keeping

U1020   *Bukhgalterskii uchet. Sbornik vazhneishikh rukovodiashchikh materialov.* [Accountancy: a collection of the major guiding materials]. Sost. V. A. Goloshchapov. Izd. 5-e, perer. M.: Gosplanizdat, 1950. 488 pp.

Earlier editions publ. 1939 (416 pp.), 1941 (402 pp.), 1947 (600 pp.), with title *Sbornik vazhneishikh rukovodiashchikh materialov po bukhgalterskomu uchetu*; 4th ed. publ. 1948 (768 pp.). 5th ed. includes material in force on 15 April 1950 covering accountancy, book-keeping, financial control, investment, wages, payments for business trips, budgets, special funds, stock-taking, etc. The documents are issued by the State Bank, the Ministry of Finance, Council of People's Commissars, Ministry of Labour, etc. Indexed.

U1021   *Bukhgalterskii uchet v promyshlennosti: spravochnik.* [Accountancy in industry: a manual]. Sost.: G. D. Verbov. M.: Finansy, 1973. 432 pp.

A collection of the major documents on the organization and methods of accountancy and book-keeping, and the rights and duties of accountants.

U1022 *Spravochnik bukhgaltera gosudarstvennoi torgovli.* [Manual for accountants in state trade organizations]. M.: Ekonomika, 1974. 502 pp.

Earlier edition with same title publ. 1969 (608 pp.). The 1958 (758 pp.) and 1960 (746 pp.) versions were called *Spravochnik po bukhgalterskomu uchetu v torgovle i obshchestvennom pitanii* and the 1964 ed. (608 pp.) was called *Spravochnik po bukhgalterskomu uchetu v gosudarstvennoi torgovle.* These volumes all include all-union and RSFSR legislation and other normative materials from a wide range of ministries and official bodies on book-keeping and accountancy procedures in shops, public catering and similar organizations.

U1023 *Spravochnik po bukhgalterskomu uchetu.* [Manual on accountancy]. Sost.: V. A. Goloshchapov. 3 izd., perer. M.: Gosfinizdat, 1961. 532 pp.

1st ed. publ. 1955 (578 pp.), 2nd ed. publ. 1957 (567 pp.). A collection of legislative and instructional materials relating to accountancy procedures in a wide range of organizations. Some documents are given as extracts, or simply listed by title with a reference to a published source. Subject index.

U1024 Verbov, G. D. *Spravochnik normativnykh dokumentov po bukhgalterskomu uchetu.* [A handbook of normative documents on accountancy, by] G. D. Verbov, P. S. Bezrukikh, pod red. P. S. Bezrukikh. M.: Finansy, 1978–.

A collection of laws, ordinances, Ministry of Finance regulations and instructions, and documents from other ministries, state committees, etc. affecting accountancy and financial management in all types of industrial and construction organizations. The handbook is planned to appear in three volumes. Vol. 1 includes material as of 1 July 1978, vol. 2 as of 1 May 1979.

Agriculture

There are three types of agricultural production units in the USSR: the kolkhoz (collective farm), sovkhoz (state farm) and the private plot. The kolkhoz is a producers' cooperative, but does not have the right to make the main decisions about farm output and its annual production plan. These are largely determined by the state procurement agency which takes a quota of what it produces, and pays the farm for it. The Ministry of Agriculture does not directly organize the work of the kolkhoz. Until 1958, however, the machine-tractor stations (MTS) were an important instrument of control over the kolkhozy, as they carried out all machine work on the farms. Technical agricultural advice to the kolkhozy is given by specialists provided by the district soviets, which also have some influence over the farms' planning. Until 1958, most collective-farmers were paid on a 'work-day' basis, but are now paid wages similar to workers on state farms. Social assistance (pensions, sickness benefit, etc.) for members of kolkhozy is poorer than that for workers and employees and until recently members of a kolkhoz were not entitled to an (internal) passport. The state farm (sovkhoz) on the other hand has the same status as an industrial enterprise, the director is appointed by the Ministry of Agriculture (not elected as the kolkhoz director is, in theory), and the workers and employees are paid in the same way as industrial workers and enjoy the same trade union and welfare benefits. Private plots are smallholdings, usually but not always worked by kolkhozniki and making an important contribution to the income of the family and the country's supply of fresh food.

Since the early 1950s, there has been increasing attention paid to agriculture, including improvements in funding, in fertilizers and equipment, and attempts to improve the living standards in rural areas.

General reference works

U1025   *Comprehensive Russian–English agricultural dictionary*, comp. by B. N. Ussovsky [et al.]. 2nd ed., revised and enlarged. Oxford [etc.]: Pergamon, 1967. xii, 470 pp.

    1st ed. publ. as *Russko-angliiskii sel'skokhoziaistvennyi slovar' = Russian–English agricultural dictionary*, comp. by B. N. Usovskii [et al.]. M.: Fizmatgiz, 1960. 504 pp. This is the most useful agricultural dictionary.

U1026   *Sel'skokhoziaistvennaia entsiklopediia.* [Agricultural encyclopaedia]. Glav. red.: V. V. Matskevich, P. P. Lobanov. Izd. 4-e, perer. i dop. M.: Sov. entsiklopediia, 1969–75. 4 vols.

    1st ed. publ. 1932–5 (4 vols.); 2nd ed. 1937–40 (4 vols.); 3rd ed. 1949–56 (5 vols.). The most authoritative encyclopaedia on agriculture, its organization and its products.

U1027   *Sel'skokhoziaistvennaia literatura SSSR: sistematicheskii ukazatel'.* [Agricultural literature of the USSR: a systematic bibliography]. (Vses. akademiia s.-kh. nauk. Tsentr. nauch. s.-kh. b-ka). M., 1948–. Monthly.

    1948–58 10 issues p.a. This bibliography is a classified listing of all the literature published in the USSR on all aspects of agriculture. Includes relevant party, government and official materials. Full name and place indexes published every six months.

Agricultural statistics

For more recent material, and data on republics not covered here, readers should consult the section 'General statistics' (sub-section 'General works and bibliographies').

USSR

U1028   *Chislennost' porodnogo skota v kolkhozakh i sovkhozakh SSSR na 1 ianvaria 1960 g.: statisticheskii sbornik.* [The number of pedigree animals in the collective and state farms of the USSR on 1 January 1960: a statistical handbook]. (TsSU SSSR). M.: Gosstatizdat, 1961. 517 pp.

Covers cattle, pigs, sheep, goats and horses, and gives a breakdown by region.

U1029　*Chislennost' skota v SSSR: statisticheskii sbornik.* [Livestock in the USSR: a statistical handbook]. (TsSU SSSR). M.: Gosstatizdat, 1957. 619 pp.

Figures on the number of cattle, pigs, sheep, goats and horses in the USSR in 1956, with some series beginning in 1916 but most in 1935 and 1941. Includes data on privately owned animals and on pedigree stock, and tables on fodder and forage crops.

U1030　*Posevnye ploshchadi SSSR: statisticheskii sbornik.* [The sown area of the USSR: a statistical handbook]. (TsSU SSSR). M.: Gosstatizdat, 1957. 2 vols.

The first volume contains general figures on sown area for 1913–56, and detailed returns for grain crops by region, 1950–65. Vol. 2 has detailed returns by region for 1950–65 for industrial crops, potatoes, vegetables and fodder crops.

U1031　*Sel'skoe khoziaistvo SSSR: statisticheskii sbornik.* [Agriculture in the USSR: a statistical handbook]. (TsSU SSSR). M.: Statistika, 1971. 711 pp.

Previous edition publ. 1960 (666 pp.). Both handbooks contain data on agricultural production, investment, equipment and organization, and on the agricultural labour force.

U1032　*Sortovye posevy SSSR (zernovye kul'tury i podsolnechnik): statisticheskii sbornik.* [High-quality crops in the USSR (grains and sunflower): a statistical handbook]. (TsSU SSSR). M.: Gosstatizdat, 1957. 423 pp.

Data for 1956 on the amount of land in the USSR sown with high-quality crops, broken down by area and type of farm, and with tables for each crop showing varieties of seed planted in each region.

U1033　*Zhivotnovodstvo SSSR: statisticheskii sbornik.* [Livestock in the USSR: a statistical handbook]. (TsSU SSSR). M.: Gosstatizdat, 1959. 252 pp.

Figures on the numbers of livestock and on the production of meat, dairy foods and other animal products. Most figures relate to 1 January 1958, with detailed figures in some tables for 1953–7 too. Some tables are broken down to oblast', krai and autonomous oblast' level.

ARMENIA

U1034　*Sel'skoe khoziaistvo Armianskoi SSR: statisticheskii sbornik.* [Agriculture in Armenia: a statistical handbook]. (TsSU SSSR. TsSU ArmSSR). Erevan, 1969. 517 pp.

Earlier edition publ. in 1961 (482 pp.). The 1970 volume has detailed figures for 1958 or 1960–7, with some tables back to 1913. The 1961 volume has more details on the 1940s and 1950s.

ESTONIA

U1035 *Osnovnye pokazateli razvitiia sel'skogo khoziaistva Estonskoi SSR za 1965–1969 gg.* [Basic indicators of the development of the agriculture of Estonia in 1965–1969]. Tallin, 1970. 160 pp. [In Estonian. Not seen].

U1036 *Osnovnye pokazateli razvitiia sel'skogo khoziaistva Estonskoi SSR.* [Basic indicators of the development of agriculture in Estonia]. Tallin, 1975. 110 pp.
　　Earlier editions, publ. 1973 (110 pp.) and 1970 (30 pp.). [Not seen].

KAZAKHSTAN

U1037 *Kolkhozy Kazakhstana: kratkii statisticheskii sbornik.* [Collective farms in Kazakhstan: a short statistical handbook]. Alma-Ata: Kainar, 1969. 165 pp. [Not seen].

KIRGHIZIA

U1038 *Sostoianie zhivotnovodstva v Kirgizskoi SSR: statisticheskii sbornik.* [Livestock in Kirghizia: a statistical handbook]. Frunze: Gosstatizdat, 1960. 205 pp. [Not seen].

LATVIA

U1039 *Sel'skoe khoziaistvo Latviiskoi SSR: statisticheskii sbornik.* [Agriculture in the Latvian SSR: statistical handbook]. Riga, 1979. 259 pp.
　　Earlier editions publ. 1970 (598 pp.), 1973 (592 pp.), 1976. [Not seen].

U1040 *Zhivotnovodstvo Latviiskoi SSR v 1970 g.* [Livestock in Latvia in 1970]. Riga, 1972. 235 pp. [Not seen].

LITHUANIA

U1041 *Osnovnye pokazateli kolkhozov i mezhkolkhoznykh organizatsii (predpriiatii) LitSSR za 1973 g.: statisticheskii sbornik.* [Basic indicators on collective farms and inter-collective farm organizations in Lithuania in 1973: statistical handbook]. Vilnius, 1974. 296 pp. [Not seen].

U1042 *Sel'skoe khoziaistvo Litovskoi SSR v ... godu: statisticheskii sbornik.* [Lithuanian agriculture in ...: statistical handbook]. Vilnius, 1966, 1968, 1971, 1973–. Annual [Not seen].

MOLDAVIA

U1043 *Nekotorye itogi khoziaistvenno-finansovoi deiatel'nosti kolkhozov i mezhkolkhoznykh ob"edinenii Moldavskoi SSR za 1970–1972 gg. i nekotorye operativnye dannye na 1-oe polugodie 1973 g.: statisticheskii sbornik.* [Some results of the economic and financial work of Moldavian collective farms and inter-collective farm organizations for 1970–1972 and some preliminary figures for the first half of 1973: a statistical handbook]. Kishinev, 1973. 276 pp. [Not seen].

U1044 *Osnovnye pokazateli razvitiia kolkhozov Moldavskoi SSR: statis-ticheskii sbornik.* [Basic indicators on the development of collective farms in Moldavia: statistical handbook]. (TsSU MSSR). Kishinev, 1969. 124 pp.
Covers 1950–68. [Not seen].

UKRAINE

U1045 *Kolhospy URSR v tsyfrakh.* [Collective farms in the Ukraine in figures]. Kyiv, 1969. 182 pp.
In Ukrainian. [Not seen].

U1046 *Radhospy Ukrains'koi RSR v tsyfrakh: statystychnyi zbirnyk.* [State farms of the Ukraine in figures: a statistical handbook]. (TsSU URSR). Kyiv: Statystyka, 1973. 322 pp.
In Ukrainian. Covers all aspects of sovkhozy in the Ukraine, mainly for 1960 and 1965–71, but some tables start in 1950, 1940 or 1913.

U1047 *Sil's'ke hospodarstvo URSR za 10 lit, 1965–1975 rr.: statystychnyi zbirnyk.* [Agriculture in the Ukraine over 10 years, 1965–1975: a statistical handbook]. Kyiv, 1975. 153 pp.
In Ukrainian. [Not seen].

U1048 *Sil's'ke hospodarstvo URSR: statystychnyi zbirnyk.* [The agriculture of the Ukraine: a statistical handbook]. Kyiv, 1969. 685 pp.
In Ukrainian. [Not seen. FDAD].

U1049 *Tvarynnystvo Ukrains'koi RSR: statystychnyi zbirnyk.* [The live-stock of the Ukraine: statistical handbook]. (TsSU URSR). Kyiv: Derzh. stat. vyd., 1960. 251 pp.
In Ukrainian. Data covers 1953 or 1954 to 1959, but some tables go back to 1941. Broken down to oblast' level.

U1050 *Valovi zbory i urozhaynist sil's'kohospodars'kykh kul'tur: statys-tychnyi zbirnyk.* [Gross yield and harvests of agricultural crops: a statistical handbook]. Kyiv, 1959. 339 pp.
In Ukrainian. [Not seen].

UZBEKISTAN

U1051 *Zhivotnovodstvo Uzbekskoi SSR v 1966 godu (spravochnik).* [A handbook on livestock in Uzbekistan in 1966]. (M-vo sel'skogo khoziaistva UzSSR). Tashkent: In-t nauch.-tekhn. informatsii i propagandy, 1967. 156 pp.
Detailed figures on the number of animals, production of animal products for 1965–6, with lists of the best farms and livestock workers.

General collections of material on agriculture

U1052 *Istoriia kolkhoznogo prava: sbornik zakonodatel'nykh materialov*

SSSR i RSFSR, 1917–1958 gg. [The history of collective farm law: a collection of USSR and RSFSR legislation, 1917–1958]. (Moskovskii gos. un-t. Iurid. fakul'tet). M.: Gosiurizdat, 1958–9. 2 vols.

A chronological collection of nearly 900 laws, government decrees and ordinances, party and government resolutions on collective farms, including material no longer in force. Most documents are given in full. About half the material in the second volume relates to the postwar period.

U1053 *Iuridicheskii spravochnik rabotnika sel'skogo khoziaistva.* [A legal manual for workers in agriculture]. Pod red. V. Z. Ianchuka. M.: Iurid. lit-ra, 1972. 565 pp.

A manual for administrators and workers in kolkhozy and sovkhozy, taking into account the 1969 Model Statute for kolkhozy and other legislation and instructions through to October 1971. Set out in a question-and-answer format. Has a useful list of all the legal and instructional materials referred to in the book (in chronological order), with a note of sources where they may be found in full. Subject index.

U1054 *Kursom martovskogo plenuma.* [Following the course of the March Plenum]. M.: Politizdat, 1975. 527 pp.

A collection of speeches and articles by party and government leaders on developments in agriculture since March 1965.

U1055 *Leninskaia agrarnaia politika KPSS: sbornik vazhneishikh dokumentov (mart 1965 g.–iiul' 1978 g.).* [The Leninist agrarian policy of the CPSU: a collection of the most important documents, March 1965–July 1978]. M.: Politizdat, 1978. 680 pp.

As well as party resolutions and decisions of the Central Committee of the CPSU, includes legislation and ordinances on the organization of agriculture and on measures to improve the standard of living in rural areas.

U1056 *Metodicheskie ukazaniia po planirovaniiu sel'skogo khoziaistva RSFSR.* [Rules and procedures for planning the agriculture of the RSFSR]. (Gosplan RSFSR). M.: Ekonomika, 1973. 375 pp.

Intended for staff in planning bodies and specialists in agriculture. Gives guidance on all aspects of the planning process in agriculture, and includes norms for the use of various materials, prices, etc.

U1057 *Metodicheskie ukazaniia po sostavleniiu proizvodstvenno-finansovogo plana sovkhoza.* [Guidance on methods of compiling a production and finance plan for a state farm]. (M-vo sel'skogo khoziaistva LatvSSR). [Riga]: Statistika, 1966. 148 pp.

Detailed instructions and norms for the use of material and other resources in compiling plans in state farms; contains material of all-union significance.

U1058 *Partiia—organizator krutogo pod"ema sel'skogo khoziaistva SSSR: sbornik dokumentov (1953–1958).* [The party as the organizer of the improvement of Soviet agriculture: a collection of documents, 1953–1958]. M.: Gospolitizdat, 1958. 520 pp.

Includes government as well as party resolutions, ordinances, etc. on agriculture during the 1950s.

U1059 *Resheniia partii i pravitel'stva po sel'skomu khoziaistvu (1965–1974).* [Party and government decisions on agriculture, 1965–1974]. M.: Kolos, 1975. 926 pp.

Earlier edition covering 1965–71 publ. 1971 (752 pp.). Both collections include party and government resolutions, legislation, etc. on agriculture and on living conditions in rural areas. Some documents are published for the first time.

U1060 *Sbornik kolkhozno-pravovykh aktov.* [A collection of legislation on collective farms]. Pod red. V. N. Dem'ianenko. Saratov: Izd-vo Saratovskogo un-ta, 1978, 396 pp.

A systematic collection of legislation, government ordinances, ministry orders and decisions of kolkhoz councils, implementing the 1969 Model Charter. Also some USSR and RSFSR Supreme Court decisions relating to collective farm matters. Many documents are in extract form, but there is a full bibliography of published sources used.

U1061 *Sbornik normativnykh aktov po kolkhoznomu pravu.* [A collection of normative acts on collective farm law]. (M-vo vysshego i srednego spetsial'nogo obrazovaniia RSFSR. Vses. iurid. zaochnyi in-t). M., 1965. 263 pp.

A collection for correspondence students. Wide-ranging, but many documents reproduced in extract only. No index.

U1062 *Sbornik prikazov i instruktsii. Gosudarstvennyi komitet zagotovok.* [Bulletin of orders and instructions of the USSR State Committee on Agricultural Procurements]. M., 1938–64. Generally fortnightly.

Title varied: 1946–56 subtitled ... *ofitsial'nyi organ M-va zagotovok.* Annual index.

U1063 *Sbornik reshenii po sel'skomu khoziaistvu.* [A collection of decisions on agriculture]. M.: Izd-vo s.-kh. lit-ry, zhurnalov i plakatov, 1963. 672 pp.

Contains party decisions and legislative and normative materials on agriculture, 1917–January 1963. The bulk of the documents included date from 1946–62, and many are given in extract only.

U1064 *Sbornik rukovodiashchikh materialov po kolkhoznomu stroitel'stvu.* [A collection of guiding materials on collective farms]. M.: Gosiurizdat, 1948. 351 pp.

A collection of material in force on 1 May 1948, intended for the practical use of collective farm chairmen.

U1065 *Sbornik zakonodatel'nykh i vedomstvennykh aktov po sel'skomu khoziaistvu.* [A collection of legislative and ministry acts on agriculture].

Pod obshchei red. V. A. Boldyreva. M.: Iurid. lit-ra, 1957–8. 3 vols.

Copy marked 'Distributed by official circulation list'. A very full collection of material in force on 1 October 1957, issued by a wide range of official bodies and covering all aspects of agriculture. Includes some material not published elsewhere. Vol. 3 has documents through to September 1958 in a supplement, and a full subject and chronological index.

U1066   *Sel'skaia zhizn'.* [Rural life]. M., 1929–. 6 per week.

Called *Sotsialisticheskoe zemledelie* 1930–April 1953 and *Sel'skoe khoziaistvo* 1953–April 1960. An organ of the Central Committee of the CPSU, and an outlet for its documents and views on agricultural matters and rural life.

U1067   *Spravochnik po zakonodatel'stvu dlia predsedatelia kolkhoza.* [A legal manual for collective farm chairmen]. M.: Gosiurizdat, 1962. 594 pp.

Includes legislation and regulations in force on 1 June 1962 relating to all aspects of the work of a collective farm. The materials are arranged in broad thematic groups and there is a subject index.

U1068   *Spravochnik po planirovaniiu sel'skogo khoziaistva.* [Manual on planning in agriculture]. Pod obshchei red. L. I. Khitruna. M.: Kolos, 1974. 736 pp.

A manual of regulations prepared by the USSR Ministry of Agriculture, including many of its instructions and regulations relating to agricultural planning, as well as more widely available legislative material, and documents from the Council of Ministers and other bodies. Includes many norms and prices currently employed in agriculture.

U1069   *Spravochnik predsedatelia kolkhoza.* [Manual for a collective farm chairman]. Pod obshchei red. A. P. Chubarova. M.: Kolos, 1972. 639 pp.

The manual includes a number of government and party documents, ministry and trade union instructions and regulations affecting the organization and day-to-day operation of a collective farm.

U1070   *Vazhneishie resheniia po sel'skomu khoziaistvu za 1938–1946 gg.* [Major decisions on agriculture, 1938–1946]. M.: OGIZ, Sel'skokhozgiz, 1948. 640 pp.

Includes legislation, normative materials and party documents on agriculture up to 10 June 1947. The collection is divided into 6 sections: general; state farms and Machine-Tractor Stations; collective farms; crops; livestock; harvesting; compulsory deliveries to the state. Original official sources are not indicated. No index.

U1071   *Veterinarnoe zakonodatel'stvo. Sbornik postanovlenii, instruktsii, nastavlenii, pravil i polozhenii.* [Veterinary legislation. A collection of ordinances, instructions, recommendations, rules and regulations]. Sost.: A. A. Poliakov, A. I. Laktionova, pod red. A. M. Laktionovoi. Izd. 4-e, perer. i dop. M.: OGIZ, 1947. 783 pp.

Earlier editions publ. 1935 (535 pp.), 1937 (790 pp.), 1941 (664 pp.). The collection includes the 1936 Veterinary Statute and other USSR and RSFSR materials on veterinary work. Indexed.

U1072 *Veterinarnoe zakonodatel'stvo. Veterinarnyi ustav SSSR. Polozh-eniia, ukazaniia, instruktsii, nastavleniia po veterinarnomu delu.* [Veterinary legislation: the USSR Veterinary Statute, regulations, recommendations, instructions and injunctions on veterinary matters]. Pod obshchei red. A. D. Tret'iakova. M.: Kolos, 1972. 2 vols.

Earlier edition publ. in 1959 (1231 pp.) with a supplementary updating volume publ. in 1962 (359 pp.). Includes material on the organization of veterinary services, staffing and salaries, as well as materials governing the diagnosis, treatment and reporting of animal diseases.

U1073 *Zakonodatel'stvo o proizvodstve, zagotovkakh i zakupkakh sel'khozproduktov. Sbornik ofitsial'nykh materialov.* [A collection of official materials on the production, procurement and purchase of agricultural produce]. Pod red. A. S. Pankratova. Sost.: D. M. Nochvin, V. P. Studentsov. M.: Iurid. lit-ra, 1967. 396 pp.

Includes legislation, government ordinances and orders and instructions from a wide range of ministries and other organizations on all aspects of the production, procurement and purchase of agricultural produce, as of 1 March 1967. It also covers incentives to workers and collective farmers. Includes some documents not previously published.

See also U1201–U1203, U1532, and U1533.

Union republics' collections of legislation on agriculture

RSFSR

U1074 *Spravochnik ekonomista kolkhoza i sovkhoza.* [Manual for the economist in a collective farm or state farm]. M.: Kolos, 1970. 791 pp.

A collection prepared by the RSFSR Ministry of Agriculture on planning and economic matters relating to agriculture. Includes many ministry instructions, letters, regulations, etc. on detailed matters of pricing, etc. not readily available elsewhere.

See also U1052 and U1056

AZERBAIJAN

U1075 *Sbornik osnovnykh zakonodatel'nykh i instruktivnykh dokumentov po finansovym voprosam i kreditovaniiu kolkhozov, sovkhozov i drugikh sel'skokhoziaistvennykh predpriiatii i organizatsii.* [A collection of basic legal and instructional materials on finance and credit for kolkhozy, sovkhozy and other agricultural organizations]. Otv. red.: K. A. Khalilov. (M-vo finansov AzSSR). Baku, 1963. 320 pp.

A very detailed collection of all-union and Azerbaijani materials.

BELORUSSIA

U1076   *Spravochnik po zakonodatel'stvu dlia rabotnikov sel'skogo khoziaistva.* [A legal handbook for agricultural workers]. Pod red. G. F. Basova, P. F. Borisova. (Iurid. komissiia pri SM BSSR. M-vo s.-kh. BSSR). Minsk: Urozhai, 1969. 547 pp.

      A collection of Belorussian and all-union legislation as of 1 January 1969, with some later material as a supplement. Some materials in abstract only. Indexed.

ESTONIA

U1077   *Põllumajandusalaseid direktive, seadusandlikke ja ametkondlikke akte.* [Directives, legislation and ministry acts on agriculture]. [Compiler: R. Antons]. (Eesti NSV Teaduste Akadeemia. Majanduse Instituudi. Õiguse Sektor). Tallin: Eesti raamat, 1960. 2 vols.

      In Estonian. Apparently up-dated by a three-volume collection publ. in 1971–2 and followed by annual volumes for 1972–6 publ. 1973–7, with the same title; these later volumes have not been seen by the compiler. The 1960 volume is a very full collection of all-union and Estonian materials on agriculture.

MOLDAVIA

U1078   *Zakonodatel'nye akty o zemle: sbornik normativnykh aktov.* [Legislation on the land: a collection of normative acts]. Kishinev: Kartia Moldoveniaske, 1977. 351 pp.

      A collection of all-union and Moldavian materials on agriculture and the land as of 1 January 1977.

TAJIKISTAN

U1079   *Sbornik zakonodatel'nykh aktov po sel'skomu khoziaistvu Tadzhikskoi SSR.* [A collection of legislation on agriculture in Tajikistan]. Dushanbe: Tadzh. gos. izd-vo, 1962. 410 pp.

      A collection of Tajik CP documents and Tajik Council of Ministers ordinances and other legislation on all aspects of agriculture, in force in April 1962.

UKRAINE

U1080   *Pravovye akty o deiatel'nosti kolkhozov.* [A collection of legislative acts on the work of collective farms]. [Sost.: V. Z. Ianchuk]. Kiev: Politizdat Ukrainy, 1978. 206 pp.

      In Ukrainian. [Not seen].

U1081   *Zbirnyk diiuchykh zakonodavchykh i normatyvnykh aktiv SRSR i URSR z kolhospnoho budivnytstva.* [A collection of current USSR and Ukraine legislation and normative acts on collective farms]. Pid red. V. Z. Ianchuka. Kyiv: Derzh. vyd. sil's`kohospodars`koi lit-ry URSR, 1962. 641 pp.

      In Ukrainian. The materials included cover organization, labour, land and forests, construction and supply, financial and economic matters, educational and cultural provision in rural areas, etc.

UZBEKISTAN

U1082 *Sbornik dokumentov po zemlepol'zovaniiu i zemleustroistvu.* [Collection of documents on land use and land tenure]. (Gl. upr. zemleustroistva M-va s.-kh. UzSSR). Tashkent, 1970. 185 pp. [Not seen].

Translations

Translations into English of legislation on agriculture and agricultural procurements can be found in the *Collected legislation* (U158), section V:5.

Land law

Land law is now regulated by the Fundamental Principles of Land Legislation of the USSR and the Union Republics passed in December 1968, on the basis of which each union republic enacted its own land code in 1970–3. Previous to the passing of the 1968 Fundamental Principles there was no general all-union act governing land tenure, land policy and land use.

Fundamental Principles and codes

U1083 *Osnovy zemel'nogo zakonodatel'stva Soiuza SSR i soiuznykh respublik.* [Fundamental Principles of Land Legislation of the USSR and the Union Republics]. M.: Iurid. lit-ra, 1969. 35 pp.
   Text of the Fundamental Principles passed 13 December 1968, in force from 1 July 1969.

U1084 *Zemel'nyi kodeks RSFSR.* [Land code of the RSFSR]. M.: Iurid. lit-ra, 1970. 80 pp.

U1085 *Zemel'nyi kodeks Armianskoi SSR.* Erevan: Aiastan, 1971. 112 pp. [Also publ. in Armenian].

U1086 *Zemel'nyi kodeks Azerbaidzhanskoi SSR.* Baku: Azgosizdat, 1971. 80 pp. [Also publ. in Azerbaijani].

U1087a *Zemel'nyi kodeks Belorusskoi SSR.* Minsk: Belarus', 1971. 142 pp. [In Russian and Belorussian].
U1087b *Kommentarii k Zemel'nomu kodeksu Belorusskoi SSR,* pod red. N. I. Krasnova. Minsk: Belarus', 1978. 223 pp.

U1088a *Zemel'nyi kodeks Estonskoi SSR.* Tallin: Eesti raamat, 1970. 213 pp.
U1088b *...: kommentirovannoe izdanie.* 1974. [Also publ. in Estonian].

U1089 *Zemel'nyi kodeks Gruzinskoi SSR.* Tbilisi: Sabchota Sakartvelo, 1973. 104 pp. [Also publ. in Georgian].

U1090 *Zemel'nyi kodeks Kazakhskoi SSR.* Alma-Ata: Kazakhstan, 1971. 124 pp. [Also publ. in Kazakh].

U1091   *Zemel'nyi kodeks Kirgizskoi SSR.* Frunze: Kyrgyzstan, 1971. 243 pp. [In Russian and Kirghiz].

U1092   *Zemel'nyi kodeks Latviiskoi SSR.* Riga: Liesma, 1970. 123 pp. [Also publ. in Latvian].

U1093   *Zemel'nyi kodeks Litovskoi SSR.* Vilnius: Mintis, 1971. 114 pp. [Also publ. in Lithuanian].

U1094   *Kodul funchiar al RSS Moldovenesht' = Zemel'nyi kodeks Moldavskoi SSR.* Kishinev: Kartia Moldoveniaske, 1971. 155 pp. [In Russian and Moldavian].

U1095   *Zemel'nyi kodeks Tadzhikskoi SSR.* Dushanbe: Irfon, 1971. 106 pp.

U1096   *Zemel'nyi kodeks Turkmenskoi SSR.* Ashkhabad: Turkmenistan, 1971. 139 pp. [Also publ. in Turkmenian].

U1097a   *Zemel'nyi kodeks Ukrainskoi SSR.* Kiev: Politizdat Ukrainy, 1970. 86 pp. [In Ukrainian].

U1097b   *..., s postateinymi materialami v red. po sost. na 1 sentiabria 1972 g.* Kiev: Politizdat Ukrainy, 1973. 211 pp.

U1097c   *Kommentarii k Zemel'nomu kodeksu Ukrainskoi SSR.* Khar'kov: Vyshcha shkola, 1973. 234 pp. [In Ukrainian].

U1098   *Zemel'nyi kodeks Uzbekskoi SSR.* Tashkent: Uzbekistan, 1970. 58 pp. [Also publ. in Uzbek].

Other material on land law

U1099   *Gosudarstvennyi kontrol' za ispol'zovaniem zemel': sbornik dokumentov.* [State control of land use: a collection of documents]. (M-vo s.-kh. SSSR. Gl. upr. zemlepol'zovaniia i zemleustroistva). M., 1975. 123 pp.

     Includes the 1968 Fundamental Principles and various USSR Ministry of Agriculture orders and instructions on land use issued 1969–75.

U1100   *Kommentarii k Osnovam zemel'nogo zakonodatel'stva Soiuza SSR i soiuznykh respublik.* [Commentary on the Fundamental Principles of Land Legislation of the USSR and Union Republics]. Pod red. G. A. Aksenenka, N. A. Syroedoeva. M.: Iurid. lit-ra, 1974. 351 pp.

     Sets out the text of the Fundamental Principles with a detailed examination of their interpretation in the codes. Other materials on land law are also examined. Subject index.

U1101   *Normativnye akty o zemle.* [Normative acts about the land]. M.: Iurid. lit-ra, 1978. 632 pp.

     Includes major laws, Council of Ministers ordinances, and enactments of various USSR and RSFSR ministries and other bodies on all aspects of land use, in force as on 1 June 1978. Many documents in extract form, but all have full references to sources for the full official text. Subject index.

U1102   *Sbornik dokumentov po zemel'nomu zakonodatel'stvu SSSR i RSFSR, 1917–1954.* [A collection of documents on land legislation in the USSR and RSFSR, 1917–1954]. M.: Gosiurizdat, 1954. 719 pp.

     A very full chronological collection of nearly 700 documents. The documents are given in their original form, with cross-references to later amendments. All the amendments to the 1922 RSFSR Land Code are listed in a separate supplement.

U1103   *Sbornik zakonodatel'nykh aktov o zemle.* [A collection of legal acts about land]. Izd. 2-e, dop. M.: Gosiurizdat, 1962. 299 pp.

     1st ed. publ. 1960 (256 pp.). Includes the main USSR and RSFSR laws, ordinances and instructions on all aspects of land use in force at the time of publication. Some material given only as extracts; includes some documents not previously published.

Translations

U1104   'Soviet conservation law: General provisions. Land'. *Soviet statutes and decisions*, vol. 9, no. 1, 1972.

     This issue of *SS&D* (*see* U164) contains translations of some major materials on land law.

See also *Collected legislation* (U158) section III:2.

Mineral resources

Until the mid-1970s, matters relating to minerals extraction and utilization were governed by the USSR Mining Statute of 9 November 1927. On 9 July 1975, the USSR Supreme Soviet adopted the Fundamental Principles on Minerals Legislation of the USSR and the Union Republics, and the union republics passed codes on this basis in 1976–8.

Fundamental Principles and codes

U1105   *Osnovy zakonodatel'stva Soiuza SSR i soiuznykh respublik o nedrakh.* [Fundamental Principles of the USSR and the Union Republics on Minerals Legislation]. M.: Nedra, 1975. 39 pp.

     The 1975 Principles.

U1106   *Kodeks RSFSR o nedrakh.* M.: Izvestiia, 1976. 47 pp.

     The other union republics issued parallel codes between 1976 and 1978.

For translations of legislation on mineral resources, see *Collected legislation* (U158), section III:3.

Water law

Water law in the USSR is now governed by the Fundamental Principles of Water Legislation of the USSR and the Union Republics passed in 1970, on the basis of which each union republic enacted its own water code.

The Fundamental Principles and codes

U1107 *Osnovy vodnogo zakonodatel'stva Soiuza SSR i soiuznykh respublik.* [Fundamental Principles of Water Legislation of the USSR and the Union Republics]. M., 1971. 31 pp.

Text of the Fundamental Principles passed 10 December 1970 and in force from 1 September 1971.

U1108 *Vodnyi kodeks RSFSR.* [Water Code of the RSFSR]. M.: Iurid. lit-ra, 1972. 55 pp.

The other union republics issued parallel codes between 1972 and 1975.

Other materials on water and water law

U1109 *Sbornik deistvuiushchikh zakonov po sel'skokhoziaistvennomu vodopol'zovaniiu respublik Srednei Azii i Kazakhstana.* [A collection of laws in force on agricultural water use in Central Asia and Kazakhstan]. (Tadzh. gos. un-t. Iuridicheskii fakul'tet). Stalinabad, 1959. 64 pp.

Includes materials from legislation on water use and from the criminal law.

U1110 *Vodnye resursy i vodnyi balans territorii Sovetskogo Soiuza=Water resources and water budget of the USSR area=Ressources en eau et bilan hydrologique du territoire de l'Union Soviétique.* (Gl. upr. meteorologicheskoi sluzhby pri SM SSSR. Mezhvedomstvennyi komitet SSSR po mezhdunarodnomu gidrologicheskomu desiatil-etiiu. Gos. gidrologicheskii in-t). Leningrad: Gidrometeorologiches-koe izd-vo, 1967. 199 pp.

Maps and statistical data on the USSR's water resources and water balance, with a lengthy methodological introduction.

Translations

U1111 'Soviet conservation law: water law'. *Soviet statutes and decisions,* vol. 9, no. 2, 1972–3.

This issue of *SS&D* (*see* U164) includes material on water law.

U1112 *Water resources law and policy in the Soviet Union,* ed. by Irving K. Fox. Madison, Milwaukee, London: University of Wisconsin Press, 1971. viii, 256 pp.

Includes translations of two Soviet studies on water law, plus the text of the 1970 Fundamental Principles, the USSR and RSFSR statutes on water use of 1960, and the section of the 1960 RSFSR Criminal Code dealing with water and air pollution. Index.

See also *Collected legislation* (U158), section III:4.

Forests and forestry

Forestry matters are the responsibility at all-union level of the State Committee on Forestry and the ministries of forestry at union republic level. However, the use of the forests is the responsibility of the all-union Ministry of Pulp and Paper Industry and the Ministry of Lumber and Wood-working Industry. In 1977, the USSR Supreme Soviet enacted Fundamental Principles of Forestry Legislation of the USSR and the Union Republics, which were followed by the enacting of codes of forestry legislation in the union republics during 1978–80.

Statistics on forests and forestry industry

U1113 *Lesnaia promyshlennost' SSSR: statisticheskii sbornik.* [The forest industries of the USSR: a statistical handbook]. (M-vo lesnoi prom. SSSR. Planovo-ekon. upr.). M., Leningrad: Goslesbumizdat, 1957. 295 pp.

Data on timber resources, timber cutting and processing, labour and costs and capital investment in the industry. Also lists of wood processing plants under the USSR Ministry of Forestries and reports on the work of the Ministry for 1956. Includes comparative data for other countries.

U1114 *Lesnoi fond RSFSR: statisticheskii sbornik (po materialam ucheta lesnogo fonda na 1 ianvaria 1961 g.).* [Forest lands of the RSFSR: a statistical handbook based on the register of forest lands on 1 January 1961]. (Gl. upr. lesnogo khoziaistva i okhrany lesa pri SM RSFSR). M.: Goslesbumizdat, 1962. 628 pp.

Data on the location of forests and woods (by oblast'), with information on the age of forests, types of trees and the bodies responsible for their management.

U1115 *Lesnoe khoziaistvo Litovskoi SSR, 1966–1970: statisticheskii sbornik.* [Forestry in Lithuania, 1966–1970: a statistical handbook]. Vilnius, 1971. 273 pp.

In Lithuanian. [Not seen].

Other materials on forestry

U1116 Lenskii, L. *Materialy po istorii sotsialisticheskogo lesnogo zakonodatel'stva (1917–1945 gg.).* [Materials on the history of socialist forest legislation, 1917–1945]. M., Leningrad: Goslestekh-izdat, 1947. 322 pp.

A chronological collection of USSR and RSFSR legislation from the government and the Commissariat of Forests, including much material in force in the postwar period. Indexed.

U1117 *Lesnaia promyshlennost'.* [Forest industry]. M., 1929–41, 1951–. 2 per week.

1929–32 called *Lesnoi rabochii.* Official newspaper of the ministries, state committees and trade unions involved in forestry, wood-processing, lumber and paper industries.

Fundamental Principles and codes

U1118   Osnovy lesnogo zakonodatel'stva Soiuza SSR i soiuznykh respublik.
         [Fundamental Principles of Forestry Legislation of the USSR and
         the Union Republics]. M.: Izvestiia, 1977. 46 pp.
             Enacted 17 June 1977 and in force from 1 January 1978.

U1119   Lesnoi kodeks RSFSR. [Forestry code of the RSFSR]. M.: Izvestiia,
         1978. 64 pp.
             The other union republics began issuing parallel codes in 1978.

Translations

U1120   'Soviet conservation law: forests'. Soviet statutes and decisions, vol. 9,
         no. 3, 1973.
             This issue of SS&D (see U164) contains translations of Soviet
         legislation on forests.

See also Collected legislation (U158), section III:5.

Fisheries

Fishing is controlled by the USSR Ministry of Fisheries and the ministries of
fisheries in the union republics.

Statistics

U1121   Osnovnye pokazateli raboty dobyvaiushchego flota rybnoi promyshlen-
         nosti SSSR za 1956–1965 gg.: spravochnik. [Handbook on the basic
         indicators of the work of the fishing fleet in 1956–1965]. Leningrad,
         1973. 371 pp. [Not seen].

U1122   Statisticheskie svedeniia po rybnoi promyshlennosti SSSR za
         1971–1973 gg. [Statistical data on the fishing industry in the USSR in
         1971–1973]. M., 1974. 38 pp. [Not seen].

Collections of official material

U1123   Sbornik rukovodiashchikh materialov po rybnomu khoziaistvu. [A
         collection of materials governing the fishing industry]. Sost.: N. S.
         Ivanchenko. (M-vo rybnogo khoziaistva SSSR. Gos. proektnyi in-t
         rybopromyslovogo flota). Leningrad: Transport, 1970–1. 3 vols. (in
         6).
             The collection covers fishing in rivers, lakes, seas and the oceans
         and deals with all aspects of the catching and processing of the fish,
         administration of the ports, procedures while at sea, etc. Includes
         some international regulations as well as Soviet documents, chiefly
         from the USSR Ministry of Fisheries.

See also the material on conservation in U1124–U1132.

Environment and conservation

Until the mid-1950s, conservation was viewed mainly in terms of preventing waste of natural resources. However, increasing ecological awareness led to the passing in 1957–63 in the union republics of legislation on the protection of nature. The coordination of environmental matters at all-union level is chiefly the responsibility of the Inter-Departmental Council on Problems of the Environment and the Rational Use of National Resources, as many ministries are involved in various aspects of the problem, including the USSR Ministry of Agriculture, the USSR Ministry of Land Reclamation and Water Management, the USSR Ministry of Fisheries, State Committee of Forestry of the USSR and the USSR Ministry of Health; Gosplan is also involved in the planning aspects of the environment and conservation. The union republics have state committees on the environment. The preservation of buildings and other man-made objects is the responsibility of the ministries of culture, aided by voluntary societies in the union republics.

U1124   *Ob okhrane okruzhaiushchei sredy: sbornik dokumentov partii i pravitel'stva, 1917–1981 gg.* [On the protection of the environment: a collection of party and government documents, 1917–81]. Izd. 2-e, dop. M.: Politizdat, 1981. 384 pp.

     Earlier edition, covering 1917–78, published 1979 (352 pp.). Documents included are arranged chronologically, with lists of nature reserves, a discussion of the organization of conservation in the USSR, and a list of party and government decisions on conservation and the use of natural resources not included in the collections, with a list of published sources where they can be found. Most of the materials included were issued at all-union level.

U1125   *Okhrana okruzhaiushchei sredy: spravochnik.* [The protection of the environment: a handbook]. Sost.: L. P. Sharikov. Leningrad: Sudostroenie, 1978. 558 pp.

     A collection of legal and other materials on the protection of land, air and water from industrial pollution. Includes details of the sanitary norms for industry, instructions from VTsSPS and other bodies as well as enactments from Gosplan and various ministries.

U1126   *Okhrana pamiatnikov istorii i kul'tury: sbornik dokumentov.* [The protection of historical and cultural monuments: a collection of documents]. M.: Sovetskaia Rossiia, 1973. 193 pp.

     A chronological collection (1917–70) of USSR and RSFSR ordinances, edicts, etc. on the protection of monuments and measures to improve public awareness of historical and cultural monuments.

U1127   *Okhrana prirody; sbornik normativnykh aktov.* [The protection of nature: a collection of normative acts]. Pod red. V. M. Blinova. M.: Iurid. lit-ra, 1978. 583 pp.

     Earlier edition, comp. by O. S. Kolbasov, publ. 1961 (384 pp.), and comp. by V. M. Blinov, publ. 1971 (407 pp.). These collections include ordinances from the USSR and RSFSR Council of Ministers, with some legal materials, party documents, and letters and circulars from various ministries. The 1978 ed. includes material in force on 1 December 1977. Subject index.

U1128   *Okhrana prirody: sbornik normativnykh aktov.* [The protection of nature: a collection of normative acts]. (Komissiia po okhrane prirody pri SM LitSSR). Vilnius: Mintis, 1976. 367 pp.

In Lithuanian. Earlier ed. called *Okhrana prirody v Litovskoi SSR* publ. 1970 (366 pp.), also in Lithuanian. [Not seen].

U1129   *Okhrana prirody: sbornik zakonodatel'nykh aktov.* [The protection of nature: a collection of legislative acts]. (Gos. Kom. SM USSR po okhrane prirody). Kiev: Urozhai, 1976. 365 pp.

In Ukrainian. Earlier edition, also in Ukrainian, publ. in 1969 (226 pp.). with title *Sbornik zakonodatel'nykh aktov po okhrane prirody.* [Not seen].

U1130   *Priroda i zakon: sbornik normativnykh aktov po okhrane prirody i ratsional'nomu ispol'zovaniiu prirodnykh bogatstv Moldavskoi SSR.* [Nature and the law: a collection of normative acts on conservation and the rational use of natural resources in Moldavia]. (Gos. komitet MSSR po okhrane prirody). Kishinev: Izd-vo TsK KP Moldavii, 1970. 536 pp.

Includes a wide range of all-union and Moldavian materials publ. up to May 1970.

U1131   Pryde, P. R. *Conservation in the Soviet Union.* London: Cambridge University Press, 1972. xv, 301 pp.

Appendices include translations of some legislation on conservation.

U1132   'Soviet conservation law'. *Soviet statutes and decisions,* vol. 9, nos. 1–4, 1972–3.

This vol. of *SS&D* (*see* U164) is devoted to legislation on conservation: no. 1 covers general provisions and the land; no. 2 covers water law; no. 3 covers forests; and no. 4 includes general materials and a 'Preliminary checklist of Soviet environmental measures, with particular reference to anti-pollution measures', comp. by J. van den Berg.

U1133   *Sovetskoe zakonodatel'stvo o pamiatnikov istorii i kul'tury: sbornik dokumentov i materialov, 1917–1972 gg.* [Soviet legislation on historical and cultural monuments: a collection of documents and materials, 1917–1972]. (Belorusskoe dobrovol'noe obshchestvo okhrany pamiatnikov istorii i kul'tury). Minsk: Polymia, 1972. 430 pp.

Includes all-union and Belorussian materials on the protection of historical, archaeological, architectural, ethnographic, artistic and folklore monuments of all types, and the penalties for infringement of this legislation. Chronological index.

U1134 *Zakonodatel'stvo o pamiatnikakh istorii i kul'tury; sbornik normativ-nykh aktov.* [Legislation on historical and cultural monuments: a collection of normative acts]. Pod red. A. N. Iakimenko. (Ukrainskoe obshchestvo okhrany pamiatnikov istorii i kul'tury). Kiev: Politizdat Ukrainy, 1970. 464 pp.
In Ukrainian. [Not seen].

For translations of legislation on conservation, see also *Collected legislation* (U158) Section III:1.

Labour

Until the end of the 1960s, labour law in the USSR was largely regulated by the RSFSR Code of Labour Laws enacted in 1922; the other republics either adopted this code or passed codes which were essentially the same. The Fundamental Principles of Labour Law of the USSR and the Union Republics were enacted on 15 July 1970 and were followed by new codes in each union republic in 1971–2. In the government, labour matters are the responsibility of the USSR State Committee on Labour and Social Problems, set up in 1955 as the State Committee on Labour and Wages; however, many matters affecting the workers' welfare and their participation in management are the responsibility of the trade unions.

Bibliographies and reference works

U1135a *Sovetskoe trudovoe pravo: ukazatel' literatury, 1917–1969.* [Soviet labour law: a bibliography, 1917–1969]. Sost.: A. K. Bezina, Zh. V. Shchelyvanova. (Kazanskii gos. un-t. Nauch. b-ka im. Lobachevskogo). Kazan': Izd-vo Kazanskogo un-ta, 1971. 391 pp.

U1135b *Trudovoe pravo: ukazatel' literatury, 1970–1975 gg.* [Labour law: a bibliography, 1970–1975]. Kazan': Izd-vo Kazanskogo un-ta, 1978. 203 pp.
These bibliographies cover material in Russian only, and exclude material from newspapers and duplicated works. They include books, articles, legal acts, collections of documents, etc. arranged in broad subject divisions.

U1136 *Trud i zarabotnaia plata: bibliograficheskii ukazatel' literatury po trudu, zarabotnoi plate i sotsial'nym voprosam, izdannoi v SSSR na russkom iazyke za 1971–1975 gg.* [Labour and wages: a bibliography of Russian-language literature on labour, wages and social matters published in the USSR in 1971–1975]. [Sost.: V. V. Grushchina i dr.]. M.: NII Truda, 1977–8. 2 parts.
A very full bibliography, including party and government official documents, as well as books and articles. Subject arrangement with author and title indexes.

U1137 *Trudovoe pravo: entsiklopedicheskii slovar'.* [Labour law: an encyclopaedic dictionary]. Gl. red.: S. A. Ivanov. 4-e izd. M.: Sov. entsiklopediia, 1979. 527 pp.

1st ed. publ. 1959 (512 pp.), 2nd ed. publ. 1963 (576 pp.), 3rd ed. publ. 1969 (593 pp.). Each edition includes definitions of terms used in labour law and short articles; 4th ed. reflects all the changes of the 1970s while the earlier editions are based on the old codes.

Statistics

USSR

U1138   *Trud v SSSR: statisticheskii sbornik.* [Labour in the USSR: a statistical handbook]. (TsSU SSSR). M.: Statistika, 1968. 342 pp.

Data on the number of workers and employees in the USSR, their distribution by type of industry, income, ages, professions and trades, etc. Also has data on scientists and on workers with higher and secondary specialized education and on technical education and training. In most sections there are tables dealing with women workers and some tables are broken down to union republic level. Most of the tables go up to the mid-1960s; some start as early as 1928.

UNION REPUBLICS

Armenia

U1139   *Trud v Armianskoi SSR: statisticheskii sbornik.* [Labour in the Armenian SSR: a statistical handbook]. Erevan: Statistika, Arm. otd-nie, 1970. 205 pp. [Not seen. FDAD].

Latvia

U1140   *Trud v Latviiskoi SSR: statisticheskii sbornik.* [Labour in the Latvian SSR: a statistical handbook]. (TsSU LatvSSR). Riga, 1960. Part 1.

Copy seen marked 'Not for publication in the open press'; no further publication details known. Contains very detailed figures, mainly from 1949 to 1959, and similar in scope to U1138.

U1141   *Trud v Latviiskoi SSR: statisticheskii sbornik.* [Labour in the Latvian SSR: a statistical handbook]. Riga, 1973. 192 pp. [Not seen].

General material on labour law

U1142   Gosudarstvennyi komitet SSSR po trudu i sotsial'nym voprosam. *Biulleten'.* [Bulletin of the USSR State Committee on Labour and Social Problems]. M., 1958–. Monthly.

1958–76, no. 8 the issuing body was called Gos. komitet SSSR po voprosam truda i zarabotnoi platy. Includes ordinances of Goskomtrud and its joint ordinances with other bodies, chiefly VTsSPS; these cover wages and bonuses, organization of labour, work-rates, working conditions, social insurance, socialist competition, etc. Annual index of ordinances.

U1143   Karavaev, V. V. *Razreshenie trudovykh sporov: kommentarii.* [The settling of labour disputes: a commentary. By] V. V. Karavaev, A. M. Kaftanovskaia, R. Z. Lifshits. M.: Gosiurizdat, 1960. 222 pp.

Text of the 1957 Statute on labour disputes, with a detailed commentary including clauses from many earlier normative acts.

U1144　*Kommentarii k zakonodatel'stvu o trude.* [Commentary on labour legislation]. (Vses. NII sovetskogo zakonodatel'stva). M.: Iurid. lit-ra, 1975. 911 pp.

Earlier editions publ. 1966 (831 pp.) and 1967 (855 pp.). The 1975 edition is a detailed commentary based on the 1970 Principles and the 1971 RSFSR Code; the earlier editions are based on the 1922 Code. The commentaries reproduce the text of the Code, with much supplementary material based on later legislation, court rulings, etc. Subject index.

U1145　*KPSS o profsoiuzakh.* [The CPSU on the trade unions]. 3 izd., dop. M.: Profizdat, 1957. 815 pp.

A very full collection of CPSU documents on the trade unions and labour matters to early 1957, supplemented by *KPSS o profsoiuzakh, 1956–1962.* 1963 (535 pp.). Together, these two anthologies are much fuller for the 1945–62 period than U1146.

U1146　*KPSS o profsoiuzakh.* [The CPSU on the trade unions]. M.: Profizdat, 1977. 471 pp.

Earlier editions publ. 1967 (666 pp.) and 1974 (503 pp.). A selective anthology of major CPSU documents on the trade unions, mainly useful for the 1960s and 1970s.

U1147　*Normativnye akty o trude: kratkii sbornik ofitsial'nykh materialov.* [Normative acts on labour: a short collection of official materials]. M.: Iurid. lit-ra, 1973. 542 pp.

A collection of basic legislative material, ordinances, etc. on labour, including the 1970 Principles and the 1971 RSFSR Code. Subject index.

U1148　*Normativnye akty po ispol'zovaniiu trudovykh resursov.* [Normative acts on the use of labour resources]. Pod obshchei red. K. A. Novikova. M.: Iurid. lit-ra, 1972. 943 pp.

Includes all-union and RSFSR legislation, ordinances and regulations on labour recruitment and placing of cadres (especially young specialists), workers' rights and duties, and material on labour mobility and the protection of special categories of workers (women, invalids and young people).

U1149　*Osnovnye zakonodatel'nye akty o trude rabochikh i sluzhashchikh.* [Fundamental legislation on the labour of workers and employees]. (M-vo iustitsii SSSR. Upr. kodifikatsii i sistematizatsii zakonodatel'stva SSSR). M.: Gosiurizdat, 1953. 111 pp.

Includes material on labour placement, transfer and dismissal, working hours and holidays, wages, labour discipline and disputes and the protection of labour.

U1150　*Osnovy zakonodatel'stva Soiuza SSR i soiuznykh respublik o trude.*

[Fundamental Principles of Labour Law of the USSR and the Union Republics]. M.: Izvestiia, 1970. 47 pp.

Text of the Principles enacted 15 July 1970.

U1151 *Raschety s rabochimi i sluzhashchimi: sbornik ofitsial'nykh materialov.* [A collection of official materials on payments to workers and employees]. Sost.: V. A. Goloshchapov. 3 izd., perer. M.: Iurid. lit-ra, 1965. 423 pp.

1st ed. publ. 1962 (390 pp.), 2nd ed. publ. 1963 (423 pp.). An earlier publication, also ed. by Goloshchapov and with the same title, was published by Gosfinizdat: 6th ed. 1946 (127 pp.), 7th ed. 1947 (167 pp.), 8th ed. 1949 (168 pp.) and 9th ed. 1954 (205 pp.). The collections all include laws, rules and regulations currently in force relating to the calculation and payment of wages, bonuses, pensions, etc. and the procedures for making deductions such as fines.

U1152 *Sbornik postanovlenii i opredelenii Verkhovnogo Suda RSFSR po trudovym delam (1953–1958 gg.).* [A collection of the ordinances and decisions of the RSFSR Supreme Court on labour matters, 1953–1958]. M.: Gosiurizdat, 1959. 244 pp.

An annotated collection of decisions in typical cases.

U1153 *Sbornik vazhneishikh zakonov i postanovlenii o trude.* [A collection of major laws and ordinances on labour]. 2 izd., ispr. i dop. M.: Profizdat, 1959. 275 pp.

1st ed. publ. 1958 (232 pp.). A handbook for trade union officials of major laws, ordinances and ministry regulations on labour and wages.

U1154 *Sbornik zakonodatel'nykh aktov o trude.* [A collection of legislation on labour]. M.: Iurid. lit-ra, 1977. 847 pp.

Earlier editions publ. in 1956 (567 pp.), 1958 (607 pp.), 1960 (732 pp.), 1961 (748 pp.), 1964 (854 pp.), 1965 (854 pp.), 1970 (936 pp.) and 1974 (1070 pp.). An important series of collections of current all-union and RSFSR legislation and normative materials relating to labour, training, holidays, wages and bonuses, work norms, labour discipline, disputes procedures, etc. Subject index.

U1155 *Spravochnik profsoiuznogo rabotnika.* [Trade-union official's handbook]. M.: Profizdat, 1948–. Annual.

Includes legislation, regulations, instructions, etc. from VTsSPS, the CPSU and various ministries on a wide range of matters relating to labour and employment.

U1156 Taits, I. A. *Kodeksy zakonov o trude soiuznykh respublik: sopostavitel'nye tablitsy.* [Comparative tables of the labour codes of the union republics]. M.: Iurid. lit-ra, 1975. 430 pp.

Includes tables based on the USSR Principles of 1970, showing the relevant articles in the labour codes of the RSFSR and the other union republics. Discussion of each article is based on the RSFSR Code, with the text of articles in other codes given where they differ significantly from the RSFSR Code or are not covered by it. Subject index.

U1157   *Trud* [Labour]. 1921–. 6 per week.

The official newspaper of VTsSPS, but also an important source of party and government official documents and authoritative views.

U1158   *Trudovye resursy SSSR: sbornik ofitsial'nykh materialov.* [Labour resources in the USSR: a collection of official material]. Sost.: M. S. Rozanov. M.: Gosiurizdat, 1950. 376 pp.

Legal materials, directives, ordinances, etc. on labour resources and technical training.

U1159   *V. I. Lenin, KPSS o sotsialisticheskom sorevnovanii.* [Lenin and the CPSU on socialist competition]. Sost. O. I. Ternovoi. 2-e izd., perer. i dop. M.: Politizdat, 1980. 512 pp.

1st ed. publ. 1973, 438 pp. Annotated collection of documents, largely from the postwar period, covering a wide range of labour organization and labour discipline materials.

U1160   *Zakonodatel'stvo o trude; kommentarii k zakonodatel'stvu o trude SSSR i Kodeksu zakonov o trude RSFSR.* [Labour legislation: a commentary to the USSR's labour legislation and the RSFSR's Labour Code]. [By] N. G. Aleksandrov [et al.]. Izd. 2-e. (Vses. in-t iurid. nauk M-va iustitsii SSSR). M.: Gosiurizdat, 1954. 468 pp.

1st ed. publ. 1947 (359 pp.). The copies seen are marked 'Distributed according to the circulation list'. Very full collections of material, thoroughly indexed.

Labour codes

RSFSR

Old

U1161   *Kodeks zakonov o trude RSFSR; ofitsial'nyi tekst s izm. na 1 oktiabria 1952 g.* M.: Gosiurizdat, 1952. 167 pp.

New

U1162   *Kodeks zakonov o trude RSFSR; ofitsial'nyi tekst.* M.: Iurid. lit-ra, 1972. 127 pp. [Republished with revisions at intervals].

ARMENIA

New

U1163   *Kodeks zakonov o trude Armianskoi SSR.* Erevan: Aiastan, 1972. 235 pp.

AZERBAIJAN

New

U1164   *Kodeks zakonov o trude Azerbaidzhanskoi SSR.* Baku: Azgosizdat, 1972. 164 pp. [Republished with revisions 1976, also in Azerbaijani].

BELORUSSIA

Old

U1165 *Kodeks zakonov o trude Belorusskoi SSR; ofitsial'nyi tekst s izm. na 1 sentiabria 1956 i s pril. sist. materialov.* Minsk: Gosizdat BSSR, 1957. 222 pp.

New

U1166 *Kodeks zakonov o trude Belorusskoi SSR.* Minsk: Belarus', 1972. 223 pp. [Republished with revisions 1976].

Commentary

U1167 *Kommentarii k Kodeksu zakonov o trude Belorusskoi SSR,* pod red. B. A. Volkova, L. Ia. Ostrovskogo, V. F. Chigira. Minsk: Izd-vo, BGU, 1978. 417 pp.

ESTONIA

New

U1168 *Kodeks zakonov o trude Estonskoi SSR.* Tallin: Eesti raamat, 1972. 174 pp. [Also publ. in Estonian]. [Republished with revisions 1975 and 1980].

Commentary

U1169 *Kodeks zakonov o trude Estonskoi SSR: kommentirovannoe izdanie.* Tallin: Eesti raamat, 1978. 526 pp.

GEORGIA

New

U1170 *Kodeks zakonov o trude Gruzinskoi SSR.* Tbilisi: Sabchota Sakartvelo, 1974. 148 pp.

KAZAKHSTAN

New

U1171 *Kodeks zakonov o trude Kazakhskoi SSR.* Alma-Ata: Kazakhstan, 1972. 151 pp. [Republished with revisions 1979].

U1172 No entry.

Commentary

U1173 *Nauchno-prakticheskii kommentarii k Kodeksu zakonov o trude Kazakhskoi SSR,* pod red. K. A. Abzhanovoi. Alma-Ata: Kazakhstan, 1978. 317 pp.

KIRGHIZIA

New

U1174 *Kyrgyz SSRinin emgek zhonundogu zakondor kodeksi = Kodeks zakonov o trude Kirgizskoi SSR.* Frunze, 1972. 235 pp. [In Kirghiz and Russian]. [Republished with revisions 1973].

LATVIA

New

U1175a *Kodeks zakonov o trude Latviiskoi SSR.* Riga: Liesma, 1972. 186 pp. [Also publ. in Latvian].

U1175b *..., s pril. postateino-sist. materialov.* Riga: Liesma, 1979. 542 pp. [Also publ. in Latvian].

LITHUANIA

New

U1176 *Kodeks zakonov o trude Litovskoi SSR.* Vilnius: Mintis, 1973. 175 pp. [Also publ. in Lithuanian]. [Republished with revisions 1977 and 1978].

Commentary

U1177 *Kommentarii k Kodeksu zakonov o trude Litovskoi SSR.* Vilnius: Mintis, 1978. 386 pp. [In Lithuanian].

MOLDAVIA

New

U1178 *Kodul munchii al RSS Moldovenesht' = Kodeks zakonov o trude Moldavskoi SSR: ofitsial'nyi tekst.* Kishinev: Kartia Moldoveniaske, 1973. 348 pp. [In Russian and Moldavian]. [Republished with revisions 1978].

TAJIKISTAN

Old

U1179 *Kodeks zakonov o trude Tadzhikskoi SSR, s izm. i dop. na 1 ianvaria 1940g.* Stalinabad: Gosizdat Tadzhikistana, 1940. 116 pp.

New

U1180 *Kodeks zakonov o trude Tadzhikskoi SSR.* Dushanbe: Irfon, 1973. 170 pp. [Also publ. in Tajik].

TURKMENISTAN

Old

U1181 *Kodeks zakonov o trude Turkmenskoi SSR; ofitsial'nyi tekst s izm. na 1 ianvaria 1955 g.* Ashkhabad: Turkmengiz, 1955.

New

U1182 *Kodeks zakonov o trude Turkmenskoi SSR.* Ashkhabad: Turkmenistan, 1973. 99 pp. [Also publ. in Turkmenian].

UKRAINE

Old

U1183 *Kodeks zakoniv pro pratsiu Ukrains'koi RSR; ofitsial'nyi tekst iz zminamy na 15 chervnia 1965 roku ta z dodatkami syst. materialov.* Kyiv: Vyd. pol. lit-ry Ukrainy, 1966. 438 pp. [In Ukrainian].

New

U1184 *Kodeks zakonov o trude Ukrainskoi SSR.* Kiev: Politizdat Ukrainy, 1972. 122 pp. [Also publ. in Ukrainian]. [Republished with revisions 1975 and 1976].

Commentary

U1185 *Kodeks zakonov o trude Ukrainskoi SSR: nauchno-prakticheskii kommentarii.* Kiev: Politizdat Ukrainy, 1977. 546 pp. [In Ukrainian].

UZBEKISTAN

Old

U1186 *Kodeks zakonov o trude Uzbekskoi SSR po sost. na 1 ianvaria 1946 g.* Tashkent, 1946. 86 pp. [Republished with revisions 1955 and 1970].

New

U1187 *Kodeks zakonov o trude Uzbekskoi SSR.* Tashkent: Uzbekistan, 1972. 124 pp. [Also publ. in Uzbek]. [Republished with revisions 1976].

Collections of union republic legislation

ESTONIA

U1188 *Akty po trudovomu pravu.* [Legislative acts on labour]. Tallin: Eesti raamat, 1969. 912 pp.
In Estonian. [Not seen].

U1189 *Tööseadusandlus: kehtivate normatiivaktide kogumik.* [Labour legislation: a collection of normative acts. 2nd, revised ed.]. (Eesti NSV Ministrite Nöukogu Juures ASUV. Juriidiline Komisjon). Tallin: Eesti raamat, 1966. 563 pp.
In Estonian. A collection of all-union and Estonian legislation in force on 1 December 1965.

U1190 *Trudovoe zakonodatel'stvo: sbornik deistvuiushchikh normativnykh aktov.* [Labour legislation: a collection of normative acts in force]. (Tartuskii gos. un-t). Tartu, 1977. 3 vols.
In Estonian. [Not seen].

LITHUANIA

U1191 *Kommentarii k zakonodatel'stvu o trude.* [Commentary on labour legislation]. Vilnius: Mintis, 1970. 624 pp.
In Lithuanian. [Not seen].

TAJIKISTAN

U1192 *Sbornik zakonodatel'stva Tadzhikskoi SSR po trudu.* [A collection of Tajik legislation on labour]. Dushanbe: Tadzh. gos. izd-vo, 1962. 324 pp.
A collection of Tajik Council of Ministers and Tajik ordinances and resolutions on labour questions, publ. 1954–61. Chronological index.

UKRAINE

U1193   *Zakonodatel'nye akty o trude; v pomoshch' rukovoditeliam predpriiatii, uchrezhdenii, organizatsii.* [Legislative acts on labour for directors of enterprises, institutions and organizations]. (M-vo iustitsii USSR). Kiev: Politizdat Ukrainy, 1976. 632 pp.

      1st ed. publ. 1974 (646 pp.). A collection of Ukrainian and all-union laws, ordinances, etc. in force on 1 January 1976, based on the 1972 Labour Code for the Ukraine. Subject index.

Protection of workers

U1194   *Okhrana truda: sbornik ofitsial'nykh materialov.* [Labour protection: a collection of official materials]. M.: Profizdat, 1977. 335 pp.

      Earlier editions publ. 1953 (471 pp.), 1958 (397 pp.), 1960 (454 pp.) and 1963 (254 pp.) with the subtitle *sbornik postanovlenii i pravil*; in 1966 called *Zakonodatel'stvo po okhrane truda* (527 pp.). 1971 edition (447 pp.) had same title as 1977 edition; another edition is planned for late 1981. This collection comprises major general legislation and trade union materials relating to labour protection. It is intended for the use of trade union officials.

U1195   *Okhrana truda i tekhnika bezopasnosti (sbornik vazhneishikh postanovlenii i pravil).* [Labour protection and safety procedures: a collection of basic ordinances and rules]. M.: Gosiurizdat, 1961. 494 pp.

      A collection of all-union and RSFSR material in force on 1 January 1961 on labour protection and safety. Subject index.

U1196   *Perechen' normativnykh dokumentov po bezopasnosti truda (po sostoianiiu na 1 ianvaria 1977 g.).* [A list of normative documents on safety at work; as of 1 January 1977]. Izd. 3-e, ispr. i dop. (VTsSPS. Vses. tsentr. NII okhrany truda). M., 1977. 204 pp.

      Lists GOST standards, regulations of other all-union agencies, and regulations of specialized ministries on safety at work.

U1197   *Sbornik vazhneishikh ofitsial'nykh materialov po voprosam gigieny truda i proizvodstvennoi sanitarii.* [A collection of major official materials on labour hygiene and industrial sanitation]. Otv. red.: L. V. Ianin. M.: Meditsina, 1962–6. 4 vols.

      Includes detailed ministry and trade union documents, arranged by branch of industry.

U1198   *Spisok proizvodstv, tsekhov, professii i dolzhnostei s vrednimi usloviiami truda, rabota v kotorykh daet pravo na dopolnitel'nyi otpusk i sokrashchennyi rabochii den'.* [List of industries, factory shops, professions and occupations with harmful working conditions, in which workers are entitled to extra holidays and a shorter working day]. (Gos. komitet SSSR po voprosam truda i zarabotnoi platy i Prezidium VTsSPS). M.: Izd-vo ekon. lit-ry, 1963. 660 pp.

      Arranged by industry and then by occupation within the industry.

U1199 *Spravochnik po okhrane truda.* [Manual on labour legislation]. Pod obshchei red. L. I. Sharikova. Leningrad: Sudostroenie, 1973–5. 4 vols.

A collection of legal materials and instructions from Gosstroi, the Ministry of Health and other ministries on health and safety at work, particularly in engineering and shipbuilding.

U1200 *Zakonodatel'stvo po okhrane truda: sbornik pravil i postanovlenii.* [Legislation on labour protection: a collection of rules and ordinances]. Vilnius: Mintis, 1971. 314 pp.

In Lithuanian. [Not seen].

Labour in particular industries: selected collections

AGRICULTURE

U1201 *Oplata truda v sovkhozakh i drugikh sel'skokhoziaistvennykh pred-priiatiiakh (sbornik osnovnykh polozhenii i ukazanii po oplate truda).* [Wages in state farms and other agricultural enterprises: a collection of basic regulations and instructions]. (M-vo proizvodstva i zagotovok s.-kh. produktov RSFSR. Upr. organizatsii truda i zarabotnoi platy). M.: Izd-vo M-va s.-kh. RSFSR, 1962 [1963 on cover]. 484 pp.

As well as normative material relating to wages, includes documents on holidays, training and staffing norms and conditions of work.

U1202 *Sbornik postanovlenii i rasporiazhenii po trudu dlia rabotnikov sel'skogo khoziaistva.* [A collection of ordinances and decisions on agricultural work]. (M-vo s.-kh. RSFSR. Upr. normirovaniia truda i zarabotnoi platy). M.: Izd-vo M-va s.-kh. RSFSR, 1958. 254 pp.

A collection of legislation, ministry instructions, Council of Ministers' ordinances, etc. governing pay and conditions for agricultural work in the RSFSR.

U1203 *Sbornik zakonodatel'nykh aktov po okhrane truda v kolkhozakh.* [A collection of legal acts on labour protection in collective farms]. M.: Iurid. lit-ra, 1971. 326 pp.

Earlier edition publ. 1963 (290 pp.). A collection of current material on safety and hygiene in agricultural work, including material on work by women and young people. Some of the documents included do not appear to have been published previously.

CHEMICAL INDUSTRY

U1204 *Sbornik rukovodiashchikh materialov po voprosam truda i zarabotnoi platy v khimicheskoi promyshlennosti.* [A collection of guiding materials on labour and wages in the chemical industry]. (Gos. komitet SM SSSR po khimii. NII tekh.-ekon. issl.). M., 1961. 408 pp.

Copy seen marked 'For official use'. A very detailed collection of material from a wide range of ministries and other organizations, some of which have not been previously published.

EDUCATION

U1205 *Sbornik rukovodiashchikh i metodicheskikh materialov po voprosam okhrany truda v uchrezhdenii sistemy Ministerstva prosveshcheniia Latviiskoi SSR.* [A collection of guidance and instructions on labour protection for institutions under the Latvian Ministry of Education]. Sost.: I. E. Vasil′ev. Izd. 2-e, dop. i perer. (M-vo prosveshcheniia LatvSSR). Riga, 1971. 257 pp.

A collection of normative acts issued by the Latvian Ministry of Education.

HEALTH

U1206 *Sbornik normativnykh aktov o rabochem vremeni i otpuskakh rabot-nikov zdravookhraneniia.* [A collection of normative acts on working hours and holidays for medical personnel]. Sost.: I. Ia. Glushchenko. M.: Meditsina, 1979. 415 pp.

Includes material in force on 1 November 1978 from the USSR Ministry of Health, the Presidium of VTsSPS and Goskomtrud.

HOUSING AND PUBLIC UTILITIES

U1207 *Okhrana truda i tekhnika bezopasnosti v zhilishchno-kommunal′nom khoziaistve: sbornik postanovlenii pravitel′stva, prikazov Ministerstva kommunal′nogo khoziaistva RSFSR i pravil tekhniki bezopasnosti.* [Protection of labour and safety procedures in housing and communal services: a collection of government ordinances, orders of the RSFSR Ministry of Communal Services and rules on safety procedures]. M.: Stroiizdat, 1969. 447 pp.

A detailed collection of all-union and RSFSR materials.

OIL AND GAS INDUSTRY

U1208 *Sbornik vazhneishikh postanovlenii i pravil po okhrane truda i tekhnike bezopasnosti v neftianoi i gazovoi promyshlennosti.* [A collection of the major ordinances and rules on labour protection and industrial safety in the oil and gas industry]. Pod obshchei red. V. P. Kusheleva. M.: Nedra, 1971. 480 pp.

Includes a wide range of government, ministry and trade union regulations.

U1209 *Spravochnik po organizatsii truda i zarabotnoi platy v neftianoi i gazovoi promyshlennosti.* [A manual on labour organization and wages in the oil and gas industry. By Ia. D. Gurevich et al.]. M.: Nedra, 1966. 641 pp.

Copy seen marked 'For official use'. The manual includes texts of some legislative materials and regulations from various periods and authorities.

PUBLISHING

U1210 *Trud i zarabotnaia plata rabotnikov izdatel'stv i redaktsii zhurnalov: sbornik ofitsial'nykh materialov.* [Labour and wages of staff of publishing houses and editorial offices of journals: a collection of official materials]. M.: Iurid. lit-ra, 1973. 344 pp.

A collection of materials from the Council of Ministers, the Ministry of Culture, Goskomizdat and other official bodies on pay and conditions in publishing and editorial work.

RIVER TRANSPORT

U1211 *Okhrana truda na rechnom transporte: sbornik rukovodiashchikh dokumentov.* [Labour protection in river transport: a collection of guiding materials]. Izd. 2-e, perer. i dop. M.: Transport, 1975. 464 pp.

1st ed. publ. 1962 (433 pp.). [Not seen].

TRADE

U1212 *Okhrana truda i tekhnika bezopasnosti v torgovle: sbornik ofitsial'nykh dokumentov.* [Protection of labour and safety procedures in trade: a collection of official documents]. Izd. 4-e, perer. i dop. M.: Ekonomika, 1972. 264 pp.

For the use of officials in the trade network.

U1213 *Okhrana truda i tekhnika bezopasnosti v organizatsiiakh i predpriiatiiakh torgovli i obshchestvennogo pitaniia.* [Labour protection and safety procedures in trade and public catering organizations]. M.: Gos. izd-vo torgovoi lit-ry, 1959. 248 pp.

For the use of trade union officials and management.

U1214 *Trud i zarabotnaia plata v gosudarstvennoi torgovle: spravochnik.* [A manual on labour and wages in state trade]. M.: Ekonomika, 1979, 247 pp.

Earlier edition publ. in 1959 (278 pp.) called *Trud i zarabotnaia plata v torgovle: sbornik rukovodiashchikh materialov*; 1961 edition (336 pp.) and 1964 edition (305 pp.) have subtitle *sbornik rukovodiashchikh materialov.* The 1979 edition includes material as of 1 April 1979. Consists of the new regulations on labour and wages issued by the USSR Ministry of Trade in December 1976 and its supplements, and older materials still in force which deal with trade and public catering.

Translations

U1215 Nash, E. *Principal current Soviet labor legislation: a compilation of documents.* (BLS report 210). Washington: US Dept of Labor, Bureau of Labor Statistics. vi, 135 pp.

Contains translations of the most important laws and decrees concerning the broader aspects of labour in the USSR. [Not seen].

U1216 'Soviet labour law'. *Soviet statutes and decisions*, vol. 15, nos. 1–4, 1978–9 and vol. 16, nos. 1–4, 1979–80.

These issues of *SS&D* (*see* U164) cover a variety of materials on Soviet law: no. 1 covers collective contracts and labour contracts; no. 2 covers job placement, working time and time off; no. 3 covers wage controls; and no. 4 deals with incentive funds. Vol. 16, no. 1 deals with recent measures on incentives, norms, production plans, monetary responsibility and the protection of women workers; no. 2 deals with agricultural labour, no. 3 with labour safety; and no. 4 with labour law in the courts.

See also *Collected legislation* (U158) section II:3.

Transport and communications

The USSR Ministry of Communications is in charge of postal, telephone and telegraph services, radio, television, and the organization of the distribution of newspapers and periodicals. Railways and roads are the responsibility of the Ministry of Transport (an all-union ministry); at union republic level most republics have combined ministries of roads and automobile transport. Aviation is administered by the all-union Ministry of Civil Aviation, and maritime transport by the all-union Ministry of the Maritime Fleet. In addition, the RSFSR also has a separate Ministry of the River Fleet. Pipelines are partly under the control of the all-union Ministry of the Gas Industry and partly under republican agencies for the transport and supply of oil. Urban transport such as trams and trolleybuses is administered by the republican ministries of municipal economy. Traffic police functions are carried out by the State Motor Vehicle Inspectorate (GAI).

Statistics

ALL-UNION

U1217 *Sviaz' SSSR za 50 let: statisticheskii sbornik.* [Communications in the USSR over 50 years: a statistical handbook]. (M-vo sviazi SSSR. Planovo-finansovoe upr.). M.: Sviaz', 1968. 191 pp.

Covers postal services, telephones, telegrams, radio and television, broken down to oblast' level. Despite the title, most of the tables start in the 1950s or 1960s, with data for earlier years largely confined to the summary tables.

U1218 *Transport i sviaz' SSSR: statisticheskii sbornik.* [Transport and communications in the USSR: a statistical handbook]. (TsSU SSSR). M.: Statistika, 1972. 320 pp.

Previous volumes publ. in 1967 (324 pp.) and 1957 (260 pp.). As well as data on roads, railways, sea and inland waterways, covers pipelines, public transport and workers in transport and communications. The section on communications deals with postal and telegraph services, telephones, radio and TV receivers. The handbooks include historical data, where appropriate.

UNION REPUBLICS

Armenia

U1219 *Transport i sviaz' Armianskoi SSR za riad let: statisticheskii sbornik.* [Transport and communications in Armenia over many years: a statistical handbook]. (TsSU ArmSSR). Erevan, 1967. 149 pp.

Covers rail and road transport from 1940, air transport from 1955, and urban passenger transport from 1933.

Latvia

U1220 *Transport i sviaz' Latviiskoi SSR: statisticheskii sbornik.* [Transport and communications in Latvia: a statistical handbook]. (TsSU LatvSSR). Riga: Latv. otd-nie izd-va 'Statistika', 1971. 154 pp.

Earlier edition publ. 1968 (115 pp.). Detailed figures on all types of transport and communication in Latvia.

General collections of documents

U1221 *Sbornik zakonodatel'nykh i vedomstvennykh rukovodiashchikh materialov po voprosam Ministerstva sviazi SSSR.* [A collection of legislative and departmental materials guiding the work of the USSR Ministry of Communications]. M., 1957. [Not seen. Apparently not publicly available].

U1222 *Transport i perevozki v torgovle: sbornik normativnykh materialov.* [Transport and freight in trade: a collection of normative acts]. Sost.: V. N. Alipov [i dr.]. M.: Gostorgizdat, 1959. 622 pp.

Includes regulations as of 1 November 1958, with a few later acts in a supplement. Covers regulations, prices etc. for freight transport by rail, road, air and ship.

Translations of legislation on transport and communications, in addition to items specifically referred to below, can be found in *Collected legislation* (U158) section IV:6.

Road transport

U1223 Bykov, A. G. *Kommentarii k Ustavam avtomobil'nogo transporta soiuznykh respublik.* [Commentary on the Statutes on Motor Vehicle Transport of the union republics, by] A. G. Bykov [i dr.]. M.: Iurid. lit-ra, 1978. 232 pp.

Commentary based on the 1969 RSFSR Statute, indicating provisions in the union republics' statutes where these differ.

U1224 Bykov, A. G. *Kommentarii k Ustavu avtomobil'nogo transporta RSFSR.* [Commentary on the RSFSR Statute on Motor Vehicle Transport. By] A. G. Bykov [i dr.]. M.: Iurid. lit-ra, 1973. 280 pp.

Commentary on the 1969 Statute.

U1225 *Sbornik zakonodatel'stva po avtomobil'nomu transportu.* [A collection of legislation on motor vehicle transport]. M.: Iurid. lit-ra, 1964. 435 pp.

USSR and RSFSR normative acts regulating motor vehicle transport, particularly lorries and public transport vehicles.

U1226 *Voditel', avtomobil', doroga: sbornik osnovnykh normativnykh aktov po dorozhnomu dvizheniiu.* [The driver, the car and the road: a collection of basic normative documents]. M.: Iurid. lit-ra, 1978. 224 pp.

A handbook for drivers and car-owners, based on laws and regulations in force on 1 July 1977. As well as the all-union regulations on the registration of vehicles, procedures for qualifying as a driver, insurance and vehicle inspection regulations and the road traffic rules, includes details of current penalties for traffic offences and excerpts from union republic legislation affecting drivers.

Railways

U1227 *Gudok.* [The whistle]. 1917–. 6 per week.

Newspaper of the USSR Ministry of Transport and the Union of Railway Workers, and a source of official materials on transport, particularly the railways.

U1228 *Kommentarii k Ustavu zheleznykh dorog SSSR.* [Commentary on the USSR Railway Statute. By] G. B. Astanovskii et al. Izd. 2-e. M.: Iurid. lit-ra, 1971. 317 pp.

1st ed., called *Ustav zheleznykh dorog SSSR: nauchno-prakticheskii kommentarii,* publ. 1966 (271 pp.). These are very detailed commentaries on the 1964 Statute.

U1229 *Zheleznodorozhnyi transport v dokumentakh Kommunisticheskoi partii i sovetskogo pravitel'stva, 1917–1957: sbornik.* [A collection of CPSU and Soviet government documents on the railways, 1917–57]. M.: Transzheldorizdat, 1957. 383 pp.

A collection of documents mainly from the prewar period, mostly given in full with references to the original official source.

Water transport

U1230 Khodunov, M. E. *Prakticheskii kommentarii k Ustavu vnutrennego vodnogo transporta.* [Practical commentary on the Statute on Internal Water Transport]. 2. izd., ispr. i dop. M.: Rechnoi transport, 1955. 181 pp.

1st ed. publ. 1952 (168 pp.). Commentary on the 1930 Statute, including all later amendments.

U1231 *Khoziaistvennye dogovory i khozraschet: sbornik postanovlenii, prikazov i instruktsii, otnosiashchikhsia k rechnomu transportu.* [Contracts and accounting in river transport: a collection of ordinances, orders and instructions]. 2 izd., perer. i dop. M.: Izd-vo M-va rechnogo flota SSSR, 1950. 259 pp.

1st ed. publ. 1941 (372 pp.). Includes a wide range of regulations affecting financial arrangements and contractual relations involving river transport, as of 1 April 1950. Fully indexed.

U1232 *Kodeks torgovogo moreplavaniia Soiuza SSR.* [The Merchant Shipping Code of the USSR]. (M-vo iustitsii SSSR). M.: Iurid. lit-ra, 1972. 62 pp.
The 1968 Code.

U1233 *Kommentarii k Kodeksu torgovogo moreplavaniia Soiuza SSR.* [Commentary on the Merchant Shipping Code of the USSR]. Pod red. A. L. Makovskogo. (Soiuzmorniiproekt. Tsentr. NII morskogo transporta). M.: Transport, 1973. 398 pp.
On the 1968 Code.

U1234 *The Merchant Shipping Code of the Soviet Union*; trans. and notes by Z. Szirmai and J. D. Korevaar, foreword by R. P. Cleveringa. (Law in Eastern Europe, 4). Leiden: Sijthoff, 1960. 151 pp.
An annotated translation of the 1929 Code.

U1235 *The Merchant Shipping Code of the USSR (1968)*; trans. and ed. by W. E. Butler and M. B. Quigley, Jr. Baltimore, London: Johns Hopkins University Press, 1970. xii, 169 pp.
As well as the Code, has some subsidiary USSR legislation in the appendices and a glossary. Selected bibliography.

U1236 *Sbornik mezhdunarodnykh konventsii, dogovorov, soglashenii i pravil po voprosam torgovogo moreplavaniia.* [A collection of international treaties, conventions, agreements and rules on merchant shipping]. (M-vo morskogo flota SSSR). M.: Morskoi transport, 1959. 475 pp.
Earlier edition: *Mezhdunarodnye konventsii i soglasheniia, otnosiashchiesia k torgovomu moreplavaniiu (sbornik).* M., Leningrad: Morskoi transport, 1951. 322 pp. A collection of documents to which the USSR is a signatory.

U1237 *Sbornik normativnykh aktov po morskomu transportu.* [A collection of normative acts on maritime transport]. Sost.: G. A. Kostylev. (Tsentr. NII morskogo flota). M.: Transport, 1968. 447 pp.
Covers the planning and organization of maritime transport, the regulation of ports and shipping in the USSR's territorial waters, safety and rescue, accidents and insurance. Most of the documents included were in force on 1 July 1967; some not previously published.

U1238 *Sbornik zakonodatel'stva po vnutrennemu vodnomu transportu.* [A collection of legislation on internal water transport]. M.: Iurid. lit-ra, 1964. 174 pp.
Includes USSR and RSFSR normative acts on internal water transport in force on 1 January 1964, with the 1955 Statute on Internal Water Transport.

U1239 *Sbornik zakonov i rasporiazhenii po morskomu transportu (rukovodiashchie materialy).* [A collection of laws, ordinances and guiding materials on maritime transport]. Sost.: V. Manzhin. (M-vo morskogo flota SSSR). M., Leningrad: Morskoi transport, 1948. 602 pp.

Earlier editions publ. 1921, 1923, 1924, 1928, 1931 and 1940. Includes the 1929 Merchant Shipping Code and other regulations on ports, shipping and workers in maritime transport. Subject index.

U1240 'Soviet maritime law'. *Soviet statutes and decisions*, vol. 6, 1969–70.
This vol. of *SS&D* (*see* U164) deals with all aspects of Soviet maritime law, including territorial waters, internal sea waters, the continental shelf and the deep seabed, and the high seas.

U1241 *Vodnyi transport*. [Water transport]. 1932–. 2 per week.
Had title *Rechnoi transport* 1940–1 and 1943–March 1953. Newspaper of the USSR Ministry of Merchant Shipping, the RSFSR Ministry of River Transport and the sailors' trade union. Useful for information on river and sea transport.

See also U912, U1211 and U1275.

Air

U1242 'Air Code of the USSR'. *Law in Eastern Europe, 14: Miscellanea II. Articles and texts*. Leiden: Sijthoff, 1967. Pp. 86–116.
The translation is accompanied by other USSR legislation on air transport, and has an introduction on the differences between the 1961 Code and the 1935 Code.

U1243 *The Air Code of the USSR*. Trans. and annotated by Denis A. Cooper. Charlottesville, Va.: Michie, 1966. xx, 298 pp.
Annotated translation of the 1961 Code, with detailed introductory notes on Soviet aviation law and an index.

U1244 *Perevozka passazhirov na vozdushnom transporte SSSR v 1968 godu*. [Passenger transport by air in the USSR in 1968]. (M-vo grazhdanskoi aviatsii SSSR. Gos. NII grazhdanskoi aviatsii). M., 1970. 307 pp.
Data for 1965–8, by quarterly periods. Covers number of passengers, distance flown, routes and airports used.

U1245 Vinogradov, A. V. *Vozdushnyi kodeks SSSR. S kommentariiami i postateino-sist. materialami*. [The USSR Air Code, with a commentary and subsidiary legislation, by] A. V. Vinogradov, A. V. Kuchel'. (Gl. upr. grazhdanskogo vozdushnogo flota SSSR). M., 1949. 219 pp.
1st ed. publ. 1938 (176 pp.). Commentary and text of the 1935 Code, with other relevant legislation.

U1246 *Vozdushnyi kodeks SSSR*. [Air Code of the USSR]. M.: Aeroflot, 1948. 52 pp.
The text of the Air Code enacted 7 August 1935.

U1247 *Vozdushnyi kodeks Soiuza SSSR*. [Air Code of the USSR]. M., 1974. 93 pp.

The text of the Air Code enacted 26 December 1971, in force from 1 January 1972, with amendments to 1 April 1974.

Trade

Internal trade

Most of the trade network is state owned, and is supervised by the Ministry of Trade of the USSR and the ministries of trade in the union republics. It also supervises the work of Tsentrosoiuz, the Central Union of Consumer Cooperatives which now serves mainly the rural areas. For translations of legal material on trade, in addition to items listed below, consult *Collected legislation* (U158) section IV:7.

STATISTICS

All-union

U1248 *Osnovnye itogi razvitiia potrebitel'skoi kooperatsii SSSR za ... gody.* [Basic data on the development of consumer cooperatives in the USSR in ...]. (Tsentrosoiuz). M.
1966–69. 1970. 98 pp.
1970–73. 1974. 100 pp.
1971–75. 1976. 130 pp.
The 1970 and 1974 volumes had title *Potrebitel'skaia kooperatsiia SSSR za. . . .* The handbooks include data, broken down to union republic level, on the volume of trade, its value, trade networks, staff, investment, etc.

U1249 *Sovetskaia torgovlia: statisticheskii sbornik.* [Soviet trade: a statistical handbook]. M.: Statistika, 1964. 503 pp.
Previous edition publ. 1956 (352 pp.). Covers all aspects of internal wholesale and retail trade, including shops, stocks, staff and profitability. Also covers kolkhoz markets and public catering, and gives price indexes. There are detailed breakdowns to union republic level. The 1964 handbook gives figures to 1963, but coverage of the 1940s and early 1950s is better in the 1956 edition.

Union republics
RSFSR

U1250 *Sovetskaia torgovlia v RSFSR: statisticheskii sbornik.* [Trade in the RSFSR: a statistical handbook]. (TsSU RSFSR). M.: Gosstatizdat, 1958. 343 pp.
Data on retail trade, broken down by regions and type of store; includes data on kolkhoz markets.

Armenia

U1251 *Sovetkskaia torgovlia v Armianskoi SSR: statisticheskii sbornik.* [Statistical handbook on trade in Armenia]. Erevan: Statistika, 1966. 212 pp. [Not seen].

Azerbaijan

U1252 *Razvitie sovetskoi torgovli v Azerbaidzhanskoi SSR: statisticheskii sbornik.* [The development of trade in Azerbaijan: statistical handbook]. Baku, 1962. 240 pp. [Not seen].

U1253 *Sovetskaia torgovlia za gody semiletki, 1959–1965 gg.: statisticheskii sbornik.* [Trade in 1959–1965: a statistical handbook for Azerbaijan]. (TsSU AzSSR). Baku, 1966. 182 pp. [For official use only. Not seen].

Latvia

U1254 *Razvitie sovetskoi torgovli v Latviiskoi SSR: statisticheskii sbornik.* [Development of trade in Latvia: a statistical handbook]. (TsSU LatvSSR). Riga: Gosstatizdat, 1968. 232 pp.
Earlier editions, publ. 1962 (374 pp.) and 1957 (144 pp.). [Not seen].

U1255 *Roznichnaia torgovlia Latviiskoi SSR v 1978 g.: statisticheskii ezhegodnik.* [Retail trade in Latvia in 1978: a statistical yearbook.]. Riga, 1979. 124 pp. [Not seen].

Lithuania

U1256 *Torgovlia Litovskoi SSR v . . . godu: statisticheskii sbornik.* [Trade in Lithuania in . . .: a statistical handbook]. Vilnius, 1970–. Annual. [Not seen].

U1257 *Torgovlia Litovskoi SSR v 1971–1975 godakh: statisticheskii sbornik.* [Trade in Lithuania in 1971–1975: a statistical handbook]. Vilnius: TsSU LitSSR, 1976. 278 pp.
150 copies printed. Covers wholesale and retail trade and the kolkhoz markets.

Ukraine

U1258 *Radians'ka torhivlia v Ukrains'kii RSR: statystychnyi zbirnyk.* [Trade in the Ukraine: a statistical handbook]. (TsSU URSR). Kyiv: Statystyka, 1971. 321 pp.
Earlier edition publ. 1963 (319 pp.). Data on state and cooperative retail trade and kolkhoz markets, with many tables broken down to oblast´ level, or by product. Figures go from 1940 to 1961 in the 1963 edition and 1940 to 1970 in the 1971 edition.

COLLECTIONS OF DOCUMENTS

U1259 *Sbornik materialov po okhrane sotsialisticheskoi sobstvennosti.* [A collection of materials on the protection of socialist property]. Sost.: N. A. Vinogradov, V. N. Sil'vanov. M.: Gosiurizdat, 1952. 251 pp.
A collection of materials in force on 1 March 1952 for accountants, auditors and legal personnel of the Ministry of Trade, covering criminal liability, weights and measures regulations, precautions against theft, staff liability, accounting, auditing and supervisory procedures to prevent and detect embezzlement, theft, etc.

U1260 *Sbornik postanovlenii i vedomstvennykh ukazanii po torgovoi rabote potrebitel'skoi kooperatsii.* [A collection of ordinances and departmental instructions on the trading activities of consumer cooperatives]. M.: KOIZ, 1948. 120 pp. [Not seen].

U1261 *Sbornik prikazov i instruktsii Ministerstva torgovli RSFSR.* [A collection of orders and instructions from the Ministry of Trade of the RSFSR]. M., 1941–9.

Frequency varied. 1941–5 title was *Sbornik prikazov, rasporiazhenii i instruktsii Narodnogo komissariata torgovli RSFSR.* Consists of letters, instructions and so on of the ministry.

U1262 *Sovetskaia torgovlia.* [Soviet trade]. 1926–41, 1953–. 2 per week.

Newspaper of the USSR Ministry of Trade and the Central Committee of the union for workers in state and cooperative trade. A source for developments in internal trade and consumer affairs.

U1263 'Soviet administrative law: administrative control of retail trade'. *Soviet statutes and decisions,* vol. 5, no. 2, 1968–9.

This issue of *SS&D* (*see* U164) deals with legislation controlling retail trade.

See also U1022, U1212–U1214, U1222 and U1295.

Foreign trade

The Ministry of Foreign Trade has the primary political responsibility for operating the USSR's state monopoly of foreign trade, and is empowered to negotiate trade and payment treaties, determine customs and tariff policy, devise foreign trade plans and determine other policy matters. It also supervises the work of the all-union foreign trade corporations, which conduct transactions with foreign buyers and sellers; each corporation deals with a particular category of goods or services. The Ministry of Foreign Trade is also responsible for the work of the All-Union Chamber of Commerce and Industry and its two tribunals which deal primarily with foreign trade disputes, the Moscow Foreign Trade Arbitration Commission and the Maritime Arbitration Commission. In addition to the translations recorded below, translations of legal material on foreign trade can be found in *Collected legislation* (U158) section V:2.

STATISTICS

U1264 *Vneshniaia torgovlia SSSR: statisticheskii sbornik, 1918–1966.* [The foreign trade of the USSR: a statistical handbook, 1918–1966]. (M-vo vneshnei torigovli SSSR. Planovo-ekon. upr.). M.: Mezhdunarodnye otnosheniia, 1967. 242 pp.

Statistical data on the USSR's foreign trade, arranged in three periods—prewar, during the Second World War, postwar—with a supplement on Russia's foreign trade in 1913. For each period, the first section gives an overall trading position and the second a breakdown by country.

U1265 *Vneshniaia torgovlia SSSR v ... g.: statisticheskii sbornik.* [The foreign trade of the USSR in ...: a statistical handbook]. (M-vo vneshnei torgovli SSSR. Gl. planovo-ekon. upr.). M.: Statistika, 1960 (publ. 1961)–. Annual.

1960–74 called *Vneshniaia torgovlia SSSR za ... g.* Published first in soft covers as a supplement to the journal *Vneshniaia torgovlia*, usually with the July issue; a hardback version is published separately later in the year. This handbook is the main source of current statistical information on the USSR's foreign trade, with tables on the volume of trade, its distribution by country and type of product, and mode of transport.

U1266   *Vneshniaia torgovlia SSSR za ... gody: statisticheskii sbornik.* [The foreign trade of the USSR in ...: statistical handbook]. (M-vo vneshnei torgovli SSSR. Planovo-ekon. upr.). M.: Vneshtorgizdat.
... *1955–59.* 1961. 623 pp.
... *1959–63.* 1965. 483 pp.
... *[1955–68].* 1969. 244 pp.

The 1969 volume had title *Vneshniaia torgovlia SSSR: statisticheskii spravochnik.* These three handbooks give similar coverage to U1265 above for the years covered; in some tables comparison is made with 1938.

DOCUMENTS ON FOREIGN TRADE

U1267   *Edinaia tovarnaia nomenklatura vneshnei torgovli.* [Unified schedule of goods in foreign trade]. Red.: V. T. Zoloev. (M-vo vneshnei torgovli. Planovo-ekon. upr.). M.: Vneshtorgizdat, 1954. 382 pp.

Detailed classification of goods and raw materials imported and exported from the USSR. The first part is the classified list, the second an alphabetical index.

U1268   *Sbornik normativnykh aktov i dokumentov po vneshnei torgovle SSSR (uchebno-metodicheskie materialy).* [A collection of normative acts and documents on Soviet foreign trade]. Sost.: L. M. Chuprunova. (Vses. akademiia vneshnei torgovli. Kafedra pravovykh distsiplin). M., 1979. 278 pp.

Only 300 copies published. A collection of basic legal and other documents on foreign trade, compiled for student use. Covers supply of goods, transport, insurance, patents and copyrights, statutes of foreign trade corporations and other official bodies involved in foreign trade. Many in extract form.

U1269   *Sbornik normativnykh materialov po voprosam vneshnei torgovli SSSR (po sost. na 1 avgusta 1956 g.).* [A collection of normative documents on Soviet foreign trade, as of 1 August 1956]. Sost.: F. M. Borisov [i dr.]. M.: Vneshtorgizdat, 1956. 670 pp.

A supplement to 1 August 1957 publ. 1957. Copy seen of the 1956 volume was individually numbered and for restricted circulation only. The documents in it, many of which had not been published elsewhere, are from the Council of Ministers, the Ministry of

Foreign Trade and other foreign trade bodies and cover the state monopoly of foreign trade, import and export, foreign currency, transport, trademarks, disputes and organizational matters.

U1270 *Sbornik normativnykh materialov po voprosam vneshnei torgovli SSSR.* [A collection of normative documents on Soviet foreign trade]. (M-vo vneshnei torgovli SSSR). M.: Mezhdunarodnye otnosheniia, 1970. 2 vols.

Earlier edition publ. 1961 (2 vols.). Although the first volume of this work is publicly available, vol. 2 is not. The first volume covers general policy matters, customs, transport, insurance, economic cooperation with socialist countries, patents and trademarks, and disputes procedure. The 1961 edition includes material as of 1 September 1960, the 1970 volume as of 10 August 1969.

U1271 *Sbornik postanovlenii pravitel'stva SSSR po voprosam vneshnei torgovli.* [A collection of ordinances of the Soviet government on foreign trade]. M.: Mezhdunarodnaia kniga, 1947. 127 pp.

Includes material in force on 1 August 1947; all have been published previously.

U1272 *Sbornik torgovykh dogovorov i soglashenii po torgovo-ekonomicheskomu sotrudnichestvu SSSR s inostrannymi gosudarstvami (na 1 ianvaria 1977 goda).* [A collection of trade treaties and agreements on trade and economic cooperation with foreign countries, as of 1 January 1977]. (M-vo vneshnei torgovli SSSR. Dogovorno-pravovoe upr.). M.: Ekonomika, 1977. 2 vols.

Earlier editions: *Sbornik torgovykh dogovorov, torgovykh i platezhnykh soglashenii i dolgosrochnykh torgovykh soglashenii SSSR s inostrannymi gosudarstvami (na 1 ianvaria 1961 goda).* M.: Vneshtorgizdat, 1961. 624 pp.; and ... *na 1 ianvaria 1965 goda.* 1965. 886 pp. These collections give the texts of all agreements signed since 1924 and still in force. Cover economic, industrial, scientific and technical cooperation as well as financial arrangements and foreign trade matters.

U1273 *Vneshniaia torgovlia: organ Ministerstva vneshnei torgovli SSSR.* [Foreign trade; organ of the USSR Ministry of Foreign Trade]. M., 1931–. Monthly.

Frequency varied in 1930s and early 1940s. Also published in English, Spanish, German and Italian. As well as authoritative articles on foreign trade by ministers and other officials, publishes news items on foreign trade, reports of the USSR Chamber of Commerce, charters of foreign trade corporations, texts of trade agreements and notes about the USSR's commercial counsellors. Annual index.

FOREIGN TRADE ARBITRATION COMMISSION

U1274 *Arbitrazhnaia praktika: resheniia Vneshnetorgovoi arbitrazhnoi komissii ... gg.* [Arbitration practice: decisions of the Foreign Trade

Arbitration Commission in . . .]. Sost.: A. I. Shpektorov. (Torgovo-promyshlennaia palata SSSR). M., 1972–.

The first four volumes, publ. in 1972, covered 1934–65; vol. 5 covering 1966–8 publ. 1975; and vol. 6 covering 1969–70 publ. 1976. Appears to be a continuing series. The collections include a selection of the most interesting and significant cases heard during the period covered. A translation of the collection is being published in the USSR, called *Arbitration practice*.

U1275   *International commercial arbitration: Soviet commercial and maritime arbitration*. Comp. and ed. by W. E. Butler. London, Rome, New York: Oceana, 1980–.

'Contains the past and present legislation governing Soviet foreign trade and maritime arbitration and an extensive selection of awards rendered by the USSR Foreign Trade Arbitration Committee from its inception in 1934'. Looseleaf format. First volume covers up to 1965. Subject index and bibliography.

CUSTOMS

U1276   *Customs Code of the USSR*. Trans. and ed. by W. E. Butler. Washington, D.C.: Hazen, 1966. 55 pp.

Includes the 1964 Code in Russian and English.

U1277   *Tamozhennyi kodeks Soiuza SSR: ofitsial'nyi tekst*. [Official text of the USSR Customs Code]. M.: Iurid. lit-ra, 1973. 32 pp.

Text of the 1964 Code.

U1278   *Tamozhennyi tarif SSSR*. [The customs tariff of the USSR]. (M-vo vneshnei torgovli SSSR. Gl. tamozhennoe upr.). M.: Vneshtorgizdat, 1962. 118 pp.

Contains the customs tariff relating to imported goods which came into force on 1 October 1961.

Standards, patents and inventions

The State Committee on Standards (Gosstandart) is responsible for the issue of state standards (usually called GOSTy), and maintains registers of its standards and those of the union republics. Patents are the responsibility of the State Committee for Inventions and Discoveries. This committee also registers trademarks.

Standards

U1279   *Gosudarstvennye standarty SSSR: informatsionnyi ukazatel'*. [State standards of the USSR: an information bulletin]. (Gos. komitet SSSR po standartam). M.: Izd-vo standartov, 1941–. Monthly.

1940–68 title was *Informatsionnyi ukazatel' standartov*; 1969–73 title was *Informatsionnyi ukazatel' gosudarstvennykh standartov SSSR*. A current list of new standards, and of Comecon standards adopted in the USSR, arranged by subject sequence. Also gives brief details on amendments to existing standards and the numbers of standards which have been replaced.

U1280 *Gosudarstvennye standarty SSSR: ukazatel' (po sost. na 1 ianvaria ...g.): izdanie ofitsial'noe.* [An official index of state standards of the USSR in force on 1 January ...]. (Gos. komitet SSSR po standartam). M.: Izd-vo standartov, [1943?]–. Annual.

Publishing history unclear. Since 1973, has appeared in three parts. A subject listing of GOSTy currently in force, with indexes by reference number and by subject, and of Comecon standards.

U1281 *Otraslevye i respublikanskie standarty: informatsionnyi ukazatel'.* [Branch and republican standards: an information bulletin]. M.: Izd-vo standartov, 1967–. Monthly.

Lists new standards for the union republics and for particular branches of industry.

U1282 *Otraslevye i respublikanskie standarty: ukazatel'.* [Branch and republican standards: an index]. M.: Izd-vo standartov, [1978?]–. [Annual?].

Starting date and frequency unclear. The 1978 edition appeared in three volumes, two listing standards by branch of industry, showing the original branch or republican index number, and the third providing a key to the first two, by branch or republican index number. Lists standards currently in force.

Patents, inventions and trademarks

U1283 *Otkrytiia, izobreteniia, promyshlennye obraztsy, tovarnye znaki.* [Discoveries, inventions, industrial designs and trademarks]. (Gos. komitet SSSR po delam izobretenii i otkrytii). M., 1924–. 48 p.a.

1924–36 called *Vestnik Komiteta po delam izobreteniia i otkrytii*; 1937–June 1946 *Ezhemesiachnyi biulleten'*; July 1946–7 *Ezhemesiachnyi biulleten' izobretenii*; 1948–62 *Biulleten' izobretenii*; 1963–5 *Biulleten' izobretenii i tovarnykh znakov*; 1966–? *Izobreteniia, promyshlennye obraztsy, tovarnye znaki.* Mainly monthly to 1958; semi-monthly 1959–67; 36 p.a. 1968–72; 48 p.a. 1973–. Gives brief details of new patents and inventions, trademarks and designs registered. Since 1967, it has had an annual index of names and index numbers.

U1284 *Sbornik zakonodatel'nykh aktov i postanovlenii po izobretatel'stvu i ratsionalizatsii.* [A collection of legislation and ordinances on inventions and rationalization]. Izd. 3-e, ispr. i dop. (Gos. komitet SSSR po delam izobretenii i otkrytii SSSR). M.: Tsentr. NII patentnoi informatsii i tekhniko-ekon. issl., 1965. 311 pp.

1st ed. publ. 1961 (144 pp.), 2nd ed. publ. 1962 (175 pp.) As well as government materials and legislation, includes ministry and trade documents. Also covers trademarks.

U1285 'Soviet patent law'. *Soviet statutes and decisions*, vol. 13, nos. 1–4, 1976–7.
This volume of *SS&D* (*see* U164) covers all aspects of patent law.

U1286 *Vnedrennye izobreteniia.* [Introduced inventions]. (Gos. komitet po delam izobretenii i otkrytii. Tsentr. NII patentnoi informatsii i tekhniko-ekon. issl.). 1968–. 6 p.a.
1968–72 published quarterly. A bulletin listing inventions and adaptations to existing processes or equipment, actually brought into use in Soviet factories.

U1287 *Zakonodatel'stvo ob izobretatel'stve i ratsionalizatsii: sbornik normativnykh materialov.* [A collection of normative materials on inventions and rationalization]. Pod red. A. N. Iakimenko. Kiev: Politizdat Ukrainy, 1973. 390 pp.
A collection of all-union material in force in December 1972, intended for the mass reader. Subject arrangement.

U1288 *Zakonodatel'stvo SSSR po izobretatel'stvu.* [Soviet legislation on inventions]. Pod red. A. I. Dvorkina. (Gos. komitet SSSR po delam izobretenii i otkrytii. Tsentr. NII patentnoi informatsii i tekhniko-ekon. issl.). M., 1979. 3 vols.
Includes material in force on 1 January 1978, in a subject arrangement. Covers all aspects of inventions, patents and trademarks.

SOCIAL AFFAIRS

This section includes material on a number of social matters: the standard cf living in general, housing and communal services, health and sport, social insurance and social security, and materials on special provision for women, children and young people. Material on working conditions and wages is in the section 'Economic affairs'.

General material on living standards

U1289 *V. I. Lenin, KPSS o povyshenii zhiznennogo urovnia trudiashchikhsia: dokumenty i materialy.* [V. I. Lenin and the CPSU on raising the workers' living standards: documents and materials]. M.: Politizdat, 1975. 375 pp.
The first third consists of Lenin's writings on workers' standard of living; the rest is made up of CPSU documents, mainly postwar, on income, housing and services, working conditions, pensions and social security, etc.

U1290 *Zabota partii i pravitel'stva o blage naroda: sbornik dokumentov.* [The concern of the party and the government for the people's welfare: a collection of documents]. M.: Politizdat.
[*Kn. 1*] *Oktiabr' 1964–1973.* 1974. 847 pp.
Kn. 2. 1974–fevral' 1980. 1980. 751 pp.

A chronological collection of party and government resolutions, decrees, regulations, etc. on living standards, incomes, public services, health care, working conditions, etc. Subject index.

See also U1000.

Housing and communal services

Housing and communal services are the responsibility of the republican ministries of housing and communal services and are administered by local soviets in the case of publicly owned facilities. In addition, housing is often built by enterprises for their own employees and some types of services are also provided by enterprises. There is also cooperatively owned housing and, mainly in rural areas, privately owned housing. The State Committee on Construction is involved in housing matters as the chief authority on building and on town planning matters. There is no ministry at all-union level responsible for housing and communal services. The trade unions, both at local level and at national level, take an active interest in the provision and allocation of housing and of other social services, such as nursery places. The law on housing is part of the civil law, and further materials dealing in part with housing will be found in that sub-section, which forms part of the section 'Law and judicial system'; documents dealing with the construction industry are in the section 'Economic affairs', as are documents dealing with trade, transport and communications.

Statistics on housing and communal services

For figures at all-union level, see the general handbooks listed in the section 'General statistics'; consult that section for those republics which have not produced any special handbooks on this topic.

ARMENIA

U1291 *Zhilishchno-kommunal'noe khoziaistvo Armianskoi SSR.* [Housing and public utilities in Armenia: a statistical handbook]. (TsSU ArmSSR). Erevan, 1967. 169 pp.

Detailed figures (broken down to town level in some cases) on housing and utilities from 1940 to 1965; some tables go back to 1921.

LATVIA

U1292 *Zhilishchno-kommunal'noe khoziaistvo i bytovoe obsluzhivanie naseleniia v Latviiskoi SSR: statisticheskii sbornik.* [Housing, public utilities and other services to the population in Latvia: a statistical handbook]. (TsSU LatvSSR). Riga, 1969. 192 pp. [Not seen].

MOLDAVIA

U1293 *Bytovoe obsluzhivanie naseleniia Moldavskoi SSR: statisticheskii sbornik.* [Services to the population in Moldavia: a statistical handbook]. (TsSU MSSR). Kishinev, 1975. 164 pp.

Figures for 1960, 1965 and 1970–4 on a wide range of services including repair facilities, laundries and dry-cleaners, photo-graphers, workshops, ateliers and the staff of such establishments. Gives an urban/rural breakdown.

U1294　*Zhilishchno-kommunal'noe khoziaistvo Moldavskoi SSR: statisticheskii sbornik.* [Housing and public utilities in Moldavia: a statistical handbook]. Kishinev, 1974. 209 pp. [Not seen].

UKRAINE

U1295　*Razvitie obshchestvennogo pitaniia v Ukrainskoi SSR: osnovnye pokazateli.* [The development of public catering facilities in the Ukraine: general indicators]. Kiev: Gosstatizdat, 1963. 63 pp. [Not seen].

Town planning, public utilities and housing in general

U1296　*Sbornik normativnykh i spravochnykh materialov po razvitiiu gorodov.* [Collection of normative and reference materials on town development]. (Tsentr. nauch.-issl. ekon. in-t pri Gosplane RSFSR). M.: Stroiizdat, 1980. 185 pp.

A wide range of official documents from the USSR and RSFSR Council of Ministers and Supreme Soviet, instructions, rules, etc. from Gosstroi, Gosgrazhdanstroi, and other ministries and organizations affecting town planning.

U1297　*Spravochnik po zakonodatel'stvu dlia rabotnikov zhilishchno-kommunal'nogo khoziaistva.* [Manual on legislation for workers in housing and public utilities]. Sost.: L. N. Andreevskii. M.: Stroiizdat, 1964. 587 pp.

Includes USSR and RSFSR legislation in force on 1 August 1963.

U1298　*Zakonodatel'stvo o zhilishchno-kommunal'nom khoziaistve.* [Legislation on housing and communal services]. M.: Iurid. lit-ra, 1972–3. 2 vols.

Contains USSR and RSFSR legislation, ordinances of the USSR and RSFSR Council of Ministers, official documents from various ministries and state committees and decisions of the USSR and RSFSR Supreme Court relating to housing, town planning and the provision of communal services. The collection includes material in force in July 1972. Subject index.

U1299　*Zhilishchno-bytovye voprosy: ofitsial'nye materialy, konsul'tatsii.* [Problems of housing and public services: official materials, consultations]. M.: Profizdat, 1971. 192 pp.

Earlier editions publ. 1960 (255 pp.) and 1964 (291 pp.). A collection for trade union and soviet officials on housing, trade, public catering, services, transport and allotments, including ordinances and other normative materials from the Council of Ministers, the All-Union Central Council of Trade Unions and various ministries.

Housing

U1300 *Pravo na zhiluiu ploshchad': sbornik rukovodiashchikh normativnykh aktov i sudebnoi praktiki po primeneniiu zhilishchnogo zakonodatel'stva. (Prakticheskoe posobie dlia iuristov).* [The right to housing: a collection of normative acts and court practice to guide lawyers in the implementation of housing legislation]. (Leningradskii obshchestvennyi NII sudebnoi praktiki). Leningrad: Lenizdat, 1973. 302 pp.

A guide intended mainly for use in the Leningrad area, and including major decisions and regulations of the Leningrad town and oblast' soviets, as well as the main USSR and RSFSR normative acts and decisions of the USSR and RSFSR Supreme Courts on housing matters. Subject index.

U1301 *Sbornik zhilishchnogo zakonodatel'stva.* [A collection of housing legislation]. M.: Iurid. lit-ra, 1963. 586 pp.

A collection of USSR and RSFSR legislation and ordinances on the construction and administration of housing. The collection includes materials in force in January 1961. Subject index.

U1302 *Zhilishchno-bytovaia rabota profsoiuzov: sbornik ofitsial'nykh materialov.* [Trade union housing work: a collection of official materials]. M.: Profizdat, 1979. 208 pp.

A collection of material for trade union officials on housing matters; as well as trade union documents, it includes a number of government documents.

U1303 *Zhilishchnoe i zhilishchno-stroitel'noe zakonodatel'stvo.* [Housing and house-construction legislation]. 3 izd., ispr. i dop. Kiev: Budivel'nyk, 1967. 272 pp.

2nd ed. publ. 1964 (355 pp.); 1st ed., called *Zhilishchnoe zakonodatel'stvo SSSR i USSR*, was publ. 1957 (238 pp.). A collection of USSR and Ukrainian normative acts relating to housing and housing construction. Subject index.

U1304 *Zhilishchnoe zakonodatel'stvo.* [Housing legislation]. (M-vo kommunal'nogo khoziaistva BSSR). Minsk: Belarus', 1968. 399 pp.

Earlier edition publ. 1961 (361 pp.). A collection of USSR and Belorussian materials on housing construction, allocation and use.

U1305 *Zhilishchnoe zakonodatel'stvo Kirgizskoi SSR: sbornik normativnykh aktov.* [Housing legislation in Kirghizia: a collection of normative acts]. (M-vo iustitsii KirgSSR). Frunze: Kyrgyzstan, 1976. 268 pp.

Kirghiz normative materials on the jurisdiction of various authorities relating to housing and spatial planning, housing allocation and individual house building. There is a supplement of USSR Supreme Court rulings and guidance on housing matters.

U1306 *Zhilishchnoe zakonodatel'stvo: sbornik ofitsial'nykh materialov.* [Housing legislation: a collection of official materials]. M.: Gosiurizdat, 1950. 579 pp.

A collection of USSR and RSFSR legislation, with cross-references to appropriate articles of union republic legislation; in some cases the text of articles from other republics is given where it differs significantly from the RSFSR or all-union material. Includes extracts from relevant Supreme Court judgements. Subject index.

U1307   *Zhilishchnoe zakonodatel'stvo: sbornik vazhneishikh zakonov, prikazov, instruktivnogo materiala s kommentariem.* [Housing legislation: a collection of the major laws, orders and instructions, with a commentary]. Sost.: A. V. Raudson. Tallin: GIZ Blankoizdat ESSR, 1949. 140 pp.

A collection mainly of Estonian material, with a supplement listing new regulations in force from 1 August 1948.

U1308   *Zhilishchnoe khoziaistvo: sbornik zakonodatel'nykh i instruktivnykh materialov po sostoianiiu na 1 oktiabria 1970 g.* [Housing: a collection of legislation and instructions, as of 1 October 1970]. Sost.: V. P. Fateev. (M-vo kommunal'nogo khoziaistva LitSSR). Vilnius: Mintis, 1971. 469 pp.

A very detailed collection of USSR and Lithuanian materials.

U1309   *Zhilishchnye zakony: sbornik vazhneishikh zakonov SSSR i RSFSR, postanovlenii, instruktsii i prikazov po zhilishchnomu khoziaistvu.* [Housing laws: a collection of the major USSR and RSFSR ordinances, instructions and orders on housing]. Sost.: T. D. Alekseev. 3 izd., dop. i ispr. M.: Izd-vo M-va kommunal'nogo khoziaistva RSFSR, 1957. 737 pp.

1st ed. publ. 1947 (240 pp.), 2nd ed. publ. 1952 (518 pp.). Includes material in force on 1 November 1957 on housing, town planning, land use, housing allocation, housing management and use, rents, exchanges and eviction. Also covers repairs and insurance. Subject index.

Health care

Responsibility for health care lies with the USSR Ministry of Health and the ministries of public health in the union republics. It is now regulated by the Fundamental Principles of Legislation of the USSR and Union Republics on Public Health, adopted by the USSR Supreme Soviet in December 1969.

Statistics on health care

For more recent figures, and more detailed figures on the union republics not listed here, consult the general handbooks in the section 'General statistics'.

USSR

U1310   *Infektsionnye bolezni cheloveka v SSSR: statisticheskii spravochnik.* [Infectious diseases of man in the USSR: a statistical handbook]. Pod red. M. N. Burgasova. (M-vo zdravookhraneniia SSSR). M.: Meditsina, 1968. 64 pp.

Data for the USSR 1913–66 on the incidence of various infectious diseases as a total number of cases registered and incidence per 100,000 population. Has a long section on the USSR's methods of fighting infectious diseases.

U1311 *Tablitsy smertnosti i srednei prodolzhitel'nosti zhizni naseleniia SSSR, 1958–1959 gg.* [Death rates and average life expectancy of the population of the USSR, 1958–1959]. M.: Gosstatizdat, 1962. 27 pp.

A short summary of figures on life expectancy and death rates, with breakdowns for men and women and urban and rural areas.

U1312 *Zdravookhranenie v SSSR: statisticheskii sbornik.* [Health care in the USSR: a statistical handbook]. (TsSU SSSR). M.: Gosstatizdat, 1960. 272 pp.

Earlier editions publ. in 1956 (130 pp.) and 1957 (179 pp.). Contains data on the provision of doctors and other medical personnel, hospitals, clinics, sanatoria, etc., and on the work of the Red Cross and the Red Crescent. Also provides some information on sport and social insurance, and basic data on the birth rate and incidence of disease.

U1313 *Zdravookhranenie v SSSR: statisticheskie materialy.* [Statistical materials on health care in the USSR]. (M-vo zdravookhraneniia SSSR. Otdel meditsinskoi statistiki). M., 1976. 62 pp.

A rather slender collection of statistics covering much the same area as U1312, but in less detail.

UNION REPUBLICS

RSFSR

U1314 *Sostoianie zdorov'ia i meditsinskoe obsluzhivanie naseleniia RSFSR: statisticheskii sbornik.* [The state of health of the population of the RSFSR and their medical services: a statistical collection]. Pod obshchei red. L. A. Brushlinskoi i M. M. Mazura. (M-vo zdravo-okhrancniia RSFSR. Nauchno-mctodicheskoe biuro sanitarnoi statistiki). M., 1963. 136 pp.

Copy marked 'For official use'. Includes general demographic data, data on disease rates, organization of medical services, services for women and children. In many tables, the oblasti are ranked according to the quality of the service provided.

Armenia

U1315 *Zdravookhranenie v Armianskoi SSR: statisticheskii spravochnik.* [Statistical handbook on health care in Armenia]. (M-vo zdravo-okhraneniia ArmSSR. Resp. nauch.-metodicheskoe biuro sanitarnoi statistiki). Erevan: Gosstatizdat, 1960. 81 pp.

Coverage similar to U1312, but limited to Armenia.

Georgia

U1316 *Zdravookhranenie v Gruzinskoi SSR: statisticheskii spravochnik.*

[Handbook of statistics on health care in Georgia]. (M-vo zdravo-okhraneniia GSSR. Otdel meditsinskoi statistiki). Tbilisi: Ganat-leba, 1966. 119 pp. [Not seen].

Moldavia

U1317 *Zdravookhranenie Moldavskoi SSR: statisticheskii spravochnik.* [Handbook of statistics on health care in Moldavia]. (M-vo zdravookhraneniia MSSR. Respublikanskii dom sanitarnogo pro-sveshcheniia). Kishinev: Gosizdat Moldavii, 1958. 80 pp.

Coverage similar to U1312, but limited to Moldavia.

Tajikistan

U1318 *Zdravookhranenie Tadzhikistana: statisticheskii spravochnik.* [Hand-book of statistics on health care in Tajikistan]. Pod red. Ia. T. Tadzhieva. (M-vo zdravookhraneniia TadzhSSR. Otdel meditsin-skoi statistiki). Stalinabad, 1960. 151 pp.

Copy marked 'Not for publication in the open press'. Has considerable data on disease rates and causes of death, but otherwise coverage similar to U1312, for Tajikistan. An unclassified handbook of the same title was publ. in 1957 (107 pp.).

Turkmenistan

U1319 *Zdravookhranenie v Turkmenskoi SSR: statisticheskii spravochnik.* [Handbook of statistics on health care in Turkmenistan]. (M-vo zdravookhranenie TurkmSSR. Otdel meditsinskoi statistiki). Ash-khabad, 1958. 63 pp. [Not seen].

Ukraine

U1320 *Zdravookhranenie v Ukrainskoi SSR: statisticheskii spravochnik.* [Handbook of statistics on health care in the Ukraine]. Kiev: Gosmedizdat Ukrainy, 1960. 251 pp. [Not seen].

Uzbekistan

U1321 *Zdravookhranenie v Uzbekskoi SSR: statisticheskii spravochnik.* [Handbook of statistics on health care in Uzbekistan]. Pod red. L. Ia. Dekhto. (M-vo zdravookhraneniia UzSSR). Tashkent, 1958. 179 pp.

Coverage similar to U1312, but covers Uzbekistan 1945–57.

Documents on health care

U1322 *Meditsinskaia gazeta.* [Medical newspaper]. M., 1938–. 2 per week.

Title was *Meditsinskii rabotnik* 1938–62. Newspaper of the USSR Ministry of Health, USSR Ministry of the Medical Industry and the medical workers' trade union, used for some official material on medical matters.

U1323 *Osnovy zakonodatel'stva Soiuza SSR i soiuznykh respublik o zdra-vookhranenii.* [Fundamental Principles of Health Legislation of the USSR and the Union Republics]. M.: Izvestiia, 1970. 32 pp.

The 1969 Principles.

U1324   *Postanovleniia KPSS i sovetskogo pravitel'stva ob okhrane zdorov'ia naroda.* [Ordinances of the CPSU and the Soviet government on the protection of the nation's health]. (In-t organizatsii zdravookhraneniia i istorii meditsiny M-va zdravookhraneniia SSSR). M.: Medgiz, 1958. 337 pp.

Contains resolutions, ordinances, etc. 1917–56 which were still in force in 1958 or which were of major importance. No material from the union republics is included and some documents are reprinted as extracts only. The documents are arranged chronologically, with a broad subject index.

U1325   *Sbornik normativnykh aktov po aptechnoi sluzhbe.* [A collection of normative acts on the pharmaceutical service]. Pod red. M. A. Kliueva. (M-vo zdravookhraneniia SSSR). M.: Meditsina, 1979. 656 pp.

A collection of over 400 regulations and instructions on the organization, management and staffing of pharmacies in the USSR. Includes regulations governing the supply of medicines to pharmacies, the quality of medicines and their storage. Most of the documents were issued during the 1970s by the USSR Ministry of Health, and the collection includes material in force on 1 April 1979.

U1326   *Spravochnik po organizatsii zdravookhraneniia. Osnovnye postanovleniia pravitel'stva i vedomstvennye materialy.* [Manual on the organization of health services. Basic government ordinances and ministry materials]. Sost.: F. Artem'ev, I. Ermolaev. Otv. red.: A. N. Shabanov. (M-vo zdravookhraneniia SSSR). M.: Medgiz, 1950. 808 pp.

Includes an enormous number of documents, mainly from the USSR Ministry of Health but also from the trade unions and the Council of Ministers, on the official organizations concerned with health care, public health, medical services to particular parts of the country or groups of people, measures relating to epidemics and the reporting of diseases, mental health and dentistry. Also covers blood transfusion services, pharmaceutics and forensic medicine. Supplements deal with staffing and with salaries.

See also U1000, U1007 and U1206.

Sport and physical training

Since 1968, sport has been regulated by the Physical Culture and Sports Committee of the USSR Council of Ministers and its counterparts in the union republics. Before that sport was controlled by the Union of Sports Societies and Organizations of the USSR. In addition, much provision for sport and physical culture is made through the trade union network.

U1327   *Fizicheskaia kul'tura, sport i turizm: sbornik rukovodiashchikh materialov.* [Physical culture, sport and tourism: a collection of guiding materials]. Izd. 2-e, perer. i dop. M.: Profizdat, 1965. 205 pp.

1st ed. publ. 1963 (223 pp.). Earlier editions, with title *Sbornik rukovodiashchikh materialov po fizicheskoi kul'ture i sportu*, publ. 1951 (144 pp.), 1952 (191 pp.) and 1953 (304 pp.). These collections include CPSU and government materials, trade union documents and instructions from the Union of Sports Societies and Organizations on all matters relating to sports facilities, equipment, the organization of sport and recreation, and the financing of these matters.

U1328   *Osnovnye postanovleniia, prikazy i instruktsii po voprosam fizicheskoi kul'tury i sporta, 1917–1957 gg.* [Basic ordinances, orders and instructions on physical culture and sport, 1917–1957]. Sost.: I. G. Chudinov. M.: Fizkul'tura i sport, 1959. 302 pp.

Contains the main party and government decrees, resolutions, etc. on sport and physical culture issued 1917–57 and also publishes for the first time much material from the Committee on Sport and Physical Culture.

U1329   *Sovetskii sport.* [Soviet sport]. 1933–. 6 per week.

1933–46 called *Krasnyi sport*. The USSR's main sports newspaper, published by the Ministry of Health with the interested trade unions and the Physical Culture and Sports Committee or the Union of Sports Societies and Organizations.

Social security and social insurance

Social security and social insurance are the responsibility of the ministries of social insurance in the union republics (there is no all-union Ministry of Social Insurance). Until 1964, collective farmers were not covered by the scheme; their benefits are now mainly financed by contributions made by the collective farm. Broadly speaking, social insurance caters for wage and salary earners, and the social security system covers those not in employment and provides for special needs. Trade union officials carry out much of the administration of social insurance schemes at local level. The collections listed here are either all-union collections, or collections in Russian; details of materials in the languages of the union republics may be found in the bibliographies on finance, U1005a–b.

U1330   Babkin, V. A. *Kommentarii k Polozheniiu o poriadke naznacheniia i vyplaty gosudarstvennykh pensii.* [Commentary on the Regulations on determining and paying state pensions]. [By] V. A. Babkin, G. B. Smirnova. Izd. 2-e, s izm. i dop. M.: Iurid. lit-ra, 1977. 527 pp.

1st ed. publ. 1975 (600 pp.); earlier versions by V. A. Babkin, O. V. Vinogradova and G. B. Smirnova publ. 1964 (459 pp.) and 1969 (536 pp.). Contains the text of the 1956 Regulations on pensions and benefits, and detailed instructions on their interpretation, including the amounts payable.

U1331   *Bibliograficheskii ukazatel' po pravu sotsial'nogo obespecheniia (1917–1975 gg.).* [A bibliography on social insurance law, 1917–1975]. (M-vo sotsial'nogo obespecheniia RSFSR. Tsentr. NII trudosposobnosti i organizatsii truda invalidov). M., 1977–8. 2 vols.

A very thorough listing of material in Russian, including normative acts, on the history of social security and social insurance, pensions, unemployment, maternity, child and welfare benefits and other social services, financial and organizational matters. Index of authors, editors and compilers.

U1332 *Gosudarstvennoe sotsial'noe strakhovanie: sbornik ofitsial'nykh materialov.* [State social insurance: a collection of official materials]. M.: Profizdat, 1963. 367 pp.

Earlier editions publ. 1948, 1949, 1953, 1954, 1957 and 1959. A handbook for trade union officials and others dealing with pensions and benefits. Includes trade union and government documents. Subject index.

U1333 Kats, R. R. *Pensii po kooperativnomu strakhovaniiu: postateinyi kommentarii.* [A commentary on cooperative insurance benefits]. [By] R. R. Kats, V. A. Acharkan, M.: Vses. kooperativnoe izd-vo, 1958. 159 pp.

A commentary on the 1956 Regulations on social insurance, including a list of industrial diseases. Indexed.

U1334 *Kommentarii k zakonodatel'stvu o pensiiakh i posobiiakh kolkhoznikam.* [Commentary on the legislation about pensions and benefits for collective farmers]. Pod obshchei red. V. N. Mikhalkevicha. (VNII sovetskogo zakonodatel'stva. TsIETIN). M.: Iurid. lit-ra, 1968. 262 pp.

Commentary on the 1964 Law on pensions and benefits for collective farmers, with later related legislation and other materials. Subject index.

U1335 *Material'noe obespechenie pri invalidnosti, starosti, za vyslugu let i po sluchaiu poteri kormiltsa: sbornik ukazov, postanovlenii i rasporiazhenii pravitel'stva, prikazov i instruktsii ministerstv i vedomstv.* [Material provision for invalids, the elderly and for long service and for loss of a bread-winner: a collection of decrees, ordinances and instructions from ministries and other authorities]. Sost. R. R. Kats pod obshchei red. A. N. Sukhova. (M-vo sotsial'nogo obespecheniia RSFSR). M., 1948. 703 pp.

Materials as of 10 February 1948 from USSR and RSFSR ministries, commissariats, etc. Many presented in extract form, but all have a reference to original sources.

U1336 *Pensii po gosudarstvennomu sotsial'nomu strakhovaniiu: sbornik postanovlenii i rasporiazhenii.* [Pensions under the state social insurance scheme: a collection of ordinances and decisions]. Sost. R. R. Kats pod obshchei red. A. N. Sukhova. (M-vo sotsial'nogo obespecheniia RSFSR). M., 1948. 232 pp.

A thoroughly-indexed collection of material as of 7 November 1947 for workers in social insurance on pensions and benefits.

U1337 *Pensionnoe obespechenie v SSSR: sbornik ofitsial'nykh materialov.* [Pensions in the USSR: a collection of official materials]. 2. izd., dop. i perer. M.: Gosiurizdat, 1960. 402 pp.

1st ed. publ. 1958 (296 pp.). A collection of materials on old-age pensions and other state benefits issued by the Council of Ministers, RSFSR Ministry of Social Insurance and other official bodies. Subject index.

U1338 *Pensionnoe obespechenie v SSSR: sbornik zakonodatel'nykh aktov po sostoianiiu na 1 oktiabria 1976 g.* [A collection of legislation on pensions and benefits in the USSR as of 1 October 1976]. M.: NII truda, 1976. 119 pp.

Includes the four basic laws governing pensions and benefits in the USSR, and some other regulations on this area.

U1339 *Sbornik normativnykh aktov o l'gotakh invalidam.* [A collection of normative acts on benefits for invalids]. Pod obshchei red. P. D. Grishina. M.: Iurid. lit-ra, 1977. 207 pp.

A collection of basic legislative and other materials on the definition and classification of invalidity, provision of work and housing, pensions and other benefits. Subject index.

U1340 *Sbornik normativnykh dokumentov po voprosam pravovoi raboty v organakh sotsial'nogo obespecheniia.* [Collection of normative materials on legal work in social security organizations]. M.: M-vo sotsial'nogo obespecheniia RSFSR, 1979. 129 pp. [Not seen].

U1341 *Sbornik ofitsial'nykh materialov o pensiiakh i posobiiakh chlenam kolkhozov.* [A collection of official materials on pensions and benefits for collective farmers]. M.: Rossel'khozizdat, 1972. 191 pp.

A chronological collection of materials (USSR and RSFSR) publ. 1964–July 1971.

U1342 *Sbornik rukovodiashchikh i instruktivnykh materialov po pensionnomu obespecheniiu.* [A collection of guidance and instructions on pensions and benefits]. Sost.: V. E. Zaitsev, pod obshchei red. I. A. Achil'bekova. (M-vo sotsial'nogo obespecheniia UzSSR). Tashkent: Frunzevets, 1949. 423 pp.

USSR and Uzbek SSR materials on pensions and social security benefits, some not previously published.

U1343 *Sotsial'noe obespechenie i strakhovanie v SSSR: sbornik ofitsial'nykh dokumentov s kommentariiami.* [Social insurance and social security in the USSR: a collection of official materials with commentary]. M.: Iurid. lit-ra, 1972. 709 pp.

Includes about 300 documents, many of them annotated. Some are in extract form, but all give an official source for the full text.

U1344 *Sotsial'noe obespechenie i strakhovanie v SSSR: sbornik normativnykh aktov.* [Social insurance and social security in the USSR: a collection of normative acts]. M.: Iurid. lit-ra, 1979. 543 pp.

A fully indexed and annotated collection of materials in force as of 1 December 1979.

U1345 *Sotsial'noe obespechenie i strakhovanie v SSSR: sbornik ofitsial'nykh materialov.* [Social security and social insurance in the USSR: a collection of official materials]. M.: Iurid. lit-ra, 1964. 462 pp.

Contains USSR and RSFSR legislation, instructions, etc. and material from the All-Union Central Council of Trade Unions in force on 1 January 1964. Subject index.

U1346 *Sotsial'noe strakhovanie v SSSR: sbornik ofitsial'nykh materialov.* [Social insurance in the USSR: a collection of official materials]. 2. izd., perer. M.: Profizdat, 1976. 255 pp.

1st ed. publ. 1971 (351 pp.); earlier edition, called *Sotsial'noe obespechenie . . .* publ. 1962 (323 pp.). The collections include laws, regulations, instructions, etc. on social security and social insurance in the USSR. The 1962 collection does not cover collective farmers and the 1971 collection contains a number of documents excluded from the 1976 one.

U1347 *Trudovoe ustroistvo invalidov v SSSR: sbornik normativnykh i metodicheskikh materialov.* [A collection of normative materials and regulations on the provision of work for invalids in the USSR]. (AN SSSR. In-t gosudarstva i prava. M-vo sotsial'nogo obespecheniia RSFSR). M.: Gosiurizdat, 1963. 471 pp.

As well as work for invalids, includes regulations on social security payments, medical services, provision of transport and other welfare measures. As well as legislation, the collection includes much material from the RSFSR Ministry of Social Security, some of which has not been previously published. Material included was in force on 1 January 1963. Chronological and subject index.

U1348 *Zakonodatel'stvo o pensiiakh i posobiiakh chlenam kolkhozov: sbornik ofitsial'nykh materialov.* [Legislation on pensions and benefits for collective farmers: a collection of official materials]. Izd. 2-e, dop. Pod obshchei red. A. S. Pankratova. M.: Iurid. lit-ra, 1966. 176 pp.

1st ed. publ. 1965 (174 pp.). A collection of legislative materials reflecting the changes in pension and social welfare provision for collective farmers in 1964.

Women, children and young people

The USSR constitution states that women and men have equal rights in the USSR. There is no government organization responsible for enforcing these rights; the Committee of Soviet Women is a voluntary body which appears to be mainly concerned with relations with international organizations, meeting foreign delegations and so on, rather than acting as a watchdog on the actual implementation of women's rights within the USSR. There is no ministry or state committee with specific responsibility for children and young people, but clearly the ministries of education, health and social security have a particular concern for them. There are in addition the three youth organizations—the Octobrists for young children, the Pioneers for children of 10–15, and the Komsomol for older teenagers and young adults—which are an integral part of the socialization process and play an important part in children's lives at school and in their leisure time.

Statistical handbooks on women and children

USSR

U1349a   *Deti v SSSR: statisticheskii sbornik.* [Children in the USSR: a statistical handbook]. (TsSU SSSR). M.: Statistika, 1979. 74 pp.

U1349b   *Zhenshchina v SSSR: kratkii statisticheskii spravochnik.* [Women in the USSR: a short statistical handbook]. (TsSU SSSR). M.: Gosstatizdat, 1960. 102 pp. Translation available as: *Women in the USSR: brief statistics.* M.: FLPH, 1960. 100 pp.

U1349c   *Zhenshchiny i deti v SSSR: statisticheskii sbornik.* [Women and children in the USSR: statistical handbook]. (TsSU SSSR). M.: Statistika, 1961 (230 pp.); 1963 (203 pp.); 1969 (207 pp.). 1963 edition available in English as *Women and children in the USSR: brief statistical returns.* M.: FLPH, 1963. 195 pp.

U1349d   *Zhenshchiny v SSSR: statisticheskii sbornik.* [Women in the USSR: a statistical handbook]. (TsSU SSSR). M.: Statistika, 1975. 135 pp.

These handbooks are the major all-union sources of statistics on women, their educational levels, employment, voluntary work, etc. and on children's health and welfare. For figures on education, see also the sub-section 'Education', in the section 'Cultural affairs'. More recent figures on women and children are sometimes published in *Vestnik statistiki*; some figures also appear in the general annual handbooks.

UNION REPUBLICS

Azerbaijan

U1350   *Zhenshchiny v Azerbaidzhanskoi SSR: statisticheskii sbornik.* [Women in Azerbaijan: a statistical handbook]. Baku, 1972. 100 pp. [Not seen].

Kirghizia

U1351   *Zhenshchina v Kirgizskoi SSR: kratkii statisticheskii spravochnik.* [Women in Kirghizia: a short statistical handbook]. (TsSU SSSR. TsSU KirgSSR). Frunze: Gosstatizdat, 1960. 96 pp.

Data on women as workers, in the administration, etc., and on mother and child health.

Latvia

U1352   *Zhenshchiny v Latviiskoi SSR: statisticheskii sbornik.* [Women in Latvia: a statistical handbook]. Riga, 1975. 110 pp.

Detailed figures on women as workers, their educational level, mother and child health, etc.; mainly 1950–74, but some series go back to the 1930s.

U1353　*Deti v Latviiskoi SSR: statisticheskii sbornik.* [Children in Latvia: a statistical handbook]. Riga, 1979. [Not seen].

Lithuania

U1354　*Zhenshchiny i deti v Litovskoi SSR: statisticheskii sbornik.* [Women and children in Lithuania: statistical handbook]. Vilnius, 1971. 103 pp. [Not seen].

U1355　*Zhenshchiny Litovskoi SSR: kratkii statisticheskii sbornik.* [Women in Lithuania: a short statistical handbook]. (TsSU LitSSR). Vilnius, 1975. 113 pp.

　　　Also publ. in Lithuanian. Earlier edition publ. 1972 (65 pp.). The 1975 volume was published for International Women's Year and shows the part women play in all spheres of Lithuanian life.

Moldavia

U1356　*Deti v Moldavskoi SSR: statisticheskii sbornik.* [Children in Moldavia: a statistical handbook]. (TsSU MSSR). Kishinev: Kartia moldoveniaske, 1979. 58 pp.

　　　Covers children's welfare, 1940–78.

U1357　*Zhenshchina Moldavii: kratkii statisticheskii spravochnik.* [Women in Moldavia: a statistical handbook]. (TsSU SSSR. TsSU MSSR). Kishinev: Gosstatizdat, 1961. 70 pp. [Not seen].

U1358　*Zhenshchiny Moldavskoi SSR: kratkii statisticheskii sbornik.* [Women in Moldavia: a short statistical handbook]. Kishinev, 1975. 66 pp.

　　　Earlier edition, in Moldavian only, publ. 1973, 45 pp. [Neither edition seen].

Tajikistan

U1359　*Zhenshchina v Tadzhikskoi SSR: kratkii statisticheskii spravochnik.* [Women in Tajikistan: a short statistical handbook]. (TsSU TadzhSSR). Stalinabad: Gosstatizdat, 1960. 95 pp.

　　　Mainly for the 1950s, but some data for 1940 and 1913.

Turkmenistan

U1360a　*Zhenshchina v Turkmenskoi SSR: kratkii statisticheskii sbornik.* [Women in Turkmenistan: short statistical handbook]. Ashkhabad, 1960. 87 pp.

U1360b　*Sovet Turkmenistanynyng aiallary = Zhenshchiny Sovetskogo Turkmenistana: kratkii statisticheskii sbornik.* [Women in Turkmenistan: a short statistical handbook]. Ashkhabad, 1973. 114 pp.

　　　In Russian and Turkmen.

U1360c　*Zhenshchiny v Turkmenskoi SSR: statisticheskii sbornik.* [Women in Turkmenistan: statistical handbook]. (TsSU TurkmSSR). Ashkhabad: Gosstatizdat, 1975. 105 pp.

The 1960 volume contains mainly current data, but the later volumes have figures for the 1960s and 1970s, with some series going back to 1940.

U1360d   *Deti v sovetskom Turkmenistane: statisticheskii sbornik.* [Children in Soviet Turkmenistan: a statistical handbook]. Ashkhabad, 1979. [Not seen].

Collections of legislation on women

U1361   *Gosudarstvennaia okhrana prav materi i rebenka v SSSR. Sbornik vazhneishikh ofitsial'nykh materialov. Spravochnoe posobie dlia med-itsinskikh rabotnikov.* [State protection of the rights of mother and child in the USSR: a collection of the major official materials for medical personnel]. (Tsentr. in-t sanitarnogo prosveshcheniia M-va zdravookhraneniia SSSR). M., 1952. 66 pp.

Selected extracts on women's work, maternity care, maternity benefits, state child-care provision and financial aid to mothers.

U1362   *Gosudarstvennaia pomoshch' mnogodetnym i odinokim materiam: sbornik rukovodiashchikh i instruktivnykh materialov.* [State aid to mothers of many children and single mothers: a collection of guidance and instructional materials]. Sost.: S. Gusev, A. Sipko, pod red. Ia. M. Koz'mina. (M-vo finansov SSSR. Upr. po gos. posobiiam mnogodetnym i odinokim materiam). M.: Gosfinizdat, 1946. 126 pp. pp.

A manual for administrators, including material in force in August 1945 and linked to the July 1944 Decree on child benefits. Covers some aspects of family law as well as financial matters.

U1363   *Okhrana zdorov'ia i prava zhenshchin v SSSR. Sbornik zakonodatel'nykh i vedomstvennykh aktov.* [The protection of women's health and women's rights in the USSR: a collection of legislation and ministry materials]. Sost.: L. I. Abramovich, E. N. Shcherbina, pod obshchei red. N. V. Manannikovoi. (M-vo zdravookhraneniia RSFSR). M., 1947. 336 pp.

The first systematized collection of USSR legislation and other normative acts on women's rights, benefits, etc., and on the health of women and children. Covers work, the family, daily life, child care, pensions and benefits. A special section deals with the legal procedures connected with claiming and enforcing these benefits and rights. The documents included were in force on 1 October 1947 and some had not been published previously. Alphabetical subject index.

U1364   *Zakonodatel'stvo o pravakh zhenshchin v SSSR: sbornik normativ-nykh aktov.* [Legislation on women's rights in the USSR: a collection of normative acts]. Otv. red.: V. N. Tolkunova. M.: Iurid. lit-ra, 1975. 222 pp.

A revised and enlarged edition was publ. in English as: *Soviet legislation on women's rights: a collection of normative acts.* M.: Progress, 1978. 215 pp. The 1975 edition was compiled for

International Women's Year, with many documents given in extract form only. It covers equal rights, maternity provision, family law, work, social insurance and benefits, and includes the major international declarations, etc. in this field to which the USSR is a signatory.

Collections of material on children and young people

U1365 *KPSS o Komsomole i molodezhi: sbornik rezoliutsii i reshenii s"ezdov, konferentsii i postanovlenii TsK, 1917–1961.* [The CPSU on the Komsomol: a collection of the resolutions and decisions of its congresses and conferences, and ordinances of the Central Committee, 1917–1961]. M.: Molodaia gvardiia, 1962. 399 pp.

Earlier edition covering 1917–56 publ. 1958 (384 pp.). A collection of party materials on the Komsomol, young people and on agitation and propaganda work among young people.

U1366 *Molodezh' i sovetskoe zakonodatel'stvo: sbornik dokumentov.* [A collection of documents on young people and Soviet law]. M.: Iurid. lit-ra, 1977. 686 pp.

A collection of government and party materials intended to: (a) give young people a knowledge of the main laws of the USSR; (b) set out those laws of particular relevance to young people in such fields as work, health, education and training, civil and criminal law.

U1367 *Naslednikam revoliutsii: dokumenty partii o Komsomole i molodezhi.* [To the heirs of the revolution: documents of the party on the Komsomol and young people]. M.: Molodaia gvardiia, 1969. 592 pp.

An annotated collection of 163 documents, dating from 1903 to 1968.

U1368 *Okhrana detstva v SSSR: sbornik normativnykh aktov.* [The protection of children in the USSR: a collection of normative acts]. Otv. red.: V. N. Tolkunova. M.: Iurid. lit-ra, 1979. 289 pp.

This collection, prepared for International Year of the Child, covers the family, mother and child health, education, child benefits and work for juveniles. It also includes the major international conventions affecting children's rights. Includes CPSU documents as well as material from the ministries of health and education.

U1369a *Polozheniia o Komissiiakh po delam nesovershennoletnikh.* [Regulations on the Commissions on the Affairs of Minors]. M.: Gosiurizdat, 1963. 165 pp.

Contains the texts of the Regulations adopted in each union republic, as of November 1962. A detailed commentary is available, based on the RSFSR Regulations, with references to those of the other union republics where they differ:

U1369b Pronina, V. S. *Kommentarii k Polozheniiam o Komissiiakh po delam nesovershennoletnikh.* [Commentary on the Regulations on the Commissions on the Affairs of Minors]. (Vses. NII sov. zakonodatel'stva). M.: Iurid. lit-ra, 1968. 143 pp.

Some of the other republics have also published commentaries on their regulations.

U1370 *Preduprezhdenie pravonarushenii i okhrana prav nesovershennolet-nikh: sbornik normativnykh aktov.* [Preventing crime and protecting the rights of minors: a collection of normative acts]. M., 1977. 568 pp.

149 documents, many in extract form, on education, the family, health, work and leisure and from the civil and criminal law particularly affecting young people or the crimes they are more likely to commit. Includes CPSU and trade union material as well as legislative documents.

U1371 *Sbornik vazhneishikh normativnykh aktov o nesovershennoletnikh.* [Collection of the major normative acts on minors]. (Iurid. komissiia SM KazSSR). Alma-Ata: Kazakhstan, 1969. 298 pp. [Not seen].

U1372 *Sbornik zakonodatel'nykh aktov o nesovershennoletnikh.* [Collection of legislation on minors]. Minsk: Belarus', 1973. 264 pp. [Not seen].

U1373 *Spravochnik po voprosam okhrany detstva. Dlia rabotnikov otdelov narodnogo prosveshcheniia.* [Manual for local education officials on the protection of children.] [Sost.: S. Zilov]. Izd. 3-e. (Upr. detskikh domov M-va prosveshcheniia RSFSR). M.: Uchpedgiz, 1956. 226 pp.

Earlier editions publ. 1947 (115 pp.) and 1951 (159 pp.). Includes general regulations affecting children, children's inspectors and the administration of child welfare, documents on children's homes, fostering and adoption, grants, benefits and other welfare provisions.

U1374 *V. I. Lenin, KPSS o partiinom rukovodstvom Komsomolom.* [Lenin and the CPSU on party guidance to the Komsomol]. M.: Politizdat, 1978. 670 pp.

Consists mainly of party resolutions on the Komsomol and work with young people, 1903–77. Subject index.

U1375 *Zakonodatel'stvo o nesovershennoletnikh: sbornik normativnykh aktov.* [Legislation on juveniles: a collection of normative acts]. Pod red. S. I. Rudika. (M-vo iustitsii USSR). Kiev: Politizdat Ukrainy, 1974. 636 pp.

USSR and Ukraine normative acts, in force 20 December 1973, affecting the health and welfare of children and young people, including grants and allowances, education, boarding schools and children's homes, work, legal rights and duties. Chronological and subject index.

For other material on young people and children, consult the sub-section Education' in the section 'Cultural affairs'.

Translations of material on health and welfare

U1376   *Fundamental Principles of Health Legislation of the USSR.* Bethesda,
Md.: US Dept of Health, Education and Welfare, Public Health
Service, National Institutes of Health, 1971. iii, 29 pp.
The 1969 Principles.

U1377   'Soviet administrative law: administration of public health'. *Soviet
statutes and decisions,* vol. 5, nos. 3 and 4, 1969.
These two issues of *SS&D* (*see* U164) contain a wide range of
Soviet law dealing with public health matters.

U1378   'Soviet social welfare law'. *Soviet statutes and decisions,* vol. 17, no. 1,
1980.
This issue of *SS&D* (*see* U164) deals with personnel involved in
social welfare work and institutions such as homes for the elderly and
invalids, rest-homes and sanatoria. The rest of vol. 17 will also be
devoted to welfare law.

See also *Collected legislation* (U158) section II:4 and II:5.

CULTURAL AFFAIRS

This section includes material on the inter-related areas of ideology, education
and science, culture and cultural organizations, the mass media, printing and
publishing, and religion.

Ideology

The formulation of the ideology of the USSR is the prerogative of the
Communist Party of the Soviet Union. It establishes the general goals of the
society, through the Party Programme, and determines which policies are
ideologically acceptable. Ideological considerations do limit the range of policy
options open to the leaders of the USSR—private schools, a free enterprise
economy, and religious broadcasting would all be precluded on ideological
grounds. Another aspect of the party's ideological monopoly is the establishment of the official system of values and the correct attitudes to be inculcated into
the mass of the population. In practice, of course, there are inconsistencies and
conflicts within the official ideology, and it changes over time in emphasis and
tone. Many observers believe that the ideology of the modern USSR is moving
further and further from the Marxist–Leninist theories upon which it is based.
However, although ideology may sometimes be meaningless verbiage, or a way
of justifying unpopular actions, it does have real importance in policy
formulation in all areas of Soviet life. Within the Central Committee, the
Department of Propaganda and Agitation is responsible for ideological matters
generally; in the context of this section, the Department of Culture and the
Department of Science, Higher Education Institutes and Schools also have
important roles in the inculcation of values.

U1379   *KPSS o formirovanii novogo cheloveka: sbornik dokumentov i materialov, 1965–76.* [The CPSU on the formation of the new person: a

collection of documents and materials, 1965–76]. M.: Politizdat, 1974. 456 pp.

A collection of CPSU documents on ideological and political education, mainly of adults, developing the concepts of the 'Moral Code of the Builder of Communism' put forward in the 1961 Party Programme and 'the new Soviet person'. Subject index.

U1380   *KPSS o kul'ture, prosveshchenii i nauke: sbornik dokumentov.* [The CPSU on culture, education and science: a collection of documents]. M.: Politizdat, 1963. 552 pp.

Includes Party Congress and Central Committee Plenum resolutions and decisions and other party documents on education, science and culture in general; does not cover the press and propaganda work. Subject index.

U1381   *Ob ideologicheskoi rabote KPSS: sbornik dokumentov.* [On the ideological work of the CPSU: a collection of documents]. M.: Politizdat, 1977. 639 pp.

Most of the documents included were published in the 1970s and relate to agitation and propaganda, culture, science and the press. Some in extract only.

U1382   *Voprosy ideologicheskoi raboty: sbornik dokumentov (1965–1973 gg.).* [Problems of ideological work: a collection of documents, 1965–1973]. 2-e izd., dop. M.: Politizdat, 1973. 524 pp.

1st ed., subtitled *sbornik vazhneishikh reshenii KPSS, 1965–1972* was publ. in 1972 (568 pp.). For similar coverage of an earlier period, see: *Voprosy ideologicheskoi raboty: sbornik vazhneishikh reshenii KPSS (1954–1961 gody).* M.: Gospolitizdat, 1961. 327 pp. These three collections include Party Plenum and Central Committee decisions and other party documents in the fields of education, science, culture, agitation and propaganda, the press, radio and television.

See also U1506, U1510, U1512 and U1554–U1556.

Statistics on education and culture

This sub-section includes general handbooks dealing with education and culture; *see* U1451–U1484 for more detailed handbooks in the field of printing and publishing. For more up-to-date but less detailed figures, and figures for republics not covered here, readers should consult the works listed under general statistical handbooks in the section 'General statistics'. More detailed figures on developments in these fields are published from time to time in *Vestnik statistiki* (U736).

USSR

U1383   *Kul'turnoe stroitel'stvo v SSSR: statisticheskii sbornik.* [Cultural construction in the USSR: a statistical handbook]. (TsSU SSSR). M.: Gosstatizdat, 1956. 332 pp.

Statistics on the development of education and culture in the USSR since the October Revolution; covers schools and other educational establishments, research institutes, libraries, clubs, museums, theatres, cinemas, circuses and publishing. English translation: *Cultural progress in the USSR: statistical returns*. M.: FLPH, 1958. 325 pp.

U1384 *Narodnoe obrazovanie, nauka i kul'tura v SSSR: statisticheskii sbornik*. [Education, science and culture in the USSR: statistical handbook]. (TsSU SSSR). M.: Statistika, 1977. 448 pp.

Previous edition publ. 1971 (403 pp.). Both editions include data from 1913 onwards for selected years on education, science and research, museums, theatres, libraries, etc. Data is broken down to republic level.

U1385 *Srednee spetsial'noe obrazovanie v SSSR: statisticheskii sbornik*. [Secondary specialized education in the USSR: a statistical handbook]. (TsSU SSSR). M.: Gosstatizdat, 1962. 155 pp.

Data on secondary specialized educational establishments, their staff and students, plus some data on higher education.

U1386 *Vysshee obrazovanie v SSSR: statisticheskii sbornik*. [Higher education in the USSR: a statistical handbook]. (TsSU SSSR). M.: Gosstatizdat, 1961. 255 pp.

Data on the development of higher education (including tekhnikumy and secondary specialized establishments), the composition of the student body, academic staff and research workers, spending on education, and the employment of people with higher and secondary specialized education. Some tables are broken down to republic level.

RSFSR

U1387 *Kul'turnoe stroitel'stvo RSFSR: statisticheskii sbornik*. [Cultural construction in the RSFSR: a statistical handbook]. (TsSU RSFSR). M.: Gosstatizdat, 1958. 459 pp.

Scope is similar to U1383, but deals only with RSFSR and has more detailed regional coverage.

Armenia

U1388a *Kul'turnoe stroitel'stvo Armianskoi SSR (statisticheskii sbornik)*. [Cultural construction in the Armenian SSR: statistical handbook]. (TsSU ArmSSR). Erevan, 1962. 121 pp.

U1388b *Prosveshchenie i kul'tura Armianskoi SSR (statisticheskii sbornik)*. [Enlightenment and culture in the Armenian SSR: a statistical handbook]. (TsSU ArmSSR). Erevan, 1970. 237 pp.

These two volumes contain detailed figures on education, culture, libraries, museums, etc. The 1970 volume has figures for 1940, 1950, 1955, 1960 and 1965–8 plus census figures from other years; the 1962 volume has more prewar figures and covers the 1940s and 1950s.

Azerbaijan

U1389   *Kul'turnoe stroitel'stvo Azerbaidzhanskoi SSR: statisticheskii sbornik.* [Cultural construction in the Azerbaijani SSR: a statistical handbook]. (TsSU SSSR. TsSU AzSSR). Baku: Az. otd-nie Gosstatizdat, 1961. 149 pp.

    Data on education, science, cultural institutions, etc. to 1960, with some tables going back to 1913. Some tables are accompanied by brief explanatory notes.

Kazakhstan

U1390   *Kul'turnoe stroitel'stvo Kazakhskoi SSR: statisticheskii sbornik.* [Cultural construction in the Kazakh SSR: statistical handbook]. (Stat. upr. KazSSR). Alma-Ata: Gosstatizdat, 1960. 116 pp.

    Coverage similar to U1383, for Kazakhstan. Most tables go back to the pre-Revolutionary period and are broken down to oblast' level.

Kirghizia

U1391   *Narodnoe obrazovanie Kirgizskoi SSR: kratkii statisticheskii sbornik.* [Education in Kirghizia: a short statistical handbook]. Frunze, 1968. 47 pp. [Not seen. FDAD].

Latvia

U1392   *Augstāka un vidēja speciaāla izglītiba Latvijas PSR: statistiko datu krājums = Vysshee i srednee spetsial'noe obrazovanie v Latviiskoi SSR: statisticheskii sbornik.* [Higher and secondary specialized education in Latvia: a statistical handbook]. (TsSU LatvSSR). Riga: Latv. gosizdat, 1964. 157 pp.

    Text in Latvian and Russian. Deals with the development of higher and secondary specialized education 1940–63.

U1393   *Kul'turnoe stroitel'stvo v Latviiskoi SSR.* [Cultural construction in Latvia]. (TsSU LatvSSR). Riga, 1972. 228 pp.

    Earlier edition in Latvian and Russian: *Latvijas PSR kulturas celtnieciba = Kul'turnoe stroitel'stvo Latviiskoi SSR: statisticheskii sbornik.* Riga, 1957. 172 pp. These two handbooks contain data on all aspects of educational and cultural development. The 1957 volume has more detailed figures on the 1940s and early 1950s than the 1972 volume, which has fuller coverage of more recent years.

U1394   *Pechat' i kul'turno-prosvetitel'nye uchrezhdeniia Latviiskoi SSR: statisticheskii sbornik.* [The press and cultural-enlightenment organizations of the Latvian SSR: statistical handbook]. (TsSU LatvSSR). Riga: Latv. otd-nie izd-va Statistika, 1967. 179 pp.

    Detailed figures on the press, museums, theatres, cinemas, clubs and libraries, broken down to town level. Figures are for 1965, with some figures going back to 1958 or 1940.

Lithuania

U1395   *Narodnoe obrazovanie, nauka i kul'tura v Litovskoi SSR: statisticheskii sbornik.* [Education, science and culture in Lithuania: a statistical handbook]. (TsSU LitSSR). Vilnius, 1976. 289 pp.

      Earlier edition publ. 1972, 317 pp. [Not seen]. The 1976 edition was issued in only 250 copies, and contains extremely detailed figures on this field for 1950–75.

U1396   *Prosveshchenie i kul'tura Litovskoi SSR: statisticheskii sbornik.* [Education and culture in Lithuania: a statistical handbook]. (TsSU LitSSR). Vilnius: Statistika, Lit. otd-nie, 1964. 207 pp.

      Covers education and culture in Lithuania 1940–63.

Turkmenia

U1397   *Kul'turnoe stroitel'stvo Turkmenskoi SSR: statisticheskii sbornik.* [Cultural construction in Turkmenia: a statistical handbook]. (TsSU SSSR. TsSU TurkSSR). Ashkhabad: Turkmen. gos. izd-vo, 1960. 131 pp.

      Data on education and culture in Turkmenia from 1940 to 1959, with some figures for 1913 and 1920.

Ukraine

U1398   *Narodna osvita, nauka i kul'tura v Ukrains'kii RSR: statystychnyi zbirnyk.* [Education, science and culture in the Ukraine: a statistical handbook]. Kyiv: Statystyka, 1973. 317 pp.

      In Ukrainian. [Not seen. FDAD].

Education

Introduction

Education at all levels in the USSR is now regulated by the Fundamental Principles on National Educational Legislation of the USSR and the Union Republics enacted on 19 July 1973 and followed by new laws on education passed by the Union republics during 1974. The previous basic law governing the Soviet educational system reflected the educational reforms initiated by Khrushchev. This was the 1958 Law on the Strengthening of Ties between the School and Life, which was also followed by laws of the same titles passed by each union republic. Education at school level is the responsibility of the USSR Ministry of Education and the ministries of education of the union republics; until the USSR ministry was set up in 1966 responsibility rested entirely with the union republics and there is still a strong emphasis on the role of the union republics in educational policy and legislation. There are considerable differences in the detail of educational law between the republics. Professional and technical education is administered by the USSR State Committee for Professional–Technical Education and its counterparts at union republic level. Higher education and secondary special schools are run by the USSR Ministry of Higher and Secondary Specialized Education; there are ministries of this title in most of the union republics, but in Kirghizia, Moldavia, Tajikistan and Turkmenistan these responsibilities are discharged by the republic's ministry of education. The supervision of the award of higher degrees (kandidat nauk, doktor nauk) is carried out by the Supreme Attestation Commission of the USSR Ministry of Higher and Secondary Specialized Education. This ministry and its union republic counterparts are responsible for the direction and administration of research work in institutes of higher education, but the USSR Academy of Science and the academies in the union republics, the USSR Academy of Pedagogical Sciences, the USSR Academy of Medical Sciences and the All-Union Agricultural Academy (all non-governmental bodies) are responsible for research work in their institutes and have a considerable influence on research by other organizations.

Much applied research is carried out in industry and in laboratories run by various Ministries and State Committees. The regulation of their work is largely the responsibility of the appropriate superior organization.

For material on pre-school education, and for works about children and young people in general, consult also the section 'Social affairs'.

Educational bibliographies and reference works

U1399 *Literatura po pedagogicheskim naukam i narodnomu obrazovaniiu.* [Literature on the pedagogical sciences and education]. (APN SSSR. Gos. nauch. ped. b-ka). M.: Pedagogika, 1951–. Quarterly.

A classified bibliography of books and journal articles in Russian, including official materials. Each issue has an author and title index, but there are no annual indexes.

U1400 *Pedagogicheskaia entsiklopediia.* [Pedagogical encyclopaedia]. Glav. red.: I. A. Kairov, F. N. Petrov. M.: Sov. entsiklopediia, 1964–8. 4 vols.

Authoritative articles, with bibliographies, on all aspects of education.

U1401 *Russko–angliiskii shkol'no-pedagogicheskii slovar'.* [Russian–English dictionary on schools and pedagogy]. Pod obshchim rukovodstvom A. I. Rozenmana. Iaroslavl´: Iaroslavskoe knizhnoe izd-vo, 1959. 455 pp.

A dictionary of words and phrases used in educational work, including educational psychology and librarianship.

Bulletins of the ministries of education

The USSR Ministry of Education and a number of the union republics' ministries publish regular collections of their orders and instructions; these are listed below. In addition, the Tajik Ministry is believed to have started publishing a bulletin in 1972, and the Estonian Ministry published a few issues of a bulletin in 1959–60, as did the Turkmenian Ministry in 1960–1. Otherwise, the republics not listed below presumably rely on an 'official use only' bulletin. The contents of the bulletins examined are similar to the RSFSR bulletin. A few sets of the USSR and RSFSR bulletins are available in the West; all the others are not available for export.

ALL-UNION

U1402 *Biulleten' normativnykh aktov Ministerstva prosveshcheniia SSSR.* [Bulletin of normative acts of the USSR Ministry of Education]. Moscow, [1980?–]. Monthly.

RSFSR

U1403 *Sbornik prikazov i instruktsii Ministerstva prosveshcheniia RSFSR.* [Bulletin of orders and instructions of the RSFSR Ministry of Education]. M.: Prosveshchenie, 1944–8, 1952–. 36 p.a.

1944–8 title was *Prikazy i instruktsii: sbornik*... and 1952–5 was *Sbornik prikazov i rasporiazhenii*.... Weekly until 1963. The bulletin includes orders, circular letters and instructions and other documents from the ministry and decisions of its presidium, with texts of orders and decisions issued jointly with other ministries. Annual index.

ARMENIA

U1404 *Sbornik prikazov i rasporiazhenii Ministerstva prosveshchenii Armianskoi SSR.* [Bulletin of orders and ordinances of the Ministry of Education of the Armenian SSR]. Erevan, 1955–. Fortnightly.

Published in Armenian only. Appeared irregularly until about 1965.

AZERBAIJAN

U1405 *Azarbaijan SSR Maarif Nazirliiinin amr va ta'limatlary majmuasi = Sbornik prikazov Ministerstva prosveshcheniia Azerbaidzhanskoi SSR.* [Bulletin of orders of the Ministry of Education of the Azerbaijani SSR]. Baku, 1954–. Monthly.

In Russian and Azerbaijani. Appeared irregularly 1954–68.

BELORUSSIA

U1406 *Zbornik zagadau i instruktsyi Ministerstva asvety BSSR = Sbornik prikazov i instruktsii Ministerstva prosveshcheniia Belorusskoi SSR.* [Bulletin of orders and instructions of the Ministry of Education of the Belorussian SSR]. Minsk, 1960–. Monthly.

In Russian and Belorussian.

GEORGIA

U1407 *Sbornik prikazov i rasporiazhenii Ministerstva prosveshcheniia Gruzinskoi SSR.* [Bulletin of orders and ordinances of the Ministry of Education of the Georgian SSR]. Tbilisi, 1937–. Monthly.

In Georgian only.

KAZAKHSTAN

U1408   *Sbornik prikazov i instruktsii Ministerstva prosveshcheniia Ka-zakhskoi SSR.* [Bulletin of orders and instructions of the Ministry of Education of the Kazakh SSR]. Alma-Ata, 1964–. Irregular (every 1–2 months).
Has separate Kazakh and Russian editions. [Not seen].

KIRGHIZIA

U1409   *Sbornik prikazov i instruktivno-metodicheskikh ukazanii Ministerstva narodnogo obrazovaniia Kirgizskoi SSR.* [Bulletin of orders and instructional materials of the Ministry of Education of the Kirghiz SSR]. Frunze, 1952–. Monthly.
1952–63 issuing body called Ministerstvo prosveshcheniia Kirgiz-skoi SSR.

MOLDAVIA

U1410   *Sbornik rukovodiashchikh i metodicheskikh materialov.* (Moldavskaia SSR. Ministerstvo narodnogo obrazovaniia). [Bulletin of instructional and methods materials issued by the Ministry of Education of the Moldavian SSR]. Kishinev: Izd-vo TsK KP Moldavii, 1966–. Monthly.
Published since 1958 in Moldavian with title *Kulezhere de direktive shi materiale metodiche.* 6 p.a. until 1970; monthly since 1971.

UKRAINE

U1411   *Zbirnyk nakaziv ta instruktsii.* (Ministerstvo prosveshcheniia USSR). [Collection of orders and instructions of the Ukrainian Ministry of Education]. Kiev, 1920–. Fortnightly.
In Ukrainian only. Some variations in title and frequency. [Not seen].

UZBEKISTAN

U1412   *Uzbekiston SSR maorif ministrligining buiruq va instruktiv-metodik kursatmalari = Sbornik prikazov i instruktivno-metodicheskikh ukaz-anii Ministerstva prosveshcheniia Uzbekskoi SSR.* [Bulletin of orders and instructions of the Ministry of Education of the Uzbek SSR]. Tashkent, 1956–. Irregular.
In Uzbek and Russian.

Other official documents on education in general and on schools

U1413   *Direktivy VKP(b) i postanovleniia sovetskogo pravitel'stva o narod-nom obrazovanii: sbornik dokumentov za 1917–1947 gg.* [Directives of the All-Union Communist Party (Bolshevik) and ordinances of the Soviet government on education: a collection of documents,

1917–1947]. Sost.: N. I. Boldyrev. M.: Izd-vo APN RSFSR, 1947. 2 vols.

Vol. 1 covers general material, schools and compulsory education, children's homes, the pioneers, and financial matters; vol. 2 covers professional training, higher education, adult education and literacy campaigns, higher degrees and research, and material provision for teachers and other workers in education. Documents included are from the USSR and RSFSR Sovnarkomy, ministries involved in education, and the Communist Party. Includes some documents no longer in force. Vol. 2 includes a bibliography of earlier collections and a full subject index.

U1414 *Dokumenty i materialy po perestroike shkoly.* [Documents and materials on the transformation of the school]. M.: Gos. uchebno-ped. izd-vo M-va prosveshcheniia RSFSR, 1960. 170 pp.

Includes legislation on education passed 1958–60, and a number of Khrushchev's speeches on the educational reforms.

U1415 *Narodnoe obrazovanie: ezhemesiachnyi zhurnal Ministerstva pro-sveshcheniia SSSR i Ministerstva prosveshcheniia RSFSR.* [Education: journal of the USSR Ministry of Education and the RSFSR Ministry of Education]. M.: Pedagogika, 1946–. Monthly.

Includes reports on the work of the two ministries, summaries of recent orders and instructions and other official documents, as well as articles by ministers and other leading officials. Annual index.

U1416 *Narodnoe obrazovanie. Osnovnye postanovleniia, prikazy i instruktsii.* [Education: the basic ordinances, orders and instructions]. Sost.: A. M. Danev. (M-vo prosveshcheniia RSFSR). M.: Gos. uchebno-ped. izd-vo M-va prosveshcheniia RSFSR, 1948. 482 pp.

Includes material in force on 1 April 1947. As well as material on schools and pre-school education, covers provision for orphans, teacher training and evening schools. Does not cover higher education and science.

U1417 *Narodnoe obrazovanie v SSSR: obshcheobrazovatel'naia shkola. Sbornik dokumentov, 1917–1973 gg.* [The general education school in the USSR: a collection of documents, 1917–1973]. [Comp. by A. A. Abakumov et al.]. M.: Pedagogika, 1974. 560 pp.

Contains the texts of about 300 laws, decrees, resolutions, etc. of the party and the government on all aspects of education. Covers all-union and RSFSR material and includes some documents no longer in force. The documents are arranged by topic, with a chronological index.

U1418 *O kommunisticheskom vospitanii i ukreplenii sviazi shkoly s zhizn'iu: sbornik dokumentov.* [On communist upbringing and the strengthening of the links between the school and life: a collection of documents]. M.: Prosveshchenie, 1964. 480 pp.

A subject collection of USSR and RSFSR legislative material and

CP documents on educational matters, 1956–June 1963. Fully indexed.

U1419 *Ob ukreplenii sviazi shkoly s zhizn'iu i o dal'neishem razvitii sistemy narodnogo obrazovaniia v SSR.* [On strengthening the links of the school with life and on the improvement of the educational system in the USSR]. (Vazhneishie zakonodatel'nye akty Soiuza SSR i soiuznykh respublik). M.: Gosiurizdat, 1961. 343 pp.

A collection of all-union legislation and ordinances on education, 1958–61, connected with the 1958 reforms, and the texts of the Law on the Strengthening of Links between the School and Life passed by each union republic in 1959.

U1420 *Osnovy zakonodatel'stva Soiuza SSR i soiuznykh respublik o narod-nom obrazovanii.* [Fundamental Principles of Legislation of the USSR and the Union Republics on Education]. M.: Izvestiia, 1973. 39 pp.

Text of the Fundamental Principles passed 19 July 1973 and in force from 1 January 1974. Also readily available in U1417; a translation is available in U159, among others.

U1421 *Sbornik rukovodiashchikh dokumentov o rabote obshcheo-brazovatel'nykh shkol-internatov.* [Collection of documents guiding the work of the general boarding school]. Riga: M-vo prosveshcheniia Latviiskoi SSR, 1979. 93 pp.

An unpriced volume in 500 copies intended for directors of boarding schools and other children's organizations. It includes documents issued by the Latvian Ministry of Education in 1978–9.

U1422 *Sbornik rukovodiashchikh i instruktivnykh materialov dlia direktorov spetsial'nykh shkol. Shkoly dlia glukhonemykh, tugoukhikh, slepykh, slabovidiashchikh, vspomogatel'nye shkoly.* [Collection of instructional materials and documents guiding the work of directors of special schools]. (Upr. shkol M-va prosveshcheniia RSFSR). M.: Uchpedgiz, 1953. 136 pp.

Covers schools for the deaf and hard-of-hearing, blind and partially sighted, and for children with mental handicaps. Most of the documents included are from the RSFSR Ministry of Education, and the volume also includes a supplement about institutions researching this field, and a bibliography.

U1423 *Sbornik rukovodiashchikh materialov a shkole.* [Collection of materials guiding schools]. (Prilozhenie k zhurnalu 'Sovetskaia pedagogika' za 1952 g., kn. 3). M.: Izd-vo APN RSFSR, 1952. 308 pp.

Consists of CP documents 1930–50, also Komsomol materials on Komsomol and Pioneer organizations in schools, and instructions, regulations, etc. from the RSFSR Ministry of Education.

U1424 *Spravochnik direktora shkoly: sbornik zakonodatel'nykh, rukovod-iashchikh i instruktivnykh materialov.* [Manual for a school director: a collection of legislative, guiding and instructional materials]. [Pod red. A. I. Shustova]. M.: Prosveshchenie, 1971. 392 pp.

Earlier editions, called *Spravochnik direktora shkoly: sbornik postanovlenii, prikazov, instruktsii i drugikh materialov o shkole* and comp. by M. M. Deineko, were publ. in 1954 (515 pp.) and 1955 (510 pp.). The 1971 edition includes only material in force at the start of 1971; material included is often presented in extract form. Has CP and Council of Ministers documents and some USSR and RSFSR ministries of education materials, arranged by broad topic with a subject index.

U1425 *Spravochnik po doshkol'nomu vospitaniiu: osnovnye zakonodatel'nye i instruktivnye dokumenty.* [Manual on pre-school education: basic legal and instructional documents]. Pod red. A. I. Shustova. Izd. 4-e, ispr. i dop. M.: Prosveshchenie, 1980. 543 pp.

Previous editions publ. 1972 (560 pp.), 1967 (471 pp.) and 1963 (400 pp.). As well as party and government documents on the public provision of care for pre-school children, the collection includes much material from the RSFSR Ministry of Education not readily available elsewhere. Covers finance, buildings and equipment, wages and working conditions and procedures for selecting children and running pre-school institutions. The 1972 edition includes material in force at the end of 1971.

U1426 *Spravochnik rabotnika narodnogo obrazovaniia: sbornik zakonodatel'nykh, rukovodiashchikh i instruktivnykh materialov.* [Manual for workers in education: a collection of legislative, directive and instructional materials]. M.: Pedagogika, 1973. 623 pp.

Includes party resolutions on education, legislation and some orders, instructions, etc. of the USSR Ministry of Education, in force in 1973. Some documents reproduced in extract only; broad subject arrangement.

U1427 *Spravochnik rukovodiashchikh materialov po narodnomu obrazovaniiu.* [Manual of directive materials on education]. Alma-Ata: Kazuchpedgiz, 1954. 340 pp. [Not seen. Presumably concentrating on Kazakh materials. A later edition publ. in 1961 is not publicly available].

U1428 *Uchitel'skaia gazeta.* [The teachers' newspaper]. M., 1924–. 2 per week.

Former title: *Za kommunisticheskoe prosveshchenie.* The newspaper of the USSR Ministry of Education and the trade union for teachers and scientific workers. As well as articles and news items, includes official material on education (mainly at school level), and to a lesser extent science and culture.

U1429 *Vecherniaia shkola: spravochnik po voprosam ochnogo i zaochnogo obucheniia rabotaiushchei molodezhi i vzroslykh.* [Evening school: a handbook on part-time and correspondence study by young workers and adults]. Pod red. N. N. Balova. M.: Pedagogika, 1973. 586 pp.

A collection of CP documents and regulations, orders, etc. from the USSR and union republics' ministries of education on the organization of evening-shift schools and correspondence schools, pupils' rights, teachers' pay and conditions, etc.

Official documents on higher education and science

U1430 *Aspirantura vysshikh uchebnykh zavedenii SSSR (po dannym na 1 iiulia 1948 g.).* [Postgraduate work in the USSR, as of 1 July 1948]. (M-vo vysshego obrazovaniia SSSR. Planovo-ekon. otdel). M.: Sov. nauka, 1949. 276 pp.

Guidance on research work in all types of higher educational institution, including lists of institutes and their special fields, regulations on grants, admissions, etc. and the syllabuses for courses in dialectical and historical materialism and foreign languages.

U1431 *Biulleten' Ministerstva vysshego i srednego spetsial'nogo obrazovaniia SSSR.* [Bulletin of the USSR Ministry of Higher and Secondary Specialized Education]. M.: Vysshaia shkola, 1933–. Monthly.

Name of issuing body varied before war; called Glavnoe upr. vysshego obrazovaniia 1953–4 and M-vo vysshego obrazovaniia SSSR 1954–9. Publication suspended April 1940–2. Frequency varied before the war; semi-monthly 1956–7, 18 issues in 1955, but otherwise monthly. This bulletin includes prikazy, instructional letters and other official documents issued by the ministry and also documents issued by the ministry jointly with other ministries or state committees. No indexes.

U1432 *Biulleten' Vysshei attestatsionnoi komissii pri Sovete ministrov SSSR.* [Bulletin of the Supreme Attestation Commission of the USSR Council of Ministers]. M.: Vysshaia shkola, 1976–. 6 p.a.

Includes reports on the work of VAK in the award of higher degrees, its orders and other instructions, reports on the validation of new courses and lists of doctoral theses to be defended. Has short abstracts of some recent theses. Annual index.

U1433 *Nauchnye kadry v SSSR: sbornik dokumentov i spravochnykh materialov.* [Scientific cadres in the USSR: a collection of documents and information]. Pod red. A. V. Topchieva. (AN SSSR). M.: Izd-vo AN SSSR, 1959. 304 pp.

A collection of Academy of Sciences and government materials on the work of postgraduate students, scientists and academic staff, covering regulations on work for higher degrees, procedures for appointment and promotion, salaries, incentives, pensions, etc.

U1434 *Novaia sovetskaia literatura po obshchestvennym naukam: nauko-vedenie.* [New Soviet literature on the social sciences: science studies]. (AN SSSR. INION). M., 1934–. Monthly.

Many variations in title 1934–51. 1952–75 called *Novaia sovetskaia literatura o nauke i nauchno-issledovatel'skoi rabote v SSSR.* Frequency varied 1934–48. Includes Soviet books and articles on all aspects of the organization of science and academic work, science policy, research and development. Includes official materials in these fields. No indexes.

U1435 *Sbornik normativnykh aktov i dokumentov po voprosam attestatsii nauchnykh i nauchno-pedagogicheskikh kadrov.* [A collection of normative acts and documents on the attestation of scientific and teaching cadres]. 2-e izd., dop. (Vysshaia attestatsionnaia komissiia. Iurid. otdel). M., 1979. 112 pp.

1st ed. publ. 1978 (111 pp.) covered 1974–1 December 1978. The 1979 edition is a chronologically arranged collection from 1974 to 1 October 1979 of party and government documents on VAK, and VAK's own regulations, circulars and instructions. Intended for supervisors and those examining higher degree candidates.

U1436 *Sbornik instruktivnykh materialov po vysshemu zaochnomu obrazovaniiu.* [Collection of instructions on higher education by correspondence]. (Vses. s.-kh. in-t zaochnogo obrazovaniia). M.: Kolos, 1965. 193 pp.

A handbook for staff involved in administering higher education courses in agricultural subjects by correspondence course, designed to deal with problems over time off and other benefits for students, the organization of their work, staff matters, finance, etc. Most of the documents included come from the USSR Ministry of Higher and Secondary Specialized Education.

U1437 *V. I. Lenin, KPSS o razvitii nauki: sbornik.* [Lenin and the CPSU on the development of science]. M.: Politizdat, 1981.

This work, announced in late 1980, is intended to cover the development of Soviet science, creation of its material and technical base, training of cadres, etc. [Not seen].

U1438 *V. I. Lenin, KPSS ob intelligentsii.* [V. I. Lenin and the CPSU on the intelligentsia]. M.: Politizdat, 1979. 295 pp.

Documents on policy towards the intelligentsia, including about 40 from the postwar period. Subject index.

U1439 *Vysshaia shkola. Sbornik osnovnykh postanovlenii, prikazov i instruktsii.* [Higher education. A collection of basic ordinances, orders and instructions]. Pod red. E. I. Voilenko. (M-vo vysshego i srednego spetsial'nogo obrazovaniia SSSR). M.: Vysshaia shkola, 1978. 2 vols.

Earlier editions, publ. in 1940 (296 pp.), 1945 (410 pp.), 1948 (616 pp.) and 1957 (655 pp.) with varying subtitles and editors. This important collection includes official material on the organization of all types of higher education institute, research work in vuzy, teacher training, working conditions, and all aspects of material provision for staff and students. Arranged by topic, with alphabetical subject index.

On education, *see also* U1000, U1007, U1008, U1205 and U1529.

Culture and the media

The CPSU takes a close interest in all matters relating to culture and the mass media, because of the ideological importance of these areas and their ability to influence people. As well as the Department of Propaganda of the Central Committee, the Department of Culture is involved in policy formulation and implementation in these areas. In the governmental structure, the ministries of culture at all-union and union republic level are responsible for cultural organizations such as libraries and museums, and for the supervision of the work of artists, musicians, actors, etc. The work of the creative intelligentsia is also deeply affected by the non-governmental organizations which act as their professional associations—the Union of Writers, Union of Composers, All-Union Theatrical Society, etc.—which confer many benefits and rights on their members, but also act as agents of control over them. Films and the cinema are administered by the State Committee on Cinematography, and radio and television by the State Committee for Radio and Television Broadcasting, which coordinates its work closely with that of the Ministry of Communications. The State Committee for Publishing, Printing and the Book Trade (formerly the State Committee on the Press, and usually called Goskomizdat) is responsible for coordinating the various organizations in this field which are directly subordinate to other administrative organizations such as ministries owning publishing houses or paper mills. Responsibility for some aspects of cultural work rests with the trade unions rather than with the government—for instance clubs, amateur theatrical societies and factory libraries are often run by the trade unions, which are formally outside the government structure. In selecting documents for this sub-section, collections consisting largely of materials from the trade unions or professional associations have been excluded. Until 1973, when the USSR signed the Universal Copyright Convention, the protection of authors' and artists' rights was a matter for the professional associations and the All-Union Administration for the Protection of Authors' Rights (VUOAP). Since 1973, the protection of artists' and authors' rights has been undertaken by the All-Union Agency for Authors' Rights (VAAP). Another important feature of the Soviet mass media and publishing process, the censorship, is not represented here; the activities of the Chief Administration for the Protection of State Secrets in the Press (still often called Glavlit) do not find expression in the open press.

General collections on the media

U1440   *O partiinoi i sovetskoi pechati, radioveshchanii i televidenii: sbornik dokumentov i materialov.* [On the party and Soviet press, radio and television broadcasting: a collection of documents and materials]. M.: Mysl', 1972. 635 pp.

An annotated collection of CPSU documents, with subject index and index of periodical publications.

U1441　*O partiinoi i sovetskoi pechati: sbornik dokumentov.* [On the party and Soviet press: a collection of documents]. M.: Pravda, 1954. 692 pp.

A very full collection of CPSU decisions and resolutions on the press, government decrees and ordinances and other documents on the press, including some not reproduced in later collections. This is particularly true of some of the important documents on ideological and cultural matters of the late 1940s originally published in *Kul'tura i zhizn'*, on the instructions of Zhdanov.

U1442　*V. I. Lenin, KPSS o pechati: sbornik dokumentov i materialov.* [Lenin and the CPSU on the press: a collection of documents and materials]. 2 izd., dop. (B-chka zhurnalista). M.: Politizdat, 1974. 383 pp.

1st ed. publ. 1970 (311 pp.). Contains CPSU resolutions on the press (particularly on newspapers), some material on Lenin as editor and journalist, and some other material on the press and ideological work.

See also U1488.

General collections on culture

U1443　*Kul'tura Moldavii za gody sovetskoi vlasti: sbornik dokumentov, v 4-kh tomakh.* [Culture in Moldavia under Soviet rule: a collection of documents in four volumes]. Gl. red.: A. M. Lazarev. Kishinev: Shtiintsa, 1975–.

A collection of Moldavian and all-union party and government materials relating to all aspects of the cultural development of Moldavia, including health care as well as literature, art, education and music. Includes much previously unpublished material. Has name and geographical indexes, and lists of archives and published works consulted.

U1444　*Kul'turnaia zhizn v SSSR, ...: khronika.* [The cultural life of the USSR in ...: a chronicle]. (AN SSSR. In-t istorii). M.: Nauka.

1941–1950. 1977. 524 pp.

1951–1965. 1979. 679 pp.

This is part of a series which began with 1917. It lists chronologically party and government decrees in the cultural field, broadly defined, and records major events and publications. A reference is given to a printed source for each item listed. There are full name, geographical and subject indexes.

U1445　*Materialy po kul'turno-prosvetitel'noi rabote: sbornik.* [Materials on cultural and educational work: a collection]. M.: Sov. Rossiia, 1959. 301 pp.

Earlier editions publ. 1947 (139 pp.) and 1948 (290 pp.). Includes documents on the organization and funding of cultural organizations such as clubs, libraries, cinemas and museums, issued by the USSR and RSFSR ministries of culture, ministries of finance, etc.

U1446 *Sovetskaia kul'tura: gazeta Tsentral'nogo komiteta KPSS.* [Soviet culture: newspaper of the Central Committee of the CPSU]. M., 1953–. Two issues per week.

Originally published by the USSR Ministry of Culture. An important source of official data on culture, the arts, libraries and museums.

Cinema

U1447 *Kinofikatsiia i kinoprokat: sistematizirovannyi sbornik zako-nodatel'nykh postanovlenii, vedomstvennykh prikazov i instruk-tsii.* [Film-making and film-distribution: a systematic collection of legislation, orders and instructions]. (Upr. kinofikatsii i kinoprokata M-va kul'tury SSSR). M.: Iskusstvo, 1959. 424 pp.

Copy marked 'For official use. Distributed according to the circulation list'. Includes material as of 1 December 1957; apparently a later supplement was issued. Contains USSR and RSFSR regulations on all aspects of the production, duplication, showing and preservation of films.

U1448 *Sovetskaia kinematografiia. Sistematizirovannyi sbornik zako-nodatel'nykh postanovlenii, vedomstvennykh prikazov i instruk-tsii.* [Soviet cinematography: a systematic collection of legislation, orders and instructions]. Sost.: A. E. Kossovskii. M.: Goskinoizdat, 1940. 917 pp.

Despite its age, this seems to be the most recent publicly available collection of regulations, legislation, etc. on the cinema. Similar in scope to U1447, but also has an alphabetical subject index.

Libraries

U1449 *Materialy k istorii bibliotechnogo dela v SSSR (1917–1959 gg.): uchebnoe posobie dlia studentov bibliotechnykh institutov.* [Materials on the history of librarianship in the USSR 1917–1959: a manual for librarianship students]. Sost.: L. A. Solov'eva i M. L. Kheifets. (M-vo kul'tury RSFSR. Leningradskii gos. in-t kul'tury im. N. K. Krupskoi). Leningrad, 1960. 236 pp.

A collection of party and government resolutions, decisions, etc., many in extract form only. Subject index.

U1450 *Sbornik rukovodiashchikh materialov po bibliotechnoi rabote.* [A collection of materials guiding the work of libraries]. (M-vo kul'tury SSSR. Glavnaia bibliotechnaia inspektsiia). M.: Vses. knizhnaia palata, 1963. 247 pp.

Earlier editions publ. 1947 (108 pp.) and 1948 (150 pp.). The 1963 collection includes CP and Council of Ministers resolutions and ordinances, orders from the USSR and RSFSR ministries of culture, and other materials relating to library work issued 1958–61. Includes many documents not previously published.

Statistics on the press

USSR

U1451 *Pechat' SSSR v . . . godu: statisticheskie materialy.* [The Soviet press in . . .: statistical materials]. (M-vo kul'tury SSSR. Vses. knizhnaia palata. Gos. komitet SSSR po delam izdatel'stv, poligrafii i knizhnoi torgovli). M.: Kniga, 1954 (publ. 1955)–. Annual.

1954 volume had title *Pechat' SSSR, 1954.* The 1956 and 1957 figures were published together in one volume in 1958. This is the main handbook for data on the publishing of books, journals, newspapers and sheet music; more recent volumes also cover maps, posters and illustrations and have some breakdown by republic. Includes some data on languages, edition size and a subject breakdown of the material published in the year covered.

U1452 *Pechat' SSSR v gody piatiletok: statisticheskie materialy.* [The press of the USSR during the five-year plans: statistical materials]. (Vses. knizhnaia palata). M.: Kniga, 1971. 96 pp.

Shows the development of the press and publishing 1928–70, in five-year periods.

U1453 *Pechat' SSSR za sorok let, 1917–1957: statisticheskie materialy.* [The Soviet press over 40 years, 1917–1957: statistical materials]. (M-vo kul'tury SSSR. Glavizdat. Vses. knizhnaia palata). M., 1957. 144 pp.

Summary of data for 1917–57; scope similar to U1451.

U1454 *Sovetskaia pechat' 1951–1955: statisticheskie materialy.* [The Soviet press 1951–1955: statistical materials]. (M-vo kul'tury SSSR. Glavizdat. Vses. knizhnaia palata). M.: Izd-vo Vses. knizhnoi palaty, 1956. 84 pp.

As well as figures for 1951–5, gives basic figures for the 1928–32, 1933–7 and 1946–50 plan periods, with some tables broken down to republic level. Coverage similar to U1451.

U1455 *Sovetskaia pechat' k 400-letiiu russkogo knigopechataniia: statisticheskie materialy.* [The Soviet press on the 400th anniversary of Russian printing: statistical materials]. (Gos. komitet SSSR po pechati. Vses. knizhnaia palata). M.: Kniga, 1964. 45 pp.

A brief summary, 1913–63.

U1456 *Sovetskaia pechat' v period mezhdu XX i XXII s"ezdami KPSS: statisticheskie materialy.* [The Soviet press in the period between the 20th and 22nd CPSU congresses: statistical materials]. (M-vo kul'tury SSSR. Vses. knizhnaia palata). M.: Izd-vo Vses. knizhnoi palaty, 1961. 168 pp.

Compares 1960 figures with those for 1955, with breakdowns by republic, type of publication and subject area.

PRESS STATISTICS OF THE UNION REPUBLICS

Nearly all the union republics publish statistics on the press and the book trade in the republic, either as occasional volumes or as annual returns. These republican handbooks generally contain far more detailed figures than the all-union ones on the output of publishing houses in the republic, language of publication, subject matter and type of publication.

Armenia

U1457   *Kniga i periodicheskaia pechat' Armianskoi SSR v ... g.* [The book and periodical press of Armenia in ...]. Erevan, 1972 (publ. 1976)–. Annual.
    In Armenian and Russian. [Not seen].

U1458   *Kniga i periodicheskaia pechat' v Armianskoi SSR za 40 let: statisticheskie materialy.* [The book and the periodical press in Armenia for 40 years: statistical materials]. Erevan, 1960. 79 pp. [Not seen].

Azerbaijan

U1459   *Pechat' Azerbaidzhanskoi SSR (1920–1956): statisticheskie materialy.* [The press of Azerbaijan, 1920–1956: statistical materials]. Baku, 1958. 47 pp. [Not seen].

Belorussia

U1460   *Druk Belaruskai SSR, ...: statystychnyia materyialy.* [The Belorussian press in ...: statistical materials]. (Dziarzh. b-ka BSSR. Kn. palata BSSR). Minsk.
    1918–1965. 1967. 92 pp.
    1966–1970. 1972. 128 pp.
    1971–1975. 1977. 114 pp.
    In Belorussian. [Not seen].

U1461   *Pechat' Belorusskoi SSR 1976: statisticheskii spravochnik.* [The press of Belorussia, 1976: statistical materials]. Minsk, 1979. 101 pp. [Not seen].

U1462   *Statistika pechati Belorusskoi SSR za 1957 g.* [Statistics of the Belorussian press for 1957]. Minsk, 1959. 28 pp. [Not seen].

Estonia

U1463   *25 aastat Nõukogude Eesti trükisona (1940–1965): statistiliste materjalide kogumik = 25 let pechati Sovetskoi Estonii, 1940–56: sbornik statisticheskikh materialov.* [25 years of Estonian publishing, 1940–1965: a collection of statistical materials]. Sost.: L. Puss. (Gos. komitet SM ESSR po pechati. Kn. palata ESSR). Tallin: Eesti raamat. 1971. 184 pp.
    In Estonian and Russian.

U1464   *Pechat' Sovetskoi Estonii v 1966–1975 gg. Sbornik statisticheskikh materialov.* [The press of Soviet Estonia in 1966–1975: a collection of statistical materials]. Sost.: L. Puss. Tallin, 1978. 146 pp.
    In Estonian and Russian. [Not seen].

U1465 *Eesti NSV trükitoodangu statistika=Statistika pechati Estonskoi SSR.* [Estonian press statistics]. (Gos. komitet ESSR po pechati. Kn. palata ESSR). Tallin, 1961/62 (publ. 1963)–. Annual.
In Estonian and Russian.

Kazakhstan

U1466 *Pechat' Kazakhskoi SSR v . . . g.: statisticheskie materialy.* [The press of Kazakhstan in . . .: statistical materials]. Alma-Ata, 1973 (publ. 1974)–. Annual?
Frequency not yet established. [Not seen].

U1467 *Pechat' Kazakhskoi SSR v deviatoi piatiletke: statisticheskie materialy.* [The Kazakh press in the ninth five-year plan: statistical materials]. Alma-Ata, 1976. 97 pp. [Not seen].

U1468 *Pechat' Kazakhskoi SSR za 50 let (1917–1967 gg.): statisticheskie materialy.* [The Kazakh press over 50 years, 1917–1967: statistical materials]. (Gos. komitet KazSSR po pechati. Kn. palata KazSSR). Alma-Ata: Kazakhstan, 1969. 51 pp.
Earlier editions: *Pechat' Kazakhskoi SSR, 1921–1957.* 1958; and *Pechat' Kazakhskoi SSR, 1920–1960.* 1960.

Kirghizia

U1469 *Pechat' Kirgizskoi SSR, 1969–1975: statisticheskie materialy.* [The Kirghiz press, 1969–1975: statistical materials]. Frunze, 1975. 178 pp. [Not seen].

U1470 *Pechat' Kirgizskoi SSR, 1926–1963: statisticheskie materialy.* [The Kirghiz press, 1926–1963: statistical materials]. Frunze, 1964. 75 pp.

Latvia

U1471 *Latvijas PSR prese 1940–1956: statistiko datu krājums = Pechat' Latviiskoi SSR, 1940–1956: statisticheskie materialy.* [The Latvian press, 1940–1956: statistical materials]. (M-vo kul'tury LatvSSR. Kn. palata LatvSSR). Riga: Latgosizdat, 1958. 124 pp.
In Latvian and Russian.

U1472 *Pechat' Latviiskoi SSR, . . .: statisticheskie materialy.* [The press in Latvia in . . .: statistical materials]. (Kn. palata LatvSSR). Riga, 1962 (publ. 1963)–1964 (publ. 1965). [Not seen].

Lithuania

U1473 *Lietuvos PSR spaudos, . . . = Statistika pechati Litovskoi SSR, . . .* [The press in Lithuania in . . .]. (Gos. komitet LitSSR po pechati. Kn. palata LitSSR). Vilnius: Mintis.
1940–1955. 1957. 116 pp.
1956–1960. 1962. 138 pp.
1961–1965. 1969. 179 pp.
1966–1970. 1972. 152 pp.
1971–1975. 1977.
In Lithuanian and Russian.

U1474   *Statistika pechati Litovksoi SSR*, ... [The press in Lithuania in ...]. (Kn. palata LitSSR). Vilnius, 1956–7 (publ. 1958)–. Generally annual. [Not seen].

Moldavia

U1475   *Pechat' Moldavskoi SSR, 1925–1960: statisticheskie materialy.* [The Moldavian press, 1925–1960: statistical materials]. (M-vo kul'tury MoldSSR. Kn. palata MSSR). Kishinev: Kartia moldoveniaske, 1962. 48 pp. [Not seen].

U1476   *Pechat' Moldavskoi SSR, 1961–1975 gg.: sbornik statisticheskikh materialov.* [The Moldavian press, 1961–1975: a collection of statistical materials]. (Gos. kn. palata MSSR). Kishinev, 1979. 72 pp. [Not seen].

Tajikistan

U1477   *Matbuoti RSS Tojikiston,* ...: *materialhoi statistiki = Pechat' Tadzhikskoi SSR,* ...: *statisticheskie materialy.* [The press in Tajikistan in ...: statistical materials]. (Komitet po pechati TadzhSSR. Kn. palata). Dushanbe: Kn. palata.
1928–1958. 1959. 74 pp.
1959–1963. 1964. 62 pp.
1964–1968. 1971. 87 pp.

Turkmenistan

U1478   *Pechat' Turkmenskoi SSR, 1927–1956: statisticheskie materialy.* [The press in Turkmenia in 1927–1956: statistical materials]. (M-vo kul'tury TurkmenSSR. Kn. palata). Ashkhabad, 1958. 52 pp. [Not seen].

U1479   *Pechat' Turkmenskoi SSR,* ... [The press in Turkmenia in ...]. (Goskomitet TurkmSSR po pechati). Ashkhabad, 1957–8 (publ. 1959)–. Annual. [Not seen].

Ukraine

U1480   *Presa Ukrains'koi RSR,* ...: *naukovo-statystychnyi dovidnyk.* [The press in the Ukraine in ...: a statistical handbook]. (Derzh. komitet RM URSR u spravakh vydavnytstv, polihrafii i knyzhkovoi torhivli). Kharkiv: Knizhkova palata URSR.
1917–1966. 1967. 146 pp.
1918–1973. 1974. 215 pp.
1918–1975. 1976. 223 pp.

Uzbekistan

U1481   *Pechat' Uzbekskoi SSR v 1976 g.: statisticheskie materialy.* [The Uzbek press in 1976: statistical materials]. Tashkent, 1977. 30 pp. [Not seen].

U1482   *Pechat' Uzbekistana v deviatoi piatiletke: statisticheskii sbornik.* [The Uzbek press during the ninth five-year plan, 1971–75: statistical handbook]. Tashkent, 1976. 66 pp. [Not seen].

U1483   *Pechat' Uzbekskoi SSR za 1964–1970 gody: statisticheskie materialy k 50-letiiu obrazovaniia Uzbekskoi SSR.* [The Uzbek press in 1964–1970: statistical materials for the 50th anniversary of the formation of the Uzbek SSR]. (Gos. komitet UzSSR po delam izdatel'stv, poligrafii i knizhnoi torgovli. Kn. palata UzSSR). Tashkent, 1973. 52 pp.

U1484   *Sovetskaia pechat' Uzbekskoi SSR za 1918–1963 gg.: statisticheskie materialy k 40-letiiu sovetskoi vlasti v Uzbekskoi SSR.* [The Soviet press of Uzbekistan in 1918–1963: statistical materials for the 40th anniversary of Soviet power in Uzbekistan]. (Gos. komitet UzSSR po pechati. Gos. knizhnaia palata UzSSR). Tashkent, 1965. 61 pp.

General materials on publishing and the book trade

U1485   *Knizhnaia torgovlia: dokumenty i materialy. Spravochnoe posobie.* [The book trade: documents and materials. A handbook]. M.: Kniga, 1980. 624 pp.

     Earlier edition published as: *Spravochnik normativnykh materialov dlia rabotnikov knizhnoi torgovli.* M.: Kniga, 1970. 432 pp. These handbooks for book trade workers cover CP and government policy on the distribution of books and periodicals, the organization of bookshops, library supply agencies, subscriptions to journals, books by mail order, and the wholesale book trade. The collection also covers planning, accountancy, wages, etc. in the book trade. It includes documents from the State Committee on the Press and about its work. Each section has a useful introduction, and there is a supplement listing instructions issued while the book was in press.

U1486   *Sbornik normativnykh aktov Goskomizdata SSSR.* [Collection of normative acts of the USSR State Committee for Publishing]. (Gos. komitet SSSR po delam izdatel'stv, poligrafii i knizhnoi torgovli). M.: Kniga, 1977–.

     Vol. 1 covers publishing activity; presumably later volumes will cover printing and the book trade. The collection is intended for workers in publishing, printing and the book trade, and includes much material not available elsewhere. It consists of instructions, orders and circulars and other documents from Goskomizdat, 1965–76, plus some earlier OGIZ material still in force. Limited edition.

U1487   *Sbornik normativnykh materialov po roznichnym tsenam na izdatel'skuiu produktsiiu.* [A collection of normative materials on retail prices for published materials]. M.: Kniga, 1974. 112 pp.

U1488   *Sovetskaia pechat' v dokumentakh.* [The Soviet press in documents]. M.: Gospolitizdat, 1961. 560 pp.

     A collection of CPSU documents on the press, covering general ideological questions, the role of the press in party work and in economic and social progress, the work of the worker and peasant correspondents and other aspects of mass work, newspapers, publishing houses and general documents. Includes material to 1960, and is annotated and indexed.

U1489   *Spravochnik normativnykh materialov dlia izdatel'skikh rabotnikov.* [A manual of normative materials for publishing house staff]. Sost.: V. A. Markus. M.: Kniga, 1977. 366 pp.

Earlier editions publ. by Iskusstvo in 1958 (481 pp.) and by Kniga in 1969 (347 pp.). A collection of regulations, mostly from Goskomizdat, on the organization of the publishing house, staff and salaries, methods of measuring output, preparation and editing of manuscripts, relations with authors, artists, outside editors and with the printer and the book trade.

Translations

For translations of some material on publishing, *see* U1496b

Copyright and authors' and artists' rights

U1490   *Avtorskoe pravo na literaturnye proizvedeniia: sbornik ofitsial'nykh materialov.* [Authors' rights in literary works: a collection of official materials]. Sost.: L. M. Azov, S. A. Shatsillo. M.: Gosiurizdat, 1953. 134 pp.

Basic USSR and RSFSR legislation on authors' rights, publishers' contracts and payments to authors. Alphabetical subject index.

U1491   *Khudozhestvennyi fond SSSR: sbornik rukovodiashchikh materialov.* [The USSR Artists' Fund: a collection of guiding materials]. Sost.: Iu. I. Savitskii, T. P. Mironova. M.: Sov. khudozhnik, 1970. 811 pp.

Documents up to March 1970 on all aspects of the work of the Artists' Fund and includes general USSR legislation and other materials on artists' rights.

U1492   Levitsky, S. L. *Introduction to Soviet copyright law.* (Law in Eastern Europe, 8). Leiden: Sijthoff, 1964. 303 pp.

The monograph is accompanied by texts of relevant legislation (as of 1962) and a full list of all Soviet legislative acts relating to copyright.

U1493   Newcity, M. A. *Copyright law in the Soviet Union.* N.Y., London: Praeger, 1978. x, 212 pp.

As well as a detailed analysis of Soviet copyright law, includes the copyright provisions of the USSR Fundamental Principles of Civil Legislation as amended in 1973, and the relevant articles of the RSFSR Civil Code, as amended to October 1976.

U1494   *Normativnye akty po avtorskomu pravu. Izdanie proizvedenii.*

Vzaimootnoshenie s inostrannymi avtorami i izdatel'stvami. [Normative acts on copyright. Relations with foreign authors and publishers]. M.: Iurid. lit-ra, 1979. 304 pp.

Includes legislation, regulations, etc. on Soviet copyright law, model publishers' agreements and the statutes of VAAP, Mezhdunarodnaia kniga and Goskomizdat. Includes the texts of various international agreements on copyright, mainly between the USSR and Comecon countries.

U1495 *Sbornik rukovodiashchikh materialov dlia otdelenii i upolnomochennykh VUOAP.* [A collection of materials guiding the work of branches and officials of the All-Union Administration for the Protection of Authors' Rights]. (Vses. upr. po okhrane avtorskikh prav). M., 1959. 86 pp.

Copy marked 'For official use'. Relates to authors' payments, authors' rights and membership of Litfond and the Muzykal'nyi fond. Includes materials published in 1958 only.

U1496a 'Soviet copyright law'. *Soviet statutes and decisions,* vol. 14, nos. 1 and 2, 1977–8.

U1496b 'Soviet copyright and publishing law'. *Soviet statutes and decisions,* vol. 14, nos. 3 and 4, 1978.

These two issues of *SS&D* (*see* U164) consist of translations of Soviet normative material on publishing and on copyright.

Religious affairs

The USSR constitution gives Soviet citizens the right to confess any religion or not to confess such, to perform religious cults, or to carry on atheistic propaganda. The church in the USSR is separated from the state and from the school. Religious affairs in the USSR are supervised by the Committee on Religious Affairs of the USSR Council of Ministers.

U1497 Gidulianov, P. V. *Otdelenie tserkvi ot gosudarstva v SSSR: polnyi sbornik dekretov, vedomstvennykh rasporiazhenii i opredelenii Verkhsuda R.S.F.S.R. i drugikh sovetskikh sotsialisticheskikh respublik: U.S.S.R., B.S.S.R., Z.S.F.S.R., Uzbekskoi i Turkmenskoi.* [Separation of the church and the state in the USSR: complete collection of decrees, administrative decisions and decisions of the Supreme Court of the RSFSR and other republics: the Ukraine, Belorussia, the Transcaucasian Federation, Uzbekistan and Turkmenistan]. Pod red. P. A. Krasikova. Izd. 3, perer. i dop. uzakoneniiami i rasporiazheniiami po 15 maia 1926g. M.: Iurid. izd-vo NKIu RSFSR, 1926. 712 pp.

With a 36-page supplement through to 1928; reprinted by Gregg International, 1971. Despite its age, this is the most complete collection of legal material on religious affairs in the USSR which is publicly available; much of the material in it is still in force.

U1498 Loeber, D. A. 'The legal position of the church in the Soviet Union'.

Studies on the Soviet Union. Vol. 9, no. 2, 1969. Pp. 16–50.

Appendix I has the Russian text and a translation of a 1945 decree on the church. Appendix II has a bibliography of RSFSR and USSR statutory material with details of translations. Appendix III is a general bibliography on the legal status of the church in the USSR.

U1499 *O religii i tserkvi: sbornik vazhneishikh vyskazyvanii klassikov marksizma-leninizma, dokumentov KPSS i sovetskogo gosudarstva.* [On religion and the church: a collection of the sayings of the classics of Marxism-Leninism, and CPSU and Soviet government documents]. Izd. 2-e, dop. M.: Politizdat, 1981. 176 pp.

First edition published 1977 (144 pp.). Earlier edition: *Kommunisticheskaia partiia i sovetskoe pravitel'stvo o religii i tserkvi.* M.: Gospolitizdat, 1959. 119 pp. The collections are annotated and include extracts from Marx and Lenin as well as party and USSR government materials, mainly from the prewar period. The 1977 edition also includes some RSFSR and Uzbek materials.

U1500 *Zakonodatel'stvo o religioznykh kul'takh: sbornik materialov i dokumentov.* [Legislation on religious cults: a collection of materials and documents]. Izd. 2-e, dop. M.: Iurid. lit-ra, 1971. 335 pp.

Copy seen marked 'For official use' and printed in an edition of 21,000 copies. Intended to be used by officials of local soviets, procuracy offices and other organizations dealing with religious matters. The first two sections of the collection include excerpts from the classics of Marxism–Leninism and party documents, all readily available elsewhere. Section 3 contains state (all-union) legislation relating to religion and the church, much of it not published in the open press. Section 4 is devoted to legislation of the union republics; most of these documents have not been published in the open press. Section 5 deals with penalties for infringing legislation on religion, mainly from the criminal codes. There is a supplement giving basic data on religions practised in the USSR, a short glossary and a subject index.

LEADERS' WORKS

Introduction

Publications by leading members of the CPSU and the Soviet government are extremely important for determining policy, providing ideological guidance and indicating priorities and problems in all areas of the nation's life. Major speeches by members of the Politburo are usually published as separate pamphlets as well as appearing in the newspapers. Leading party and government officials also contribute articles to general journals and to specialist journals dealing with their particular field of responsibility. Until the early 1970s, it was usually only the Party Secretary who had collections published of his speeches and articles, but in the last decade this distinction has been conferred on other members of the Politburo.

This section lists only collections of articles and speeches, and major monographs. Where English translations of these volumes are known, they are listed; for other translations, *CDSP* (U853) and *Soviet news* (U858) should be consulted. Translations of speeches at party congresses can be found in the translations of the proceedings of those congresses (see the section 'Communist Party'). Lenin is included in this section; although he died in 1924 his ideas and policies still constitute the guiding ideology of the USSR and his works cannot be ignored when studying the postwar USSR. However, for reasons of space only the latest edition of his collected works is included here; some selections of his writings on various topics, together with CPSU documents, are also included, but are to be found in the appropriate sections of this bibliography. Anthologies which deal with Lenin alone are excluded.

General

U1501   *XXIV s"ezd KPSS: edinstvo teorii i praktiki.* [The 24th Congress of the CPSU: unity of theory and practice]. M.: Politizdat, 1974–6. 3 vols.
    A collection of speeches and articles publ. 1972–5 by members of the Central Committee of the CPSU and other senior officials, showing how the decisions of the 24th Party Congress are being carried out. They are mainly reprinted from *Pravda, Kommunist* and *Partiinaia zhizn'*.

U1502   *XXV s"ezd KPSS: edinstvo teorii i praktiki.* [The 25th Congress of the CPSU: unity of theory and practice]. M.: Politizdat, 1977–81. 8 vols.
    Similar to U1501, containing articles from 1976 to 1980.

U1503   *A documentary history of Communism.* Edited, with an introduction, notes and new translations, by Robert V. Daniels. N.Y.: Vintage Books, 1960. 2 vols.
    Vol. 1 deals with the USSR to 1928, and includes translations of some of Lenin's and Stalin's policy statements. Vol. 2 covers international communism 1919–57 and the USSR 1929–59. It includes Stalin's speeches and other documents relating to the Second World War, some of his speeches and articles from 1945 to 1953, and some of Khrushchev's speeches and articles 1955–9, including extracts from the 'Secret Speech'. Many of the documents included are given in extract form only.

U1504   *Lenin, Stalin, Khrushchev: voices of Bolshevism.* Ed. by Robert H. McNeal. Englewood Cliffs, N.J.: Prentice-Hall, 1963. viii, 180 pp.
    A selection of major speeches and articles, briefly annotated.

Collections of individual leaders' works

Andropov

U1505 Andropov, Iu. V. *Izbrannye stat'i i rechi.* [Selected speeches and articles]. M.: Politizdat, 1979. 318 pp.

Chairman of the Committee of State Security since 1967. This collection covers 1942–79 and deals with party organization, international and ideological matters; there is also some material on the work of the KGB. The collection includes some items not previously published.

Brezhnev

Member of the Politburo since 1957; Party Secretary since 1966.

U1506 Brezhnev, L. I. *Aktual'nye voprosy ideologicheskoi raboty KPSS.* [Current problems in the CPSU's ideological work]. M.: Politizdat, 1978. 2 vols.

Covers 1964–78 and includes *Malaia zemlia* and *Vozrozhdenie* as well as works on ideology, education, culture and the arts. Subject index.

U1507 Brezhnev, L. I. *KPSS v bor'be za edinstvo vsekh revoliutsionnykh i miroliubivykh sil.* [The CPSU in the struggle for the unity of all revolutionary and peace-loving forces]. 2 izd., dop. M.: Mysl', 1979. 493 pp.

1st ed. publ. 1972 (303 pp.). Includes speeches 1967–79 at foreign CP congresses, international meetings, etc.

U1508 Brezhnev, L. I. *Leninskim kursom: rechi i stat'i.* [On a Leninist course: speeches and article]. M.: Politizdat, 1970–. Vol. 1–.

The main collection of Brezhnev's works, from 1964; some material is published in an abbreviated form. His memoirs, *Malaia zemlia*, *Vozrozhdenie* and *Tselina* are all included in vol. 7 (1979).

U1509 Brezhnev, L. I. *Mir sotsializma—torzhestvo velikikh idei* [The socialist world is a triumph of great ideas]. M.: Politizdat, 1978. 656 pp.

Works 1964–78 on international friendship among socialist states, including many speeches at meetings abroad. Subject index.

U1510 Brezhnev. L. I. *Molodym—stroit' kommunizm.* [Young people will build communism]. 3 izd., dop. M.: Politizdat, 1978. 736 pp.

Earlier editions publ. 1970 (400 pp.) and 1974 (527 pp.). Works on the Komsomol, party education, international youth movements and ideology.

U1511 Brezhnev, L. I. *Na strazhe mira i sotsializma.* [In the defence of peace and socialism]. M.: Politizdat, 1979. 663 pp.
On foreign policy and disarmament, 1964–78.

U1512 Brezhnev, L. I. *O kommunisticheskom vospitanii trudiashchikhsia: rechi i stat'i.* [On the communist upbringing of the workers: speeches and articles]. 2 izd., dop. M.: Politizdat, 1975. 639 pp.
1st ed. publ. 1974 (559 pp.). Covers various aspects of education, agitation and propaganda, and ideological work. Subject index.

U1513 Brezhnev, L. I. *O vneshnei politike KPSS i sovetskogo gosudarstva.* [On the foreign policy of the CPSU and the Soviet state]. Izd. 3-e, dop. M.: Politizdat, 1978. 759 pp.
1st ed. publ. 1973 (599 pp.), 2nd ed. publ. 1975 (879 pp.). Covers foreign policy and world affairs since 1964.

U1514 Brezhnev, L. I. *Ob aktual'nykh problemakh partiinogo stroitel'stva.* [On current problems of party construction]. Izd. 2-e, dop. M.: Politizdat, 1976. 775 pp.
1st ed. publ. 1973 (456 pp.). Covers various aspects of party work, 1964–76, including the nomenklatura, CPSU relations with the armed forces, voluntary organizations and the state apparatus. Subject index.

U1515 Brezhnev, L. I. *Ob osnovnykh voprosakh ekonomicheskoi politiki KPSS na sovremennom etape: rechi i doklady.* [Basic questions of the current economic policy of the CPSU: speeches and reports]. Izd. 2-e, dop. M.: Politizdat, 1979. 2 vols.
1st ed. publ. 1975 (2 vols.). All areas of economic policy are covered.

U1516 Brezhnev, L. I. *Selected speeches and writings on foreign affairs.* Oxford [etc.]: Pergamon, 1979. vii, 305 pp.
Covers 1970–8.

U1517 Brezhnev, L. I. *Socialism, democracy and human rights.* Oxford [etc.]: Pergamon, 1980. xi, 247 pp.

U1518 Brezhnev, L. I. *Sovetskie profsoiuzy v usloviiakh razvitogo sotsializma.* [Soviet trade unions under full socialism]. M.: Politizdat, 1978. 575 pp.
Works on the trade unions, 1964–77. Subject index.

U1519 Brezhnev, L. I. *Voprosy upravleniia ekonomikoi razvitogo sotsialisticheskogo obshchestva: rechi, doklady, vystupleniia.* [Managing the economy in a developed socialist society: speeches, reports, addresses]. M.: Politizdat, 1976. 600 pp.
Materials on economic matters, 1964–76. Subject index.

U1520 *Leonid Il'ich Brezhnev: kratkii biograficheskii ocherk.* [Leonid Il'ich Brezhnev: a short biographical sketch]. Izd. 2-e, dop. (In-t marksizma-leninizma pri TsK KPSS). M.: Politizdat, 1977. 192 pp.

1st ed. publ. 1976 (208 pp.). This is the official biography of Brezhnev, prepared by the Institute of Marxism–Leninism of the Central Committee of the CPSU. An English translation of the first edition appeared as: *Leonid Il'ich Brezhnev, General Secretary of the Communist Party of the Soviet Union: a short biography*. M.: Novosti, 1976. 109 pp.; and of the second as: *Leonid Ilyich Brezhnev: a short biography*. Oxford [etc.]: Pergamon, 1977.

Chernenko

U1521 Chernenko, K. U. *Nekotorye voprosy tvorcheskogo razvitiia stilia partiinoi i gosudarstvennoi raboty*. [Some problems of the creative development of party and state work]. M.: Politizdat, 1978. 255 pp.

1st ed. publ. 1977 (95 pp.). Member of the Politburo since 1978. Monograph on ideology and the links between the party, the government and the people.

Grishin

U1522 Grishin, V. V. *Izbrannye rechi i stat'i*. [Selected speeches and articles]. M.: Politizdat, 1979. 654 pp.

Member of the Politburo since 1971 and First Secretary of Moscow City Party Organization since 1967. Collection covers all fields, 1952–79.

Gromyko

Minister of Foreign Affairs since 1957 and a member of the Politburo since 1973.

U1523 Gromyko, A. *Lenin and the Soviet peace policy: articles and speeches, 1944–1980*. M.: Progress, 1980. 496 pp.

U1524 Gromyko, A. *Only for peace: selected speeches and writing*. Oxford [etc.]: Pergamon, 1979. x, 277 pp.

As well as material written in the 1960s and 1970s, includes an autobiographical introduction.

U1525 Gromyko, A. A. *Vo imia torzhestva leninskoi vneshnei politiki: izbrannye rechi i stat'i*. [In the name of the triumph of Lenin's foreign policy: selected speeches and articles]. M.: Politizdat, 1978. 599 pp.

Covers 1964–78.

Kalinin

Head of state, 1919–46; several collections of his works have been published, of which this is the fullest:

U1526 Kalinin, M. I. *Izbrannye proizvedeniia*. [Selected works]. (In-t marksizma-leninizma pri TsK KPSS). M.: Politizdat, 1960–75. 4 vols.

Vols. 1–3 were publ. 1960–2; vol. 4 appeared in 1975 with the title *Stat'i i rechi*. Each volume is annotated and has a chronology of

Kalinin's life; vol. 4 has a chronological and alphabetical index to the whole collection.

Khrushchev

Khrushchev (1894–1971) was First Secretary of the Central Committee of the CPSU, 1953–64, and also Chairman of the USSR Council of Ministers, 1958–64, thus occupying both the key party and government posts.

For editions of his 'Secret Speech', see the material on the 20th Party Congress in U563a–h.

U1527 *Khrushchev speaks: selected articles and press conferences, 1949–1961.* Ed. with commentary by Thomas P. Whitney. Ann Arbor: University of Michigan, 1963. vi, 466 pp.

17 documents, each with a short introduction.

U1528 Khrushchev, N. S. *Kommunizm—mir i schast'e narodov.* [Communism is peace and happiness for the people]. M.: Gospolitizdat, 1962. 2 vols.

On foreign policy matters. Also publ. in English as: *Communism—peace and happiness for the peoples.* M.: FLPH, 1963. 2 vols.

U1529 Khrushchev, N. S. *O kommunisticheskom vospitanii.* [On communist upbringing]. M.: Politizdat, 1964. 349 pp.

Speeches and articles, 1956–64, on education and moral development, including speeches to the Komsomol. Subject index.

U1530 Khrushchev, N. S. *O vneshnei politike Sovetskogo Soiuza, 1960 god.* [On the USSR's foreign policy in 1960]. M.: Gospolitizdat, 1961. 2 vols.

Selected speeches and articles.

U1531 Khrushchev, N. S. *Predotvratit' voinu, otstoiat' mir!* [To prevent war and defend peace!]. M.: Gospolitizdat, 1963. 447 pp.

Speeches and articles on foreign affairs.

U1532 Khrushchev, N. S. *Sovremennyi etap kommunisticheskogo stroitel'stva i zadachi partii po uluchsheniiu rukovodstva sel'skim khoziaistvom.* [The present stage of building communism and the tasks of the party in improving the management of agriculture]. M.: Gospolitizdat, 1962. 448 pp.

Speeches October 1961–March 1962 on agriculture.

U1533 Khrushchev, N. S. *Stroitel'stvo kommunizma v SSSR i razvitie sel'skogo khoziaistva.* [The building of communism and the development of agriculture]. M.: Politizdat, 1962–4. 8 vols.

Covers a wide range of his speeches and writings from September 1953 to March 1964, including a few items not previously published elsewhere.

U1534 *Khrushchev remembers*; trans. and ed. by Strobe Talbott with an introduction, commentary and notes by Edward Crankshaw. Boston, Mass.: Little, Brown; London: Deutsch, 1970–4. 2 vols.

An illustrated translation of Khrushchev's reminiscences, as constructed from 'material emanating from various sources at various times and in various circumstances'. There have been doubts about the authenticity of the memoirs, but they are now generally accepted as genuinely originating with Khrushchev and largely his work. The memoirs confirm many hypotheses held by Western scholars and give a detailed and vivid picture of life under Stalin and some impression of events after Stalin's death. In his reminiscences of life after 1956, Khrushchev is less illuminating on domestic affairs but devotes some space to foreign affairs and his visits abroad.

Kirilenko

Member of the Politburo since 1962.

U1535 Kirilenko, A. P. *Izbrannye stat'i i rechi*. [Selected speeches and articles]. M.: Politizdat, 1976. 511 pp.
Material 1965–76 on social and political questions, and the economy.

U1536 Kirilenko, A. P. *Politika sozidaniia i mira: izbrannye rechi i stat'i*. [A constructive and peaceful policy: selected speeches and articles]. M.: Politizdat, 1980. 759 pp. [Not seen].

Kosygin

Chairman of the USSR Council of Ministers, 1964–80, and a member of the Politburo, 1948–52 and 1960–80.

U1537 Kosygin, A. N. *Izbrannye stat'i i rechi*. [Selected speeches and articles]. M.: Politizdat, 1974. 783 pp.
Mainly economic affairs and foreign economic policy, 1939–74.

U1538 Kosygin, A. N. *K velikoi tseli: izbrannye rechi i stat'i*. [Towards a great goal: selected speeches and articles]. M.: Politizdat, 1979. 2 vols.
Documents 1939–78, but mainly from the post-1964 period, on economic affairs and foreign economic policy.

Kulakov

U1539 Kulakov, F. D. *Izbrannye stat'i i rechi*. [Selected speeches and articles]. M.: Politizdat, 1978. 463 pp.
Member of Politburo, 1965–78, mainly responsible for agriculture. This collection covers his works during that period on agriculture, foreign affairs and party policy in general.

Kunaev

U1540 Kunaev, D. A. *Izbrannye stat'i i rechi*. [Selected speeches and articles]. M.: Politizdat, 1978. 511 pp.
Member of the Politburo since 1971 and Party Secretary of the

Kazakh CP since 1964. Collection covers 1965–78 and deals with agriculture, relations between the peoples of the USSR and domestic issues in general, and some speeches made while heading Soviet delegations abroad.

Lenin

U1541 Lenin, V. I. *Polnoe sobranie sochinenii*. [Complete collected works]. 5 izd. (In-t marksizma-leninizma pri TsK KPSS). M.: Gospolitizdat, 1958–70. 55 vols. plus indexes.

The fullest edition available; some material not included may be found in the irregular serial *Leninskii sbornik*. An alphabetical index appeared in 1966 and a two-part *Spravochnyi tom* in 1969–70, which includes a full subject index, title index, and various other indexes. A translation is available of the 4th ed.: Lenin, V. I. *Collected works*. London: Lawrence and Wishart, 1960–70. 45 vols.

Molotov

U1542 Molotov, V. M. *Voprosy vneshnei politiki: rechi i zaiavleniia, aprel' 1945 g.–iiun' 1948 g.* [Problems of foreign policy: speeches and announcements, April 1945–June 1948]. M.: Gospolitizdat, 1948. 587 pp.

Minister of Foreign Affairs, 1939–49 and 1953–6.

Pel'she

U1543 Pel'she, A. Ia. *Izbrannye stat'i i rechi.* [Selected speeches and articles]. M.: Politizdat, 1978. 671 pp.

Member of the Politburo since 1966 and for many years First Secretary of the Latvian CP. Covers 1940–77, mainly in the fields of nationality policy, agitation and propaganda. Subject index.

Ponomarev

U1544 Ponomarev, B. N. *Izbrannoe: rechi i stat'i.* [Selected speeches and articles]. M.: Politizdat, 1977. 624 pp.

An alternate member of the Politburo; on the CPSU Central Committee secretariat since 1961. This collection covers 1934–76, mainly in the fields of ideology, party organization and party history.

Romanov

U1545 Romanov, G. V. *Izbrannye stat'i i rechi.* [Selected speeches and articles]. M.: Politizdat, 1980. 615 pp.

Member of the Politburo since 1976 and First Secretary of the Leningrad Obkom of the CPSU since 1970. This collection covers materials publ. 1971–80 in all areas, but especially on the economy.

Shcherbitskii

U1546 Shcherbitskii, V. V. *Izbrannye stat'i i rechi*. [Selected speeches and articles]. M.: Politizdat, 1978. 624 pp.

Member of the Politburo since 1971 and, since May 1972, First Secretary of the Ukrainian CP. Covers from mid-1960s to 1978, mainly party organization, political and ideological work, the economy.

Shelest

U1547 Shelest, P. E. *Idei Lenina pobezhdaiut*. [Lenin's ideas are victorious]. Kiev: Politizdat Ukrainy, 1971. 395 pp.

Also publ. in Ukrainian. Speeches and articles on party work in the Ukraine by its Party Secretary until his fall in 1972. [Not seen].

Stalin

Joseph Stalin was General Secretary of the CPSU from 1922 until his death in 1953; he was the dominant political figure during most of the postwar decade and the consequences of his rule and reactions to it coloured much of the political life of the later 1950s, 1960s and 1970s. During his lifetime his speeches and writings were assiduously published in the USSR, but the publication of his collected works ceased shortly after his death and it was left to Western scholars to complete the bibliographical listing of his works and publish the major ones from his last twenty years.

U1548 *The essential Stalin: major theoretical writings, 1905–1952*. Ed. and with an introduction by Bruce Franklin. London: Croom Helm, 1973. 511 pp.

Translations of a number of Stalin's works, including *Marxism and linguistics, Economic problems of socialism in the USSR, Foundations of Leninism* and his reports to the 17th, 18th and 19th party congresses.

U1549 McNeal, R. H. *Stalin's works: an annotated bibliography*. (Hoover Institution Bibliographical Series, 26). Stanford, Calif.: Hoover Institution on War, Revolution and Peace, 1967. 197 pp.

Covers Stalin's works from 1895 to 1952, including the many documents excluded from the official Soviet *Sochineniia*. Gives a reference to the place where a work was first published and records its location (if any) in the *Sochineniia*. There is an introduction discussing previous bibliographies of Stalin's works, problems of attribution and authenticity, and the ways in which the versions in the *Sochineniia* differ from the originals. Includes the text of two documents, and an index.

U1550 Stalin, I. V. *Sochineniia*. [Works]. (In-t Marksa-Engel'sa-Lenina pri TsK VKP(b)). M.: Gospolitizdat, 1946–53. Vols. 1–13.

An English translation is available as: *Works*. M.: FLPH, 1952–5. Vols. 1–13. The collection includes some of Stalin's works up to

1934; later items are available in the American edition, *see* U1551. No Soviet index was published, but one was prepared by the US Department of State: Matlock, J. F. *An index to the collected works of J. V. Stalin.* (External Research Paper No. 118, Jan. 15 1955). [Washington]: External Research Staff, Office of Intelligence Research, Dept. of State, [1955]. [Reprinted 1973 by Kraus Reprint]. 193 pp. The index covers personal names and names of organizations; titles of publications; major subject categories.

U1551   Stalin, I. V. *Sochineniia = Works,* ed. by R. H. McNeal. Stanford, Calif.: Hoover Institution on War, Revolution and Peace, 1967. vols. 1(14)–3(16).

Continues the Russian edition by publishing work of 1934–53; does not include any of the pre-1934 items omitted from the Soviet collection. Text is in Russian, with an English introduction.

U1552   Stalin, I. V. *Voprosy Leninizma.* [Problems of Leninism]. 11 izd. M.: OGIZ, Gospolitizdat, 1952. 651 pp.

Previous editions publ. 1929–38; the 11th ed. was reprinted several times 1945–52. A number of English translations exist based on the different editions. The work is in fact a selection of Stalin's writings and his speeches at party congresses and plenums, and to other organizations.

U1553   *Iosif Vissarionovich Stalin: kratkaia biografiia.* [J. V. Stalin: a short biography]. Sost.: G. F. Aleksandrov, [i dr.]. 2 izd., ispr. i dop. M.: OGIZ, 1947. 243 pp.

1st ed. publ. 1940 (87 pp.); many different versions of both editions were publ. 1940–52, and several English translations are available. One based on this 2nd ed. is: *Joseph Stalin: a short biography,* comp. by G. F. Alexandrov. M.: FLPH, 1952. 206 pp. This work is the official biography of Stalin.

Suslov

Member of the Politburo, 1952–3 and since 1955 and is particularly influential in ideological matters.

U1554   Suslov, M. A. *Izbrannoe: rechi i stat'i.* [Selected speeches and articles]. M.: Politizdat, 1972. 695 pp.

Covers 1941–72 in the fields of ideology, economy and culture.

U1555   Suslov, M. A. *Marksizm-leninizm i sovremennaia epokha: sbornik vystuplenii.* [Marxism-leninism and the modern world: a collection of speeches]. 2 izd., dop. M.: Politizdat, 1980. 198 pp.

1st ed. publ. 1979 (95 pp.). Includes speeches, etc. 1977–9, mainly on ideology.

U1556   Suslov, M. A. *Na putiakh stroitel'stva kommunizma: rechi i stat'i.* [On the road to the building of communism: speeches and articles]. M.: Politizdat, 1977. 2 vols.

Covers 1938–76, especially in ideological and cultural fields, but also the economy. Subject index.

U1557 Suslov, M. A. *Selected speeches and writings*. Oxford [etc.]: Pergamon, 1980. 368 pp. [Not seen].

Tikhonov

U1558 Tikhonov, N. A. *Izbrannye stat'i i rechi*. [Selected speeches and articles]. M.: Politizdat, 1980. 448 pp.

Member of Central Committee since 1966 and since 1980 Chairman of the Council of Ministers (he was Deputy Chairman 1965–80). This collection covers 1941–80 and is mainly concerned with the economy, foreign trade and party policy and organization.

Ustinov

U1559 Ustinov, D. F. *Izbrannye stat'i i rechi*. [Selected speeches and articles]. M.: Politizdat, 1979. 519 pp.

USSR Minister of Defence and, since 1976, member of the Politburo. This collection covers 1942–70, with the emphasis on recent materials, international relations and defence. Subject index.

Voznesenskii

U1560 Voznesenskii, N. A. *Izbrannye proizvedeniia, 1931–1947*. [Selected works, 1931–1947]. (In-t marksizma-leninizma pri TsK KPSS). M.: Politizdat, 1979. 606 pp.

Chairman of Gosplan, 1938–47. This collection includes some postwar material.

X INTERNATIONAL AND MULTINATIONAL OFFICIAL PUBLICATIONS

Gregory Walker

INTRODUCTION

This chapter aims to include the most important publications in the following categories:

Bibliographies providing significant coverage of official publications issued in more than one European socialist country, and/or by one or more of the international organizations set up by the socialist states.

Collections of official publications issued by more than one European socialist state or ruling communist party.

Collections of statistics issued by more than one European socialist state or under the auspices of a socialist international organization.

Official publications concerning the CMEA and other forms of international economic cooperation between socialist states.

Official publications concerning the Warsaw Treaty Organization.

CMEA

The Council for Mutual Economic Assistance (abbreviated in English to CMEA or Comecon; in Russian, Sovet Ekonomicheskoi Vzaimopomoshchi or SEV) was set up on 8 January 1949 after a conference on economic affairs attended by representatives of the USSR, Bulgaria, Czechoslovakia, Hungary, Poland and Romania, which all became founder members, with Albania joining the following month. The German Democratic Republic was admitted in 1950, Mongolia in 1962, Yugoslavia to a form of associated status in 1964, Cuba in 1972 and Vietnam in 1978. Certain other states have been invited to Council Sessions as observers: China was so invited until an undetermined point in the mid-1960s, and those attending in 1980 were Afghanistan, Angola, Ethiopia, North Korea, Laos, Mozambique and the People's Democratic Republic of Yemen. Albania has not participated in the CMEA's activities since 1961. From shortly after its foundation until 1954, the CMEA was virtually dormant as an organization, and its work gained in tempo only gradually after that date. It acquired a charter as late as December 1959, which was amended in 1962 and again in 1974.

The CMEA's overall aim is to strengthen the solidarity of its member states through economic cooperation to foster development and improve living standards. Coordination has made a good deal of progress at the level of some individual industrial branches, and in certain infrastructural services such as transport and statistics; but although the CMEA adopted the 'Basic Principles of the International Socialist Division of Labour' in 1962, subsequent resistance by some members—notably Romania—to Soviet pressure for a greater degree of supranational economic management has allowed all members to retain what J. M. van Brabant has called 'their prerogative to formulate national economic plans autonomously and to embrace uncoordinated policies'. Even the 'Comprehensive Programme' of 1971, although it envisaged a much broader basis for planning coordination than previously, did not alter this principle.

Although the main policy decisions affecting the CMEA are taken at meetings of party and government leaders of the member states, either outside the formal framework of the organization or as 'Special Sessions' of the Council, it is in principle directed by Sessions of the Council, which have taken place annually since 1962. National delegations to each Session are usually led by the Chairman of the Council of Ministers of each country. The Executive Committee (which replaced the Conference of Representatives in 1962) is responsible to the Council Session, and meets about once a quarter, with a Deputy Chairman of the Council of Ministers heading each delegation. The CMEA's Secretariat, based in Moscow, is the Council's permanent administrative organ. There are three Committees reporting to the Council on major areas of cooperative effort: planning; scientific and technical cooperation; and material and technical supplies. Twenty-two Standing Commissions and seven Standing Conferences, most linked to a department in the CMEA Secretariat, deal with matters affecting separate branches of the economy and other specialized matters such as standardization and statistics.

In looser association with the CMEA, but operating in coordination with it under agreements, are a wide and rather disparate range of other specialized agencies (described in detail in X23). They include the International Bank for Economic Cooperation, the International Investment Bank, organizations for cooperation in rail freight transport, power systems, the ball-bearing, metal and chemical industries, and the International Centre for Scientific and Technical Information in Moscow.

In comparison with most major international organizations, the CMEA issues to the public a very limited range of publications arising from its activities. Many items published by its Secretariat have appeared in extremely small numbers and are apparently intended for restricted circulation. Nevertheless, the Secretariat is responsible for the bulk of the CMEA's printed output, while a small number of important documents, collections and some other items intended for a wide readership, are entrusted to regular publishing houses (almost always Soviet, but sometimes with translations published in other countries). Shorter public announcements, such as the communiqués on Council Sessions, are printed in *Pravda* and other leading dailies in member states.

Warsaw Treaty Organization

The Warsaw Treaty was signed on 14 May 1955 as a basis for military cooperation between the USSR and the socialist states of Eastern Europe, a few days after the Federal Republic of Germany was admitted to membership of NATO. The signatories of 1955—the USSR, Albania, Bulgaria, Czechoslovakia, the German Democratic Republic, Hungary, Poland and Romania—still constitute the membership of the WTO today, with the exception of Albania, which withdrew in September 1968 as a protest against the invasion of Czechoslovakia. China held observer status at meetings of the WTO's Political Consultative Committee from 1955 to 1961, as did Mongolia and North Korea in 1960–1; but since 1962 there have been no observers at PCC meetings, although Mongolian, North Korean and Cuban observers attend the joint manoeuvres.

At the head of the WTO is the Political Consultative Committee, which normally meets in formal session only at one- or two-year intervals. It consists of party and government heads, usually accompanied by Foreign and Defence Ministers. Its meetings are followed by communiqués, and sometimes by 'resolutions', 'declarations' or other documents directed at the general public. A separate Committee of Defence Ministers of WTO member states was set up in 1969, and a Committee of Foreign Ministers in 1976. The communiqués following the latter's meetings have been described by an authoritative Soviet source as 'documents of great political significance' (*Mezhdunarodnye organizatsii sotsialisticheskikh gosudarstv* (M.: 1980), pp. 36–7). The 'professional' military structure of the organization is headed by the Military Council, set up in 1969, which is believed to meet about twice a year. It consists of the Commander-in-Chief and the Chief of Staff of the Joint Armed Forces, and Deputy Ministers of Defence of the member states.

The Warsaw Treaty Organization does not itself act as a publisher of material for open distribution; and the WTO's Secretariat, unlike that of the CMEA, produces no public documentation on the organization's work. Important documents intended for public consultation are either issued by regular publishing houses in the USSR and other member states; or, in the case of shorter items such as communiqués on PCC or other committees' meetings, they appear in *Pravda*, *Krasnaia zvezda* and other major dailies. The main authorized collection of published documents is X39, but several collections in English with Western-orientated commentaries have also appeared and are listed below.

BIBLIOGRAPHIES

X1 Leideritz, P. M. *Key to the study of East European law.* Deventer: Kluwer, 1978. xviii, 168 pp.

Part 1 is a bibliography of bibliographies for the study of East European law, Part 2 a location guide to Dutch libraries' holdings of relevant periodicals and series.

X2 *Razvitie mirovoi sotsialisticheskoi sistemy khoziaistva i ekonomiche-skoe sotrudnichestvo evropeiskikh sotsialisticheskikh stran-uchastnits SEV. Bibliografiia. (Knigi i stat'i 1957–1962 gg.).* [The development of the world socialist economic system and the economic cooperation of the European socialist member-states of the CMEA. (Books and articles 1957–1962)]. (AN SSSR, FBON). M.: 1964. 167 pp.

Lists 1922 items published in the area dealt with, chiefly journal articles and documents, with a limited amount of newspaper material. Name/title indexes.

X3 *Novaia sovetskaia i inostrannaia literatura po obshchestvennym naukam. Evropeiskie sotsialisticheskie strany: obshchie problemy.* [New Soviet and foreign literature in the social sciences. The European socialist countries: general problems]. M.: INION, 1976–. Monthly.

Continuation of *Novaia literatura po obshchim problemam evropeiskikh sotsialisticheskikh stran,* M.: FBON, 1964–75, monthly. Lists books, articles, documents and reviews on a wide range of matters affecting more than one European socialist country, and on the CMEA and WTO. Western publications are also represented. Short descriptive annotations. No indexes.

X4 *Ekonomicheskoe i nauchno–tekhnicheskoe sotrudnichestvo evropeiskikh sotsialisticheskikh stran. Kompleksnaia programma sotsialisticheskoi ekonomicheskoi integratsii. Ukaz. lit. [. . .] 1969–1973 gg.* [Economic and scientific–technical cooperation of the European socialist countries. The comprehensive programme of socialist economic integration. Bibliography . . . 1969–1973]. M.: INION, 1975. 2 vols. and supplement.

4,432 entries in the two main volumes with common name/title index. Primarily journal articles, but with documentary publications well covered. Limited to material published in the countries dealt with. The supplement covers Yugoslav cooperation with the CMEA, with the title *Ekonomicheskoe i nauchno–tekhnicheskoe sotrudni-chestvo SFRIu s evropeiskimi stranami–chlenami SEV.* Continued by annual volumes as follows:

X5 *Ekonomicheskoe i nauchno–tekhnicheskoe sotrudnichestvo stran-*

chlenov SEV i SFRIu. Razvitie sotsialisticheskoi ekonomicheskoi integratsii. Bibliogr. ukaz. [Economic and scientific–technical cooperation of the member states of the CMEA and the SFRY. The development of socialist economic integration. Bibliography.] M.: INION, 1976–. Annual.

Series begins with the volume for 1974 (publ. 1976). Some volumes (e.g. that for 1975) are in more than one part. Coverage similar to that of X4.

X6 *Sovet Ekonomicheskoi Vzaimopomoshchi XXX let. Ukazatel' literatury 1969–1978 gg.* [Thirty years of the CMEA. Bibliography 1969–1978]. M.: MISON/INION, 1979. 257 pp.

897 items published in CMEA countries, chiefly monographs and 'sborniki' of a documentary or academic character, but including documents published in newspapers. Partially annotated. Name/title index.

X7 Teich, G. *Der Rat für gegenseitige Wirtschaftshilfe 1949–1963. Bibliographie.* [The CMEA 1949–1963. A bibliography]. (Kieler Schrifttumskunden zu Wirtschaft und Gesellschaft, 14). Kiel: Institut für Weltwirtschaft, Bibliothek, 1966. 445 pp.

2,032 items, mainly journal articles from both East and West but listing some documents. Some non-evaluative annotation. Name index.

OFFICIAL PUBLICATIONS OF MORE THAN ONE STATE OR PARTY

X8 *Constitutions of the Communist-Party states.* Ed. J. F. Triska. (Hoover Institution publications, 70). Stanford, Calif.: Hoover Institution, 1968. xiii, 541 pp.

English translations of the texts and amendments of all constitutions adopted since the establishment of communist rule in the states concerned (both in Europe and elsewhere).

X9 *Konstitutsii zarubezhnykh sotsialisticheskikh gosudarstv Evropy.* [Constitutions of the other socialist states of Europe]. Red. B. N. Toporin. M.: Progress, 1973. 741 pp.

Russian texts of all East European socialist states' constitutions (including Albania's) as at 1 November 1972. General introduction for each country, with notes on amendments in the texts.

X10 *The constitutions of the communist world.* Ed. W. B. Simons. Alphen aan den Rijn: Sijthoff & Noordhoff, 1980. xvii, 644 pp.

Intended as a successor to Triska (X8), giving texts as amended up to the (unspecified) time of compilation. Index.

X11 *Highlights of current legislation and activities in Mid-Europe.* Washington: Library of Congress Mid-European Law Project, 1953–60. Monthly (but many issues combined).

Project founded by the Free Europe Committee. Carries summaries of, and comment on, recent legislation, and includes some translated texts of laws. Deals with the USSR and all East European socialist states except the German Democratic Republic.

X12 *WGO. Monatshefte für osteuropäisches Recht.* [WGO. Monthly [*sic*] publication on East European law]. Hrsg. G. Geilke. Hamburg: 1958–. 6 issues p.a.

Each issue lists recent significant published legislation from the USSR and all East European socialist states, with German translations of selected laws, and articles, notes and reviews. Annual survey of court decisions and international agreements. *Generalregister 1958–1978* publ. 1979.

X13 *Documents in communist affairs.* Ed. B. Szajkowski. Cardiff: University College Cardiff Press, 1978–. Annual?

The first two volumes appeared in 1978 and 1979, containing material which became available in the preceding year. Not restricted to 'official' documents (some dissident material is printed), and includes much material from Western and other non-ruling communist parties. Details of sources not always fully stated. Many of the documents are not available in English elsewhere.

X14 Meissner, B. *Die 'Breshnew-Doktrin'. Dokumentation.* [The 'Brezhnev Doctrine'. Documentation]. Köln: Wissenschaft und Politik, 1969. 189 pp.

After a 41-page introduction, prints German translations of Soviet statements, speeches and articles on developments in Czechoslovakia during 1968, Czechoslovak statements of the invasion period, and reactions from other socialist states.

X15 *Plany razvitiia narodnogo khoziaistva stran narodnoi demokratii.* [National economic development plans of the people's democracies]. Vstup. stat'ia. I. V. Dudinskogo. M.: Izd-vo inostr. lit-ry, 1952. xxxix, 469 pp.

Russian text of the first five-year (in Poland six-year) plans of Albania, Bulgaria, Czechoslovakia, Hungary, Poland and Romania, with data on plan fulfilment up to the date of compilation.

STATISTICS

X16 *Narodnoe khoziaistvo sotsialisticheskikh stran v 1961 [etc.] godu. Soobshcheniia statisticheskikh upravlenii.* [The national economies of the socialist countries in the year 1961 [etc.]. Reports of the statistical administrations]. M.: Statistika, 1962–. Annual.

Reports on plan fulfilment for the year preceding publication. Countries included vary: China is omitted, as is Albania from 1965.

X17 *Ekonomika sotsialisticheskikh stran v tsifrakh 1964 [etc.] god.* [The economies of the socialist countries in figures for the year 1964 [etc.]]. (AN SSSR. In-t ekon. mir. sots. sist.) M.: Mysl', 1964–6. Annual.

Volumes relate to the years 1963, 1964 and 1965. Includes data on China, North Korea, Cuba and Yugoslavia.

X18 *Statisticheskii ezhegodnik stran-chlenov Soveta Ekonomicheskoi Vzaimopomoshchi 1970 [etc.].* [Statistical yearbook of member states of the CMEA 1970 [etc.]]. M.: Sekretariat SEV, 1971–3. Statistika, 1974–. Annual.

Basic statistical yearbook for comparison between CMEA members. Base year is rarely earlier than 1960 (but *see* X19). English translation (title as above) published for the years 1976 onwards, London: IPC Industrial Press.

X19 *Narodnoe khoziaistvo stran-chlenov Soveta Ekonomicheskoi Vzaimopomoshchi. Statisticheskii sbornik 'K 30-letiiu obrazovaniia SEV'.* [The national economies of member states of the CMEA. Statistical collection for the 30th anniversary of the CMEA's foundation]. M.: Sekretariat SEV, 1979. 410 pp.

Only 1,800 copies printed. Issued outside the annual series (X18), and including figures for 1950 in many tables. Latest figures are for 1978.

CMEA AND INTERNATIONAL ECONOMIC COOPERATION

X20 *Mnogostoronee ekonomicheskoe sotrudnichestvo sotsialisticheskikh gosudarstv. Sbornik dokumentov.* [Multilateral economic cooperation between the socialist states. Collection of documents]. Izd. 2-e. Pod obshch. red. P. A. Tokarevoi. (In-t gosudarstva i prava AN SSSR). M.: Iurid. lit-ra, 1972. 648 pp.

Supersedes 1st edition of 1967. The principal collection of public documents on the CMEA and its associated organs. Supplemented by X21.

X21 *Mnogostoronee ekonomicheskoe sotrudnichestvo sotsialisticheskikh gosudarstv. Dokumenty za 1972–1975 gg.* [Multilateral economic cooperation between the socialist states. Documents for 1972–1975]. Pod obshch. red. P. Tokarevoi. (In-t gosudarstva i prava AN SSSR). M.: Iurid. lit-ra, 1976. 407 pp.

Supplements X20. A further volume, covering 1975–80, was scheduled for publication in 1981.

X22 *Nauchno–tekhnicheskoe sotrudnichestvo sotsialisticheskikh stran. Sbornik mezhdunarodnykh dokumentov i materialov.* [Scientific and technical collaboration between the socialist countries. A collection of international documents and materials]. (Gosud. komitet SM SSSR po nauke i tekhnike). M.: 1971. 436 pp.

Covers the period 1956–70. Sections on the organizational,

economic and legal bases of scientific and technical collaboration; international organizations and agreements; and bilateral agreements. [Not seen].

X23 Szawlowski, R. *The system of the international organisations of the communist countries.* Leiden: Sijthoff, 1976. xxix, 322 pp.

Main text is a history and analysis of the operation of the organizations concerned, most attention being given to the CMEA and WTO. Annexes give English translations of the Warsaw Treaty, Comecon Charter, certain other CMEA and WTO documents, and statutes and agreements relating to many specialized organizations. Amendments to 1975 are indicated.

X24 *A source book on socialist international organisations.* Ed. and transl. W. E. Butler. Alphen aan den Rijn: Sijthoff & Noordhoff, 1978. xxiv, 1143 pp.

Agreements, statutes, protocols, charters and other documents relating to, or issued by, the CMEA and other socialist organs of economic, industrial, scientific and technical cooperation. Two documents only on the WTO. All translated afresh into English.

X25 *Recueil des législations des pays socialistes européens sur la coopération économique.* Genève: Institut de Hautes Études Internationales/ Leiden: Sijthoff & Noordhoff, 1974–. Annual?

Loose-leaf format. [Not seen].

X26 *Osnovnye dokumenty Soveta Ekonomicheskoi Vzaimopomoshchi.* [Basic documents of the CMEA]. Izd. 3-e. M.: Sekretariat SEV, 1976–7. 2 vols. [Not seen].

X27 *Ekonomicheskoe sotrudnichestvo stran-chlenov SEV.* [Economic cooperation of CMEA member countries]. M.: Sekretariat SEV, 1975–. 6 issues p.a. (4 in 1975).

Carries a selection of reports and speeches presented at CMEA meetings, besides articles and news of CMEA activities.

X28 Faddeev, N. V. *Sovet Ekonomicheskoi Vzaimopomoshchi 1949–1974.* [The CMEA 1949–1974]. M.: Ekonomika, 1974. 375 pp.

Faddeev has been Secretary of the CMEA since 1958. His account of its foundation, aims, structure and operations is the most substantial 'official' treatment. Earlier editions appeared in 1964 and 1969.

X29 *Dvadtsat' piat' let deiatel'nosti organov Soveta Ekonomicheskoi Vzaimopomoshchi. (Khronologiia zasedanii organov SEV).* [25 years of CMEA activity. (A chronology of the meetings of CMEA organs)]. Red. L. I. Lukin. M.: Sekretariat SEV, 1974. 426 pp. [Not seen].

X30 *Obzor deiatel'nosti SEV za 1968 [etc.] god.* [Survey of CMEA activities in 1968 [etc.]]. M.: Sekretariat SEV, 1969?–. Annual.

Length varies between about 60 and 200 pp. English translation published for years 1968 onwards (title as above, except for 1972 and 1977 volumes, entitled *Information on activities of the CMEA in . . .*). [Russian ed. not seen].

X31 *Sbornik informatsii o deiatel'nosti organov SEV v 1973g. [etc.].* [Collected reports on various activities of bodies of the CMEA in 1973 [etc.]]. M.: Sekretariat SEV, 1974–. Annual?

Reports prepared for international organizations and meetings. English editions (title as above) have been traced for 1973 and 1976.

X32 *Letopis' Soveta Ekonomicheskoi Vzaimopomoshchi.* [Chronicle of the CMEA]. M.: Sekretariat SEV, 1979. [Not seen].

X33 *Kommiunike o soveshchaniiakh predstavitelei kommunisticheskikh i rabochikh partii i glav pravitel'stv stran-chlenov Soveta Ekonomicheskoi Vzaimopomoshchi i o zasedaniiakh sessii Soveta. 1949–1978 gg.* [Communiqués of the meetings of representatives of communist and workers' parties and heads of government of member states of the CMEA, and of sessions of the Council. 1949–1978]. M.: Sekretariat SEV, 1979. [Not seen].

X34 *Kommiunike o zasedaniiakh Ispolnitel'nogo komiteta Soveta Ekonomicheskoi Vzaimopomoshchi.* [Communiqués of sessions of the Executive Committee of the CMEA]. M.: Sekretariat SEV, 1979.

Most such communiqués have also appeared, though not always in full, in X27 since it began publication in 1975. No communiqué appears to be issued for Executive Committee meetings which take place during Council Sessions. [Not seen].

X35 *Kompleksnaia programma dal'neishego uglubleniia i sovershenstvovaniia sotrudnichestva i razvitiia sotsialisticheskoi ekonomicheskoi integratsii stran-chlenov SEV.* [Comprehensive programme for the further extension and improvement of cooperation and the development of socialist economic integration by the CMEA member countries]. M.: Politizdat, 1971. 119 pp.

Separate publication of the CMEA's first substantial 'development programme'. Also published in X20. Official English translation (title as above) publ. M.: CMEA Secretariat, 1971, and in another translation in X24.

X36 *Ukazatel' standartov SEV i rekomendatsii SEV po standartizatsii.* [List of CMEA standards and recommendations on standardization]. M.: Sekretariat SEV, 1972. 415 pp.

Continued by: *Standarty SEV i rekomendatsii SEV po standartizatsii: ukazatel',* M.: Sekretariat SEV, 1975?–. Annual. [Not seen].

WARSAW TREATY ORGANIZATION

X37 *Moskovskoe soveshchanie evropeiskikh stran po obespecheniiu mira i bezopasnosti v Evrope. Moskva, 29 noiabria–2 dekabria 1954 goda.* [The Moscow conference of European countries on the safeguarding of peace and security in Europe. Moscow, 29 November–2 December 1954]. M.: Pravda, 1954. 159 pp.

Speeches, declarations and communiqués of the conference of future WTO members.

X38 *Varshavskoe soveshchanie evropeiskikh gosudarstv po obespecheniiu mira i bezopasnosti v Evrope. Varshava, 11–14 maia 1955 goda.* [The Warsaw conference of European states on the safeguarding of peace and security in Europe. Warsaw, 11–14 May 1955]. M.: Gosud. izd-vo polit. lit-ry, 1955. 142 pp.

Speeches, communiqués and the text of the treaty.

X39 *Organizatsiia Varshavskogo Dogovora. Dokumenty i materialy 1955–1980 gg.* [The Warsaw Treaty Organization. Documents and materials 1955–1980]. (Min. inostr. del SSSR). M.: Politizdat, 1980. 296 pp.

83 documents in chronological order, including the treaty itself, declarations and communiqués. Earlier edition (with 62 documents) publ. 1975.

X40 Jain, J. P. *Documentary study of the Warsaw Pact.* N.Y.: Asia Publishing House, 1973. 413 pp.

39 pages of introduction followed by 210 documents in English, mostly from the WTO side (official statements, communiqués, speeches and editorials), but including some Western comment. Covers the period 1954–65 only.

X41 Remington, R. A. *The Warsaw Pact: case studies in communist conflict resolution.* Cambridge, Mass.: MIT Press, 1971. xix, 268 pp.

Fifteen translated documents (pp. 201–8) include the treaty, some communiqués and declarations, and the Soviet–Romanian and Soviet–Czechoslovak bilateral treaties of 1970.

INDEX

SEQUENCE

There is a single name/title sequence of entries, regardless of language or original alphabet. (On transliteration, see the section 'Language and transliteration' in the Introduction.)

COVERAGE

The index includes the *titles* of all works mentioned in the bibliography, whether in main entries or annotations, except for slight title variations given in annotations only, and for the titles of leaders' works. It includes the *names* of all authors, editors and compilers given before a title, and normally also the first or only such name following any title.

FILING ORDER

Arrangement is alphabetically word-by-word, with hyphenated combinations treated as two or more separate words.

Personal initials in titles (e.g. *V. I. Lenin . . .*) are each treated as a separate word, but other sets of initials or similar contractions (e.g. AVNOJ, KazSSR) are treated as single words.

Titles beginning with a cardinal or ordinal number or a date, if shown in figures, are filed *last*, in *numerical* order.

Definite and indefinite articles are disregarded for filing purposes where they occur at the beginning of a title.

All diacritical marks are ignored in the filing order (inevitable when 26 languages are represented!).

ABBREVIATIONS

Because of the great length of many titles, abridgements have been made where possible, with omissions shown by . . . . Established abbreviations have also been used extensively.